MUHAMMAD
AND THE
PEOPLE
OF THE
BOOK

MUHAMMAD
AND THE
PEOPLE
OF THE
BOOK

SAHAJA CARIMOKAM

To order additional copies of this book, contact:
Xlibris Corporation
1-888-795-4274
www.Xlibris.com
Orders@Xlibris.com
83176

CONTENTS

FOREWORD TO MUHAMMAD AND THE PEOPLE OF THE BOOK: OUR QUESTION AND METHOD

This book is an enquiry into the life of one of the most important human beings of world history, Muhammad, the Prophet of Islam. Within fifty years, this religion will be the largest world religion not only encompassing the Middle East, but also expanding into regions where Muslims have never been a population factor before. In the face of this worldwide demographic and ideological expansion, it is essential for Westerners to understand this religion in terms of its earliest sources. It is to these sources that Muslims are turning in their search for a true expression of Islam. Malise Ruthven points out that the "sociological reductionism" of present Western analysis, which sees the current crisis as merely a "revolt against national secular elites," misses the true nature of this revival. He states, "Much of what was happening in the Muslim communities today could only be understood in terms of the unfolding and implementing of theology."[1]

Theology is not important in the Western world today. Therefore, Westerners have few tools with which to analyze the thinking of Muslims. The West doesn't "get it" because the West seems to be able to analyze only within a secular framework. This study is the product of a group of theological students who are looking at Muhammad through the lens of theology. Specifically, we want to understand Muhammad's vision of the nature of God and how that affected his relations with fellow monotheists. We are studying this chronologically through the life of the Prophet.

This research is based on some of the early documents on the life of Muhammad. We wanted to understand Muhammad in terms that would be most relevant for a Western reader and Western society in general. The main question we are seeking to answer is this: What was the nature of Muhammad's relations with non-Muslims from the beginning of his prophetic work, and how did it change during his lifetime? The phrase "People of

---

[1]   Lloyd Ridgeon, ed. *Islamic Interpretations of Christianity*, New York: St. Martin's Press, 2001, p. xii.

7

the Book" is the Qur'an's (Islam's holy book) most frequent title for Jews and Christians and therefore relates to how the Muslims regarded other monotheistic communities. However, we have not ignored Muhammad's relations with other non-Muslims, such as the pagans of Mecca. We have studied this in a chronological fashion to determine what shifts occurred in the Prophet's view of these communities over time. These shifts have to do primarily with theological conceptions. David Marshall points out that this historical progression is largely a conflict between the "ideal" Christianity (and Judaism) which Muhammad understood as precursors to Islam and the "real" Christianity that he encountered gradually over the course of his work.[2] Marshall does an excellent job of describing this progression in the Prophet's viewpoint. This study is an attempt to spell out the nature of this progression in the early Islamic historical and Qur'anic context.

Our primary source for this research has been an early biography of Muhammad. The work is entitled *The Life of Muhammad*, and was authored by Ibn Ishaq around 750 CE. It is available from Oxford University Press in English translated by Alfred Guillaume. In our opinion, this book should be on the reading list of everyone in the Western world because it presents an early interpretation of Muhammad's life by a Muslim. Further, it is much more understandable than the Qur'an, as it is written in chronological order with dates, places, and individuals clearly identified. As is true of all the early biographies of Muhammad, the aspect of his relationship to non-Muslims is primary from the very first page. Ibn Ishaq's work dates from around CE 750 or from about one hundred and twenty years after the events that it describes. It should be noted that the original text is only known from the version edited by Ibn Hisham around 810, 178 years after the death of the Prophet. As we have studied Ibn Ishaq's biography, we followed two methodological principles. First, we have emphasized the things that Ibn Ishaq emphasizes. We allow the text to set the agenda. Some of the material appears to be eulogy/hagiographic; stories of the miracles of Muhammad or the signs of his appearing. Nevertheless, these stories reflect Muslim opinions of Muhammad and are, therefore, included. We have also consulted three other early biographers of Muhammad, Al-Waqidi, Al-Tabari, and Ibn Kathir.

When writers, Western or Muslim, have commented directly on the historicity of particular events, we have consulted them, though we do not pretend to be comprehensive. The major issues of the historicity of the texts

---

[2]   David Marshall "Christianity in the Qur'an," *Islamic Interpretations of Christianity*, pp. 24-5.

are considered primarily in chapter 13. It should be kept in mind that all of these "histories" are polemic works intended to demonstrate the superiority of Islam and the perfections of the Prophet. To use an American analogy, they are like a history of the Indian wars written by George Armstrong Custer. The history they present is sanitized and highly slanted. Opponents of the Prophet are generally presented in the worst possible light.

In this context, when atrocities by heros are admitted, we have every reason to believe that they are historical. These events became foundational to Islamic law (*sharia*). That is the issue of the twenty-first century; not that such things happened 1,450 years ago, but that those events are now considered canonical as expressions of theology and therefore exemplary for modern Muslims. The Prophet's *sunnah* or "practices" are the practical outworkings of Islamic theology and are the primary source of the present ideological struggle between the West and the Muslim world.

Our second source is the Qur'an itself, the holy book of Islam. While the book contains little in terms of historical information, it is the only source that can reasonably be traced to Muhammad himself. We have read it in chronological order, according to the outline of Theodore Nöldeke, which is generally accepted by Muslims, rather than in its textual order. This is a part of our effort to see the progression of the text's viewpoint on non-Muslims. Where Muslim commentators have mentioned a specific historical context relating to non-Muslims we have noted that, though this is often inaccurate. Critical issues with regard to the text of the Qur'an are also discussed in the final chapter. An excellent brief summary of the Western chronological views on the progression of the Qur'an is found in Gerhard Bowering's article, "Recent Research on the Construction of the Qur'an."[3] The importance of the chronology of the Qur'an lies in the issue of abrogation (*naskh*), by which Muslims interpreted certain earlier passages in the Qur'an as abrogated or cancelled by later contradictory passages. All of this relates to the unfolding of Muhammad's relationship with Jews and Christians and with non-Muslims in general.

Finally, we have read through three of the canonical collections of Sunni Muslim Hadith (traditions of the Prophet) looking specifically at all references to non-Muslims. Practically, this has meant Jews and Christians (the "People of the Book") as polytheists' figure in a relatively minor way in the Hadith. Historically, by the time the Hadith were compiled the polytheist community

---

[3]   Gerhard Bowering, "Recent Research on the Construction of the Qur'an," *The Qur'an in its Historical Context*, Routledge, 2008, pp. 70-83.

in Arabia had ceased to exist and pragmatically the main non-Muslim religious communities were the Jews and Christians. In the history of Islam, rules that applied to the "People of the Book" also were sometimes applied to other religious groups that were conquered by Muslim armies. This includes Zoroastrians, Buddhists, and Hindus. Historically, "People of the Book" can mean, "non-Muslims," or even "non-Arabs," since some Arab Christians were forcibly converted to Islam in spite of being "People of the Book." We have studied the Hadith of Bukhari, Muslim, and Dawud, all collected during the third century of Islam. It should be noted that Hadith literature relates largely to the Medinan period of the Prophet's life. The events of this period were analyzed to determine legal principles for the law courts of the Muslim empire. Once again we will consider the historical issues relating to this literature in chapter 13.

In order to better understand the text of the Qur'an, we have consulted with several collections of commentary literature (*tafsir*). Primary is the *Tafsir Ibn Kathir*, a ten volume work translated in Saudi Arabia and available in most mosques and Muslim bookstores across the United States. Ibn Kathir was born in 1302 CE in Syria. He was famous as a "mufassir" or interpreter of the Qur'an and wrote a history of the Prophet that was also consulted for this work. We have also utilized the commentary of Al-Tabari (d. 923 CE) concerning chapter 2 of the Qur'an. These are older traditional commentaries on the Qur'an that form the bedrock of how Muslims interpret the Qur'an today. The modernist viewpoint in commentary is represented by Abdullah Yusuf Ali's own copious notes on his translation of the Qur'an dating from 1938. This is still the most popular English translation of the Qur'an in the Muslim community in the English speaking world.

In the course of our study, another aspect of Islam was deemed important enough in light of the texts to give it special emphasis. This is the aspect of Islam as a fusion of religion with political-military policies. During the Medinan period of Muhammad's life, it becomes clear that the prophet's main goal was to establish a political state based on the *Shahada* (confession of faith) as an obligatory oath of allegiance taken by his army. We decided that tracing the evolution and formation of this concept from the earliest times was essential to understanding the nature of Islam as a practical theology of the kingdom of God on earth. It seemed to us that Muhammad formed Islam in the mold of a new theocracy on earth like the early Israelite nation with Muhammad filling the role Moses occupies in the Old Testament. The difference, of course, lay in its universality. While the Jews sought to establish a kingdom only in their "promised land," the Muslim kingdom was meant to encompass the whole earth. The first hundred years of Islam, which witnessed one of the most rapid series of military conquests in world history, demonstrated the political and military genius of the Prophet. It seems that Westerners have for too long regarded Muhammad primarily as a religious leader. That he was. But religion or perhaps more accurately, theology, in the conception of Muhammad provided the glue and rationale for an empire; the only empire in world history established from the beginning on the basis of religion. This viewpoint is obvious in all of the Muslim texts. Islam, which claims to be a "complete code of life," as a political and military concept, needs greater illumination and that forms an initial assumption in our study of the Prophet's life.

What other assumptions underlie our study? The question of the historicity of the texts is extremely important for Westerners. We are skeptics by nature. However, we would caution that this issue is largely irrelevant for Muslims. Muslims believe these accounts to be historically true. For the purposes of dialogue, this assumption must simply be accepted. There are major historical problems presented by all of our sources; we have nevertheless assumed that there is a historical core to these texts. They are sanitized versions of history meant primarily for propaganda purposes. We will note contradictions and issues of historicity as we move along.

The assumption that a historical core can be demonstrated from the texts underlies our thesis. We believe that some of the information provided is historically true if for no other reason than that many of the stories, though sanitized, are distasteful in the extreme. History demonstrates that when loyalists tell unpleasant stories about their heros, those stories have a strong claim to credibility. The tragedy of modern historical critical writings on Islam in the late twentieth century is that they tend to sanitize the Islamic texts. They produce a sanitized version of an already sanitized version of history. In other words, they produce propaganda. We would invite anyone to compare Karen Armstrong's *Life of Muhammad* with Ibn Ishaq's history (which is supposedly her source) to see how this works. Not surprisingly, her book is sold on Islamist propaganda web sites. For the Western skeptic, we would, again, refer to chapter 13, where this issue is discussed in depth.

Our third assumption is that the preponderance of certain historical descriptions indicates their relative importance. This seems fairly obvious. The Battle of Badr receives far more attention than the brief uneventful raid of Al-Kadid. This level of focus seems to correspond to a certain degree with the relative historical certainty of the event. All of the biographical literature about Muhammad follows a similar pattern with the same basic events presented. It is possible that we have left some important, but little noted, events out. It remains for the reviewers of this work to identify our areas of neglect and for subsequent researchers to evaluate their importance in relation to our central thesis.

A final assumption is that this material is relevant for understanding Muslim relations with non-Muslims today. Muhammad is the paradigm for all Muslims. For them, he is the last and the best and the seal of the Prophets. He is the perfect exemplar in all circumstances for the Muslim community. Everything he did is to be imitated. We shall trace his example in the first twelve chapters of this book. Chapter one covers Muhammad's life before his call as a Prophet. The following eleven chapters divide the remaining twenty-three years of his life in approximately two-year segments. This is not arbitrary. Muslims typically divide the revelations during the Meccan period of Muhammad's life into three chronological periods, early, middle, and late. This provides a natural division for this period. Because of some complexities, we have further subdivided the late period into two chapters. In a similar way, the Medinan period can be divided into segments corresponding to important historical events leading up to the death of the Prophet. Chapter 13 is concerned with the historical critical, and source critical issues that relate to our documents and their reliability. Chapter 14 concludes the book with a brief study of one controversial area of Qur'anic teaching and its relevance in modern Muslim practice.

What is the relevance of this study? First, we consider it essential that Westerners have an opportunity to look at a version of the Prophet's life that includes the elements that early Muslims thought important as expressions of theology. It is to these theological sources that Muslims are returning. It is equally important to hear the Muslim interpretation of these events as they appraise the significance of the Prophet's life. These materials, particularly the biographies, are polemic in nature and set out to prove that Muhammad was, indeed, the Prophet of God. In light of the Islamic revival sweeping the planet, these texts are growing in importance today as they point the way back to the true path for Muslims.

In the course of these studies, we have not avoided showing applications of the Prophet's behavior to the modern world. We have not, overlooked, ignored, or attempted to explain away certain difficult events, as it seems many Western researchers now do, in the name of pluralistic relativism. They sanitize an already sanitized version of history. It is as if they took as their primary rule that any aspect of the Prophet's life that seems crude to a Westerner will simply be left out of the description or explained away with rationalizations that fly in the face of the canonical, theological nature of the texts. This is merely a reverse form of value judgment, as if certain items must be sanitized for fear they will inspire judgment. These events are clearly emphasized by the Muslim authors themselves. Since the nineteenth century many orientalists have cautioned against judging the Prophet in terms of modern concepts of right and wrong. However, in the interconnected world of today, ideas have direct consequences, and ideals that apply in the Muslim world are now being argued for the West, such as the application of Sharia law. The actions of the Prophet need to be understood in their historical context, and their consequences for the modern world must also be understood. At the very least, it will help us to appreciate the struggle of moderate Muslims to find a tolerant man of peace in a history of warfare and empire building.

The final chapter will simply discuss an important question that Muslims need to answer for themselves as they ask the question, how is Islam and its theology to relate to the modern world, and even more importantly, how are Muslims to relate to non-Muslims in the modern world?

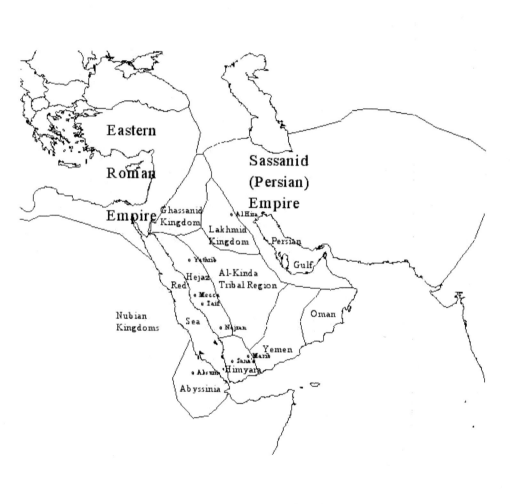

Eastern

Roman

Empire   Ghassanid
      Kingdom

Sassanid
(Persian)
Empire

○ Al Hira

Lakhmid
Kingdom

Persian

○ Yathrib

Hejaz   Al-Kinda
        Tribal Region

Gulf

Red

○ Mecca

○ Taif

Nubian
Kingdoms

Sea

○ Najran

Oman

Yemen

○ Marib

○ Sana'a

○ Abyssinia

Himyar

Abyssinia

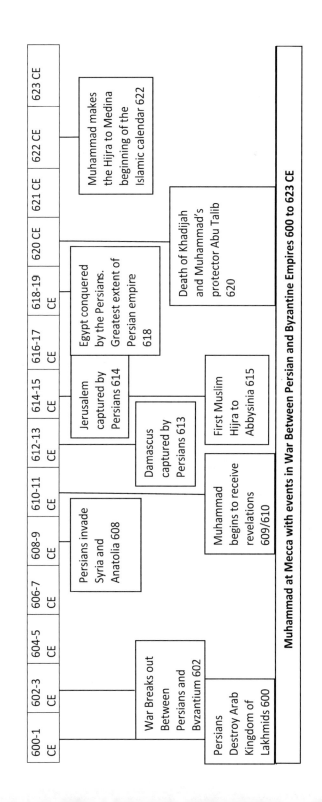

600-1 CE	602-3 CE	604-5 CE	606-7 CE	608-9 CE	610-11 CE	612-13 CE	614-15 CE	616-17 CE	618-19 CE	620 CE	621 CE	622 CE	623 CE

War Breaks out Between Persians and Byzantium 602

Persians Destroy Arab Kingdom of Lakhmids 600

Persians invade Syria and Anatolia 608

Muhammad begins to receive revelations 609/610

Damascus captured by Persians 613

Jerusalem captured by Persians 614

First Muslim Hijra to Abbysinia 615

Egypt conquered by the Persians. Greatest extent of Persian empire 618

Death of Khadijah and Muhammad's protector Abu Talib 620

Muhammad makes the Hijra to Medina beginning of the Islamic calendar 622

Muhammad at Mecca with events in War Between Persian and Byzantine Empires 600 to 623 CE

CHAPTER 1

THE EARLY LIFE

OF MUHAMMAD

A. Introduction to the Issue of Historicity

The early life of the Prophet of Islam is a paradox. From the early Muslim writings, we would seem to know a great deal. All the early Muslim biographers include extensive stories and descriptions of the period leading up to the Prophet's birth and his early life to age forty in Mecca. Yet much of this material is patently mythological. It mixes eulogy and polemic with tidbits of possibly historical material. This can be illustrated through the tradition of Muhammad's birth date, associated with the "Year of the Elephant," which has been traditionally ascribed to 570 CE. According to Arab traditions recorded in Ibn Ishaq's biography, in that year an Abyssinian/ Axumite Christian King named Abraha, who controlled Yemen, invaded the Hijaz (area of modern Mecca and Medina). He made an attempt to conquer Mecca with his army that included a large war elephant (hence, the name, "Year of the Elephant"). Ibn Ishaq records that the elephant refused to enter the Meccan domains when told that it was "God's holy land." The elephant retreated toward Yemen and God, according to Ibn Ishaq, sent birds who pelted the Abyssinians with pebbles and drove them away.[4]

Just when we are about to dismiss the entire story as fanciful and invented, we discover that Abraha was not only a historical person, but several ancient inscriptions in his name have been discovered.[5] The so-called "dam inscription of Abraha" from Yemen establishes him as an Abyssinian King in Yemen around

---

[4]   Ibn Ishaq, *The Life of Muhammad*, trans. Alfred Guillaume, Pakistan: Oxford University Press, 2003, pp. 21-7.

[5]   K. A. Kitchen lists three such inscriptions, p. 10.

the year 539 CE.[6] Recent research has shown that the date of the "Year of the Elephant" is more likely around 550 CE. too early for Muhammad's birth date. Thus the story is a mixture of the mythological (God talking to elephants and birds dropping pebbles)[7] and the historical (there was a king named Abraha who lived about this time in Yemen) and simple inaccuracy (the date of the "Year of the Elephant"). The inaccuracy has a probable explanation. Early Muslim biographers probably tried to associate Muhammad's birth with this auspicious date in an effort to demonstrate another of the many miraculous signs that supposedly accompanied the birth of the Prophet. The overlays of the mythological find their echoes in many other events both in the early and later life of the Prophet, such as his throwing pebbles at his enemies at the start of the Battle of Badr.[8] All the early biographers affirm that Muhammad was forty years of age when he began his prophetic work around 609/610 CE.,[9] and the assignment of his birth date to around 570 CE is possibly accurate.

It will be our purpose in this chapter to work our way through the stories of Muhammad's life up to age forty with our primary thesis in mind. What influence did Jews and Christians have upon him, and what was the nature of his relationship to them? What were the religious, political, and social circumstances during this period, and how might they have influenced Muhammad's theological views of those followers of other monotheistic religions? Even the mythological elements will teach us a great deal about Muslim borrowings from other religious traditions particularly as it was appropriated to their own veneration of Muhammad.

B. The Religious, Political, and Economic Circumstances in Arabia

By the beginning of the sixth century CE, polytheism was a dying phenomenon in the Middle East. The Eastern Roman empire had made

---

6   Sidney Smith, "Events in Arabia in the 6th Century CE.," *Bulletin of the School of Oriental and African Studies*, Vol. 16, 1954, pp. 437-41.
7   Al Waqidi describes this also as a smallpox epidemic though using the same words and fanciful tale. Muir, 1975, p. cxvii.
8   Ibn Ishaq, 2003, p. 301.
9   It is possible that the attribution of forty years has more to do with stylistic and cultural associations as to the appropriate age of a person called to such an office. Yet these same cultural considerations would have made it unlikely for a younger man to attempt to do what Muhammad did. An age of around forty makes a lot of sense in terms of the rest of the chronology of early Islam.

Christianity its official religion. Most of Egypt, Palestine, Syria, and Turkey had been converted, at least nominally, to the Christian faith. In the north and east of Arabia lay the Persian Empire with its organized Zoroastrian faith, interspersed with communities of Nestorian Christians. Zoroastrian communities also existed in Arabia.[10] Spread among these two empires were large communities of Jews. Abyssinia/Axum (modern Ethiopia/Eritrea) across the Red Sea from Arabia had become Christian. The bordering Nubian kingdoms were converted to the Christian faith during the middle of the sixth century. Sizeable groups of Jews and Christians existed in Yemen.

Ibn Ishaq tells the story of the conversion of a Yemeni King to Judaism. Hassan b. Tiban, the king of Yemen, came under the influence of two Jewish rabbis in Yathrib (Medina) during an invasion. He was converted to Judaism, and on his return to Yemen, his pagan people opposed him. A trial by fire was arranged between the rabbis and the pagan priests:

> So his people went forth with their idols and sacred objects, and the two rabbis went forth with their sacred books hanging like necklaces from their necks until they halted at the place whence the fires used to blaze out . . . the fire covered them and consumed their idols and sacred objects and the men who bore them. But the two rabbis came out with their sacred books, sweating profusely but otherwise unharmed. Thereupon the Himyarites accepted the king's religion. Such was the origin of Judaism in the Yaman.[11]

The story is clearly a fable and bears a strong resemblance to the story of the three young men in the book of Daniel in the Bible. Nevertheless, after extensive review of ancient Arabian inscriptional materials, Smith concludes, "A strong case can be made out for believing that . . . the dynasty (in Yemen) was Jewish in faith, and connected with Yatrib."[12] Indeed a large Jewish community existed in Yemen until 1948.

The early Muslim biographers emphasize about the large and influential communities of Jews and Christians in Arabia, and the wars that were fought

---

[10]   Samuel Zwemer, *The Influence of Animism on Islam*, New York: Macmillan Company, 1920, pp. 158-9. Some interpreted this as being a temple of the thunder god though Zoroastrian influence cannot be discounted.

[11]   Ibn Ishaq, 2003, pp. 6-12.

[12]   Smith, 1954, p. 462.

between them. Ibn Ishaq describes the conversion of Najran in Yemen to Christianity and the killing of a large number of Christians of Najran[13] by the Jewish Yemeni King Dhu Nuwas.[14] There is considerable inscriptional evidence in favor of the veracity of some events although certainly not the details.[15] Virtually, every tribe in Arabia had members who converted to one of the major monotheistic religions or slaves who had come from a monotheistic background. Stories about Christian monks, priests, and Jewish rabbis abound in these early histories. After the suppression of the Jewish Kings of Yemen by the Christian Abyssinians, the gradual trend in Arabia was toward conversion to Christianity.[16] F. E. Peters notes, "In CE 600 an observer might easily have predicted that within three or four decades the Arabs would be as Christian as the Celts or later Slavs."[17]

Aside from the religious divisions, Arabia and its northern extension into modern Iraq was a political football passed between the Persian and Roman empires. The tribes were variously aligned with the Byzantines or the Persians, and the wars between these two empires were fought back and forth across these territories. M. J. Kister comments as follows:

> The rivalry between the Persian and Byzantine empires over the control of the reigns of the Arab peninsula at the end of the sixth and the beginning of the seventh century is reflected in a number of traditions attributed to the Prophet . . . The struggle between the two empires, in which the two vassal kingdoms of al Hira and Gassan took active part, was closely watched by the unbelievers and Muslims in the different stages of their context.[18]

---

[13]   Christians in Saudi Arabia are to this day referred to as "Najrani."

[14]   Ibn Ishaq, 2003, pp. 14-20. Guillaume mentions that an inscription was found in Arabia by Professor Ryckmans in 1952 that demonstrates the historicity of some of this material and provides a date of 518 CE.

[15]   Smith notes an early Christian manuscript which tells the story of the "martyrs" of Najran.

[16]   One of the signs of this growing Christian influence is the large number of Axumite coins that have been retrieved from Yemen dating from this period.

[17]   F. E. Peters, *The Arabs and Arabia on the Eve of Islam*, Brookfield: Ashgate, 1999, Introduction xi.

[18]   M. J. Kister, "Al-Hira: Some notes on its relations with Arabia," *The Arabs and Arabia on the Eve of Islam*, Brookfield: Ashgate, 1999, pp. 143-4.

An example of a Hadith or historical tradition of this type is found in the collection of Sahih Muslim from the third Islamic century:

> I heard the Apostle of Allah (may peace be upon him) say: you will make a secure peace with the Byzantines, then you and they will fight an enemy behind you, and you will be victorious, take booty, and be safe. You will then return and alight in a meadow with mounds and one of the Christians will raise the cross and say: the cross has conquered. One of the Muslims will become angry and smash it, and the Byzantines will act treacherously and prepare for the battle.[19]

Muslim biographical and traditional literature reflects this sense of conflict between the surrounding empires and the religions they represented. When the Jews suppressed the Christians in Najran, the Abyssinian Christians invaded Yemen to suppress the Jews. The aforementioned attack of Abraha was probably turned back by an outbreak of smallpox.[20] The occasion of Abraha's invasion of Mecca arose according to Ibn Ishaq out of his desire to destroy the temple of the Ka'ba established by Abraham. Abdu'l-Muttalib, the grandfather of the Prophet prays "O God, a man protects his dwelling, so protect Thy dwellings. Let not their cross and their craft overcome Thy craft."[21] Monologues of this type are polemic inventions and the story contains many elements that anticipate Islam and Islamic conceptions such as the "religion of Abraham." But it also reflects the attitude of the Arabs toward outside domination, whether by Christians or Zoroastrians. Muhammad was aware of these events and mentioned them in the Qur'an. Surah Al Fil (the Elephant), one of the early Meccan surahs states the following:

> Seest thou not how thy Lord dealt with the people of the Elephant? did he not make their treacherous plan go astray? And he sent against them flights of birds striking them with stones of baked clay.[22]

---

[19] Abu Dawud, *Hadith*, v. 3, p. 1194.
[20] Ibn Ishaq, 2003, pp. 20-30.
[21] Ibn Ishaq, 2003, p. 26.
[22] *The Meaning of the Holy Qur'an*, trans. Yusuf Ali, Maryland: Amana Publications, 1999, p. 1700, surah 105:1-4.

Later, the Persians invaded Yemen and captured Sana'a from the Abyssinians. Arabia had become a neutral zone between the great Roman and Persian empires. Conflicts between these two empires were often settled in battle in this neutral zone. Each empire had its client states that it supported as surrogates in the ongoing struggle. Arab soldiers fought on opposite sides, and religious conversion as a sign of loyalty was often expected. The movement from one foreign domination to another is summarized by Ibn Ishaq as follows:

> The period of Abyssinian domination from the entry of Aryat to the death of Masruq ibn Abraha at the hands of the Persians and the expulsion of the Abyssinians was seventy-two years.[23]

There is an interpretive element in these stories. It is possible that the expression of empire associated with monotheistic religion, in the early Muslim writings, is meant as a precursor to Islam, the last and the "best" of the empires based on religion. The Muslim biographers include citations from the Qur'an, concerning these events and thus use their "history" in the task of exegesis, explaining the Qur'an. When Dhu Nuwas the Jewish king of Yemen slaughtered the Christians of Najran, Ibn Ishaq notes, "Concerning Dhu Nuwas and that army of his, God revealed to his apostle . . ." and Ishaq goes on to cite surah 85:4-8. The Christians mentioned are presented as "Muslims" of the previous revelation also fitting Islamic conceptions that all true believers of history were actually Muslims.[24] These events seem to provide the backdrop illustrating the Muslim view of history and their idea of the establishment of the kingdom of God on earth. It is a political kingdom associated with empires.

The Jewish presence in Arabia is also quite significant. A tombstone at Al-Hijr from as early as 45 BCE mentions the occupant as "Yehudaya." Samuel Kurinsky notes that Jewish traders in Arabia of this period were able to keep Roman historians and traders in the dark about their sources of cinnamon and East Indies spices. Jewish agents and scouts were involved in the Roman invasion of Arabia in 24-25 BCE. Jewish settlers apparently established many of the communities of Arabia such as Yathrib and Khaybar, and their very names may be etymologically related to Hebrew.[25]

---

23   Ibn Ishaq, 2003, p. 34.
24   Ibn Ishaq, 2003, p. 17.
25   Samuel Kurinsky, *The Arabs and the Jews Part I: The Pre-Islamic Period*, www.hebrewhistory.info/factpapers/fp043-1_preislam, pp. 9-16.

The economic circumstances of the period are not what they appear. Until recently, Western scholars followed the lead of the early Muslim historians in describing Mecca as the center of thriving overland trade routes.[26] These historians also described Mecca as a bustling urban center. Modern scholarship has shown that Mecca was not the important economic center that Arab tradition claimed. Patricia Crone's in-depth discussion of the trade routes of the time indicates that Arabia was a declining economic backwater and certainly not the center of any major spice trade in the period of Muhammad's life. Greek and Roman geographers show no indication of Arabia containing significant urban centers either. Peters mentions this as follows:

> There is no notice by Procopius of the fugitive "Makoraba" sited in Arabia by the Greek geographer Ptolemy, and neither mentions nor even has space for the Quays who are as invisible as Mecca itself in subsequent Byzantine interest in the region.[27]

Crone notes that perfume was possibly one of the few significant trade items moving though Arabia, probably because it was popular locally. Ibn Ishaq describes an event that seems to confirm this as follows:

> The B. 'Abdu Manaf brought out a bowl full of scent (they assert that some of the women of the tribe brought it out to them) and they put it for their allies in the mosque beside the Ka'ba and they dipped their hands into it and they and their allies took a solemn oath. Then they rubbed their hands on the Ka'ba strengthening the solemnity of the oath. For this reason they were called the Scented Ones.[28]

Crone also notes that trade had long since bypassed Arabia in favor of sea routes through the Persian Gulf and the Red Sea. This is obliquely confirmed by the early Muslim writers. Both Ibn Ishaq and Ibn Kathir mention a Byzantine merchant ship wrecked off the coast of Arabia whose wood was used in the reconstruction of the Ka'ba prior to Islam, a work supervised

---

[26] Although it should be frankly admitted that Muir in the nineteenth century was aware that Mecca had fallen into obscurity due to the switching of trade routes to the Red Sea. Patricia Crone's thesis is well anticipated in his writings. See Muir, 1975, pp. lxxxix-xci.

[27] F. E. Peters, *Muhammad and the Origins of Islam*, Brookfield: Ashgate, 1999, p. 64.

[28] Ibn Ishaq, 2003, pp. 56-7.

by a Coptic Christian.[29] We can see no reason to invent a story like this and it seems to confirm the economic circumstances of the time. Arabia was declining and economically depressed as well as a political football. The trade carried on from Arabia was largely in food and leather products on a subsistence level.

> The Nessan papyri show us a group of Ismaelites who were active at Nessana, some sixty kilometers from Gaza, and who traded in wool, camels, donkeys, grain, and the like, that is, in commodities similar to those handled by Quraysh at very much the same place and time. For what it is worth, the evidence does not suggest that the Meccans dominated the exchange of goods between north Arabia and south Syria, let alone that they enjoyed a monopoly of it.[30]

These would be factors that could have encouraged a nativist movement of the type that Crone suggests, a movement to elevate Arabia from its intermediary position on the political stage, and to provide new opportunities for economic gain to the impoverished Arab tribes. Muir posited a similar thought in the nineteenth century.[31]

One final element in the economic structure of Arabia is worthy of note, the intertribal cooperative confederation of *hums*. *Hums* was a cooperative system between the tribes that reduced tribal raiding by enlisting the Bedouin in the process of trade.

F. E. Peters says that the tribe to which Muhammad belonged, Hashim, invented the *hums* to activate the Meccan economy in reaction to the limitation created by Persian and Byzantine monopoly of trade.

> The Hums, as we shall see, was a confederation of tribes pledged to guarantee the security of Mecca, its House, and the Holy Quraysh. And because trade on any scale in Arabia was rendered difficult by the presence everywhere of predatory bedouin tribes, the agreements (ilaf) negotiated by Hashim with the bedouin provided the final link in the chain of commercial opportunity . . . He

---

[29] Ibn Ishaq, 2003, p. 84.
[30] Patricia Crone, *Meccan Trade and the Rise of Islam*, New Jersey: Princeton University Press, 1987, p. 141.
[31] Muir, 1975, p. xciv.

managed it (hostile bedouin), according to this same source by engaging the bedouin in the commerce, using their camels, and taking their goods on consignment in return for a share in the profits.[32]

Ibn Ishaq describes the *hums* largely as an exploitative system of taxation utilized by the major tribe in Mecca, the Quraysh.[33] Nevertheless, there are striking similarities between this system and the pattern that Muhammad utilized in creating the *ummah* or congregation of the faithful.[34] The *ummah* functioned as a supratribal confederation for both military and economic cooperation bound together by the common bond of Islam. This was a confederacy motivated by theology. The harsh Arab environment precluded mutual plunder, and so the idea of *ummah* (*hums*) became one of important economic innovation and set the stage, through intertribal unity, for the Islamic wars of expansion during the seventh and eighth centuries. The military element also followed a pattern that already existed among northern Arab tribes. These tribes established military and economic treaties with the Byzantines to circumvent the decline in Arabian trade. These treaties were often facilitated by the tribes converting to the Christian faith. Peters notes the following:

> Arab units were incorporated into the Roman army, and in the fourth century CE the Romans (after this period often called Byzantines in modern scholarship) began to conclude formal treaties (spondai, faedera) with the leaders of various tribal groups, probably those already converted to Christianity, to serve where the needs of the empire dictated.[35]

As the power of the Byzantines faded around the time of the Prophet, economic problems triggered by the breakdown of established tribal alliances perhaps inspired Muhammad to advance the idea of a uniquely Arab monotheism as a new basis for tribal unity as well as economic and military advance.

> In 575, when Muhammad was small boy . . . the Byzantines had lost control of the eastern Maritimes and were carrying Indian

---

[32] F. E. Peters, *Muhammad and the Origins of Islam*, p. 69.
[33] Ibn Ishaq, 2003, pp. 87-9.
[34] Ibn Ishaq, 2003, pp. 87-9.
[35] F. E. Peters, The Arabs on the Eve of Islam, Introduction xix.

goods only to Sassanian ports. The overland spice trade through
Arabia was dead. International trade through Mecca was even
less likely in the lifetime of Muhammad than in the time of
Hashim.[36]

The division of Arab society with its different tribal units, each with its own
tribal idols, precluded the creation of a unified economic and military power.
It seems possible that Muhammad conceived Islam, faith in "One God," as
the glue to hold together this new *hums*; this new military confederation of
Arabian tribes.

C. Elements in the Biographical Tradition on the Early Life of the Prophet

1. The Religion of Abraham as Distinct from Judaism and Christianity

The early life of Muhammad in the biographical literature is a product
of a thoroughly polemic tradition. Its purpose is to demonstrate that
Muhammad is the last Prophet, and that Islam is the final revelation. It arose
largely out of a need to define Islam as something different, better, and yet
somehow primeval with regard to the other monotheistic traditions. This is
accomplished in a number of ways. The Muslim writers defined Islam as
the primeval monotheistic religion, the "religion of Abraham." The Qur'an,
of course, was the foundation of this conception. In Muhammad's theology,
all true believers are Muslims, whether they are called Christians or Jews or
not. There is an implicit syncretistic element in this meant to appeal to Jews
and Christians while yet exalting Islam as both final and primeval. Ibn Ishaq
describes how the Arabs had fallen away from their primeval monotheism.

They say that the beginning of stone worship among the sons
of Ismail was when Mecca became too small for them and they
wanted more room in the country. Everyone who left the town took
with him a stone from the sacred area to do honor to it. Wherever
they settled they set it up and walked round it as they went round
the Ka'ba. This led them to worship what stones they pleased and
those which made an impression on them. Thus as generations

---

[36] F. E. Peters, *Muhammad and the Origins of Islam*, p. 71.

passed they forgot their primitive faith and adopted another religion for that of Abraham and Ismail. They worshipped idols and adopted the same errors as the peoples before them.[37]

This is a backreading into history, a myth created to connect Arabia and Abraham, while at the same time side stepping Judaism and Christianity. This enabled the early Muslim biographers to deny influence of other religions upon Islam by claiming that Islam was the original monotheism restored by revelation from Allah through Muhammad. Ibn Ishaq's work begins with a genealogy of Muhammad through Abraham back to Adam which, from Abraham, is an exact copy of the Gospel of Luke 3:34-38 with the exception that the name Cainan, mentioned twice in Luke, is only mentioned once by Ibn Ishaq.[38] Muhammad established a pedigree for Arab primitive monotheism based on ideas already widely circulated in the Middle East.

> As regards history, they took up an idea that had circulated at least since the time of the Jewish historian Josephus (d. c. CE 110), that the Arabs were descendants of Ishmael (Ant. 1.214, 2210). With it, they fashioned a religious pedigree for themselves, narrating how Ishmael and his father Abraham had gone to Mecca together and founded the original Muslim sanctuary.[39]

Various aspects of Arab culture were preserved and glorified by this means. The Meccan sanctuary that had been protected and preserved by the Quraysh is now seen as the creation of Abraham. Quraysh were the purest descendants of Ishmael. As a device for "Arabism," it was exquisite. It is possible that Muhammad was aided in this device by pre-Islamic notions of monotheism not directly connected to the monotheistic religions. Watt comments on a group referred to as the "Hanafiya" that was defined by the biographers as "the religion of Abraham."

> It has been recognized by various writers from Julius Wellhausen onward that there is evidence in the Quran that some persons in Mecca, while continuing to recognize the pagan deities

---

[37]   Ibn Ishaq, pp. 35-6.
[38]   Ibn Ishaq, p. 3.
[39]   Robert G. Hoyland, *Arabia and the Arabs: From the Bronze Age to the Coming of Islam*, New York: Routledge, 2001, p. 243.

and to worship them, regarded Allah or God as creator of the world and a "high god" superior to the other deities (29:61-65; 39:38-39 . . . even though God is acknowledged as creator, some men set up "peers" (andad) or "partners" (shuraka) for him (sura 40:12).[40]

Wensinck pointed out that this term, *hanif*, is closely related to the term *ummah*, referring to the community of believers. He considers that it was originally a derogatory term used by the Jews of Medina to refer to Muhammad and his group. Muhammad adopted the term as an *epithet* for Abraham and those of his community.[41] The Muslim biographers paint this in much clearer terms. Ibn Kathir relates a pre-Islamic tradition of the Arab search for a (monotheistic) religion.

> Waraqa b. Nawfal told them, 'By God, you all know that your people have no religion. They have made an enormous mistake and abandoned Abraham's religion . . . O my people, adopt a religion!' And so thereupon they left, traveling all over asking about the Hanifiyya, the religion of Abraham.[42]

In a similar way, the sanctuary at Mecca was appropriated to this primeval religion of Abraham. As a member of the Quraysh tribe, Muhammad must have been well prepared to serve the sanctuary at Mecca, for he had experienced paganism first hand.[43] Rubin notes that the Prophet's daughters were married to pagans with the approval of the Prophet, and his sons were given pagan names according to Ibn Qutayba (d. AH 276) in his Tawil Mukhtalif al-Hadith.[44] Peters also recognizes Muhammad's early life in paganism of the Quraysh tribe. "Muhammad was immersed in the same cult practices in which the Quraysh persisted even after God had sent the Guidance 'to them as well.'"[45] The incident later in Mecca of the "satanic

---

[40]   Watt W. Montgomery, "Belief in a '"High God'" in pre-Islamic Mecca," *The Arabs and Arabia on the Eve of Islam*, Peters, F. E., pp. 307-9.

[41]   A. J. Wensinck, "Muhammad and the Prophets," *The Life of Muhammad*, Uri Rubin, p. 19.

[42]   Ibn Kathir, *Al-Sira al-Nabawiyya*, trans. Trevor Le Gassick, UK: Garner Publishing, 1998, Vol. 1, p. 257.

[43]   Hoyland, Robert G., 2001, p. 121.

[44]   Uri Rubin, *The Life of Muhammad*, Brookfield: Ashgate, 1998, p. 73.

[45]   F. E. Peters, 1999, p. 131, see also Qur'an 93:7.

verses"[46] is a further indication of the internal struggle that went on inside Muhammad concerning how much of the cultic practices of Mecca he would adopt to his new faith. We shall return to that particular event later. Hawting notes the following:

> It seems that the Muslim sanctuary at Mecca is the result of a sort of compromise between a preexisting pagan sanctuary ideas that had developed first in a Jewish milieu. I envisage that Muslim sanctuary ideas originated first in a Jewish matrix, as did Islam itself. At a certain stage in the development of the new religion, the need arose to assert its independence, and one of the most obvious ways in which this could be done was by establishing a specifically Muslim sanctuary.[47]

Muhammad had frequent contact with Jews in his family and with people whom he possibly encountered in the city of Mecca. Lecker shows the evidence of a Jewish heritage in his family line.

> The book of Muhammad b. Habib (d. 245/860) has a special section on "the Qurashis who were sons of Jewish women" (pp. 506-7) . . . The first names on the list of Qurashis who were born to Jewish women in Ibn Habib's Kitab al munammaq are Safi and Abu Sayfi, the sons of Hashim b. Abd Manaf. Firstly, no one would dare invent such a story concerning the prophet's great grandfather. Secondly, there is some corroborative evidence to this effect . . . Hashim and al-Muttalib, sons of Abd Manaf, had children from the same woman.[48]

Muhammad was thus distantly related to the Jewish community in Yathrib (Medina)! This may have been one of the factors that influenced the Hijra "migration" to Yathrib. This also accounts for the preponderance of Jewish oral traditions in the earlier chapters of the Qur'an. In a similar way, Montgomery

---

[46] We will explain this incident in the next chapter. This refers to several verses located at Qur'an 53:21-22 that were removed from the Qur'an and replaced by other verses.

[47] G. R. Hawting, *Origins of the Muslim Sanctuary at Mecca*, South Illinois University Press, 1982, pp. 27-8.

[48] Michael Lecker, *Jews and Arabs in Pre-and Early Islamic Arabia*, Brookfield: Aldershot, 1999, pp. 1, 18, 29, 30.

Watt mentions Muhammad's possible encounters with Christians in Mecca and on his business trips.

> There were a few Christians in Mecca, of whom one, Khadijah's cousin, Waraqah b. Nawfal, may have influenced Muhammad considerably; but the majority were probably Abyssinian slaves and not well instructed in the faith. Muhammad would also have seen something of Christianity while trading in Syria.[49]

This is testified to in the early Muslim biographers. They, however, give this influence a different interpretation. All of the early mentions of Jews and Christians in the life of Muhammad are meant to demonstrate that they recognized Muhammad was the true Prophet of God. They are a polemic device meant to show that Islam is the true fulfillment of the previous revelations and to demonstrate the perniciousness of those believers, particularly Jews, who despite what they knew, refused to follow Muhammad.

2. Muhammad as the Prophet Predicted by Jewish and Christian Sources

The birth and early life of Muhammad is deeply embellished with hagiographic and miraculous stories derived from Jewish and Christian sources. The Jewish rabbis of the tribe of Banu Qurayza, who effected the conversion of the Yemeni King previously mentioned, are made in Ibn Ishaq's history into sentinels of the coming Prophet.

> When lo from Qurayza came a rabbi wise, among the Jews respected. 'Stand back from a city preserved;' he said, 'for Mecca's prophet of Quraysh true-guided.' . . . 'I hope thereby for a reward from Muhammad's Lord. I knew not that there was a pure temple devoted to God in Mecca's vale.[50]

Thus the Jews, according to this account, were aware long before Muhammad's birth of his name, his birth city, his hijra (migration) to Medina, and that the true temple would be in Mecca. The Qur'an, as we shall see

---

[49]   Watt W. Montgomery, *Muhammad at Medina*, p. 315.
[50]   Ibn Ishaq, 2003, p. 11.

later, constantly accuses the Jews of ignoring what was already present in their scriptures, namely, predictions of the coming of Muhammad. This is a polemic device putting words in the mouths of the Jews.[51] Banu Qurayza is the Jewish tribal group that Muhammad had destroyed in Medina after the Battle of the Trench. So the passage also serves as anticipatory indictment of the Jews who knew who Muhammad was and yet conspired against him. These polemic "prophesies" often serve multiple purposes. Ibn Kathir tells the story of the "appearance of a star at the birth of the messenger of God." A Jew living among the Banu Qurayza named Ibn al-Hayyiban predicted the coming of the Prophet based on this, but then said as follows:

> His time is near for you but don't hasten to him, O Jews, for he is sent to shed blood and capture the women and children of those who oppose him.[52]

Ibn Kathir goes on to mention two young men of Banu Qurayza who had heard this prophecy and saved their lives by converting to Islam at the time of the execution of the males of the tribe. Ibn Ishaq tells a similar tale of a star interpreted by a Jew as announcing the birth of Muhammad: "Tonight has risen a star under which Ahmad is to be born."[53]

These are thinly veiled borrowings of the star of Bethlehem story that serve the dual purpose of demonstrating signs of the Prophet in keeping with the story of Jesus and showing the culpability of the Jews. It anticipates that which the early Muslims felt needed explaining.

The early biographers affirm that all the previous holy books foretold the coming of Muhammad. Ibn Kathir states the following:

> The rabbis and the priests found in their books descriptions of him and of his time along with inferences relating to him from their prophets.[54]

---

[51] It is worth noting that the Torah does record in Deuteronomy 18:15 "The Lord your God shall raise up a Prophet like me from your midst," although the passage goes on to qualify that only a Prophet who makes predictions that come true is to be considered a true Prophet of God. This may explain why later Islamic writers were at pains to put predictions that have come true into the mouth of the Prophet.

[52] Ibn Kathir, *al-Sira*, Vol. 1, p. 213.

[53] Ibn Ishaq, 2003, p. 70.

[54] Ibn Kathir, *al-Sira*, Vol. 1, p. 207.

Kathir also notes from the book of Daniel that Muhammad is regarded as final conqueror through the faith of Islam.

> He relays an Arab tradition about Daniel's response to Nebuchadnezzar's dream concerning the gold, silver, brass, iron, and clay statue. The stone which struck down this idol is God's final prophet who will strike down all other religions and nations.[55]

Islam now supersedes the Christian faith in that the final world ruler, a Messianic role, is attributed to the Prophet. To connect the prophetic lineage it is claimed that Muhammad shared the role of shepherd with two main biblical figures, Jesus from the New Testament and Moses from the Old Testament. "The apostle of God used to say, There is no prophet but has shepherded a flock. When they said, 'You, too, apostle of God?' He said, 'Yes.'." Muhammad states that he is "what Abraham my father prayed for and the good news of Jesus."[56]

Ibn Kathir goes on to quote several verses from the Qur'an that asserts the Bible predicts the coming of Muhammad:

> And remember, Jesus, the son of Mary, said, 'O Children of Israel! I am the messenger of Allah (sent) to you confirming the Law (which came) before me, and giving glad tidings of a messenger to come after me, whose name shall be Ahmad. But when he came to them with clear signs, they said, 'this is evident sorcery!' Who doth greater wrong than the one who invents falsehood against Allah, even as he is being invited to Islam.[57]

Ibn Ishaq is the first Muslim writer to cite John's gospel concerning the coming of the "comforter" or paraclete as referring to Muhammad.

---

[55] Ibn Kathir, *al-Sira*, Vol 1. p. 207.

[56] Ibn Ishaq, 2003, p. 72. It is interesting to note that Muhammad misunderstood the role of Jesus as "shepherd" at this point, for the early Christian writings give no indication that Jesus ever functioned as an actual shepherd. He was a carpenter (Matt. 13:55). He did, however, use the image for himself in his parables (John 10:11-16). It is possible that this is a genuine tradition of Muhammad since later Muslims would not have been so naïve about the background of Christ.

[57] Surah 61:6, Ibn Kathir also cites surah 7:157, 48:29, 3:81, and 2:129.

But when the comforter has come whom God will send to you from the Lord's presence, and the spirit of truth which will have gone forth from the Lord's presence . . . The Munahhemana (God bless and preserve him!) in Syriac is Muhammad; in Greek he is the paraclete.[58]

These additions to the text are probably in response to early Muslim debates and discussions with the Christians of the Middle East. These debates provided them with the information required to write back into history what was needed to respond to Christian criticisms. This interpretation of the "paraclete" has remained a stock-in-trade of Muslim apologists down to the present day even though Muhammad patently does not fit the figure described as the paraclete,[59] and the interpretation requires an impossible alteration of the Greek word. History is written as anticipating the content of the Qur'an and to demonstrate its veracity. It is history written as exegesis of the Qur'an.

In a similar way, various Christian figures from the early life of the Prophet function as foretellers and confirmers. In Ibn Kathir's biography Abdul Muttalib, the grandfather of the Prophet is made to say as follows:

O Baraka, do not neglect my son. I found him with some boys close to the lote tree; and the people of the book (i.e., Christians and Jews) claim that my boy will be the Prophet of this nation.[60]

Muhammad's earliest contact with Christians, according to Ibn Kathir occurs when his wet-nurse Halima passed a caravan of Christians. They wanted to take him with them to be their king as he was "a person of great importance."[61] Ibn Ishaq spends four pages telling the story of the Christian monk Bahira who receives a vision that the promised Prophet of God is coming in a caravan to him. Muhammad is left watching the baggage so that Bahira must summon him specifically to see the marks of apostleship "which he knew and found in his books." Having examined Muhammad Bahira says to Abu Talib:

---

[58]   Ibn Ishaq, 2003, p. 104. The story is also told in Ibn Kathir, Vol. 1, p. 238.
[59]   From the biblical text, the paraclete is clearly a spiritual entity that is alive and active in the Church. Muhammad, even by Muslim estimations, is dead. John 14:15-17.
[60]   Ibn Kathir, *al-Sira*, Vol. 1, p. 173.
[61]   Ibn Kathir, *al-Sira*, Vol. 1, p. 166.

Take your nephew back to his country and guard him carefully against the Jews, for by Allah! If they see him and know about him what I know, they will do him evil; a great future lies before this nephew of yours, so take him home quickly.[62]

Ali Dashti, commenting on these prophecies notes:

Muhammad's protector and guardian Abu Talib, who died without embracing Islam, must certainly have heard nothing and seen nothing. Muhammad himself did not know before his appointment that he was going to be a prophet, as verse 17 of sura 10 (yunos) eloquently attests as follows: "Had God so willed, I should not have recited it to you, and He would not have made it known to you. I dwelt among you for a lifetime before it."[63]

This is a reflection of the kind of contradictions that polemic literature of this type often falls into. Ibn Kathir tells a similar story of an unnamed Christian monk who meets Muhammad while he is leading a caravan for Khadija and he affirms that Muhammad is a Prophet. Khadija's cousin Waraqa bin Nawfal is a Christian, and he also affirms that Muhammad is the promised Prophet. Another story concerns Salman, the Persian, who was converted to Christianity, but was sold into slavery in Arabia to the Jewish tribe of Banu Qurayza.[64] He recognized Muhammad as the Prophet predicted by the Christian bishop who had cared for him. He was manumitted from his slavery after his conversion to Islam with help from the Prophet and fought at the Battle of the Trench. Salman also claimed to have met Jesus.[65] Though formerly a Zoroastrian, he becomes a Christian, and then later, converts to Islam on the remembered advice of his Christian mentor. He asks of his bishop "But what if he tells me to abandon your faith and practices." The

---

[62] Ibn Ishaq, 2003, pp. 80-1.

[63] Ali Dashti, *23 years*; *A study of the prophetic career of Mohammad*, trans. from the Persian by F. R. C. Bagley. Costa Mesa, California: Mazda, 1994, p. 2.

[64] It is remarkable how often the Banu Qurayza are mentioned in the early stories of Muhammad's life, and always in a negative context. It is as if the early Muslim authors understood the importance of explaining this event of the Medinan period of the Prophet. It is equally remarkable how little modern Western writers have focused on this event and the precedents it sets.

[65] Ibn Kathir, *al-Sira,* Vol. 1, pp. 214-9.

Bishop replies "no matter what he orders you, he brings the truth with him."[66] These stories reflect Muhammad as the last Prophet who would always be recognized by true Christians. The polemic purpose is amusingly obvious. Both Ibn Ishaq and Ibn Kathir include a lengthy poem by Waraqa in praise of the Prophet and what he would accomplish. Ibn Ishaq concludes his section on the prophecies of Jews and Christians with this eulogy:

> The apostle of God grew up, God protecting him and keeping him from the vileness of heathenism because he wished to honor him with apostleship, until he grew up to be the finest of his people in manliness, the best in character, most noble in lineage, the best neighbor, the most kind, truthful, reliable, the furthest removed from filthiness and corrupt morals, through loftiness and nobility, so that he was known among his people as 'The Trustworthy' because of the good qualities which God had implanted in him.[67]

The Qur'an contains numerous references to the perfections of the Prophet, and the necessity of Muslims to imitate his behavior.[68] It is also true that the Qur'an mentions the sins of Muhammad, and these passages are largely ignored by the Muslim commentators or explained away.

There is probably little in these stories that is historical. These accounts were written, at the earliest, one hundred and thirty years after the time of Muhammad and only exist in editions dating from far later than that. They are a backreading into history designed to anticipate certain verses in the Qur'an, to demonstrate the superiority of that faith over others and to indict those, particularly Jews, who refused to believe in Muhammad. They are formed from a position of hindsight to create in the "history" of Muhammad those elements that were by then understood to be lacking in the story. In a backhanded way, they do demonstrate the reality of the Jewish presence in Arabia and the Jewish rejection of Muhammad as the Prophet of God.

---

66   Ibn Kathir, *al-Sira*, Vol. 1, p. 221.
67   Ibn Ishaq, 2003, p. 81.
68   See 33:21: Apart from the practices (sunna) of the Prophet it would be impossible to follow Islam. None of the five pillars of Islam is explained in its canonical form in the text of the Qur'an. Even the confession of faith of Islam (*shahada*) is found nowhere in the Qur'an in its canonical form.

3. Miraculous Signs of Prophethood

Miraculous signs are a common feature of all the hagiographic material of this period, whether Jewish, Christian, or Islamic. In the Islamic tradition, some of these elements are clearly borrowings from Jewish and Christian literature while others seem unique to Arab traditions. An example of the latter is the stories of shooting stars that are one of the significant signs of Muhammad's prophethood in Arab tradition.

> As to the Arab soothsayers they had been visited by satans from the jinn with reports which they had secretly overheard before they were prevented from hearing by being pelted with stars . . . When the prophet's mission came the satans were prevented from listening and they could not occupy the seats in which they used to sit and steal the heavenly tidings for they were pelted with stars, and the jinn knew that that was due to an order which God had commanded concerning mankind.[69]

The story of the shooting stars anticipates Muhammad's ministry that would bring about Satan's fall. The shooting stars tradition was associated with supernatural signs for the collapse of the old order and the emergence of a new one. In Sunni tradition, it was related to the prophetic mission.[70] This tradition initially conceived of Muhammad as a mere man, who is elevated to the prophetic ministry. Thus, the stars appeared at the time the prophetic revelations began, around 610 CE. As time went on, Muhammad's role was augmented by the concept of ontological prophethood. The shooting stars described in the biographies of Muhammad focused more on emerging preexistent attributes of Muhammad. Consequently, the time of the shooting stars moves back to the time of Muhammad's birth, some forty years earlier.

> The combined evidence of Ibn Ishaq's report, Al Waqidi's two reports, Ibn Sa'd's report and that of Ibn Abi Shayba shows that the association of the shooting stars tradition with the beginning of the prophetic mission existed at an early stage of Sunni tradition. On the other hand, the occurrence of the Ibn Kharrabudh report

---

69 Ibn Ishaq, 2003, p. 90.
70 Adrien Leites, "Sira and the Question of Tradition," in *The Biography of Muhammad* by Motzki, Harald, Brill, 2000, p. 55.

in Ibn Bakkar shows, in view of the reconstruction just indicated, that the association of the view of the shooting stars tradition with the birth of Muhammad was integrated into Sunni tradition by the turn of the second/eight century.[71]

Thus, the initially human Prophet of the earliest Muslim writings is replaced by a superhuman Prophet who is the firstborn of creation. Ibn Sa'd quotes Muhammad as saying, "I was the first at the creation, and I was already a prophet while Adam was still between spirit and body." The Muhammad of Islam, over time, gradually bifurcates into two separate entities, the Muhammad of devotion and the Muhammad of history. Wensinck notes that "Muslim teachings emerge directly from Christian concepts at this point."[72] Adam himself asks for forgiveness for his sins for Muhammad's sake. Allah asks him how he knew of Muhammad, and he responded with the *Shahada* that is written on God's throne. God forgives Adam because of his confession of Muhammad as the final Prophet and states as follows:

> Adam was created in Muhammad's likeness . . . Were it not for Muhammad I would not have created you . . . This is a recognition and affirmation of his honor and high stature among all religions and upon the tongues of all the Prophets.[73]

Thus, during in the first one hundred years of Islam, the human prophet is superceded by the glorified Prophet as Muhammad is successively glorified into a superhuman figure. He has become a Christ-figure for the Muslim world. This is ironic given that Muhammad emphatically denies such a role for himself in the Qur'an.[74]

There is an exegetical purpose as well. The Qur'an mentions shooting stars and explains them as missiles launched by angels at the satans in the heavenly realm who were trying to eavesdrop on the revelations being sent down by God to Muhammad.

---

[71] Adrian Leites, 2000, p. 61.

[72] Wensinck, 1999, p. 14.

[73] Ibn Kathir, *al-Sira*, Vol. 1, pp. 209, 231.

[74] Qur'an 5:19, 7:184, 11:2, 13:7 and numerous other passages. There are several instances where God rebukes the Prophet for his behavior, which we will note later (such as 80:1-10). Muhammad's favorite title for himself is "merely a warner."

And we have (from of old) adorned the lowest heaven with lamps,
and we have Made such (lamps) as missiles to drive away the evil
ones, and have prepared for them the penalty of the blazing fire.[75]

This literature thus explains the content of the Qur'an.

Many other signs are mentioned in the biographical literature. At the time
of Muhammad's birth, the fires go out in the Zoroastrian fire temples. Idols
among the pagans fell over or announced the coming of Muhammad. An
exhausted donkey becomes lively at the mere touch of the baby Muhammad.
There is a miraculous lactation of an aged camel and Muhammad's wet nurse
Halima during a famine.[76] Trees and rocks bow down before Muhammad as
he travels in Khadija's caravan.[77] The Arab soothsayers receive anguished
messages from their familiar spirits that the time of idolatry is coming to an
end. When a calf is sacrificed at the Ka'ba just before Muhammad begins
his ministry:

> . . . a voice more penetrating than I have ever heard coming out
> of the belly of the calf (this was a month or so before Islam),
> saying, "O blood red one, the deed is done, a man will cry beside
> God none."[78]

There is also the story of the cleansing of Muhammad's heart. This, like the
shooting star story, is found both in the early life of Muhammad and at the time
of his Miraj, or night journey to Jerusalem and heaven. Ibn Kathir records fully
four different versions of the event. In each, his chest is opened and a black clot
of blood is removed representing sin. In one, two men dressed in white carry
out the operation, in another two birds, in a third two angels, and in the fourth
Gabriel himself.[79]

---

[75]   Qur'an 67:5, see also 37:6-10, 72:8-9.

[76]   Ibn Kathir, *al-Sira*, Vol. 1, pp. 161167. Part of the purpose of this story is to
       explain why Muhmmad was merciful to the tribe of Hawazin after the battle of
       Hunayn. He was in the process of separating the male and female prisoners when
       a woman pointed out to him that Halima his wet-nurse was a member of their
       tribe. In response to this, Muhammad did not carry out any executions of the male
       prisoners, and after they were induced to accept Islam, the women of the tribe
       were returned to their men.

[77]   Ibn Kathir, *al-Sira*, Vol. 1, p. 175

[78]   Ibn Ishaq, 2003, p. 93

[79]   Ibn Kathir, *al-Sirar*, Vol. 1, pp. 162-165.

The borrowing of prophetic or Messianic images from the Jews or Christians is also augmented by designed Messianic motifs that may have a Jewish or Christian source or may simply indicate events in Muhammad's background that have been interpreted in a messianic light. The story of discovering the well of Zamzam by Muhammad's grandfather seems like a prelude of the life of Muhammad. It is the well of Zamzam that God provided water to Ishmael through Hagar's prayer in the wilderness. Somehow this well was lost later by the Arab tribes as they fell back into idolatry. Therefore, finding the lost well in the holy sanctuary implies the character of the coming ministry of Muhammad. Muhammad was to restore the Meccan Sanctuary that had been lost since the time of Ishmael. The story is designed to emphasize Muhammad's divine ministry and his outstanding position. Hawting suspects that

> The tradition about the finding of Zamzam is a reworking of a tradition found in Judaism about the loss and rediscovery of certain sanctuary vessels or treasures. In its Jewish versions the story has Messianic overtones . . . Zamzam does function as a symbol for the sanctuary as a whole note how, in the Muslim versions of the story of Hagar and Ismael, the appearance of Zamzam in effect begins the history of the Meccan sanctuary.[80]

Abu al Muttalib's vow before the Ka'ba is a similar story.

> The story of Abu al-Muttalib's vow is linked in the Sira with the story of the discovery of Zamzam. The vow was made because at the time when he was digging Zamzam, and Quraysh contested his right to it, Abu al-Muttalib had only one son and felt that he needed more to support him; he, therefore, vowed to God that he would sacrifice one of them if He would give him ten. This does not make obvious sense, and the story of the son selected for sacrifice, and subsequently freed, is the father of the Prophet himself.[81]

The story seems to borrow the motif of the sacrifice of Isaac as applying to the father of the Prophet. Many more examples exalting the Meccan sanctuary could be cited. Muhammad wanders away from his family and is discovered

---

[80]   Gerald R. Hawting, *The 'Sacred Offices' of Mecca from Jahiliyya to Islam.* JSAI 13(1990): p 81.

[81]   Ibid., p. 81.

in Mecca circumambulating the Ka'ba, which seems a borrowing of Jesus in the temple at age of twelve. During the rebuilding of the Ka'ba, a syriac inscription is found that a Jew translates. There God declares, "Mecca is God's holy house."[82] Wensinck has traced the extensive borrowings from Christian notions of Christ. Muhammad will cleanse his people from their sins (Matt. 1:21), Jews are murdered at the birth of Muhammad (Matt. 2:16-18). Waraqa explains that he can now die because he has seen the promised one (Luke 2:29-31). Abd al-Muttalib blesses the newborn in the Ka'ba (Luke 2:28). The miracle of the feeding of the multitudes (Mark 6:30-44), which imitates the NT passage down "to the smallest details." Muhammad's teaching on the signs of the end of the age (Matt. 24). Muhammad riding a donkey (Matt. 21:1-5), Muhammad as the cornerstone (Ephesians 2:20), number of disciples, 12 and 70 (Matt. 10:1 and Luke 10:1), the similarity of Umar and Peter and many more examples.[83]

4. Stories Created in Anticipation of Later Events in Muhammad's Life

In the Muslim historical tradition, Muhammad is proved to be the last prophet promised by God both through the Qur'an and through the previous revelations. If one who knows the older revelations denies the prophethood of Muhammad, he is, in a sense, more sinful than polytheists who have never had access to the earlier revelations.

> We were at that time polytheists and worshipped idols, while they, the Jews, were people with scriptures who had knowledge we did not. There was always enmity between us and them. They predicted the coming of a prophet and even prayed for victory in battle over their enemies by the name of the prophet, yet later when Muhammad came they rejected him. These words were revealed. They formerly prayed for victory against those who disbelieved.[84]

---

[82] Ibn Ishaq, 2003, p. 86.

[83] Wensinck, 1999, pp. 21-25. It is possible that some of the similarities noted by Wensinck are merely coincidental, but the extent of the borrowings is so massive that it is entirely accurate to say that the Islamic biographers and Hadith collectors in the first three centuries of Islam appropriated the entire corpus of Christian devotional notions about Christ and applied them to Muhammad. This syncretism was applied, it would seem, to facilitate the conversion of the largely Christian population of the Middle East to Islam.

[84] Ibn Kathir, al-Sira, Vol. 1, p. 211.

Similar anticipatory hostility is noticed in the following story. Abu Karib, as we noted earlier, was a Yemeni King who embraced Judaism through two rabbis in Medina from the tribe of Banu Qurayza. These rabbis predicted the emigration of Muhammad, the Prophet, and persuaded the king not to destroy Yathrib (Medina) to avenge the killing of his son. They also predicted that the coming prophet would demolish the two tribes that killed Abu Karib's son. "In rage against two Jewish tribes who live in Yathrib who richly deserve the punishment of a fateful day."[85] This story seems to originate in a later event in Muhammad's life: the Prophet's revenge on two Jewish tribes in Yathrib, the Al-Nadir and the Banu Qurayza. In Ibn Ishaq's writing, through the mouth of Jewish rabbis, Muhammad's judgments on the Jews are legitimized while demonstrating that the Jewish rejection of Muhammad's prophethood was without excuse. This concern to create a matrix of justification is a strong sign of the historicity of the later events.

G. R. Hawting makes an even more novel thesis in his book *The Idea of Idolatry and the Emergence of Islam*. He sees the passages in the Qur'an that purportedly deal with idolaters as actually referring to other monotheists. His thesis is that the primary arguments of the Qur'an against disbelief and associating others with God were directed not at polytheists, but against Jews and Christians. He states the following:

> This book questions how far Islam arose in arguments with real polytheists and idolaters, and suggests that it was concerned rather with other monotheists whose monotheism it saw as inadequate and attacked polemically as the equivalent of idolatry.[86]

Hawting's point is an interesting one. He calls Islam the "result of an intra-monotheist polemic."[87] The stories of the early life of Muhammad do seem to contain far more material directed at the Jews as the enemies of the Prophet than against the Meccan "idolaters." Perhaps the real struggle of early Islam was against other competing forms of monotheism that were non-Arab. This study is not attempting to answer that question, but perhaps it will generate material that relates to it.

---

[85]   Ibn Ishaq, p. 8.
[86]   G. R. Hawting, *The Idea of Idolatry and the Emergence of Islam*, Cambridge University Press, 1999, p. xiii.
[87]   Hawting, p. 7.

5. Possible Historical Points in These Narratives

Other than a probable birth date around 570 CE, very little in these narratives has any sort of a historical basis. Their main interest lies in how they indicate the historicity of some later events in the life of the Prophet, as well as showing us the mentality of backreading into history. There are a few points that have merit as possible historical events.

One of these are the many stories told about Muhammad's wet-nurses. This seems a trivial point, but the respect shown by Muhammad for certain tribes he conquered due to having been suckled by a member of that tribe (he had several wet-nurses according to traditions) would seem to indicate the reality of this. Also the fact that at least one wet-nurse declined to suckle Muhammad because he was an orphan, and there was little economic benefit. It is hard to imagine something like that being made up. Also, the idea that Muhammad suffered from epilepsy has emerged from the stories of his fits told by the wet-nurses. This could be hagiography at work, but it may also explain the stories of Muhammad's trance-like states on some occasions when he received revelation in the later traditions. There could be some kernel of truth to this.

It is also likely that Muhammad was an orphan as this is described in the early histories (and they are quite consistent on this point), and this is also inferred in the Qur'an (surah 93:6). The names and roles of the pagan relatives who cared for Muhammad as an orphan, his grandfather Abdul Muttalib, and uncle Abu Talib, seem likely historical as neither converted to Islam and yet retain a high standing in the Muslim writings albeit with interpolations we have noted earlier.

Some of the stories of Muhammad's travels with Arab caravans seem likely historical though without the fantastic interpolations of meetings with monks and priests. Even a cursory reading of the Qur'an shows the heavy influence of apocryphal stories that circulated in the Jewish and Christian communities of that time so we must posit that the Prophet was meeting people and hearing stories from those communities. Muhammad may have been an Arabian Jew who, because of his later political involvements and their rejection of him as Prophet, broke with the Jewish community. This would explain his much higher level of hostility to Jews than to Christians. No backreading into history could explain something like this, since the Jews after the time of Muhammad were not a significant obstacle for Islam.

Having thus set the stage for the emergence of Islam, the biographers now begin to tell the story of the first revelations of the Qur'an. We shall begin with a study of the Qur'anic content from the earliest chapters of the Qur'an.

CHAPTER 2

THE EARLY REVELATIONS
609-612 CE

This chapter concerns the first two years of Muhammad's prophetic activity. The period is approximately dated from 609/610 to 612 CE. It includes Muhammad's initial call to transmit the "recitations" of the Qur'an and some notion of the response he received. Since the Qur'an is the only document dating from the period, we begin with an analysis of its earliest chapters.

A. The Content of the Qur'an, Early Meccan Period

1. Hellfire, Judgment, and the Bliss of Paradise

There is some debate as to the exact order of the earliest chapters of the Qur'an. We are following the order established by Nöldeke, which, though debated at certain points, is generally based on a system accepted by Muslims.[88] Forty-eight chapters of the Qur'an were revealed during this period, close to half the total number of chapters though less than 10 percent of the total volume of the Qur'an because both the verses and the chapters are much shorter on average than later chapters.[89] These early chapters comprise

---

[88] Theodor Nöldeke, Geschichte des Qorans, Leipzig: Dieterich'sche Verlagsbuchhandlung, 1909, p. ix. The Encyclopedia of Islam has an extensive article on the dating of the Surahs of the Qur'an and the basis for the dating in subject matter and use of words.

[89] These chapters in order from earliest to latest are: 96, 74, 111, 106, 108, 104, 107, 102, 105, 92, 90, 94, 93, 97, 86, 91, 80, 68, 87, 95, 103, 85, 73, 101, 99, 82, 81, 53, 84, 100, 79, 77, 78, 88, 89, 75, 83, 69, 51, 52, 56, 70, 55, 112, 109, 113, 114, and 1. Generally speaking shorter chapters are older and are grouped toward the end of the Qur'an.

a total of 1,197 verses or about 19 percent of the total 6,236 verses in the Qur'an.

What is striking about the early verses of the Qur'an is their preoccupation with the subject of hellfire and judgment. Of the 1,197 verses of these initial forty-eight chapters, four hundred and thirty nine concern descriptions of the coming judgment and the punishments of hell. There is also a limited variation in the literary forms used to express this. "Soon I will cast him into hell-fire!" (74:26), "Burnt soon will he be in a fire of blazing flame" (111:3), "Ye shall certainly see hellfire!" (102:6), "Therefore do I warn you of a fire blazing fiercely" (92:14), "On them will be a fire vaulted over (all round)" (90:20), "Who will enter the great fire, in which they will then neither die nor live" (87:12-13). "Those who persecute the believers . . . will have the penalty of hell, they will have the penalty of the burning fire" (85:10).

Accompanying these verses on hell are apocalyptic descriptions of the destruction of creation. "The day of noise and clamor . . . it is a day whereon men will be like moths scattered about and the mountains will be carded like wool" (101:1, 4-5). "When the earth is shaken to its (utmost) convulsion" (99:1). "When the sky is cleft asunder; when the stars are scattered" (82:1-2). "When the sun . . . is folded up, when the stars fall . . . when the mountains vanish" (81:1-3). "When the sky is rent asunder, . . . when the earth is flattened out" (84:1, 3).

A further strong association is the concept of the weighing of good and bad deeds; "He bears witness (by his deeds)" (100:7), "separate them one from another . . . for the day of sorting out (77:4, 13). "He whose balance (of good deeds) will be (found) heavy, will be in a life of good pleasure and satisfaction. But he whose balance (of good deeds) will be found light will have his home in a (bottomless) pit . . . a fire blazing fiercely" (101:6-9, 11). Angels are appointed "kind and honorable writing down (your deeds): . . . the righteous . . . will be in bliss . . . the wicked . . . in the fire" (82:10-14), "verily the day of sorting out is a thing appointed" (78:17). The idea of two angels recording one's deeds is reminiscent of the earlier Christian work "The Shepherd" by Hermas.[90]

God's judgment in these early chapters is based upon human moral decisions. Primary among the moral failings of man is his self-sufficiency

---

[90]   This early Christian devotional work mentions two angels, one who tempts to do evil and one who tempts to do good. Their location is "in the heart" not on the shoulders as in later Islamic texts. Shepherd of Hermas, Second Book, Command Five, The Angels.

and lack of humility toward God; "man doth transgress all bounds, in that he looketh upon himself as self-sufficient" (96:6-7); "man is to his Lord ungrateful" (100:6); man is condemned as a "scandalmonger and backbiter, who pileth up wealth and layeth it by" (104:1-2); he "repulses the orphan (with harshness) and encourages not the feeding of the indigent" (107:2-3); man is enjoined to "freeing the bondman; or the giving of food in a day of privation to the orphan," (90:13-15). Muhammad himself is encouraged to care for orphans, "Did he not find thee an orphan and give thee shelter (and care)?" (93:6). The day of judgment will come "when the female (infant) buried alive, is questioned—for what crime she was killed" (81:8-9). The Qur'an reflects at this point a deep concern for orphans and the economically oppressed, perhaps as a reflection of Muhammad's own background as an orphan. The Qur'an calls for the reform of Arab society, the forbidding of female infanticide, and, most importantly, the exalted view of Allah as the one true God.

In another segment of these early chapters, man is condemned for rejecting the truth, "Ah woe, that day, to the rejecters of truth" (77:45); those who "treated our signs as false," (78:28); "he gave nothing in charity, nor did he pray!—But on the contrary, he rejected truth and turned away," (75:31-31). The "truth" in this sense refers primarily to the message of the Qur'an. This kind of concern about rejection of the truth would seem to indicate a longer process than seems possible from these early chapters. This is reinforced by the mention of the persecution of believers mentioned above. The fact that the Qur'an seems to open to a conflict already in progress indicates that the Prophet had already been involved in religious dialogue and teaching for some time, to which the Qur'an was really the beginning of the second stage of the conflict. It seems hard to imagine the Prophet threatening people with hell-fire for rejecting the truth, when according to the traditions of Islam he had not even begun preaching Islam publicly.

Accompanying these passages are a number of descriptions of the heavenly bliss which awaits the true believers; "the companions of the right hand (they will be) in gardens (of delight)" (74:39-40). "For those who believe and do righteous deeds, will be gardens, beneath which rivers flow: That is the great salvation (the fulfillment of all desires)" (85:11); "As for the righteous they will be in bliss" (82:14). "Their abode will be the garden" (79:41); a little later the descriptions of the garden become more elaborate. "As to the righteous, they shall be amidst (cool) shades and springs (of water), and (they shall have) fruits—all they desire. Eat ye and drink ye to your heart's content" (77:41-41). "Gardens enclosed and grapevines; companions (feminine) of "equal age" (Ali mistranslates at this point, the phrase means 'round breasts'[91])." (78:33). "We will join them to companions with beautiful, big and lustrous eyes" (52:20). "We have created (their companions) of special creation, and made them virgin-pure (and undefiled)—beloved (by nature), equal in age for the companions of the right hand," (56:35-38). The word *"beloved"* Ibn Kathir points out is *"urub"* meaning desirous of their husbands "like a she-camel in heat."[92] "In them will be (maidens), chaste, restraining their glances, whom no man or jinn before them has touched" (55:56).[93] The phrase uses the Arabic verb "tamatha" that means "to deflower" or "expand the hymen through intercourse."[94] Ibn Kathir in his commentary on the Qur'an describes these young women as being "delightfully passionate with their husbands." When asked about the men's staying power, At-Tirmidhi records the following: "O Allah's Messenger. Will we have sexual intercourse with our wives in paradise?" He said, "The man will be able to have sexual intercourse with a hundred virgins in one day."[95] While these descriptions are clearly addendums to the text, the point of the text itself is clear.

It may be worthwhile to briefly mention the theory of Christoph Luxenberg concerning Aramaic words in the Qur'anic text where he claims that houris, the celestial virgins are really "white grapes." As can be seen from the context above, the interpretation requires many other transformations in order to make sense. Devin Stewart does an excellent job of demonstrating

---

[91]   Ibn Kathir, *Tafsir Ibn Kathir*, trans. Shaykh Safiur-Rahman al-Mubarakpuri, New York: Darussalam Publishers, Vol. 10, p. 333. Ibn Kathir goes on to explain, "They meant by this that the breasts of these girls will be fully rounded and not sagging because they will be virgins, equal in age. This means that they will only have one age."

[92]   Ibn Kathir, *Tafsir*, Vol. 9, p. 430.

[93]   Yusuf Ali is at pains to tone down the sexual content of the imagery here. He states, "Lest grosser ideas of sex should intrude, it is made clear that these companions for heavenly society will be of special creation—of virginal purity." In contrast, the text is plainly sexual. These damsels have not been touched before by jinns or men, the implication being that they will be now. Later, Muslim exegetes whose followers are found down to the modern period describe how these vestal virgins regrow their hymens after every sexual event to insure that the companions of the right hand experience a deflowering with every intercourse. Ali, Abdullah Yusuf, *The Meaning of the Holy Qur'an*, Amana Publications, Note 5240, p. 1411.

[94]   Hanna Kassis, *A Concordance of the Qur'an*, Los Angeles: University of California Press, 1983, p. 1238. This verb occurs in two locations in chapter 55 at verses 56 and 74.

[95]   Ibn Kathir, *Tafsir*, Vol. 9, p. 429.

the implausibility of this interpretation, and how it requires a mass of other emendations in the text. We might point out how difficult it is to explain, among other things, what sort of hymens white grapes have? Stewart also points out that the text has a parallel concept of the young men and servants who will also be available in the garden (ghilman, wildan) that makes the grapevine analogy far-fetched.[96]

It is worth noting some other textual problems in the Qur'an that Stewart discusses in regard to the garden concept. In chapter 56, verse 29, we are introduced to the "talha" trees in the garden, which Ali transliterates "talh," but the noble Qur'an calls "banana trees." These are certainly not typical of the Arabian context. Stewart points out that the text is probably a corruption of the word *tal'in* meaning "date clusters" and that this parallels the Qur'an at 50:10. As to why such simple changes are not discussed more Stewart notes, "one senses that this topic confronts in a tangible fashion widely held Muslim beliefs about the Qur'an, and so produces a certain unease with taking up a line of criticism that potentially questions the basic assumptions of Muslims."[97] We shall note other problems like this as we go along.

When these three categories are put together, descriptions of hell, judgment, and heavenly bliss, they account for the majority of the early verses of the Qur'an. Muhammad was deeply affected by this apocalyptic vision. It supersedes all other aspects in the early revelations.

2. Muhammad's Self-Conception

The second emphasis in the early Qur'an concerns Muhammad's view of himself. This moves clearly through stages that reflect self-doubt gradually giving way to increased confidence in the prophetic call. God plays a direct role in this as he addresses the Prophet directly, either to give him instructions or to encourage, defend or even rebuke him. God initially is the one to define the role of the Prophet as he addresses him directly. "Arise and deliver thy warning! And thy Lord do thou glorify and thy garments keep free from stain! And all abominations shun!" (wa ar rujza fahjur) (74:2-5). This seems

---

[96]   Devin J. Stewart, "Notes on the Emendation of the Qur'an," in *The Qur'an in its Historical Context*, London: Routledge, 2008, pp. 242-4.

[97]   Stewart, 2008, pp. 233-4. If the Qur'an is considered to be the word-for-word dictation of God, then there is no room in such a rigid conception of revelation for even the slightest variation in the text or in the history of its transmission. In fact, the Qur'an has as many textual variations as the New Testament.

to be a direct command to the Prophet to abstain from idolatry. It is apparent again that Muhammad had conflicts early on, at least with members of his own clan. God, in one of the earliest chapters, seems to quote the attitude of those rejecting Muhammad saying, "This is nothing but the word of a mortal" (74:25) in reference to Muhammad's recitation. God defends the Prophet saying, "Soon will I cast him into hell-fire" (74:26).[98] The third chapter to be revealed (111) is supposedly a reference to Muhammad's uncle, Abu Lahab, who opposed Muhammad's teaching. The title and first verse is actually a play on the uncle's name that means "flame"; "Perish the hands of the father of flame! Perish him! . . . Burnt soon will he be in a fire of blazing flame! His wife shall carry the (crackling) wood as fuel!" (111:1, 3-4). It is hard to imagine that such a level of conflict would emerge from just the first two chapters of the Qur'an.

Is it possible that Muhammad had been teaching in this way for some time, and had already attracted the ire of his relatives? Perhaps the Qur'an represents a new effort at self-identification in which Muhammad begins to borrow patterns familiar to him from the other religions present in Arabia. Ibn Kathir's explanation of the event is that Muhammad called the Quraysh out to a mountain where he would declare God's Word to them. After gathering the people Muhammad said, "I am a warner sent to you before the coming of a severe torment." To which Abu Lahab dusted himself off with his hands and said, "Have you gathered us for this? May you perish!"[99] God's response is to declare that the hands of Abu Lahab will perish instead. The story has a strong resemblance to Moses at Sinai.[100] These background explanatory stories are the inventions of a later age. Nevertheless, Allah functions for Muhammad as a defender and even mouthpiece in expressing the Prophet's feelings toward his enemies. Clearly, conflict was present from before the beginnings of the Qur'an.

---

[98]   Ibn Kathir notes that this verse refers to Al-Mughira who, in the early Meccan period, plotted to defame the Qur'an by claiming that its power was simply the power of magic. *Tafsir*, Vol. 10, pp. 246-250.

[99]   Ibn Kathir, *Tafsir*, Vol. 10, p. 623.

[100]   The early commentators and historians are rife with stories about the first preaching done by Muhammad to the Quraysh. The stories are highly contradictory and mutually exclusive. Inevitably, they emphasize a period of special preparation followed by a dramatic announcement that leads to general rejection. Sometimes Muhammad is portrayed as delivering the first sermon, sometimes Abu Bakr, and sometimes others. These backreadings into history perhaps disguise the fact that Muhammad's religious dialogue with the Quraysh had begun long before the Qur'an began to be revealed.

Some of these earliest revelations do not follow the pattern typical in most of the Qur'an. Muhammad acting as a mouthpiece for Allah is less evident here. Muir, as early as the 1860s, asserted that surahs 91, 100, 102, and 103, "do not seem to be intended as revelations at all."[101] These early surahs show evidence of Muhammad developing his approach to revelation perhaps in response to an already ongoing conflict. Some of the material is initial responses to his enemies and some of it seems to be for personal encouragement.

A similar passage regarding conflict with the members of Muhammad's tribe of Hashim is chapter 108. This chapter is thought to be the fifth revealed and it records God's comfort to Muhammad at some insult he had suffered.

> To thee have we granted the fount (of abundance).
> Therefore to thy Lord turn in prayer and sacrifice.
> For he that hateth thee—he will be cut off (from future hope).
> (Chapter 108)

Yusuf Ali interprets this verse as referring to Abu Jahl, Muhammad's greatest opponent in the tribe. According to Ali, Abu Jahl had mocked Muhammad at the death of two of his infant sons.[102] The implication was that Muhammad lacked the "life-force" to bring male children to adulthood, and thus preserve his family line. It is clear that Muhammad had enemies from the very beginning of his work for these boys were actually given pagan names, a clue to how little Islam was defined at the time they died. It is interesting to note the disagreements of Muslim interpreters on this text. Ibn Kathir makes the passage much later, revealed at Medina, and claims, based on Tabari, that it refers to a later enemy of the Prophet, Al-As bin Wa'il.[103] Another interpreter mentions the passage as referring to Uqbah bin Abi Mu'ayt[104] whom Muhammad had killed after he was captured at the Battle of Badr.[105] These conflicts show just how opaque the Qur'anic text remains for Muslim commentators. This also argues for the age and originality of the text.

---

[101] William Muir, *The Life of Mohammad*, New York: AMS Press, 1975, p. xiv.
[102] Ali, Yusuf, Note 2688, p. 1706.
[103] Ibn Kathir, *Tafsir*, Vol. 10, p. 610.
[104] Ibn Kathir, *Tafsir*, p. 610.
[105] Ibn Ishaq, *The Life of Muhammad*, ed. by Alfred Guillaume, Oxford University Press, 2003, p. 308: "When the apostle ordered him killed Uqba said, 'But who will look after my children, O Muhammad?' 'Hell', he said, and Asim b. Thabit . . . killed him."

In some of the early chapters, God addresses the Prophet directly to provide encouragement. "Have we not expanded thee thy breast? And removed from thee thy burden . . . Verily with every difficulty there is relief" (94:1-2, 6). This entire chapter seems to be addressed to Muhammad himself.[106] The chapter 93 is similar, "Thy guardian Lord hath not forsaken thee, nor is He displeased" (93:3). In later passages, God extols the virtues of his Prophet, "verily this is the word of a most honorable Messenger, endued with power, with rank before the Lord of the throne with authority there and faithful to his trust" (81:19-21).

Occasionally, God seems to correct the Prophet. In early chapter 86, he tells Muhammad to tone down his rhetoric and be patient while God plots schemes on his behalf, "As for them, they are but plotting a scheme, and I am planning a scheme. Therefore, grant a delay to the unbelievers: Give respite to them gently (for a while)" (86:15-17). The interpreters of the Qur'an do not see this, however, as calling for respite on the unbelievers. Ibn Kathir states, "This means that you will see what befalls them of torment, punishment, and destruction."[107] The later commentators do seek to radicalize the text at times. Elsewhere God directs the Prophet concerning the speed of revelation; "Move not thy tongue concerning the (Qur'an) to make haste therewith. It is for us to collect it and to recite it: But when we have recited it, follow thou its recital" (75:16-18). Ibn Kathir makes this into a description of the process of revelation. The Prophet is instructed to be patient as God collects the Word into his "chest."[108] After this, Muhammad was to recite the verses and then interpret what they mean. Al-Bukhari interpreted this to mean that Jibrail would first recite the verses to Muhammad, who was to remain silent, and then, when he left, Muhammad was to first recite the verses and then interpret their meaning.[109]

Sometimes the correction seems a clear rebuke as in chapter 80 that is entitled "He frowned." The background to the passage is that Muhammad, according to Yusuf Ali,[110] was presenting the Qur'an to the larger tribe of Quraysh, when a blind man came asking questions. The Prophet apparently

---

[106]   Ibn Kathir emphasizes the high standing of the Prophet in God's eyes. He points out that wherever God's name is remembered so also is the name of the Prophet, alluding to the confession of faith (shahada). Vol. 10, p. 525.
[107]   Ibn Kathir, *Tafsir*, Vol. 10, p. 443.
[108]   Ibn Kathir, *Tafsir*, Vol. 10, p. 269.
[109]   Ibn Kathir, *Tafsir*, Vol. 10, p. 270.
[110]   Ali, Yusuf, p. 1600.

frowned and turned away. God rebukes him for showing preference to the powerful men of the tribe over a blind man. "(The Prophet) frowned and turned away because there came to him the blind man (interrupting) . . . But as to him who came to thee striving earnestly and with fear (in his heart), of him wast thou unmindful" (80:1-2, 8-10). Yusuf Ali is at pains to explain that this does not imply any sin on the Prophet's part even though "they seemed to reprove him . . ."[111] Ibn Kathir mentions the event without explanation. Perhaps even more astonishing is God's command to the Prophet in chapter 74:9 "And all abomination shun." Ibn Kathir interprets this as, "Verily it is the idols."[112] God is calling the Prophet to leave behind idolatrous practices.[113] Hawtings thesis that God was only addressing monotheists seems to be inaccurate, for why would God rebuke the Prophet for monotheistic practices?

That Muhammad came from a background of polytheism is simply ignored by the Muslim commentators. Clearly, Muslim interpreters are at pains to find no sin in the Prophet's character, even when the Qur'an itself mentions this. The passage also indicates a wider level of discussion of the Prophet beyond his immediate tribe. It does not seem that Muhammad's teaching was particularly secretive at this stage as the early Muslim historians indicate.[114]

3.   Muhammad and the Holy Book

Muhammad's self-conception seems to have experienced considerable turmoil in these early stages of his work. In surah 68, God addresses the Prophet concerning who he is, "Thou art not, by the grace of thy Lord, mad or possessed" (68:2). This is in reference to accusations made against the Prophet by his detractors. God responds to the detractors saying, "(oh people)! Your companion is not one possessed" (81:22). The Arab soothsayers (Kahin) of this time were believed to be possessed by spirits whose inspiration led to poetic utterances. God says, "What is the matter with you? How judge

---

[111]   Ali, Yusuf, p. 1599.

[112]   Ibn Kathir, *Tafsir*, Vol. 10, p. 243. This is reinforced in Bukhari's description of the first revelations of the Prophet. When the second chronological chapter is revealed, God commands him, "desert the idols" (Sahih al-Bukhari, Vol. 6, no. 478, p. 453.

[113]   This would seem a very strange reference for Hawting's thesis that The Qur'an is written only to criticize other monotheists.

[114]   Ibn Ishaq, *The Life of Muhammad*, p. 117.

ye? Or have ye a book through which ye learn?" (68:36-37). The implied answer is "yes," Muhammad is different from the soothsayers because he is receiving a holy book. This first mention of the holy book concept perhaps marks a new point in the progression of Muhammad's self-conception. His words are not merely the poetic utterances of a Kahin possessed by a familiar spirit, but a holy book in the process of being revealed. God encourages Muhammad throughout this chapter and concludes, "So wait with patience for the command of thy Lord, and be not like the companion of the fish—when he cried out in agony" (68:48).[115] This message God says, "is nothing less than a message to all the worlds" (68:52). This idea is developed further in chapter 85 where God declares, "Nay this is a glorious Qur'an (inscribed) in a tablet preserved" (85:21-22). Ali's translation at this point is inaccurate, "a tablet preserved" should be translated "high and guarded from error."[116] Ali's translation indicates the later Muslim conceptions of the nature of the holy book as coeternal with God and preserved on golden tablets. The concept of a unique new holy book seems to have emerged out of a need to distinguish Muhammad's revelations from the polytheistic utterances of the soothsayers. Later, this need to deny the influence of spirits in the generation of the Qur'an leads to God's most emphatic defense of the Prophet.

> This is verily the word of an honored messenger; it is not the word of a poet: Little it is ye believe! Nor is it the word of a soothsayer: Little admonition it is ye receive. (This is) a message sent down from the Lord of the worlds. And if the messenger were to invent any sayings in Our name, we should certainly then cut off the artery of his heart.[117]

This thinly veiled aspect of Muhammad speaking in his own defense through the mouthpiece of Allah is highly idiosyncratic and argues for the integrity of this text as a product of the Prophet. Chapter 51 is even more exemplary of this tendency. God illustrates the reality of the day of judgment through those prophets who had come before. Suddenly, at verse 51, Muhammad begins speaking in the first person, "Hasten ye then (at once) to Allah: I am from him a warner to you, clear and open! And make not another an object of worship with Allah: I am from him a warner to you, clear and open!"

---

[115]   An apparent reference to Jonah.
[116]   Ibn Kathir, *Tafsir*, Vol. 10, p. 436.
[117]   Qur'an 69:40-46.

(51:50-51). Just as suddenly God is once again speaking in verse 55, "But teach (thy message): For teaching benefits the believers. I have only created jinns and men that they may serve me." The passage is unified and follows a distinct theme, culminating in Muhammad's defense of his prophethood. It is also complicated involving several switchbacks concerning who is speaking. It is hard to imagine that this is a product of an editorial process as Wansbrough, Crone, and Cook have maintained.

God functions as Muhammad's mouthpiece at times. On other occasions, Muhammad speaks himself to explain the nature of his revelations. After developing the earlier arguments of holy books revealed from heaven and the line of the Prophets, in surah 53, Muhammad describes the actual process of revelation. Here again, God is his very thinly veiled mouthpiece:

> Your companion is neither astray nor being misled, nor does he say (aught) of (his own) desire. It is no less than inspiration sent down to him: He was taught by one mighty in power, endued with wisdom: For he appeared (in stately form) while he was in the highest part of the horizon: Then he approached and came closer, and was at a distance of but two bow-lengths or (even) nearer; so did Allah convey the inspiration to his servant—(conveyed) what he (meant) to convey. The (Prophet's) (mind and) heart in no way falsified that which he saw. Will ye then dispute with him concerning what he saw? For indeed he saw him at a second descent, near the lote-tree beyond which none may pass. (53:2-14)

This is the closest we have in the Qur'an to an actual description of the process of revelation. The Qur'an argues that Muhammad reveals nothing of his own will. Later commentators interpret this to mean that "every word that comes out of me is the truth,"[118] that is, God is speaking the Qur'an. These sayings are accompanied with stories about scribes sitting around Muhammad recording his every word. These stories are an invention of later Islam. In the context of the passage, God seemingly tries to explain what had happened to Muhammad when some kind of heavenly being conveyed the message. Ibn Kathir states that Muhammad only saw Gabriel twice, although some claim his vision was only of "light." The traditional literature (Hadith) goes on to describe spectacular scenes, including Jibrail

---

[118] Ibn Kathir, *Tafsir*, Vol. 9, p. 307.

having "six hundred wings."[119] There are quainter stories as well such as the one when Muhammad sees Gabriel, but Khadija does not so she puts the angel to the test. Muhammad sits on the right and then on the left of Khadija, and each time she asks if he can still see the angel. Muhammad says "yes". Then when she asks him to sit in her lap, the angel disappears. By this she knows "he is an angel and not a satan."[120]

The nature of these revelations and how they took place remains a topic about which Muhammad is highly defensive. In this very passage, Muhammad is led to make a conciliatory concession to the Meccan tribes. He states the following, "for truly did he see of the signs of his Lord, the greatest! Have you seen Lat and Uzzah, and another, the third (goddess), Manat?" (53:18-19). It seems clear that Muhammad is directly appealing for acceptance to the Meccans and concludes his appeal with recognition of three deities of the Ka'ba, "These are the gharaniq (high flying cranes) whose intercession is approved."[121] These are the so-called "satanic verses" that we will return to later. What is evident is that Muhammad is under some kind of pressure to explain his revelations, and this leads him to make a concession to the polytheists, which is later revoked.[122]

It is worth noting that one passage of the Qur'an often cited by Muslims as describing the "descent" of the first chapter of the Qur'an, may well be a Christian hymn concerning the birth of Christ. This is chapter 97, and the use of the word "peace" in verse 5 is different from most usual functions of this word, and very similar to the announcement of peace by the angels at the birth of Christ.[123]

Toward the end of the early Meccan period, Muhammad's conception of the Qur'an as a holy book, pure and perfect in its text and preserved with God has become clear, "this is indeed a Qur'an most honorable, in a book well-guarded, which none shall touch but those who are clean: A revelation from the Lord of the worlds" (56:77-80).

---

[119] Ibn Kathir, *Tafsir*, Vol. 9, pp. 313-4.

[120] Ibn Ishaq, p. 107.

[121] Verse 20 has been removed from the Qur'an and replaced with a verse condemning the idols of the Ka'aba.

[122] The actual mention of the deities by name makes Hawting's argument that the Qur'an is not addressing polytheism, but rather various forms of monotheism a bit contrived. I do not accept the argument that they are merely female angels. Hawting gives an exhaustive discussion of viewpoints with regard to the incident of the satanic verses (pp. 130-149).

[123] Claude Gilliot, "On the Origins of the Informants of the Prophet," from Ohlig and Puin, 2010, p. 162.

4. The Prophet's Mission

In the early stages of the Qur'an, Muhammad did not conceive of his mission as having a political element. God encourages Muhammad to "keep in remembrance the name of thy Lord and devote thyself to him wholeheartedly . . . have patience with what they say, and leave them with noble (dignity). And leave me (alone to deal with) those in possession of the good things of this life who (yet) deny the truth" (73:8, 10-11). At this stage of Islam, it is God who deals with the rebellious, not the Islamic state. This viewpoint of the role of the Prophet is most clearly expressed in chapter 88.

> Therefore do thou give admonition, for thou art one to admonish. Thou art not one to manage (men's) affairs. But if anyone turns away and rejects Allah—Allah will punish him with a mighty punishment. (88:21-24)

This passage is a startling contrast to Medinan revelations such as 4:89:

> They would have you disbelieve as they themselves have disbelieved, so that you may be all like alike. Do not befriend them until they have fled their homes for the cause of God. If they desert you seize them and put them to death wherever you find them. Look for neither friends nor helpers among them . . . [124]

The progressive nature of the Qur'anic revelation with its deep contradictions engendered in a short period of twenty-three years is one of the most problematic aspects of studies of the Qur'an. Equally disturbing is the fact that many early verses that contain fairly innocuous concepts take on a distinctly more militant meaning in later commentaries. One of these is chapter 70 that initiates Muhammad's legal pronouncements. There is a section on sexual purity which states as follows:

---

[124] I have taken this quotation of the Qur'an from Ibn Warraq's *Leaving Islam*, New York: Prometheus Books, 2003, p. 17, because it is more accurate to the text of the Qur'an. Yusuf Ali substitutes "turn renegades" for "desert" in an effort to make the apostates seem as common criminals. There is no such implication in the Qur'anic text. Yusuf Ali is often guilty of sanitizing the Qur'anic text for a Western audience.

> Those who fear the displeasure of their Lord—for their Lord's
> displeasure is the opposite of peace and tranquility—and those
> who guard their chastity, except with their wives and the (captives)
> whom their right hand possess—for (then) they are not to be
> blamed. (70:27-30).

This passage is meant to condone sexual intercourse with women captured
in tribal raiding, a not uncommon practice. Ibn Kathir, however, refers the
reader to the much later Medinan passage from chapter 23:6-7. In the later
conception of Islam, this was taken to justify the rape of women prisoners
captured in war. "Do not approach anyone except the wives whom Allah has
made permissible for them or their right hand possessions from the captives."
One common Hadith concerns the rape of the women captives of war where
Muhammad gives this reaction to his questioners:

> "O Allah's apostle! We get female captives as our share of booty,
> and we are interested in their prices, what is your opinion about
> coitus interruptus?" The Prophet said, "Do you really do that? It is
> better for you not to do it. No soul that which Allah has destined
> to exist, but will surely come into existence."[125]

Yusuf Ali tries to doctor this up as "marriage" even though the early sources
record many instances where women so "consummated" refused to marry
their rapists.[126] The best-known case is Raihana bint Amr, the Prophet's
concubine captured from the Jewish tribe of Banu Qurayzah, who refused
to marry the Prophet after being "consummated." The injunction mentioned
against al-azl or coitus interruptus should not be thought of as forbidding rape.
Rather it indicates that when one rapes, one should also try to impregnate
the victim in order to make her a "mother of a believer." This will be dealt
with further in the final chapter.

5. Textual Emendations and the Satanic Verses

Contradictions in the text were recognized even in the lifetime of the
Prophet. Occasionally, this led to efforts at emending the older textual

---

[125]   Al-Bukhari, *Translation of the Meanings of Sahih Al-Bukhari*, trans. Dr. Muhammad
Muhsin Khan, Chicago: Kazi Publications, 1977, Vol. 3, no. 432, p. 237.
[126]   Ali, Yusuf, Note 5694, p. 1528. A further sanitizing of the text.

materials with interpolations clearly from the Medinan period. It is interesting that some verses are interpolated at the end of chapter 73 that Yusuf Ali admits were an addition to the passage from the Medinan period. This passage mentions those "fighting (*jihad*) in Allah's cause."[127] This is an obvious attempt to downplay the earlier self-concept of the Prophet and to read back into history a more militant interpretation of Islam. What is significant is that this backreading interpolation is done by the writer of the Qur'an, we are not dealing with later interpretation. The accompanying verses also read back into history many of the practices of prayer, fasting, and almsgiving, which did not exist at this stage in Islam's development.

It is fairly easy to spot the interpolations in these early texts of the Qur'an. They are stylistically very different. The verses from the early chapters are usually very short, usually no more than three to eight words, and highly poetic. The interpolations are versified prose, sometimes fifteen to twenty lines long and showing a much later conception of Islam. The earliest interpolation is in the second chronological chapter 74, verse 31. The previous verse made obscure mention of nineteen (angels), and verse 31 seems to be an answer to Jews who disputed over the number and nature of these angels; "we have fixed their number only as a trial for the unbelievers—in order that the People of the Book may arrive at certainty, and the believers may increase in faith—and that no doubts may be left for the People of the Book and the Believers." This is, therefore, not the earliest mention of the People of the Book in the Qur'an. It is, however, indicative of the kinds of debates that must have been going on in Medina between Muhammad and the Jews, over the meanings of the early verses in the Qur'an. We shall return to this subject.

The most important interpolation in the early passages of the Qur'an is in chapter 53 just after verse 20. This is the location of the so-called satanic verses. Verses 19 and 20 state, "have ye seen Lat and Uzza, and another, the third goddess, Manat." We know from Ibn Sa'd that this passage originally was completed in verse 21 as, "these are the gharaniq whose intercession is approved."[128] A gharaniq is a kind of high-flying migratory bird (commonly called the Hopoe) that was a symbol of these Arab goddesses. Muhammad was allowing for intercession to the three primary idols of the Ka'ba. He made a compromise at this point with Meccan paganism in an effort to gain

---

[127] Ali, Yusuf, p. 1555, cf. footnote no. 5774.
[128] Ibn Sa'd, Vol. 1, p. 237.

acceptance. Al-Tabari gives an extensive description of these so-called "Satanic verses."

> When he came to the words: "have you though upon al-Lat and al-Uzzah and Manat, the third, the other?" Satan cast upon his tongue, because of his inner debates and what he desired to bring to his people: "These are the high flying cranes; verily their intercession is accepted with approval." When Quraysh heard this, they rejoiced and were happy and delighted at the way in which he spoke of their Gods.[129]

The text of the present Qur'an has been extensively tampered with at this point. In place of and following verse 21, eleven verses of entirely different prose-like style have been substituted which declare concerning the goddesses, "these are nothing but names which ye have devised—ye and your fathers—for which Allah has sent down no authority (whatever)" (53:23). So the text of the Qur'an is not only highly opaque, but it has also obviously been tampered with at a later time to make earlier passages congruent with later ones. This would seem to be emendation of the text by the Prophet himself. These stories have a significant level of credibility. One cannot imagine that anyone could have made this up and gotten the story accepted by the larger Muslim community.

6. Historical Passages in the Early Qur'an

There is only one passage in the early chapters of the Qur'an that seems to comment on a historical event directly. Chapter 105 tells the miraculous story of how God sent birds with clay stones[130] to pelt and drive off invaders and their war elephant. This is generally associated with the events of the so-called "Year of the Elephant." "Seest thou not how thy Lord dealt with the people of the elephant. Did he not make their treacherous plan go astray?" (105:1-2). Typically, there is virtually no historical data to be retrieved from this. Neither Mecca, nor the Abyssinians, nor their leader is mentioned by name. There is no date provided either. Were it not for later biographies, and

---

[129]   Al-Tabari, *History of al-Tabari*, ed. W. Montgomery Watt and M. V. McDonald, State University of New York Press, 1988, Vol. 6, p. 108.

[130]   These stones of hard clay "sijjil" are later described as the stones with which God overthrew the people of Sodom and Gomorrah.

exegetic works on the Qur'an, this reference would be as opaque as much of the remainder of the book. Ibn Ishaq claims that 85:4 refers to the killing of the Christians of Najran by the Jewish King Dhu Nuwas, although there is nothing in the passage that even hints at that.[131] Ibn Kathir includes six pages of fanciful stories about the killing of the Christians of Najran by "the people of the ditch."[132] Sahih Muslim tells an entirely different apocryphal story about a boy and a monk who by a very strange set of tests are executed for their faith.[133]Once again, there is nothing in the passage itself that indicates who it is about or what the time frame was.

7. The Cosmology of the Early Qur'an

Another curious feature of the early chapters of the Qur'an is their descriptions of the creation of man. It is first mentioned in the two initial verses of the Qur'an. "Read! In the name of thy Lord and Cherisher, who created—created man out of a (mere) clot of congealed blood" (96:1-2). Later, chapter 86 expands on this idea, "now let man think from what he is created! He is created from a drop emitted" (86:5-6). Ibn Kathir spells this out in no uncertain terms.[134] The implication seems to be that humility is in order for a creature created from this unclean substance: "From what stuff has he created him? From a sperm drop" (80:18-19). Later chapter 77 makes this clearer. "Have we not created you from a fluid held despicable—that which we placed in a place of rest, firmly fixed for a period (of gestation)." Semen and menstrual blood were considered most unclean substances, pollution with which required a full bath to remove one from the taboo state of being "junub" (unclean). These earlier animistic conceptions are utilized in the Qur'an as inspiration to humility and submission to the creator.

It is also possible that certain animistic myths of creation lie behind the Qur'an's descriptions of conception. Overall, however, animistic elements and aspects of magic are rather sparse in the text at this point. Perhaps the best examples of magical verses are chapters 113 and 114, which come at the end of this period in the Prophet's life. It must be noted that we understand the magical aspect of these verses only through the biographies and exegetical works that describe their background. According to some

---

[131]   Ibn Ishaq, *The Life of Muhammad*, p. 17.

[132]   Ibn Kathir, *Tafsir*, Vol. 10, pp. 427-432.

[133]   Sahih Muslim, Vol. 4, *Hadith*, no. 7148.

[134]   Ibn Kathir, *Tafsir*, Vol. 10, p. 439.

traditions, Muhammad was bewitched in this period in Mecca by a Jew who had succeeded to obtain eleven strands of hair from the Prophet's comb that he tied to a date palm branch and threw into a well. Ibn Sa'd in the Tabaqat mentions that the Prophet was bewitched for a year during which time he lost interest in food and sex. Eventually, the eleven verses of chapters 113 and 114 were revealed and as each verse was revealed a hair was released from the fetish, and the Prophet was delivered. The passages themselves give no hint of this interpretation though 113:1, 4 states, "Say: I seek refuge with the Lord of the dawn . . . from the mischief of those who practice secret arts." The mythical aspect here is obvious as is the attitude of hostility to Jews. The story is repeated in the Medinan period according to both Muslim and Bukhari:

> A Jew from among the Jews of Banu Zuraiq . . . cast spell upon Allah's Messenger with the result that he had been doing something whereas, in fact, he had not been doing that . . . During one night Allah's Messenger made supplication, (during the night two angels came and said) "What is the trouble with the man?" He said: "The spell has affected him." He said: "Who cast that?" He said: "It was Labid (the Jew)." He said, "What is the thing by which he transmitted its effect?" He said: "By the comb and by the hair stuck to the comb and the spathe of the date palm." He said: "Where is that?" He said: "In the well of Dhi Arwan."[135]

8. Jewish Words, Concepts, and Stories in the Early Meccan Period

Finally, we return to our thesis, examining the nature of Muhammad's relationship with the "People of the Book" and how it changed over time. The amount of material with allusions to biblical ideas is quite limited in these first 48 chapters, a total of only forty-four verses. These seem to be derived from oral traditions. About twenty of these verses concern the story of Moses and Pharaoh, and about fourteen concerns with Abraham. If we add in those verses that Geiger considers references to Eber and the Tower of Babel (Genesis 10-11), the story of Daniel's three friends, and the earlier potential mention of Jonah, we would add another seventeen verses. The allusions are vague in the extreme.

---

[135] Muslim, Vol. 3, p. 1193, Bukhari, Vol. 4, p. 266.

The earliest use of cognates to Hebrew words is in verse 7 of chapter 107, where the word *Maun* for "refuge" is used. It does not seem to be related to any Jewish traditions.[136] The same is true of the reference to inspiration by the "spirit" in 97:4 that may be related to Jewish concepts of the inspiration of scripture.[137] This later became associated with the angel Gabriel, although Christian influence of the idea of a "Spirit of God" is not impossible at this point. The earliest reference to the traditions of the Jews and the Christians is probably chapter 68, which is the seventeenth in Nöldeke's order of chapters. There is an oblique reference to the "people of the garden," whose fruits were destroyed because they forgot to say, "if it be Allah's will" (68:17-18). In verse 34, reference is made to the Garden of Eden, as the word used to describe this place is a cognate of Hebrew *Jannatu*. Shortly after, Muhammad challenges his opponents as to whether they have a holy book through which they can learn. The word for deep learning is another Hebrew cognate *durasa*.[138] Ibn Kathir claims that it is merely a parable.[139] There is also a brief reference to idolatry as follows: "have they some 'partners' (in Godhead)? Then let them produce their 'partners' if they are truthful!" (68:41). Yusuf Ali immediately makes reference to the Christian trinity, but that is almost certainly not what Muhammad is referring to.[140] Rather, he is arguing against the "partners" of Allah in rival idols and gods of the Arabs. This is indicated by Ibn Kathir as well.[141]

Muhammad is also concerned to establish a new concept of the holy book as something that distinguishes his activities from the other Arab soothsayers. It may well be that he was initially drawn to the books of the "People of the Book" because they provided a new paradigm of revelation that reinforced his gradually emerging prophetic consciousness. This passage also contains an oblique reference to Jonah, "be not like the companion of the fish—when he cried out in agony." It is clear that Muhammad had a vague awareness of some tales from the Hebrew Scriptures and particularly apocryphal stories explaining the Hebrew Scriptures, but in almost every case he gets the details wrong. In the case of Jonah, he states, "Had not the grace of His Lord reached him, he would indeed have been cast off on the naked shore in disgrace"

---

136   Abraham Geiger, *Judaism and Islam*, New York: Ktav Publishing House, 1970, p. 42.
137   Geiger, 1970, p. 62.
138   Geiger, 1970, p. 36.
139   Ibn Kathir, *Tafsir*, Vol. 10, p. 112.
140   Ali, Yusuf, p. 1512, note no. 5621.
141   Ibn Kathir, *Tafsir*, Vol. 10, p. 118.

(68:49). But this was, according to the Hebrew Scriptures, exactly what did happen to him, and it was not a disgrace, but deliverance in answer to a prayer when he was vomited from the belly of the fish to the shore.

Ibn Kathir shows greater sophistication than Yusuf Ali by interpolating into the text "left in the stomach of the fish, but we forgave him,"[142] to make the passage fit the Hebrew Scriptures. The very next chapter in chronological order, chapter 87, reinforces this impression. Muhammad cites the writings of the Jews as if to prove the truthfulness of what he is saying, "And this is in the books of the earliest (revelations)—the books of Abraham and Moses" (87:18-19). Yusuf Ali is immediately at pains in his footnotes to demonstrate what the "book" of Abraham was, since the Jews did not regard Abraham as the author of any of the books of scripture.[143] From the Jewish perspective, Muhammad repeats the mistake later in 53:36-37. Muhammad is appealing to previous revelations as proof of what he is saying and as a paradigm for what he is doing, but in the process he commits textual/historical blunders that will eventually ensure his rejection by the Jews.

This progression of thought concerning the holy books culminates in the twenty-first chronological chapter 85, where the idea of the eternal word preserved in heaven is recorded. Closely related to this is the concept that the revelations are God's great "signs" given to the Prophet (78:28-29). As we noted earlier, the golden tablet idea is a later interpretation.

The very next chapter, chapter 73 introduces the work of Moses and Pharaoh, "We have sent you, (O men!) a messenger to be a witness concerning you, even as we sent a messenger to pharaoh. But pharaoh disobeyed the messenger" (73:15-16). Muhammad's understanding of Moses' work is completely wrong from a Jewish perspective. Instead of the deliverer of Israel who thunders "let my people go," Moses is made a Prophet to Egypt! This is further explained in the later chapter 79.

> "Has the story of Moses reached thee? Behold thy Lord did call
> to him in the sacred valley of Tuwa—Go thou to Pharaoh, for he

---

[142]   Ibn Kathir, *Tafsir*, Vol. 10, p. 123.

[143]   Ali, Yusuf, p. 1638, footnote no. 6094. It is interesting that Ali disagrees with Nöldeke on the order of this chapter, claiming that it was the eighth in succession, not the nineteenth. It should be noted that Geiger thinks this verse is in reference to non-scriptural Jewish traditions that Abraham was the author of the Sepher Jazirah, Abraham Geiger, *Judaism and Islam*, New York: Ktav Publishing House, 1970, p. 96.

has indeed transgressed all bounds: And say to him, wouldst thou that thou shouldst be purified (from sin)? And that I guide thee to the Lord, so thou shouldst fear Him? Then did Moses show him the great sign. But (Pharaoh) rejected it . . ."

Ibn Kathir interprets this to mean that Moses invited the pharaoh to accept Islam![144] It was inevitable that the Jews would find Muhammad's "revelations" inaccurate. The stage was being set for a great confrontation with Judaism in Medina.

There are other allusions to Moses in this earliest section of the Qur'an. Mount Sinai is mentioned, using the probably syriac term *tur* for "mountain" in 95:2 and in chapter 52, where it is the chapter title.[145] In both cases, it is used as a symbol of God's judgment and fear. Ali's translation makes it the mount of revelation, but that does not seem to be the Qur'an's meaning of the term at this point. If *tur* refers to Mount Sinai and the giving of the law, clearly Muhammad was unaware of it. Later, a different word is used of the place where Moses received his call from God, *tuwa*, which Stewart interprets as a poetical take on the word *tur* to "exhibit end rhymn."[146] If *tuwa* is, indeed, a form of *tur*, then it is another confusion from the Jewish perspective since Mount Horeb, where Moses received his call, is quite distinct from Sinai where the law was given. Muhammad seems to consistently mix up these details.

Later chapters explain the Qur'anic conception of the Prophets as messengers to different peoples and how these people were destroyed when they rejected the message. Some of these peoples are biblical; he mentions Noah being sent to "the people of Noah" and that "he destroyed the overthrown cities (of Sodom and Gomorrah") (53:52-53). Here Muhammad seems to mix up the story of Noah with a later story of Abraham. Others are extra biblical, such as the peoples of Ad and Thamud (53:50-51) though Geiger associated these with the judgment on the Tower of Babel.[147] A similar litany covering the same characters is recorded in the first eleven verses of chapter 69.

Chapter 51 expands on these earlier themes as Muhammad details the "signs" or means of judgment on these peoples. Sodom and Gomorrah are destroyed, "and we left there a sign for such as fear the grievous penalty" (51:37). The sign shown over Pharaoh was that "we took him and his forces

---

[144] Ibn Kathir, *Tafsir*, Vol. 10, p. 346.
[145] Stewart, 2008, p. 226.
[146] Stewart, 2008, p. 236.
[147] Geiger, 1970, pp. 88-93.

and threw them into the sea" (51:40). The sign to Ad was a devastating wind and to Thamud an earthquake (51:41, 44). Preliminary to the story of Sodom and Gomorrah, however, we find the story of Abraham's angel visitors who bring the promise of a son (unnamed). For once, the story seems to fairly accurately reflect the Old Testament text even recording that "His wife came forward (laughing) aloud: She smote her forehead and said: 'A barren old woman'" (51:29). Most Muslim exegetes insist that the child of promise was Ishmael, not Isaac. This in spite of the fact that Isaac means "laughter" reflected in the Qur'anic passage. It is ironic that the one time the Qur'an gets the story correct from a Jewish perspective, Muslims reject the clear implication of the text. It seems clear that Muhammad followed the Jewish interpretation at this point, and, indeed, names Isaac later in the same passage. Ishmael, the supposed father of the Arabs, does not appear until much later and in such a way that it seems, initially, Muhammad did not connect him with Abraham at all.

In summary, the early passages of the Qur'an belong to the genre of literature known as apocalyptic. The images and allusions used are of a limited range that perhaps indicates direct borrowing from other sources. In translation, it is distinctly unimpressive. Conflicts with members of his own tribe and the larger tribe of Quraysh seem to be indicated from the very beginning. May we posit that Muhammad had an initial pre-Islamic period of advocating change in Meccan society that was opposed? Is it possible that he turned to the avenue of revelation as a way of trumping his detractors? This is speculation, but clearly, the early biographers do not have the whole picture. It does seem clear that when Muhammad's initial revelations were rejected or mocked, he began to cite earlier revelations, particularly from oral Jewish traditions, as support for his prophetic role. Shortly, this led to his adopting the argument that his was a holy book being revealed from heaven like the earlier revelations. That Muhammad conceived of himself as a mouthpiece through whom Allah spoke is clear from the complex interchanges between God and Prophet. It is also clear that Muhammad himself lost track of who was talking at points and began speaking himself. His textual faux pas presented no problems in Mecca, where there was no Jewish community that we know of; it would prove a disaster in his dealings with the Jews in Medina.

B. Biographer's Descriptions of the Early Meccan Period

The early Muslim biographers focus on four main events in the early period. First, they describe the nature of the earliest revelations and the process by which Muhammad came to accept his call. The role of Christians in confirming this call and the reaction of Jews is an interesting side note. The second relates to the names and circumstances of the earliest converts to Islam. The third concerns the beginning of what we may call Muhammad's public ministry. The final concerns the response Muhammad received and the earliest persecution that he and his followers experienced.

1. The Call of Muhammad

We begin with Muhammad's call as described in Ibn Ishaq. He starts his narrative with a description of the devotions Muhammad was engaged in during the pre-Islamic period in a cave on Mount Hira. As he traveled to the cave at Hira, Muhammad was performing a ritual month of seclusion, the same religious path along which he had walked many times before.

> Wahb b. Kaisan a client of the family of al-Zubayr told me: I heard Abdullah b. al-Zubayr say to Ubayd b. Umayr b. Qatada the Laythite, 'O Ubayd tell us how began the prophethood which was first bestowed on the apostle when Gabriel came to him.' And Ubayd in my presence related to Abdullah and those with him as follows: The apostle would pray in seclusion on Hira every year for a month to practice *tahannuth* as was the custom of Quraysh in heathen days. *Tahannuth* is religious devotion.[148]

The purpose of Muhammad's journey to Hira was to fulfill a ritual of religious devotion (*tahannuth*). Kister cites Watt's opinions about the meaning of *tahannuth*:

> Muhammad's going to Hira " . . . might be a method of escaping from the heat of Mecca in an unpleasant season for those who could not afford to go to al-Ta'if': 'Judaeo-Christian influence, such as the example of monks, or a little personal experience," continues Watt, "would show the need and desirability of solitude." "The precise meaning and derivation of *tahannuth*," says Watt, "is uncertain, though it is evidently some sort of devotional practice." The best suggestion is perhaps that of H.

---

148   Ibn Ishaq. *The Life of Muhammad*, trans. A. Guillaume. London: Oxford University Press, 1955, p. 105.

Hirschfeld, that it comes from the Hebrew *tehinnot* or *tehinnoth,* meaning prayers for God's favor.[149]

What is of particular interest is that the call described here bears no resemblance to the Qur'anic description of the process of revelation mentioned above. Ibn Ishaq relates as follows:

> "He (Gabriel) came to me," said the apostle of God, "while I was asleep, with a coverlet of brocade whereon was some writing, and said, 'Read!' I said, 'What shall I read?' He pressed me with it so tightly that I thought it was death; then he let me go and said, 'Read!' I said, 'What shall I read?' He pressed me with it again so that I thought it was death . . . I said, 'What then shall I read?'—and this I said only to deliver myself from him, lest he should do the same to me again. He said the following: 'Read in the name of the Lord who created, who created man of blood coagulated. Read! Thy Lord is the most beneficent, who taught by the pen, taught that which they knew not unto men.' So I read it, and he departed from me. And I awoke from my sleep, and it was as though these words were written on my heart."[150]

It is apparent that this first revelation occurred in a dream. Bukhari's Hadith also indicates that Muhammad's earliest revelations were in dream form.

> Narrated Aisha: The commencement of the Divine Inspiration to Allah's apostle was in the form of good righteous (true) dreams in his sleep. He never had a dream, but that it came true like bright day light.[151]

Muhammad's later explanation in the Qur'an seems to indicate meeting an angel at a distance on the horizon. It is possible that Muhammad was describing the event of a later revelation. Ibn Ishaq includes a story of Muhammad's later meeting with Gabriel when he is deeply discouraged

---

[149] M. J. Kister, *Studies in Jahiliyya and Early Islam.* "Al-Tahannuth: An Inquiry into the Meaning of a Term." London: Variorum Reprints, 1980. p. 229
[150] Ibn Ishaq, p. 106. The Qur'anic citation is from the first revealed chapter 96:1-5.
[151] All-Bukhari, Vol. 9, no. 111, p. 91.

about his calling and is preparing to commit suicide: "I will go to the top of the mountain and throw myself down that I may kill myself and gain rest." The angel meets him astride the horizon and declares, "O Muhammad! Thou art the apostle of God and I am Gabriel."[152] Muhammad is, nevertheless, still unsure of his calling. Al-Tabari quotes him as saying, "Woe is me, poet or possessed."[153]

Al-Tabari seems to indicate that the first revelations came before the initial revealing of the Qur'an. In his description, it seems that 53:1-18 refers to an initial vision the Prophet had that leads to his drawing aside to meditate regularly on Mount Hira after which the first chapter of the Qur'an was given.

> "The first form in which the revelation came to the Messenger of God was true vision; this used to come to him like the break of dawn. After that, he grew to love solitude and used to remain in a cave on Hira engaged in acts of devotion."[154]

Is it possible that Muhammad's work of reforming Meccan society really began after this initial vision and before the formal revelations of the Qur'an began?

There is significant debate in the biographical and commentary literature as to which revelation of the Qur'an came first. Some maintain that chapter 96 that begins with "recite!" was first while others argue chapter 74, which begins with "O you enveloped in your cloak."[155] These stories are also accompanied by descriptions of the purification of Muhammad for his prophetic task. His chest is opened and a black clot is removed from his heart and replaced by a white substance called the *sakinah,* a borrowing from the Hebrew *Shekhinah,* for "glory."[156] This story repeats a similar process described in Muhammad's childhood in Ibn Ishaq. Like the night flight to Jerusalem (*miraj*), it is a story that seems to be repeated to function symbolically at different stages in the Prophet's life.

---

[152]   Ibn Ishaq, p. 106.
[153]   Ibn Ishaq, p. 106.
[154]   Al-Tabari, *The History of Al-Tabari,* trans. W. Montgomery Watt, State University of New York Press, 1988, Vol VI, p. 67.
[155]   Al-Tabari, Vol. VI, p. 74. Ishaq. p. 107.
[156]   Al-Tabari, Vol. VI, p. 75.

The Role of Jews and Christians in Confirming His Call

The early biographical literature goes to great lengths in showing that Muhammad received much encouragement from early Christians. Among these is a supposed cousin of Khadija named Waraqa. In Ibn Ishaq's work, it is Waraqa who identifies the angel of revelation as Gabriel and then declares, "He is the Prophet of this people."[157] In Ibn Kathir's version, Waraqa wants first to question Muhammad closely because "I am afraid it may be someone other than Gabriel, for certain devils imitate him and by so doing can mislead and corrupt some men."[158] When Khadija mentions this to Muhammad, God himself reveals 63:1 to indicate that Muhammad was not "mad." Waraqa later confirmed his revelation to the distress of his own people.[159]

Waraqa stories are many and varied. In another, he meets Muhammad while circumambulating the Ka'aba, calls him "cousin," and delivers a similar confirmation of his prophetic call.[160] Other Christian characters are mentioned as confirming Muhammad. Abdul Shams was a Christian from Ninevah who, on hearing of Muhammad's revelation, identified that the angel was Gabriel and that Muhammad was the prophet to his people.[161] Ibn Kathir tells the story of a Christian monk in Busra who spoke of Muhammad in the month he began his prophetic work.

> "Has Ahmad come forth yet?" I asked, "Who is Ahmad?" He responded, "He is the son of Abd Allah . . . this is the month during which he will appear. He is the last of the prophets. He will come forth from the holy quarter and go into exile to a place of date palms, stony tracts and salty earth."[162]

A deeper study of the supposed informants of the Prophet is found in Claude Gilliot's *On the Origin of the Informants of the Prophet*, in Ohlig and Puin's 2010 work, *The Hidden Origins of Islam.* It is surprising that all of these early stories about Christians are positive in great contrast to the

---

[157] Ibn Ishaq, p. 107.
[158] Ibn Kathir, *Al-Sira al-Nabawiyya*, trans. Trevor Le Gassick, UK: Garner Publishing, 1998, Vol. 1, pp. 296-7.
[159] Ibn Kathir, *Sira*, p. 298.
[160] Ibn Kathir, *Sira*, p. 293.
[161] Ibn Kathir, *Sira,* p. 294.
[162] Ibn Kathir, Sira, p. 318.

stories of the Jewish response to the advent of Muhammad that is universally negative.[163] Ibn Kathir relates the story of Abu Sufyan's journey to Yemen shortly after Muhammad began to proclaim himself the messenger of God. One of his companions, Al-Abbas got into a conversation with a rabbi about Muhammad. The rabbi asked whether Muhammad can write. When Abbas said no, "The rabbi jumped up and his loose robe fell down as he exclaimed, 'Jews will be slaughtered, Jews killed!'" The Jews of Hijaz were terrified of Muhammad, Ibn Kathir notes.[164] While these stories are clearly a backreading into history, they do illustrate an interesting point. If all these stories were merely a reflection of later conflicts from the first and second centuries of Islam when Muslims were primarily at war with Christians, then one would expect the reverse of this pattern. Jews would be a safe group to call friends, and Christians would be the evil people who rejected Muhammad because Christians were the ones Muslims were at war with. These backreadings occur because there was an early conflict between Muhammad and the Jews, which Muslims sought to explain by backreadings into history, however irrelevant they may have been to the contemporary circumstances of the Muslim world at the time they were writing. There may have also been an appeal to the largely Christian population of the Middle East at the time.

For the first three years after the revelations began, according to Ishaq, Muhammad kept his newfound faith a secret between himself and his early followers, allowing only Ali into his personal times of prayer. Ishaq records as,

> A traditionist mentioned that when the time of prayer came the apostle used to go out to the glens of Mecca accompanied by Ali, who went unbeknown to his father, and his uncles and the rest of his people. There they used to pray the ritual prayers, and return at nightfall. This went on as long as God intended that it should, until one day Abu Talib came upon them while they were praying, and said to the apostle, "O nephew, what is this religion which I see you practicing?" [165]

---

[163] There is a political aspect to this. We must not forget that these biographies were written as tracts for the Muslims who then ruled over a largely Christian population in the Middle East. The purpose was to attract Christians to convert to Islam.

[164] Ibn Kathir, *Sira*, p. 226.

[165] Ibid., p. 114

This depiction is clearly at odds with the earliest chapters of the Qur'an that seem to begin with a conflict already in progress. Ibn Ishaq is insistent on this point and returns to it through the various stories that he tells of the early days of Islam. One such story is the mention of the cessation of revelations that so disturbed Muhammad that he considered suicide. After a period, estimated as about six months, Gabriel reveals chapter 93 of the Qur'an, according to Ibn Ishaq, with this intent, "God's kindness to him and to his servants in the matter of prophecy to everyone among his people whom he could trust."[166] Thus the Qur'an is meant to be revealed only to those who the Prophet could trust. Strangely, the traditions (Hadith) record an entirely different situation with regard to the cessations of the revelations. When Muhammad goes without revelations for a time, Al-Bukhari notes that the people of Mecca said, "His Shaitan has deserted him."[167] Once again, this indicates a public aspect to the early revelations and an ongoing conflict. When the apostle invites Ali to Islam, his initial response is noncommittal to which Ibn Ishaq notes as follows:

> Now the apostle did not want his secret to be divulged before he applied himself to the publication of his message, so he said, "If you do not accept Islam, then conceal the matter."[168]

In a similar way, the conversion of Abu Dharr is cloaked in secrecy as special arrangements are made for enquirers to meet with Muhammad.[169]

There are several possible explanations to these conflicts in the stories of early Islam. Primary among these is the desire to read back into history of Islam as a complete phenomenon. The idea of it gradually taking shape through a historical process was perhaps seen as denigrating its revelation as a complete code by Allah. Thus, Muhammad and Khadija receive very early on the instructions for ritual prayer five times a day.[170] This prayer procedure is not described in its canonical details anywhere in the Qur'an. Of course, other traditions record these rules as being revealed during the Prophet's

---

[166] Ibid., p. 112.
[167] Al-Bukhari, Vol. 4, p. 232.
[168] Ibn Ishaq, p. 115.
[169] Ibn Kathir, p. 325.
[170] Ibn Ishaq, pp. 112-3.

miraculous night journey to Jerusalem (*miraj*) during the middle Meccan period, three or four years later. The *miraj* itself is recorded as occurring in two separate time periods. Al-Tabari records it as taking place immediately after the first chapters of the Quran are revealed. Part of the reason for this is to enable the Prophet to be instructed in ritual prayer and fasting at the very inception of Islam.[171] Islam is revealed as complete, and so the Prophet must make careful preparation for its initial public proclamation. It is stated that there were thirty-nine secret Muslims at the time Abu Bakr made the first public proclamation of Islam on behalf of the Prophet.[172] It is also possible that the writers mixed up a later period of secrecy (from 613 to 614) and attributed it to the earliest period. The stories about Islam being kept secret in the early years are pervasive. Ibn Kathir notes, "The believers were concealing their Islam at this time."[173] In any case, these stories are highly contradictory. Muranyi, on reviewing them, maintains that initially the Quraysh "had no objections to the movement," but that when Muhammad began to criticize paganism there was a strong reaction which led to an initial period of persecution. After this, Muhammad began to teach secretly in the "House of Al-Arqam."[174] Based on the earliest passages of the Qur'an, we may posit that there were several waves of negative reaction. Some generated almost immediately, which perhaps led to the initial revelations of the Qur'an as a rebuttal with new authority. After further persecution, Muhammad began to develop a system of secret believers that enabled him to spread his teachings without raising public ire. This was also the beginning of the political side of Islam.

2. Muhammad's First Converts
Khadija

There are varying traditions regarding the first converts to Islam. Differences in these traditions can yet be seen in the sects of Islam today. For example, Shi'ite Muslims believe that Ali was Muhammad's first male convert to Islam, while Sunni Muslims hold fast to their tradition that Abu Bakr was first to convert to Islam. Ibn Ishaq identifies Khadija, the first wife of Muhammad, as the very first convert to Islam:

---

[171] Al-Tabari, Vol. VI, pp. 78-80.
[172] Ibn Kathir, *al-Sira*, Vol. 1, p. 319.
[173] Ibn Kathir, *al-Sira*, Vol. 1, p. 321
[174] Muranyi, p. 103.

She was the first to believe in God and His apostle, and in the truth of his message. By her God lightened the burden of His prophet. He never met with contradiction and charges of falsehood, which saddened him, but God comforted him by her when he went home. She strengthened him, lightened his burden, proclaimed his truth, and belittled men's opposition.[175]

Despite this description by Ibn Ishaq, as a woman she didn't "count" as the first convert.

Ali

The second convert to Islam, or the first male convert, is surrounded by a bit of controversy. Traditions differ regarding the sequence of conversions. Ali, a young boy taken under Muhammad's care, was identified by Ibn Ishaq as the second convert to Islam.[176] Ali b. Abu Talib was actually Muhammad's cousin, the son of Muhammad's uncle Abu Talib. Ali was placed under Muhammad's care when it seemed that Muhammad was in a better position to provide for his upbringing than was his birth father. About Ali's conversion to Islam, Ibn Ishaq describes,

Ali was the first male to believe in the apostle of God, to pray with him and to believe in his divine message, when he was a boy of ten. God favored him in that he was brought up in the care of the apostle before Islam began.[177]

There is some discrepancy among Muslim tradition as to whether Ali or Abu Bakr was the second convert to Islam. Ibn Kathir identifies Khadija as the first to accept Islam, followed by Ali, with Abu Bakr being the third (or the second male) convert.[178] Ibn Kathir also notes that there is considerable disagreement with the Shia over whether Ali or Abu Bakr was the first one to accept Islam.[179] Interestingly, both of these Sunni writers affirm that Ali was the first male to accept Islam. However, Al-Tabari mentions several scholars

---

[175] Ibid., p. 111
[176] Ibid., pp. 113-5.
[177] Ibid., p. 114.
[178] Ibn Kathir, *Sira,* pp. 312-3
[179] Ibid.

who maintained that Abu Bakr was the first male convert to Islam.[180] The disagreements are of interest only as they illustrate the tendency of polemicists to read back into history what they wanted to find in the interest of sectarian debate. There may also be an effort to imitate the Christian stories about the disciples of Jesus, and how they were called as a means of appealing to the Christian community to convert to Islam.

3. The Public Proclamation of Islam and the Reactions

Various stories are told of the first public proclamation of Islam. Ibn Ishaq credits Abu Bakr with being the first to openly espouse Islam, though primarily to his own close friends. What is interesting is that the initial confession that Muhammad requires of his followers in Ibn Ishaq's version is a shortened form of *Shahada*. "Bear witness that there is no God but Allah alone without associate, and disavow Al-Lat and Al-Uzza, and renounce rivals." Muhammad as the Prophet of God is left out.[181]

Al-Tabari maintains that Muhammad was secretive for the first three years of his prophethood, though he cites chapters of the Qur'an in support of this that clearly came during the middle Meccan period (15:94, 26:214-216).[182] It is said that the first bloodshed in Islam was when a group of polytheists happened upon the Muslims in prayer before their religion had been revealed. In the resulting altercation, one Muslim struck a polytheist in the head with a jawbone.[183]

Two distinct stories occur concerning the first proclamation. One has it that Muhammad calls the tribe of Quraysh together at a mountain outside the city where he tells them that he is "a warner to you in the face of a terrible doom." Abu Lahab responds angrily to this that leads to chapter 111 of the Quran.[184] Another states that Muhammad invited members of the Quraysh to a feast. After intensive preparations and a great feast, Muhammad is about to address those gathered:

> When the apostle wanted to address them Abu Lahab got in first
> and said, "Your host has bewitched you," so they dispersed before

---

[180] Al-Tabari, Vol. VI, pp. 81, 84-5.
[181] Ibn Ishaq, p. 115.
[182] Al-Tabari, Vol. VI, p. 88.
[183] Al-Tabari, Vol. VI, p. 89.
[184] Al-Tabari, Vol. VI, p. 89

the apostle could address them. On the morrow he said to me, "This man spoke before I could, and the people dispersed before I could address them, so do exactly as you did yesterday."[185]

The feast is repeated and Muhammad is able to give his call. Ibn Ishaq notes that his message is generally well received until, "he spoke disparagingly of their gods. When he did that they took great offence and resolved unanimously to treat him as an enemy."[186] Later, a large number of opponents come to Muhammad's uncle and protector, Abu Talib, to call for him to silence Muhammad or allow them to silence him. "Your nephew has cursed our gods, insulted our religion, mocked our way of life and accused our forefathers of error."[187] Ibn Ishaq goes on to note how Abu Talib protected Muhammad from Quraysh and obtained commitments from his own tribe of Banu Hashim to not give Muhammad over to his detractors. The text notes that everyone in the tribe followed his call with the exception of Abu Lahab who functions as the Judas of the text.[188] The protection of Abu Talib does not extend to the followers of Muhammad in other tribes and Ishaq notes, "Every tribe fell upon the Muslims among them, beating them and seducing them from their religion."[189]

The Muslim accounts mention this initial persecution in a way that signals the end of the first period of Qur'anic revelations. It is as if we have jumped from a secret faith to a sudden period of public ministry and conflict followed by the Prophet withdrawing into a more secretive period again. Al-Tabari jumps immediately from this initial persecution to the story of the emigration to Abyssinia, thus nearly skipping the middle Meccan period.[190] Ibn Ishaq records only a few stories from this period that we shall consider in the next chapter.

What is significant to note here is that the early texts present a picture of the early work of Muhammad that is not congruent with the text of the Qur'an. Clearly, dialogue, arguments, and polemic at various levels went on over a period of years in the early Meccan period. Indeed, the arguments had begun before the Qur'an began to be revealed. It does not seem that

---

[185]   Ibn Ishaq, p. 118.
[186]   Ibn Ishaq, p. 118.
[187]   Ibn Ishaq, p. 119.
[188]   Ibn Ishaq, p. 120.
[189]   Ibn Ishaq, p. 120.
[190]   Al-Tabari, Vol. VI, pp. 97-8.

there was an initial secretive period, but that a secretive period of sorts did occur during the middle Meccan period of revelations probably as a result of a build up of resentment toward Muhammad and his new religious ideas. This period of seclusion must have been highly formative for the Muslim community, and yet it is virtually ignored by the Muslim historians. It is to this period that we now turn our attention.

CHAPTER 3

THE MIDDLE MECCA PERIOD
613-614 CE

The period from 613 to 614 CE represents a change in the method and message of the Prophet. Muhammad is experiencing the rejection of his message by Quraysh and even members of his own tribe. He, therefore, withdraws from more public activities and begins to teach privately those who are his closest associates. This, at least, is the view of tradition. The content of the Qur'an from this period reflects some aspects of this. It is clear, however, that Muhammad was involved in dialogue, not only with his disciples, but also with the Meccans, perhaps even publicly. To understand this further, we turn to the content of the Qur'an from this period.

A. The Content of the Qur'an 613-614

About twenty chapters of the Qur'an were revealed during this period comprising 1,671 verses.[191] The volume, however, is more than double that of the previous forty-eight chapters. There is a stylistic change that partly explains this. Whereas the early chapters are poetry and the verses are short, the verses of these chapters tend to be versified prose, and are longer, and there is a marked emphasis on storytelling. The content of the Qur'an also changes significantly. About 286 verses deal with God's judgment or 17 percent of the total and 106 with hellfire verses, comprising about 6 percent of the text. There are a smaller number of verses on the pleasures of heaven. The total for these three categories is now about 25 percent of the text, down

---

[191] These are, in approximate order of revelation, 54, 37, 71, 44, 50, 20, 15, 19, 38, 36, 43, 72, 67, 23, 21, 25, 17, and 27.

from more than 50 percent of the earlier chapters. In contrast, Jewish and Christian apocryphal traditions, which were only 2 percent of the verses in the first forty-eight chapters now jump to 32 percent of the text or five hundred and forty three verses.[192] Thus, both the content and the style of the Qur'an change significantly during this period. Does this reflect a period of internal reflection on Muhammad's part as he seeks out Judeo-Christian traditions to explain his conception of himself and his faith?

There seems also to be a dialogical aspect to these chapters. Numerous questions are answered as if put to the Prophet by others; some are hostile in nature, and others seem to reflect questions of his followers. The tone of the chapters also varies widely. Sometimes the tone is conciliatory. At other times, railing judgments are pronounced. Gradually, a political sentiment begins to emerge, partly as a result of biblical models that Muhammad seems to adopt as types of himself. The prophetic self-image gradually takes form in the light of previous traditions and the controversies he is involved in. Gradually, we see the formation of Islamic doctrines and practices as these are hammered out in distinction to local ideas that the Prophet reacts against. A number of stories are told of an apocryphal nature, some of them quite fantastic. Supernatural elements also emerge involving spirits, omens, and magic. Finally, views of the People of the Book begin to take shape, perhaps through direct contact with members of the Jewish and Christian faiths.

A word should be said about the influence of the commentators like Ibn Kathir on the interpretation of the Qur'an. One is struck by the fact that Ibn Kathir has a radicalizing way of interpreting the text. He is continually backreading into the text elements that simply did not exist in Islam at this point. At times, he seems to ignore what is clearly stated in the text and simply launches off into stories and interpretations that have little or nothing to do with the text. Inevitably, he is more militant. He is interpreting the older texts in the light of what Islam had become. Ibn Kathir also provides fifteen or so historical contexts, as explanations of the background of the chapters, some of these quite dubious. The flavor and direction of the text is discernable, but its historical context is almost totally opaque. Yusuf

---

[192] There is a disagreement as to which stories are derived from biblical sources. I have included in this total those verses dealing with the stories of Ad and Thamud, which may or may not have Jewish/Christian sources. These two stories though cited often are only a minor portion of the verses associated with biblical sources.

Ali, by contrast, is more direct in his interpretation and simply follows the leading of the text.

1. The Development of the Prophetic Self-Image

In an average of three times in each chapter, God explains who the Prophet is. This is divided into declarations made by God concerning the Prophet and answers provided by God to various accusations made against the Prophet. We begin with those titles that God himself uses to identify the Prophet.

a. Muhammad a "Warner"

By far the most common title for the Prophet in this section of the Qur'an is "a warner." This title occurs eleven times in the twenty chapters. In chapter 38:65, he is called a warner, and God follows up by stating on behalf of the Prophet, "No knowledge have I of the chiefs on high . . . only this has been revealed to me, that I am to give warning plainly and publicly."[193] At times, it is so clear that Muhammad is explaining himself that one must remind oneself that these passages are prefaced with "Say!" indicating rather transparently that God is the one making the statement. While Muhammad gets mixed up in the earlier passages, he has become fairly consistent by this stage of the Qur'an. At times, the title seems to express the limitations of Muhammad's work. He is often referred to as "only a warner." The Muslim commentators tend to ignore this humility. Sometimes the title is used to beg off from difficult questions. When, it seems, his disciples ask him "They ask, when will this promise be fulfilled?" apparently referring to eschatological matters, he responds, "The knowledge is with Allah alone, and I am only a plain warner."[194] Elsewhere God himself explains the Prophet's role to the Prophet, "We have sent you only as a bearer of good news and a warner."[195] The agenda here does not seem coercive and God states, "whosoever wills may take a path to his Lord."[196] God's role for the Prophet is as "only one of the warners" since many other Prophets were sent to declare the imminence of God's judgment.[197]

---

[193]   Qur'an 38:69-70.
[194]   Qur'an 67:20.
[195]   This title is repeated in Qur'an 17:105.
[196]   Qur'an 25:56-57.
[197]   Qur'an 27:91.

Warnings of judgment are interspersed throughout these twenty chapters. Muhammad declares that the judgment of God is on all the "sects."[198] This seems to be the paradigm for all the Prophets according to the Qur'an. The first verse of the chapter entitled, "The Prophets" begins, "draws near for mankind their reckoning, while they turn away in heedlessness."[199] God tells the Prophet to be patient for the judgment will come to the disbelievers. God himself is the guarantor of the coming judgment.[200] Sometimes questions about the end times seem to come from the unbelievers, and Muhammad is quick to relate this to the coming judgment. The unbeliever's ask, "When this promise?" to which Muhammad responds that everything for judgment is written in "a clear book," and what "you wish to hasten on may be close behind you."[201] When the Qur'an rails that the unbelievers "will be cast down on their faces in the fire" on the day of judgment, Muslim commentators, like Ibn Kathir quickly fill in the details from traditional (Hadith) stories of the judgment. Ibn Kathir states that on the day of judgment 999 out of 1,000 will be condemned. Stories of the angel Israfil blowing on the trumpet to awaken the dead and how the bodies of the dead are rejoined with their souls fill three pages of commentary on this single verse.[202]

b. Muhammad Brings Good News

Muhammad is also called a messenger bearing good news. More importantly, he is called "a mercy to the worlds" providing a means for escape from the coming judgment by calling to the unbelievers, "will you then be Muslims?"[203] This verse is revealed in the midst of a passage describing the rolling up of the heavens, and how in the midst of the judgment, the righteous would inherit the land. Verse 105 of this passage seems to quote directly

---

[198] Qur'an 19:68.
[199] Qur'an 21:1.
[200] Qur'an 21:37-38.
[201] Qur'an 27:72-81.
[202] Ibn Kathir, *Tafsir*, Vol. 7, pp. 366-368. His descriptions remind me of the thesis put forward by Raymond Ibrahim as to what motivates suicide bombers. His thesis was the Muslims may be just as much motivated to "martyrdom" by the fear of the punishments of the grave and not just the supposed delights of heaven. See Jihad, Martyrdom, and the Torments of the Grave, Raymond Ibrahim, Pajamas Media, March 14, 2009.
[203] Qur'an 21:107. The word *Muslim* means one who is submitted. It seems to me that the word at this stage does not have the religious affliative meaning which it has later in the Medinan period.

from the Psalms according to Ibn Kathir, "My servants the righteous will inherit the land."[204]

In a number of passages, God comforts the Prophet in the midst of the struggle he faces with the Meccan tribes. In chapter 21 entitled, "The Prophets" God addresses the Prophet concerning the mockery he faces. God's assurance is that judgment is coming. Muhammad seems distressed that every other prophet seems to have failed at their task. All the examples given from the previous prophets' end with the nation of that prophet being destroyed, or later going astray. God addresses Muhammad directly and commands him to put his trust in God for his name is Ar-Rahman, the gracious.[205] Elsewhere God commands the Prophet not to grieve for the idolaters, for the earth is a place of judgment.[206] The three stories that follow in the passage are illustrations of God's righteous judgment.

c. Muhammad's Signs in the Heavens

As in the first period of Qur'anic revelations, Muhammad focuses many of his arguments on the wonders of creation and the power of God as he seeks to reason with the Meccans. Although these signs are not cited as evidence that Muhammad is the Prophet of God, these passages came to be interpreted that way in later Islam. In the chapter entitled, "Noah," he argues, "See ye not how Allah has created the seven heavens one above another, and made the moon . . . and made the sun."[207] Often Muhammad takes recourse in the power of God to justify the idea of resurrection, a belief which the Meccan's apparently held in contempt. "What! When we die and become dust (shall we live again?) That is a (sort of) return far (from our understanding)" To this criticism Muhammad affirms that God has a record of all who have died and then says, "But they deny the truth when it comes to them: So they are in a confused state. Do they not look at the sky above them?—How we have

---

[204] This does not directly correspond to any biblical text. Psalm 37:29 and 69:36 seem to come the closest. This passage is typical of Qur'anic material, which approximates biblical antecedents, but never exactly corresponds. It is as if Muhammad is hearing oral traditions and then trying to fit them into his poetic constructions. The material is an approximation of the biblical text twisted to fit his particular sectarian views.

[205] Qur'an 25:58.

[206] Qur'an 18:6-8.

[207] Qur'an 71:15-16.

made it and adorned it, and there are no flaws in it?"[208] God's power and glory expressed in the heavens is the assurance of his ability to recreate life. God's power also functions as a source of comfort for the Prophet. The stubborn Meccan disbelief prompts God (or the Prophet?) to muse.

> But never came a messenger to them but they mocked him . . . even if we opened out to them a gate from heaven and they were to continue all day ascending therein they would only say: Our eyes have been intoxicated: Nay, we have been bewitched by sorcery. It is we who have set out the Zodiacal signs in the heavens and made them fair-seeming to (all) beholders.[209]

Muhammad was particularly impressed with the signs of the heavens and astrology, the movement of the heavenly spheres, sun, moon, and stars as aspects of God's decrees. "And the sun runs its course for a period determined for it; that is the decree of (him) the exalted in Might, the All-Knowing."[210] Shooting stars are further examples of this divine power whose display is interpreted thus, "We have adorned the lowest heaven with lamps, and we have made such (lamps as) missiles to drive away the evil ones and have prepared for them the penalty of the blazing fire."[211] Ibn Kathir struggles to explain how "lamps" meaning "stars" could also be "missiles" as he points out "the stars in the sky are not thrown."[212] The answer is simply that the Prophet saw no difference between these lights in distinction to the viewpoint of the more astronomically sophisticated Arabs of later generations. Ibn Kathir concludes, "Allah knows best." As we have seen earlier, these shooting stars later became interpreted as signs of Muhammad's advent.

d. Muhammad's Signs: The Qur'an and Man's Humility

All of these natural phenomena are "signs" (ayat), indications of God's sovereignty and power just as each verse of the Qur'an is also a "sign."[213] This argument is related to the Prophet's reasoning about the lack of miraculous

---

[208] Qur'an 50:3-6.
[209] Qur'an 15:11, 14-16.
[210] Qur'an 36:38.
[211] Qur'an 67:5.
[212] Ibn Kathir, *Tafsir*, Vol. 10, p. 83.
[213] Qur'an 17:12.

signs accompanying his ministry. Like the constancy of the sun and moon, so the Qur'an is his ultimate "sign":

> Truly thou canst not cause the dead to listen, nor canst thou cause the deaf to hear the call, when they turn back in retreat. Nor canst thou be a guide to the blind (to prevent them) from straying: only those wilt thou get to listen who believe in our signs, and they will bow in Islam.[214]

This "sign of revelation" is "a Qur'an that makes things clear."[215] Perhaps the fact that it was in Arabic was the ultimate demonstration of its clarity for the Arabs. "Thus have we sent this down—an Arabic Qur'an—and explained therein in detail."[216] An appeal to nationalistic or tribal linguistic sentiments is implicit.

Another theme to which the Prophet returns regularly is the theme of the humble origins of man and his debt of gratitude to God. Man is the *nutfah*, the product of the combination of the two despicable male and female seminal fluids. Man's humble origin is as a drop of "mingled sperm." But he is put to the test as to whether he will be "grateful or ungrateful." God expresses a sentiment of incredulity that man of such humble origins would even dare to oppose the creator of the universe, "Doth not man see that it is We who created him from a sperm drop, yet behold! He (stands forth as an open adversary!)"[217] On one occasion, the Qur'an utilizes this image as the basis for social equality. The poor man and the rich man alike are created from this humble *nutfah*. "More wealth have I than you, and more honor and power . . ." to which the poor man replies, "Dost thou deny Him who created thee out of the dust, then out of a sperm drop, then fashioned thee into a man?"[218]

At times, the tone of the Qur'an is plaintive. In chapter 71, Noah pleads with his people to turn back from rebellion against God. "What is the matter with you, that ye place not your hope for kindness and long-suffering in Allah."[219] It seems to me that this is a type of Muhammad's pleading with his

---

[214]   Qur'an 27:80-81.
[215]   Qur'an 15:1.
[216]   Qur'an 20:113.
[217]   Qur'an 36:77.
[218]   Qur'an 18:34, 37.
[219]   Qur'an 71:13.

own nation, although spoken through the mouth of Noah. Elsewhere, when Muhammad condemns the greedy among his people God encourages him, "even if thou hast to turn away from them in pursuit of the mercy from thy Lord which thou dost expect, yet speak to them a word of easy kindness."[220] Muhammad was a man of little political power at this point. God admonishes, "We know best what they say; and thou art not one to overawe them by force. So admonish with the Qur'an such as fear my warning!"[221]

Chapter 72 concerning the jinn has one of the longest sections regarding Muhammad's conception of himself as mediated through the mouth of God.

> Say: "It is not in my power to cause you harm, or to bring you to right conduct." Say: "No one can deliver me from Allah . . . Mine is only to convey what I receive From Allah . . . Then they will know who it is that is weakest in (his) helper and least important in numbers."

The Qur'an explains the lack of signs from the Prophet in another way, "And we refrain from sending the Signs, only because the men of former generations treated them as false," and again, "we only sent the signs by way of terror."[222]

Over time, the Prophet's tone becomes more militant. Chapter 37 entitled, "Those Ranged in Ranks" refers to the angels who "are so strong in repelling (evil) and thus proclaim the message."[223] The analogy is a military one, and most of the chapter relates biblical stories of Prophets who proclaimed the coming judgment, and in the end, their nations were destroyed. At the end of the chapter, Muhammad returns to the image of the angels ranged in ranks and indicates their military purpose in carrying out the will of Allah. "Already has our Word been passed before (this) to our servants sent (by us), that they would certainly be assisted, and that our forces—they surely must conquer."[224] Stories of angels helping the Muslims in actual battles abound in the later chapters of the Qur'an and biographical stories.

---

[220] Qur'an 17:28.
[221] Qur'an 50:45.
[222] Qur'an 17:59.
[223] Qur'an 37:2-3.
[224] Qur'an 37:171-173.

In chapter 43, God comforts the Prophet in regard to the Meccan mockers saying, "And never came there a Prophet to them but they mocked him. So we destroyed (them)—stronger in power than these."[225] This tone grows stronger in chapter, "Al-Mulk—The Kingdom" where God represents Himself in military terms, "Nay, who is there that can help you (even as) an army, besides (Allah) Most Merciful."[226] The theology of a kingdom of God on earth emerges in this section of the Qur'an. Nevertheless, Muhammad's personal role affirmed at this point is simply as a "warner."

e. Muhammad's Growing Self-Conception: The Prophet Kings

The seeds of this military conception are also found in the paradigm of Prophet Kings that Muhammad finds in his biblical allusions. Chief among these is the example of Sulayman (Solomon) and to a lesser degree his father Dawud (David). Chapter 27, "The Ant" seems to represent a significant addition to Muhammad's conception of his prophetic station based on Jewish stories. Key among these is the story of Solomon's conflict with the Queen of Sheba. Loosely based on the Targum Sheni (second Targum) of Esther (or an oral tradition antecedent to it),[227] Muhammad transforms this Jewish fable of male superiority into a parable of Solomon's political hegemony over a pagan queen. We shall have occasion to return to this story in greater depth later. The main point is that Solomon forces the Queen's submission by his superior military force, after which the glory of his palace leads to her conversion to Islam. "O my Lord! I have indeed wronged my soul: I do (now) submit (in Islam), with Solomon to the Lord of the Worlds."[228]

In the midst of the Meccan resistance to Muhammad's message, the facility of political power in effecting change by force must have seemed both an attractive option and a paradigm well represented in the previous holy books. Ibn Kathir, going well beyond the text, reads these meanings in where there is no reference to it in the text. In chapter 17:80-81, he claims that the verses refer to the Hijra, which they clearly do not, and concludes, "alongside the truth he also needed power and authority in order to suppress those who opposed and

---

225 Qur'an 43:7-8.
226 Qur'an 67:20.
227 Jacob Lassner, *Demonizing the Queen of Sheba*, Chicago: University of Chicago Press, 1993.
228 Qur'an 27:44.

resisted him."[229] Yusuf Ali, the moderate Muslim, is in agreement with the need for political power in Islam.

The level of Muhammad's frustration can also be seen in the frequent outbursts against the Meccan opposition to his message. In chapter 25, "The Criterion" (Al-Furqan)[230] God says concerning the Prophet's opponents, "The Messenger will say: 'O my Lord! Truly my people took this Qur'an for just foolish nonsense.' Thus we have made for every Prophet an enemy among the criminals."[231], [232] It is remarkable how tolerant Meccan society was permitting Muhammad to preach that they were criminals to whom he was an enemy. Perhaps this passage was revealed quietly only to Muhammad's followers. Later in the same passage, God commands the Prophet, "Therefore listen not to the unbelievers, but strive against them with the utmost strenuousness, with the (Qur'an).[233] The word "strive" is jihad though here it still refers only to warfare on the level of ideas. In Chapter 15, after a litany of judgments upon biblical and nonbiblical peoples, Muhammad calls down God's wrath, "(of just such wrath) as we sent down on those who divided (scripture into arbitrary parts)—(so also on such) as have made the Qur'an into shreds."[234] Ibn Kathir goes on to highlight Muhammad's prayer against some individuals of Quraysh who had so mocked his book, and all of them died untimely accidental deaths.[235] There is a growing intolerance of any critique of the content of the Qur'an.

Muhammad's words were being dissected and mocked in poetic form, perhaps even in poetic debates between the Prophet and his detractors. Some traditions indicate this and also note Muhammad's disdain for poetry.[236] During the Medinan Period, Muhammad took severe action against those who mocked him and the Qur'an, having several people assassinated.[237] We do not gain any insight into what was being done to the Qur'an by the Quraysh

---

[229] Ibn Kathir, Tafsir, Vol. 6, p. 71.
[230] This title later became virtually synonymous with the Qur'an itself. Qur'an is furqan, "the Criterion" by which all things are judged.
[231] I use Kathir's translation at this point since the word is stronger than "sinners" which Yusuf Ali employs.
[232] Qur'an 25:30-31.
[233] Qur'an 25:52.
[234] Qur'an 15:90-91.
[235] Ibn Kathir, Tafsir, Vol. 5, pp. 423-4.
[236] Muslim, Vol. 4, p. 1221, Bukhari, Vol. 8, p. 113.
[237] Ibn Ishaq, p. 364-369.

in Ibn Kathir's commentary. It is symptomatic of Ibn Kathir that most of his commentary at this point is directly against the later use of the word *yaqin* or "certainty" by Sufis who used to justify the idea that anyone who had attained higher knowledge or certainty no longer needed to follow the strictures of ritual law. The passage has nothing to do with this. Ibn Kathir is dealing with theological issues that arose hundreds of years later.[238]

f. Muhammad's Self-Perception: The Sinless Prophets

Although the Qur'an records several cases of Muhammad's own moral failings in the eyes of God, as the Qur'an incorporates more and more biblical allusions, it becomes less and less willing to mention the failings of the Prophets. David's sin with Bathsheeba, though mentioned, is fairly glossed over.[239] Later commentators exclude consideration of the story.[240] Aaron (Harun) is exonerated in the matter of the golden calf, all blame being laid on a mysterious figure as-Samiri. This would seem to be a Samaritan and as such would constitute another anachronism for the Jews. The Samaritans emerged after the destruction of the Northern Kingdom of Israel in 722 BCE, and thus in Jewish thinking could have nothing to do with the events of the Exodus around 1400 BCE

Ibn Kathir goes on to explain that Harun had tried to prohibit the worship of the calf and was nearly killed for it.[241] It seems that Prophets in Muhammad's changing conception were capable of oversight and forgetfulness, but not of direct sin. Ibn Kathir mentions that Muhammad was so engrossed with his war preparations that he missed a prayer time during the Battle of the Trench, considered a major oversight. He mentions that they prayed the *asr* prayer after the sun had set without further comment.[242] The question of whether the

---

[238] Ibn Kathir, *Tafsir*, Vol. 5, p. 426-7.

[239] Qur'an 38:21-25. Ibn Kathir does not understand the story at all, and merely notes that David prostrated in repentance and that Muslims, following the example of the Prophet, should prostrate when this passage is read. Yusuf Ali, aware of his Western audience, deals with the obvious issue of King David's sin. He rejects the biblical passages stating "passages like these are mere chroniques scandaleuses, that is, narratives of scandalous crimes of the grossest character." (Ali, no. 4178, p. 1167). In this sense, he follows traditional Muslim thinking that the Prophets were above sin.

[240] as noted in the footnote above.

[241] Ibn Kathir, *Tafsir*, Vol. 6, p. 379.

[242] Ibn Kathir, *Tafsir*, Vol. 8, p. 329.

Prophet was sinless or became sinless through God's forgiveness is a point of some contention. Ibn Kathir notes in regard to night prayers mentioned in chapter 17 that

> "an additional prayer" means the night prayer has been made an extra prayer specifically for the Prophet because all his previous and future sins had been forgiven. But for other members of his Ummah, offering optional prayers may expiate for whatever sins they may commit."[243]

It seems that the office of Prophet conferred with it the automatic forgiveness of sins and does not necessarily indicate that the Prophet never sinned, only that he was completely forgiven. We may note the Qur'an's increasing unwillingness to attribute sin to any of the Prophets, and that this formed a crucial aspect of Muslim thinking about Muhammad himself. This ultimately has a devastating impact on Muslim culture by negating the ability to question and criticize those in authority, particularly the religious clergy. The secularism of the West is largely a result of the freedom to criticize the Bible, Jesus, and the clergy.

g. Questions by the Disciples

Finally, we should note some teaching that seems to be the result of questions raised by disciples of the Prophet. In chapter 17, God notes the response of the Prophet's enemies to his followers: "They listen when they listen to thee; and when they meet in private conference, behold the wicked say, ye follow none other than a man bewitched!"[244] Muhammad responds to this accusation and a further concerning the resurrection and then concludes, "Say to my servants that they should (only) say those things that are best. For Satan doth sow dissensions among them: For Satan is to man an avowed enemy."[245] Some of the Prophet's followers were apparently discouraged by both the lack of miraculous signs as well as some of the fantastic claims that Muhammad made. We noted earlier that signs were withheld according to the Qur'an, because men "treated them as false" or "we only sent the signs by way of terror." Muhammad's claim that he had made a night journey to

---

[243] Ibn Kathir, *Tafsir*, Vol. 6, p. 62.

[244] Qur'an 17:47.

[245] Qur'an 17:53.

Jerusalem on a winged horse and his description of the Zaqqum tree of hell occasioned some of his followers to doubt. Ibn Kathir mentions that because of these two stories, "some people gave up their Islam."[246] Apparently, Muhammad tries to explain these earlier revelations saying, "We granted the vision which we showed thee but as a trial for men—as also the cursed tree (mentioned) in the Qur'an: We put terror (and warning) into them, but it only increases their inordinate transgression."[247]

2. Arguments That the Meccans Put to Muhammad

Much of the prophetic self-image was formed in the context of discussion and argument with those who did not accept Muhammad's visions and had their own explanations for who he was. These are far more numerous than arguments which seem to be the result of discussions with his followers. On the basis of this, one is hard pressed to believe that Muhammad was only teaching privately during most of this period. Clearly, the debate was still going on.

The Meccan's made many accusations against Muhammad, some more frequently than others. They claimed that he was insane or possessed, "They say: O thou to whom the message is being revealed, truly thou art mad or possessed, why bringest thou not angels to us if it be that thou hast the truth?"[248] Muhammad's response is that angels were not sent because then they would have no respite from God, nor would they believe even if he were to cause them to ascend to a gate in heaven. To the signs in the heavens, which the Qur'an points out the Meccans say, "this is nothing but evident sorcery" and of Muhammad they say, "Shall we give up our gods for the sake of a poet possessed?"[249] This particular accusation elicits a direct response later, "We have not instructed the (Prophet) in poetry, nor is it meet for him: This is no less than a message and a Qur'an making things clear."[250] This culminates

---

[246] Ibn Kathir, *Tafsir*, Vol. 6, p. 43.
[247] Qur'an 17:60.
[248] Qur'an 15:6-7.
[249] Qur'an 37:15, 36. Hawting notes these and other direct mentions of "gods," but argues that these are examples of "monotheistic polemic" addressing other monotheists. It is a novel argument and clearly the context of the Qur'an is deeply influenced by monotheistic groups. I find it hard to accept that the range and multitude of references are only between monotheists. Nevertheless, it is a thesis worth considering. Hawting, G. R. *The Idea of Idolatry and the Emergence of Islam*, Cambridge University Press, 1999, pp. 50-56.
[250] Qur'an 36:69.

in a whole litany of accusations recorded in chapter 21, "The Prophets." The Meccans state, "will you go to witchcraft with your eyes wide open." The Qur'an then illustrates their contradictory explanations, "'Nay', they say, '(these are) medleys of dreams!—Nay, he forged it!—Nay, he is but a poet!' Let him then bring us a sign like the ones that were sent to (Prophets) of old!'" This reference indicates that the Meccans were aware of other revelations, such as the Jewish and Christian scriptures.

In commentary on the slightly later chapter 17, Ibn Kathir describes a delegation of Quraysh that came to Muhammad to offer him wealth, power, or exorcism so that he would stop slandering their ancestors and gods. "You have slandered our forefathers . . . slandered our gods and caused division."[251] Attacks on the ancestors and their gods apparently infuriated the Meccans more than anything else. Earlier they had accused Muhammad of being of low status and wealth, "The unbelievers say to those who believe, 'Which of the two sides is best in point of position? Which makes the best show in council?'" To this Muhammad responds that God would ultimately reveal "who is worst in position, and (who is) weakest in forces!"[252] The Meccan's call his Qur'an a "made-up tale" and snivel, "What! Has the message been sent to him—(of all persons) among us?' . . . But they are in doubt concerning my (own) message! Nay, they have not yet tasted my punishment!"[253]

At times, God seems to question the Prophet concerning material desires, "or is it that thou askest them for some recompense? But the recompense of thy Lord is best."[254] Was this a temptation or merely a rhetorical question? Elsewhere the Prophet affirms, "Say: 'No reward do I ask of you for this (Qur'an). Nor am I a pretender.'"[255]

a. Meccan Questions: Resurrection

Among the many questions put to Muhammad by the Meccans, three stand out as far more frequent than any others. These are the question of resurrection, the issue of the lack of signs accompanying the Prophet's work, and the accusation that he was tutored by others. We begin with the question of resurrection.

---

[251] Ibn Kathir, *Tafsir*, Vol. 6, p. 81.

[252] Qur'an 19:73, 75.

[253] Qur'an 38:7-8.

[254] Qur'an 23:72.

[255] Qur'an 38:86.

Apparently, the pagan Arabs did not believe in a physical resurrection of the body. They had animistic concepts about the ancestors and spirits, but the concept of a physical resurrection was apparently held in contempt by them. This would argue against the idea that Muhammad was dealing primarily with monotheists, as Hawting maintains. Christians and Jews were generally strong believers in the resurrection of the body. The argument about resurrection winds its way through most of the chapters in this section of the Qur'an. Early in this period the Qur'an asserts:

> As to these (Quraysh) they say forsooth: "There is nothing beyond our first death and we shall not be raised again. Then bring back our forefathers, if what ye say is true."[256]

Muhammad does not argue the point, but merely rebuts that the day of judgment is coming. The question is repeated in the next chapter 50:3: "What! When we die and become dust (shall we live again?)" to which Muhammad responds by pointing out the glories of creation and God's power. After an interlude of one chapter, the question is raised again with a slightly more sophisticated answer: "Man says: 'What! When I am dead, shall I then be raised up alive?' But man does not call to mind that we created him before out of nothing."[257] In chapter 36:33, he uses the analogy of the renewal of the dead earth as a "sign" of how life is restored. Ibn Kathir provides a historical context in which this discussion took place. Ubayy bin Khalaf, one of the unbelievers, held up a dry bone and asked how it could be resurrected.[258] To this, according to Ibn Kathir, Muhammad replies with verse 78: "And he makes comparisons for us and forgets his own (origin and) creation: He says, 'Who can give life to (dry) bones and decomposed ones (at that)?' Say, 'He will give them life who created them for the first time!'"[259]

Perhaps the most powerful interchange on this subject comes in chapter 23, "The Believers." After relaying various examples from biblical Prophets, Muhammad quotes the Quraysh:

> "Does he promise that when ye die and become dust and bones, ye shall be brought Forth (again)? There is nothing but our life in

---

[256] Qur'an 44:34-36.
[257] Qur'an 19:66-67.
[258] Ibn Kathir, *Tafsir,* Vol. 8, p. 222.
[259] Qur'an 36:78.

this world! We shall die and we live! But we shall never be raised up again! He is only a man who invents a lie against Allah, but we are not the ones to believe in him!' (The Prophet) said: 'O My Lord! Help me: For that they accuse me of falsehood.' (Allah) said: In but a little while, they are sure to be sorry!'"[260]

Shortly after in the same chapter:

"They say things similar to what the ancients said. They say, 'What! When we die and become dust and bones, could we really be raised up again? Such things have been promised to us and to our fathers before! They are nothing but tales of the ancients!' Say: 'To whom belong the earth and all beings therein?'"[261]

Once again Ibn Kathir provides a dubious historical context for this verse. He claims that Muhammad had prayed for seven years of famine on the Quraysh just like the seven years of famine in the time of Joseph.[262] It does not seem to bother him that none of the Muslim historians records such a famine taking place. There is an element of anger at this rejection of faith in resurrection. Toward the end of this period under consideration Muhammad calls down the fires of hell on those who reject the message of resurrection:

Their abode will be hell: Every time it shows abatement we shall increase for them the fierceness of the fire. That is their recompense because they rejected our signs. And said, "When we are reduced to bones and broken dust, should we really be raised up (to be) a new creation?" See they not that Allah who created the heavens and the earth, has power to create the like of them (anew)?[263]

b. Meccan Questions: Signs.

A second category of criticisms from the Meccans relates to the lack of signs demonstrating Muhammad's prophetic office. These signs are expected

---

[260] Qur'an 23:35, 37-40.
[261] Qur'an 23:81-84.
[262] Ibn Kathir, *Tafsir,* Vol. 6, p. 677.
[263] Qur'an 17:97-99. Kathir lists three other passages with similar content: 40:57, 46:33, 36:81-2.

to be miraculous events that would show God's power. This critique finds an echo in the near preoccupation of the Qur'an with the "signs" of God. This also shows the influence of Judeo-Christian ideas. Indeed certain miraculous signs are put forward by the Prophet as demonstrating his office. Yet these seem to have no impact on the criticism of the Meccans. This raises the question, what does Muhammad mean by the word *sign* (ayat)? In chapter 20, the Meccans ask,

> They say: "Why does he not bring us a sign from his Lord?" Has not a clear sign come to them of all that was in the former books of revelation? And if we had inflicted upon them a penalty before this, they would have said: "Our Lord! If only thou hadst sent us a messenger, we should certainly have followed."[264]

Here it seems that "signs" refer to the content of previous revelations of which the Qur'an is a confirmation. Now that a messenger has been sent with similar "signs" they are without excuse. Most of the content of this chapter relates to the story of Moses, Aaron, and Pharaoh now explained in "an Arabic Qur'an." There is a sense that Muhammad is relating a tradition that he has received, and that this is the "sign" of his prophethood. The idea of Jews tutoring Muhammad comes immediately to mind.

We noted earlier the Meccan question "why bringest thou not angels to us" as another example of the demand for signs. There Muhammad argues that signs have been given in the astrological lights and, in particular, the shooting stars. In chapter 21, they demand, "Let him bring us a sign like the ones sent to Prophets of old!" Muhammad appeals that past generations who saw those signs, nevertheless, did not repent: "(As to those) before them, not one of the populations that we destroyed believed: Will these believe?"[265] He argues that they should ask those "who possess the message." This clearly refers to the Jews and Christians and regards those previous messages of their scriptures as signs to be consulted for confirmation. Ibn Kathir ignores this appeal to previous revelations as signs[266] and completely distorts the thrust of the passage stating: "Why do you ask the People of the Book about what they

---

[264] Qur'an 20:133-134.

[265] Qur'an 21:5-6.

[266] In my way of thinking, this is the strongest argument against Hawting's thesis. If Muhammad's tirades against idolatry were really against other monotheists, why would Muhammad appeal to the scriptures of those groups he was austensibly criticizing?

have, which has been altered and distorted."[267] The commentator at this point essentially negates the thrust of Muhammad's argument by backreading later controversies with Christians into the text of the Qur'an. Yusuf Ali does not engage in these polemics, but simply avoids the issue, making no comment on the clear thrust of the passage.

Angels as an aspect of the signs of God come up regularly in the text. "Why has not an angel been sent down to him"[268] the Meccans ask at one point and claim that Muhammad is bewitched. Muhammad seems to regard this as idolatry. The question is repeated, "Why are not angels sent down to us, or (why) do we not see our Lord." To this Muhammad replies, "Indeed they have arrogant conceit of themselves and mighty is the insolence of their impiety! The day they see the angels no joy will there be . . ."[269]

c. Muhammad's Miraculous Signs in Qur'an and Commentary

Elsewhere commentators claim miraculous signs. These are primarily two: The splitting of the moon and the night journey, or *isra/miraj*, to Jerusalem. The first occurs at the very beginning of this second period of the Qur'anic revelations. Chapter 54, entitled "The Moon" begins: "The hour (of judgment) is nigh, and the moon cleft asunder." But if they see a sign, they turn away and say, "This is (but) transient magic." In actual fact, this passage is merely a repetition of the apocalyptic visions recited in the earlier chapters of the Qur'an. It has nothing to do with any miracles of Muhammad. Nevertheless, Ibn Kathir relates eight different traditions concerning how Muhammad split the moon as a demonstration of his "signs" to the Meccans.[270] It is obvious that this was not the case because Muhammad never raises this as an argument later when the Meccans accuse him of lacking "signs."[271] Yusuf

---

[267] Ibn Kathir, *Tafsir,* Vol. 6, pp. 423-4.
[268] Qur'an 25:7.
[269] Qur'an 25:21-22.
[270] Ibn Kathir, *Tafsir*, Vol. 9, pp. 345-9.
[271] The story of the splitting of the moon has taken on a life of its own throughout the Muslim world. Modern examples of the power of this story can be found in the many urban legends that circulate about how the Americans never landed on the moon because Muhammad had split it. This is backed up with factual sounding stories about how the moon landing was staged in Algeria. Elsewhere the pervasive and equally false rumor that Neil Armstrong was converted to Islam after hearing the call to prayer on the moon probably has its basis in the desire to cover up the fact that no split moon was discovered by the astronauts.

Ali mentions three different interpretations of the split moon, but mentions nothing of a miracle of Muhammad.

The other clear "sign" of Muhammad does have a basis in the Qur'an. This is a verse concerning his night journey to Jerusalem. Typically the Qur'anic material itself is quite limited:

> Glory to (Allah) who did take his servant for a journey by night from the sacred mosque to the farthest mosque, whose precincts we did bless—in order that we might show him some of our signs: For he is the one who heareth and seeth (all things).[272]

This brief notation has been generously filled out by the commentators. Based on this highly obscure verse Ibn Kathir produces twenty-six pages of isogetical content. Muhammad rides on the back of the winged horse, burak, to Jerusalem. After visiting the sacred precincts, he climbs a ladder up into heaven and, after passing through the seven heavens and meeting various prophets, he is ushered into an audience with Allah himself. There he receives the commands for daily prayer and fasting during Ramadan after an interesting process of reducing the requirements to a more manageable level. Ibn Kathir intersperses this narrative with various "proofs" of the historicity of the event, as well as elements of the Prophet's guided tour of hell. The story of Muhammad's chest being split and his heart being cleansed, found at two other periods of his life, is repeated here as well.[273] Interestingly, Ibn Kathir also records the contempt with which the Meccans responded to this fantastic story. Abu Jahl[274] says about the night journey and Muhammad's description of hell. "Muhammad is trying to scare us with the tree of zaqqum; bring some dates and butter and let us have some zaqqum!"[275] As was noted earlier, apparently some Muslims left their faith at this time in disbelief.[276] Yusuf Ali has very little to say about this verse and includes nothing of the fantastic stories that permeate the earlier commentary literature. Moderate Muslims tend to ignore

---

[272] Qur'an 17:1
[273] Ibn Kathir, *Tafsir,* Vol 5, pp. 550-576.
[274] The name Abu Jahl means "promoter of ignorance." He was given this name by the Muslims due to his resistance to Muhammad. His real name was Amr b. Hesham, and he was killed by the Muslims at the battle of Badr. Dashti, Ali, *23 Years*, Mazda Publishers, 1992, p. 211.
[275] Ibn Kathir, *Tafsir,* Vol. 5, p. 566.
[276] Ibn Kathir, *Tafsir,* Vol. 5, p. 566.

material like this. They do not engage in historical-critical methodology and in that sense are still pre-modern dogmatists.

It seems that Muhammad did desire some kind of a sign with which to demonstrate his prophethood. Exactly what this "sign" was will probably never be known. It does seem that Muhammad claimed here to have taken part in something miraculous. That the event contained none of the content claimed for it by later commentators is indicated by the fact that neither a clear detailed description of the rules for prayer or fasting in line with traditions is included in this chapter or in any later chapter of the Qur'an. Further, Muhammad never uses this as an argument for a miraculous sign when the Meccan's make the same accusation later. This attempt to generate a "sign" backfired and Muhammad perhaps lost credibility through it. The event is never again mentioned in the Qur'an, nor is it raised in response to later questions about the Prophet's lack of "signs." The fanciful tales associated with this event in the writings of the commentators have no basis in the Qur'an, and contain massive problems in chronology, including widely disparate stories about its date and circumstance and invariably backread an Islam as it existed two hundred years after the death of the Prophet.

d. Meccan Questions: The Tutors of the Prophet

The final criticism that the Meccans leveled against Muhammad was that he was tutored by others. This is an extremely significant criticism, because it may indicate something of the process by which Muhammad obtained his primarily Jewish legendary and apocryphal materials. We have already noted that this second section of the Qur'an contains a quantum leap in terms of Jewish content. The first accusation of this type occurs in chapter 44, "The Smoke," "yet they turn away from him and say, 'tutored by others, a man possessed!'." To this accusation, God responds through the Prophet, "One day we shall seize you with a mighty onslaught: We will indeed (then) exact retribution."[277] Chapter 20:133, we noted earlier, indicates Muhammad pointed to the authority of the earlier holy books and affirms them as signs. Ibn Kathir feels constrained to state in contradiction to the text itself: "This means the Qur'an which Allah revealed to him while he was an unlettered man who could not read or write well, and who did not study with the people of the book."[278] It is a point of some sensitivity to the early Muslim commentators.

---

[277] Qur'an 44:14, 16.
[278] Ibn Kathir, *Tafsir,* Vol. 6, p. 418.

Yusuf Ali twists the text to make it say that they should have been convinced of the truth of the Qur'an from "what was in their own books"![279] He thus turns this into an address to the Christians and Jews even though the rest of the chapter is addressed to the Meccans, and there is no critique of Jewish or Christian concepts anywhere in the chapter. Muhammad, at this point in his career, was not aware of any differences between what he was teaching and what Jews and Christians taught. Indeed, the chapter is based primarily on the story of Moses, and this argues for a confidence on his part that Jews would back him up. Muslim commentators, whether radical or moderate, seem to be constrained to provide certain traditional interpretations even if these are in direct contradiction of the text they are supposedly interpreting.

In the chapter, entitled "The Criterion" (Furqan) a longer accusation takes place:

> "But the misbelievers say,'Naught is this but a lie which he has forged, and others have helped him at it.' In truth it is they who have put forward an iniquity and a falsehood. And they say, "Tales of the ancients which he caused to be written: And they are dictated before him morning and evening." Say, "The Qur'an was sent down by him who knows the mystery (that is) in the heavens and the earth."[280]

Ibn Kathir points out that Muhammad was illiterate, and thus, could not have studied under others and further his character was so honest that he could not ever engage in such falsehood.[281] What Ibn Kathir does not seem to understand is that this has nothing to do with being taught or studying written documents. We are almost certainly dealing with oral traditions being interchanged in a process of dialogue. To "cause to be written," the Meccan accusation seems, potentially, to indicate illiteracy. Yusuf Ali avoids the question of outside help entirely.

A final accusation occurs in the midst of Meccan calls for "signs" from the Prophet:

> "They say, 'We will not believe in thee, until thou causest a spring to gush forth for us from the earth, or (until) thou hast a garden of date

---

[279]   Ali, Yusuf, p. 792, footnote 2658.
[280]   Qur'an 25:4-6.
[281]   Ibn Kathir, *Tafsir,* Vol. 7, p. 143.

trees and vines and causest rivers to gush forth in their midst, carrying abundant water, or thou causest the sky to fall in pieces, as thou sayest (will happen), against us, or thou bring Allah and the angels before (us) face to face; or thou have a house of gold or thou mount a ladder right into the skies. No, we shall not even believe in thy mounting until thou send down to us a book that we can read." Say: "Glory to my Lord! Am I aught but a man—a messenger?"[282]

The final accusation is the most potent. What is the source of Muhammad's revelation? Is it the heavenly book that he claims is being recited to him? If so, show us a copy. Ibn Kathir explains this as being part of a Quraysh delegation that tried to dissuade Muhammad. In his rendition, they say, "We have heard that the one who is teaching you this, is a man in Al-Yamamah called ar-Rahman. By Allah, we will never believe in ar-Rahman."[283] It may be that Kathir is mocking at this point, making a play on a name of God. Nevertheless, the accusation that Muhammad was borrowing traditions from elsewhere was important enough to find significant space both in the Qur'an and in the apologetics of the later interpreters. These accusations of borrowing do seem to be linked with Muhammad's increasing usage of Hebrew words, Jewish traditions, and biblical and apocryphal allusions.

3. The Emerging Theology of Islam

The second period of Qur'anic revelation involves a considerable development in Muhammad's conception of God. Islamic theology, it seems, was born during this period, largely in the light of previous revelations. In the earliest period, Muhammad seems to have struggled with the reality of a coming judgment and settling his own questions concerning the oneness of God. In this second period, the revelations work out the parameters of the absolute oneness (tauhid) of God, what this oneness means, and how it relates to the power, immanence, and sovereignty of Allah. Concepts concerning God's Word, the spirits, and the means of forgiveness emerge. Prophecies concerning the end of time fill out the Prophet's concept of God's judgment. Finally, man's proper response to God is described in the ubiquitous term "taqwa" meaning "fear" or "awe."

---

[282]   Qur'an 17:90-93.
[283]   Ibn Kathir, *Tafsir,* Vol. 6, p. 84.

a. God's Unity

In chapter 37, the first phrase of the Islamic confession of faith begins to emerge, primarily as a reaction against idolatry, "for they, when they are told that there is no God except Allah, would puff themselves up with pride."[284] His oneness is defined primarily in terms of lacking a pantheon of other gods who relate to Him in a familial fashion. Thus, the jinn affirm that God has neither wife nor son.[285] In a fashion similar to the interpolation placed over the satanic verses of chapter 53, God declares, "What! Has he taken daughters out of what he himself creates and granted to you sons for choice?" Thus, God has no daughters.[286] Further, God has no "offspring" of any kind, which Ibn Kathir interprets as a rejection of the pagan Arab concept of angels as god's children.[287] The invocation that God has no sons is the most frequent of all. In chapter 19, "Mary" in addition to containing several stories about Jesus and his mother includes, "They say: '(Allah) most gracious has begotten a son!' Indeed they have put forth a thing most monstrous."[288] Later in chapter 43, he records apparent arguments with sects of the Christians: "When Jesus the son of Mary is held up as an example . . . they say, 'are our gods best, or he?' This they set forth to thee, only by way of disputation: yea, they are a contentious people."[289] Muhammad was in contact with Christians at this point. Their belief in Christ as the Son of God becomes a primary point in Muhammad's rejection of their faith even as he goes on to define a very high position for Christ as the one who will return on the day of judgment.[290] Muhammad rejects the concept of any kind of partners with God using the logic that this would create chaos in the universe between a multiplicity of conflicting gods:

> No son did Allah beget, nor is there any god along with him. (If there were many gods), behold, each god would have taken away what he had created, and some would have lorded it over

---

[284]   Qur'an 37:35.
[285]   Qur'an 72:3.
[286]   Qur'an 43:16.
[287]   Qur'an 21:26, Ibn Kathir, *Tafsir,* Vol. 6, p. 438. Similar verses he notes are found at 43:81 and 39:65.
[288]   Qur'an 19:88-89. Ibn Kathir considers this to be a sin that virtually rips creation apart. "There is no coequal for Him in his creation, because all creatures are His slaves," Vol. 6, p. 315.
[289]   Qur'an 43:57-58.
[290]   Similar statements are found in 25:1, 17:111.

others! Glory to Allah! (He is free) from the (sort of) things they
attribute to Him! . . . Too high is He for the partners they attribute
to Him![291]

It is this conception of the absolute unity of God that underlies the concept
of *Shirk,* the attributing of partners to God, which is the ultimate sin in Islam.
The Christian concept of an eternal relationship within God's nature, as taught
by the concept of trinity, is vehemently denied. One of the consequences of
this is that the idea of relationship on any sort of a personal level with God is
impossible. As Isma'il Faruki points out, "God does not reveal himself. He does
not reveal himself to anyone in any way. God reveals only His will."[292]

b. God's Decrees

Along with God's unity, the second section of the Qur'an defines
his sovereignty and absolute power. This begins the development of the
doctrine of God's decrees, that nothing happens apart from his will. Allah, in
Muhammad's conception, was not only the prime mover of the universe, but
was, in essence, the only movement in the universe. The *qadr* or "fate" that
God has determined cannot be changed. Perhaps Muhammad developed this
conception of God's control as a means of comfort in the face of the compact
resistance he encountered from the Meccan tribes. The first inkling of this
comes in the first chapter of this period, chapter 54, "The Moon":

> The day they will be dragged through the fire on their faces (they
> will hear) 'Taste ye the touch of Hell!' Verily all things have we
> created in proportion and measure. And our command is but a
> single (act)—like the twinkling of an eye.[293]

Kathir goes on to explain the concept of God's decrees at some length in
refuting the views of the vanished Qadariyyah sect.

> Verily we have created all things with Qadar. They are the worst
> members of this Ummah. Do not visit those who fall ill among

---

[291] Qur'an 23:91-92.
[292] Al-Faruki, Isma'il R., *Islamic Da'wah Its Nature and Demands*, American Trust
Publications, p. 17.
[293] Qur'an 54:48-50.

them or pray the funeral prayer for those among them who die. If I saw one of them, I would pluck out his eyes with these two fingers of mine . . . everything is predetermined, even laziness and intelligence . . . 'O my son! Know that you will not taste the delight of faith or earn true knowledge in Allah until you believe in al-Qadar . . . when you know that what has missed you, would never have come to you and what has befallen you would never have missed you.'[294]

Yusuf Ali does not reflect on the earlier vanished sect, but notes that Qadr is "another phase of the philosophy of unity."[295] The absolute unity of God ultimately leads to a kinetology in which God is the only actor in the universe. "Relationship" between Him and his puppets is an utter absurdity.

Chapter 76 "Al-Insan (Man)" states, "This is an admonition: Whosoever will, let him take a (straight) path to his Lord. But ye will not, except as Allah wills. For Allah is full of knowledge and wisdom'.[296] The response or rejection of Quraysh is completely dependent on the will of Allah. This does not function to dissuade the Prophet from his task, and he is confirming by his invitation that which God has already determined. Ibn Kathir includes another explanation of this in his commentary on Adam and Eve's sin at the instigation of the serpent. When rebuked by Moses for leading mankind into sin, Adam responds; "Are you blaming me for a matter that Allah wrote upon me before he created me?"[297] The passage in the Qur'an, however, has nothing to do with qadr. In fact, many of the passages that Kathir uses to illustrate qadr really do not refer to it at all. Rather something in the traditions of Islam that refers to qadr relates superficially to an event or person in the Qur'an and this becomes an occasion to give teaching unrelated to the direct teaching of the text. In chapter 19, the story of Jesus giving a speech immediately after his birth is told. Jesus announces, "He has enjoined on me prayer and almsgiving as long as I live," to which Kathir adds, "Allah informed him of what would be his affair until his death. This is the firmest evidence against the people who deny Allah's preordained decree."[298]

---

[294]   Ibn Kathir, *Tafsir,* Vol. 9, pp. 369-371.
[295]   Ali, Yusuf, p. 1394, footnote 5164.
[296]   Qur'an 76:29-30.
[297]   Ibn Kathir, *Tafsir,* Vol. 6, p. 404. Qur'an 20:116-123.
[298]   Ibn Kathir, *Tafsir,* Vol. 6, p. 255.

The decrees of God are most clearly illustrated by his acts of judgment on a rebellious humanity:

> We shall gather them together, and (also) the evil ones (with them). Then we shall bring them forth on their knees round about hell. Then shall we certainly drag out from every sect all those who were worst in obstinate rebellion against (Allah) most gracious. And certainly we know best those who are most worthy of being burned therein. Not one of you but will pass over it: This is with thy Lord, a decree which must be accomplished.[299]

The word for decree that must be accomplished is stated by Ibn Kathir to be a "hatman decree." "Hatman" is translated as "preordained." He does not explain the concept of a "preordained" form of a decree. This can indicate levels of surety in the fixed decrees of God. What Ibn Kathir focuses on is the obscure phrase "Not one of you but will pass over it," which he takes to refer to the bridge over hell that is "like the sharp edge of a sword."[300]

Perhaps the most classic statement of God's decrees is found in Qur'an in 17:13 that states, "Every man's fate we have fastened on his own neck: On the day of judgment we shall bring out for him a scroll, which he will see spread open."[301] Once again we see how clearly decrees are connected with judgment. Later in the same chapter he goes on to say,

> It is he whom Allah guides, that is on true guidance but he whom he leaves astray—for such wilt thou find no protector besides him. On the day of judgment we shall gather them together, prone on their faces, blind, dumb and deaf: Their abode will be Hell: Every time it shows abatement, we shall increase for them the fierceness of the fire.[302]

Ibn Kathir notes that God leads astray who he wills and "whomever he leaves astray can never find any helpers."[303] God is the sole source of action in the

---

[299] Qur'an 19:68-71.
[300] Ibn Kathir, *Tafsir,* Vol. 6, p. 296.
[301] Qur'an 17:13.
[302] Qur'an 17:97.
[303] Ibn Kathir, *Tafsir,* Vol. 6, p. 91.

universe and thus, as Kathir puts it, he "has no need of his servants or their worship."[304]

This aspect of God's decrees also underlies the preoccupation of the Qur'an with saying "if God wills." In the final chapter of the middle Meccan period, the Qur'an describes a group of young men who slept in a cave for hundreds of years. We shall return to this story later, but in the conclusion of the story we find this admonition; "Nor say of anything I shall be sure to do so and so tomorrow—without adding, 'So please Allah!'"[305] In Ibn Kathir's discussion of this chapter, he draws parallels to the life of Solomon. Solomon declared his intention to sleep with seventy, or ninety or one hundred of his wives in a single night to birth new warriors for Islam. However, because he failed to say "if Allah wills," only one half-formed child was born for the effort.[306] The epithet "Insha' Allah" has become ubiquitous in all Muslim cultures.

This concept of the absolute decrees of Allah indicates also God's absolute transcendence. There is no immanence here for God. His distance from his creation is absolute. Ibn Kathir goes on to deny one of the most popular verses in the Qur'an which is often used to indicate the concept of God's immanence and presence in His creation. In chapter 50:16 we read, "Indeed we have created man, and we know what his self whispers to him. And we are nearer to him than his jugular vein." Ibn Kathir goes on to interpret the verse:

> "The statement of Allah the exalted means, His angels are nearer to man than his jugular vein . . . for Allah did not say, 'and I am closer to him than his jugular vein' . . . Thus the angels are closer to man than his own jugular vein, by the power and leave of Allah. Consequently the angel touches mankind, just as the devil touches them."[307]

The translator notes that Ibn Kathir's view is not held by most scholars though it indicates the degree to which Islamic scholars have a problem with a transcendent God coming near to man in any way. Yusuf Ali does speak of a "limited free will" for humankind and interprets the nearness of God as referring to his knowledge of human inner motivations.[308]

---

[304] Ibn Kathir, *Tafsir,* Vol. 7, p. 235.
[305] Qur'an 18:23-24.
[306] Ibn Kathir, *Tafsir,* Vol. 6, p. 138.
[307] Ibn Kathir, *Tafsir,* Vol. 9, pp. 227-8.
[308] Ali, Yusuf, p. 1348, footnote 4952.

c. God's Word and Abrogation

The commentators, we have noted, often engage in anticipatory interpretation, reading something into an early text of the Qur'an that does not really emerge until later. This seems to serve the function of justifying the viewpoint on the later text by creating an artificial matrix of similar passages to give the impression of uniformity; that the Qur'an fits into the box of its later interpreters. One such function is the early introduction of the concept of abrogation (*naskh*). In surah 37, the story of Abraham's sacrifice of his son is told. When Abraham is about to strike, Allah intervenes and provides a ram in the boy's stead. Reflecting on this, Ibn Kathir notes, "Allah commanded Ibrahim, peace be upon him, to sacrifice his son, then he abrogated that and pointed out the ransom."[309] A principle of abrogation is developed from this that does find a more explicit form in later passages of the Qur'an. Abrogation in the later chapters of the Qur'an was meant primarily to enable Muhammad to get away from contradictions that arose between his earlier and later revelations. In Muslim apologetics, however, the concept of abrogation takes on a much wider function and is applied primarily to the scriptures of the Jews and Christians, which are considered "abrogated" by the Qur'an. The Qur'an itself never states this.

One of the early Qur'anic verses that are later abrogated is found in chapter 19 where again Abraham is conversing with his idolatrous father. When the father rebukes him for reviling his gods, Abraham says, "Peace be on you! I will ask forgiveness of my Lord for you."[310] This statement is repeated in the late Meccan chapter 14, "Our Lord! Forgive me and my parents." Ibn Kathir notes,

> "From this tradition, during the beginning stages of Islam, the Muslims used to seek forgiveness for their relatives and family members who were polytheists . . . Then Allah explains that Ibrahim abandoned this statement and retracted it."[311]

He goes on to cite the Qur'anic verse from the next to last chapter revealed in the Qur'an, "It is not proper for the Prophet and those who believe to ask

---

[309] Ibn Kathir, *Tafsir,* Vol. 8, p. 275.
[310] Qur'an 19:47
[311] Ibn Kathir, *Tafsir,* Vol. 6, pp. 269-270.

Allah's forgiveness for the idolaters."[312] Thus, Abraham functions as a device to abrogate a custom initiated in the early stages of the Islamic community. The purpose seems to have been to remove all sense of familial solidarity toward those who refused conversion to Islam. Even in the modern age, this idea of rejection is codified in all schools of Islamic law primarily with reference to Muslims who leave the Islamic faith.

d. Spirits, Forgiveness, and End Times

One entire chapter of the Qur'an from this period concerns Muhammad's communication with spirit beings. Thus, the Qur'an itself not only affirms the reality of these nonangelic spirits, but also clearly teaches that Muhammad was able to communicate with them. In chapter 72, entitled "Al-Jinn," Muhammad speaks of the reaction of the spirits to his recital of verses from the Qur'an:

> "Say: It has been revealed to me that a company of Jinns listened (to the Qur'an). They said, 'We have really heard a wonderful recital! It gives guidance to the right, and we have believed therein: We shall not join (in worship) any (gods) with our Lord. And exalted is the Majesty of our Lord: He has taken neither a wife nor a son.[313]

According to Yusuf Ali, this chapter was revealed at the time of Muhammad's preaching journey to Taif about two years before the hijra. The mission ended in failure and rejection of the Prophet. Yusuf Ali considers that this was given to encourage the Prophet that great spiritual forces were responding to his message.[314] This interpretation is out of sequence with the chronology of the Qur'an. The passage repeats the familiar story of the pelting of the jinn with shooting stars to prevent their stealing of the heavenly tidings. What is remarkable about this passage is that it records the discourse of the jinn themselves. Muhammad, speaking in their place, essentially reports their internal debate over the nature of the revelations they had heard. Like men, some had responded and others had rejected: "Amongst us are some that submit their wills . . . but those who swerve—they are (but) fuel for

---

[312] Qur'an 9:113.
[313] Qur'an 72:1-3.
[314] Qur'an, p. 1624 Yusuf Ali's introduction to the chapter.

hell-fire."[315] The remainder of the passage moves back from the first person on the part of the jinn to God addressing the pagans of Quraysh.

This passage is remarkable for several reasons. First, Muhammad clearly speaks for the jinn in the first fifteen verses. Is this an indication of spirit possession? Muhammad is made party to the internal debates of the jinn. Further, by means of this discussion, the Qur'an introduces a structure in the spirit world of believing and nonbelieving spirits. This opened the door for the enormously complex later cosmologies of Islam concerning Christian, Jewish, Muslim, and pagan jinn with their respective kingdoms and kings. Ibn Kathir's *tafsir* emphasizes that the jinns were in league with men particularly in the matter of *shirk* whereby God was believed to have a wife and a son.[316] This communion between jinns and men led later in Islamic jurisprudence to an entire genre of legal rules binding the relations of men and jinn, including matters of marriage and bearing of children (product of human and jinn sexual interaction). We have ethnographies of modern Arabs believing in such things here in the United States.

Verse six goes on to say, "Verily, there were persons among mankind who took shelter with persons among the jinns, but they increased them in folly." Ibn Kathir interprets this to mean that men feared the jinn. They sought refuge in the spirits which is why the spirits turned against man "afflicting them with insanity and madness."[317] This would seem to indicate spirit possession. That humans could be possessed by jinns is clearly indicated by the interpretation of the following verses. God expels the jinn from their former "seats" to prevent them from stealing the revelations of the Qur'an. The rationale for this according to Ibn Kathir is the following:

> "The devils were then expelled from the places where they used to sit prior to that. This was so that they could not steal anything from the Qur'an and tell it to the soothsayers, thereby causing matters to be confused and mixed up."[318]

The process of telling was the process of possession, of communication between familiar spirit and adept. Similarly, when the jinn heard the Prophet reciting the Qur'an, "they almost mounted on top of him due to their zeal.

---

[315] Qur'an, 72:14, 15.
[316] Ibn Kathir, *Tafsir,* Vol. 10, p. 196.
[317] Ibn Kathir, *Tafsir,* Vol. 10, pp. 196-7.
[318] Ibn Kathir, *Tafsir,* Vol. 10, p. 198.

When they heard him reciting the Qur'an they drew very near to him." The view that God was revealing the content of the jinn discourse does not remove the possibility that this is an analogy of possession. The terminology of Islamic revelation and possession are similar. The end of the passage is a discourse on the role of Muhammad as messenger. He is merely the one who receives inspiration and passes it on. "Mine is only to convey what I receive from Allah."[319] The focus is entirely on transmission of a message. This reinforces the view that the process of revelation was one of a type of spirit possession. The angel Gabriel "pressing upon Muhammad" that we noted in the previous chapter in the early descriptions of the process of revelation also affirms this interpretation.

The Qur'an also teaches that the spirits could be harnessed for productive activities. Solomon was considered the master of jinn manipulation. "They worked for him as he desired (making) arches, images, basins as large as reservoirs."[320] In one case, a jinn has the title of "Afrit" that indicates levels of power and authority among them. The Afrit is able to conjure the throne of the queen of Sheba, bringing it to Solomon's court. Five passages in the Qur'an attest to Solomon's relationship to the jinn.[321] The creation of the jinn from fire free of smoke as well as various tales about their mischief and power contribute to a strong basis for a cosmology of the spirit world.

Jinns are associated with trees and various living things. According to Bukhari, Muhammad was informed about the jinns listening to his recitation of the Qur'an by a tree. Trees thus function as an animistic spirit focus.[322] Jinns are also associated with certain animals, particularly snakes, which are considered to be spirit incarnations.[323] Other traditions state that the Prophet taught that there are three categories of jinns, those with wings (associated with ravens and owls), those that crawled on the ground (associated with snakes), and those that walk (associated with wolves and hyenas). Even the angel of revelation, Gabriel, is attributed the power of assuming the form of a particular person.[324] It is this ability of the spirits to incarnate themselves in

---

[319]   Qur'an 72:23.
[320]   Qur'an 34:13.
[321]   Qur'an 21:82, 27:17, 39, 34:12-14, 38:37-38.
[322]   Bukhari, Vol 5, p. 125-6, no. 199.
[323]   Sahih Muslim, trans. Abdul Hamid Siddiqi, Lahaore: Muhammad Ashraf, 1990, Vol. 4, pp. 1211-13.
[324]   Bukhari, Vol. 4, p. 531 and Vol. 5, pp. 308-9: In both cases Gabriel assumes the form of one of Muhammad's followers named Dihya.

human form or to abide within human beings that forms the basis for another class of spirit beings in the Qur'an, the Qarina.

Qarina means "companion" and the term is used six times in the Qur'an. The meaning, however, is not human but spirit companion. Modern translations of the Qur'an tend to gloss this over.[325] It seems to be the basis of the familiar spirits of the pre-Islamic "Kahins" or soothsayers. The concept seems to be that every human has a familiar spirit, an alter-ego, of the opposite sex. The process of divination, as Ibn Ishaq presents it, is one of sexual intercourse between the kahin and his/her familiar spirit. At the time of Muhammad's advent, the Qarinas are portrayed as distraught because the Prophet's teaching would end the process of adultery with the spirits[326] (although not perhaps of legally binding marriages with the spirits). The Qarina is presented in the Qur'an as a deceiving spirit intending to bring about the destruction of the human counterpart:

> "One of them will start the talk and say, "I had an intimate companion (on the earth, who used to say, What! Art thou amongst those who bear witness to the truth (of the message)? When we die and become dust and bones, shall we indeed receive rewards and punishments?"[327]

Al-Tabari noted that the Qarina is everyone's personal devil. This demonic spirit seeks the eternal damnation of its human counterpart.[328] The concept of the Qarina is further developed in chapter 41:25:

> "And we have assigned for them intimate companions (in this world), who have made fair seeming to them, what was before them, and what was behind them. And the word is justified against them as it was justified against those who were among the previous generations of jinns and men that had passed away before them. Indeed, they (all) were the losers."

---

[325] Ali, Yusuf, Qur'an, note 4067, p. 1143. Yusuf Ali presents the Qarina as a human "intimate companion."

[326] Ibn Ishaq, p. 91.

[327] Qur'an, 37:51-53.

[328] Al-Tabari, 22:357 cited in Ibn Kathir, *Tafsir,* Vol. 9, p. 236.

In Ibn Kathir's commentary, this verse is explained as exemplifying the absolute sovereignty of God in appointing destruction to whom he will by appointing devils as companions of the damned:

> "Allah tells us that He is the One who sends the idolaters astray, and that this happens by his will and decree. He is the All-Wise in his actions, when he appoints for them close companions from among the devils of men and jinn."[329]

This is reinforced in chapter 43:36 where Allah declares, "And whosoever Ya'shu (turns away blindly) from the remembrance of the Most Gracious, we appoint for him Shaytan to be a Qarin (a companion) for him." The idea is further developed in Qur'an 50:23-27:

> "And his companion will say, "here is (his record) Ready with me!" (The sentence will be): "Both of you throw into hell every stubborn disbeliever, hinderer of good, transgressor, doubter, who set up another God with Allah. Then both of you cast him in severe torment." His companion will say, "Our Lord! I did not make him transgress, but he was (himself) far astray."[330]

In the light of these passages one might consider that all forms of spirit possession were seen by the Prophet as demonic and inherently evil. This would seem to be reflected in the negative view of the kahins, the Arab adepts at spirit possession, in the Hadith literature. But the picture is not entirely clear.

There does seem to be another concept of "spirit" in the Qur'an. Spirits, in terms of jinns, are a fairly clear concept. The spirit of revelation by which Muhammad received the Qur'an is assumed by Muslims to be an angel, Gabriel. Then in chapter 17, we encounter another spirit:

> "And they ask you concerning the Ruh (the spirit).
> Say: "the Ruh (the spirit) is one of the things, the knowledge of which is only with my Lord. And of knowledge, you (mankind) have been given only a little."[331]

---

[329] Ibn Kathir, *Tafsir,* Vol. 8, pp. 533-4.
[330] Qur'an 50:23-27.
[331] Qur'an 17:85.

Ibn Kathir declares the context of this verse to be Medina, claiming that this is in response to a question by a Jew. The stage is set for this interpretation by his earlier interpretation of verses 80-81 as referring to the hijra. The phrase "truth has come and falsehood has vanished" is even taken to refer to Muhammad's statement when the Ka'aba was cleansed of idols near the end of his life.[332] All of this is incorrect. The question clearly comes either from Christians/Jews or perhaps from Muhammad's disciples who wonder what the members of these other religious communities meant by "spirit." This verse is another indication that Muhammad and/or his disciples were dialoguing with members of other religious communities during this period in Mecca. It seems most likely that the idea came from Christian sources because the Jewish conception of spirits, both angels and jinn, was the same as the Muslim. The concept of the Holy Spirit as Christians conceived him seems to have remained a mystery to Muhammad. Thus the concept of trinity in the Qur'an is father, mother (not Spirit), and son.

God's forgiveness is affirmed in these early sections of the Qur'an, even forgiveness for those who were idolaters, as the prayer of Abraham has shown. The idea of ransom, particularly in the animal sacrifice of Abraham is also affirmed though not with the concept of vicarious atonement attached, as it was in the Christian community. Later, we will see that the Qur'an denies the concept of vicarious atonement, declaring that no man can die for another's sin. The cross of Christ is denied later in the Qur'an both as a historical event and as a theological necessity.[333] Nevertheless, Ibn Kathir and some of the collectors of Hadith maintain a bizarre form of atonement that echos the Christian concept. In his interpretation of the duties of Muslim believers from chapter 23, Muslim states,

> Some of the Muslims will come on the day of resurrection with sins like mountains, but Allah will forgive them and put (their burden of sin) on the Jews and Christians . . . When the day of resurrection comes, Allah will appoint for every Muslim a Jew or Christian, and it will be said, "this is your ransom from the fire."[334]

---

[332] Ibn Kathir, *Tafsir,* Vol. 6, pp. 70-6.
[333] Todd Lawson does a great job of reviewing Muslim views of the crucifixion both in the Qur'an and through history. He questions whether the Qur'an actually teaches that Jesus was not crucified. The majority of Muslim opinion throughout the last fourteen hundred years has been that Christ was not crucified. See; Todd Lawson, *The Crucifixion and the Qur'an*, Oxford: One World Press, 2009.
[334] Muslim, 4:2120, 2119 quoted in Ibn Kathir, *Tafsir,* Vol. 6, p. 634.

The point seems to be that God would comfort the Muslims. Even if they were unable to fulfill all the obligations of the ritual law, God would provide a means of ransom for them; Christians and Jews will burn in hell in their place.

Finally, we must consider the developing notion of last days and eschatology, which came to influence Muhammad's apocalyptic thinking. Here we see the influence of the People of the Book on Muhammad. We noted earlier that when asked "when will this promise be fulfilled," Muhammad begs off stating, "I am only a plain warner." Yet later, in chapter 21, "The Prophets," he introduces the story of Gog and Magog as an example of the unity in teaching of all the Prophets:

> "Verily this brotherhood of yours is a single brotherhood . . . but there is a ban on any population which we have destroyed: that they shall not return. Until the Gog and Magog (people) are let through (their barrier) and they will swiftly swarm from every hill. Then will the true promise draw nigh."[335]

Muhammad's quotation here is little more than a citing of the name of Gog and Magog with some awareness of the apocalyptic attached to the names. The concept derives from Ezekiel, chapters 38 and 39, where the hordes of these two nations attack Israel and are destroyed by the hand of God. These verses are later interpreted as referring to the apocalyptic age for the return of Christ in Revelations 20:8. Both elements may be present in the Qur'anic text, but the reference is obscure and unclear. Both the traditions and commentary literature richly fill in this largely obscure reference. Ibn Kathir associates the two nations with the Turks who in his days were ravaging the Middle East. He also cites various traditions that essentially tell the story of Ezekiel with a Muslim twist. The armies of these two nations are wiped out by pestilence and the Muslims are vindicated. Other traditions are citing concerning the Dajjal, or antichrist, who will rule for 14 ½ months. Jesus returns to kill him and, in this case, Gog and Magog are wiped out by insects and their bodies are carried away by birds with necks like dromedary camels. Jesus kills a pig, breaks the cross, performs the hajj, and converts the world to Islam.[336]

In surah 27, Muhammad provides a number of details of the end times derived again from biblical sources. The Qur'an begins this section by

---

[335]   Qur'an 21:92-97.
[336]   Ibn Kathir, *Tafsir,* Vol. 6, pp. 491-8.

stating, "Verily this Qur'an doth explain to the Children of Israel most of the matters in which they disagree."[337] Muhammad sees himself as the arbiter of disagreements among the People of the Book, and he seems to consider himself as part of their movement. Muhammad gains assurance from Allah that "only those wilt thou get to listen who believe in our signs and they will bow in Islam." He then begins to describe in obscure terms one sign of the end times. First, God will produce "a beast" from the earth who will speak to mankind (27:82). This beast seems to be used of God to declare to mankind that they have not believed in the signs of God. This allusion seems to be based on the book of Daniel chapter 7 with possible influence from Revelation 13. The allusion is extremely obscure and actually reverses the biblical viewpoint, making the beast an agent of God's message to mankind. Ibn Kathir cites numerous traditions that purport to give the Prophet's interpretation of the beast. Along with the various signs of the end, the sun rising in the west, smoke from the burning, and the *Dajjal*, the interpreters see the beast as a righteous servant of Allah who marks out the believers from the unbelievers:

> A beast will emerge from the earth, and with it will be the staff of Musa and the ring of Sulayman, peace be upon them both. It will strike the nose of the disbelievers with the staff, and it will make the face of the believer bright with the ring, until when people gather to eat, they will be able to recognize the believers from the unbelievers.[338]

This is an exact reversal of the biblical image where the beast is an agent of Satan and marks the unbelievers with the sign of the beast without which no one can buy or sell.[339] Yusuf Ali, who is more knowledgeable of the Christian teachings, reverses this imagery back in keeping with the Bible, seeing the beast as a servant of materialism.[340]

The final apocalyptic sign considered in the middle Meccan period occurs in the last chapter revealed during that time. In it, we are introduced to the mysterious Prophet Dhu al Qarnayn whom some scholars have identified with Alexander the Great. He comes to a people in a valley who beg him to

---

[337] Qur'an 27:76.
[338] Ibn Kathir, *Tafsir,* Vol. 7, p. 360.
[339] Revelation 13:11-18.
[340] Ali, Yusuf, p. 956, footnote 3313.

receive their tribute and erect a barrier against the hordes of Gog and Magog. He builds a barrier to their valley against the horde made of blocks of iron soldered together with molten lead. Thus, the horde is restrained until the day that the Lord would make the barrier into dust. Then, "On that day we shall leave them to surge like waves on one another; the trumpet will be blown, and we shall collect them all together."[341] The background of the passage gives the commentators considerable trouble for Dhu al Qarnayn travels to the place of the setting of the sun, in the spring of Hami'ah, where he finds this people. Ibn Kathir interprets this figuratively to mean the sun setting in the western sea and not being able to find a suitable analogy for Qarnayn reaching the western most place on earth says, "The stories told by storytellers that he traveled so far to the west that the sun set behind him are not true at all. Most of the stories come from the myths of the People of the Book and the fabrications and lies of their heretics."[342] It would seem that the Qur'an regards the earth as flat, and the only place where these "myths" have been preserved is in the Qur'an itself. In fact, this flat earth conception is essential to two of the five pillars of Islam, prayer and fasting.[343]

All of the passages from this period that deal with end-times signs are obscure and indicate that Muhammad repeated oral traditions that he had heard as best he could remember them. Not being sure of the details, references were left fleeting and unclear. The commentators try to fill out these holes with what they were able to glean at a later stage of history from Jews and Christians. In order to keep their descriptions consistent with the Qur'an, they were often forced to reverse the original meaning of the biblical material. The cosmology expressed in these chapters is of an extremely primitive

---

[341] Qur'an 18:94-99.
[342] Ibn Kathir, *Tafsir*, Vol. 6, p. 205.
[343] Islamic law is unable to accommodate the reality that in polar regions, at certain times of the year the sun either never comes up or never sets. It is physically impossible to follow Islam in those regions and no Islamic scholar is willing to promulgate a new set of laws to control the most holy and complete aspects of Islamic legislation, for that would be innovation (bid'a) in the revealed religion. Bid'a is synonymous with "heresy." Some suggestions have been made including following the times in Mecca, but these have only increased the problem as it is impossible to assign where in world geography the dividing line would be drawn. Most scholars say that such laws exist, but no one is willing to define them. We have a copy of a book of timings for prayer and fasting from Kazan, Russia, quite far north, and it continues to maintain the timing according to the rising and setting of the sun. It is as if the God of Islam was unaware of salient features of world geography.

sort and creates the kind of interpretive problems that force commentators into a total lack of discipline in hermeneutical principles. Sometimes they interpret figuratively, sometimes literally. Often they read far more into the text than is really there. No system is established by which certain passages are interpreted one way and others in the opposite way. The *tafsir* literature is polemic wishful thinking.

e. The Punishments of Hell and the Delights of Heaven

The second period of Qur'anic revelations contains a somewhat reduced focus on heaven and hell and the day of judgment. Nevertheless, the emphasis on an apocalyptic day of judgment is still strong, and the images, particularly of the punishments of hell are more varied and nuanced.

Hell continues to be characterized as a place of fire where the unbelievers will be continuously tortured and experience deep regret:

> "Nay, they deny the hour (of the judgment to come): but we have prepared a blazing fire for such as deny the hour: when it sees them from a place far off, They will hear its fury and its raging sigh. And when they are cast, bound Together, into a constricted place therein, they will plead for destruction there and then! This day plead not for a single destruction: plead for a destruction oft repeated."[344]

Ibn Kathir interprets, "Allah threatens the idolators who denied and opposed his messenger Muhammad."[345] This fire will cling to the faces of the unbelievers who are unaware of their grave danger: "If only the unbelievers knew (the time) when they will not be able to ward off the fire from their faces, nor yet from their backs, and when no help can reach them."[346] This agony of torment will lead them to beg for destruction:

> "The sinners will be in the punishment of Hell, to dwell therein (for aye): nowise will the (punishment) be lightened for them. And in despair will they be there overwhelmed . . . They will cry: "O Malik! Would that thy Lord put an end to us!" He will say, "Nay, but ye shall abide!"[347]

---

344 Qur'an 25:11-14.
345 Ibn Kathir, *Tafsir,* Vol. 7, p. 171.
346 Qur'an 21:39.
347 Qur'an 43:74-5, 77.

After their deeds are weighed in the balance, the Qur'an describes the disfigurement and agony that the fires of hell will cause in their bodies:

> "But those whose balance is light, will be those who have lost their souls; in Hell will they abide. The fire will burn their faces, and they will therein grin, with Their lips displaced. They will say . . . "Our Lord! Bring us out of this: if ever we return (to evil), then shall we be wrongdoers indeed!" He will say: "Be ye driven Into it (with ignominy)! And speak ye not to me."[348]

The grinning disfigurement may be seen as either the grimacing of pain, or perhaps more accurately the burning away of the flesh exposing the bone like a grinning skull. The Qur'an also uses the analogy of a furnace to describe hell:

> "For those who reject their Lord (and cherisher) is the penalty of Hell: And evil is (such) destination. When they are cast therein, they will hear the (terrible) drawing in of its breath even as it blazes forth, almost bursting with fury: Everytime a group is cast therein, its keepers will ask, "Did no warner come to you?" They will say: "Yes indeed; a warner did come to us, but we rejected him and said, 'Allah never sent down any (message): Ye are in nothing but an egregious Delusion!'" They will then confess their sins: But far will be (forgiveness) from the companions of the blazing fire!"[349]

The content of these passages was highly expedient in demonstrating what Muhammad's enemies would ultimately confess. Once within this worldview, believers could come to no other conclusion concerning their family members still outside the faith. This kind of teaching must have had a profound impact in terms of breaking normal family and tribal loyalties on the part of those who followed Muhammad. Those who remained outside the faith were now without excuse. This is a highly polarizing viewpoint that set the stage for more direct confrontation.

A number of new forms of torture in hell are also described in this section of the Qur'an. "For the rejecters, we have prepared chains, yokes, and a blazing fire."[350] Those trapped in hell will be made to drink various

---

[348] Qur'an 23:103-4, 107.
[349] Qur'an 67:6-11.
[350] Qur'an 76:3.

kinds of boiling mixtures. "They will be given a mixture made of boiling water."[351] Ibn Kathir describes this as a mixture of water with "blood and bodily discharges."[352] Elsewhere these substances are described as alternating between boiling hot and intensely cold: "Then shall they taste it—a boiling fluid, and a fluid dark, murky and intensely cold!"[353]

> "For the wrongdoers we have prepared a fire whose (smoke and flames), like the walls and roof of a tent, will hem them in: If they implore relief they will be granted water like melted brass that will scald their faces. How dreadful the drink!"[354]

Ibn Kathir describes this drink as "Al-Muhl" that is a mixture of boiling blood and pus.[355]

The most oft-repeated image is the Zaqqum tree that abides in the core of hell whose horrid fruit the unbelievers are made to eat. To the question of judgment after death, Muhammad outlines what the unbelievers say and then responds:

> "Is it (the case) that we shall not die, except our first death and that we shall not be Punished? Verily this is the supreme achievement! For the like of this let all strive, who wish to strive. Is that the better entertainment or the tree of Zaqqum? For we have truly made it (as) a trial for the wrongdoers. For it is a tree that Springs out of the bottom of hellfire: The shoots of its fruit-stalks are like the Heads of devils: truly they will eat thereof and fill their bellies therewith."[356]

Ibn Kathir interprets that the zaqqum tree is made from fire whose roots are in the core of hell and the shoots of which are the heads of Satan.[357] The fruit of the zaqqum tree will be the food of the sinners in hell, and it will boil the innards of them like molten brass.[358]

---

351 Qur'an 37:67.
352 Ibn Kathir, *Tafsir,* Vol. 8, p. 259.
353 Qur'an 38:57.
354 Qur'an 18:29.
355 Ibn Kathir, *Tafsir,* Vol. 6, p. 146.
356 Qur'an 37:58-66.
357 Ibn Kathir, *Tafsir,* Vol. 8, p. 258.
358 Qur'an 44:43-45.

The delights of heaven also occupy a significant place in this section of the Qur'an. Early in the period Muhammad describes the liquor of heaven as well as the chaste virgins:

> "In gardens of felicity facing each other on thrones (of dignity):
> Round will be Passed to them a cup from a clear-flowing fountain,
> crystal white, of a taste Delicious to those who drink (thereof),
> free from headiness; nor will they Suffer intoxication therefrom.
> And besides them will be chaste women; restraining their glances,
> with big eyes (of wonder and beauty) as if they were (delicate)
> eggs closely guarded."[359]

Ibn Kathir describes the liquor of heaven as a wine that does not intoxicate. The women of heaven will only be interested in their men, and they will possess bodies which are "bayd maknun" which, according to Kathir, means "the membrane which is between its outer shell and its inner contents" which is not touched "by human hands."[360] These are "chaste women restraining their glances (companions) of equal age."[361] Along with beautiful women with lustrous eyes they will be provided with gardens of "every kind of fruit in peace and security."[362] The visions of heavenly bliss are always presented as a contrast to the agonies of hellfire. The images seem to be related to the court concept which informs the Muslim view of heaven:

> "For them will be gardens of eternity; beneath them rivers will
> flow: They will be Adorned therein with bracelets of gold, and
> they will wear green garments of fine silk and heavy brocade; they
> will recline therein on raised thrones. How good the Recompense!
> How beautiful a couch to recline on!"[363]

f. The Moral Concerns of Muhammad

We noted in the early Meccan period some of the moral concerns of Muhammad; for widows, orphans, and the poor, for female infanticide.

---

[359] Qur'an 37:43-49.
[360] Ibn Kathir, *Tafsir*, Vol. 8, pp. 251-2.
[361] Qur'an 38:52.
[362] Qur'an 44:54-55.
[363] Qur'an 18:31.

Surprisingly, this moral concern is less evident in the middle period. We could find only three brief allusions to these universal moral concerns. Heaven's reward is given to those who "feed, for the love of Allah, the indigent, the orphan and the captive saying 'we feed you for the sake of Allah alone: No reward do we desire from you nor thanks'."[364] In the context of encouraging generosity we read: "render to the kindred their due rights, as (also) to those in want, and to the wayfarer: But squander not (your wealth) in the manner of a spendthrift."[365] A little later in the same passage we read: "Kill not your children for fear of want: We shall provide sustenance for them as well as for you. Verily the killing of them is a great sin . . . come not nigh to the orphan's property except to improve it."[366] These admonitions are part of a passage concerned with overall moral behavior, sexual mores, honest balances, humble attitudes, and avoiding idolatry.

In the area of proper behavior Ibn Kathir's commentary records a failing of Muhammad in not saying, "if God wills." The context is chapter 18 that records three apocryphal stories. Ibn Kathir explains that these stories were obtained from the Jews in Yathrib (Medina) by a delegation of Quraysh in order to put Muhammad to the test as to whether he was the true "messenger" who could answer the riddles. Initially, Muhammad gives the assurance that he will receive revelation to answer the riddles, but he neglects to say, "if God wills." God delayed sending the revelation for fifteen days, subjecting Muhammad to great humiliation and mockery by Quraysh before He finally sent Gabriel to reveal the riddles. This sounds like a borrowing of Daniel and Nebuchadnezzar's dream. The story is remarkable in that it seems to record an act of presumption on the part of the Prophet for which God puts him in his place. There is no hint of this background in the Qur'an, and we may assume that this is a further example of isogetical backreading of history into the Qur'an to explain an otherwise thoroughly opaque passage.

g. The Duties of Muslims

We have already noted that the *tafsir* literature tries to backread much of later Islam into the earlier passages of the Qur'an. This is particularly true with regard to Muslim duties. Nowhere in these passages are the five pillars explained in their canonical forms. Indeed, nowhere in the Qur'an do we find

---

[364] Qur'an 76:8-9.
[365] Qur'an 17:26.
[366] Qur'an 17:31, 34.

them fully explained. This is one of the reasons why the traditional literature became so important in describing the practices of Islam.

Of all the duties mentioned of Muslims during this period, the most pervasive is attitudinal. The key word is "*taqwa*" meaning fear, awe, or piety in regard to God. The term occurs several times in virtually every chapter of this period. The term often appears in passages describing the judgment, as in 19:68-72 in which sinful humanity, particularly of the "sects" will be cast into hell, but "we shall save those who had *taqwa* (72)." In some cases, awe of creation is the source to true fear:

> "Say: 'Who is the Lord of the seven heavens, and the Lord of the Throne (of glory) supreme?' They will say '(they belong) to Allah.' Say: 'Will ye not then be filled with awe (taqwa)?'"[367]

The prophets, such as Abraham, argue for the value of *taqwa* over gold (43:35). Jesus declares, "Have *taqwa* and obey me" (43:63). Taqwa is also the attitude associated with prayer and the duties of believers.

> "And the servants of (Allah) most gracious are those who walk on the earth in humility, and when the ignorant address them, they say, 'Peace!' Those who spend the night in adoration of their Lord prostrate and standing; those who say: 'Our Lord! Avert us from the wrath of hell, for its wrath is indeed an affliction'."[368]

This concept of the fear of God is a primary characteristic of the community (*ummah*) Muhammad wanted to establish.

The duty of the Muslim that is next most often spoken of in this period of the Qur'an is prayer. Nearly, ten separate passages discuss this most important of all Islam practices. The earliest mention of prayer order in worship is in chapter 37, "Those Who Set the Ranks." There the angels state, "And verily we (angels), we stand in rows; and verily, we (angels) indeed are those who glorify."[369] It may be argued that this does not actually refer to postures in prayer. However, the commentators draw a direct connection to the practical:

---

[367] Qur'an 23:86-7.
[368] Qur'an 25:63-65.
[369] Qur'an 37:165-166.

"We have been favored above mankind in three things: our rows have been made like the rows of the angels; the whole earth has been made a place of prayer for us; and its soil is a means of purification for us."[370]

There is, as has been noted, a courtly, indeed, military flavor to this arrangement. Later, in chapter 76, Allah commands prayer at certain times: "Celebrate the name of thy Lord morning and evening and part of the night prostrate thyself to him; and glorify Him a long night through."[371] This earliest passage on times of prayer seems to indicate three periods of prayer each day, morning, evening and night. Shia Islam continues to follow this pattern. This is defined a bit more in the later passage 50:39-40:

"Celebrate the praises of thy Lord, before the rising of the sun and before (its) setting, and during the part of the night (also), celebrate his praises and (so likewise) after the postures of adoration."

The time is further defined as before the rising of the sun, which corresponds to *fajr* prayer, before its setting, the *asr* prayer and in the evening, corresponding to *Maghrib* and *Isha* prayer. This description is repeated several times such as 20:130 that adds "at the sides of the day." Yusuf Ali and Ibn Kathir interpret this as the *Zuhr* or midday prayers.[372] However, later passages are less clear. Chapter 17 which is the actual Isra passage states:

"Establish regular prayers at the sun's decline till the darkness of the night and the morning prayer and reading for the prayer . . . and pray in the small watches of the morning: an additional prayer for thee: Soon will thy Lord raise thee to a station of praise and glory."[373]

Here only three times of prayer are specified, in the very event that supposedly defined the canonical number and times for prayer. Postures in prayer are mentioned, though not defined, as a means of adoration. Prayer is not a personal communication with God, but a ritual act of formulaic adoration, stylized to set times and postures. Ibn Kathir admits that there existed an earlier form of prayer,

---

[370] Muslim 1:371.
[371] Qur'an 76:25-26.
[372] Ali, Yusuf, footnote 2655, p. 791, Ibn Kathir, *Tafsir*, Vol. 6, p. 404.
[373] Qur'an 17:78-9.

but claims that this was abrogated by Muhammad's *Isra* journey to heaven.[374] The *Isra* and similar events became a sort of device by which standardized practices were introduced authoritatively in the Muslim community, after the death of the Prophet. It is probable, given the descriptions in the Qur'an, that these practices corresponded largely to the actual prayer pattern of the Prophet. The vagueness of the Qur'an simply made it essential to spell this out.

Aside from prayer, no other pillars of Islam are mentioned as duties of believers. Almsgiving is mentioned on several occasions as a characteristic of righteous men. Ishmael is mentioned: "He was a messenger and a prophet. He used to enjoin on his people prayer and charity."[375] Ishmael is a very minor figure in this period of the Qur'an, Muhammad is unsure even of his chronology. Given his importance in later Islam, however, the commentators find in this brief reference both an example of the pillar of Zakat and a demonstration of Ishmael's superiority over Isaac:

> "In this is proof of Ismail's favored status over his brother, Ishaq. Ishaq was only described as being a prophet but Ismail was described with both prophethood and messengership."[376]

In later Islam, this is a technical distinction, messengership, indicating one who received a holy book. Yet Ishmael received no holy book that Muslim scholars are aware of. This is exemplary of the foggy thinking of the commentators who often contradict their own teachings in an effort to make an apologetic point. Similarly, almsgiving is used here in only a generic sense. Both Jesus and John the Baptist possess this same quality in the same chapter![377] Nevertheless, Yusuf Ali is moved to write, "The ummah and the Book of Islam reflect back the prophethood on Ismail."[378] All of this reflects the tendency of the commentators to read back later interpretations into the early chapters of the Qur'an. He notes that Zakah is mentioned in chapter 23 from Mecca, but that Zakah as a system was not instituted until a year or two after Hijra. Here he allows that the principle of Zakah was established in Mecca and its specifics as to who was responsible to pay and how much in Medina.[379]

---

[374] Ibn Kathir, *Tafsir,* Vol. 9 p. 244.
[375] Qur'an 19:55.
[376] Ibn Kathir, *Tafsir,* Vol. 6, p. 277.
[377] Qur'an 19:13 and 31.
[378] Ali, Yusuf, footnote 2506, p. 755.
[379] Ibn Kathir, *Tafsir,* Vol. 6, p. 630.

The commentators mention several other practices: the night of power, call to prayer, and the fast of Ashura, none of which were actually present during this period of the Qur'an. The fast of Ashura was not instituted until Muhammad moved to Medina, in imitation of the Jews there, and then was later abrogated (although Shia Islam has maintained the practice).

The Qur'an does provide a list of duties for the Muslims during this period:

> "The believers must eventually win through—those who humble themselves in their prayers; who avoid vain talk; who are active in deeds of charity; who abstain from sex, except with those joined to them in the marriage bond, or (the captives) whom their right hands possess—for (in their case) they are free from blame."[380]

This early list of Islamic duties receives very little attention from the commentators. When Ibn Kathir describes the most important duties of Islam in this passage, he affirms that prayer is the most important, followed by respect of parents, and then "*jihad* in the way of Allah."[381] Only the first has anything to do with the actual passage. This is understandable as the passage does not define Islam in terms typical of the later period.[382]

---

[380] Qur'an 23:1-6.

[381] Ibn Kathir, *Tafsir,* Vol. 6, p. 632.

[382] The only part of the passage that causes modern commentators some problems is the permission to rape female "captives" given in verse 6. Numerous Hadiths deal with this "right" of capture (Bukhari, Vol. 3 no. 432, p. 237). Ibn Kathir mentions this without reference to marriage. Yusuf Ali, writing for a Western audience, finds the need to sanitize this by making the relationship analogous to marriage. He states, "It will be seen there that the status of the captive when raised to freedom by marriage is the same as that of a free woman as regards her rights, but more lenient as regards the punishment to be inflicted if she falls from virtue." This clever construct makes it sound like the woman has special privileges. If the woman had sex without the permission of her owner, then she was to be beaten, rather than stoned to death, which is apparently what Ali is referring to (Bukhari, Vol. 3, no. 363, p. 204). In fact, the use of captive women in prostitution is something allowed under Islamic law. In the Hadith, Muhammad seems to decry the practice of forcing slave girls into prostitution, but allows for their forgiveness if such takes place (Bukhari, Vol. 3, no. 482). One of the Medinan chapters refers to this, "Force not your maids to prostitution when they desire chastity, in order that ye may make a gain in the goods of this life. But if anyone compels them, yet after such compulsion is Allah oft-forgiving, most merciful" (Qur'an 24:33).

h. Christian and Jewish Oral Traditions

It has been known since the time of Abraham Geiger that a significant portion of the stories included in the Qur'an have their origins in Jewish oral traditions. These are far more numerous than Christian oral traditions and this indicates the primary Jewish influence on the thinking of Muhammad. Many of these traditions were interpretations and background stories concerning the text of the Old Testament. These were not scriptural texts in the eyes of the Jews. Some may not even have been considered historical. Teaching parables in the genre of Aesop's fables would be the closest analogy. To repeat such stories with minor variations as holy writ must have seemed to the Jews something ludicrous and insured the rejection of Muhammad by the vast majority of Jews. It is during the middle Meccan period of revelations that this tendency is most pronounced.

Not surprisingly, there is a significant increase in the use of Hebrew loan words during this period. Words such as "jannatu" for paradise (37:42, 20:133, 26:85, 19:62, 38:50, 18:30, 107), "masani" for repetition which is a synonym for Qur'an (26:85), "Malakut" for government or the rule of God (36:83, 23:90), "paradiso" (Greek for paradise (23:11), "furqan" for deliverance, redemption and criteria (21:49), the phrase "throne of God" (27:26) etc., . . . It is in the apocryphal stories themselves, however, where the greatest influence is seen.

1. Adam

We shall consider the biblical characters in the chronological order that they are found in the Old Testament, and trace them as they gradually emerge in the order of the chapters of the middle Meccan period of the Qur'an. Adam is first among the Prophets, and is mentioned in two passages in this section. In the first, the creation of Adam is told and how God commands the angels to do obeisance before him. Adam is the paradigm of man in the Qur'an, a weak and forgetful creature, "but he forgot: and we found on his part no firm resolve" (20:115). Satan (Iblis) refuses to bow down to Adam and resolves to tempt him. Unlike the biblical text, he tempts Adam to eat of "the tree of eternity" to receive a kingdom "that never decays" (20:120). Adam is expelled from the garden and, as a result, all of mankind is subjected to the test of whether they will follow the guidance of God or not. This passage comes early in the period and then a similar brief passage is repeated in the last chapter of this section:

> "We said to the angels, "Bow down to Adam": They bowed down except Iblis. He was one of the jinns, and he broke the command of his Lord. Will ye then take him and his progeny as protectors rather than me? And they are enemies to You."(18:50)

Ibn Kathir gleans from this that Muhammad is a great Prophet above the rest because he was informed of Iblis' unwilliness to bow down to Adam. This story is one which has clear antecedents in Jewish traditions. From the Jewish Haggadah we have the following story:

> "After Adam had been endowed with a soul, God invited all the angels to come and pay him reverence and homage. Satan, the greatest of the angels in heaven, with twelve wings instead of six like the others, refused to pay heed of the behest of God, saying, 'Thou didst create us from the splendor of the Shekinah, and now thou dost command us to cast ourselves down before the creature that thou didst fashion out of the dust of the ground!' God answered, 'Yet this dust of the ground has more wisdom and understanding than thou.' Satan demanded a trial of wit with Adam, and God assented thereto saying: 'I have created beasts, birds and reptiles. I shall have them all come before thee and before Adam. If thou art able to give them names, I shall command Adam to show honor unto thee, and thou shalt rest next to the Shekinah of my glory. But if not, and Adam calls them by the names I have assigned to them, then thou wilt be subject to Adam, and he shall have a place in my garden and cultivate it.'"[383]

Clearly Muhammad has borrowed this earlier story although not completely. In these earliest passages, he does not mention the aspect of naming the animals as being part of the test. This comes later, and once again, demonstrates the accuracy of the chronology of the surahs. Muhammad is always adding new information as we move forward chronologically. For an example of how

---

[383] Louis Ginzberg, *The Legends of the Jews*, Johns Hopkins University Press, Vol. 1, pp. 62-63.

closely he mirrors the Jewish passage, consider this quote from chapter 15 from the middle of this period:

> "Behold, the Lord said to the angels: 'I am about to create man, from sounding clay from mud molded into shape; when I have fashioned him and breathed into him my spirit, fall ye down in obeisance unto him.' So the angels prostrated themselves, all of them together: Not so Iblis: He refused to be among those who prostrated themselves. (Allah) said: 'O Iblis! What is your reason for not being among those who prostrated themselves?' (Iblis) said: 'I am not one to prostrate myself to man, whom thou didst create from sounding clay, from mud molded into shape.' (Allah) said: 'Then get thee out from here: for thou art rejected, accursed.'"[384]

The similarities are obvious and require no further commentary. Ibn Kathir could find no explanation to give substance to the story and the lengthy passage is left virtually unexplained.[385] The Jewish traditions and legends that Muhammad had been steeped in had been eradicated or ghettoized by Ibn Kathir's day. Yusuf Ali is similarly in the dark about the origins of these stories.

2. Noah

Noah is another prominent figure in this period. He was also the first biblical character mentioned in the early Meccan period. In the middle period, he is mentioned six times beginning in the first chapter of the period. There Muhammad speaks of a strange sign in the moon, the so-called splitting of the moon. He notes that unbelievers mock at such signs, declaring the Prophets insane and relates this to the sign of the Ark of Noah. Namely, that the unbelievers would be destroyed even as the believers escaped on the Ark (54:1-15). Clearly, Muhammad sees in Noah a type of himself, and declares that his book the Qur'an is easy to "understand and remember" in apparent contrast to the Hebrew scriptures.

In the next chapter, Muhammad returns to the story of Noah, declaring that he had cried out to God and was saved when "the rest we overwhelmed in the flood" (37:82). The following chapter is entitled "Noah" and is the first

---

[384] Qur'an 15:28-34.
[385] Ibn Kathir, *Tafsir*, Vol. 5, p. 393.

entire chapter dealing with a biblical character. Noah addresses the people in a form which exactly reproduces the form of Muhammad's revelations, even though Noah addresses the people directly without indicating that God is speaking through him. By this device of speech, Muhammad himself is able to address his hearers directly:

> "O my people! I am to you a warner, clear and open: That ye should worship Allah, fear Him, and obey me . . . O my Lord! I have called to my people night and day. But my call only increases (their) flight (from the right) . . . They have (only) thrust their fingers into their ears . . . What is the matter with you, that ye place not your hope for kindness and long-suffering in Allah?" (71:2-3, 5-7, and 13)

Noah goes on to decry their commitment to their idols, which he names as "Wadd, Suwa, Yaghuth, Yauq and Nasr" (71:23). In the end, Noah called for the extermination of all the unbelievers that none of the true believers be led astray. He prays for the salvation of his parents and his own house. Noah is also briefly mentioned in Chapter 19.

After a long hiatus, Muhammad returns to the theme of Noah in chapter 23, "The Believers." Once again, Noah functions as a paradigm of Muhammad who pleads with the people to repent and worship Allah. They accuse him of being possessed. God now gives instruction for the gathering of a male and a female of every creature on earth to be preserved in the Ark as humanity "shall be drowned." (23:27) Once again, the emphasis is on the "signs" of God as shown in the destruction. It is as if Muhammad is declaring, wait and see, my signs will come in the judgment that approaches.

As we move through the Qur'an chronologically, Muhammad gradually gains greater clarity regarding his biblical characters. This indicates both the accuracy of the chronological pattern of the chapters and also the fact that Muhammad was interacting with Jews in a way that gradually increased the accuracy of his descriptions. One need only compare the earliest descriptions of Noah and their inaccuracies in the previous period with the materials we find here in the middle Meccan period to see this. Finally, in chapter 21 he declares,

> "(Remember) Noah, when he cried (to us) aforetime: We listened to his (prayer) and delivered him and his family from great distress. We helped him against people who rejected our signs: Truly they

were a people given to evil: so we drowned them (in the flood) all together." (21:76-77)

3. Idris (Enoch) and Ishmael

Another biblical character briefly mentioned in the Qur'an is Enoch, known in the Qur'anic text as Idris. Surprisingly, he occurs in the context of the first mention of Ishmael. Muhammad relates briefly the story of Moses, after which he states, "Also mention in the Book (the story of) Ishmael." Then, "Also mention in the book the case of Idris, he was a man of truth" (19:54, 56). One gets the distinct impression that Muhammad was quite unclear about the relative chronology of these figures, and his way of relating them is obscure and indefinite. The only other mention is in 21:85 where once again he is connected with Ishmael: "And (remember) Ismail, Idris and Dhu al kifl" (21:85). The last figure has sometimes been associated with Ezekiel.

4. Abraham, Isaac, Jacob, and Lot

The stories of Abraham, Isaac, and Jacob form a particular locus in the Qur'an. Often, the three names are mentioned together imitative of the Jewish traditional pattern. Abraham is the most important Prophet in Muhammad's conception. Muhammad, however, seems to consider Jacob to be a son of Abraham. Muhammad tells the story of Abraham's early life in a way quite in keeping with Jewish traditions. Abraham grows up as the son of an idol maker. As a lad, he comes to an understanding that the idols are not the creator since they can do nothing by their own power. He decides to smash all the idols in the local sanctuary. When asked what he has done, he blames the deed on the largest idol, as an illustration of its true impotence. The people of the town determine to have him burned for the crime: "They said, 'Build him a furnace and throw him into the blazing fire!'"[386] This story is repeated nine times in the Qur'an.[387] Geiger points out, "The whole story is taken from rabbinical writings."[388] He points out that the only part of the story not in rabbinic writings is the rejection by Allah of the intercession of Abraham

---

[386] Qur'an 37:97.
[387] Qur'an 6:74-82, 19:42-51, 21:52-69, 22:43, 26:69-105, 29:15-23, 37:81-95, 43:25-28, 60:4-6.
[388] Geiger, Abraham, *Judaism and Islam*, New York: KTAV Publishing, 1970, p. 96.

on behalf of his father in hell.[389] Geiger points out that this was because Muhammad was opposed to prayer for the ancestors. However, this denial comes later in the Qur'an and contradicts the earlier revelations where such intercession is accepted. Muhammad may well have been a kind of convert to Judaism, but possessing only second hand and fragmentary knowledge of that faith.

There then follows in chapter 37 the second rendition of the promise of God concerning a son and his sacrifice. Abraham begs for a son and God provides him with a son, but then commands him to sacrifice the child. When Abraham is obedient to the command, God spares the boy's life and provides a ram in his place. The son remains unnamed until the end of the story when Muhammad, recapitulating the main point states, "And we gave him the good news of Isaac—a prophet—one of the righteous."[390] In spite of the clear force of the text, Muslim commentators almost universally identify the child sacrificed as Ishmael. Yusuf Ali and Ibn Kathir are in agreement on this point.[391] It is ironic that when the Qur'an gets the details correct, Muslim commentators deny it and backread into the Qur'an later interpretations. In context it is not even clear if Muhammad recognizes that Ishmael was a son of Abraham. He seems to locate him in the time of Idris (Enoch), and does not mention him at all until eight chapters later.[392] In a way, this story indicates the integrity of the Qur'anic text. Muslims could have easily added the name of Ishmael earlier in the story and gotten themselves out of an interpretive pickle. That they didn't is a testimony to the respect they had for the text and their unwillingness to deliberately tamper with it. It is also worth noting that God's abrogation of the command to sacrifice the son forms the basis according to Ibn Kathir of the Islamic doctrine of abrogation (*naskh*) by which earlier commands of God are abrogated by later ones.[393] This becomes a key element in later political and social pronouncements of the Prophet.

The story of Lot (*Lut*) and his escape from Sodom is told, but with interesting variations. God himself prophesies that Lot's wife will prove disobedient, and the city is destroyed not by fire and brimstone, but with pebbles (*sijjil*), the same pebbles with which Abraha had been driven from

---

[389] The following passages relate Abraham's intercession for his father in Hell: 9:115, 26:86-104, 60:4.

[390] Qur'an 37:112.

[391] Ibn Kathir, *Tafsir,* Vol. 8, p. 271, Yusuf Ali, Footnote no. 4101, p. 1150.

[392] Qur'an 19:55-6.

[393] Ibn Kathir, *Tafsir,* Vol. 8, p. 275. See also Dawud's Hadith on *naskh*: Vol. 2, p. 550.

Mecca.[394] Ibn Kathir maintains that the city was destroyed with stones, but Yusuf Ali, mindful of his Western audience, states that the city was destroyed by fire and brimstone.[395]

5. Moses, Aaron, and Pharaoh

Muhammad makes some significant corrections in this section of the Qur'an, regarding his earlier view of the Prophet Moses. The early chapters of the Qur'an define Moses as a Prophet called to the land of Egypt to call their people to repent of their idolatry. He communicates directly with their king for that purpose. In chapter 44, early in the middle Meccan period, he gets it more accurately. "Restore to me the servants of Allah," Moses declares.[396] The remainder of the story is highly truncated. Moses declares that he has sought safety with God, and that the Egyptians should keep away from him. God then calls him to march away by night "and leave the sea as a furrow (divided): For they are a host (destined) to be drowned."[397] The entire story of the miracles of Moses and the plagues of Egypt is left out. Muhammad has corrected the most glaring error from his previous description of these events, but it is clear that his notion of what happened in the Exodus is quite fuzzy and unclear.

In the very next chapter of the Qur'an, the story of Moses is significantly clarified. The story of Moses at the burning bush is told, but the details are very different. Moses is called to "establish regular prayer" and to announce "the hour (of judgment) is coming."[398] God gives him the signs of the rod that turns into a snake and a shining white hand. He also provides Aaron as spokesperson to "remove the impediment from my speech."[399] God then reminds him of his protection from Pharaoh by his mother who put him "into the chest" on the river. God says, "fear not: for I am with you: I hear and see everything."[400] Moses and Aaron then approach Pharaoh who asks who their Lord is, and they respond, "He who gave to each thing its form." Pharaoh asks the condition of previous generations to which "he" replies, "the

---

[394] Qur'an 54:33-39.
[395] Ibn Kathir, *Tafsir*, Vol. 9, p. 362, Yusuf Ali's footnote, p. 1392 #5154 and p. 532, #1579.
[396] Qur'an 44:18.
[397] Qur'an 44:24.
[398] Qur'an 20:14-15.
[399] Qur'an 20:27.
[400] Qur'an 20:46.

knowledge of that is with my Lord."[401] There then follows a description of the competition with the magicians of Egypt who are defeated and "thrown down to prostration" and declare their faith in the God of Moses and Aaron. Pharaoh declares, "I will cut off your hands and feet on opposite sides, and I will have you crucified on trunks of palm trees."[402] Ibn Kathir notes that Pharaoh was the one who invented crucifixion, and the biographical literature notes that Muhammad used this exact method of execution in the affair of the shepherds of the Ukl Tribe also mentioned in chapter 5:33[403] Yusuf Ali, perhaps aware of the anachronism of this description (crucifixion was invented many centuries later), makes no comment at all.[404]

There follows the story of the parting of the Red Sea, and how the people are led astray by "the Samiri" while Muhammad is on the "mountain." He creates the golden calf by throwing their ornaments in the fire. Moses interrogates Aaron who affirms his innocence. The Samiri is banned from the camp with the expression "touch me not," reminiscent of the mark of Cain.[405] Yusuf Ali attempts to connect the name with the Egyptian "shemer," which is inaccurate. A more likely candidate is the Samaritans although this would involve a massive anachronism which is probably why Yusuf Ali goes in search of something Egyptian. Ibn Kathir does not explain who the Samiri was, but includes the absurdity of the early Israelites despoiling the "Copts" at the time of the Exodus.[406] The story ends here. There is a certain level of detail accurate to the biblical text, and yet there are inaccurate innovations (from a Jewish perspective) and again, large portions of the story are left out, primarily the plagues.

It seems to me that Muhammad repeats these stories over and over adding gradually more detail each time because he is in the process of learning the story himself. The difference between the obscure references in chapter 44

---

[401] Qur'an 20:51-52. This is the same question that the animistic Arabs asked Muhammad, and this seems to be a transparent answer by Muhammad through the mouth of Moses. Muhammad had not yet come to the place of declaring that the previous pagan generations were burning in hell. The text follows the Hebrew scriptures remarkably well with the exception of several inclusions like the above which were of direct interest to Muhammad's listeners.

[402] Qur'an 20:71.

[403] Ibn Kathir, *Tafsir*, Vol. 6, p. 362. This is also noted in various Hadiths.

[404] Ali, Yusuf, p. 778.

[405] Qur'an 20:83-97.

[406] Ibn Kathir, *Tafsir*, Vol. 6, p. 377. The terminology "Coptic" would not have existed until more than fifteen hundred years later.

and the sharp images of chapter 20, coming a short time after, indicates that Muhammad was in a process of assimilating oral traditions. Some stories he obtained only as a vague awareness. In some cases, this obscurity is exchanged for considerable clarity later. Some sections he changes to fit his theological viewpoint (the sinlessnes of prophets such as Aaron). He adds some elements, such as demonstrating the oppression of Pharaoh, that are highly anachronistic (crucifixion one thousand years out of context). Some sections remain obscure or entirely absent. This is the kind of spotty understanding one would expect through learning by oral tradition and poetry. There is none of the discipline of studying historical prose here. These are stories being picked up and fashioned to fit, as Wansborough put it, an as yet not fully formed new doctrine.[407] There is no doubt in our minds that Muhammad appropriated, through Jewish contacts, oral traditions which he then fashioned in accordance with his emerging theological views.

The pattern for the emergence of Muhammad's understanding of the plagues follows a similar pattern of gradually increasing clarity. They are first mentioned about halfway through the chapters of the middle Meccan period. The reference is typically obscure: "We showed them sign after sign, each greater than its fellow, and we seized them with punishment . . . But when we removed the penalty from them, behold, they broke their word."[408]

The Qur'an does not return to the subject of the plagues again until near the end of this period. In chapter 17:101, it states, "To Moses we did give nine clear signs." Muhammad does not define what the clear signs are, and this seems to remain obscure for him during the remainder of this section of the Qur'an. The lists that the commentators provide of what these nine plagues were all differ significantly from the Hebrew text. The most glaring difference being that all of them leave out the most important story of the final plague and the Passover. In fact, in the entire Qur'an the story of Moses and Pharaoh is told twenty-seven times, each time with slightly greater clarity, but always missing the main point. It seems hard to imagine that Muhammad could have gleaned so many details of the story from oral tradition and yet somehow missed the main point. One must assume that there was an emerging theological reason for this oversight. The gradually increasing clarity, in any case, indicates that Muhammad had informers who would give him new information to make his "revelations" more accurate over time. This tends to confirm the general existing chronological structure of the chapters of the

---

[407]   Wansbrough, John, *Quranic Studies*, Oxford University Press, 1977.
[408]   Qur'an 43:48, 50.

Qur'an. We have found no clear anachronisms where Muhammad's growing understanding of the stories suddenly decays.

Another topic that emerges strongly in this middle period is Muhammad's view of previous revelations. Muhammad affirms that a holy book was given to Moses to provide guidance: "And we gave Moses the Book, in order that they might receive guidance."[409] This remarkable affirmation of the Hebrew scriptures is completely ignored by Ibn Kathir who affirms instead that when the Holy Book came down, "He commanded the believers to fight the unbelievers."[410] Yusuf Ali also ignores this. Muhammad affirms the holy book even as he constructs a view of its contents derived from oral tradition. He refers to the *furqan* of Musa[411] in the following chapter, utilizing a Hebrew word and giving further indication of his high view of the Hebrew scriptures. In the following chapter, entitled the "Children of Israel" he affirms again, "We gave Moses the book, and made it a guide."[412] He also affirms in the same chapter the Psalms as a book that "we wrote after the message."[413] It should be noted that there is much confusion over what *Adh-Dhikr* and *Az Zubbur* actually mean in this context. The fact that he was dealing with nonauthoritative oral tradition meant that he had freedom to amend and edit in accord with his developing theology without reference to the actual content of the Hebrew scriptures.

It is worth noting that each time Muhammad affirms the Hebrew scriptures and calls them either "Holy Book" or "furqan" the Muslim commentators quickly downplay the reference. Ali notes that this Holy Book "was violated

---

[409] Qur'an 23:49.

[410] Ibn Kathir, *Tafsir,* Vol. 6, p. 654. Yusuf Ali also completely ignores the implications of this momentous verse, p. 852.

[411] Qur'an 21:48.

[412] Qur'an 17:2.

[413] Qur'an 21:105. Ali interprets this passage as giving a chronological order. First the *Taurat,* then the *Zabbur* to affirm what a Western audience would regard as a correct chronological pattern. However, this is not clear in the commentaries. Adh-Dhikr, which Yusuf Ali interprets as *"Taurat"* really means remembrance and Ibn Kathir lists three interpretations, including the "mother of the book" that would be the original copy of the book of God in heaven (making it earlier than the *Taurat*). *Zabbur* is also variously interpreted, including the idea that it referred to all three Holy Books, "the *Tawrah,* the *Injil,* and the *Qur'an.*" The understanding of these terms had not emerged even at this period in which Ibn Kathir was writing (fourteenth century). Ibn Kathir, *Tafsir,* Vol. 6, pp. 509-510.

by the very people who claimed to be its custodians."[414] This was clearly not Muhammad's view at this point in history, nor did it ever become his view. It seems also that Muhammad is adopting the typology of these various Hebrew Prophet's as an indication of himself and his role. This is only stated obliquely in the Qur'an. After referring to Jesus and Mary the Qur'an states, "Verily this brotherhood of yours is a single brotherhood, and I am your Lord."[415] He notes that there has been a separation, but eventually "will they all return to us." Ibn Kathir translates this more literally, "Truly this your *ummah* is one."[416] The commentators affirm it over and over: "We have already noted that Allah often mentions Musa and Muhammad together—may the peace and blessings of Allah be upon them both—and he often mentions their books together as well."[417] Muhammad is similar to Noah in warning of the coming judgment and similar to Abraham, Moses, and Jesus in being the recipient of a holy book. He is like David and Solomon in the establishing of God's political kingdom on earth.

6.   Elijah, Elisha, Jonah, and Job

Several minor biblical characters are mentioned during this period. Jonah (Yunus) had been mentioned more extensively in the earlier period as a type of prophet declaring God's approaching judgment. He is like Noah in that regard. In chapter 21, he is briefly mentioned as "Dhu al Nun," the man of the fish. He cries out from the depths an approximation of the first part of the Muslim confession, and declares, "I was indeed wrong!"[418] Muhammad is still unclear about what it is that Jonah did wrong. The issue is not clarified until chapter 37, where the entire story is told in fairly accurate detail. It is worth noting that this kind of pattern is repeated over and over again in the Qur'an. The initial stories about Bible characters begin highly obscure and inaccurate, and then are gradually clarified in later chapters, although always remaining somewhat different from the Hebrew Bible whether by theological design or simple oversight. We have not found a single story that reverses this pattern when the Qur'an is read in chronological order. The same is true of all the chronologies in the Qur'an. They begin utterly mixed up from a

---

[414]   Ali, Yusuf, footnote no. 2170, p. 673.
[415]   Qur'an 21:92.
[416]   Ibn Kathir, *Tafsir,* Vol. 6, p. 489.
[417]   Ibn Kathir, *Tafsir,* Vol. 6, p. 456.
[418]   Qur'an 21:87.

Jewish or Christian perspective and are only partially corrected by the end of the book. The present chapter order of the Qur'an disguises this reality.

Job (Ayyub) is mentioned twice in this period. In chapter 38, the story is told that Ayyub called on God for deliverance from the affliction of Satan. God says, "Strike the ground with your foot. This is water to wash in, cool and a drink." His family is restored to him, "and along with them the like thereof," indicated perhaps double the number of the original. Finally, he is commanded to "strike his wife" with a bundle of grass.[419] This story has certain elements of the biblical text, Job's afflications, and the restoration of his family. But two elements are strange. The story of the spring of water is nowhere in the biblical texts. The beating of his wife would seem to be a reflection of the biblical statement she made "curse God and die."[420] Both of these odd elements give rise to a whole mass of traditions and interpretive stories. In Ibn Kathir, they stretch for six pages. The story of the spring becomes a fable of God's miraculous provision of a spring of healing waters for Job, which cleansed his body "inside and out."[421] This bears no resemblance to the biblical story though it may have a basis in certain Jewish fables and oral traditions. The older commentators all reverse the imagery of the wife beating. They affirm the righteousness of the wife, her "service, mercy, compassion and kindness" based on various traditions. They affirm that he had declared he would beat his wife simply because "he was upset about something she had done."[422] This confusion results from the inaccuracy of the traditions and leads Ibn Kathir to reverse the actual meaning of the Qur'an. Yusuf Ali manages to correct this by simply citing the Bible text.[423] Many times the Qur'an is simply incomprehensible without reference to the Bible. When Job is later mentioned in chapter 21, the previous inaccuracies of healing springs and wife-beating are absent. Did someone correct Muhammad as he went along?

Elijah and Elisha (Ilyas[424] and Al-Yasa) are both briefly mentioned although only Elijah receives any particular attention.[425] The Qur'an describes

---

[419] Qur'an 38:4-144.

[420] Job 2:9.

[421] Ibn Kathir, *Tafsir,* Vol. 8, p. 336.

[422] Ibn Kathir, *Tafsir,* Vol. 8, p. 339.

[423] Ali, Yusuf, footnote no. 4202, p. 1171.

[424] It should be noted that the Muslim commentators are unsure if Ilyas is another name for Idris (Enoch), which is the view that the most renowned Qur'anic commentator, Tabari, held. Ibn Kathir, *Tafsir,* Vol. 8, p. 281. It is a further example of how mixed up the chronologies and interpretations are.

[425] Al-Yasa: Qur'an 38:48 and Ilyas: Qur'an 37:123-132.

how Ilyas calls the people to Allah and to turn away from the "ba'l."[426] Ibn
Kathir's explanation of this verse indicates the total confusion of the early
Muslim commentators:

> Allah sent him to the children of Israel after Hizqil (Ezekiel) . . . They
> had started to worship an idol called ba'l, and he called them to
> Allah . . . They persisted in their misguided ways . . . So he prayed
> to Allah against them, and Allah withheld the rain . . . Then they
> asked him to relieve them . . . So he prayed to Allah for them, and
> the rains came, but they persisted in their evil ways . . . So Ilyas
> was commanded to go to such and such a place, and whatever
> mount came to him he was to ride on it and not give it away. A
> horse of fire was brought to him and he rode it, and Allah clothed
> him with light and covered him with feathers, and he used to fly
> with the angels.[427]

This fantastic story combines elements of three events in the life of Elijah
from the Hebrew Bible, with a mixed up chronology of Ezekiel (a postexilic
prophet), and the Greek fable of Icarus. Yusuf Ali straightens this out in the
modern period by making reference to the Hebrew Bible to make sense of
the obscure Qur'anic references.[428]

7. David and Solomon

We have noted earlier that David and Solomon provide a paradigm for
the emerging self-image of the Prophet. They are Prophet kings who combine
priestly and political power. The first mention of David in the Qur'an occurs
in chapter 38, concerning David's sin with Bathsheeba and Nathan's rebuke
(verses 20-26). David is extolled as one to whom the birds assembled and
with whom the mountains praised God. He was a man of sound judgment,
but no mention is made of a holy book. The story is then told of the poor man
whose only lamb is taken by his rich brother. It is clearly Nathan's parable
to David. The passage then states, "And Dawud guessed that we have tried
him and he sought forgiveness from his Lord." We have already noted how
all the commentators bend over backward to show that this has nothing to

---

[426] Qur'an 37:125.
[427] Ibn Kathir, *Tafsir,* Vol. 8, p. 282.
[428] Ali, Yusuf, footnote no. 4112, p. 1152.

do with any sin with Bathsheeba or the murder of her husband. Muhammad, during this period, speaks often of the repentance of the prophets, "and he fell down prostrate and turned (to Allah) in repentance."[429] It is clear that later commentators try to impose their theological viewpoints on these early texts. The concept of the sinless Prophets is gradually emerging in the Qur'an, but in this early period it seems there was still room for true confession and repentance even on the part of Prophets. Yusuf Ali refers to the "scandalous" stories of the Bible as an indication of its inaccuracy.[430] Ibn Kathir is aware that a repentance on the part of David is implied here. He does not, however, explain why.[431] This has tragic consequences for Muslim culture as we have noted earlier. The Bible is realistic about the sins of human beings, even exalted ones. The Qur'an and particularly later Muslim interpretations of the Qur'an gradually negates this area of critical thinking.

The next mention of David comes in chapter 21, "The Prophets." Here Muhammad tells another story of God's judgment on David: "Remember David and Solomon, when they gave judgment in the matter of the field into which the sheep of certain people had strayed by night: We did witness their judgment."[432] This story bears a resemblance to that of the earlier disputants, yet it has no counterpart in the Hebrew Bible. Muhammad simply does not understand what is in the Hebrew Bible, and it seems like he is trying to explain what the earlier obscure reference was about. Both Ibn Kathir and Yusuf Ali explain this story as referring to a group of sheep that had trampled a vineyard, a story that seems to be a pure invention of the commentators.[433] The passage goes on to explain that David invented "metal chain mail," an anachronism as the earliest known examples of chain mail date from the fourth century BCE and are Celtic. The mention of David's singing leads Ibn Kathir to interpret this as referring to the Psalms. "This refers to the beauty of his voice when he recited his book, Az-Zabur."[434] In fact, the book is not mentioned at all. Yusuf Ali clarifies this by actually citing the Psalms. The first mention of the word *Zabur* is later in the passage and not connected with David at all. "Before this we wrote in the *Zabur* after the message; my servants the righteous shall inherit the earth." The commentators disagree as

---

[429]   Qur'an 38:24.
[430]   Ali, Yusuf, p. 1223, footnote no. 4178.
[431]   Ibn Kathir, *Tafsir*, Vol. 8, pp. 322-323.
[432]   Qur'an 21:78.
[433]   Ibn Kathir, *Tafsir*, Vol. 6, pp. 472-3, Ali, footnote no. 2732, p. 811.
[434]   Ibn Kathir, *Tafsir*, Vol. 6, p. 475.

to what the word *Zabur* actually means particularly in relation to "the recited message" (*Adh-Dhikr*).

> He said, "Az-Zabur means the Tawrah, the Injil and the Qur'an." Mujahid said, "Az-Zabur" means the book." . . . others said, "Az-Zabur is that which was revealed to Dawud, and Adh Dhikr is the Tawrah." Mujahid said: "Az Zabur means the books which came after adh-Dhikr and Adh-Dhikr is the Mother of the Book (umm Al-Kitab) which is with Allah."[435]

The reason for this confusion is that *Zabur* may also refer to "scrolls" or "scriptures" in the plural (*Zubur*) where David is clearly not indicated.[436] The final mention of David in this period is in chapter 27:15-16 where his wisdom is extolled.

Solomon receives a more extensive treatment in this period of the Qur'an. He is mentioned first in the same context in chapter 38 as David's son. The passage is very obscure. Solomon is presented with horses in the evening. Then the translators disagree on the next verse. Yusuf Ali translates it, "Truly do I love the love of good, with a view to the glory of my Lord." Ibn Kathir reverses the meaning. "I did love the good instead of remembering my lord." There then follows a verse about how Solomon patted the horses and that God tried him. This obscurity leads Ibn Kathir into several pages of traditions about Solomon neglecting his evening prayers while admiring the horses and this leads him to slaughter them in repentance. He mixes this with a story of Aisha playing with her toy horse after the Battle of Khaybar or Tabuk.[437] Yusuf Ali's reverse interpretation begins with the telling statement, "The story is not found

---

[435]   Ibn Kathir, *Tafsir,* Vol. 6, p. 509.

[436]   Qur'an 26:196 Where Ali notes that the Zabur here is referred to in plural, ie. "books" (Zubur) (footnote no. 3226, p. 931), which is the same as the plural for "sects." See also Qur'an 54:43, 52.

[437]   Ibn Kathir, *Tafsir,* Vol. 8 p. 328. It is worth noting that the Hadith about Aisha further indicates her young age. She was married in the year following the hijra. Khaybar took place in 628 about five years later, and Tabuk in 630. If she was still playing with toys like doll horses, as this passage indicates, then she must have been extremely young at the time of the consummation of her marriage. The Hadith universally claim an age of eight or nine, and this is substantiated by these kinds of collateral unintended confirmations. The low legal age for marriage found in Arabia and Iran to this day has its basis in the fact that this is canonical behavior to be imitated by all Muslims.

in the Old Testament." His interpretation is the exact opposite of Ibn Kathir: "Solomon was also the most meticulous in not allowing the least motive of self to be mixed up with his spiritual virtues."[438] Yusuf Ali indicates that Solomon had no fault in this. Perhaps he represents the final stage of "sinless Prophets" theology that now completely controls Muslim theology.

The Qur'an goes on to note that Solomon had occult powers. "We subjected the wind to his power, to flow gently to his order . . . as also the evil ones, every kind of builder and diver—as also others bound together in fetters."[439] Yusuf Ali tries to make the "divers" into something human, "The divers were probably those employed in pearl fisheries."[440] Ibn Kathir's translation is more direct: "We subjected to him the wind; it blew gently by his order wherever he willed and the shayatin, from every kind of builder and diver." Ibn Kathir then takes this story of Solomon's power over the spirits and shows how Muhammad had the same powers. When Muhammad is bothered by an "Ifrit" among the jinn, he overpowers it.

> An Ifrit from among the jinn came and bothered me last night—trying to stop me from praying. Allah enabled me to overpower him, and I wanted to tie him to one of the pillars in the Masjid so that you could see him this morning. Then I remembered what my brother Sulayman said, "My Lord! Forgive me and bestow upon me a kingdom such as shall not belong to any other after me" . . . so he let him go humiliated . . . the enemy of Allah Iblis came with a flame of fire to throw in my face . . . Then I wanted to seize him. By Allah if it were not for the words of our brother Sulayman, he would have been chained up and he would have become a plaything for the children of the people of Al-Madinah.[441]

The purpose of this fantastic story seems primarily to indicate that Muhamad is a new Sulayman with the same power over spirits who would also establish a kingdom "such as shall not belong to any other after me" (verse 35). Yusuf Ali interprets the Qur'anic verse in an entirely different way, "Grant me a kingdom which (it may be) suits not another after me." The first interpretation

---

438 Ali, Yusuf, footnote no. 4185, p. 1168.
439 Qur'an 38:36-38.
440 Ali, Yusuf, footnote no. 4194, p. 1170.
441 Ibn Kathir, *Tafsir,* Vol. 8, pp. 332-333.

exalts the political kingdom of Muhammad, the second maintains the focus on Solomon alone.

It should be noted at this point that the Qur'an also strongly resembles Jewish occult literature. The "Testament of Solomon" contains numerous similar references to Solomon's occult powers in the control of various kinds of spirits, and even how he put them to work in his building projects. Mordecai Margalioth in his edited *Sefer ha-Razim,* a manual of fifth to sixth century Jewish magical rites, states,

> "Solomon is characterized as having acquired authority 'over all the spirits and demons' and, in one sort of relation or another with these, as having 'imprisoned and released . . . sent out and brought in . . . built and prospered.'"[442]

Solomon is credited in the Qur'an with power to cause the Jinns to march in battle order (27:17), to conjure thrones from distant places (27:39), to bind spirits in fetters, and to use them as divers and builders (38:37-38). The two Jewish works are part of a common field of Jewish writings of this period that clearly find their reflection in the text of the Qur'an. Klutze dates the earliest versions of the Testament of Solomon as no later than the fifth century CE and possibly as early as the third century. He lists the probable place of origin as Egypt,[443] where there was a large Jewish community until modern times. Though the work has a Jewish origin it also contains significant later additions of a Christian nature purporting to show the fall of Solomon and thereby the superiority of Christ.[444] Klutz states,

> An important implication of this hypothesis is that the envisaged document . . . would be the result of a process of Christianizing interpretation and redactional activity that was later perpetuated and intensified by the various editors who produced the fuller versions of the Testament preserved in manuscripts.[445]

---

[442]   Cited in Klutz, Todd E., *Rewriting the Testament of Solomon*, New York: T & T Clark International, p. 82.

[443]   Klutz, pp. 35-36.

[444]   Klutz, p. 67.

[445]   Klutz, p. 108, Klutz also notes the connection of some of this imagery to the text of the Qur'an, p. 86.

This kind of borrowing of other groups writings that are then reworked as polemic tracts seems to be a regular feature of this period. Klutz notes that the "Jewish-Christian debates of late antiquity included disputes about who really fulfilled select biblical promises and prophecies—Solomon or Jesus."[446] These debates may be reflected in the way the Qur'an also borrows and reworks materials from Jewish and Christian sources for Muhammad's polemic purposes. This was a pattern typical of the time period.

One of the longest individual stories told in the middle Meccan period is the story of Solomon and the queen of Sheba. As we noted earlier, the story is a virtual quotation from the second Targum of Esther, a sixth century Jewish didactic fable. The major difference aside from some details is that the Jewish version of the fable is meant to demonstrate the superior wisdom of men over women. The Qur'an makes this into a story of the conversion of the Queen to Islam. A brief rendition of the story's contents follows.

Solomon is introduced as in the earlier passages as the son of David, a man endued with great wisdom who "understood the speech of birds" and who "marshaled his hosts—of Jinns and men in battle order." Solomon also understands the language of ants and is amused when they call to seek cover from his approaching army, "lest Solomon and his hosts crush you."[447] Solomon calls for a muster of his birds and discovers that his Hoopoe bird is missing. He is enraged and threatens to "execute him." Yusuf Ali explains this outburst as Solomon's insistence on discipline in the ranks. Ibn Kathir notes that a certain man questioned the reality of this story and was silenced by the threats of Ibn Abbas.[448] From the beginning, Islam has forbidden critical thinking as this leads to doubt that is considered a "Satan." Suicide bombers could use a little doubt.

In due time, the Hoopoe returns and explains his absence as resulting from his discovery of a land (Saba) where a woman with a great throne rules over the people and idolatry is unbridled. "I found her and her people worshipping the sun."[449] Solomon tests the bird by sending it back with a letter to the Queen. He calls the Queen to come "to me in submission." Solomon's political threat leads her counselors to advise preparations for war. She, instead, decides to send a gift to placate Solomon. Solomon rejects the gift, stating he has been

---

[446] Klutz, p. 77.
[447] Qur'an 27:16-19. The chapter takes its name, "The Ant" from this episode.
[448] Ibn Kathir, *Tafsir,* Vol. 7, p. 312, Ali, footnote no. 3262, p. 943.
[449] Qur'an 27:24.

given something better than what was given them, and we "shall come to them with armies that they cannot resist and we shall drive them out." Yusuf Ali interprets the "something better" as being the religion of Islam, while Ibn Kathir interprets this as better "troops." Ibn Kathir concludes, "We shall accept nothing from you except Islam or the sword."[450]

Solomon calls his chiefs to ask who could bring the queen's throne to him. A powerful spirit comes forward, "Said an Ifrit of the Jinns: 'I will bring it to thee' . . . Said one who had knowledge of the Book, 'I will bring it to thee within the twinkling of an eye'."[451] The Ifrit conjures the throne of the Queen, and Solomon orders that he transform it so that she cannot recognize it as her throne.[452] The Queen recognizes its similarity and declares, "we have submitted to Allah." After this, she is shown Solomon's palace, which looks like a lake though actually paved with "slabs of glass." The Queen again declares, "I do submit with Solomon to the Lord of the Worlds."

The story is fragmentary. How the Queen arrived at Solomon's palace is not explained. Indeed the commentators add considerable material in an effort to arrive at a smooth story line. Yusuf Ali notes that this sometimes leads to alternative constructions as to the meaning of Qur'anic verses.[453] Indeed, knowing the source in the second Targum of Esther would have clarified the actual meaning of the story considerably. This is typical of the fragmented nature of many Qur'anic passages. One thing is clear, such a long passage directly cited from a Jewish text indicates that Muhammad was either in direct dialogue with Jews or was a sort of Jewish convert himself. Under what circumstances will never be known, but the fragmentary nature of the texts preserved indicates an oral tradition passed on by word of mouth where certain details could be preserved with remarkable clarity even when the story line in general was left obscure. Muhammad was in poetic dialogue with Jews, perhaps even poetic debates such as the one described by Bukhari:

> I ask you by Allah, did you hear Allah's apostle saying (to me),
> "retort on my behalf O Allah! Support him (i.e., Hassan) with the

---

[450] Ali, Yusuf, footnote no. 3272, p. 946, Kathir, Vol. 7, p. 321.
[451] Qur'an 27:39-40.
[452] Ibn Kathir considers that these two verses refer to two different individuals, one a Jinn ruler and the other a scribe knowledgeable in the scriptures named Asif. The story is considerably embellished (p. 324).
[453] Ali, Yusuf, footnote no. 3280, p. 948.

Holy Spirit?" Abu Huraira said, "Yes." The Prophet said to Hassan, "Lampoon them (i.e., The pagans) and Gabriel is with you."[454]

Muhammad adapted the material he gleaned from the Jewish poets and storytellers to fit his particular doctrinal purpose. At this stage, there is no sense of conflict with the Jews. They are providing important background information on the role of Prophets in a literary context in which borrowing and adapting is quite acceptable. Debates and discussions with another poet were no threat to the Jews. It is only when Muhammad usurps the role of king, states his Qur'an as scripture, and pretends to interpret the Jewish Pentateuch that conflict with the Jews became unavoidable. What is important to note from a developmental standpoint, is the degree to which political and spiritual, even occult, power is combined toward the end of this period. The viewpoint, not untypical for the time, was one of coercive political/military power harnessed in the cause of religion. This paradigm surely moved Muhammad closer to the religiopolitical state concept that Islam was to become.

8. John the Baptist (Yahya)

The first clear reference to John (Yahya)[455] is found in the chapter entitled "Mary." John's father Zachariah (Zakariya) pleads with Allah for a son, and there follows a fairly accurate rendition of the New Testament story. The differences are slight. Zachariah's unbelief in the promise of a son results

---

[454] Bukhari, no. 434-435, Vol. 4, p. 292-293. The circumstance seems to be a poetic debate between the Muslims and the pagans, in which Muhammad called on one of his followers to make fun of the pagans in verse. Later, Muhammad took a very negative view of those who lampooned him in verse, ordering them to be assassinated. Compare Ibn Ishaq, *The Life of Muhammad*, p. 367.

[455] There is an earlier passage that sounds like the description of John in Luke quoting from Isaiah. The Qur'anic passages reads, "They ask thee concerning the Mountains: say, 'My Lord will uproot them and scatter them as dust. He will leave them as plains smooth and level; nothing crooked or curved wilt thou see in their place. On that day will they follow the caller: no crookedness him" (20:105-108). The picture here is apocalyptic, representative of God's judgment, arguably the same context for the emergence of John in the New Testament: "The voice of one calling in the desert, prepare the way of the Lord, make straight paths for Him. Every valley shall be filled in, every mountain and hill made low. The crooked roads shall be made straight, the rough ways smooth" (Luke 3:4-6, Isaiah 40:3-5).

in his receiving a sign from God, at his own request, of being struck dumb for three days (rather than the duration of the pregnancy). John is told after his birth to "Take hold of the book with might." This seems to indicate that John also was the recipient of a Holy Book, though this is never defined in the Qur'an. It seems that the orthodox view of four revealed holy books could be potentially expanded by at least three or four other supposed texts mentioned in the Qur'an. On John, the Qur'an makes a blessing that is repeated concerning several Prophets including Christ: "So peace on him the day he was born, the day that he dies, and the day that he will be raised up to life" Once again, Yusuf Ali fills out the details on John by making reference to the New Testament.[456] Ibn Kathir is in the dark about the "sign" of Zachariah's dumbness and so includes several pages of details relating how this sign was at his own request, not as a result of God's rebuke of his lack of faith.[457] John's relation to the advent of Christ is not developed though the order in the chapter seems chronological and the story of Jesus follows immediately after.

9. Jesus and Mary

After not being mentioned at all in the early Meccan period, Jesus and his mother Mary are second only to Moses in frequency of mention during the middle Meccan period. Jesus appears as a fantastic figure, speaking at the time of his birth and evidencing various miracles.

The first mention of Jesus occurs about halfway through the middle period in a chapter appropriately named for his mother, "Mary." Mary is the only woman mentioned by name in the Qur'an. The passage begins with God declaring, "Relate in the Book Mary when she withdrew from her family to a place in the east." There an angel appears to her, and she responds in fear. Ibn Kathir interprets that she thought he was a man and feared he would rape her. The location of her withdrawal has evinced considerable speculation by the commentators. Ibn Kathir thinks Jerusalem and Yusuf Ali agrees.[458] Mary is promised a son and she questions, "How shall I have a son, seeing that no man has touched me, and I am not unchaste?" This parallels Luke 1:26-37 although it is much abbreviated. The angel declares that this is what is decreed and "that is easy for me." Mary withdraws again to "a remote place." Again

---

[456]   Ali, Yusuf, footnote no. 2468, p. 747.
[457]   Ibn Kathir, *Tafsir,* Vol. 6, pp. 232-234.
[458]   Ibn Kathir, *Tafsir,* Vol. 6, pp. 239-241, Yusuf Ali, footnote no. 2471, p. 747.

the terminology is obscure both in reference to time and place. These verses elicit much discussion from the commentators concerning the decrees of God that cannot be "avoided" and God's power to create what He wills as being thoroughly distinct from the idea of Christ being the Son of God. It does seem likely that Muhammad is establishing a separate identity for Jesus that fits his theological system. He maintains the concept of the virgin birth while denying any implication of sonship to God. "Many scholars differed over its location" Ibn Kathir notes as he discusses the birthplace of Jesus. He finds no problem in identifying this obscure place as Bethlehem, and Yusuf Ali notes more specifically that it must have been under a palm tree in Bethlehem.[459]

Mary cries out in the pain of childbirth and suddenly a voice speaks to her "from below." There is considerable disagreement among the commentators as to who is speaking. Some say it was Gabriel, others the newborn Jesus lying on the ground.[460] Yusuf Ali avoids comment. A rivulet of water is provided, and she shakes the palm tree to get some dates. Some interpret the rivulet "Sariy" to refer to Jesus. God instructs her to a vow of silence, and she returns to her people. They address her "O sister of Aaron," indicating that Muhammad had mixed up the two Miriams of the Old and New Testaments.[461] When they accuse her of immorality she points to the baby and Jesus speaks, giving a speech about his prophethood "I am indeed a Prophet of Allah," and concluding with the same adage as John the Baptist, "Peace is on me the day I was born, the day that I die, and the day the I shall be raised to life." The commentators include quaint details of the suckling Jesus releasing his mother's breast to speak. The fact that Jesus is "enjoined" by God to his task becomes a further demonstration of God's decrees. He is also mentioned as a receiver of "revelation" though it is not defined what this is.

Immediately following this speech, the Qur'an launches into an attack on the Christian doctrines based on the virgin birth. "Such is Isa . . . It befits not Allah that he should beget a son, glorified be he. When he decrees a thing, He only says to it: 'Be!'—and it is . . . So worship him. That is the straight path. The sects differed, so woe unto the disbelievers . . ." It seems clear that Muhammad is addressing either his disciples in response to their

---

459   Ibn Kathir, *Tafsir*, Vol. 6, p. 244, Ali, footnote no. 2475, p. 748.
460   Ibn Kathir, *Tafsir*, Vol. 6, p. 247.
461   We will discuss this later. "Mary" is a latin form of her Hebrew name which would have been "Miriam" in Arabic and thus identical to the name of the sister of Aaron in the Old Testament. Muhammad consistently assumes that they are the same person.

questions about Christian teaching, or perhaps Christians themselves. It seems plausible that Muhammad received revelations in response to issues raised by his disciples, such as questions about the beliefs of other monotheistic religions in Arabia. As an oracle, Muhammad would be expected to provide answers direct from his "familiar spirit." His answers are obscure, in the style of the kahins, because that style makes it hard to discern actual errors. Such material is, however, ideal for determining theological views. Later in the same passage, Muhammad returns to the subject of God having a son and states that this is "something monstrous." Those who believe such things are not true Christians, but "unbelievers."

The next passage to mention Jesus is chapter 43, the "Ornaments of Gold." The passage is primarily refuting the pagan belief in "daughters of Allah." The idea that God would exalt woman, "a creature who is brought up in adornments and who, in a dispute, cannot make itself clear," is something that the Qur'an lampoons. The misogynist viewpoint aside, the remainder of the passage illustrates from the lives of the Prophets the rejection of polytheism in any form. In verse 57, Muhammad seems to address Christians directly:

> "When the son of Mary is held up as an example, behold thy people raise a clamour there at! And they say, "Are our gods best, or he?" To thee, only by way of disputation: yea they are a contentious people. He was not more than a servant . . . And when Isa came with clear proofs, he said: "I have come to you with wisdom, and in order to make clear to you some of that in which you differ. Therefore fear Allah and obey me. Verily, Allah! He is my Lord and your Lord. So worship him. This is the straight path." But the sects from among themselves differed.[462]

The passage seems the clearest example of an address to Christians directly: "thy people," and could also reflect some of the theological differences of Christian groups. Muhammad seems to address a Christian sectarian environment in which the nature of Christ and his mother is being debated. The phrase "your Lord and my Lord" is reminiscent of John 20:17, which was used by certain sects to justify a separate identity for Jesus and God. It is, perhaps, addressed to a single person with whom Muhammad was in dialogue. It seems possible that the form of address indicates an answer to a question raised by one of Muhammad's disciples who was himself a Christian. Perhaps

---

[462] Qur'an 43:57-59, 63-65.

there had been an argument in Muhammad's presence between members of two different Christian sects. In any case, the Qur'an seems dialogical at this point as stories appropriated by Muhammad in his interchanges are then reworked to fit into his emerging theological framework. Jesus is also referred to as: "he shall be a known sign for the hour." This seems to be an eschatological reference indicating that Jesus would return at the end of the age and this is affirmed by both Ibn Kathir and Yusuf Ali.[463] Toward the end of the passage Muhammad affirms again, "If most gracious had a son, I would be the first to worship," but he concludes "Glory to the Lord . . . from the things they attribute, so leave them to babble and play until they meet that day of theirs which they have been promised." Muhammad's theology of tawhid, or the absolute unity of God, puts him on a collision course with anyone advocating complexity in the godhead.

Three chapters later in chapter 23, "The Believers'," Muhammad mentions again the story of Mary and Jesus who are called "a sign." God says, "We gave them shelter on high ground, affording rest and security and furnished with springs." This seems to be a repetition of the previous description in abbreviated form. Muhammad goes on to say that "this ummah of yours is a single ummah." He conceives of all the Prophets as being servants of the same God, and thus representative of the same community. He contrasts this with the disunity of these religions now: "But people have cut off their affair between them into sects." So Islam begins to emerge as an effort to reestablish that unity.

In the next chapter, "The Prophets," Muhammad makes reference to the other monotheistic communities. In answer to the accusation that he is a dreamer, forger, and poet, Muhammad responds in verse 7 stating, "Before thee, also, the messengers we sent were but men, to whom we granted inspiration: If ye realize this not, ask those who possess the message." Ibn Kathir affirms that this refers to the Jews and Christians, although Yusuf Ali is silent on the subject.[464] Muhammad is saying that his followers should consult the Jews and the Christians and their "message" to confirm what he is saying. At this stage, Muhammad is convinced that the Jews and Christians would back him up in his claims of being an inspired Prophet. He is regarding their scriptures as uncorrupted sources of revelation. This seems to indicate a more indirect relationship to those communities, or perhaps that a number of his followers were from those backgrounds, and he reasonably expected

---

[463]   Ibn Kathir, *Tafsir,* Vol. 8, p. 654, Ali, footnote no. 4662, p. 1276.
[464]   Ibn Kathir, *Tafsir,* Vol. 6, p. 427.

that those communities would support him. There is very little negative said about either of these communities at this point in the Qur'an. Shortly after in verse 21, he says, "Or have they taken gods from the earth who can raise (the dead). This seems to be an oblique reference to Christ, as one who raises the dead, though it is obscure. Muhammad includes it under a series of arguments against associating anything with God. He returns again to the subject of Mary and Jesus in verse 91: "And (remember) her who guarded her chastity: We breathed into her of Our Spirit, and we made her and her son a sign for all peoples." Here Muhammad goes further than in the earlier passage. Now it is not merely a decree, but the actual breathing out of the "Spirit" that leads to the conception of Jesus. This is a step closer to Christian teaching and creates an anomaly in Islam that has never been explained. If God has a "Spirit" that He can breathe out, are there then two parts to God? As was noted earlier, the subject of the "Spirit" is something that, according to the commentators, Muhammad avoided discussing. The "spirit" is not Gabriel as some commentators maintain. Gabriel is not an agent of creating life.

We have now considered the general trends in the second period of the Qur'an. We can say several things about Muhammad's view of the People of the Book at this stage in his career. He did not see his message as separate from theirs. There is one God so there must be only one message. The word *Islam* does not really have a specific meaning at this stage. It is simply a description of how all believers "submit" to almighty Allah. Muhammad is aware of the divisions among the People of the Book, but considers that they will recognize him as one of their own and the unity of his message with theirs. The fact that he finds Christians contentious must indicate some kind of personal contact. His followers at this stage do not see themselves as separate from the other monotheistic communities, and it seems likely that members of other communities were among his followers, perhaps moving from one group to another and asking questions along the way. Muhammad was also clearly a public person during this period. He is in dialogue, and then, perhaps at times, he is withdrawn in personal discussion with his followers. Clearly, however, this is not a secretive group, and there is plenty of room for the interchange of religious poetry from many sources, some of which emerges in the text of the Qur'an. Muhammad's reinterpretations of other religious ideas seem to be an Arabization, a contextualization of Christian/ Jewish ideas to the Arabian circumstance. The stage is set for the gradual appropriation of much of the cultures and beliefs of the People of the Book into the rubric of an entirely new community.

B. The Muslim Biographical Literature

When we consider the *sira* literature of this period, we find very little information. This is interesting in and of itself. The middle Meccan period must have been one of the most foundational periods in the development of the Prophet, in terms of his self-image and his growing confidence in the message and how to present it. Twenty-one chapters of the Qur'an are revealed during this period. Yet this period in Al-Tabari occupies six short pages. The entire section deals with how Abu Talib, Muhammad's uncle protected Muhammad. It contains the usual adage that Muhammad's followers practiced their religion "in secret."[465] The passage affirms that Abu Talib refused to leave the religion of his ancestors, but protected Muhammad out of a genuine affection. There is a brief mention of persecution of those who followed Muhammad. Finally, several occasions of revelation (Asbab al-Nazul) are mentioned. One is God's Word to Muhammad when Abu Talib refuses to accept Islam (28:56) and God states, "You guide not whom you will, but God guides whom he will." This passage is actually from the late Meccan period and may refer to a word of comfort at the death of Abu Talib. Two other passages are cited that do come from the middle period. In the heat of an argument in Abu Talib's house the Word comes, "They have not yet tasted my doom" (38:5-8). Similarly, in the midst of argument the Meccans attack Muhammad's religion, "naught but an invention" (38:6-7). There are also some anachronisms. Muhammad several times offers the Quraysh rule over the Arabs and non-Arabs (forcing the latter to pay the jizya) if they will but say "there is no God but God."[466] This may well have been part of the later motivation of Islam, but was probably not conceived of at this point, unless we are to believe that Muhammad was a militarist from the start. The seeds are there, but the direct teaching is not at this stage of the Qur'an.

Ibn Ishaq, similarly, devotes only twenty-one pages out of his eight hundred page tome to this period. He describes incidents of persecution against Muhammad. Apparently, this harassment ceased when his uncle, Hamza, accepted Islam, as he was "the strongest man of Quraysh."[467] Ibn Ishaq tells various stories concerning debates between Muhammad and members of Quraysh, questions of who he is and what is the nature of his revelations.

---

[465] Tabari, Vol. 6, p. 93.
[466] Tabari, Vol. 6, p. 93-98.
[467] Ibn Ishaq, p. 131.

This follows the pattern of the middle Meccan period, but tells us nothing of actual events. It reads more like a catalogue of questions and answers. Most of the passages cited by Ibn Ishaq do belong to the middle Meccan period, although there are some inconsistencies. Aside from these stories of questions and answers and persecutions, we gain no insight into the period that we couldn't have derived from the Qur'an itself, which is not much. It seems to us that this period is avoided by the historians because it was clearly a time of dialogue with the People of the Book. There is almost no mention in the biographies of Muhammad dialoguing with Jews or Christians. We shall look at one exception shortly. This is despite the fact that the Meccan's accusations that Muhammad was being tutored in his stories by Jews or Christians are recorded throughout the Qur'an during this period. Clearly, this was a matter too sensitive to pass on to posterity.

In the later biographies, particularly of Ibn Kathir, a fiction of Muhammad secretly preaching Islam and then being commanded at a certain time to preach openly is developed. According to this story, a three-year period of secretly preaching in the countryside ended around 613. Ibn Kathir notes that Muhammad then received a revelation that it was time for him to start publicly proclaiming God's message, "God then orders his messenger after three years of his mission, to announce it openly and to remain firm against the evil of the polytheists."[468]

Ibn Kathir records sura 63:44 as God's command for Muhammad to preach Islam openly. However, according to Nöldeke, sura 63 is placed in the Medinan period between 622-623 CE. Ibn Kathir also believes sura 26:85, "Make me one of the inheritors of the Garden of Bliss" and 15:92-3, "Therefore, by thy Lord, We will, of a surety, call them to account for all their deeds," also have the same thrust for Muhammad to publicly proclaim Islam.[469] The latter two are at least in sync chronologically. Ibn Kathir then recounts the stories we looked at from the early Meccan period as if they had occurred in the middle period. In particular, he focuses on the feast, which Muhammad held to make his initial proclamation to the Quraysh. The purpose of these stories is also clearly polemic and intended to attract the largely Christian population of the Middle East to Islam. In Ibn Kathir's story, the feast that was prepared resembled Jesus's miracle of feeding five thousand with two loaves of bread and five fish. This gathering consisted of about

---

[468]   Ibn Kathir, *Al-Sira Al-Nabawiyya*. Trans Trevor Le Gassick Sr., UK: Garner Publishing. 1998, p. 330.
[469]   Ibn Kathir, p. 331.

forty-five men. Then he (Muhammad) said, "Take, in the name of God." They ate until they could eat no more, and yet the food was as it had been, except for where their hands had been. I swear by God in whose hand "Ali's soul rests, that a single man could have eaten the amount of food which I put before all of them." Then he said, "Give them something to drink." "So I brought them that bowl and they drank from it until they had drunk their fill, and swear by God that one man could have drunk that amount."[470] Watt interprets this as miracle that was invented later by Muslim scholars to show that Muhammad was a prophet and performed miracles since one of the reasons Christians rejected Muhammad was because he had not performed any miracles.[471] In Ibn Ishaq's account, there is no indication of any miracle of this nature.

There are numerous other stories recorded from this period that seem quite invented, sometimes running parallel stories with different characters. Abu Jahl planned to assassinate Muhammad by crushing him with a stone while he was praying. The Quraysh had given their approval to this action.[472] As Abu Jahl moved toward Muhammad he became frightened and dropped the stone because his hand had become withered. He said a "camel stallion" got in his way, "by God," he said, "I have never seen anything like his head, shoulders, and teeth on any stallion before, and he made as though he would eat me."[473] This was not the only occasion that someone planned to kill Muhammad by crushing his head in with a rock. Abu Lahab is also recorded to have planned to kill Muhammad in this way.[474]

Watt gives two possible reasons for the opposition toward Muhammad. First, Muhammad's teachings went against the Quraysh's way of life.[475] His teachings were now attacking the upper class and their way of life. "It must have stung them to be called "niggardly" and to have it asserted that they were not the lords of creation they thought they were."[476]

If Muhammad continued in his current direction, attacking the wealthy, it could lead to political support. If people started to believe that God spoke through him, people would start to think he was a man who possessed great "wisdom,

[470] Watt, Montgomery, W. and McDonald, MV (translated). *The History of al-Tabari.* New York: State University of New York Press. P. 90.

[471] Watt, Montgomery, W. and McDonald, MV (translated), P. 90, footnote no. 142.

[472] Ibn Ishaq, p. 135.

[473] Ibn Ishaq, p. 135.

[474] Ibn Kathir, *Al-Sira*, p. 337.

[475] Watt, Montgomery, W. *Muhammad Prophet and Statesman* p. 59.

[476] Watt, Montgomery, p. 59

prudence, and judgment."[477] If this became the case, people would start to look for him to be a leader and would upset the current political structure.[478] However, as we have noted, there was not a great deal of emphasis on economic justice in this period of the Qur'an. The arguments recorded over Muhammad's insults of the pagan gods and disrespect of the ancestors seems a much better candidate for causing the growing opposition to Muhammad in Mecca.

This brings us to the one story of dialogue with the People of the Book. It is, however, not Muhammad who has the dialogue, but the Quraysh. The Quraysh recognized the Jews as people of the scriptures according to Ishaq. They also recognized that the Jews understood issues pertaining to Prophets. So the Quraysh send a delegation to the Jews to inquire if Muhammad might indeed be a Prophet. The Jews responded by giving them three questions to ask Muhammad: (1) "Ask him what happened to the young man that disappeared in ancient days, for they have a marvelous story." (2) "Ask him about the night traveler who reached the confines of both East and West." and (3). "Ask him what the spirit is?"[479]

If Muhammad was able to answer these questions then the Quraysh would consider him a Prophet, otherwise he should be considered a fake. Muhammad responded that he would return the answers to the questions on the following day. Instead it took Muhammad fifteen days for the answers to be revealed by God, for reasons we have spoken of earlier.[480] Over the fifteen-day period, the people started to spread many lies and rumors about Muhammad. Finally, Gabriel, the Angel, appears to Muhammad and reproaches him for his sorrow. Then Gabriel revealed the answers to the questions, which are recorded in sura 18. Frankly, this quaint story strikes me as a cover-up of what would seem a much more plausible explanation that Muhammad derived these stories from his interaction with the Jews, or at least awareness of their oral traditions. The fact that the story parallels the story of Daniel explaining Nebuchadnezza's dream in the Old Testament makes it further suspect.

Ibn Ishaq and Ibn Kathir both record the questions posed to Muhammad by the Quraysh which they received from the Jewish Rabbis in Medina. However, Ibn Kathir records the first question as "What happened to the warriors who die in earlier time?"[481] While Ibn Ishaq records the first question

---

[477]   Watt, Montgomery, p. 59.
[478]   Watt, Montgomery, p. 59.
[479]   Ibn Ishaq, p. 136.
[480]   Ibn Ishaq, p. 136.
[481]   Ibn Kathir, *Al-Sira*, pp. 350-351.

as "Ask him what happened to the young man that disappeared in ancient days, for they have a marvelous story." They record the same questions for the other two questions. Sura 18:9-16 is given as the answer to question number one by Yusuf Ali, but this does not seem to answer the question recorded by Ibn Kathir. Sura 18 deals with the story of seven youths who hide in a cave to escape persecution by a king who reigned in the year 249-251 CE. The boys awoke during the reign of a new king from 408-450 CE after the age of persecution of Christians had ended. Muhammad records this as a period of three hundred or three hundred and nine years in the cave.[482] This is a well-known Christian story, which even Yusuf Ali admits was identified from Christian sources by Gibbon.[483] Ibn Kathir places the answer to the third question regarding the spirit in sura 17. Sura 17:85 says "They ask thee concerning The Spirit (of inspiration)." Say: "The Spirit (cometh) by command of my Lord: Of knowledge it is only a little that is communicated to you (O men!)" How can the answer for the third question come chronologically well before chapter 18? Ibn Kathir also explains that when Muhammad was in Medina, the Jews had asked the same question. Aside from chaos in chronology and details, there is a distinct sense that Muhammad was in dialogue with the People of the Book and the Muslim writers use the various details to disguise that reality.

If the opposition of the Quraysh was becoming more obvious toward Muhammad, this may be the time period when the Quraysh started to meet with Abu Talib in hopes he could persuade Muhammad to stop his teaching.[484] The Quraysh also tried to persuade Muhammad by bribing him with power, wealth, or position. Utba b Rabi'a says,

> "O my nephew, you are one of us as you know, of the noblest of the tribe and hold a worthy position in ancestry. You have come to your people with an important matter, dividing their community thereby and ridiculing their customs, and you have insulted their gods and their religion, and declared that their forefathers were unbelievers, so listen to me and I will make some suggestions, and perhaps you will be able to accept one of them."

---

[482] Qur'an 18:25.
[483] Ali, footnote no. 2337, p. 709.
[484] Muranyi, M. "The First Muslim in Mecca: a Social Basis for a New Religion" in *The life of Muhammad*. ed. By Uri Rubin. 1998, p 102.

He offers him money, honor, kingship or, if possessed by a spirit, he offers to find a doctor and use all their wealth to make him better. Muhammad says no and responds by saying,

> "Now listen to me, "In the name of God, the compassionate and merciful, a revelation from the compassionate, the merciful, a book whose verses are expounded as an Arabic Qur'an for a people who understand, as an announcement and warning, though most of them turned aside not listening and say 'Our hearts are veiled from that to which you invite us.'"[485]

Muhammad's refusal of these offers seems to have impressed Utba, and he gives the Quraysh a warning not to touch Muhammad for the time being. He said,

> "that he had heard words such as he had never heard before, which were neither poetry, spells, nor witchcraft.
> "Take my advice and so as I do, leave this man entirely alone for, by God, the words which I have heard will be blazed abroad. If (other) Arabs kill him, others will rid you of him; if he gets the better of the Arabs, his sovereignty will be your sovereignty, his power your power, and you will be prosperous through him."
> They said, "He has bewitched you with his tongue."
> To which he answered, "You have my opinion, you must do what you think fit."[486]

Utba's response indicates a political bent in Muhammad, but this may just be further backreading into history.

Does Muhammad's refusal of the gifts show he has alternative plans for his future? Do we see an example of some early hints to Muhammad's plan to build a brotherhood bound together through religion not blood ties? Al-Tabari records that the leaders of the Quraysh went to Abu Talib to encourage him to speak to his nephew about not attacking their gods, and they would leave him alone to his god.[487] Abu Talib talks with Muhammad, but Muhammad claims something better for them than their gods. Muhammad says,

---

[485]   Ibn Ishaq. pp. 132-133.
[486]   Ibn Ishaq. pp. 132-133.
[487]   Watt, Montgomery, W. and McDonald, MV, p. 95.

"Uncle, he said, "shall I not summon them to something which is better for them than their gods?"

"What do you summon them to?" he asked.

He replied, "I summon them to utter a saying through which the Arabs will submit to them and they will rule over the non-Arabs."[488]

The Quraysh left in anger when Muhammad claimed the sole deity of Allah. It is interesting that Muhammad seeks unity among the Arabs, but with a political and ruling overtone.

The persecution against Muhammad was lighter than what came later to his followers of lower social class. Muhammad's social class and family connection protected him from much harm according to the biographers. Abu Talib, Muhammad's uncle, was concerned for Muhammad's safety and extended his protection over Muhammad. Abu Talib protected Muhammad since Muhammad was a family member, but did not convert to Islam. However, there is one story told that Talib encouraged his son to convert to Islam, in spite of the fact he himself rejected it.

"Mohammad is praying with his cousin Ali when his Uncle Abu Talib over heard them. He asks, "My nephew! What is this new faith I see thee following?"

"O my uncle!" he replied. "This is the religion of God, and of his angels, and of his prophets; the religion of Abraham. The lord hath sent me an Apostle unto his servants; and thou, my uncle, art the most worthy of all that I should address my invitation unto, and the most worthy to assist the Prophet of the Lord."

Abu Talib answered, "I am not able, my nephew, to separate from the religion and the customs of my forefathers, but I swear that so long as I live no one shall dare to trouble thee."

Abu Talib tells his son, "He will not call thee to aught but that which is good; wherefore thou are free to cleave unto him."[489]

Muhammad's family ties offer him protection, but his followers from the lower class and slaves were not protected. Ishaq records some of the types of persecution they faced. They might be put outside during the hottest part

---

488   Watt, Montgomery, W. and McDonald, MV, p. 95.
489   Ibn Ishaq, p. 142.

of the day with a large rock on their chest until they would denounce Islam and turn back to the polytheist gods, Al-Lat and Al-Uzza. Also, "every clan that contained Muslims attacked them, imprisoning them and beating them, allowing them no food or drink, and exposing them to the burning heat of Mecca, so as to seduce them from their religion."[490]

Muhammad was questioned, "Why he associated with slaves?" They asked Muhammad why he did not free stronger people who could protect him. Muhammad responds, "I am only trying to do what I am attempting for God's sake," Then Muhammad received the verse "As to him who gives and fears God and believes in goodness," up to the divine words, "none is rewarded by God with Favor but for seeking his Lord's most sublime face and in the end he will be satisfied."[491]

Due to the hardships Muslims faced concerning persecution, it is reported that apostasy was acceptable in times of persecution. Ibn Ishaq records, Hakim b. Jubayr from Sa 'id b Jubayr told: I said to 'Abdullah b. 'Abbas, "Where the polytheists treating them so badly that apostasy was excusable?"

"Yes, by God, they were."[492]

The persecution against Muhammad and his followers help set the stage for the first Hijra (emigration) to Abyssinia that we will consider in the next chapter.

---

[490] Ibn Ishaq, p. 143.
[491] Ibn Ishaq. p 144.
[492] Ibn Ishaq. p 145.

CHAPTER 4

LATE MECCAN PERIOD
615-619 CE

The late Meccan period of the Qur'an dates from approximately CE 615 to 622. It is a period bookended with two "Hijras" or emigrations. The first Hijra involved a group of about eighty believers who left Mecca for relative safety in Abyssinia. Muhammad did not accompany that group. The second emigration involved the entire Muslim community in Mecca, included the Prophet himself, and marks the formal beginning of the Islamic era. According to tradition, it was a time of grave testing both for the Prophet and his community. Muhammad's first and only wife up to that point died during this time. His uncle and protector, Abu Talib also died. It was a period of crisis that moved the Prophet from the role of religious teacher gradually into the role of political and military leader.

About twenty-one chapters were revealed during this period, comprising 1,568 verses or about 25 percent of the verses of the Qur'an. One of those chapters, chapter 34, may well belong to an earlier period. The content of this period only changes marginally compared with the middle Meccan period. There are two hundred and sixty one verses concerning the coming day of judgment, about 17 percent of the text. There are eighty verses about hellfire (5 percent of the text) with less graphic description of the tortures of hell, though this is not entirely absent. Verses about heaven are also comparatively few, forty-six, comprising about 3 percent of the text. These generally follow the same simple formula comprising a verse or two, and there is nothing of the elaborate description of sexual partners that was found in the early Meccan period. Allusions to extrabiblical and Jewish traditions remain a very important part of the text. There are three hundred eighty five verses with this content making up about 25 percent of the text. Chapter 12 (entitled "Joseph") of this period is of considerable interest as it is one chapter of the Qur'an that focuses on a single biblical story, the story of Joseph loosely based on Jewish traditions relating to Genesis 37-50. Moses's life also encompasses most of chapter 28. There are also a few references to historical events that enable us to clearly designate these chapters to the historical period at hand.

Because this is a long period with a number of significant events, we have divided the material into two chapters. This division is arbitrary, but will enable us to look at the relative progression of the text and see whether there are connections to events that the traditions describe. The first period we will look at is 615-619 CE, including the events of the first Hijra as well as, possibly, the deaths of Khadijah and Abu Talib. We will begin by considering the first eleven chapters of this period, chapters 32, 41, 45, 16, 30, 11, 14, 12, 40, 28, and 39.

A. Content of the Qur'an 615-619 CE

1. Concepts of Gratitude and Controversies About Christians Teaching Muhammad

The content of the Qur'an from this period remains largely the same as the middle Meccan period. It is monotonous in its renditions of the same questions and formulaic answers. An example of this is found in the similitude that man is ungrateful when blessed of God and falls into despair when God removes the blessing. It is a similitude used fifty-three times in the Qur'an and numerous times in this section (11:9-10, 39:8, 39:49, etc., . . .). Renditions of the blessings of God also follow a formulaic pattern with few variations. God provides man with cattle and crops, mates, rain, the heavens, and the earth, and the stars, ships, and sleep. These elements are mixed in various ways and retold in every chapter from this period. A typical example is 14:32-4:

> "It is Allah who hath created the heavens and the earth and sendeth down rain from the skies, and with it bringeth out fruits wherewith to feed you: it is He who hath made the ships subject to you, that you may sail through the sea by His command; and the rivers hath He made subject to you. And he hath made subject to you the sun and the moon, both diligently pursuing their courses: and the night and the day hath He made subject to you."[493]

---

[493] Qur'an 14:32-34. Similar passages are 16:10-18, 30:19-26, 46-53, 40:61-68, 79-82, 39:5-6.

The main point in each case is that man is ungrateful for this provision. One welcome respite from these monotonous repetitions is the brief passage on the blessings of honeybees, which provides the title for chapter 16, "Al Nahl":

> "And thy Lord taught the bee to build its cells in hills, on trees, and in habitations; then eat of all the produce and find with skill the spacious paths of its Lord: there issues from within their bodies a drink of varying colors, wherein is healing for men."[494]

Is it possible that Muhammad did not originally conceive of his utterances as something that would be saved for posterity? It is hard to imagine why the Qur'an would repeat so many similar statements in a monotony that is absolutely grinding for the modern student. Perhaps Muhammad responded to the same questions that were put to him using his favorite arguments again and again over a period of thirteen years. The monotony of the dialogue and the uniformity of the responses only become apparent when the various sections are collected together chronologically. In our understanding, this demonstrates the integrity of the Qur'anic text as an actual product of Muhammad. When read in chronological order there is a remarkable level of similarity that shows clearly the periodization of Muhammad's thought.

If Muhammad was continuing in dialogue and arguments with the Meccans, it is clear that the dialogue was not making much progress. The questions and issues raised remain the same. Muhammad calls mankind to humility because they are created from the despicable *nutfah* fluid.[495] The same arguments about resurrection are repeated. God has power by his decrees to resurrect the dead.[496] Often the answer seems to be given in response to a real or imagined critique:

> "And they say: 'What! When we lie, hidden and lost, in the earth, shall we indeed be in creation renewed?' Nay, they deny the meeting with their Lord!"

Say: "The angel of death, put in charge of you, will take your souls. Then shall ye be brought back to your Lord."[497]

[494] Qur'an 16:68-9.
[495] Qur'an 32:8, 16:4.
[496] Qur'an 16:40.
[497] Qur'an 32:10-11, similar passages are: 32:10, 41:39, 45:25-26.

Questions concerning the nature of the Qur'an follow the same pattern from the middle Meccan period. The Meccans accuse him of forgery, "do they say, 'he has forged it.'"[498] The response is partly to indicate that the book comes from God and then partly to challenge the critics "Bring ye then ten surahs forged, like unto it."[499] A more significant challenge is presented in 16:103. Here the Meccans specifically accuse Muhammad of being taught by a foreigner.

"We know indeed that they say, 'It is a man that teaches him.' The tongue of him they wickedly point to is notably foreign, while this is Arabic, pure and clear."[500] What is particularly significant about this is that it occurs in the context of people accusing Muhammad of substituting verses in the revelation. Muhammad was often getting into trouble through problems either of internal logic in his stories or by someone pointing out how they were inconsistent with previous stories he had told. An example of this is the various versions of the destruction of Madyan provided in the Qur'an. The destruction of these people is attributed in various chapters to an earthquake, a powerful rain, and a loud cry from heaven. Ibn Kathir in his commentary on the Qur'an reconciles this by saying, "All of these punishments were gathered on the day of their destruction,"[501] that is, all three things happened. Clearly, though, Muhammad made adjustments as he went along. He explains this, speaking on behalf of God.

> "When we substitute one revelation for another—and Allah knows best what He reveals they say, 'Thou art but a forger': but most of them understand not. Say. The Holy Spirit has brought the revelation from thy Lord in truth, in order to strengthen those who believe, and as a guide and glad tidings to Muslims."[502]

The commentators wrestle with this in various ways. Yusuf Ali maintains that Muhammad is referring here to previous holy books, which are now being set aside by a new revelation. This is nonsense. Nowhere in the Qur'an does Muhammad teach that the earlier holy books have been replaced or

---

[498] Qur'an 32:2.
[499] Qur'an 11:13.
[500] Qur'an 16:103.
[501] Ibn Kathir, *Tafsir*, Vol. 5, p. 105.
[502] Qur'an 16:101-102.

abrogated.[503] The reference is to verses in the Qur'an itself that are being replaced. Ibn Kathir gets this point correctly and points out that this verse is in keeping with the later verse 2:106, where Muhammad again refers to changing verses in the Qur'an through new revelations.[504] Moderate Muslims like Yusuf Ali seem at pains to cover up this aspect of the Qur'an from prying western eyes. The older commentaries are more reliable on this point.

What is important here is that Muhammad is accused of consulting with a foreigner at the very time he is also accused of changing the revelation. Both Yusuf Ali and Ibn Kathir respond to the accusation with incredulity based on the Prophet's own reasoning. How could a foreigner write the beautiful poetry of the Qur'an? But that is not the point. The changes have nothing to do with composing poetry. They have to do with emending content. That requires neither poetic skill nor deep knowledge of Arabic. Muhammad was dealing in oral tradition and probably did not regard listening to or borrowing content from others as forgery. It is only a small mental sleight of hand to gain details of a story and then transform them into new poetic revelatory content that one would see as original to oneself, or, in this case, original to God. It is also clear in Muhammad's telling of the stories of the Prophets that he is constantly upgrading his understanding as he goes along. If one traces each individual Prophet chronologically through the Qur'an you find that Muhammad is regularly making emendations and corrections to his own previous notions concerning the Prophets. This also demonstrates the correctness of the chronology of the Qur'an as outlined by various scholars.

In Ibn Ishaq we find several references to individuals Muhammad was thought to have consulted in regard to his revelations. He states,

> "According to my information the Prophet used often to sit at al-Marwa at the booth of a Young Christian called Jabr, a slave of the B. al-Hadrami, and they used to say, "The one Who teaches Muhammad most of what he brings is Jabr, the Christian, slave of B. al-Hadrami."[505]

---

[503] Ali, Yusuf, footnote 2140, p. 664. This seems to be a follow-up on Ali's earlier footnote where he states that the Qur'an has been given to supercede the other scriptures "already corrupted in the hands of their followers," footnote 2070, p. 648.

[504] Ibn Kathir, *Tafsir*, Vol. 1, pp. 323-332.

[505] Ibn Ishaq, p. 180.

This seems unlikely given the relative lack of Christian content in the Meccan surahs, although it could be indicative of the kinds of influences Muhammad had, coming from people not very knowledgeable in the faith. This particular story seeks to explain surah 16:105. There is much evidence that Muhammad consulted the followers of the earlier faiths and this is backed up by the extent of apocryphal literature reflected in the pages of the Qur'an. This is further demonstrated by Muhammad's consistent improvements over time upon the apocryphal stories that he tells.

It is interesting to note that Muhammad often discusses similar accusations made against other prophets. Noah is accused of having forged his holy book.[506] Every argument Muhammad makes seems to raise new problems. What holy book did Noah receive? Responding to the people of his day, who are arguing with him, he says, "Or do they say, 'He has forged it?' Say: if I had forged it on me were my sin! And I am free of the sins of which ye are guilty."[507] On several occasions, Muhammad uses prophets as mouthpieces, defending all holy books and by extension his own:

> "Can they be those who accept a clear sign from their Lord, and whom a witness from himself doth teach, as did the book of Moses before it—a guide and a mercy? They believe therein; both those of the sects that reject it—the fire will be their promised meeting place."[508]

Muhammad declares in this passage that those who deny the earlier holy books as well as his book will find their place in hell! The other arguments that Muhammad deals with we have seen before. He is accused of following magic (30:58), and his belief in resurrection is called "sorcery" (11:7). He is challenged to show signs to demonstrate that he is from God (28:48). This latter challenge is interesting since Muhammad does not make reference at all to the miraj trip to Jerusalem mentioned much earlier in 17:1. Muhammad no longer used this as a argument for a sign granted to him. The Meccans ask him when the day of judgment will occur (32:28) and ask that an angel should be sent down to demonstrate the truthfulness of his assertions (11:12). These are all questions and challenges that we have heard before, extending back to the earliest revelations of the Qur'an. If anything, we may note a

---

[506] The Qur'an mentions many more holy books than actually make it to the canonical list of four. We have already noted the books of Ishmael and Abraham.
[507] Qur'an 11:35.
[508] Qur'an 11:17.

gradual decrease in the number of questions asked as if this period of dialogue between Muhammad and the Meccans is gradually drawing to a close. One other aspect is noticeable during this period; stories of the supernatural, of jinn, and the fantastic are largely absent from the text with the exception of chapter 34 and chapter 41, which mention the Qarina or alter-ego demons (41:25). This is one reason that one may consider that these two passages perhaps belong to an earlier period.

2. Concepts of Hell and Heaven

The threat of hellfire remains an important aspect of Muhammad's teaching during this time. The imagery used is stock-in-trade. There are descriptions of the idolaters and jinn being led into hell and their remorse.[509] Hell's fire, boiling putrid substances, yokes and chains and betrayals are all described in some detail.[510] It is a place for mockers and the interrogation of the dead. Satan speaks here and betrays those who followed him.[511] It is a place that everyone will fear. Ibn Kathir takes 45:28 and expands it to include all the "sects." Moses and Jesus are in deep fear of the fires of hell.[512] Even the unbelievers skin will testify against them.[513]

Descriptions of heaven, by contrast, are much more subdued in this period. There is none of the sensual revelry of the early Qur'an. The primary imagery is that of gardens well stocked with fruits and with rivers flowing through it.[514] Generally speaking a single verse suffices for the description. In one case, the Greek word for "paradise" is used, in another, mansions are mentioned.[515] The earlier other worldly emphasis seems to be becoming less important to the Prophet.

3. Islamic Doctrines

There are few new doctrines introduced during this period. Muhammad continues to rail against polytheism, warning of the day of judgment, and

---

[509] Qur'an 11:19, 32:13, 20-21, 45:10-11, and 11:96-107.
[510] Qur'an 14:42-50, 40:46-50, 71-76, and 39:16.
[511] Qur'an 45:34-35, 16:29, and 14:22.
[512] Ibn Kathir, *Tafsir,* Vol. 9, p. 35
[513] Qur'an 40:30-31.
[514] Qur'an 32:19, 11:23, 11:108, and 14:23.
[515] Qur'an 41:30-31 and 39:20.

calling for repentance.[516] Man is guilty of forgetfulness and ungratefulness. Man is called to holy fear, or taqwa, which is one of the key themes of the entire Qur'an.[517] The nature of God is also defined in familiar terms. His foreknowledge is affirmed as well as the absolute power of His decrees. This is often combined with the denial that he could have any partners: "Thy Lord does create and choose as He pleases: no choice have they: glory to Allah! And far is He above the partners they ascribe."[518] The element of the absolute nature of God's decrees is evident as well. There are a number of verses relating to the Spirit of God, Ruh-ul Quddus. Sometimes this Spirit is associated with the spirit of man (32:9), elsewhere it is associated with the coming down of revelation (16:2). Ali translates this as "inspiration," which has none of the theological content of the Arabic word.[519] Ibn Kathir refers to the Spirit as something sent with the angels to convey revelation.[520] As we have noted earlier in 16:102, the spirit is that which brings down the Qur'an. Ali interprets this as the angel Gabriel, but this is not at all clear from the Qur'anic text. It seems that this topic is as much a mystery for Muslims through the ages as it was for Muhammad in his day.

There is one mention of *jihad* during this period. It is found in 16:110. This seems to be referring to a period of persecution through which the followers of the Prophet were passing and may relate to the Hijra to Abyssinia: "To those who leave their homes after trials and persecutions—and who thereafter strive and fight for the faith and patiently persevere."[521] It is impossible to tell what is being referred to here. The word *jihad* as used in this case seems to be referring to the "striving" of perseverance. Further, there is an element of pacifism in the teaching of the Prophet during this period. He calls for his followers to forgive those who do not follow their way: "Tell those who believe, to forgive those who do not look forward to the days of Allah: it is for him to recompense each people."[522] One even finds the unusual command for believers to overcome the evil of their oppressors with good and so to win

---

[516] Qur'an 41:37, 16:51, 73, 40:73, and 39:60-75.
[517] Qur'an 32:14, 41:51, 30:51-2, 41:18, and 16:125. Note the similarity to the Old Testament concept of the "fear of the Lord," which is the "beginning of wisdom."
[518] Qur'an 28:68.
[519] Ali, Yusuf, p. 637.
[520] Ibn Kathir, *Tafsir* Vol. 5, p. 431.
[521] Qur'an 16:110.
[522] Qur'an 45:14

their enemies into friends: "Nor can goodness and evil be equal. Repel with what is better: Then will he between whom and thee was hatred become, as it were thy friend and intimate."[523] This is the first time I have encountered such sentiments in the Qur'an. Was Muhammad's attitude softened by the harsh experiences of losing a wife and an uncle/protector? Chronologically, we may be too early for that and the text is too opaque to indicate, but there are tantalizing elements to speculate about.

4. Moral Issues and God's Relationship to the Prophet

The five pillars of Islam are still very unclear during this period. Muhammad speaks of the importance of prayer (32:16) and makes allusions to the times of prayer (30:17, 31, and 11:114), but the exact format of this is still not spelled out despite the efforts of later commentators to fit pronouncements into the orthodox system.[524] Mention is made of "charity" in two locations, but this is not spelled out in any way.[525] Aside from these brief mentions, nothing is said concerning the practices of Islam during this period.

The definition of Muhammad and his role in the revelation is similarly weak. There are few direct references. Muhammad is called a "warner" and a witness against idolaters on the Day of Judgment.[526] There are more references where God seems to address the Prophet directly, but these are also few in number. God tells the Prophet that he is but a warner and that he is called as a witness to the unbelievers.[527] God warns the Prophet that he may die before God's promise is fulfilled.[528] This is one of the few times in the Qur'an when such a pessimistic viewpoint is expressed. There is also a strange passage where God seems to ask the Prophet about aspects of the revelation that he is "giving up" because of what his opponents are saying.[529] Neither Yusuf Ali nor Ibn Kathir attempt to explain this strange statement, and it remains an illustration of how little even Muslims understand the background and content of the Qur'an. This seems to have been a period of deep discouragement for the Prophet.

---

[523] Qur'an 41:34.
[524] Ali, Yusuf, p. 541.
[525] Qur'an 41:7, 14:31.
[526] Qur'an 32:3 and 16:89.
[527] Qur'an 16:126-7, 16:89.
[528] Qur'an 40:77.
[529] Qur'an 11:12.

The moral and social concerns of the Prophet are also fairly infrequently mentioned during this period. There is a brief mention of female infanticide that Muhammad maintains will be an important question on the day of judgment.[530] Justice and kindness is enjoined upon Muslims as is the importance of fulfilling oaths.[531] There are some brief notations about Kosher laws concerning forbidden meats and a mention about telling the truth and the importance of like punishment for like crime (eye for an eye).[532] There is one verse in chapter 16 that addresses for the first time the issue of apostasy from Islam.

> Anyone who, after accepting faith in Allah, utters unbelief—except under compulsion, his heart remaining firm in faith—but such as open their breast to unbelief—on them is wrath from Allah, and theirs will be a dreadful penalty.[533]

Of all the world religions, Islam has developed the most strict system of punishments for those who leave the faith. This system of legal punishments for apostasy remains one of the greatest hindrances in the modern age for the acceptance of freedom of religion in Muslim countries. The foundations of the law of apostasy in Islam clearly extend back into the Meccan period. One may also combine this concept with various other legal pronouncements concerning the value of believers versus those who are not believers. This seems to reflect that the Prophet was losing some followers during this period, and he is moving in the direction of coercion to maintain believers within the ranks.

Muhammad states that women captured in raiding should not be regarded as having equal rights with women one has married.

> "Allah has bestowed his gifts of sustenance more freely on some of you than on others: those more favored are not going to throw back their gifts to those whom their right hands possess, so as to be equal in that respect. Will they then deny the favors of Allah?"[534]

Although this verse is meant to illustrate the difference between Allah and those "partners" attributed to him, the effect is to establish a form of religious

---

[530] Qur'an 16:59.
[531] Qur'an 16:90-91.
[532] Qur'an 16:115.
[533] Qur'an 16:106.
[534] Qur'an 16:71.

apartheid. Those captured in war have no rights to be compared with those among the conquerors. There is an immense distinction in Islam between the rights of Muslims and non-Muslims, and this distinction is established early on. The discrimination that God establishes between people is restated in several places (16:76 and 30:28).

5. Muhammad's View of the People of the Book

There are a few references during this period to the People of the Book. In 16:118, there is a direct mention of the Jews: "To the Jews we prohibited such things as we have mentioned to thee before: We did them no wrong, but they were used to doing wrong to themselves." The context of this passage is some pronouncements on hallal food, where swine, blood and meat of dead animals is forbidden. What is significant is Yusuf Ali's mistranslation of the first part of the verse. Ibn Kathir renders it: "for those who are Jews we have forbidden."[535] This would seem to indicate that Jews were among Muhammad's followers, and that he made pronouncements concerning their customs. "Have Forbidden" indicates an ongoing reality in distinction to Yusuf Ali's rendition that is intended to refer only to the past.[536] The passage also indicates that Muhammad was allowing different traditions for different ones among his followers. Clearly, Islam and Judaism were not distinguished at this point except in the matter of food laws. The obscure reference to "doing wrong to themselves" may be simply a reference to the many stories in the Old Testament of God's punishments on the Jews for their disobedience. The passage also refers extensively to Abraham and contains an anachronistic reference to the Sabbath by which one would "follow the ways of Abraham."[537] Sabbath laws were given in the time of Moses, not Abraham. From a Jewish perspective, Muhammad's chronology and sense of when certain laws were given was hopelessly confused. In that sense, it is hard to imagine Jewish followers of Muhammad, unless they were people with little connection to Jewish traditions, unable to discern what Jewish tradition would regard as Muhammad's errors.

---

[535] Ibn Kathir, *Tafsir*, Vol. 5, p. 539.
[536] Ali, Yusuf, p. 688, Ibn Kathir, *Tafsir*, Vol. 5, p. 538. See also *The Noble Qur'an*, p. 398.
[537] Qur'an 16:124, 123. The law of the Sabbath, while mentioned in the time of creation and Noah, is actually only clearly defined in the law of Moses.

Muhammad also does not seem to recognize any difference between his revelations and the previous Jewish and Christian scriptures. He makes the following statement:

> "And before thee also the messengers we sent were but men, to whom we granted inspiration: if ye realize this not, ask of those who possess the message. We sent them with clear signs and scriptures and we have sent down unto thee the message."[538]

This seems to indicate that Muhammad believed that his new revelation was completely in keeping with previous scriptures. He anticipates that followers of the other monotheistic faiths will support his views from their own scriptures. He could not have been in contact with knowledgeable members of other religions and held this inaccurate notion. It would seem that his awareness of oral tradition was mediated either by those only vaguely aware of the Old Testament, or followers who did not feel it necessary to correct Muhammad's notions.

It seems also that Muhammad used the supposed acceptance of his revelation by the Jews and Christians as an argument to the Meccans. In the context of arguing that his scripture was not forged, he makes the following claim:

> "Those to whom We sent the Book before this—they do believe in this (revelation); and when it is recited to them, they say: We believe therein, for it is the truth from our Lord: Indeed we have been Muslims (bowing to Allah's will) from before this."[539]

Both Yusuf Ali and Ibn Kathir argue that this shows that many believers in the other religions recognized Muhammad's revelation and affirmed that they had always been Muslims, and thus began to follow the new revelation. There are two problems with this. The term "Muslim" at this stage probably did not designate a separate religion, but the condition of being "submitted" to God. There may not have been a perceived distinction at this stage. According to Muslim tradition, Muhammad was not well received by the Jews of Medina, so who were these people from among the People of the Book? It seems to me that they were either those only nominally familiar with

---

[538]   Qur'an 16:43-44.
[539]   Qur'an 28:52-3.

previous revelations and/or individuals who did not perceive that Muhammad was calling to anything other than following their own creeds. Hawtings' viewpoint that Muhammad was primarily criticizing other monotheists does not fit this ethos. It seems that Muhammad sees his struggle in alliance with Jews and Christians against the polytheists. It is a constant struggle to read the Qur'anic interpreters, as they continually read back into the Qur'an the religious circumstances of a later age. At this stage, Muhammad thinks he is preaching the unified teaching of Judaism and Christianity.

There are just two references during this period that seem to refer to theological beliefs of the People of the Book with which Muhammad disagrees. In one reference, Allah declares that he has no son, "Had Allah wished to take to Himself a son, He could have chosen whom He pleased out of those whom he does create: But glory be to Him."[540] The implication is that the idea is rejected although not in a harsh way. This would seem to refer to Christian beliefs. Shortly after in verse seven, there seems to be a reference to vicarious atonement, "No bearer of burdens can bear the burden of another."[541] Ali interprets this as a rejection of the Christian concept of vicarious atonement, and given the context, this certainly seems possible. What is notable is that Muhammad never seems to mirror any questions coming back from these statements, such as what we find from Meccan animistic ideas. There does not seem to be any kind of dialogue going on here with the People of the Book, but rather an occasional reference to an idea that perhaps arrived via some oral transmissions. Muhammad was also clearly aware that he didn't have the entire picture. There is a remarkable reference to this in 40:78:

> "We did aforetime send messengers before thee: of them there are some whose story we have related to thee, and some whose story we have not related to thee. It was not for any messenger to bring a sign except by the leave of Allah."[542]

Muhammad here seems to be providing reasons for his own lack of understanding of previous revelations. This is complemented by a brief reference to God sending other Prophets with revelations in other languages: "We sent not a messenger except in the language of his (own) people, in order

---

[540]   Qur'an 39:4
[541]   Qur'an 39:7.
[542]   Qur'an 40:78.

to make clear to them."[543] It is not clear what Muhammad is arguing here, although he may be arguing for a paradigm that supports his own revelation in Arabic. It does seem to restrict the universal view of Muhammad's revelation that seemed stronger in the earlier period. Can one detect a loss of confidence here, perhaps a search for allies from among other religious groups? Possibly, but the evidence is very subtle, not something that we can say anything definitive about. Muhammad says concerning his book, "Allah has revealed the most beautiful message in the form of a book consistent with itself."[544] Aside from the self-complementary aspect, it indicates a question that was indeed being raised concerning his book and his more conciliatory tone indicates a weakness in the face of his external critics.

6. Historical Allusions in the Qur'an

For a period that, according to the traditions, contained such emotional events, it is astonishing how little can be discerned from the Qur'anic text during this period. There is no reference to the death of Khadija, Muhammad's wife. The death of Abu Talib which, according to traditional literature, left Muhammad in such a vulnerable position is also not mentioned. Other events, such as the boycott of Hashim, are also absent. We have already noted mention of the first Hijra in 16:41. The reference is, however, completely opaque, and we would have no understanding of its meaning apart from the commentators discussion. The same can be said of 16:110, which supposedly refers to the same event.

There is one clear historical reference in this period. Chapter 30, "The Romans," makes the following reference: "The Roman Empire has been defeated—in a land close by: but they, after this defeat of theirs, will soon be victorious."[545] The verse possibly refers to a defeat of Byzantium, by the Persian empire around 614-615 CE, possibly referring directly to the conquest of Jerusalem by the Persians at about that time. It is one of the few external reference points in the Qur'an and it is certainly not above dispute. I doubt that it is an interpolation, for surely a back writing into the text would have included more specific information. It does connect this chapter to the approximate timetable that has been suggested.

---

[543]   Qur'an 14:4.
[544]   Qur'an 39:23.
[545]   Qur'an 30:2-3.

7. Apocryphal Stories of This Period

As already noted, about 25 percent of the text from this period is comprised of Jewish and Christian stories and allusions. Most are brief, but a number comprise large segments of certain chapters and one entire chapter is dedicated to the story of Joseph and another to Moses. I begin in biblical chronological order.

There are numerous highly repetitive stories of the Prophet Hud, sent to Ad and Prophet Salih, sent to Thamud. Salih's story includes the provision of a she-camel by Allah that the wicked people of Thamud hamstring (or slaughter in another interpretation).[546] These stories are told apparently as types of Muhammad. Noah has an extended story that details the loss of his son in the flood, the accusation that he is a forger, and that he is threatened with being driven out of the land as God's messenger. These seem to function as types of the Prophet Muhammad, and potentially, reflect the Prophet's own struggles in Mecca.[547]

a. Abraham

The Prophet Abraham and his sons gain a much better focus during this period. It is during this period that Muhammad links Isaac and Ishmael together for the first time.[548] In previous descriptions, it was not at all clear that Ishmael was even related to Abraham. Abraham undergoes a number of transformations from earlier passages. For the first time, Muhammad seems to link Abraham to the city of Mecca and the Ka'aba, although the reference is oblique.[549] Of course, the commentators run wild with these obscure references.[550] Muhammad records Abraham's prayer for his pagan parents, a concept that is considered abrogated (*naskh*) by later passages in the Qur'an.[551] Abraham is also identified as a member of the "ummah," the true community of believers, and he is identified at the head of the traditional

---

[546] Qur'an 11:50-60, 61-68.
[547] Qur'an 11:25-49, 14:10-13.
[548] Qur'an 14:39.
[549] Qur'an 14:37, The reference to the "Valley without Cultivation" and the "sacred house" does seem to refer to Mecca.
[550] Ibn Kathir, *Tafsir* Vol. 5, p. 359, Ali, references 913-917, p. 614.
[551] Qur'an 14:41.

Jewish appellation of "Abraham, Isaac, and Jacob."[552] In general, however, Abraham does not figure largely in the texts from this period.

b. Joseph

One character who does figure prominently is Joseph, called Yusuf, in the Qur'an. One entire chapter of the Qur'an from this period deals entirely with the life of Joseph, essentially retelling the story of Genesis chapters 37-50. We may begin by reflecting on why this particular story receives so much attention. Joseph is sold into slavery and, after much suffering, experiences vindication and exaltation to the position of Vizier to the court of Pharaoh. It is one of the most familiar stories of the Old Testament. It would seem to me that this story takes on such importance because it mirrors, in some senses, the circumstances of Muhammad. Three chapters of the Qur'an were revealed consecutively that deal with similar biblical images, the story of Hud, and the story of Abraham in chapter 11 revealed just slightly before chapter 12. Like many believers through the ages, Muhammad sees himself in the story and draws comfort from the ultimate victory of Joseph. In the final two verse, he states,

> "when the messengers give up hope, and think that they were treated as liars there reaches them our help, and those whom we will are delivered into safety . . . There is, in their stories, instruction for men endued with understanding" . . . [553]

That being said, the story of Joseph in Muhammad's rendition deviates in many significant ways from the biblical text. Some of these differences are trivial, and others are quite substantial. Any Jew at all conversant with the Old Testament story (and that would be most) would find Muhammad's story both inaccurate and, at times, thoroughly absurd. In the beginning of the chapter, God addresses the Prophet directly: "We do relate unto you the best of stories through our revelations unto you of this Qur'an. And before this you were among those who knew nothing about it."[554] Muslim commentators do not deal with the issue of revelation. The text is simply saying that God told the story directly to Muhammad. Speculations about how influences

---

[552] Qur'an 12:38.
[553] Qur'an 12:110-111.
[554] Qur'an 12:3

came and under what circumstances are unimportant. To the Westerner, this simply begs the question and the transparent intent of the claim made by God that Muhammad "knew nothing about" the story beforehand is altogether too obvious.

What is even more fascinating is how Ibn Kathir deals with this verse. He reflects on an event apparently from the early Medinan period when Umar was reading a Jewish holy book:

> "There is a Hadith that is relevant upon mentioning this honorable Ayah, which praises the Qur'an and demonstrates that it is sufficient from needing all books beside it . . . Umar bin Khattab came to the Prophet with a book that he took from some of the People of the Book. Umar began reading it to the Prophet who became angry. He said, "Are you uncertain about it Ibn Khattab? By the one in whose hand is my soul! I have come to you with it white and pure. Do not ask them about anything, for they might tell you something true and you reject it, or they might tell you something false and you believe it. By the one in whose hand is my soul! If Musa were living, he would have no choice but to follow me."
>
> Imam Ahmad also recorded . . . Umar came to Allah's messenger and said, "O messenger of Allah! I passed by a brother of mine from Qurayzah, so he wrote some comprehensive statements from the Tawrah for me, Should I read them to you?"
>
> The face of Allah's Messenger changed (with anger). So I said to him, "Don't you see The face of Allah's Messenger?"
>
> Umar said, "We are pleased with Allah as our Lord, Islam as our religion, and Muhammad as our Messenger." So the anger of the Prophet subsided, and he said, "By the one in whose hand is Muhammad's soul, if Musa appeared among you and you were to follow him, abandoning me, then you would have strayed. Indeed you are my share of the nations, and I am your share of the Prophets."[555]

Two points are significant in this interpretation. First, it is meant to dissuade Muslims from reading other religious literature that might provide a balance to the Qur'an. Ibn Kathir and other commentators often find fault with the writings of the People of the Book even though they are dependent on those books for their understanding of the Qur'an. It is as if they want to know what

---

[555] Ibn Kathir, *Tafsir* Vol. 5, pp. 135-6.

the Qur'an means, yet they don't want their readers to know how they found out what the Qur'an means. We see an example of this just a few verses later. In verses 8-10, we are introduced to the plot of the brothers against Joseph, with intention to kill him. One of the brothers speaks up on Joseph's behalf that he should not be killed. The Qur'an does not state who this brother was. Ibn Kathir lists three different Muslim theories about who the brother was, Reubin, Judah, and Simeon. Without explanation, he continues with the narrative that the brother was Reubin.[556] How does he know this? Since the Qur'an never says, the only explanation is that he read it in the Jewish Torah. Nevertheless, he is quick to point out that Muslims should not read these other holy books, as they are distorted. It is a hermeneutical absurdity and universally practiced across the Muslim world.

The second key point in the above Hadith is the prominent place that it gives to the Jewish tribes in Medina. It is clear that Muhammad did not have to deal extensively with the viewpoints of other religions than paganism while in Mecca. There are very few references to Jews or Christians, or People of the Book that are directly negative during the entire Meccan period of the Qur'an. We shall see that this situation changes radically in the text of the Qur'an once the Medinan period begins. It is clear that the stories that Muhammad told in Mecca did not stand up well to the scrutiny of knowledgeable Jews in Medina. One tribe, the Banu Qurayzah, is mentioned specifically. This is the very tribe that Muhammad had slaughtered in 627 CE.

The problems with Muhammad's story of Joseph are many. First, the brothers plot against Joseph. They request that Jacob send him out to accompany them. Jacob seemingly prophesies that his son may be eaten by wild animals: "I fear lest a wolf should devour him."[557] After throwing Joseph in a well, they return with his cloak soaked in blood and an explanation they seem to sense their father will not believe:

> "They said, 'O our father! We went racing with one another, and left Yusuf by our belongings and a wolf devoured him; but you will never believe us even when we speak the truth.' And they brought his shirt stained with false blood. He said: 'Nay, but your own selves have made up a tale. So patience is most fitting. And it is Allah whose help can be sought against that which you describe'."[558]

---

[556] Ibn Kathir, *Tafsir*, Vol. 5, p. 141. Yusuf Ali makes no comment on this.
[557] Qur'an 12:13.
[558] Qur'an 12:17-18

The Qur'anic text at this point is patently absurd. First the father predicts what may happen. Then, when his sons tell the very thing he feared with a caveat that could only indicate their culpability, what does the father do? He decides "patience is most fitting." That is to say, he decides to sit on his hands and do nothing. Imagine what this means? A father's favorite son is missing, his brothers are lying about it, and he knows this, so he decides to do nothing? Ibn Kathir, in his explanation of the sons' words and the father's incomprehensible reaction, can do no more than to repeat them and marvel at the "strange coincidence and the amazing occurrence." To knowledgeable Jews of Medina this must have been a delicious piece of nonsense to satirize.

The next problem concerns what is done with Joseph. According to the Qur'anic text, the brothers throw him down in a well and leave him there in anticipation that he will be found and kidnapped. In due course, he is found by a party of traders in the well:

> "And there came a caravan of travelers and they sent their water-drawer, and he let down his bucket. He said: 'What good news! Here is a boy.' So they hid him as merchandise . . . And they sold him for a bakhs price,-a few dirhams. And they were of those who regarded him insignificant. And he from Egypt who bought him, said to his wife: 'Make his stay comfortable'."[559]

This part of the story makes no sense at all. The brothers left Joseph in a well anticipating that he would eventually be kidnapped? Who would do such a thing in their own home area? Would it not be more likely that someone who knew Joseph would come first and release him to go back and tattle on the brothers? The Muslim commentators recognize the absurdity of this. So they twist the Qur'anic text to make it fit the story line of the Bible. Ibn Kathir makes the claim that the verse "they hid him as merchandise" refers to the brothers, claiming that they sold him to the travelers.[560] The obvious meaning of the text is that the travelers were merchants who hid Joseph in their merchandise because they were kidnapping him![561] Joseph is only sold once in the Qur'anic text and this simply could not be true. Here we arrive

---

[559] Qur'an 12:19-21.

[560] Ibn Kathir, *Tafsir,* Vol. 5, p. 148.

[561] Ali, Yusuf at least gets this right and can only opine, "the circumstances were peculiar," p. 550.

at the second rule of Qur'anic interpretation; when the Qur'an's version of a Bible story does not make sense, twist it to make it fit the Bible story.

Muhammad's mix-ups with the story of Joseph may also be connected to his sources. It is certain that Muhammad was more conversant with Jewish traditions and legends than with the actual biblical text. When reading the Qur'an legends one finds bits and fragments of these Jewish legends but put together in a way that misses the point of the earlier Jewish stories. For instance, in one Jewish story Joseph is thrown in a pit while his brothers debate his fate. While they are discussing this, a group of Midianites comes to the pit and discovers Joseph, a comely lad, crying in the pit. Then the story states:

> "They all joined together and dragged him up, and took him along with them when they continued on their journey. They had to pass his brethren, who called out to the Midianites: 'Why have you done such a thing, to steal our slave and carry him away with you?'"[562]

Following an altercation the brothers agree to sell Joseph to the Midianites for a paltry price; "The sum paid was too low by far." Clearly, Muhammad had fragments of the story, but he missed segments that tied it together so that it made sense. It would seem that Muhammad was picking up fragments of Jewish oral tradition and reproducing them in Arabic, including the gaps where his own sources had been deficient. I find it astonishing that he was not more concerned about the fact that his version of the story did not make sense. Perhaps this reflects his conviction that he really was reciting the very Word of Allah, which could not be corrected once given except by way of a new revelation.

Beyond these obviously absurd elements, the text contains many errors from a Jewish perspective. Joseph is vindicated when Potiphar's wife tries to seduce him and Potiphar rebukes his wife. This leaves no rational reason for Joseph's subsequent imprisonment. The wife throws a banquet for her court ladies to admire Joseph. There she admits her guilt not only with the excuse of his exquisite beauty, but also says that Joseph should be imprisoned for not doing her bidding. Joseph refuses publicly to do so and the Qur'an states, "Then it occurred to the men after they had seen the signs to imprison him for a time." Potiphar has vanished from the text. All of this makes absolutely no

---

[562] Louis Ginzberg, *The Legends of the Jews*, The Johns Hopkins University Press, Vol. 2, p. 15.

sense at all. Once in prison Joseph predicts that the baker will be crucified. This is about a 1,500-year anachronism since crucifixion was invented by the Romans. In verses 52-3, we seem to have a speech by Joseph, but the inclusion of the words, "Nor do I absolve my own self: The soul is certainly prone to evil" causes both Ali and Ibn Kathir to consider it an interpolation of the wife. This seems to be a part of the concern to present Prophets as sinless. In Ibn Kathir's words, as recognized by their "virtues, great ability, brilliance, good conduct and perfect mannerisms."[563] Later, Joseph is said to take "his parents to himself" when according to the biblical story his mother had been dead for years.

It may be argued that these anomalies, internal contradictions, and logical fallacies were unimportant to the overall thrust of the story from a poetic perspective and that is true. But Muhammad is reinterpreting Jewish Bible stories. Jews were called People of the Book because their culture was profoundly textual. To have played so fast and loose with one of the key stories of Jewish culture insured that Muhammad would be completely rejected as a Prophet by the vast majority of Jews he came in contact with. While in Mecca, this was apparently not a problem. There are no Meccan period verses that condemn or attack Jews. But one senses deeply in this period of the Qur'an that Muhammad is unaware how much his revelations were to bring him into conflict with the very people he thought would support him most.

c. Moses

The story of Moses also figures significantly during this period. Of particular interest is Muhammad's confidence in the holy book, revealed through Moses. He states,

> "Can they be those who accept a clear sign from their Lord, and whom a witness from himself doth teach, as did the book of Moses before it—a guide and a mercy? They believe therein; but those of the sects that reject it—the fire will be their promised meeting place. Be not then in doubt thereon: for it is a truth from thy Lord" . . . [564]

All the references to the holy books in the Meccan period indicate their reliability and authority from God and of God's judgment on those who did

---

[563] Ibn Kathir, *Tafsir* Vol. 5, p. 179.
[564] Qur'an 11:17.

not accept their authority. Of course, some books named, such as those of Abraham, would not be recognized by Jews. The book of Noah is not known in the Old Testament, but is found in Jewish legends:

> "Now, when God resolved upon bringing the flood on the earth, He sent the archangel Raphael to Noah, as the bearer of the following message: "I give thee herewith the holy Book, that all the secrets and mysteries written therein may be made manifest unto thee, And that thou mayest know how to fulfill its injunction in holiness, purity, modesty and Humbleness."[565]

It should be noted that the Jewish concept of this book was that it was the holy book originally given to Adam and then periodically lost or hidden in a cave due to the unrighteousness of men. This conception of a hidden book that later gets revealed by an angel and which is in keeping with the other holy books may have been foundational to Muhammad's conception of the nature of his holy book. The Jewish ethos seems pervasive.

There are numerous references to God giving a holy book to Moses, and indicating that this book is true.[566] Some references to the book of Moses do contain some notion of disagreements:

> We certainly gave the Book to Moses, but differences arose therein: had it not been that a word had gone forth before from the Lord, the matter would have been decided between them: but they are in suspicious doubt concerning it.[567]

The picture that seems to arise from this is that Muhammad felt his revelation was given to solve some of the controversies among the People of the Book, but that they were suspicious of his revelations. This is about the closest we get to a sense that Muhammad had some dialogue with members of other religious communities, and that they did not receive his revelations positively. This does not appear to be a significant conflict at this stage. Clearly, Muhammad had no conception at this point that Jewish Holy Books had been changed or corrupted.

---

[565]   Louis Ginzberg, *The Legends of the Jews*, The Johns Hopkins University Press, Vol. 1, p. 156.

[566]   See also, Qur'an 32:23.

[567]   Qur'an 11:110.

One large section of the next to last surah of this period retells the story of Moses's life. Chapter 28 is entitled "The Narrations (Al Qasas)," and its title is a cognate of the word for the storytellers so prominent in contemporary Arab culture. All but ten of eighty-eight verses have to do with the life of Moses. The story follows with some accuracy the accounts of Exodus-Deuteronomy. Details, however, significantly differ from the biblical text, and this occurs primarily in the way Muhammad mixes stories up from various parts, not only of the Pentateuch, but also the entire Old Testament. Thus, Haman (from the book of Esther) is Pharaoh's official mentioned several times (28:6, 8 and 38).[568] The story of Moses' marriage to two women is mixed up with the story of Jacob's marriage to Leah and Rachael. Haman appears again on Moses's return to Egypt as the agent Pharaoh commissions to build "a lofty palace, that I may mount up to the god of Moses." This mixes Moses with the story of the Tower of Babel in Genesis 11. This repeats the, in Jewish eyes, error of the previously revealed chapter 40:36.

What is really striking, however, is the way in which Muhammad relates the calling of Moses to his own circumstances. The giving of the holy book to Moses elicits an immediate connection not only to Muhammad's book, but also the struggles of the two are related as a kind of theology of "sent ones" or "messengers."

> "We did reveal to Moses the Book after we had destroyed the earlier generations, insight to men, and guidance and mercy, that they might receive admonition. Thou wast not on the western side when we decreed the commission to Moses, nor wast thou a witness. But we raised up generations, and long were the ages that passed over them; but thou wast not a dweller among the people of Madyan, rehearsing our signs to them; but it is we who send messengers. Nor wast thou at the side of Tur[569] when we called to Moses. Yet, as a mercy from thy Lord, to give warning to a people to whom no warner had come before thee: in order that they might receive admonition. If—in case a calamity should seize them for that their hands have sent forth, they might say: "Our Lord! Why

---

[568] A study of the book of Esther shows that the names mentioned in it are clearly derived from Persian and fit the chronology of the fifth century BCE. The connection of Haman to Egypt at the time of the Exodus is simply a patently false anachronism. This will be discussed later.

[569] In Islamic thinking, the site of the burning bush.

didst thou not send us a messenger? We should then have followed
the signs . . ."[570]

Interestingly, the Quraysh seem to question why Muhammad does not
receive the same signs, meaning miracles, which Moses did, and which are
described in the story Muhammad tells. "They say, 'Why are not (signs) sent
to him, like those which were sent to Moses.'"[571] Muhammad's response is,
"Do they not reject (the signs) which were formerly sent to Moses?" This
seems to indicate that he sees the Pagan Arabs as descendants of Abraham
and thus ones who have fallen away from the true faith. He then returns to
the argument that the Qur'an is his sign, "then bring me a Book from Allah
which is a better guide than either of them that I may follow it."[572] This is an
old argument but Muhammad follows it up with a startling assertion:

> "Those to whom we sent the Book before this—they do believe
> in this (revelation); and when it is recited to them, they say: "We
> believe therein, for it is the truth from our Lord: Indeed, we have
> been Muslims from before this."[573]

We have noted this assertion before. What is significant by way of additional
notation is that these believers say they were "submitted" before the coming
of Muhammad. Clearly, "Islam" here only refers to the nature of submitted
relationship to God. This seems to indicate that there were some Jews
and perhaps Christians in Mecca who had an affinity for Muhammad as
monotheists in the context of a hostile pagan society. Under pressure, groups
with a similar belief structure may support one another. It is also possible to
read the statement this way: these believers emphasized that they followed
God long before Muhammad came along; that is, Muhammad's message
was not new to them. In either case, Muhammad picks up their statement as
a source of support for his position. Muhammad goes on to compliment this
group: "Twice will they be given their reward, for that they have persevered,
that they avert evil with good, and that they spend (in charity) out of what we
have given them." There is an implicit sense of alliance building here. The
response of the group to Muhammad is cordial if nevertheless noncommittal:

---

[570] Qur'an 28:43-47.
[571] Qur'an 28:48.
[572] Qur'an 28:48-49.
[573] Qur'an 28:52-53.

"They turn away therefrom and say, 'To us our deeds, and to you yours; peace be upon you: we seek not the ignorant.'"[574]

Moses functions in Muhammad's thinking as a type of himself and as a bridge to the other monotheistic communities that he hoped to relate to, particularly the Jews. This does seem to back up the notion found in the early Muslim historians that this was a period of his life when Muhammad vigorously sought out those he could be allied with. What is also clear is that there weren't very many of them in Mecca, and they provided little support other than tacit agreement to some aspects of his message. Muhammad apparently took encouragement from this and used their acceptance in his arguments with the Meccans. Did he think eventually that a center of Jewish life in Arabia might be the most fertile ground for his message? One senses that he also read too much into their responses.

The theology of Islam arose in a weak Jewish ethos. There is strong influence from the traditions of the Jews. However, from the perspective of the Jews, Muhammad's understanding of Jewish holy writ, particularly the Torah, was limited and fumbling and full of incredible inaccuracies. Knowledgeable Jews could not have done anything other than reject Muhammad as a Prophet. Before we even get to the Medinan period, we sense the gathering clouds of unavoidable conflict.

B. Historical Literature

It is difficult in the early literature to demarcate exact transitions in the time line. Ibn Ishaq's work is essentially a collection of stories intermixed with poetry and a weak chronology. These writers are also hampered by a concern to demonstrate the superiority of Islam and an obvious tendency to backread into the stories the sentiments of a later age. As we noted earlier, most of these early writers consider that Muhammad hid Islam up until the time when he began making public proclamation. The evidence of the Qur'an is that the dialogue and arguments had been going on before and are evident from the very first surahs of the Qur'an through to our present point.

The conflict with the Meccans must have led to some instances of physical violence. Mention of this is pervasive in all the early historical writings and is certainly reflected in the argumentative tone of the Qur'an. The Meccans are presented in these texts as the aggressors, attacking Muhammad because "he had declared their mode of life foolish, insulted their forefathers, reviled

---

[574]   Qur'an 28:54-55.

their religion, divided their community, and cursed their gods."[575] There seems to be some indication that Muhammad responded in kind. "He stopped and said, 'Will you listen to me, O Quraysh? By him who holds my life in his hand, I bring you slaughter.'"[576] There is also an evidence of Muhammad's seeking out powerful protectors and that his movement was gradually gaining supporters. This provided Muhammad with some measure of protection. When Muhammad is insulted by Abu Jahl, his uncle Hamza comes to his aid. His uncle, Ibn Ishaq, tells us was considered, "the strongest man of Quraysh and most unyielding." After striking the insulter, Hamza gains a measure of protection for the Prophet. Ibn Ishaq notes,

> Hamza's Islam was complete and he followed the apostle's commands. When he became a Muslim the Quraysh recognized that the apostle had become strong, and had found a protector in Hamza, and so they abandoned some of their ways of harassing him.[577]

There are also numerous stories of lower-class people and slaves converting to Islam who suffered greatly for their allegiance to Muhammad. Several cases where Abu Bakr manumitted slaves that had become Muslims are recorded including Bilal, who had been tortured by his owner for his new faith.[578] There is also mention that apostasy from Islam was allowable under the duress of physical abuse. Another account relates the story of Umar b. al-Khattab punishing a slave in order to "make her give up Islam." At that time, he was a polytheist. He beat her until he was tired and said, "I have only stopped beating you because I am tired." The slave replied, "May God treat you in the same way." After hearing the confirmation of her faith, Abu Bakr purchased and manumitted her[579] (Ibn Ishaq, 144).

There are also many stories of the Quraysh, trying to seduce Muhammad from his Islam by means of offering riches or positions of influence. Many of these would seem to be pious stories as the Qur'an makes no direct mention in this period of any offerings of money or power. Given the more harsh accusations repeated in the Qur'an, one would expect such things to also be

---

[575]   Ibn Ishaq, pp. 130-131.
[576]   Ibn Ishaq, p. 131.
[577]   Ibn Ishaq, p. 132.
[578]   Ibn Ishaq, p. 143-144. Bilal later kills his former owner after he is captured at the battle of Badr. These kinds of details create a matrix that indicates historicity.
[579]   Ibn Ishaq, p. 144.

recorded, albeit by way of God's response. Some of the dialogues of Ibn Ishaq, however, do reflect issues that were also raised in the Qur'an. Of particular interest is the accusation that Muhammad was instructed in his stories by Al-Rahman from Al-Yamama.[580] Many of the requests for demonstrations of power, of signs by the angels, etc . . . parallel Qur'anic passages from this period. They are also several tales of plots to have Muhammad murdered.

Some of these stories give interesting details of Muhammad's behavior that may accurately reflect his practices. Ibn Ishaq notes that Muhammad at this time prayed facing toward "Syria," which was also his practice during his first year in Medina (this notion would have probably included the region of Palestine). The statement that Muhammad began to preach when he developed grey hairs may also be accurate to the contemporary cultural notions of timing for leadership.[581] Ishaq also records interesting controversies over storytelling and how others imitated Muhammad's style:

> Al Nadr b. al Harith had been to al-Hira and learnt there the tales of kings of Persia, the tales of Rustum and Isbandiyar. When the apostle had held a meeting in which he reminded them of God, and warned his people of what had happened to bygone generations as a result of God's vengeance, al-Nadr got up when he sat down and said, "'I can tell a better story than he, come to me.' Then he began to tell them about the kings of Persia, Rustum and Isbandiyar, and then he would say, 'In what respect is Muhammad a better storyteller than I?'"[582]

The passages from the Qur'an that Ibn Ishaq cites to back up these stories all fall among the Meccan surahs though they follow no clear chronological pattern.

Ibn Ishaq also tells the story of the Meccans sending emissaries to the "Rabbis in Medina" to find questions that Muhammad would be unable to answer and this leads to the revelation of the middle Meccan surah 18, and the story of the young men who spent three hundred and nine years in a cave.[583] There are numerous references to discussions with Jewish rabbis in Medina. Sometimes rabbis questioned the Prophet about the interpretation of

---

[580] Ibn Ishaq, p. 134.
[581] Ibn Ishaq, p. 135.
[582] Ibn Ishaq, p. 136.
[583] Ibn Ishaq, p. 137.

Meccan surahs. Ishaq states, "When the Apostle came to Medina, the Jewish rabbis said, 'When you said, "And you have only a little knowledge about it," did you mean us or your own people." He said, 'Both of you.'"[584] I find no reference to rabbis in Mecca and this points to the accuracy of the Islamic historians in noting that Old Testament related content was not questioned while Muhammad was in Mecca.

1. The Hijra to Abyssinia

The growing opposition from all sides pressured Muhammad to seek refuge for his persecuted followers. Al-Tabari states, "When the Muslims were treated in this way, the Messenger of God commanded them to emigrate to Abyssinia. In Abyssinia, there was a righteous king called Negus in whose land no one was oppressed and who was praised for his righteousness."[585] "The first migration occurred in the fifth year of the mission (615 CE) in the month of Rajab". One source reports a total of eleven men and four women departing Mecca, another cites eighty-three, not including women and children. Muhammad had the protection of Abu Talib in Mecca, but his followers were suffering. He told them, "There is a king in whose realm no one is harmed, where truth prevails, stay there until God gives you relief."[586] Thus, the majority of Muslim pilgrims sought refuge from the abuse of the Quraysh in Abyssinia. Abyssinia (modern Eritrea) was a frequented place of trade and commerce for the Quraysh tribe. While Muhammad decided to remain in Mecca, the majority of Muhammad's followers heeded his command to flee to Abyssinia.

There is linguistic evidence of an Ethiopian influence based on Ethiopic words in the Qur'an, particularly the words *gibt*, *taghut*, and *ma'ida*, which are all found in Medinan chapters of the Qur'an corresponding to the time after the migrants returned to Arabia.[587] These, as well as odd stories of Muslims in Ethiopia converting to Christianity, would seem to show the historicity of these events. The question arises, why exactly did they leave Mecca? Was Muhammad's command for them to flee solely for their safety? William Montgomery Watt has a few suggestions. "There are strong grounds

---

[584]   Ibn Ishaq, p. 139.
[585]   Al-Tabari, p. 98.
[586]   Al-Tabari, pp. 99-100.
[587]   Manfred Kropp, "Beyond Single Words," *The Qur'an in its Historical Context*, Routledge, 2008, pp. 204-214.

for thinking that these Muslims went to Abyssinia to avoid persecution. This can hardly be the whole reason for migration, however, since it does not account for some of them staying on in Abyssinia after the Muslims had settled in Medina and were no longer troubled by persecutors." Watt presents possible political and religious motives for this move. It is clear that this first immigration provides something of a paradigm for later Muslim actions.

There are reasons to consider this story, at least in part, historical. First, it contains details that are not favorable to Islam, and one cannot imagine any reason for including such details other than the fact that they were simply historical. We have the story of one Muslim in Abyssinia who converts to the Christian faith and dies in that faith while still in Abyssinia. His widow later returns to Mecca and becomes one of the wives of the Prophet. We have other occasions later in the Medinan period where women who had returned make references positively to the images and icons in the churches in Abyssinia. This elicits a clear rebuke from the Prophet. Even the story of how the Ethiopian monarch protects the followers of Muhammad contains elements that could be true. Ibn Ishaq's record of their apology for Islam contains nothing that Christian Abyssinians would find offensive.[588] When their Meccan persecutors use the denial of the divinity of Christ as a means to attack the exiles in the king's presence, the followers of Muhammad are careful to say only positive things about Jesus from the Qur'an. The only problem is that some of the verses cited were clearly revealed in the Medinan period. One of the Muslims, when recounting the faith of Islam to the Negus, points out that nonviolence was the basis of their faith. This clearly changes in the Medinan period and is a strange point to include in a rendition of the faith, unless it were true and accurate to that period of Islam. Clearly, pious fictions are mixed in, but the overall thrust of the story does not seem implausible.

The Muslims remained in Abyssinia for several years (it is not certain how long). Various historians record that several of the Muslims returned to Mecca after they heard a rumor stating that the Meccans had accepted Islam. For example, Ibn Ishaq states, "The apostle's companions who had gone to Abyssinia heard that the Meccans had accepted Islam and they set out for the homeland. But when they got near Mecca they learned that the report was false, so that they entered the town under the protection of a citizen or by stealth. Some of those who returned to him stayed in Mecca until they migrated to Medina and were present at Badr and Uhud with the apostle;

---

[588] Ibn Ishaq, pp. 151-2. Watt, p. 67.

others were shut away from the Prophet until Badr and other events were passed; and others died in Mecca."[589] Another historian, Ibn Kathir records, "Some Muslims returned from Abyssinia after hearing that the polytheists had accepted Islam. This was wrong, some then turned around and returned to Abyssinia and some others joined them. Jafar b. Abu Talib 'acted as their spokesman and translator before the Negus and others.'"[590]

2. Boycott of Hashim

Shortly after the Hijra to Abyssinia, Ibn Ishaq tells the story of the conversion of Umar, who later became the second caliph. Umar was, like Hamza, considered to be a powerful man and his conversion was considered a great support to Muhammad. Ibn Ishaq indicates that shortly after his conversion the Quraysh undertook their most powerful actions against the Prophet and his tribe. The Quraysh gathered together to confer and decided to draw up a document in which they undertook not to marry women from the Banu Hashim and the Banu al-Muttalib (Muhammad's specific tribal group), or to give them women in marriage, or sell anything to them or buy anything from them. They drew up a written contract to that effect and solemnly pledged themselves to observe it."[591] The writer of the boycott against the Muslims was Mansur b. Ikrimab, Amir b. Hashim, and Abdu Manaf b. Abdu'l-Dar b. Qusayy. Ibn Ishaq notes that Muhammad, "Invoked God against him and some of his fingers withered."[592] The Quraysh hung this pledge up on the interior of the Ka'bah. This pledge brought forward an official division. "The Banu Hashim and the Banu al-Muttalib joined with Abu Talib, went with him to his valley and gathered round him there; but Abu Lahab 'Abd al-Uzza b. Abd al-Muttalib left the Banu Hashim and went to the Quraysh, supporting them against Abu Talib."[593] The Muslims survived only because of friends who would smuggle material goods into them. They lived in quarters designated to them by the Quraysh.[594] To illustrate the intensity of the boycott, Ibn Ishaq tells this story.

---

[589]   Ibn Ishaq, p. 167.
[590]   Ibn Kathir, *The Life of the Prophet Muhammad*, trans. Trevor Le Gassick, Garnet Publishing, 2000, Vol. 2, pp. 2-3.
[591]   McDonald & Watt, p. 105.
[592]   Ibn Ishaq, p. 159.
[593]   McDonald & Watt, pp. 105-106.
[594]   Ibn Ishaq, p. 172.

"Abu Jahl met Hakim b. Hizam b. Khuwaylid b. Asad with whom was a slave carrying flour intended for his aunt Khadija, the prophet's wife, who was with him in the alley. He hung on to him and said, 'Are you taking food to the B. Hashim? By God, before you and your food move from here I will denounce you in Mecca.' Abu'l-Bukhtari came to him and said, 'What is going on between you two?' When he said that Hakim was taking food to the B. Hashim, he said, 'It is food he has which belongs to his aunt and she has sent to him about it. Are you trying to prevent him taking her own food to her? Let the man go his way!' Abu Jahl refused until they came to blows, and Abu'l-Bakhtari took a camel's jaw and knocked him down, wounded him, and trod on him violently . . ." [595]

Thus, it is evident that the boycott brought about sharp divisions and even bloodshed. It seems that Abu Jahl is defeated at every turn in these stories and one senses an element of pious fiction and embellishment.

It is not difficult to find contradictions in these stories. Who issued the decree? Which people were involved in the confederacy? What was said at the meeting? There seems to be an assumption in western thinking that if contradictions can be demonstrated in the sources, then we may safely assume that the meeting did not take place. This assumption is false. In fact, we can expect contradictions, and in many ways, this demonstrates historicity. One should be very suspicious of stories with carefully maintained uniformity of content. History does not happen that way. Differing and contradictory viewpoints are a demonstration that the event actually took place and that event by its very nature generated various conflicting viewpoints.

The boycott continued for about three years until some of the Quraysh gathered together to reverse the boycott. The leader of this movement was Hisham b. Amr. According to Ibn Ishaq, he was moved to compassion at the suffering of the Muslims. Secretly, he had been sending food and supplies to the hungry families of Muslim pilgrims.[596] Hisham gathered together others who felt the same way. He asked them, "Are you content that two clans of the B. Abdu Manaf should perish while you look on consenting to follow Quraysh? You will find that they will soon do the same with you." They met together at al-Hajun north of Mecca. Zuhayr spoke and said, "O people

---

[595]   Ibn Ishaq, p. 161.
[596]   Ibn Ishaq, p. 172.

of Mecca, are we to eat and clothe ourselves while the B. Hashim perish unable to buy or sell? By God I will not sit down until this evil boycotting document is torn up!" Abu Jahl of the Quraysh tribe outspokenly opposed him. "You lie by Allah. It shall not be torn up." One of Hisham's cohorts said, "We are not satisfied with what is written and we don't hold with it . . ." Another said, "We take Allah to witness that we dissociate ourselves from the whole idea and what is written in the document." Interestingly enough, when al-Mut'im approached to destroy the document, he discovered that worms had already devoured it.[597] A similar story was recorded by Al-Tabari. The only variation was that the document was determined to be eaten by termites except for the words, which had been written, "In your name, O God." These are surely pious fictions in the details, but the very flourish of debate and tribal relationships illustrated in these stories certainly fits the pattern of Arab society of the time.

There are also various stories in Ibn Ishaq about Muslims receiving and then rejecting the protection of polytheist leaders.[598] While one may interpret these as glorifications of some of the early Muslims (Uthman, Salama, and Abu Bakr are prominently mentioned), it fits the pattern of establishing a new community not based on tribal loyalties. If Muhammad was going to unify the Arabian tribes, this was a transition that he logically would have to make. The stories make sense from a historical perspective.

There are other stories that are clearly inventions. One tells of the Prophet's wrestling match with a pagan named Rukana. After defeating him twice, Muhammad commands a tree to move from its place to the Prophet and then to move back. Astonishingly, the pagan is not converted.[599] There is no mention of these kinds of miracles in the Qur'an, and they serve only the purpose of attracting converts to Islam after Islamic political hegemony had been established in the Middle East. There are similar pious stories of Christians from Abyssinia and Najran meeting Muhammad in Mecca and accepting Islam. These are used to explain verses from this period we have already discussed (28:53-55). These are sometimes mixed with Medinan verses.

In the midst of these discussions, Ibn Ishaq throws in the earlier story we have considered about the Prophet's Miraj to Jerusalem and thence to heaven. He emphasizes that wine was forbidden to the Muslims. It is clear

---

[597]	Ibn Ishaq, pp. 172-174.
[598]	Ibn Ishaq, pp. 169-172.
[599]	Ibn Ishaq, p. 178.

from the later story of Hamza's drunkenness after the Battle of Badr, that wine drinking was only forbidden later in the Medinan period. The story does not fit the chronology of the surah's of the Qur'an, and it demonstrates that the stories of the Miraj, like that of the shooting stars, migrates throughout the history of the Prophet as a kind of typology. In other early Muslim writings, this trip is emphasized as the birthplace of the prayer and fasting practices of Islam. Ibn Ishaq provided at the very start of the Prophet's career a story of how the angel Gabriel introduced him to the practices of prayer. Thus, there are constant contradictions in these texts. Interestingly, Ibn Ishaq does admit that many left Islam at this time because of the "absurdity" of some stories, such as the Miraj.[600]

3. The Deaths of Khadija and Abu Talib

The year 619 CE has been recognized as an emotionally difficult year for Muhammad. It was during this year that Khadija, his wife of nineteen years, died. Soon after this, his uncle Abu Talib died as well. These two great losses proved to weigh heavily on him. Al-Tabari's account comments on these deaths. "Their death was a great affliction to the Messenger of God."[601] Khadija had born a number of children to the Prophet from before the time of Islam, including two sons with pagan names (all deceased in infancy). Abu Ubayda cites the tradition about Khadija's conversation with the Prophet concerning the fate of their deceased children. "The Prophet assured her that their infants were in Paradise but added that the children born by her to her former husband the unbeliever were in hell."[602] During her lifetime, she was his only wife. She had been very instrumental in encouraging belief in his revelations and in his call as a prophet. Nothing is recorded of the circumstances of her death. Soon after Khadija died, Muhammad married a widow named, Sawdah. Sawdah was one of the early converts to Islam. Her previous husband had also been a Muslim. W. Montgomery Watt believes that Muhammad's marriages after Khadija's tended to be politically motivated. Furthermore, W. M. Watt states, "There are signs that deepening religious experiences were taking the place of human companionship."[603] Ibn Kathir

---

[600] Ibn Ishaq, pp. 182-183.
[601] McDonald & Watt, *The History of al-Tabari*, New York: State University of New York Press, p. 115. Hereafter cited as Al-Tabari.
[602] Rubin & Kister, p. 74.
[603] Watt, p. 79.

records that Muhammad married Sawdah soon after Khadija died. He also mentions that Muhammad is engaged to Aisha at this time, possibly even before his marriage to Sawdah.[604] The death of Abu Talib was even more difficult to bear than his wife's and receives more attention in the Muslim literature. For years, his uncle had watched over him. He had provided for him when he was young and protected him from his opponents. Ibn Ishaq comments:

> With the death of Abu Talib he lost a strength and stay in his personal life and a defence and protection against his tribe. Abu Talib died some three years before he migrated to Medina, and it was then that the Quraysh began to treat him in an offensive way which they would not have dared to follow in his uncle's lifetime.[605]

After Abu Talib's death, the opposition to Muhammad's movement and his followers became even stronger. The Messanger of God used to say, "Quraysh never did anything unpleasant to me until Abu Talib died."[606] In three years, the opposition would drive Muhammad and his followers once again from Mecca. This time they would be "emigrate" to Yathrib, later named Medina by the Prophet.

4. Muhammad and the People of the Book

There are many references to debates between the Meccans and Muhammad concerning the Christian teaching that Jesus is the Son of God. The Meccans use this as an excuse; if Christians who are People of the Book may worship Jesus, why can't Meccans worship Al-Lat and Al-Uzzah.[607] Nowhere in the Medinan surahs of the Qur'an do we find this kind of detailed discussion reflected. It is interesting to note, however, that these stories show that Muhammad's notions about the Christian faith were not based on direct interaction but by way of third parties arguing using references to other beliefs not their own. This might account for the occasional verses during the Meccan period that seem to deny specifically Christian doctrines.

---

[604]   Ibn Kathir, p. 97
[605]   Ibn Ishaq, p. 191.
[606]   Al-Tabari, p. 115.
[607]   Ibn Ishaq, p. 163.

We have already noticed the positive views of the biographers to the Christians of Abyssinia who took in and protected the Muslim immigrants. Further, the Prophet's direct mention of the Romans in a positive sense, as being at war with the Persians, indicates that the overall sentiment of the Qur'an and the historical literature for this period was quite positive to the Christians and not negative to the Jews. We now move to the critical time of change that led up to the Prophet's migration to Medina.

CHAPTER 5

MUHAMMAD EXTENDS
HIS APPEALS CE 619-622

The period from CE 619-622 marked a significant transition for Islam. During this time, Muhammad experienced many challenges in his relationships. Muhammad was greatly influenced by the lives of Abu Talib and Khadija. His uncle, Abu Talib, gave Muhammad a source of protection in Mecca while his wife, Khadija, was his first convert to Islam. He was equally affected by their deaths, both occurring in the same year according to the Muslim historians. The removal of these two influences changed Muhammad's relationship with the Quraysh and birthed a new strategy for Islam. Muhammad was left in a vulnerable and uncertain position. Life in Mecca became unstable as conversions were minimal and conflict increased. The loss of Abu Talib's security heightened Meccan hostility, forcing Muhammad to establish relationships outside of Mecca. Due to this opposition, Muhammad began to extend his support base to surrounding tribes and cities. Resistance from the Quraysh propelled Muhammad to make appeals with other clans and finally to flee to Yathrib (Medina) in 622 CE. In this chapter, we will look at the historical documents first and then conclude with a review of the content of the Qur'an during this period.

A. Muslim Biographical Traditions

The three years prior to the Hijra signify a transfer of loyalties from the local Quraysh tribe to the Islamic family.[608] We have noted this in the previous chapter where various Muslims rejected the protection of their own pagan

---

[608] William Montgomery Watt, *Muhammad at Mecca*, Oxford: Clarendon Press, 1953, 77-78.

relatives. Given the existing situation, Montgomery Watt comments on the need for a new approach:

"In such circumstances, if Islam was not to fade away, some fresh line of activity was urgently required. All that could be done in Mecca had been done; therefore, the chief hope lay in advances elsewhere."[609]

Muhammad made the necessary adjustments in order to sustain Islam during this trying time. Commitment to the Quraysh clan was now compromised for the greater religious cause. This, in effect, instituted a new association with non-Muslim people. Consequently, Muhammad's mission to Ta'if and his pledges at Aqaba defined the evolution of this relationship. Examining these two events, as well as local reactions to Islam, will reveal how Islam was impacted during this time.

B. Responses to Islam

Various conditions in Mecca signaled a subtle, but steady orientation toward monotheism. Christianity and Judaism were already being introduced among Arab tribes, threatening existing polytheistic beliefs. Mecca was situated along trading crossroads and was home to a sanctuary area, considered holy by the Arabs.[610] Pilgrims would come to visit the shrines and traders circulated stories from other tribes. Though polytheism had historical roots, it was already being challenged by monotheism before Muhammad arrived on the scene. There were very few Jews in Mecca, and perhaps only a bit more of a Christian presence at some level according to Watt.[611] On the other hand, as we have seen, the influence of Judaism seems preeminent in the Qur'an during this period. Did the early historians want to cover that up by ignoring evidence of a Jewish presence? The point remains that the movement to monotheism was already taking place. Muhammad's interest in the Jewish faith may have resulted from its lack of connection to the world empires that dominated Arabia at this time.

There are numerous accounts of both positive and negative reactions to Muhammad. The spiritual climate of Mecca both facilitated and hindered

---

[609] Watt, 138.
[610] Watt, 2-3.
[611] Watt, 27.

the spread of Islam. As monotheism gained a foothold in Mecca, individuals were prepared for Muhammad's revelations. At the same time, however, Muhammad was perceived as dangerous to the balance of power in Mecca. This contributed to a greater threat to the cause of Islam and a larger rift between Muhammad and the Quraysh.

In the earlier Meccan periods, there were several favorable responses to Muhammad's appeals. Muhammad's first convert was his wife, Khadija. It is debatable whether the first male Muslim was Abu Bakr, Zayd, or Ali. Other important conversions include Hamza and Umar. Although there were several conversions to Islam during Muhammad's time at Mecca, his later years in particular were a dry period. There is little record of conversions, apart from the initial ones mentioned, until Muhammad met with the people of Yathrib. Some of these converts had interaction with Jews from Medina. They heard about the coming of a prophet, so when Muhammad invited them to Islam, they said, "This had to be the Prophet the Jews foresaw; we should not let them get to him first."[612] This kind of dialogue is undoubtedly invented, but the presence of a large monotheistic Jewish community must have seen a possible power base for Muhammad to appeal to.

Montgomery Watt lists three categories of early Muslim converts. First, Muhammad aimed to include younger sons of the best families. Second, he targeted young men from other families. Third, he aimed for men without close relationships to their tribe.[613] Most of the men, with the exception of only a few, were under the age of thirty. Watt adds:

> "The most important point which emerges from this survey is that the young Islam was essentially a movement of young men . . . it was not a movement of "down and outs," of the scum of the population, of "hangers-on" with no strong tribal affiliations who had drifted into Mecca. It drew its support not from the bottom layers of the social scale, but from those about the middle who, becoming conscious of the disparity between them and those at the top, were beginning to feel that they were underprivileged. It was not so much a struggle between "haves" and "have nots" as between "haves" and "nearly hads."[614]

---

[612] Ibn Kathir, *Al-Sira Al-Nabawiyya vol. 2,* translated Dr. Trevor le Gassick, U.K.: Garner Publishing, 1998, 118.

[613] Watt, 95.

[614] Watt, 96. Islam continues to be an excellent religion for angry young men.

Muhammad not only promised his followers Paradise in the afterlife, "but also a thoroughly material special social position following the Hijra."[615] There was added incentive both in the here and now as well as in the future. It is disputable to what extent Muhammad initially intended to gain followers outside of the Quraysh. Was this Muhammad's goal all along? Watt comments,

> "Muhammad had originally regarded himself as a prophet sent solely or primarily to Quraysh, and there is no way of telling whether prior to the death of Abu Talib he had thought of an expansion of his mission to the Arabs in general. The deterioration in his position, however, now forced him to look further afield, and during his last three years in Mecca we hear only of dealings with nomadic tribes and with the citizens of at-Ta'if and Yathrib.[616]

Muhammad faced significant contention as a result of his uncompromising commitment to his message. Ibn Ishaq illustrates the ill treatment he experienced from his neighbors:

> I have been told that one of [the neighbors] used to throw a sheep's uterus at him while he was praying; and one of them used to throw it into his cooking-pot when it had been placed ready for him. Thus the apostle was forced to retire to a wall when he prayed. Umar . . . told me on the authority of his father that when they threw this objectionable thing at him the apostle took it out on a stick, and standing at the door of his house, he would say, 'O Banu Abdu Manaf, what sort of protection is this?' Then he would throw it into the street.[617]

Muhammad also continued to confront strained relationships with the Quraysh. An example of this was his relationship with Abu Lahab. Ibn Kathir recounts that Abu Lahab protected Muhammad following the death of Abu Talib, but withdrew his protection when Muhammad declared to him that all their dead ancestors were burning in hell.[618]

---

[615] Uri Rubin, ed., *The Life of Muhammad.* (Brookfield, VT: Ashgate, 1998), *The First Muslims in Mecca: A Social Basis for a New Religion?* by Miklos Muranyi, 97.

[616] Watt, p. 138.

[617] Ibn Ishaq, *The Life of Muhammad*, ed. Alfred Guillaume (Karachi: Oxford University Press, 1955), p. 191.

[618] Ibn Kathir, History, pp. 98-99.

Muhammad reacted to the Meccan pressures with political strategies and perhaps began to look elsewhere for companions for the cause. It is with this intention that it is said Muhammad journeyed to Ta'if in an effort to build a larger support base beyond the Quraysh. A similar strategy had taken part of the Muslim community to Abyssinia in 615CE. Finally, the strategy resulted in the Hijra to Medina in CE 622.

1. Mission to Ta'if

Following the death of Abu Talib, Muhammad went up to the nearby city of Ta'if in approximately 620 CE. Ta'if was a competing trading town similar to Mecca. In addition to traveling to Ta'if for trade, wealthy Meccans bought property in Ta'if to use as summer retreats.[619] Ta'if sat seven thousand feet higher than Mecca and was famous for raisins and cereals, available due to the fertile land of the region and the moderate climate. Muhammad anticipated potential supporters from the tribe of Thaqif, the dominant tribe residing in this area.[620] It was Muhammad's ambition in this mission to gain both converts to Islam and helpers for his cause.

Ibn Ishaq describes Muhammad's mission as twofold, "the apostle went to Ta'if to seek help from Thaqif and their (defense) against his tribe. Also he hoped that they would receive the message that God had given him."[621] It is debatable whether Muhammad traveled alone or with other companions. Ibn Ishaq and Al-Tabari state Muhammad went alone, whereas other sources mention Zayd, Abu Bakr, or his manumitted slave accompanying him on the journey.[622] After arriving in the city, Muhammad met some of the leaders of Thaqif and asked them for help against the Quraysh. Ibn Ishaq recounts the event as follows:

> When the apostle arrived at al-Ta'if he made for a number of Thaqif who were at that time leaders and chiefs, namely three brothers . . . The apostle sat with them and invited them to accept Islam and asked them to help him against his opponents at home.

---

[619] Watt, 138-139.
[620] Al-Tabari, *Muhammad at Mecca vol. 6,* trans. W. M. Watt and M. V. McDonald, Albany, NY: State University of New York Press, 1988, p. 115. Hereafter cited as Al-Tabari.
[621] Ibn Ishaq, 192.
[622] Ibn Ishaq, 192. Al-Tabari, p. 115.

One of them swore that he would tear up the covering of the Ka'ba if God had sent him. The other said, "Could not God have found someone better than you to send?" The third said, "By God, don't let me ever speak to you. If you are an apostle from God as you say you are, you are far too important for me to reply to, and if you are lying against God it is not right that I should speak to you!" So the apostle got up and went, despairing of getting any good out of Thaqif.[623]

Muhammad's arrival in Ta'if was most disappointing. Watt and McDonald note that the Thaqif "had been forced into an alliance with the Meccans, and Muhammad may have hoped that anti-Meccan feeling would lead (them) to support him."[624] Instead, Muhammad received rejection and insults. Ibn Ishaq continues the story:

I have been told that [Muhammad] said to them, "Seeing that you have acted as you have, keep the matter secret, 'for he was loath that his people should hear about it, so that they would be still further emboldened against him. But they did not do so and stirred up their louts and slaves to insult him and cry after him until a crowd came together, and compelled him to take refuge in an orchard belonging to Utba b. Rabi'a and his brother Shayba who were in it at the time."[625]

Interestingly, Muhammad asked for his request to remain a secret. Ibn Kathir comments that Muhammad "did not want his people to hear about this, since it would have encouraged them to oppose him."[626] The tribe "sent Muhammad away with nothing accomplished and even encouraged the town rabble to fling stones at him."[627] Some traditions claim that Muhammad was stoned, others that an angel offered to destroy the city,[628] and Ibn Ishaq omits both.

It was at this point that Muhammad found shelter in the garden of two opponents. Ibn Ishaq, Al-Tabari, and Ibn Kathir all record the story of Muhammad's interaction with a Christian slave while resting there:

---

[623] Ibn Ishaq, pp. 192-193.
[624] Watt and McDonald, footnote in Tabari, p. 115.
[625] Ibn Ishaq, pp. 192-193.
[626] Ibn Kathir, *al-Sira,* p. p. 99.
[627] Watt, 139.
[628] Ibn Kathir, *al-Sira,* p. 102.

"When Utba and Shayba saw what happened they were moved with compassion and called a young Christian slave of theirs called Addas and told him to take a bunch of grapes on a platter and give them to him to eat. Addas did so, and when the apostle put his hand in the platter he said, 'In the name of God' before eating. Addas looked closely into his face and said, 'By God, this is not the way the people of this country speak.' The apostle then asked, 'Then from what country do you come, O Addas? And what is your religion?' He replied that he was a Christian and came from Nineveh. 'From the town of the righteous man Jonah son of Mattal,' said the apostle. 'But how did you know about him?' asked Addas. 'He is my brother; he was a prophet and I am a prophet,' answered the apostle. Addas bent over him and kissed his head, his hands, and his feet. 'The two brothers were looking on and one said to the other, 'He's already corrupted your slave!' And when Addas came back they said to him: 'You rascal, why were you kissing that man's head, hands, and feet?' He answered that he was the finest man in the country who had told him things that only a prophet could know. They replied, 'You rascal, don't let him seduce you from your religion, for it is better than his.'"[629]

This dialogue is polemic fiction. Utba and Shayba, originally "moved with compassion" toward Muhammad, later accused him of corrupting Addas. The author likely assumed to know the heart attitude of these two brothers, who later fought at the Battle of Badr against the Muslims. Their presence on the opposing side at that battle gives a level of credibility to this story.

After the account of Addas, Ibn Ishaq records that Muhammad left Ta'if and met the seven jinns in the middle of the night at Nakhla.[630] The jinns listened to Muhammad and departed believing. Watt suggests the probability of this encounter being fictitious, a result of "later editing." During this time of rejection, he turned to God in his weakness.[631]

There are several reasons why it would be logical for Muhammad to plan this mission to Ta'if. It is widely held that Muhammad had hopes of spreading Islam and gaining protection from the Quraysh. Watt also adds two

---

[629]   Ibn Ishaq, p. 193.
[630]   Ibn Ishaq, pp. 193-194.
[631]   Al-Tabari, p. 116.

other reasons. It is possible that Muhammad also was looking for a place of refuge for his followers, who were facing persecution in Mecca. In addition, Muhammad may have aspired to act on "the idea of inaugurating an Islamic community, such as the one that later came into existence at Medina."[632] This last suggestion should be considered more carefully.

Muhammad entered Ta'if with a religious agenda and a political purpose. This is first seen in Muhammad's search for a protector. The Thaqif tribe was considered weaker than the Quraysh.[633] Muhammad's goal seems to have been to appeal to the Thaqif in a way that would strengthen them politically through the addition of the Muslims to their community. Moreover, Muhammad's urge for secrecy protected his political pursuits more than his religious persuasions.[634] The fact that his mission was secretive, accompanied by few if any followers, shows a shift to a different political strategy. Monotheism was used as a unifying tool for the widening of Muhammad's influence. It is doubtless that Muhammad had a religious motivation for traveling to Ta'if, but his ensuing activities divulge a greater agenda. This was not the end of his relationship with Ta'if. Muhammad returned to Ta'if in 630 CE at the head of an army.

Muhammad was protected by Al-Mutim on his return back to Mecca where he appealed to Arab tribes during the fairs of pilgrimage.[635] He sought supporters from various tribes, including the clans of Kinda, Kalb, Hanifa, and Amir. Ibn Ishaq writes,

> The apostle offered himself to the tribes of Arabs at the fairs whenever opportunity came, summoning them to God, and telling them that he was a prophet who had been sent. He used to ask them to believe in him and protect him until God should make clear to them the message with which he had charged his prophet.[636]

Muhammad was rejected by each of these clans. "The first three rejected Muhammad outright, the last rejected him after Muhammad had refused to promise them the political succession to his own position."[637] When he made

---

[632] Watt, p. 139.
[633] Watt, pp. 138-139.
[634] Ibn Kathir, *al-Sira*, p. 115.
[635] Ibn Kathir, *al-Sira*, pp. 102-103.
[636] Ibn Ishaq, p. 194.
[637] Watt, pp. 140-141.

his appeals to the tribes, he recited the Qur'an and invited them to Islam. "Whenever men came together or the apostle heard of anyone of importance coming to Mecca he went to them with his message."[638] The initial success of these appeals was limited. Ibn Kathir records why the tribes rejected Muhammad. Muhammad would,

> "present himself to the Arab tribes at each fair speaking with each tribal leader but asking them only for their protection and support. He would say, "I don't wish to force any one of you to do anything. Any of you who agree to what I ask may do so, but I would not compel anyone not so wishing. All I want is to guard myself against those wanting to kill me, so that I may fulfill my Lord's mission and carry out whatever decree he wishes' . . . But not one of them accepted him . . . 'How could we accept as suitable for us someone who has subverted his tribe and whom they have expelled.'"[639]

Considering the centrality of the tribal relationship, it is likely that this response is indeed accurate. Many Arab tribes would have viewed Muhammad as a disgrace to the Quraysh since loyalty was a primary virtue. Despite this general rejection, however, there was a future for Islam when Muhammad found an opportunity with some visitors around this time. Responses improved upon meeting with residents of Yathrib where Muhammad was given a hearing and the men of Yathrib responded positively to his message. I think it is also worthwhile to consider the issue of the Jews of Medina. The Muslim biographies leave them entirely out of the picture of this initial approach to the people of Medina. Yet they were one of the largest groups in Yathrib and had the same religious views, seemingly, as the Prophet himself. Most significantly, as we will see later, they are included in provisions of the so-called "Constitution of Medina" and are considered as part of the "Umma" along with pagans. It would seem logical to assume that part of Muhammad's motivation in approaching Yathrib (Medina) was the fact that a large Jewish community would have seemed a potential source of support to this monotheistic Prophet who had already borrowed so extensively from Jewish oral traditions.

---

[638] Ibn Ishaq, pp. 195-196.
[639] Ibn Kathir, al-Sira, p. 106.

2. Treaty of Aqaba

Muhammad's arrangement of "secret meetings" with the Medinans has been referred to as the "beginning of Islam."[640] Aqaba, meaning "mountain road," was located two miles east of Mecca on the route to Mina.[641] The passageway and the surrounding area were traveled by pilgrims on route to Mecca and were known for "strange religious ceremonies" and annual marketplaces.[642] Muhammad met a party of Medinans at Aqaba, whom he later dubbed as the "Ansar," or helpers. It was here "that Muhammed took the decisive step to break with his fellowmen in Mecca, and instead, to join a number of Medina's inhabitants, who received him with welcome."[643] Originally, the town was known as Yathrib, but was later named Medina in honor of the Prophet. Surprisingly, the Qur'an fails to mention the events at Aqaba. Ibn Kathir refers to the pledge as "revelation that was not recited."[644]

The traditional account of the Aqaba meetings records Muhammad making two pledges with the Medinans. Twelve helpers attended the first meeting in 621 CE, known as the Pledge of Women. Some of these individuals may have been pilgrims that Muhammad met previously in 620 CE. Ishaq quotes one of the helpers,

> "I was present at the first Aqaba. There were twelve of us and we pledged ourselves to the prophet after the manner of women and that was before war was enjoined, the undertaking being that we should associate nothing with God; we should not steal; we should not commit fornication; nor kill our offspring; we should not slander our neighbours; we should not disobey him in what was right; if we fulfilled this paradise would be ours; if we committed any of those sins it was for God to punish or forgive as He pleased."[645]

---

[640] Uri Rubin, ed., *The Life of Muhammad,* Brookfield, VT: Ashgate, 1998, *The Meetings at Al-Aqaba,* by Gertrude Melamede, pp. 105-106.

[641] Michael Lecker, *Jews and Arabs in Pre-and Early Islamic Arabia,* Aldershot, Hampshire: Ashgate, 1998, p. 163.

[642] Gertrude Melamede in Uri Rubin, p. 105.

[643] Gertrude Melamede in Uri Rubin, p. 105.

[644] Ibn Kathir, *al-Sira,* p. 121.

[645] Ishaq, p. 199.

The allegiance made with Muhammad was called the Pledge of Women "because in surah 60:12 Muhammad is told to require something like this from believing women wanting to become Muslims."[646] This does not fit the chronology of the Qur'an and exemplifies the chaos found in Tafsir chronology of the Qur'an. Ibn Ishaq states that, "This was before the duty of making war was laid upon them."[647] Clearly, the early Muslim writers recognized the Hijra and the events that led up to it marked a significant turning point in the strategy of Islam. Muhammad is working on political alliances that can only lead to violent conflict. Coercive violence in the propagation of the faith is moving into the forefront of the Prophet's thinking.

Following this meeting, Muhammad sent Mus'ab to Medina. He was responsible for reciting the Qur'an to the converts and teaching them about Islam. He became known to them as "the Reader."[648] Tabari says, "Muhammad sent an agent to al-Madinah with them, ostensibly to teach them Islam, but probably also to gain detailed information about political trends in al-Madinah and to avoid a repetition of the fiasco at al-Ta'if."[649] Watt adds,

> "It is clear that there must have been long and careful negotiations between Muhammad and the Medinans. When he sent Mus'ab to Medina, it was not merely to instruct the new converts, but also to report on the situation there . . . The first effective contacts were with the Khazraj, but Muhammad insisted on meeting a more representative group, since he could not trust himself to one of the rival clans without the other. At this meeting, whatever the exact details may have been, there must have been a provisional agreement between Muhammad and the Medinans which included some acknowledgement of Muhammad as prophet" . . . [650]

The following year, in CE 622, a larger group of Medinans met Muhammad at Aqaba. Like the previous meeting, Muhammad met them secretly at night. This second meeting is known as the Pledge of War. According to Ishaq, there were seventy-three men present and two women. Ibn Ishaq reports,

---

[646] Watt and McDonald, footnote in Tabari, p. 126.
[647] Ishaq, p. 198.
[648] Ishaq, p. 199.
[649] Al-Tabari, p. xlv.
[650] Watt, pp. 146-147.

"Then Mus'ab returned to Mecca and the Muslim Ansar came to the fair there with the pilgrims of their people who were polytheists. They met the apostle at al-Aqaba in the middle of the days of Tashriq, when God intended to honour them and to help His apostle and to strengthen Islam and to humiliate heathenism and its devotees."[651]

Muhammad arrived on the scene with his uncle, Abbas. Abbas stood up at the commencement of the meeting and addressed the Medinan Ansars saying,

"O people of al-Khazraj . . . You know what position Muhammad holds among us. We have protected him from our own people who think as we do about him. He lives in honour and safety among his people, but he will turn to you and join you. If you think that you can be faithful to what you have promised him and protect him from his opponents, then assume the burden you have undertaken. But if you think that you will betray and abandon him after he has gone out with you, then leave him now. For he is safe where he is."[652]

Watt maintains that the account was a result of later invention.[653] This is an example of interpolation because Abbas was honored as the ancestor of the Abbasid caliphs under which the Muslim historians wrote. Abbas later fought against Muhammad and was captured at the Battle of Badr. This is indicative of the kinds of political concerns that influenced the Muslim historians leading to the contradictions inherent in these texts.

After this scene with Abbas, the following takes place:

"The apostle spoke and recited the Quran and invited men to God and commended Islam and then said, "I invite your allegiance on the basis that you protect me as you would your women and children."

Al-Bara took his hand and said, "By him who sent you with the truth we will protect you as we protect our women. We give our allegiance and we are men of war possessing arms which have been passed on from father to son."

---

[651] Ishaq, p. 201.
[652] Ishaq, p. 203.
[653] Watt, p. 147.

Abu l-Haytham . . . interrupted him and said, "O apostle, we have ties with other men (he meant the Jews) and if we sever them perhaps when we have done that and God will have given you victory, you will return to your people and leave us?"

The apostle smiled and said, "Nay, blood is blood and blood not to be paid for is blood not to be paid for. I am of you and you are of me. I will war against them that war against you and be at peace with those at peace with you."[654]

Even though this dialogue passage is clearly a polemic invention of a later age, what kind of war was Muhammad suggesting? What did this pledge of war mean? Ibn Kathir believes the pledge "seems to advocate defensive war."[655] Michael Lecker is of the opinion that the pledge of war did not promote bloodshed. He holds that later source documents portray a more accurate view of history, associating the pledge with tribal loyalty, not war. He believes the older sources include added interpolation. He also concludes that there was no intention of breaking relationship with the Jews at the second pledge.[656] On the other hand, Al-Tabari explains that the pledge "was to wage war against all men."[657] Watt and McDonald add, "that is, on anyone who injured or killed Muhammad."[658] The text, however, does not specify this limitation. Muhammad may have sent his followers to Medina with a defensive strategy, anticipating attack from the Jews, and upon finding a secure position, turned the tables to an offensive position.[659] Many of the seventy-three participants mentioned by Ibn Ishaq went on to fight in the Battle of Badr. Several were also killed as martyrs.[660] As history unfolds, it seems that the pledge gave greater freedom to participate in and initiate war. It does not seem that Muhammad had any negative feelings toward the Jews at this point, he probably saw them as potential allies.

---

[654] Ishaq, pp. 203-204.
[655] Ibn Kathir, al-Sira, p. 132.
[656] Harald Motzki, The Biography of Muhammad: The Issue of the Sources, Boston: Brill, 1999, Did the Quraysh Conclude a treaty with the Ansar Prior to the Hijra? by Michael Lecker, 157-166.
[657] Al-Tabari, p. 138.
[658] Watt and McDonald, footnote in Al-Tabari, p. 138.
[659] Julius Wellhausen, Muhammad and the Jews of Medina. Trans. A. J. Weinsinck. Klaus Schwarz Verlag, 1975, 33.
[660] Ibn Ishaq, pp. 208-211.

While taking the oath of allegiance, one participant said,

> "People of the Khazraj, do you know what you are pledging yourselves to in swearing allegiance to this man . . . you are pledging yourselves to wage war against all mankind. If you think that when your wealth is exhausted by misfortune and your nobles are depleted by death you will give him up, then stop now, for by God, it is disgrace in this world and the next if you later give him up. But if you think that you will be faithful to the promises which you made in inviting him, even if your wealth is exhausted and your nobles killed, then take him, for by God, he is the best thing for you in this world and the next." They answered, "We shall take him even if it brings the loss of our wealth and the killing of our nobles.[661]

Such monologues are pious inventions. Paradise was then promised as a reward, and this certainly fits the pattern of Qur'anic promises.[662] It seems that the treaty prepared the way for a more purely political establishment of Islam. It is interesting to note the events that followed. After they had given their oaths, one testified, "Satan shouted from the top of al-Aqabah in the most piercing voice I have ever heard. He said, 'People of the stations of Mina, do you want a blameworthy person and the apostates with him who have gathered together to wage war on you?'"[663] The people were ready to go to war the next day at Mina, but Muhammad did not give the command.[664] The representatives replied, "We are of you and you are of us. Whoever comes to us of your Companions, or you yourself if you come to us, we shall defend you as we would defend ourselves."[665] Muhammad then appointed twelve leaders, or *nuqaba*, to lead this new community. The fictional dialogues do illustrate for us the backreading of the Muslim interpreters into history, and what they considered important in their understanding of early Islam.

There is considerable controversy over the number of meetings at Aqaba. The traditional view, according to Ishaq and Tabari, is that there were two meetings with the Ansar. The first meeting was known as the Pledge of

---

[661] Al-Tabari, p. 134.
[662] Al-Tabari, p. 134.
[663] Al-Tabari, p. 135.
[664] Al-Tabari, p. 135.
[665] Al-Tabari, pp. 136-137.

Women and the second meeting was known as the Pledge of War. Some classify the meetings, however, as three encounters and others as only one. Gertrude Melamede argues that the first two meetings never took place.[666] There are also discrepancies over who attended the meetings and what was said. Despite the differences among the accounts, the results of the treaty were monumental. The pledge was an oath of commitment to a new type of community, a loyalty that transcended all tribal loyalties.

The significance of these events is threefold. First, Muhammad gained a new support base and greatly expanded the number of his followers. Muhammad's perspective continued to shift to political pursuits. Second, Muhammad set up a system of alliances leading to the so-called Constitution of Medina that, at this time, included Jews and even pagans in the "Ummah" or community. This may explain the early use of the term "millat Ibrahim" or "religion of Abraham" for the first time in the Qur'an from the late Meccan period.[667] Debates between Christians and Jews as to who was a true descendant of Abraham may have motivated Muhammad to find ways of bringing the various monotheistic groups together in a new "Ummah" based on a common ancestor. Later, Muhammad identifies his own religion as the true restoration of the "religion of Abraham" and uses it as polemic against the Jews in the Medinan period particularly in his first ultimatum to the Jews in the first chapter of the Medinan period (Qur'an 2:130-136).

Finally, there was a change in the early Muslim code of law as a result of the pledges of Aqaba. Prior to these events in 615 CE, Ja'far described Islam to the Negus saying, "The prophet . . . (forbid) the shedding of blood."[668] The early confession included teachings in regards to the confession of faith, almsgiving, rights of kinship, lying, immorality, hospitality, and fasting.[669] Now that the law against bloodshed had been repealed, the Islamic confession began to take on a more political/military nature than before. Many Qur'anic passages of the late-Meccan period echo this thought. For example, sura 39:51 says, "Nay, the evil results of their deeds overtook them. And the wrongdoers of this (generation)-The evil results of their deeds will soon overtake them (too), and they will never be able to frustrate (Our Plan)!" Yusuf Ali comments as follows:

---

[666]   Gertrude Melamede in Uri Rubin, pp. 130-133.
[667]   Qur'an 6:161, 16:123, Qur'an 12:38.
[668]   Ibn Kathir, *al-Sira,* p. 12.
[669]   Ibn Kathir, *al-Sira*, p. 12.

"It is the same story through the ages. People laugh at Truth, persecute Truth, and try to destroy Truth. But Allah's Plan is never to be frustrated. It will be carried out, and only the enemies of Truth will accomplish their own undoing. So it happened in Arabia: so will it happen always and everywhere."[670]

What was the nature of Muhammad's new orders? The treaty with the Medinans at Aqaba highlights new principles for spreading the religion. Ibn Ishaq says as follows:

"The apostle had not been given permission to fight or allowed to shed blood before the second Aqaba. He had simply been ordered to call men to God and to endure insult and forgive the ignorant. The Quraysh had persecuted his followers, seducing some from their religion, and exiling others from their country. They had to choose whether to give up their religion, be maltreated at home, or to flee the country, some to Abyssinia, others to Medina. When Quraysh became insolent toward God and rejected His gracious purpose, accused His prophet of lying, and ill treated and exiled those who served Him and proclaimed His unity, believed in His prophet, and held fast to His religion, He gave permission to His apostle to fight and to protect himself against those who wronged them and treated them badly."[671]

The definition of being "wronged," however, could be subject to change over the years to come. Muhammad initially responded to this permission to fight with a defensive posture in protecting his community as it emigrated to Medina. Once that position became secure, the "offence" became any unwillingness to confess the Prophet as the messenger of God. This, coupled with the need to provide financial support to the newly transplanted community, moved the Prophet's policy from one of defense to one of offense. Though war did not start immediately, peaceful relations had certainly come to an end.

---

[670] Yusuf Ali, p. 1252, footnote #4322.
[671] Ibn Ishaq, pp. 212-213.

It is in this spirit that the Muslims emigrated to Medina. Watt concludes,

> "Muhammad must have realized that his migration to Medina would lead sooner or later to fighting with the Meccans. How much of this did he communicate to the Medinans and in what form? And how much did they realize of themselves? Much more, we may suspect, than our sources indicate."[672]

The Hijra was made possible by the pledges at Aqaba. Tabari summarizes,

> "Muhammad encouraged those who wanted to go to make the journey in small groups. After about two months, over seventy men with their wives and families had reached al-Madinah. Some Muslims chose to remain in Mecca, but it is difficult to know how many. The leading opponents apparently had some awareness of what was happening, and realized that it could create problems for themselves, though, despite some of their alleged remarks, they could hardly have anticipated the precise nature of their problems.
>
> So long as he remained in Mecca Muhammad was presumably still under the "protection" of the clan of Nawfal. On leaving Mecca, however, he would have no "protection" until he reached al-Madinah. This was the reason for the secrecy of his departure" . . . [673]

Summary

Muhammad's final season in Mecca began with tragedy and ended with strategy. The opposition from the Quraysh could have extinguished the Muslim presence altogether. Instead, Muhammad made appeals to surrounding tribes and began his wider campaign. Bernard Lewis describes Muhammad as a powerful and innovative man. He was able to adapt to his circumstances and make adjustments that furthered his religious and political agendas. Lewis says,

---

[672] Watt, p. 148.
[673] Al-Tabari, p. xlv.

"Muhammad attained not martyrdom but power. During his lifetime he became a head of state, commanding armies, collecting taxes, administering justice, and promulgating laws. The resulting interpenetration of faith and power, of religion and authority, has remained characteristic of Islam throughout most of its history."[674]

Muhammad's success and influence grew as he appealed to the Medinans. Watt discusses the new concept of the "Ummah," or community, as established in Medina and states,

"These thoughts and conceptions doubtless only received their full development some time after the Hijra, but they must have been present in embryo when Muhammad began his negotiations with the men of Medina. That Muhammad should have had in mind—albeit in rudimentary form—an ideology capable of being elaborated to form the basis of the great movement of Arab expansion, is a measure of the width of his perception of the needs of his time and the vastness of his achievement during the Meccan period."[675]

Muhammad's tolerance toward non-Muslims decreased as he acquired the capability and authority to fight. It is clear that Muhammad's motives for Islamic propagation stemmed from a political rationale. His initial quest for protection evolved to a greater pursuit of power, driving Muhammad to extend his appeals beyond Mecca.

Inclusion of Others in the Treaty

It is also worth noting that the treaty of Aqaba made provisions for Jews and even non-Muslims to be part of Muhammad's new "ummah." This remarkable fact is so startling as to cause even a skeptic like Patricia Crone to declare the substance of this treaty to be fully historical. Muhammad shows a consummate political skill in this. His actions bind together quite disparate units for the time being when he is most vulnerable. Once the position of the

---

[674] Bernard Lewis, *The Jews of Islam,* Princeton, NJ: Princeton University Press, 1984, pp. 4-5.

[675] Watt, p. 153.

community had been strengthened, particularly after the Battle of Badr, he could afford to begin to more narrowly define this new community.

Content of the Qur'an

We will consider ten surahs as reflecting the final stages of Muhammad's time in Mecca, surahs 29, 31, 42, 10, 34, 35, 7, 46, 6, and 13 in that relative order.

Historical allusions are nonexistent in these chapters. There is not the slightest indication of the deaths of either Abu Talib or Khadija. No allusions to a trip to Ta'if or of an agreement with individuals from Medina. There are no allusions to any planned migrations either. It is astonishing how unbiographical the Qur'an is. This is also a testimony that the early followers made no emendations to the text. Given the importance of the practice and example of the Prophet, if there was any scope for interpolations of a biographical sort, surely this would be a place to find them. There is nothing.

We find all the same accusations from earlier surahs made against the Prophet with the stock in trade responses. He is accused of forgery, of lacking signs, of being a sorcerer, his book is a product of magic, it is a product of falsehood, he is seized by a spirit, and he is insane.[676] Two new arguments appear that seem to reflect Jewish objections, or perhaps pagan reflections on what was available from the Jews. One is the critique that the Qur'an is not written down on paper; "even if we had sent down unto you a message written on paper so that they could touch it with their hands, the disbelievers would have said, "This is nothing but obvious magic."[677] God seems to be comforting the Prophet at this point for the mockery he was suffering. The reference to written books, however, would have had little meaning for a pagan society steeped in oral traditions. The tradition of a holy book collected in written form is clearly Jewish and one wonders whether this was a thought put to him by Jewish sources. This is reinforced by another argument that the revelation should have been revealed as something complete. "If thou bring them not a revelation, they say, 'Why hast thou not got it together?' Say, 'I but follow what has been revealed to me from my Lord.'"[678] Neither Yusuf Ali nor Ibn Kathir comments on the phrase "got it together." This would

---

[676] Qur'an 42:24, 46:8, 10:38, 10:2, 46:7, 34:43-4, 6:7, 7:184, 69:50-51, 6:37, 13:7, 27, 6:8-9.

[677] Qur'an 6:7.

[678] Qur'an 7:203.

seem to be a collection of signs, or perhaps a holy book that is collected. Muhammad's book is both unfinished and uncollected in written form. Does this also represent Jewish influence? While this seems a minor point, as one approaches the end of this section of the Qur'an there are palpably more references to Jews, dialogues with Jews, and Jewish dietary regulations. These are so frequent in the last several chapters that one is tempted to consider that they might actually have been revealed in the earliest part of the Medinan period. We shall return to similar evidence shortly.

Islamic doctrines and moral concerns are also quite familiar. God's decrees and the fact that He leads and misleads who He will are strongly emphasized.[679] God's unity and that He has no partners is emphasized over and over.[680] Prayer and charity are enjoined, as is respect for parents, justice for orphans, and not killing children.[681] God's power in creation and the ubiquitous concept of the signs of God and man's ungratefulness are well represented.[682] Muhammad does spend more time in this section discussing kosher laws, particularly in the last chapters of this period.

> "So eat of meats on which Allah's name hath been pronounced,
> if ye have faith in His signs. Why should ye not eat of (meats) on
> which Allah's name hath been pronounced when he hath explained
> to you in detail what is forbidden to you" . . . [683]

Some of these injunctions clearly refer to various pagan taboos while others are explicitly in keeping with Jewish law.

> Say: "I find not in the message received by me by inspiration any
> (meat) forbidden to be eaten by one who wishes to eat it, unless it
> be dead meat, or blood poured forth, or the flesh of swine . . . For
> those who followed the Jewish law, we forbade every (animal)
> with undivided hoof, and we forbade them the fat of the ox and
> the sheep . . ." If they accuse thee of falsehood, say, "Your Lord
> is full of mercy."[684]

---

[679]   Qur'an 35:11, 7:178, and 6:39.
[680]   Qur'an 6:21-24, 56-7, and 13:16.
[681]   Qur'an 31:4, 46:15-18, 6:152, 6:137, 140, and 151.
[682]   Qur'an 31:10-11, 6:95-99, 13:2-5, 42:32, 10:22, 31:32, and 10:12.
[683]   Qur'an 6:118-119, 138-9, 143-6.
[684]   Qur'an 6:145-47

This passage seems to reflect a dialogue with Jews over the nature of the kosher laws. It would seem that Muhammad is trying to work out some common legal views that would bind his community with the Jewish community. He refers to the Jewish community as if they are a part of his "ummah" with some smaller variations in practice. This could reflect negotiations for those going to Medina or perhaps discussions between Muhammad and the Jews shortly after his arrival in Medina. It certainly fits the pattern of the community concept as it is expressed in the treaty of Aqaba. It should be noted that by the time we arrive at surah 2 of the Qur'an, which is considered the first from the Medinan period, Muhammad has already experienced a clear break with the Jews. These late Meccan chapters may be our only snapshot of the initial contact and conflicts between Muhammad and the Jews of Medina. There is more evidence like this.

References to the "millat Ibrahim" noted above could also be explained either as a device of unity to the Jews or as a preliminary point of contrast though the language is not strongly polemic. He mentions "the religion of Abraham" in the context of critique toward "those who divide their religion and break up into sects, thou has not part in them in the least" (Qur'an 6:159-161). Muhammad is arguing for unity on the part of monotheists. Given the pressure in Mecca upon Muhammad, it would seem logical that he sought the support of all monotheists, and there was no polemic purpose in this statement. This would change.

Toward the end of the final Meccan period, we find God admonishing the Prophet not to dispute with the "People of the Book":

> "Recite what is sent of the Book by inspiration to thee . . . And dispute ye not with the People of the Book, except with means better, unless it be with those of them that inflict wrong; but say, 'We believe in the revelation which has come down to us and in that which has come down to you; Our God and your God is One; and it is to Him we bow. And thus (it is) that we have sent down the Book to thee. So the People of the book believe therein."[685]

This is the clearest indication that Muhammad had some dialogue probably with Jews and felt that their books were the same and that they worshipped the same God. Although Muhammad speaks of the Qur'an as unique in Arabic,

---

[685] Qur'an 29:45-47.

he also claims that it confirms the book of Moses. He believes in the book of Abraham (which he seems to assume the Jews knew about). Indeed, God enjoins that he should read the other holy books.

> "If thou wert in doubt as to what we have revealed unto thee, then ask those who have been reading the book from before thee: The truth hath indeed come to thee from thy Lord: So be in no wise of those in doubt."[686]

And further God states the following:

> "Moreover, we gave Moses the Book, completing our favor to those who would do right, and explaining all things in detail—and a guide and a mercy, that they might believe in the meeting with their Lord . . . Lest ye should say: "The book was sent down to two peoples before us, and for our part we remained unacquainted with all that they learned by assiduous study."[687]

Elsewhere the unbelievers are threatened with punishment for not believing in the books sent down previously.[688] These remarkable statements as to the truthfulness and efficacy of the previous revelations are further backed up by statements concerning the immutability of God's Word. Muhammad notes that others suggested that he change the revelations he had received, to which he responds that he has no authority to do so. Further, in the same chapter, he makes the statement, "No change can there be in the Word's of Allah."[689] He goes on to say in surah 6: "The Word of thy Lord doth find its fulfillment in truth and justice: None can change his words."[690] If other holy books are the Word of God, then they must be equally immutable, which is why God enjoins their reading. One senses that Muhammad is appealing to a Jewish community here, emphasizing the similarity of their holy books and their common monotheistic viewpoint.

   In contrast, the only book that Muhammad refers to where changes are made is the Qur'an itself in its progressive revelation (occasions of *naskh* or

---

[686]   Qur'an 10:94.
[687]   Qur'an 6:154-156.
[688]   Qur'an 34:31.
[689]   Qur'an 10:15, 66.
[690]   Qur'an 6:115.

abrogation of earlier revelations). This figures much more prominently in the Medinan surahs, particularly chapter 2, where many previous revelations are abrogated. These final Meccan chapters not only seem to be an appeal to the Jewish community, but also an intimation of brewing conflict.

There are a number of verses that indicate disputes between Muhammad and the People of the Book during this period. Chapter 42 records several lengthy verses that indicate such a dispute as follows:

> "The same religion has he established for you as that which he enjoined on Noah . . . and that which we enjoined on Abraham, Moses and Jesus: Namely, that ye should remain steadfast in religion, and make no divisions therein . . . but truly those who have inherited the Book after them are in suspicious doubt concerning it. Now then, for that, call and stand steadfast . . . say: "I believe in the Book which Allah has sent down; And I am commanded to judge justly between you. Allah is our Lord and your Lord . . . There is no contention between us and you. Allah will bring us together, and to Him Is (our) final goal."[691]

Muhammad seems to conceive of his religion as a correction by way of a return to the unity of the faith that has somehow been broken by the recipients of the previous revelations. In 6:159, he states as follows: "As for those who divide their religion and break up into sects, thou hast no part in them in the least." It would make sense that Muhammad would appeal for unity in the different monotheistic groups in anticipation of the coming conflict with Mecca.

Elsewhere he seems to accuse the Jews of hiding things in their revelations in apparent response to Muhammad's own conception of revelation:

> "No just estimate of Allah do they make when they say: 'Nothing doth Allah send down to man.'"Say: "Who then sent down the Book which Moses brought?—A light and a guidance to man: But ye make it into separate sheets for show while ye conceal much: Therein were ye taught that which ye knew not."[692]

---

[691] Qur'an 42:13-15.
[692] Qur'an 6:91-92.

The disagreement seems to be over the concept of revelation. In Islam, the Qur'an is a "tanzil kitab" literally "let down" book from heaven in dictated form. This rigid conception of revelation apparently is rejected by the Jews in this discourse as a way of rejecting Muhammad's revelation. Muhammad's argument, however, is correct. The books of Moses were considered to be dictated by God within Jewish thought, thus the Torah was revealed in ways very similar to the Qur'an.[693] This must have been one argument that Muhammad won. Nevertheless, Muhammad refers to the books of Moses as being confirmed by his new Arabic revelation. Though there is conflict and disagreement here, Muhammad is clearly trying to incorporate the Jews and their holy books into his own community as a grand alliance. There is no indication of this kind of effort in the earlier periods of the Qur'an and this textual evidence, I believe, indicates that the final Meccan chapters actually record some of the initial discussions with the Jews in Medina or perhaps Jewish individuals from Medina who came to discuss with Muhammad in Mecca. Further, I think it lays to rest the arguments of Hawting that the polemic of the Qur'an is not focused on idolaters but upon groups with differing views on monotheism. Clearly, Muhammad makes a distinction in treatment toward Jewish monotheists. He does not view them as the enemy at this point. The seeds of conflict are there, but he is trying to fit them into his monotheistic alliance. Their Word is from God and immutable. He is preaching the same word.

In this final Meccan period we do have three miraculous stories briefly recorded. One concerns Solomon's power over the jinns.[694] Another concerns Muhammad preaching to the jinn:

> "Behold, we turned toward thee a company of Jinns listening to the Qur'an: when they stood in the presence thereof, they said, "Listen in silence!" When the reading was finished, they returned to their people to warn. They said, "O our people! We have heard a book revealed after Moses, confirming what came before it: it guides to the truth and to a straight path."[695]

---

[693]   Torah in Jewish practice is the actual Word of God directly revealed to Moses. The other two sections of the Old Testament, Neviim and Ketuviim (prophets and writings) are considered to have lesser authority and are not revealed in the same way as Torah.

[694]   Qur'an 34:12-14.

[695]   Qur'an 46:29-30.

This is very similar to the earlier surah 72 and seems to indicate Muhammad's supernatural power and ministry as well as his affinity to the Jews and earlier holy books. It is also interesting that the Jewish revelation figures importantly while other holy books such as the Injil of Jesus are not mentioned. It seems that Muhammad was dealing extensively with a Jewish community at this point and had little contact with Christians.

One final miraculous story is told, which is a retelling of a Jewish fable apparently current at that time. People living in a town by the sea were tempted to go fishing on the Sabbath, for the fish would only appear on that day when work was forbidden "openly holding up their heads" to be caught. In the Jewish version of the story, the people break the Sabbath and as a curse are turned into "apes." Muhammad's version of the story is a little unclear as to what the disobedience was, but it concludes as follows: "We said to them: be ye apes. Despised and rejected."[696] In this context, the story fits into the homilies of disobedience and punishment that Muhammad utilizes as types of his own work. He seems to be appealing to certain Jews he feels will accept his teaching. Ibn Kathir turns this into a story that is virtually genocidal in its intentions to the Jews. He states, "In the future the Jews will support the Dajjal (false messiah); and the Muslims, along with Isa son of Mary, will kill the Jews."[697] Muhammad's statement at this point does not have this genocidal meaning at all. Just before telling the story, he says, "Of the people of Moses there is a section who guide and do justice in the light of truth."[698] In chapter 2, at the beginning of the Medinan period, the story is briefly retold. However, this time, it is in the context of Muhammad condemning the Jews for their disbelief.

Biblical Stories

Adam and Eve

Toward the end of this period, Muhammad dedicates one of the last Meccan chapters as a direct appeal to the Jewish community in Medina. Chapter 7 runs through the stories of the Pentateuch beginning with creation and ending with the story of Moses. He corrects his earlier mention of creation, taking eight days and mentions creation in six days.[699] He provides one of the longest renditions of the

---

[696] Qur'an 7:166.
[697] Ibn Kathir, *Tafsir*, Vol. 4, p. 193.
[698] Qur'an 7:159.
[699] Qur'an 7:54.

story of Satan's (Iblis) fall for not prostrating before Adam and his temptation of Adam and Eve. The first story is derived from a Jewish apocryphal story.[700] The second follows the biblical text somewhat though with significantly different details. The garden seems to be heaven, for after the fall, God commands them to go down to the earth, "On earth will be your dwelling place."[701]

Lot and Others

Abraham is not mentioned in this passage, but the story of Lot and his arguments with the wicked men of Sodom are detailed.[702] Other Prophets that may be connected to certain early Genesis personalities are mentioned, Hud, Salih, and Shuayb.[703] These seem to be Arabian personalities known to the people of Muhammad's time as they are mentioned in some pre-Islamic poetry and inscriptions.[704] There is a brief allusion to the Tower of Babel where God seems to say that human unity should have been maintained, in contrast to the biblical text where God commands linguistic cultural diversity. Much of the monocultural approach of Islam can be explained by the lack of a theology explaining cultural diversity.

Moses

Moses continues to be the most prominent figure with the story of his life retold in two extensive passages. Chapter 10 is entitled "Yunus" referring to Jonah. In spite of the title, there are only a couple of verses of a repetitive nature dealing with Jonah and the fact that the people he preached to were distinguished by the fact that they actually repented. Verses 75-94 retell the story of Moses with only one startling new detail. Pharaoh repents at the Red Sea and becomes a Muslim.

> "We took the children of Israel across the sea: Pharaoh and his hosts followed them in insolence and spite. At length, when overwhelmed with the flood, he said, "I believe that there is no

---

[700]   Ginzberg, Legends of the Jews, Vol. 1, pp. 62-64.

[701]   Qur'an 7:24.

[702]   Qur'an 7:80-84.

[703]   Qur'an 7:67-9, 73-79, 85-93.

[704]   Roberto Tottoli, *Biblical Prophets in the Qur'an and Muslim Literature*, London: Routledge, 2002, p. 47.

god except Him whom the children of Israel believe in: I am of those who submit . . . This day shall we save thee in thy body, that thou mayest be a sign to those who come after thee."[705]

There is little mention of the ten plagues, only the snake/staff conflict with the sorcerers of Egypt. Muhammad never really gets the complete story of the Exodus. He invariably leaves out the main point of the Passover. This coupled with his new twist of the conversion of Pharaoh would make his scriptures and his preaching highly offensive to Jews.

In surah 7, it seems he tries to correct what was missing in the earlier story of Moses. This is his final lengthy rendition of the story of Moses. It is his strongest appeal to the Jewish community. As the saying goes, the devil is in the details. Muhammad's rendition goes fatally astray from the biblical text and must have sounded thoroughly ludicrous to Jewish listeners. The story of the staffs follows the biblical text, but then when the sorcerers repent, Pharaoh threatens them with crucifixion, repeating an earlier anachronism. Yusuf Ali makes no comment on this. Ibn Kathir claims that they became martyrs for Islam.[706] Then Pharaoh decides to kill all the male babies of Israel, mixing up an early story from the life of Moses with the final plague on the first born of Egypt and perhaps the story of the killing of the innocent children in Bethlehem (Matt. 2:16). Yusuf Ali claims that this is the same pharaoh who had made the original ruling before the birth of Moses for the killing of the male children.[707] That would make his reign at least eighty years long by Jewish traditional chronology. Ibn Kathir makes the same interpretation[708] and this is clearly to explain away the inaccuracies of the text. Pharaoh is punished with years of drought and famine, mixing up the story of Moses with Joseph. Beginning at verse 133, God sends plagues. He sends only five, not the ten of Exodus, and only three follow the Exodus account, but not in the correct order. Locusts, frogs, and blood are listed. The first plague is an ambiguous calamity (tufan) and "lice" are another plague. There is no mention of either the final plague or the institution of Passover. This aspect of the plagues is also ignored by Yusuf Ali and Ibn Kathir. From a Jewish perspective this is a disastrously inaccurate rendition

---

[705]　Qur'an 10:90, 92.
[706]　Ibn Kathir, *Tafsir*, Vol. 4, p. 141 referring to Qur'an 7:124.
[707]　Ali, Yusuf, p. 379, footnote no. 1084.
[708]　Ibn Kathir, *Tafsir*, Vol. 4, p. 143.

of their most sacred story. It was inevitable that Muhammad would be rejected by most Jews.

The remainder of the story changes significant details from Muhammad's earlier rendition, making them more accurate from a Jewish perspective. The mysterious Samiri who led the people astray in the affair of the golden calf has disappeared from the text, and Aaron seems to need to repent, although he claims the people made him do it by threatening his life. Yusuf Ali, nevertheless, maintains that the "Samiri" led the people astray in spite of the thrust of the text, and Ibn Kathir also maintains that Aaron was "innocent."[709] The commentators do not understand Muhammad's effort to correct the earlier revelation. naskh (abrogation) seems to imply that even historical narratives may be altered by later revelations.

There are other aspects that are replicated such as Moses's request to see God's glory and the giving of the law on tablets of stone. Muhammad ends his story with what can only be described as an appeal to the members of the community who were Jewish and perhaps Christian to believe in and follow Muhammad.

> "Those who follow the messenger, the unlettered Prophet, whom they find mentioned in their own (scriptures)—in the law and the Gospel—for he commands them what is just and forbids them what is evil; he allows them as lawful what is good and prohibits from what is bad; he releases them from their heavy burdens and from the yokes that are upon them. So it is those who believe in him, honor him, help him and follow the light which is sent down with him—It is they who will prosper. Say: "O men! I am sent unto you all, as the Messenger of Allah . . ."[710]

It is clear that Muhammad expected at this stage of his work that the Jews would work together with him and he appeals to them directly to support him. He seems to truly believe that both the Christian and Jewish scriptures predict his coming. Moses does mention a Prophet to come, but, tragically, Muhammad's thoroughly confused and contradictory rendition of the sacred

---

[709] Yusuf Ali, p. 387, footnote no. 1118, and Ibn Kathir, Tafsir, Vol. 4, p. 167.
[710] Qur'an 7:157-158.

history of the very people he was appealing to insured his rejection. The stage is set for major conflict in Medina.

Abraham and the Final Appeal to the "Confederates"

In the last two surahs (6 and 13) of this period, Muhammad returns to the person of Abraham as the paradigm of himself. He tells the story of Abraham's rejection of the idols in the house of his father "Azar." The details in the Qur'an follow the pattern of Jewish apocryphal literature.[711] He then provides a list of the biblical prophets who emerge from Abraham.

> "We gave him Isaac and Jacob: all we guided: and before him Noah and among his progeny, David, Solomon, Job, Joseph, Moses and Aaron: thus do we reward those who do good: and Zakariya and Yahya, and Jesus and Elias: all in the ranks of the righteous: and Ismail, and Elisha, and Jonah, and Lot: and to all we gave favor above the nations."[712]

It is not clear whether Muhammad intended this as a chronological list, with Noah placed before and Abraham's progeny after. Ismail is once again not even placed in conjunction with Abraham, and this is the first time that we find a reversal of knowledge that Muhammad had apparently gained earlier. However, that is based on the assumption that the list is intended to be chronological. In any case, the list is both incomplete of biblical prophets and shows no schematic or organizational grouping. Once again, in the midst of an appeal to the People of the Book Muhammad displays his ignorance of the scope and structure of Jewish salvation history. The inclusion of Jesus and John the Baptist certainly would have done nothing to ingratiate him with Jews. It is in the same passage that Muhammad accuses the Jews of rejecting the contents of their holy books. "These were the men to whom we gave the Book and the authority, and Prophethood: If these reject them, behold! We shall entrust their charge to a new people who reject them not."[713] In the final chapter of the Meccan period, Muhammad makes reference to the Jews as being part of his "confederates" (ahzab) in spite of the fact that they do not fully believe in his revelations.

---

[711] Ginzberg, *Legends of the Jews*, Vol. 1, pp. 209-217.
[712] Qur'an 6:84-86.
[713] Qur'an 6:89.

> "Those to whom we have given the Book rejoice at what hath been revealed unto thee: but there are among the clans (ahzab: confederates) those who reject a part thereof. Say: "I am commanded to worship Allah, and not to join partners with Him."[714]

Yusuf Ali interprets this to mean merely that some will accept and some will reject. He sees nothing of a reference to the allies to Muhammad. Ibn Kathir, however, recognizes that this refers to "Jews and Christians" though he does not see a connection to Medina.[715] In my opinion, this is a reference to the confederates that Muhammad had become allied with as he began to make his move to Medina. He recognized that some of them were not in full agreement with his revelations. But it seems he thought that such differences were not significant. At the very least, they could "do their religion" even as he did his in the context of a wider alliance. It was a false hope.

---

[714] Qur'an 13:36.
[715] Ibn Kathir, *Tafsir*, Vol. 5, p. 295.

Timeline 622-635

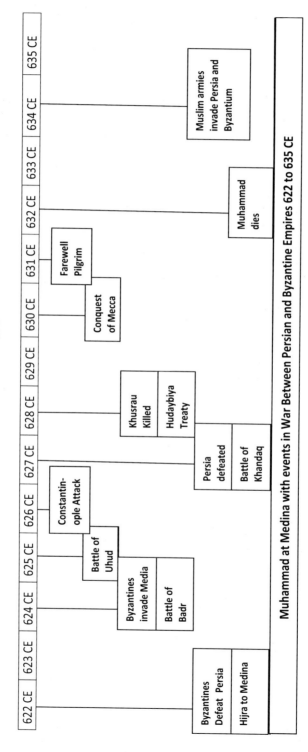

| 622 CE | 623 CE | 624 CE | 625 CE | 626 CE | 627 CE | 628 CE | 629 CE | 630 CE | 631 CE | 632 CE | 633 CE | 634 CE | 635 CE |

Byzantines Defeat Persia

Hijra to Medina

Byzantines invade Media

Battle of Badr

Battle of Uhud

Constantin-ople Attack

Persia defeated

Battle of Khandaq

Khusrau Killed

Hudaybiya Treaty

Conquest of Mecca

Farewell Pilgrim

Muhammad dies

Muslim armies invade Persia and Byzantium

Muhammad at Medina with events in War Between Persian and Byzantine Empires 622 to 635 CE

CHAPTER 6

THE HIJRA: IMMIGRATION
TO YATHRIB (MEDINA)

Why was the Hijra such a pivotal moment in the history of Islam? There is no intimation of such a planned movement in the late Meccan chapters of the Qur'an. As we shall see, the Qur'an's Medinan chapters only refer to it in an oblique way. Yet it becomes the start of the Muslim calendar and also marks major changes in the content and direction of the Qur'an. Simply put, according to the later Muslim writings, the Hijra marks the move of Islam from a purely prophetic religion to a political religion. Nearly all the Hadith literature, which really defines what Islam is, ostensibly emerged during the Medinan period. The Prophet moves from preaching his austere vision of absolute monotheism to insisting upon its supremacy by means of political and military coercion. One key question needs to be answered before moving on to a description of the events of the Hijra; why Yathrib (Medina)?

We have noted in the previous chapter the many stories of Muhammad's treaties and confederacies with tribes in Medina. The so-called "Constitution of Medina" that even the minimalist Patricia Crone regards as solidly historical indicates that Muhammad was seeking a new political base for his religion. There is clearly another reason for the choice of Medina; its large population of monotheistic Jews. Yathrib had been established primarily by Jewish refugees from the diasporas of Roman persecution in the first and second centuries CE. Muhammad must have seen this Jewish center as a natural place for him to find allies to build his political base. Muhammad had at least two Jewish aunts from this city. At this stage, Muhammad did not perceive his religion as being any different from the religion of the Jews (and indeed, theologically speaking there was and is very little difference). There are no strong negative comments about the Jews in any of the Meccan chapters of the Qur'an. Yathrib must have seemed the ideal place to set up the religio-political-military confederation that the Jewish oral traditions of kings, prophets, and holy wars had encouraged in the Prophet's mind.

Because we have no chapters of the Qur'an occurring immediately around the time of the Hijra, we shall reverse order in this chapter and begin with the Muslim historical writings about it. Officially, "the Hijra" dates from Muhammad's own flight to Yathrib, which I will hereafter refer to as "Medina" (he had sent some of his followers on beforehand), and took place in CE 622. There are many accounts and traditions concerning Muhammad's flight from Mecca to Medina. The accounts are an admixture of what has probably historic content and what are embellishments designed to reinforce the heroic view of the Prophet and his companions.

There are two incidents mentioned in Ibn Ishaq that need to be recounted. The first is the threat against Muhammad by the Quraysh.

> "Thereupon Abu Jahl said that he had a plan which had not been suggested hitherto, namely that each clan should provide a young, powerful, well-born, aristocratic warrior; that each of these should be provided with a sharp sword; then that each of them should strike a blow at him and kill him. Thus they would be relieved of him, and responsibility for his blood would lie upon all clans . . . Having come to a decision the people dispersed."

Muhammad was able to learn of the attack ahead of time and placed Ali in his bed, wrapped in his mantel. By the time, the Quraysh had learned of their mistake, Muhammad was safely on his way with Abu Bakr. [716] These kinds of substitutionary stories are typical of the heroic literature of this time (even the Qur'an tells a substitutionary tale of someone else being crucified in the place of Christ) and the substitution of Ali for Muhammad is entirely fictitious. Even the plan for representative members of the tribes to kill him simultaneously is a well-know typological form in heroic literature of this period. The level of resistance to his message that is recorded in the Qur'an seems to indicate that the danger was, however, real.

The second incident is the account of Muhammad's departure. There is a citation in Ibn Ishaq[717] as well as a Hadith detailed by Aisha that refers to

---

[716]   Ibn Ishaq. *The Life of Muhammad*: a translation of Ishaq's Sirut Rasul Allah with Introduction and notes by A. Guillaume. New York, NY: Oxford UniversityPress, 1980, pp. 222-223.

[717]   Ibn Ishaq, p. 223.

Muhammad's flight.[718] According to these accounts, Muhammad had been visiting Abu Bakr's house on a daily basis in the mornings or evenings while he awaited Allah's permission to migrate. One day, he came in the middle of the day with some urgency. "As soon as he saw him Abu Bakr realized that something had happened to bring him at this hour . . ."[719] "The Prophet said, 'I feel that I have been granted the permission for migration.' Abu Bakr said, 'I will accompany you O Allah's Apostle! . . . I have two she-camels I have prepared specifically for migration.'"[720]

According to Ibn Kathir, Abu Bakr was instrumental in protecting Muhammad on the journey. They had to hide out in a cave for three days. There are several "miracles" mentioned concerning Muhammad's flight. It is said that God provided a spider whose web caused the Quraysh not to search within. It is also said that two doves with eggs also aided in the process of discouraging the pursuers.[721] These are hagiographic inventions, but certainly, Muhammad had lost the protection of the tribes in Mecca and was vulnerable on his own. Stories of the pursuit of the Quraysh are probably also embellishments of a later age. It may well be that the Meccans were happy to be rid of the contentious Prophet, and it is clear that it was his own free choice to go. This was not a banishment but a "migration."

Muhammad arrived safely in Medina. "By the preceding *isnad* . . . Muhammad b. Ishaq told me that the apostle came to Medina on Monday at high noon on the 12th of Rabi'u'l-awwal. The apostle on that day was fifty three years of age, that being thirteen years after God had called him."[722] The first one to spot the appearance of Muhammad on this day was a Jew who had been on the lookout from the roof of his house.[723] Even though accounts of Muhammad's arrival vary, it does appear as if the inhabitants of Medina were eagerly expecting his arrival.[724] To have a Jew to be the first to spot him is strange, and I think potentially a true detail. Perhaps it is a hint of an initial hope on the part of the Prophet for Jewish support.

Following Muhammad's successful migration to Medina, the remainder of the believers continued to come from Mecca. "The emigrants followed one

---

[718] Al-Bukhari, Vol III, pp. 196-197.

[719] Ibn Ishaq, p. 223.

[720] Al-Bukhari, Vol III, p. 197.

[721] Ibn Kathir, Vol II, pp. 154-55.

[722] Ibn Ishaq, p. 281.

[723] Julius Wellhausen, and A. J. Wensinck, *Muhammad and the Jews of Medina*. Berlin: W. H. Behn, 1982., p. 6. Ibn Kathir, Tafsir, Vol II, p. 177.

[724] Julius Wellhausen, p. 39.

another to join the apostle, and none was left in Mecca but those who had apostatized or been detained . . . their houses in Mecca were locked up when they immigrated, leaving no inhabitant."[725] This would seem to indicate that at least some believers were left behind in Mecca. As Muhammad moved into political strategies, having spies in Mecca was helpful.

Medina: City of the Prophet

What kind of city was Medina? How did Muhammad regard it? What was Muhammad entering into? Muhammad said, "The Prophet Abraham made Mecca a sanctuary, and asked for Allah's blessing in it. I made Medina a sanctuary as Abraham made Mecca a sanctuary and I asked for Allah's blessing in its measures . . ."[726] Another Hadith states, "Whenever the Prophet returned from a journey and observed the walls of Medina, he would make his mount go fast, and if he was on an animal (i.e., a horse), he would make it gallop because of his love for Medina."[727] Medina, as we have noted, was described "like an oasis created by wadis with palm groves, orchards and gardens."[728]

"Medina was a Jewish settlement . . . Then after the bursting of the dam (in Yemen), displaced Arab groups moved north and settled in Medina . . . The roles were reversed and the Arabs became the "patrons" of the Jews . . ."[729] At the time of the Hijra, the Banu Qaylah maintained control of Medina. The Banu Qaylah was composed of two different groups: the Banu al-Aws and the Banu al-Khazraj.[730] "The Khazraj were divided into five main clans: Banu Awf, Banu al-Harith, Banu Saida, Banu Jusham, and Banu al-Najjir . . . the Aws were grouped in the following clans: Amr ibn Awf in Quba, Aws Allah to the north of al-Nadir, and Qurayzah and al-Nabit east of the town"[731] (see the diagram on the following page). The al-Aws and Khazraj were "polytheists worshipping idols knowing nothing about paradise and hell . . ."[732] There were three main types of idols used among these groups: "clan idols worshipped by the whole clan and probably used in the public cult . . . idols held by each

---

[725] Ibn Ishaq, p. 230.
[726] Al-Bukhari, Vol III, p. 192-193.
[727] Al-Bukhari, Vol. III, p. 61.
[728] Wellhausen, p. 8.
[729] Wellhausen, p. 24-25.
[730] Wellhausen, p. 24.
[731] Wellhausen, p. 38.
[732] Ibn Ishaq, p. 253.

nobleman of the Aws and the Khazraj . . . lesser idols of the domestic family cult which were presumably part of every household in Medina . . ."[733]

Please note the chart of tribal allegiances below:

Tribal Structure of Medina at the Time of the Prophet, CE 622

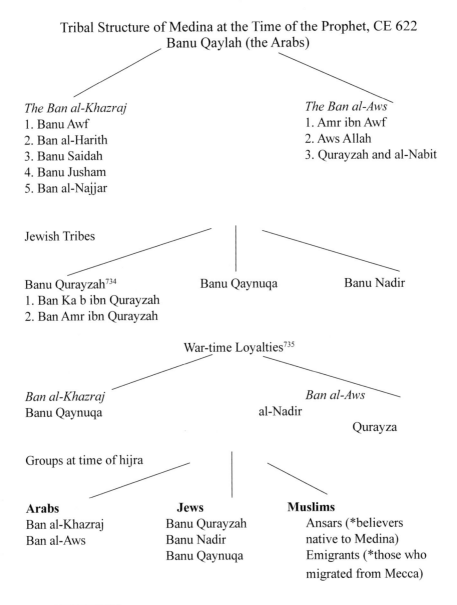

Banu Qaylah (the Arabs)

The Ban al-Khazraj
1. Banu Awf
2. Ban al-Harith
3. Banu Saidah
4. Banu Jusham
5. Ban al-Najjar

The Ban al-Aws
1. Amr ibn Awf
2. Aws Allah
3. Qurayzah and al-Nabit

Jewish Tribes

Banu Qurayzah[734]
1. Ban Ka b ibn Qurayzah
2. Ban Amr ibn Qurayzah

Banu Qaynuqa

Banu Nadir

War-time Loyalties[735]

Ban al-Khazraj
Banu Qaynuqa

Ban al-Aws
al-Nadir
Qurayza

Groups at time of hijra

Arabs
Ban al-Khazraj
Ban al-Aws

Jews
Banu Qurayzah
Banu Nadir
Banu Qaynuqa

Muslims
Ansars (*believers native to Medina)
Emigrants (*those who migrated from Mecca)

---

733 Michael Lecker, *Idol Worship in Pre-Islamic Medina (Yathrib). Le Museon* 106 Louvain-la-Neuve, 1993, p. 342.

734 Lecker, p. 32.

735 Ibn Ishaq, p. 253.

Jews were the second major population group in Medina at the time of the hijra. "Though thirteen Jewish tribes are mentioned at this period, the Prophet in his day apparently took direct political action only against three."[736] The three main Jewish tribes are the Banu Qaynuqa, Banu Qurayza, and the Banu Nadir. Although the Jews were no longer the primary political power in Medina, they were a formidable force due to their large numbers and economic prowess.[737] The Jews were the owners of both weapons and house fortresses in Medina.[738] The large number of weapons owned by the Jews is confirmed by the stories of the spoils of the Nadir and Qurayza, which are described in detail.[739] While the Al-Nadir and the Qurayza were fortified, they were also farmers who were able to live off the products of their lands.[740] The Qaynuqa were not as closely associated with the Qurayza and the al-Nadir and were at times viewed as a separate entity from the larger Jewish clans.[741] The Qaynuqa were the owners of two fortresses ideally located next to their market, which obtained notice from Muhammad's immigrants.[742] The Hadith notes the following: "On our arrival in Medina, I asked whether there was a market of trading. Somebody said, 'There is the market of the Qainuqa.'"[743] The Prophet's lands were close to the market of the Qaynuqa.[744] In addition to their market, the Qaynuqa were also noted for making their living as goldsmiths.[745]

Relations in Medina were far from harmonious among the various groups at the time of the arrival of the Prophet. Tensions existed among the al-Aws

---

[736] R. B. Serjeant, The Sunnah Jami'ah, pacts with the Yathrib Jews, and the Tahrim of Yathrib: analysis and translation of the documents comprised in the so-called "Constitution of Medina" in *The Life of Muhammad* by Uri Rubin. Brookfield, VT: Ashgate, 1998, p. 3.

[737] Wellhausen, p. 28.

[738] Michael Lecker, Waqidi's account on the status of the Jews of Medina: a study of the combined reports. *Journal of Near Eastern Studies* 54. Chicago, 1995, p. 18.

[739] Michael Lecker, *Muslims, Jews and Pagans: Studies on Early Islamic Medina.* Leiden, New York: E. J. Brill, 1995, p. 10.

[740] Wellhausen, p. 27.

[741] Wellhausen, p. 32.

[742] Michael Lecker, *On the Markets of Medina (Yathrib) in Pre-Islamic,* p. 139.

[743] Al-Bukhari, Vol III, p. 186.

[744] Michael Lecker, On the Markets of Medina (Yathrib) in pre-Islamic and early Islamic times. *Jerusalem Studies in Arabic and Islam* 8. Jerusalem, 1986, p. 139.

[745] Wellhausen, pp. 27-28.

and the al-Khazraj. There was a minor war prior to the hijra,[746] which Ibn Ishaq describes as follows:

> When there was war between Aus and Khazraj the B. Qaynuqa went out with Khazraj, and al-Nadir and Qurayza with Aus, each side helping his allies against his own brethren so that they shed each other's blood, while the Torah was in their hands by which they knew what was allowed and what was forbidden them.[747]

This quote reflects the polemic viewpoint held that the Jews were often acting against the knowledge that was revealed to them even prior to their interaction with the Muslims. The Jews were faithlessly fighting against other monotheists in these wars. The message of this polemic seems to be that the Jews failed because of their disunity, and the Muslims would win because of their superior unity. Muslim commentators were forever finding fault with everything the Jews did so, while these stories may be made up, they do indicate the level of hostility that was felt toward the Jews. In spite of the polemic taint, it seems clear the Jews were an active part of some of the existing conflicts in Medina. These conflicts also reached closer to home within the three main Jewish tribes. Watt states the following: "there was little unity among the Jews of Yathrib. In their political relationships they behaved in much the same way as Arab clans and smaller groups."[748]

Muhammad: His Message and His Mission

With all the various divisions and tensions within Medina, Muhammad's task of settling his followers and establishing a community was a tremendous challenge. He must have been aware of the divisions among the various groups in Medina, but he maintained a clear vision of a united Medina with the ultimate purpose of the conquest of Mecca. His vision was birthed into a document referred to as the Constitution of Medina. Muhammad's motivation for writing the constitution centers on his desire to use politics to bring peace to the internal conflicts in Medina. His hope in doing this was to be able to

---

[746] Wellhausen, p. 32.
[747] Ibn Ishaq, p. 253.
[748] Watt, W. Montgomery. *Muhammad at Medina*. Oxford, Clarendon Press 1977, 1956, p. 195.

strengthen the Medinans against outside threats and to prepare for his war for the conquest of Mecca.[749]

There are several differences concerning the exact date of the constitution. Ibn Ishaq and al-Waqidi both date the constitution as occurring not immediately after the hijra, but before the Battle of Badr.[750] Others have placed the constitution in the middle of the year AH 2 or 623 CE.[751] The writing of the document can be seen as an attempt to develop cooperation between the Muhajirun (those believers who came from Mecca to Medina) and the Ansar (believers who originated in Medina) that occurred five to eight months after the arrival of the Prophet and to include in this other groups not actually believers in Muhammad.[752] The constitution was a testimony of Muhammad's growing authority as well as his initial limitations and need for outside support.

In spite of the differences in the exact dating of the constitution, it is clear that one of the ways in which Muhammad was able to use the constitution to unite the community is through the creation of a new concept of *ummah*. Muhammad was able to breathe new life into a concept that had been referred to as a religious community, prior to the time of Islam. "It is the community under the protection of Allah. He is the ruler, and Muhammad is his deputy. The faith is the bond, and the believers are the bearers of this unity. They have the main obligations and rights in the community."[753] This new concept of a united *ummah* of believers helped to weaken the role of the clans in military and political matters.[754] The *ummah*, as led by Muhammad, became the deciding factor and force of action.

Although some of the functions formerly held by the individual clans were now attributed to the *ummah*, Muhammad incorporated the structure of the clans into his new community of believers. "By keeping the believers within the organization of their clans, they became not only the bond which united the clans, but also the leaven which in time was to influence the rest of them. In the beginning the *ummah* was a rather loose heterogeneous political entity; but since the Muslims were its soul, this entity naturally tended to create a unity of the faith and was strengthened on account of this."[755]

---

[749]   Wellhausen, pp. 68, 134.
[750]   Wellhausen, p. 134.
[751]   Wellhausen, pp. 48, 71.
[752]   Gil, Moshe. "The Constitution of Medina: a Reconsideration" in *Israel Oriental Studies*, Volume IV. Tel Aviv University. Jerusalem, Israel: Central Press, 1974, p. 49.
[753]   Wellhausen, p. 129.
[754]   Gil, Moshe, p. 53.
[755]   Wellhausen, pp. 130-131.

Though the notion of *ummah* was a beginning point for uniting the clans, further changes were necessary to bring lasting change and peace to the community. There were many clauses written into the constitution for this very purpose. One of these clauses is the following: "A believer shall not slay a believer for the sake of an unbeliever, nor shall he aid an unbeliever against a believer . . . Believers are friends one to the other to the exclusion of outsiders."[756] In regards to this clause, " . . . the purpose . . . was to prevent the renewal of old intertribal intrigues, based on alliances with foreign elements."[757] What exactly is a "believer" at this point is not very clearly defined. It seems to include Jews and even pagans allied to the Prophet. There were also clauses written to help against internal strife among the clans. An example of one of these clauses is the following: "If any dispute or controversy likely to cause trouble should arise it must be referred to God and to Muhammad the apostle of God."[758] This clause served to encourage the clans to give up their rights to vengeance and learn to settle their differences peacefully. If the internal peace was broken it became the duty of the community, rather than an individual, to take action against the offender. In the more serious cases of bloodshed, the criminal could be handed over to the one who had the right to revenge, who could then claim blood money.[759] The clans became responsible for the payment of the blood money and ransoming of captives when a community purse was not available for use.[760] The community became responsible for dealing with the redemption of prisoners. "The usual ransom (fida) for a captive was a hundred camels, whereas the blood-money (diya) was a hundred she-camels."[761] All of these factors aided in bringing tribes out of their chaos and strife into more peaceful relations with one another.

There are three areas of controversy in regards to the Constitution of Medina. The first is the debate as to what groups were included in the constitution, and in particular if the Jews were part of the agreement. The strongest arguments for the fact the Jews were a part of the constitution is Muslim tradition. Muslim tradition accuses the Qaynuqa, Nadir, and Qurayza of breaking the constitution. "If the three Jewish clans had not been part of

---

[756]   Ibn Ishaq, p. 232.
[757]   Gil, Moshe, pp. 52-53.
[758]   Ibn Ishaq, p. 233.
[759]   Wellhausen, p. 132.
[760]   Wellhausen, p. 131.
[761]   Gil Moshe, p. 53.

this contract, tradition would not have needed to defend Muhammad's later actions against these three clans with such far-fetched arguments." These three groups comprised such a significant portion of the population that it would have been ridiculous if he had excluded them from it.[762] The second chapter of the Qur'an criticizes the Jews for their fighting with each other rather than unifying under the Prophet's banner. One of the arguments used for the idea of the Jews not being included in the constitution is the lack of mention of the three main Jewish tribes by name. Because the Banu Nadir and Banu Qurayza lived among the Aws and Khazraj, they could have been included with those groups. Only the weaker Jewish clans were mentioned by their names.[763] The term "believer" as mentioned above was probably very generic and unspecific. The evidence is more in favor of the Jews being a part of the constitution than being excluded from it. Clearly, Muhammad would have wanted all monotheists united in the struggle to come so it seems logical that the Jews were part of the initial Constitution of Medina. Crone considers this so counterintuitive to later anti-Jewish sentiment in the traditions that she is convinced that this constitution must be a historical reality.

The Jews are undoubtedly treated differently than the Arabs within the constitution. They were made a part of the constitution only as secondary parties who were subject to their Arab superiors.[764] This secondary status was due to Muhammad's desire to remove the Arab clans from their associations with their Jewish neighbors and allies. "The Prophet only refers to them (Jews) in as far as they are allies of the Islamized clans." The constitution aided in reducing their political and economic independence.[765] "They were prohibited to feud with the believers; they had to refer matters to Muhammad, assist against those who attacked Yathrib, and contribute financially to those wars of the believers in which they were not obliged to support actively. The Jews did not lose the right to feud with external enemies completely but, except in minor affairs, they could not make war without the permission of Muhammad."[766]

The second area of controversy in regard to the Constitution of Medina is the unity of the constitution—whether it is composed of several documents or whether it is one cohesive document. R. B. Serjeant maintains the

---

[762]   Wellhausen, p. 69.
[763]   Moshe Gil, p. 61.
[764]   R. B. Serjeant, p. 165.
[765]   Moshe Gil, pp. 64-65.
[766]   Wellhausen, p. 133.

viewpoint that the Constitution of Medina is composed of eight separate documents.[767] This viewpoint may come from the various representations of the "Constitution" in periods of Islamic tradition after Muhammad's death. Moshe Gil and Julius Wellhausen are two proponents of the contrasting viewpoint that the constitution is one document. This viewpoint is "based upon a strong connection between its elements. This becomes clear when the contents are analyzed. The various short phrases and paragraphs concentrate on a limited number of ideas, representing the immediate political aims of the Prophet." The truth of this statement is reflected in the following extraction:

> "No separate peace shall be made when believers are fighting in the way of God. Conditions must be fair and equitable to all. In every foray a rider must take another behind him. The believers must avenge the blood of one another shed in the way of God. The God-fearing believers enjoy the best and most upright guidance. No polytheist shall take the property or person of Quraysh under his protection nor shall he intervene against a believer."[768]

Another argument for the unity of the constitution is the Hadith literature. The Hadith were classified according to legal needs; therefore, it is probable that parts of the document would be divided up and located in different sections of the Hadith according to legal subject area. "Rather than separate agreements, they are vestiges and echoes of one and the same document. They have that fragmentary and often deteriorated form in which components of the document, whose original text was hidden during several generations, were preserved in oral tradition."[769] It seems that the evidence for the constitution being one document is stronger.

The third area of controversy is the historicity of the Constitution of Medina. The controversy centers around who was included in the constitution as well as whether the document itself ever existed. The controversy arises from Arab historians who have omitted the constitution and replaced it with a censored content under another name. The most compelling reason for the omission is that Muhammad included Jews and polytheists as partners with

---

[767]   R. B. Serjeant, p. 159.
[768]   Ibn Ishaq, p. 232 including the previous quote.
[769]   Moshe Gil, pp. 44-45, 48.

the believers.[770] One example of the omission is Ibn Kathir's account. He states Muhammad "established a pact between the emigrants and helpers in the house of Anas b. Malik," which makes no mention of the major Jewish tribes. He also mentions "Whatever Jews follow us shall receive help and equality," but this is in reference to a different group separate from the Jewish tribes.[771]

There are several arguments that explain the omission of the constitution from many Muslim accounts and which speak for the validity of the document. Historians record statements from Muhammad that are practically quotes from the constitution as late as the conquest of Mecca. As we have seen, there is some recognized documentation of the constitution within Muslim sources. There is an account by Al Waqidi that includes elements of the constitution in a speech by Muhammad. However, other Muslim historians do not record this account. There are Hadiths by Bukhari and Muslim that contain fragments of the constitution.[772] The strongest argument for the constitution is that "no true Muslim writing under the Umayyads or the Abbasids would have included non-Muslims in the *ummah*; no one would have dwelt to such an extent on the hate for the Quraysh as the true enemies of God; and no one would have fabricated an ordinance in which the Prophet made so little direct use of his divine authority.[773] They would not have recorded it if it weren't true. I believe the constitution was a historical document that was a significant factor in establishing intertribal peace in Medina as well as furthering the political goals of the Muslim community.

Another important element in establishing the Muslims in Medina was Muhammad's message. It was not enough to establish peace; Muhammad also needed to establish credibility and a pattern of life that distinguished his believers. One of the ways he sought to do this was through his teaching, at least according to traditions. In his first sermon at Medina, he emphasized cultivating a relationship with Allah and fearing Him. He also made references to "oppose his enemies and strive energetically for God," "strive for what comes after death."[774] In his second sermon, he attempted to address issues relevant to the community and the struggle between those who believed

---

[770] Wellhausen, p. 63.
[771] Ibn Kathir. Vol II, pp. 212-213.
[772] Wellhausen, p. 66-67.
[773] Wellhausen, p. 135.
[774] Ibn Kathir. Tafsir, Vol II, p. 198.

and those who were not of the faith. "He whom God guides none can lead astray; and whom He leads astray none can guide . . . The finest speech is the book of God. He to whom God has made it seem glorious and made him enter Islam after unbelief, who has chosen it above all other speech of men, doth prosper . . . Verily God is angry when His covenant is broken."[775] These sermons are pious inventions of a later age and provide a conception of Islam only present at a later time, but may reflect needs that would have been evident in the nascent Muslim community.

The early historians and Hadiths tell only a little about Muhammad's relations with the Jews during his first year in Medina. There are some generalized stories of Jews covering up what their books said, of Muhammad forbidding his followers to read or handle Jewish books, and of debates between Jews and the Prophet's followers. None of these is localized to this first year of interaction. In my opinion, this first year was a period of intense conflict on an intellectual level with the Jewish tribes followed by an increasing sense on the part of the Prophet that the Jews, in general, would reject him as a Prophet. It could not possibly have been any other way. The words of the Qur'an, now clearly labeled as the very speech of God, were an absolute hodgepodge of distorted and thoroughly inaccurate and unhistorical gibberish from a Jewish perspective. Jews are a profoundly textual people whose sense of history is legendary. Thirty percent of the Qur'an up to this point is made up of borrowed Jewish oral traditions, mixed up in ways that must have both amused and outraged the Jews. It is clear when we come to chapter 2 of the Qur'an dated as the first surah of the Medinan period that Muhammad has decided to make a final and permanent break with the Jews.

A key element in this break was Muhammad's effort to establish practices to distinguish his emerging community of believers from the Jews. Some of his pronouncements included saying prayer five times a day, giving alms to the poor, and taxes to the Muslim state.[776] Ibn Ishaq gives an account of this as follows:

"When the apostle was firmly settled in Medina and his brethren the emigrants were gathered to him and the affairs of the helpers were arranged Islam became firmly established. Prayer

---

[775] Ibn Ishaq, p. 231.
[776] Ibn Kathir. *Al-Sira*, Vol I, pp. 228-229.

was instituted, the alms tax and fasting were prescribed, and Islam took up its abode with them . . . When the apostle first came, the people gathered to him for prayer at the appointed times without being summoned. At first, the apostle thought of using a trumpet like that of the Jews who used it to summon to prayer. Afterward he disliked the idea and ordered a clapper to be made, so it was duly fashioned to be beaten when the Muslims should pray.[777]

The clapper was probably only used for a short period of time. Ishaq records the account of the call to prayer in which Abdullah b. Zayd b. Tha'laba b. 'Abdu Rabbini and Umar had the same dream, instructing them about how to call people to prayer. In the dream, they were provided with the words to say, which are still used today. This is hagiographical myth. Following this revelation, Bilal was commissioned to give the first call to prayer.[778] He made the pronouncement from the rooftop of al-Nuwar's house, the mother of Zayd ibn Thabit, until the completion of the first mosque.[779] More important than the form for the call to prayer, of course, was the direction of prayer. The direction of the *qiblah* had been toward Jerusalem.[780] "People used to pray toward Jerusalem when the Prophet came to Medina, and for eighteen months after his emigration."[781] Muhammad during this period changes that direction from Jerusalem to Mecca in what must have been seen as a direct rejection of Jewish practices that Muhammad had previously followed. This is discussed at length in chapter 2 of the Qur'an, so we will return to that later.

Although Muhammad strove to distinguish his believers from the Jews, Judaism still influenced many of the practices that were incorporated into early Islam. For example, the Prophet modeled the times of prayer after the Jews. The Qur'an states in 2:238, "Guard strictly Your (habit) of prayers, especially the middle prayer; and stand before Allah in a devout (frame of mind)."[782] The middle prayer occurred during the midday service. The

---

[777] Ibn Ishaq, p. 235.
[778] Ibn Ishaq, p. 236.
[779] Wellhausen, p. 86.
[780] Wellhausen, pp. 95-96.
[781] Al-Tabari, Vol VII, McDonald, p. 69.
[782] Ali, Yusuf, *The Meaning of the Holy Qur'an*, Beltsville, MD: Amana. Publications, 1997, p. 98.

morning, noon, and evening prayers that were held followed closely the Jewish prayers of *shaharit, minhah,* and *marib.*[783] Another practice that was influenced was that of the Friday prayer. "In the year before the Hijrah, when Mus'ab b. 'Umayr was acting as Muhammad's emissary in Medina, he asked permission to hold a meeting of the believers, and was told he might do so provided he observed the day on which the Jews prepared for the Sabbath (i.e., Friday, the *paraskeue* or preparation). Thus the Friday worship, which became a distinctive feature of Islam, was somehow connected with Judaism. Muhammad himself does not seem to have observed it until his first Friday in Medina." The Friday service had aspects that corresponded with the Sabbath, including prohibition against fasting, wearing of one's best clothes, use of perfumes, and the celebratory incorporation of eating and drinking.[784]

The final practice that was influenced by Judaism is the feast of Ashura. The feast of Ashura is observed on the tenth of the Jewish month *Tishri.*[785] The fasting occurred from one evening until the next.[786] This fast was observed in order to celebrate the day in which God drowned Pharaoh's armies thereby saving Moses and the Israelites. Muhammad noticed the Jewish celebrations of this day and inquired about why they celebrated. When he heard the answer, he felt the Muslims had more claim to Moses than the Jews did, so he fasted on that day and ordered his followers to do the same.[787] "The Prophet observed the fast on the tenth of Muharram (Ashura) and ordered (Muslims) to fast on that day."[788] The direct inclusion of a Jewish festival into the Muslim community shows clearly the degree of influence of Judaism on Islam. It is interesting to note that over the centuries this fast has gradually faded from Muslim practice perhaps as Islam has grown distant from its Jewish roots over time.[789]

Rejection of the Prophet

Muhammad's prophethood was thoroughly rejected by the Jews of Medina, and this rejection is the only sensible way to explain the pervasively

---

[783]   Wellhausen, p. 77.
[784]   Wellhausen, pp. 81-82.
[785]   Watt, W. Montgomery, 1977, p. 199.
[786]   Wellhausen, p. 88.
[787]   Al-Tabari, Vol VII, McDonald, p. 26. and Bukhari, Vol III, p. 124.
[788]   Al-Bukhari, Vol III, p. 65.
[789]   A similar trend can be seen in the Passover seder and the Lord's supper in Christianity.

negative and violent attitude toward Jews expressed in the Medinan chapters of the Qur'an. The difference between Meccan and Medinan chapters of the Qur'an at this point could not be clearer.

There was another group that was less than receptive to his new religion. "In Medina, however, a party arose who, although ostensibly converted to Islam, actually could be considered neither among Muhammad's disciples nor among those who had been converted."[790] This group is known as "munafiqun" or hypocrites. There are many Medinan passages referring to these hypocrites. Ibn Kathir's references 9:74 in regards to the Aws hypocrites who apostatized after Tabuk and 3:86 in regards to their apostasy. He also notes that 9:61 and 33:12 were revealed about "those hypocrites from Aws and Khazraj who joined the Jews antagonistic to Islam."[791] Ishaq describes the Aws and Khazraj as follows:

> "hypocrites, clinging to the polytheism of their fathers denying the resurrection; yet when Islam appeared and their people flocked to it they were compelled to pretend to accept it to save their lives. But in secret they were hypocrites whose inclination was toward the Jews because they considered the apostle a liar and strove against Islam."[792]

Clearly, the Jewish arguments against the Prophet and his revelations went home with some. There are also references to the Jews who were considered to be part of the group of hypocrites. Ibn Kathir provides names of nine rabbis who hypocritically adhered to Islam. These Jews were said to have gone to the mosque to listen to the Muslims only to ridicule what they had heard afterward.[793] Ibn Kathir records that a fight happened at the Prophet's mosque, centering on some of the hypocrites who were forcibly expelled.[794] The Muslims were understandably frustrated with this group for their lack of clear alliance with them or against them. This story strikes me as historical for we could assume just such activities of the Jews in the early days of the Prophet's residence in Medina. That they would go to listen to his sermons

---

[790]   Wellhausen, p. 39
[791]   Ibn Kathir, *Tafsir*, Vol II, p. 231.
[792]   Ibn Ishaq, p. 239.
[793]   Wellhausen, p. 41
[794]   Ibn Kathir, *Tafsir*, Vol II, p. 232.

to figure out where he stood and also listen to the recitations of the Qur'an makes absolute sense given the pact that they had already engaged with him in. They may have even gone as Jews, not false converts, at a time when Muhammad perhaps was courting them. It would be an easy thing to label them as hypocrites and false converts at a later time. Clearly, any sort of coercive violence in the name of religion will automatically produce "hypocrites."

In the minds of Muslim historians, it should have been natural for the Jews to accept Muhammad and his teachings. They saw Muhammad's teachings as a continuation of the previous revelations made to the Jews. Therefore, the Jews should have recognized that Muhammad was continuing their revelation.[795] Only a handful of Jews accepted Islam. Abd Allah b. Salam was the only significant one of the Jews said to have converted. He was a Jewish leader who converted to Islam just after Muhammad's arrival in Medina.[796] In spite of the conversion of this leader, it remains true that "Islam made few inroads on the Jewish population in Medina."[797]

Initially, there was a positive relationship with the Jews. "Ibn Ishaq shows us that the Jews actually permitted Muhammad to participate in the activities of their community during the first few months after his arrival in Medina. The scenario presented by Ibn Ishaq shows Muhammad pass sentence on a Jewish couple, raise the value of the blood price of the B. Qurayza to equal that of the B. Nadir and become involved in religious arguments with them . . . Unfortunately, the activity led to much religious conflict . . . and . . . Jewish rejection of Muhammad."[798]

There are different accounts of the rejection of Muhammad by individual Jews. "Huyayy b. Akhtab, at that time the leader of the Jews . . . sat and listened to the messenger . . . (he) insisted no, by God, I will never obey you!" His daughter Safiyya heard them speak against Muhammad. She was later forcibly married to Muhammad after the Battle of Khaybar when her father was killed.[799] The rejection by the rabbis is described in both Ibn Ishaq and Ibn Kathir. Ibn Kathir states, "All these men were rabbis and men of evil intent and full of antagonism toward Muhammad . . . There were those who

---

[795] Wellhausen, p. 43.
[796] Ibn Ishaq, pp. 240-241 and Ibn Kathir, Vol II, p. 182.
[797] Wellhausen, p. 43.
[798] Ibn Ishaq and al-Waqidi, p. 171.
[799] Ibn Kathir, *Tafsir*, Vol II, p. 197.

asked Muhammad many questions in their desire to confuse and to express their obstinacy and disbelief."[800] Although told from the Muslim perspective, these stories ring of historical truth. We only get to hear the Muslim side of the argument, but it is easy to reconstruct the Jewish issues with Muhammad as we consider the distorted versions of Jewish traditions, which his Qur'an presents. This conflict was unavoidable.

According to Ishaq, there were three questions that were asked of Muhammad that the Jews provided answers to. This story has been considered earlier and it is typical of the way these typological confrontations get moved around in the chronology. However, on the fourth question the Jews differed significantly enough that they used it as an excuse not to follow Muhammad. The fourth question was about Gabriel, whom they saw as an enemy "who comes only with violence and the shedding of blood."[801] This argument is false, for the Jews had no sure enmity to the biblical angelic figure of Gabriel. Sura 2:97-98 addresses this controversy: "Say: Whoever is an enemy to Gabriel—for he brings down the (revelation) to thy heart by Allah's will, a confirmation of what went before and guidance and glad tidings for those who believe—Whoever is an enemy to Allah and His angels and prophets, to Gabriel and Michael—Lo! Allah is an enemy to those who reject faith."[802] This supposed event is an exegetical reading back into the text. The context of this particular statement is quite opaque, but reflects not a Jewish rejection of Gabriel, but a rejection that Muhammad's revelations had come down from Gabriel. It reflects the attitude of Jews who found Muhammad's teachings unnecessarily hostile and violent as well as highly inaccurate to their Jewish scriptures and traditions.

Another way that the Prophet dealt with the rejection of the Jews was his formulation of a new myth, the development of the "religion of Abraham" (*millat Ibrahim*). Close to the time the change of the *qiblah* was made, it was taught that Abraham founded the Ka'bah and the Hajj.[803] Abraham was set before the Muslims as an example. They deemed him the first Muslim. "When it came to a break with the Jews, Abraham had two great advantages: he was in a physical sense the father of the Arabs (according to local traditions we have mentioned earlier) as well as of the Jews; and he lived before the

---

[800] Ibn Kathir. *Tafsir*, Vol II, pp. 226-227, and Ibn Ishaq, p. 239.
[801] Ibn Ishaq, p. 255.
[802] Ali, Yusuf, pp. 43-44.
[803] Wellhausen, p. 95-96.

Torah had been revealed to Moses and the Gospel to Jesus (as the Jews had to admit), and was, therefore, neither a Jew nor a Christian." The concept of Abraham as the first Muslim also helped to aid the believers in feeling distinct from the Jews and the Christians. It also served to give Muhammad new grounds for attacking the Jews and their lack of adherence to the religion of Abraham. [804]

The third notable change occurring in chapter 2 of the Qur'an was the downgrading of the importance of the feast of Ashura in favor of and the implementation of the Ramadan fast. This change occurred in the month of Ramadan AH 2.[805] "There is not the least reason to depart from the consensus of tradition . . . we can conclude that Muhammad established the fast of Ramadan in AH 2 in order to distinguish Islam from Judaism also in ritual matters."[806] The Qur'anic passage regarding this change is sura 2:183-188. Sura 2:183 supports the idea that Muhammad was trying to distinguish Islam—"O ye who believe! Fasting is prescribed to you as it was prescribed to those before you, that ye may (learn) self-restraint." The tafsir states, "*As it was prescribed*: this does not mean that the Muslim fast is like other fasts previously observed, in the number of days, in the time or manner of the fast, or in other incidents; it only means that the principle of self-denial by fasting is not a new one."[807] Yusuf Ali tries to explain this aspect of borrowing through this rationale. Another reason for the establishment of fasting in the month of Ramadan is in 2:185 which states, "Ramadan is the (month) in which was sent down the Qur'an as a guide to mankind, also clear (signs) for guidance and judgment (between right and wrong). So every one of you who is present (at his home) during that month should spend it in fasting . . ."[808] So this change in fasting practices was also tied into the story of the revelation of the Qur'an, clearly to bolster the book against the criticisms of the Jews. Even though Ramadan became the primary Islamic feast, Muhammad did not prohibit others from observing Ashura.[809]

---

[804]   Watt, W. Montgomery, 1977, pp. 205-206.
[805]   Wellhausen, p. 96.
[806]   Wellhausen, pp. 98-99.
[807]   Ali, Yusuf, p. 73.
[808]   Ali, Yusuf, p. 73.
[809]   Al-Bukhari, Vol III, p. 65 and al-Tabari, Vol VII, McDonald, p. 26.

Acceptance of the Prophet

Although Muhammad faced a lot of opposition from the Jews, he had a great deal of support from the Ansar and the emigrants, the remaining composite of Medinan society. The Jews, although they opposed Muhammad, had helped to lay the foundation for his coming. They had prepared the tribes with a sense of expectation concerning the coming Messiah.[810] Although the people readily accepted what Muhammad had to say, there was still a clear distinction between those believers that had come from Mecca and those who were native to Medina. Muhammad was very intentional about uniting the two groups. He made many statements in hopes of drawing the emigrants and the Ansars into a close community.

He spoke very highly of the Ansar referring to them "as an undergarment," "my household and my family."[811] He addresses both groups in 9:100. "The vanguard (of Islam) the first of those who forsook (their homes) and of those who gave them aid, and (also) those who follow them in (all) good deeds—well-pleased is Allah with them, as are they with Him: for them hath He prepared gardens under which rivers flow, to dwell therein forever: that is the supreme felicity." The tafsir states, "The vanguard of Islam—those in the first rank—are those who dare and suffer for the Cause and never flinch. The first historical examples are the *Muhajirs* and the *Ansar*. The *Muhajirs*—those who forsook their homes in Makkah and migrated to Madinah, the Holy Prophet being among the last to leave the post of danger, are mentioned first. Then come the *Ansar*, the helpers, the citizens of Madinah who invited them, welcomed them, and gave them aid, and who formed the pivot of the new Community . . ."[812] His efforts toward uniting the groups were not without result. The tribe that Muhammad stayed with in the process of building the first mosque became Muslims. In addition, "every house of the Ansar accepted Islam except Khatma, Waqif, Wa'il, and Umayya who were the Aus Allah, a clan of Aus who clung to their heathenism."[813]

---

[810]   Watt, W. Montgomery, *Muhammad: Prophet and Statesman,* New York: Oxford University Press, 1980, 1961, p. 89.
[811]   Ibn Kathir. *Tafsir*, Vol II, p. 184.
[812]   Ali, Yusuf, p. 467.
[813]   Ibn Ishaq, p. 230.

The Ansars did not merely convert but, according to tradition, went out of their way to help their Meccan brothers. There was a distinct economic difference between the two groups. "Anas bin Malik said, 'When the emigrants came to Medina, they had nothing whereas the Ansar had land and property."[814] Sura 59:9 details their generosity: "But those who before them, had homes (In Madinah) and had adopted the Faith—show their affection to such as came to them for refuge, and entertain no desire in their hearts for things given to the (latter), but give them preference over themselves, even though poverty was their (own lot) . . ." The tafsir states, "This refers to the *Ansar* (the Helpers) . . . the Hijrah was possible because of their good will and their generous hospitality . . . The most remarkable ties of full brotherhood were established between individual members of one group and the other. Until the Ummah got its own resources,[815] the helpers regularly gave and the Refugees regularly received."[816]

The Muhajirun were able to establish themselves economically by taking one of two approaches. The first approach was to resume their former trades. The second approach was to take part in profitable raids against the Quraysh caravans from Mecca.[817] In the month of Ramadan, Muhammad gives Hamza permission "to interfere with Quraysh caravans."[818] It is important to note that the Muslims took the offensive. There are eight raids noted by Muslim tradition before the Battle of Badr. Only one of those raids was not directed against the Meccan caravans.[819] Raiding of this type was typical of the Arab culture of this time. The increasing attacks served to make tensions worse between Muhammad and the Quraysh. The emigrants were the predominant participants in these earlier raids. Their involvement flowed from a desire to bring in economic provision for the Muhajirun as well as a determination to weaken the Meccans. Below is a listing of some of these early raids according to the Muslim historians.

---

[814] Al-Bukhari, Vol III, p. 481.

[815] Through raiding and warfare.

[816] Ali, Yusuf, p. 59.

[817] Henri. Lammens, "Fatima and the Daughers of Muhammad" in *The Quest for the Historical Muhammad* by Ibn Warraq. Amherst, NY: Prometheus Books, 2000, p. 245.

[818] Ibn Kathir. *Tafsir*, Vol II, p. 224.

[819] Watt, W. Montgomery, 1977, p. 2.

A Working Chronology of the Raids of Muhammad

al-Abwa	Safar, AH 2[820]
Thaniyyat	al-Murra Not dated Ibn Ishaq[821]
Buwat	Rabi al-Awwal, AH 2[822]
al-Ushayra	Jumada l-Akira, AH 2[823]
al-Kharrar	Not dated Ibn Ishaq[824]
Badr al-Ula	Jumada l-Akira, AH 2[825]
Banu Kinana	Rajab AH 2[826]
Nakhl	Rajab AH 2[827]

Events of the Raids

al-Abwa   ⟶   First raid against the city of Waddan. Muhammad made peace with the Banu Damra. No conflict occurred.[828]

Thaniyyat al-Murra ⟶ Led by Ubayda. No conflict occurred. Abu Waqqas shot "the first arrow shot for God's cause after the coming of Islam."[829]

Buwat   ⟶   Hamza was sent with thirty emigrants to the territory of Juhayna. The Quraysh numbered three hundred. A man named Amr al-Juhani was a peacekeeper between the two groups and fighting was avoided.[830]

---

[820] J. M. B. Jones, "The Chronology of the Maghazi: a textual survey" in *Life of Muhammad* by Uri Rubin. Brookfield, VT: Ashgate, 1998, p. 227.

[821] Ibn Kathir. *Tafsir*, Vol II, p. 235 and Ibn Ishaq, p. 281.

[822] Jones, JMB, p. 227.

[823] Jones, p. 227.

[824] Jones, p. 227.

[825] Jones, p. 227.

[826] Ibn Kathir. *Tafsir*, Vol II, p. 239.

[827] Jones, JMB, p. 227.

[828] Ibn Ishaq, p. 281 and Ibn Kathir, *Tafsir*, Vol II, p. 235.

[829] Ibn Kathir, *Tafsir*, Vol II, p. 235 and Ibn Ishaq, p. 281.

[830] Ibn Ishaq, p. 283 and Ibn Kathir, *Tafsir*, Vol II, p. 237.

al-Ushayra	&rarr;	The Prophet returned to the region of Banu Damra and makes peace with a related tribe named Banu Mudlij.[831]
al-Kharrar	&rarr;	The apostle sent eight men with Sa'd b. Abu Waqqas. They returned without fighting.[832]
Badr al-Ula	&rarr;	Muhammad pursued Jabir al-Fihri who had raided Medina. He was not able to capture him and he returned to Medina. This is the first expedition of Badr.[833]
Banu Kinana	&rarr;	Muhammad sent one hundred men to raid the Banu Kinana. His men were overwhelmed and outnumbered. They sought refuge with their allies the Juhayna.[834]
Nakhla	&rarr;	Abdullah b. Jahsh was sent with eight emigrants to spy on the Quraysh. They attacked, killing one person, and taking two prisoners to Medina. This was the first blood shed and it occurred in a holy month.[835]

Of all of the raids, the one in Naklah seems to have sparked a move toward broad warfare. Ibn Ishaq gives a picture of the circumstances surrounding this raid as follows:

"Abdullah b. Jahsh was sent with eight emigrants (once again excluding the Ansar) in Rajab . . . Muhammad ordered him to essentially spy on the Quraysh at Nakhla (which was between

---

[831] Ibn Kathir, *Tafsir*, Vol II, p. 239.
[832] Ibn Ishaq, p. 286.
[833] Ibn Kathir, *Tafsir*, Vol II, p. 239 and Ibn Ishaq, p. 286.
[834] Ibn Kathir, *Tafsir*, Vol II, pp. 239, 241.
[835] Ibn Ishaq, pp. 287-288.

Mecca and al-Ta'if). Abdullah relayed Muhammad's orders and conveyed that all who were not willing to be martyred should stay behind. Abdullah and his band attacked. They killed one person and took two prisoners back to Medina. The apostle made it clear that he did not authorize the fighting in the holy month. Soon after a Qur'anic revelation came to him (2:217) and said that driving out God's people and unbelief were more serious crimes than fighting in the holy month. After this revelation the people were at ease and the booty was divided up. One prisoner returned to Mecca and the other became a believer.[836]

The difficulty for the Quraysh was not just in the loss of life or captured prisoners. They could not believe that Muhammad would choose to disdain an agreement that had been historically sacred among Arabs. Warfare was supposed to be forbidden in the "sacred months," and Muhammad received special revelation to set aside this Arab custom in favor of permanent warfare. This attack led the Quraysh in Mecca to take the Muslims more seriously and encounter them with greater force. Through this act, Muhammad established himself and his believers as a political threat as well as being a formidable religious threat. This threat could no longer be ignored. Through Nakhla and his teaching on *jihad*, Muhammad prepared the way for the greater battles to come. This was offensive, not defensive, warfare, and it was warfare on a permanent basis. We now turn our attention to the first revelation of the Qur'an during this period.

The Most Important Chapter of the Qur'an Revealed in Medina

It seems to me that the occurrence of the verses concerning the forbidden months in the context of the raid against Nakhla creates an historical matrix that establishes the approximate time for the revealing of the first Medinan surah of the Qur'an. This is in keeping with the Muslim historians mentioned earlier. This chapter is also considered the most important large chapter in the Qur'an and is placed second in order for that reason. The dating seems reasonably to be around eighteen months after the Hijra. Most Muslims, while they occasionally mention certain verses as being later, date the chapter to between sixteen and twenty months after the Hijra. It is also the time of the change of the *qibla,* and the Muslim policy of raiding Meccan caravans

---
[836]   Ibn Ishaq, pp. 287-288.

has drawn its first blood. There is a need to draw lines as to who may be trusted and who may not be. Clearly, war is on the horizon and Muhammad throws down a gauntlet before the Jews while extolling the virtues of *jihad*. He also provides a new set of appeals to the Arabs, for this new religion will incorporate much of the practices of Arab paganism. He also begins to take for himself the pattern of a lawgiver. He is becoming Prophet, priest, and king.

In terms of comparative content, the Qur'an incorporates from this point some very significant changes from the earlier chapters. About seventy-three verses out of two hundred and eighty six in the chapter contain Jewish narrative material. But now this material is being used in an entirely new way. For the first time, this Jewish narrative material is being used to attack the Jews. Out of seventy-one verses that attack the beliefs or practices of Jews and Christians, sixty-six occur in the initial one hundred and fifty verses of the chapter where most of the Jewish narrative material is also found. The material is also being used in another unique new way. The stories of the Jewish religious wars lead by Saul and David are now being used to justify the Muslim concept of *jihad*. The religio-political state of the children of Israel with its kings and prophets and holy wars is now appropriated to the emerging Muslim *ummah*. About fifteen verses also refer to the fires of hell and the joys of heaven. For the first time, Jews are threatened with hell for not embracing the Prophet in seven out of these fifteen verses.

Section 1: Prologue: Verses 1-7 of Surah al-Baqarah (The Heifer)

Allah begins with a commendation of the Qur'an as a "sure guidance" to those who believe it as "revelation," who believe in prayer and alms and in the revelation "sent before thy time." He condemns "those who reject faith" and points out that warning them is useless because "Allah has set a seal on their hearts." Ibn Kathir focused attention in this section on verse 2, which says that this book is a guidance without "Rayb" meaning "doubt." He explains, "This ayah—2:2—contains a prohibition meaning, 'Do not doubt the Qur'an.'"[837] This kind of prohibition is found throughout the Qur'an. Doubt, in Islam, is a Satan. It is something to be avoided at all costs, and the holy book must never be subjected to any sort of critical scrutiny. This becomes, I believe, a system at this stage because Muhammad is dealing with Jews who

---

[837] Ibn Kathir, *Tafsir*, Vol. 1, p. 106.

are knowledgeable about their own traditions, and it is obvious to them where Muhammad has borrowed many of his ideas. There is evidence in the Hadith of Jewish critiques of the Qur'an based on the many errors (from a Jewish perspective) in the text. The historical-critical theories that have assailed the Bible for the last two hundred years have made virtually no headway in the Muslim world for this reason. Because of the Jewish critique of the Qur'an, Muhammad forbids all critical thinking with regard to his book. Ibn Kathir made the following interesting comment in the introduction to his Tafsir:

> "The Israelite accounts and stories should only be used as supporting evidence, not as evidence themselves . . . Such examples of things that Allah kept unexplained in the Qur'an do not carry any daily or religious significance for responsible adults."[838]

The Qur'an is brimming with Jewish stories and tales as we have seen. Certain sections of the Qur'an simply cannot be understood without reference to these Jewish materials, and one sees this tacitly in how the commentators arrive at their interpretations. Yet they deny that this is occurring and deny the value of consulting outside materials. Muhammad's emphasis on not doubting must have been particularly acute as he came into direct contact with Jewish rabbis who could not only identify the sources for many of his stories, but also poke holes in the mistakes, contradictions, and fragmentary reproductions in his supposedly divine revelations. Forbidding doubt and silencing critics would soon become part of state policy, and it remains a part of Muslim state policy in many Muslim countries today.[839]

Section 2: Verses 8-20—The Hypocrites

In this section, Allah describes a new group for the first time. He says, "Of the people there are some who say: 'We believe in Allah and the last day'; but they do not believe." These are the hypocrites or *munafiqun*, and they had not been a factor in the Meccan period.[840] Clearly, Muhammad's

---

[838] Ibn Kathir, *Tafsir*, Vol. 1, p. 31.

[839] It would seem that this has now become a part of Western policy as well. Bernard Lewis, the noted British historian of Islam, has pointed out that on the BBC today one can say anything about the Bible, but no critique of the Qur'an is allowed.

[840] Ibn Kathir states this directly, "there were no hypocrites in Makkah" (*Tafsir* Vol. 1, p. 125).

followers are not being persecuted, rather they are growing in political power and stature such that it is becoming advantageous to pretend to be a follower of the Prophet. The Qur'an then lists typical statements by members of this group: "Why we only want to make peace!" and "Shall we believe as the fools believe?" Clearly, these people felt there were reasons to doubt Muhammad, but it was politically expedient to pretend not to. This political aspect comes through in the final statement: "When they meet with those who believe, they say, 'We believe' but when they are alone with their evil ones (Shayatin), they say: 'We are really with you.'" Ibn Kathir states that this attitude emerged after the Muslims had won the Battle of Badr: "After the battle of Badr took place . . . he (Ibn Sallul) pretended to be a Muslim . . . as well as many among the People of the Book.[841] This does not fit even Ibn Kathir's own chronology for the surah. Clearly, the power factor emerged well before the Battle of Badr. There is an entire chapter 63 revealed later that deals exclusively with this topic. The emergence of the hypocrites from the early Medinan period indicates that Muhammad's intentions from the beginning were political and military. Coercive violence becomes the cornerstone on which the Islamic state will be built. Such a policy will automatically create "hypocrites."

The Qur'an then describes these hypocrites as suffering from a disease. Ibn Kathir explains, "They are the hypocrites and the disease is the doubt that they brought to Islam."[842] This hypocrisy is also a function of the fact that Muhammad and his revelations were being subjected for the first time to knowledgeable scrutiny. There was reason to doubt. Ibn Kathir goes on to describe the "rabbis of the Jews" as the "Shayatin (devils) with whom the hypocrites conferred."[843] But politics and fear now created an atmosphere in which free thought was subjected to expediency. It seems remarkably like the atmosphere in the West today.

Section 3: Verses 21-29—Address to Mankind

Allah briefly addresses all mankind in these verses. First, man is called upon to "adore" the guardian Lord for his provision of rain to the earth. Ibn Kathir uses this as an opportunity to introduce how to adore the Lord. Interestingly, he uses a story about John the Baptist giving the command for the five pillars of Islam to the children of Israel.[844] All believers from the past were Muslims

---

841   Ibn Kathir, *Tafsir*, Vol. 1, p. 125.
842   Ibn Kathir, *Tafsir*, Vol. 1, pp. 128-129.
843   Ibn Kathir, *Tafsir*, Vol. 1, p. 135.
844   Ibn Kathir, *Tafsir*, Vol. 1, p. 154.

following the same commands as those Muhammad had laid down. It is possible that these devices were used to justify Muhammad imitating the practices of the Jews or Christians by claiming that they had their origin in actual Muslim practice from the beginning. Then there is a brief word about the uniqueness of the Qur'an with the typical challenge to produce another *surah* (chapter) like it (Qur'an 2:23). This elicits several pages from Ibn Kathir on the perfections of the Qur'an, which "mentioned the stories of the people of the past; and these accounts and stories occurred exactly as the Qur'an stated."[845] This is, of course, false and is meant to dissuade Muslims from considering what other holy books may actually teach. Here again, the word "doubt" appears concerning those "in doubt as to what we have revealed from time to time to our servant." Ibn Kathir makes clear this word is addressed to Christians and Jews.[846] Muhammad uses God as a mouthpiece to justify himself, and it provides us with an interesting self-portrait. Doubt is forbidden as is critical thinking.

He seems to answer a word of critique concerning the simple similies, which the Qur'an uses, "What means Allah by this similitude?" Frankly, he never really answers this question. There is also a brief mention of the fire reserved for those "who reject faith" and the gardens with rivers and pure wives (azwajun mutahharatun) reserved for believers. Ibn Kathir explains that these women will be pure from menstruation and pregnancies as well as feces, urine, spit, and semen.[847]

Section 4: Verses 30-39—The Story of Adam and Iblis

Allah then begins again to tell the story of Adam. This time, however, he adds the significant detail of naming the animals in the garden. This figures in the biblical account, but even more prominently in the Jewish legends about Satan as was noted earlier. When Satan refused to prostrate before Adam, the Jewish legend explains that God put him to the test by challenging him to a naming contest with Adam. Satan failed the test, being unable to name the animals and was banished along with his hosts of angels who also refused to prostrate before Adam.[848] The story is reproduced in

---

[845] Ibn Kathir, *Tafsir*, Vol. 1, p. 160.
[846] Ibn Kathir, *Tafsir*, Vol. 1, p. 156.
[847] Ibn Kathir, *Tafsir*, Vol. 1, p. 169. One must remember that the Qur'an considers that there is both male and female "semen," impure fluids that combine in pregnancy. The holy whores of heaven will make no impure fluids.
[848] Ginzberg, *Legends of the Jews*, Vol. 1, pp. 62-64.

the Qur'an here, including the story of naming the animals as a contest between the angels and Adam. Again, Muhammad seems to pick up new and more accurate details as he moves along. This interchange indicates that he was still picking up information, perhaps through Jewish contacts or intermediaries, and this section may be seen as a prologue to the more direct address to the Jews, which begins in the next section. That the Jews would not ultimately respond to Muhammad's appeals is admitted by all the Muslim historians and commentators. Ibn Kathir states the following: "Only a few Jews embraced Islam, such as Abdullah bin Salam."[849] The reasons for this are always said to be Jewish wickedness. But how could Jews respond positively to something that was so obviously a half-baked replay of their own apocryphal traditions?

Section 5-11: Verses 40-94—Muhammad's Address to Jews and Christians

I have grouped these seven sections together because they seem to be a unified address appealing directly to Jews and secondarily to Christians. That Jews are the primary intended audience is indicated by the fact that most of the sections begin with a direct address to Jews, and that the material covered is entirely from Jewish oral traditions. There is only one direct reference to Christians, which indicates that they were an afterthought in this address, perhaps added later.

This section begins with Allah calling to the Jews:

> "O Children of Israel! Call to mind the favor which I bestowed upon you and fulfill your covenant with me as I fulfill my covenant with you, and fear none but me. And believe in what I reveal confirming the revelation which is with you, and be not the first to reject faith therein . . . And cover not Truth with falsehood, nor conceal the Truth when ye know."

This introduction is repeated in the next section, and throughout the passage, the Jews are requested to "remember" their covenant with God. The call to remembrance is accompanied by lengthy renditions from the life of Moses with application to the present law that Muhammad is promulgating. All this

---

[849] Ibn Kathir, *Tafsir*, Vol. 1, p. 125.

will be very familiar to Jewish readers. The Prophets of the Old Testament were continually calling the wayward Hebrews to return to the covenant and remembrance of the Exodus deliverance figured large in their writings. Muhammad is clearly well acquainted with Jewish culture at this point and is appealing to them to accept him as the new Prophet. God functions as the mouthpiece calling them to believe what "I reveal" and affirming that this confirms the earlier revelations. He also opens with accusations that the Jews are "selling their signs," which seems to indicate selling the knowledge of the holy books for a price and that they are concealing what they know. The Muslim commentators indicate that the Jews knew their books predicted the coming of this new Prophet, and they covered up what they knew out of jealousy.

The Sira literature and Hadiths are full of similar accusations. There is an astonishing level of projection and reversal in the logic of these accusations. For instance, Ibn Kathir notes in his commentary on verse 40 that Israel was also known as "Jacob." He then cites a Hadith where Muhammad tells the Jews this fact and they agree: "Do you know that Israel is Jacob?" They (the Jews) said, "Yes, by Allah."[850] The indication is that Muhammad is the fountainhead of all wisdom and the Jews can only, but agree. This simply covers up the fact of the reverse that the knowledge was flowing the other way. What Jew doesn't know that Jacob was also called Israel? Similarly, Ibn Kathir points out how all the holy books predicted the coming of Muhammad: "'O People of the Book! Believe in what I have sent down that conforms to what you have.' This is because they find the description of Muhammad recorded in the Tawrah and the Injil." The problem with this argument is that Allah himself never provides the stories of these descriptions in the holy books. Muhammad is speaking of legal pronouncements regarding charity and prayer, not predictions of himself. But the Muslim commentators are constantly projecting their later theological views onto the text of the Qur'an. When Ibn Kathir explains "And mix not truth with falsehood" he interprets this to mean, "Do not mix Judaism and Christianity with Islam, that the religion of Allah is Islam, and that Judaism and Christianity are innovations that did not come from Allah."[851] These kinds of distinctions date from a later age and are projected back on the Qur'an. This is nearly a universal in Muslim commentary literature. Muhammad had no such conceptions. He is

---

[850]   Ibn Kathir, *Tafsir*, Vol. 1, p. 205.
[851]   Ibn Kathir, *Tafsir*, Vol. 1, p. 210.

appealing to a belief structure that he believes is the same as his own, but not being properly practiced. There is nothing in the Qur'an that questions the veracity of either Old or New Testament revelation. Verse 44 states this clearly: "Do ye enjoin right conduct on the people, and forget yourselves. And yet ye study the scripture? Will ye not understand." At no time does he attack these scriptures, only their lack of application. Ibn Kathir ignores the obvious meaning of the text, as does the modernist Yusuf Ali.[852]

In the next section, Allah reminds Israel of the deliverance that he accomplished for them over Pharaoh. Here, however, rather than providing a detailed story line, such as was found in the Meccan period, Muhammad only touches on the high points. Pharaoh's oppression of the Israelites, the parting of the Red Sea, Moses' absence for forty nights, the calf, manna, and quail, these things are merely touched upon as examples of God's favor. Muhammad is avoiding potentially contentious details. Still, he gets several significant details correct; the slaying of those out of control after the golden calf incident,[853] the Israelites desiring to draw near to the mountain to see God, the plague (perhaps referring to the incident of Baal Peor in Numbers 25). His discussions in this chapter are significantly more accurate to the biblical text than previous discussions in the Meccan period. Does this indicate direct interaction with knowledgeable Jewish Rabbis? One senses a contrast to the Meccan period whose sources seem to be primarily Jewish oral legends picked up haphazardly and largely (from a Jewish perspective) inaccurately. The legends are still present here, but actual scriptural accounts show through the text. An echo of this is seen in verse 61.

> "'Oh Moses! We cannot endure one kind of food; so beseech thy Lord for us to produce for us of what the earth growth—Its pot-herbs, and cucumbers, its garlic, lentils and onions.' He said, . . . 'Go ye down to any town and ye shall find what ye want.'"

---

[852] Ali, Yusuf, p. 27. Ali makes no comment on Muhammad's clear statement of the veracity of the Jewish scriptures for it is a viewpoint nearly universally rejected by Muslims in direct contrast to what the Qur'an actually says.

[853] It is striking that the later commentators and Hadith found on these incidents are far less accurate to the biblical text than the Qur'an itself. Ibn Kathir's commentary on the golden calf strays far away from the biblical text. Vol. 1, pp. 229-230.

Compare this to the text of Numbers 11:4-5:

> "The people of Israel also wept again and said, 'Oh that we had meat to eat! We remember the fish we ate in Egypt that cost nothing, the cucumbers, the melons, the leeks, the onions and the garlic. But now our strength is dried up, and there is nothing at all but this manna to look at.'"

There are significant differences, but the texts are close enough to indicate a new level of interchange between Muhammad and his Jewish interlocutors.

There are still some very strange elements in the Qur'anic text. Verses 55 and 56 indicate that when the people drew near to see God at Sinai they were struck dead by lightening and then raised from the dead. This seems to be the inclusion of a Jewish legend. We also have Ibn Kathir's discussion of the Jewish fast of Ashura, which he claims Muhammad adopted after discussing it with the Jews of Medina.[854] The event of Passover is still remarkable by its total absence from the text. Why does Muhammad avoid this topic, which is so near and dear to the Jewish heart? Perhaps it is because following this tradition really means being part of the Jewish community in the same way that baptism functions for Christians. It is just a little bit too Jewish.

Muhammad's relationship to Jews and Christians is still not entirely negative. It seems that commentators easily become uncomfortable with the continual emphasis on the People of the Book. Ibn Kathir takes two long sections in his commentary to explain that the *ummah* of Muhammad is better than the *ummah* of the Children of Israel, and later that the virtues of the companions of Muhammad were much greater than the virtues of the followers of other prophets.[855] The Qur'an does not seem to be making that kind of distinction at this point. At the beginning of the next section, Allah states the following (verse 62):

---

[854]   Ibn Kathir, *Tafsir*, Vol. 1, p. 227.

[855]   Ibn Kathir, *Tafsir*, Vol. 1, pp. 219, 236. Interestingly, one of the reasons Ibn Kathir feels the companions of Musa were unworthy was because of their unwillingness to pursue *jihad* to the degree that Allah required. They were "weak and exhausted," which is why God allowed them to wander in the desert. He launches into a long Hadith-based discussion, which has no relation to any biblical or Jewish legend text, some of it frankly ridiculous (see page 240 if you want a good laugh.). The Qur'an, for all its faults, tends to be far more accurate than the later commentators.

"Verily, Those who believe and those who are Jews and Christians, and Sabians, whoever believes in Allah and the last day and does righteous good deeds shall have their reward with their Lord, on them shall be no fear, nor shall they grieve."

This passage is interesting in its acceptance of other religious communities. This exact formulation will be used in a very different way later in the Qur'an. Sadly, the Muslim commentators invariably downplay or outright ignore the passage. Ibn Kathir states in exact contrast to the text he is interpreting: "Allah does not accept any deed or work from anyone, unless it conforms to the law of Muhammad."[856] Even Yusuf Ali finds it necessary to downplay the significance of this. He states, "Islam existed before the preaching of Muhammad on this earth: The Qur'an expressly calls Abraham a Muslim (3:67). Its teaching (submission to Allah's will) has been and will be the teaching of religion for all time and all people."[857] What is remarkable here is that Muhammad clearly sees these groups as being part of his *ummah* of faith. Islam or "submission" was not really a word denoting a separate religion at this point in time, but rather an attitude that could be common to any monotheistic groups. Muhammad is still trying to build a grand alliance of monotheists. Later, this formulation will change, and true believer's from these groups will be defined in terms of their acceptance of Muhammad as the Prophet of God. That is not the case here.

Having appealed to his hearers by declaring that Jews, Christians, and Sabians who keep the law shall have their reward from Allah, Muhammad then begins to accuse his listeners of unfaithfulness. He mentions the Jews trespassing Mount Sinai (verse 63), their transgression of the Sabbath that he claims turned some of them into apes (verse 65), their insincerity in offering a heifer to God (verses 67-71) and their growing hardness of heart (verses 72-74). It seems to me that many of these brief vignettes are derived from Jewish oral traditions and several have parallels in the Ginzberg's *Legends of the Jews*.[858]

Beginning at verse 75, Muhammad accuses the Jews of "perverting the Word of Allah . . . knowingly after they understood it." This indicates a dialogue between these Jews and "men of faith" that seems to be a new term for believers in the message of Muhammad. Muhammad says that these (Jews) are seeking "to engage in argument" with the men of faith. Clearly,

---

[856] Ibn Kathir, *Tafsir*, Vol. 1, p. 249.

[857] Ali, Yusuf, p. 34, footnote no. 77.

[858] Ginzberg, *The Legends of the Jews*, Vol. 3.

this suggests ongoing debate between the followers of Muhammad and members of the other "party" in Medina. Ibn Kathir sees these stories as a clear indication of an ongoing debate between the Jews and the Muslims in Medina even though the text does not explicitly state that the group is Jewish. The context of Jewish oral tradition and allusions to the Old Testament makes that abundantly clear, however. Ibn Kathir focuses on their deliberate distortion of the holy book in their attempt to argue with the Muslims.[859] This becomes the universal paradigm of Muhammad's response to the Jews. Wherever Jewish and Muslim books disagree, the Jews must have distorted the interpretation of their books. The Qur'an does not accuse the books themselves of becoming corrupted. Al-Tabari argues that this was the result of earlier generations of Jews who had altered the book, and now they disagreed with Muhammad bringing the correct story of their sacred history through the Qur'an.[860] But the Qur'an does not make this accusation.

It is easy to see why the Jews would reject Muhammad's argument. From the Jewish perspective, Muhammad was bringing a corrupted version of their own stories back to them as the true version. To be accused of being the ones who were covering up the true meaning of the scriptures must have seemed intolerable. This raises an interesting issue because in three separate places in the Qur'an the promise is given that Allah's Word cannot be changed.[861] So does this mean misinterpreted or actually altered? Al-Tabari indicates that there were two parties: one who had distorted a book and one who had not.[862] The book is seen as distinct from the "Torah," which is declared in many places to be the Word of Allah. Apparently, Muhammad's respect for Allah's Word indicated an uncorrupted Torah, though other law books perhaps were corrupted. Al-Tabari goes on to state that there was a group among the Jews who found the description of Muhammad in their scriptures and were rebuked by the other Jews for revealing this to the Muslims. This could be a reference to the promised Prophet in Deuteronomy 18:15. Muhammad's (from a Jewish perspective) many mistakes and inaccuracies in his new holy book would have made Jews regard him as a false Prophet, far more extensively described in the Old Testament (see Deuternomy 13:1-5).

---

[859]   Ibn Kathir, *Tafsir,* Vol. 1, pp. 268-9.
[860]   Al-Tabari, *Tafsir*, Vol. 1, pp. 402-403
[861]   Qur'an 6:34 and 115: "There is none that can alter the Words of Allah," and "None can change His Word." This shows again that God's Word cannot be changed. Similar statement is found in 10:64.
[862]   Al-Tabari, *Tafsir*, Vol. 1, pp. 403.

The text goes on to declare "woe" on "those who write the book with their own hands and then say, 'this is from Allah'" (verse 79). Al-Tabari interprets this "woe" (wailun) to be the pus that unbelievers drink or the river in hell into which they sink.[863] Muhammad calls them illiterate and goes on to threaten these people with becoming "companions of the fire, therein shall they abide" (verse 81). True believers who follow Muhammad are "companions of the garden" (verse 82). Ibn Kathir argues that Muslims should never ask Jews about the contents of other holy books since they have altered them, and their teachings are untrustworthy. But this is not nor does it ever become the viewpoint of the Qur'an. He then goes on to describe the eternity these Jews will spend in hell as taught by the Prophet. Nevertheless, none of these passages actually accuses the Jewish scriptures of being perverted or changed, only that the Jews wrote other books that were perverted.[864]

The Qur'an then goes on to accuse the Jews of backsliding (verse 83), unlawful killing, and driving members of their own community out, only receiving them back at the price of a ransom (verses 84-86). Ibn Kathir explains this as relating to how the Jews treated each other prior to the time of Muhammad and did not follow their own book when they fought in the civil wars in Medina against other Jews allied with other pagan tribes. The killing of monotheists by other monotheists was a great sin in the Jewish scriptures, Ibn Kathir opines.[865] Al-Tabari agrees with this interpretation, Muhammad is criticizing the Jews for aligning themselves with different segments of the Arab pagan population and actually fighting against other Jews aligned with the opposing Arab tribes.[866] The lesson is that they should align with Muhammad who is a fellow monotheist. Yusuf Ali, however, changes the story in his explanation completely. He accuses the Jews of "treacherously" breaking the agreement of the "Constitution of Medina" referred to earlier.[867] This is apparently a late modern interpretation designed to make the condemnation of the Jews more palatable. The lack of such a rationale in the earlier writings indicates they are probably more accurate.

---

[863] Al-Tabari, *Tafsir*, Vol. 1, p. 412.

[864] This discussion between Muhammad and the Jews may well have taken place over the nature of the apocryphal legends that were the basis of Muhammad's stories in the Qur'an. The Jews would have accused these of being a different sort of literature, and not part of scripture at all.

[865] Ibn Kathir, *Tafsir*, Vol. 1, pp. 284-285.

[866] Al-Tabari, *Tafsir*, Vol. 1, pp. 431-433.

[867] Ali, Yusuf, p. 39, footnote no. 88.

The next section of chapter 2, verses 87-96, is an all-around condemnation of the Jews. They have received a succession of messengers, including Moses and Jesus, but they refuse to believe in this latest messenger because of envy (verse 90). They are puffed up with pride and cursed by Allah for their blasphemy of disbelief (verses 87-88). Even though they prayed for victory over those "Without faith," which must here refer to the pagans, yet they refuse Allah and his messenger who are sent to fulfill that victory. They are accused of slaying the prophets, worshipping the golden calf, and disobeying the law. If they truly believe, they should be willing to die, "seek ye death if ye are sincere" (verse 94), but they know their deeds are evil before Allah, and therefore, they are "most greedy of life—even more than the idolators" (verse 96). The words here are very militaristic. Muhammad expects the Jews to aid him in his military campaigns against the pagan Arabs, and they apparently refused. The ethos here is earlier than the Battle of Badr, and Muhammad is less confident. We begin to see the source of modern radical challenges to "moderate" Muslims. If one is a genuine believer, one should be willing to fight and die in *jihad*. This would be the time of the early raids against the Meccans. Furthermore, there is a clear distinction made in this passage between Jews and Christians and the "unbelievers" that can only refer to a pagan Arab community separate from them. This contrasts with Hawting's thesis mentioned earlier that the Qur'an only really addresses various monotheistic groups.[868]

Sections 12-16: Verses 97-141—The Condemnation of the Jews

In the next section, Muhammad deals with the truthfulness of his revelation through the angel Gabriel and the fickleness of the Jews. These five sections are an ongoing condemnation of the Jews with brief mention also of the Christians. In the previous section, there was an allusion to the Jews believing what was "sent down to us." Muhammad argues here that his revelation is genuine, for it was given "to his heart" by Gabriel (verse 99). Whoever is an enemy to God, his prophets, and the angels Gabriel and Michael, God is an enemy to them. Muhammad calls the Jews faithless for making a covenant and then throwing it aside (verse 100). This could be a reference to the Constitution of Medina in which Muhammad wrote a treaty with certain tribes, including the Jews, and which he now says the Jews are

---

[868]   G. R. Hawting, *The Idea of Idolatry and the Emergence of Islam*, Cambridge University Press, 1999. See page 5 for brief rendition of his thesis.

violating. Is this because they were unwilling to engage in military operations with the Muslims? He accuses the Jews of throwing aside their own holy books and includes a legend of the Jews selling their souls to the magic of Harut and Marut in Babylon (verse 102). It is also interesting to note the rejection of the angel Gabriel by the Jews that is stated again in this section. Ibn Kathir makes a major point of this claiming, "The Jews are the enemies of Jibrail" and spending five pages concluding with proofs of Muhammad's prophethood.[869] Al-Tabari does the same as does Yusuf Ali. What is really reflected here is not a rejection of Gabriel. The Jews believed in this angel. What they do not believe is that this angel has given Muhammad new revelations. This is the clearest indication that Muhammad's key conflict with the Jews was in regard to his claim of receiving a new holy book. The Muslim commentators, whether Islamist or modernist, have no understanding of this.

The next section of the chapter seems to be addressed to the Muslims "O ye of faith" (verse 104). Here Muhammad seems to be encouraging his followers (troops?) that good times are coming "for Allah is the Lord of grace abounding." He then deals with the issue of abrogated verses in the Qur'an. "None of our revelations do we abrogate or cause to be forgotten but we substitute something better." (verse 106) This verse continues the Muslim doctrine of *naskh*, or abrogation. It raises the immediate question, what has been abrogated that has led to this questioning on the part of Muhammad's followers? I would argue that the issue is Muhammad's going over to the pathway of violence in seeking to subjugate his enemies by force. Abrogation of earlier revelations was clearly raising doubts in the Muslim ranks. Muhammad may have been forced to promulgate this doctrine when the Jews pointed out contradictions in the text of the Qur'an. Muhammad argues simply that Allah can change his mind. He then vaguely threatens that they are starting to question him the way the Jews used to question Moses. He points out that their enemies among "the people of the Book" would like to turn them back to "infidelity" because of their envy (verses 104-109). He encourages them to reject these temptations, to be steadfast in prayer and charity, and to reject what the Jews and Christians say about who will go to paradise. Muhammad is clearly conceiving of his community as at least separate from a significant party among the Jews and the Christians. The sentiment has not become total enmity yet.

---

[869] Ibn Kathir, *Tafsir*, Vol. 1, p. 306. al-Tabari, *Tafsir*, Vol. 1, p. 469.

Muhammad then turns again to condeming the Jews and the Christians. First, he points out the arguments between Jews and Christians who claim to follow the same holy book. Verse 114 is very significant. Here Muhammad says, "And what is more unjust than he who forbids that in places for the worship of Allah, his name should be celebrated?—Whose zeal is to ruin them?" He then goes on to say that Allah belongs to the "east and the west" such that wherever one turns "there is Allah's countenance" (verses 114-115). This would seem to refer to the direction of prayer, which according to the biographical literature was changed from Jerusalem to Mecca about this time. Ibn Kathir interprets it this way.[870] Perhaps this was the abrogated rule that gave rise to the earlier questioning? But the passage is maddeningly opaque. Whose zeal is it to ruin "them?" What destruction is being referred to? What places "for the worship of Allah" is he referring to? Yusuf Ali makes this a reference to the pagan Arabs in Mecca, refusing entry for the Muslims to worship to which Ibn Kathir agrees.[871] In verse 116, Muhammad attacks the Christians for stating that God "has begotten a son" and that all creation should worship him. He states that the Jews and the Christians will never be satisfied, unless "you follow their form of religion." Ibn Kathir takes this opportunity to attack the concept of "innovation" (bid'ah) stressing that every bid'ah is a heresy.[872] Nevertheless, Muhammad seems to have a respect for those who study their holy book stating they read it "as it should be studied" and "they believe in it." Once again, Muhammad has faith in the other holy books, and clearly indicates that they are uncorrupted. Indeed, he claims that those who "disbelieve in it . . . are the losers" (verse 121). Both Ibn Kathir and Yusuf Ali interpret this to refer only to those Jews and Christians who have accepted Muhammad as the new Prophet.[873] Thus, their books can only be considered true if they are led by those books into becoming Muslims. At this stage, Muhammad does not seem to be saying this at all. He is calling the Jews to follow him apparently believing that if they read their own books they would be convinced of his truthfulness. He seems to be unaware of just how different his revelations are from the Jewish scriptures.

Section 15 of chapter 2 introduces a completely new topic in the narrative of the Qur'an. Up to this point, Ishmael was a shadowy character, in most of the earlier Qur'an not even connected to Abraham. Here Ishmael emerges

---

[870]   Ibn Kathir, *Tafsir*, Vol. 1 p. 347.
[871]   Ali, Yusuf, p. 49 and Ibn Kathir, *Tafsir*, Vol. 1, p. 343.
[872]   Ibn Kathir, *Tafsir*, Vol. 1, p. 354.
[873]   Ibn Kathir, *Tafsir*, Vol. 1, p. 363.

not just as the son of Abraham, but as the source along with Abraham of an entirely new sanctuary narrative. The section is directly addressed to the "Children of Israel." Muhammad notes that Abraham was called "imam to the nations" (verse 124). Then it is stated that Abraham and Ishmael were called to make "the house," to do their prostrations there, to make it a "city of peace" and to raise its "foundations" (verses 125-7). All of this would seem to refer to Jerusalem, but no, the new sanctuary established for the nations is in the land of "the new messenger" who would "rehearse the signs" (verse 129). Muhammad is shifting the focus from Jerusalem to Mecca. Muhammad puts these words into the mouths of Ishmael and Abraham, "show us our places for the celebration of rites." Mecca now supplants Jerusalem as the house for the nations, the new center of Allah's universe. They both cry out as "submitted ones" literally Muslims bowing to the will of Allah. I think for the first time the word "Muslims" is being used in its final sense, as a descriptive of those who follow Allah and his Prophet Muhammad (verse 128). Here Muhammad is making a clear break with both Judaism and Christianity. He is establishing a new religion, even though he is claiming that this is the original religion of Abraham. This places him on a permanent collision course with both of those earlier religions.

Section 16 continues this transformation of the whole of Jewish and Christian salvation history into an actual narrative of the original religion, Islam. Muhammad calls this "the religion of Abraham" (*millat Ibrahim*, verse 130). This term appeared first in the late Meccan chapters of the Qur'an, but now it takes on a new meaning establishing a separate prophetic pedigree for the religion of Muhammad. Abraham and Jacob both "bowed" in "submission" to Allah and called their children to do the same. In verse 133, Muhammad changes the very core trifold fathers of the faith terminology of Judaism by stating, "The God of thy fathers, of Abraham Ismail and Isaac." No longer are the fathers of the faith "Abraham, Isaac, and Jacob," now Ismail is regarded as the true father of the faithful, thus including the Arabs in the salvation history. On the face of it, this would seem to be a gauntlet thrown down before the Jews implying a major rejection/revision of the whole thrust of Jewish salvation history. What did Muhammad hope to gain by this? Surely, he must have known that the Jews would utterly reject such a notion?

Some might say that this is an interpolation added later, perhaps after Muhammad's time, to seal the distinction between Judaism and Islam. I reject that notion. The passage begs to be read as a unified whole, a discourse moving fairly logically through a process of reinterpretation and revision of previously known facts. It is known that the idea that Ishmael was the father of the Arabs was a Jewish invention of the first century CE. It may well have been an invention of Jewish refugees to Arabia at the time of the revolts against Rome who were seeking common ground with the Arab tribes in order to gain asylum. It seems clear that Muhammad and the Arabs of his day were very aware of these Jewish ideas and approaches. We have already seen that Muhammad was very well steeped in the Jewish and Christian oral traditions of the time. There would seem to be no reason not to assume that many Arabs were equally well versed in the other monotheistic oral traditions. Thus, Muhammad's appeal here, I believe, is primarily to them. His inclusion of Ishmael in the trinity of the fathers of the faithful is one of many devices meant to appeal to Arabs to abandon Jewish traditions and come to the original religion of Abraham, the original Arab monotheism.

Two verses later, he makes this abundantly clear: "They say: 'Become Jews or Christians if ye would be guided'. Say thou, 'Nay, the religion of Abraham, the true" (verse 135). Conversion to Judaism or Christianity was regarded as cultural unfaithfulness to the Arab tribal spirit. Muhammad is appealing to that spirit to turn to a new interpretation that is uniquely Arab and not associated with the outside political powers of the day. Yet he maintains the continuity of all these faiths declaring, "We believe in Allah and the revelations given to us, and to Abraham, Ismail, Isaac and Jacob and the descendants and that given to Moses and Jesus and to Prophets from their Lord and we make no difference between one and another" (verse 136). Muhammad is still appealing to these other faiths as equally valid, but he is now including his revelations as part of the scriptures and himself as one of the prophets and Ishmael as a new father of the faithful. The Qur'an here is functioning liturgically. One can almost see a chorus line of Muslims lining up to recite this verse in unison as a rebuttal to Jewish criticism of their new holy text. He throws the Jewish criticisms back at them, "If they believe as you believe, they are indeed on the right path, but if they turn back, it is they who are in schism" (verse 137). With this verse, Muhammad makes his revelations the arbiter of truth. If the other religions disagree with what he says, it is they who are schismatic.

There seems to be a pattern in these verses. Powerful attacks on these other faiths are interspersed with statements like, "We make no difference" and "We are responsible for our things and ye for yours" (verses 136, 139). Yet the conciliation is always followed by another accusation or rebuttal. "Do ye say that Abraham, Ismail, Isaac and Jacob and the descendants were Jews and Christians?" Obviously, those who came before the formal religions of Judaism and Christianity were something other than Jews and Christians, and Muhammad is claiming that this is what Islam is. It is a highly specious though an effective argument. He repetitiously concludes with a word of judgment on them, "Of their merits there is no question in your case" meaning, you were not as meritous as they were, that is, in their submission (Islam). The constant repetition of the concept of submission is rapidly becoming the name of the religion.

Sections 17-18: Verses 142-152—The Climax of Muhammad's Shift in Religion

The next section (verses 142-152), I believe, is the climax of the entire chapter for it is here that Muhammad deals with the issue that has led to his major break with the Jews and Christians. It is this very passage that defines Islam as a separate religion from Judaism and Christianity, and it is here that Muhammad separates himself and his faith forever from "The People of the Book." This is the passage where Muhammad gives the explanation for the change of *qiblah*, the direction of prayer.

According to Muslim traditions, up till about one year after the Hijra, Muslims prayed in the direction of Jerusalem, in imitation of Jewish and Christian practice of the time. For Jews, this practice had an obvious meaning. The final verse of the Hebrew Bible states, "Who is among you of all his people? May the Lord his God be with him, and let him go up!" (2 Chronicles 36:23). Jerusalem was the center of the Jewish kingdom of God concept; it was here that God had established His worship. This was the place to which the nations would come with their offerings acceptable on God's altar. Christians, partly in imitation of the Jewish practice, looked to Jerusalem as the place of Christ's ultimate sacrifice and the place to which he would return to establish the kingdom of God forever. Muhammad had, up to this point, joined the Jews and the Christians in this common devotion to Jerusalem as the center of the kingdom of God on earth.

Something happened in Medina during that first year after the Hijra that lies behind the decision being made here. It is something about which we only get very small intimations about in the Hadith literature, the Sira literature, and the Tafsir writings. The events that lead to this change of Qibla are founded of five key realities:

1. For the first time, Muhammad's "revelations" were subjected to the knowledgeable critique of those who knew the other holy books well, primarily the Jewish tribes of Medina.

2. Muhammad's followers for the first time were in discussions with other Arabic speaking people who could find fault with the supposedly divine utterances of Muhammad. The very trust of his own movement was at risk.

3. For the first time, Muhammad met stiff resistance to his plans from others who were just as monotheistic and pure in their absolute rejection of paganism as he was. What was wrong with Judaism that they should not be following it?

4. Muhammad's plan for a monotheistic center unified in its drive to subjugate paganism was now threatened from within. Who could he now trust with his militaristic plans?

5. Ultimately, Muhammad had to formulate the most important question of all, where was his movement going? Was he headed for inclusion in Judaism or Christianity or could his movement "go it alone."

In order to survive as a prophet, Muhammad had to reject his erstwhile partners in monotheism and invent an entirely new sanctuary myth. Up to this point, Muhammad had borrowed most of his salvation history from the oral traditions of Jews and Christians. It is here that he begins to write an entirely new salvation history with a new focal point for the kingdom of God, Mecca. He continues to borrow, particularly Jewish terminology, but the story line now departs completely from the pattern of previous revelations. They are now only footnotes meant to buttress this new story of God's plan for the nations.

Muhammad changes the *qiblah* or direction of prayer from Jerusalem to Mecca. This has already taken place as chapter two began so the explanation is in the past tense. Muhammad asks rhetorically, "The fools among the people say, 'What hath turned them from the Qiblah to which they were used'" (verse 142). Muhammad's response is to say that this was in order to establish his followers as "witnesses over mankind," and that the new *qiblah* was established by God to test whether the followers of the Prophet were true to him or would turn away. Thus, the new sanctuary to which they would turn would be the center of a new religion testifying over all the nations and distinguishing between those who would follow the new Prophet and those who would not. He goes on to define who these were, "Even if thou wert to bring to the People of the Book all the signs, they would not follow thy Qiblah; nor art thou going to follow their Qiblah" (verse 145). Muhammad has essentially given up on trying to convince the Jews of the truthfulness of his call. His Qur'an should have been sufficient to convince them. He intimates that they knew themselves that his book was true. "The People of the Book know this as they know their own sons; but some of them conceal the truth" (verse 146). He goes on to state that the ones who conceal what is in their books are "the ones cursed by Allah and cursed by the cursers" (verse 159). Only those who repent (how is not clearly defined, but the commentators indicate that they must accept Muhammad's revelations) will be accepted by God, and the others will suffer severe punishment. Indeed, they are cursed of God if they do not follow the new revelation. As we have seen, it was the Qur'an, which primarily turned them away.

The last fifteen hundred years have witnessed the playing out of this epistemological rupture. Muhammad intimates another reason for the change of the *qiblah*; "now shall we turn thee to a Qiblah that shall please thee" (verse 144). Part of the reason for this change was to appeal to the Arab followers of the Prophet setting their sanctuary as the new center of the religious universe. He encourages his followers to "be not at all in doubt" (verse 147).

Section 18 completes these thoughts for the believers in Muhammad. They are repeatedly encouraged to turn their direction toward the "sacred mosque" no matter where they are or what direction they are travelling in. The analogy is that even when they are marching out to battle their faces should be turned toward the "sacred mosque." They are called on to remember that they have received the blessing of "a Messenger of your own . . . instructing you in scripture and wisdom and new knowledge" (verse 151). Interestingly, the aspect of prayer toward Mecca is never mentioned here although it is inherent in the concept of *qiblah*. The analogy is military, and this is spelled out in the next section.

Sections 19-40:Verses 153-286—Muhammad the Lawgiver

The remaining sections of the chapter promulgate the new laws of his religion. *Jihad* is the first subject he takes up. Muhammad calls his followers to be patient and "not say of those who are slain in the way of Allah: 'They are dead.' Nay, they are living though ye perceive not" (verse 154). Part of the purpose of the shift of the *qiblah* is to create a new army of undivided loyalty, removing from its midst those of the People of the Book whose loyalties were divided. The believers are encouraged to persevere even in the loss of goods, or affliction and calamity. Muhammad is preparing his people for war. Clearly, this passage is before the time of the Battle of Badr for there is no recitation of previous victories at this point. Muslim historians speak of this early period of *jihad*, where Muhammad's soldiers carried out raids against the Meccans, as a time of deep frustration where little was accomplished. Chapter 2 reflects these sentiments and reinforces the sense of the historicity of the early Arab narratives of this period.

Muhammad then begins to incorporate the elements of the Mecca sanctuary into his salvation history narrative as he promulgates the laws of pilgrimage. He mentions the hills of Safa and Marwah and the pagan rites of walking between them. To do so is "no sin" he says as Allah knows their "impulse to good." Behind this lies the question of how one is to revere the Meccan sanctuary when it is full of pagan idols? This question has probably come from the Jews as Muhammad responds, "We have made it clear for the People of the Book—on them shall be Allah's curse" (verse 159). Ibn Kathir notes that curses on disbelievers are allowed, and these are probably considered to have magical power.[874] Muhammad did not appreciate these kinds of questions that implied inconsistency in this new way of life. Yusuf Ali, as he so often does, points to the Bible as also containing curses and that the Qur'an offers a superior type of cursing here.[875] Muhammad offers freedom from the curse to "those who repent," but those who reject faith in the Prophet shall be covered with "Allah's curse and the curse of angels and of all mankind" (verse 161). Cursing in animistic Arab thinking carried a direct spiritual power to inflict harm on others and the text intimates that God's curse is the fire of hell. To say that Jews and Christians are "cursed" if they do not accept Muhammad is saying more than that they will go to hell. It really means that they are now objects of Muhammad's military campaign and must be subjugated. Muhammad is drawing the line between his followers and the Jews and Christians from a military perspective.

The next section is essentially a mediation on the blessings of Allah in the natural world much like similar passages from the Meccan period and ending with a severe warning to cut off all relations with those who "take others besides Allah as equal" (verse 165). Muhammad is trying to break tribal loyalties in favor of loyalty to the one true God. Those not loyal to him will suffer eternal punishment "nor will there be a way out for them from the fire" (verse 167).

The next sections of chapter 2 is something like Moses on Sinai, Muhammad details other laws for his new community. He calls them to eat the good things of the earth, but forbids "dead meat, blood and the flesh of swine" as well as anything over which some other name than Allah has been invoked. He goes on to condemn those who "conceal Allah's revelations in the book" and purchase them for profit. He accuses them of being the cause of dispute over the book, which Allah sent down and says that they will be tormented in the place of fire. It would seem that he is referring to the Bible rather

---

[874]   Ibn Kathir, *Tafsir*, Vol. 1, p. 455ff.
[875]   Ali, Yusuf, p. 63, footnote no. 163.

than the Qur'an, and his logic here shows that he regards the actual Bible as an unchanged and uncorrupted book, but that the (unnamed) Jews and Christians are hiding its true content. Yusuf Ali makes no connection to Jews and Christians, but Ibn Kathir tells of the "Jews" who "concealed what Allah revealed." As will be repeated innumerable times in the coming chapters of his Tafsir, Ibn Kathir accuses the Jews of "concealing their book's descriptions of Muhammad, all of which testify to his truth as a Messenger and a Prophet."[876]

Muhammad then goes on to define what his community must believe in; Allah, the last day, angels, the book, and messengers. This is very close to a canonical rendition of the six points of faith for a Muslim, missing only faith in the decrees of Allah. What is interesting is that the book is mentioned as one document. Muhammad regards all the books of Jews, Christians, and his own book as one and the same. Later, Islamic theology would call this the "mother of the book" (*umm al-kitab*). All the revelations have been derived and brought down from this original book. He also lists prayer, charity, and steadfastness in trouble as characteristics of his community. He continues with rules concerning murder; free men shall be executed for freemen killed, women for women, and slaves for slaves. Killing across those categories is not defined, and Muhammad also leaves place for the payment of blood money to cover guilt. There is a brief section on inheritance pledges and honesty of the witnesses.

Muhammad then goes on to define some of the rules for fasting. What is remarkable here is that he defines the rules "as it was prescribed to those before you" (verse 183). This is an ongoing tradition though never before clearly defined in the Qur'an. The month of Ramadan is defined as the month for fasting because it was the month "in which was sent down the Qur'an" (verse 185). As noted earlier, this is a key step in distinguishing his new religion from Judaism and reinforcing faith in the Qur'an as the new holy book. Ways of making up for missed fasting days are mentioned. Eating and sexual relations are permitted "until the white thread of dawn appear to you distinct from the black thread" (verse 187[877]). Rules are given against bribery

---

[876]   Ibn Kathir, *Tafsir*, Vol. 1, p. 475.

[877]   Muhammad and his God do not seem to be aware of the salient features of world geography. This law of fasting, as well as timings for prayer cannot be followed in the polar regions because the sun either never comes up (in the winter) or never sets (in the summer). This is not a small problem for Muslims because all the innovative ideas on how to keep the law in these regions end up being a denial of the clear teaching of the Qur'an. They are *"bid'ah,"* innovations. Innovations are heresy. These are the two most important pillars of Islam.

of judges, the significance of new moons (perhaps an attack on animistic practices), and going in through the front door of a house not the back.

Verse 190 takes up again the rules for *jihad*. He begins by stating, "Fight in the cause of Allah, those who fight you" (verse 189). Some Muslim exegetes define this as strictly "self-defence" (Yusuf Ali, p. 76). Others clearly state that one must fight against those who resist coming under Islamic rule. The command is to "slay them wherever ye catch them and turn them out from where they have turned you out." Ibn Kathir cites this verse from chapter 9, which was revealed later, as modifying this verse. The verse here could be interpreted to indicate primarily defensive warfare.[878] This verse refers to the Meccans who Muhammad regards as oppressors because they turned him out of Mecca, even if the Hijra was his own decision. He commands fighting even in the sacred mosque of Mecca if they should resist. In this sense, Muhammad's rules of *jihad* are offensive warfare. He is not describing the defence of Medina, but rather the conquest of Mecca. "Slay them. Such is the reward of those who suppress faith" (verse 191). The fight is to continue until there is "no more tumult of oppression and there prevail justice and faith in Allah" (verse 193). Clearly, the vision is one of conquest where the religion of Allah is established as supreme over the pagans of Mecca.

He then goes on to describe the rules of the prohibited months, the months during which warfare was forbidden. The Qur'an later abrogates this rule in the follow up to the Battle of Badr as Muhammad advocates warfare even during the months prohibited for warfare. He encourages his followers to spend their "substance in the cause of Allah," which would seem to be contributions toward the warfare. This is strongly reinforced in later chapters and shows why Muslim charities in the twenty-first century have a strong tendency to get involved in the support of military and terrorist organizations. There then follows rules for the *Hajj* and *umra,* the greater and lesser pilgrimages to Mecca. These are defined at a time when Muhammad and his followers did not have access to Mecca. Perhaps this is in anticipation of the eventual subjugation of Mecca. Muhammad then details other rituals of Hajj, including fasting, maintaining a pure lifestyle, celebrating Allah's praises on Mount Arafat, and so forth . . . (verses 196-200). Muhammad is reinterpreting the pagan rituals of the Hajj, transforming them into the new Islamic ritual. He captures the significant points of Arab pagan culture transferring them into the realm of his new religion and adopting primarily biblical names and

---

[878]   Ibn Kathir, *Tafsir*, Vol. 1, p. 527.

terms to the previously pagan locations and deities. Muhammad concludes the section with warnings about those who pretend to be followers of Allah, but practice "mischief." He calls the believers to "wholeheartedly enter into Islam" and warns them not to "backslide" for Allah will "come to them in canopies of clouds" (verses 208-210).

In the following section, Muhammad addresses both "the Children of Israel" and the "People of the Book." Muhammad uses the second term as a collective term for both Jews and Christians. Was there some kind of representation of Christians in Medina? The verse would seem to indicate this. He claims in this section that they did not differ among themselves except as a matter of selfishness. Muhammad seems to believe in the truthfulness of their revelations, reserving his critique for their "selfish" interpretations. The tafsir literature consistently ignores that meaning. He calls the believers to be steadfast in suffering and to spend in charity adding, "fighting is prescribed upon you, and ye dislike it." From Muhammad's perspective, giving to the *jihad* and particularly giving oneself to the fighting of *jihad* is a form of charity. This leads into a further discussion of the duty of *jihad* and the prohibited month, which can now be violated since they are oppressed and kept from the "sacred mosque" in Mecca (verse 217). Clearly, again, this is an offensive form of *jihad* for the conquest of Mecca. There is deceptiveness in the way these verses are written. They could be interpreted as defensive, yet the cause they espouse could not be accomplished apart from the conquest and subjugation of those who "resist" the Prophet. Mecca's "offense" is that it is controlled by non-Muslims, and thus, its conquest is "defensive" in Muhammad's terminology. Those who are attacked are guilty by virtue of the fact that they have not confessed the prophethood of Muhammad.

This event is very important to the interpreters. Ibn Kathir spends six pages, explaining the events of the raid to Naklah, and its importance in revoking the sacred months during which fighting was prohibited.[879] Yusuf Ali, the moderate Muslim, hypes the supposed crimes of the Meccans and concludes that their activities "are deservedly called worse than slaughter."[880] In fact, the Meccans have done nothing against the Muslims in Medina at all, according to all the Islamic sources. Their aggressive "crime" was not providing access to their enemies to Mecca. The Muslims are the aggressors and that during months that were normally considered months of truce. The event also serves to date

---

[879]   Ibn Kathir, *Tafsir*, Vol. 1, pp. 598-603.
[880]   Ali, Yusuf, p. 85, footnote 238.

the chapter too shortly after the Naklah raid and explains why Muhammad is throwing down the gauntlet to the Jews. He has set events in motion that will lead to a broader war, and he needs to establish who is in his army.

Muhammad then goes on to define gambling and wine as "great sin" and sets rules for orphans "do what is for their good" (verses 219-220). He concludes the section by forbidding his followers to marry unbelievers or to give their daughters to them. This seems to indicate the pagans of Mecca since Muhammad later allows his men to marry wives from the People of the Book. This again makes a clear distinction in Muhammad's mind between pagans and fellow monotheists in contrast to the thesis of Hawting.

Muhammad then defines laws of purity, particularly how to deal with women who are menstruating. They are considered unclean, and one should not have intercourse with them because "they are a hurt and a pollution." He states, once purified, one may have intercourse with them "in any manner, time, or place." He likens them to farmland that one may approach "when or how you will" (verses 222-223). He defines rules concerning oaths, particularly oaths of divorce from women. After divorce, women are not allowed to hide their pregnancy for the child belongs to the father, and there is the possibility of reconciliation in that case. Women have similar rights to men, but "men have a degree over them" (verses 226-228). There follows a long section of rules about divorce. Divorce is to be "equitable," and husbands are not allowed to take back gifts given to their wives. Wives, however, may give back gifts as a way of buying themselves out of a marriage; "she gives something for her freedom," the indication being that the husband does not want to dissolve the union (verse 229). There is also the strange law that if a husband divorces his wife, "he cannot remarry her until after she has married another husband and he has divorced her." Women are allowed to marry "persons of their choice" after a divorce. In the case of divorce, women are allowed to retain their children for two years of breast-feeding before giving them up to their former husbands (verses 232-233). Rules for the remarriage of widows are also defined. Men who divorce before the marriage is consummated shall receive half of the determined dowery back. There is one interesting conflict in the text. Verse 234 and verse 240 give contradictory accounts of how widows are to be maintained after the death of a husband. Ibn Kathir states that verse 234 "abrogates" verse 240 according to "the majority of scholars."[881] This is logically absurd since the text is clearly

---

[881] Ibn Kathir, *Tafsir*, Vol. 1, p. 675. Yusuf Ali, p. 96.

a chronological progression. Yusuf Ali's explanation is short and muddled. These are the kinds of internal conflicts that arise when a fallible human being is the mouthpiece of God.

The habit of prayer is also encouraged "in the manner which he has taught you." This seems to be Allah referring to what Muhammad has taught his people about the postures and timings of prayer. One is to particularly maintain the midday prayer, a possible borrowing from Judaism as we noted earlier. None of the five pillars of Islam is ever fully described in its canonical form in the Qur'an. This is why the traditions of the Prophets and his personal example are so important in understanding Islamic practices. Whatever Muhammad did is canonical for the behavior of Muslims. The Qur'an anticipates and, indeed, teaches this as we shall see.

The next section of chapter 2 contains an apparent attempt of Muhammad to encourage the children of Israel to join his army. Verse 243 seems to be an allusion to Ezekiel's Valley of Dry Bones that is resurrected as a great army. He uses various other Bible stories from the Old Testament as a way to motivate the necessity of utilizing holy war. Unfortunately, Muhammad so mixes up the details of three very different stories that he insured that Jews would find his confused chronology and tale a laughingstock. He argues for fighting in the cause of Allah, stating, "Hast thou not turned thy vision to the chiefs of the Children of Israel after Moses?" (verse 246). The story is the appointing of Israel's king to "fight in the cause of Allah." He then mixes together the story of Gideon during the period of the judges and the choosing of three hundred, with the story of the appointment of Saul (called Talut). Saul tests the army by drinking at a stream and selecting "a few." Then they advance to fight the army of "Goliath and his forces" mixing in a story of David. There is even a hint of the bringing of the Ark of the Covenant into Jerusalem (verse 248). Yusuf Ali tries to reconcile this mishmash of stories by breaking them apart as if Muhammad meant it to be three separate stories.[882] That is clearly not the thrust of the text. Ibn Kathir interprets it as one single story with Saul testing and reducing his army, carrying the Ark of the Covenant into Jerusalem and joining with David to kill Goliath.[883] This must have seemed an impossible parody of scripture to knowledgeable Jews. God concludes the story by stating to Muhammad, "Verily thou art one of the messengers," in the same train as Moses and Jesus who were given similar

---

[882] Ali, Yusuf, pp. 98-99.
[883] Ibn Kathir, *Tafsir*, Vol. 1, pp. 691-695.

"signs" and "strengthened with the Holy Spirit" (verse 252-253). Allah will fulfill his plan. The Jews, if they heard this, must have been incredulous.

There follows a lengthy meditation on the sovereignty of Allah, "the self-subsisting, eternal, who never sleeps" (verse 255 is known as the "throne verse"). Given the power of Allah over all things, Muhammad concludes, "Let there be no compulsion in religion" (verse 256). How this notion fits in with the coercion inherent in the violent *jihad* prescribed earlier is hard to see. Modern Islamic radicals interpret this to mean that Islam's political power must be established by force, but that once Islam's hegemony is established the non-Muslims living under Islamic power as second-class citizens will have freedom of choice. Sayyid Qutb describes it in the following way:

> "Islam has the right to take the initiative. Islam is not a heritage of
> a particular race or country; this is God's religion and it is for the
> whole world. It has the right to destroy all obstacles in the form
> of institutions or traditions which limit man's freedom of choice.
> It does not attack individuals nor does it force them to accept its
> beliefs."[884]

This is a remarkable piece of double-talk that follows in the exact stream of the Qur'an itself. When Yusuf Ali states that Islam must establish its political power, he is, moderate or not, essentially stating the same thing.

Muhammad includes a brief dialogue between Abraham and the pagans about the preeminence of Allah borrowed from Jewish apocryphal stories about Abraham.[885] There is another story about a man caused to die by Allah who is brought back to life after one hundred years. His donkey's bones are also brought back together and filled with life to demonstrate Allah's power to resurrect. These are followed by proverbial similitudes, Abraham and some birds (whose point about the resurrection is unclear), the importance of charity through the similitude of barren stone that does not respond to rain (possibly a borrowing of parable of the soils by Jesus), and the similitude of a garden cared for by an aged man that is "burnt up." Further stories of charity include one enjoining that it is better to "conceal" charity, also reminiscent of the sermon on the mount (verse 271). Muhammad is enjoined by Allah not to set people on the right path, for Allah is the one who "sets on the right path"

---

[884]   Sayyid Qutb, *Milestones*, The Mother Mosque Foundation, p. 75.
[885]   See Ginzberg, *Legends of the Jews*, Vol. 1, pp. 216-217.

(verse 272). In contrast to charity, the Qur'an then forbids usury threatening those who practice it with being "companions of the fire" (verse 275).

In the final two sections of the chapter, Muhammad enjoins the writing down of transactions through the facility of scribes with witnesses. Two men are required for any contract or one man and two women in keeping with the position of a woman's testimony being worth half that of a man (verse 282). He concludes by repeating what the believers must believe in; Allah, angels, books, and messengers, the power of Allah "over all things" and that every soul will receive the "good that it earns" and the "ill that it earns" (verses 284-286). Finally, he cries out to God for help "against those who stand against the faith."

Conclusion

Chapter two of the Qur'an fits very well into the chronology of events posited by the Muslim historians. The points of connection cannot be simple backreading into history. Though opaque at many points, chapter 2 of the Qur'an clearly reflects the historical progression of Islam found in the early Arab historians. The Hijra marks a key turning point in Muslim and world history. Islam is now being defined as the new kingdom of God based on political and military coercion. Warfare for the subjugation of non-Muslims becomes essential to the system. It is a clearly related to the duty of charity (*Zakah*). Judaism and to a lesser degree, Christianity, are rejected in favor of a new sanctuary myth and new practices incorporating what Muhammad found worthy in the old practices of pagan Mecca. A new *ummah* has been established with a strategy for future conquests. If Jews and Christians continue to refuse to recognize Muhammad and his book as the new Prophet and the new Revelation, they now become objects for *jihad*.

CHAPTER 7

THE BATTLE OF BADR
AND ITS AFTERMATH

Introduction

The Battle of Badr was a watershed event in the life of Muhammad, and its effect upon Islamic theology and practice cannot be underestimated. The Battle of Badr is referred to as the *furqan* (salvation or deliverance) in Islamic theology because it was the first showdown between forces of "good" and "evil" for the newfound faith,[886] drawing parallels to the importance of the parting of the Red Sea by Moses in Jewish theology. It is also seen as the battle that paved the way for Muslims to set off on their conquest and domination of a large part of the Middle East, Africa, Asia, and Europe.[887]

We shall follow traditional dating in this section even though the supposed accuracy here is illusory. The details provided and the conversations that supposedly took place are clearly the inventions of a later age. However, in all the early Muslim histories, this engagement was the first major one, and the general dating is fairly consistent, and it clearly was a victory for Muhammad. Badr is not the invention of a later age. The Battle of Badr took place on Ramadan 17, AH 2,[888] or November 18, CE 623. It was to be another raid upon a Meccan trade caravan, however, on a much larger scale.

---

[886] Ali, Yusuf, *The Holy Qur'an,* Brentwood: Amana Corporation, 1991, p. 421 note 1202. The dating for the Battle of Badr has been placed variously at the 17, 19, and the 21 of 2 AH. The exact dating cannot be known due to intercalation problems.

[887] Bashumail, Muhammad, *The Great Battle of Badr*, Delhi, India: Islamic Book Service, 1997, p. 120.

[888] Ali, Yusuf, 413.

The merchants of Mecca engaged in regular trade with Syria that involved caravans traveling up the western coast of Saudi Arabia along the Red Sea. Apparently, due to the onslaught of raids upon their caravans over the previous several months by the Muslims living in Medina, the merchants of Mecca felt the need to band together, sensing perhaps that there would be strength in numbers. The result was a very large caravan of one thousand camels worth fifty thousand dinars in which nearly everyone in Mecca had a financial interest.[889] Again, many of these details are later inventions. According to Ibn Ishaq, when Muhammad heard of this large caravan returning from Syria to Mecca, he declared, "Go attack it, perhaps God will give it as a prey."[890] About three hundred and fourteen volunteers, eighty-three emigrants,[891] and two hundred and thirty-one helpers[892] agreed to go on the raid, although some went reluctantly alarmed that Muhammad would go to war on this scale.[893] This group of Muslim raiders had only two horses and seventy camels that they took turns riding to Badr.[894] The helpers had not engaged in any of the previous raids, being bound only to help the emigrants if they were to be attacked in Medina, however, the prospect of a share of this large booty was perhaps a motivating factor.

Abu Sufyan, the leader of the caravan, apparently had his own agents stationed in Medina and when he received word from them of Muhammad's planned attack he immediately sent a person ahead of the caravan to warn the Meccans and to rally up a protection force. Originally, the Meccans were reluctant to send out an army because of an ongoing feud they had with the Kinana, a neighboring tribe. The Meccans feared the Kinana would seize this opportunity to mount a rear attack while they were fighting the forces of Muhammad, thus leaving them in the vulnerable position of a two-front battle. However, the leader of the Kinana assured them that they would not attack, and therefore, a large force left Mecca to protect the caravan of Abu Sufyan. Muslim historians and theologians have traditionally

---

[889] Watt Montgomery, *Muhammad: Prophet and Statesman*, Oxford, London: Oxford University Press, 1960, p. 119.

[890] Ibn Ishaq, *The Life of Muhammad* trans. Alfred Guillaume, Karachi: Oxford University Press, 1955, p. 289.

[891] Ibn Ishaq, p. 330.

[892] Ibn Ishaq, p. 336.

[893] Ibn Ishaq, p. 289.

[894] Barakat Bashumail, *Muhammad and the Jews,* New Dehli, India: Vikas Publishing House, 1979, p. 57.

interpreted this leader of the Kinana to be the devil himself, sent to deceive the Meccans.[895]

The roads to Mecca, Medina, and Syria converge at Badr, which is approximately ten miles inland from the Red Sea.[896] Sufyan, aware that Badr was the most likely place for an attack from Muhammad, traveled instead along the seacoast, and thereby slipped past the attacking force from Medina. Once the Meccan force received word that the caravan had avoided Muhammad and was safe, many wanted to return to Mecca, sensing there was now no need to fight. However, Abu Jahl, the leader of the Meccan force, insisted that they must go on to Badr to show that they were not intimidated[897] and to hopefully dissuade the Muslims from further raids on their caravans. Again, all of these details are words put into the mouths of the participants to indicate God's controlling hand over the events.

The Muslims, meanwhile, unaware that the caravan had slipped past them, were the first to arrive in Badr. Muhammad seized this opportunity for some strategic battle planning. He sent spies out to obtain a report on the caravan and the force coming from Mecca. The spies captured two water carriers from the Meccan force, who were out looking for water. They brought them back to camp to interrogate them, assuming they were from the caravan. When the water carriers reported that they were from the Meccan force, the Muslims beat them mercilessly, believing that they were lying. The water carriers changed their story to state that they were from the caravan and the Muslims stopped beating them. Muhammad was watching this and rebuked his followers saying, "When they told you the truth you beat them; and when they lied you let them alone."[898] Muhammad wanted to know the size of the force his men would be facing. When the water carriers said they did not know the number, Muhammad asked them how many camels they killed per night to eat. When the water carriers responded that nine to ten camels were slaughtered a night, Muhammad estimated the size of the army to be 900-1,000 strong. Muhammad listened to the advice of one of his men, al-Hubab bin al-Mundhir, and stopped up all the wells in Badr except the one closest to Mecca. The Muslims then surrounded this one well, securing their supply of water and leaving the Meccans in the desperate situation of being in the desert with no access to water. Muhammad

---

[895]   Ibn Ishaq, p. 292.

[896]   Muhammad Hamidullah, *The Battlefields of the Prophet Muhammad*, Hyderabad, 1973, p. 15.

[897]   Ibn Ishaq, p. 296.

[898]   Ibn Ishaq, p. 295.

also strategically massed his army in such a way that when the battle began, the sun would be shinning in the eyes of the enemy instead of their own.[899] These two deft actions allowed Muhammad to dictate the exact location of the battle and secured for him and his army a strategic advantage.

The Battle

The actual battle was short with few casualties by today's standards. It is also certain that the narratives of what happened are the stuff of pious legend and heroic literature. Nevertheless, it is worth looking at these narratives as they give us a picture of how later generations interpreted these events. The battle began with hand-to-hand combat by individual warriors, which Watt states was a normal prelude to Arab battles.[900] A man from Mecca, named al-Aswad, who seeing the only functioning well in Badr being guarded by the Muslims, stepped forward and boasted, "I swear to God that I will drink from their cistern or destroy it or die reaching it."[901] As he approached the well, Hamza Ibn Abd al-Muttalib rushed up to him with his sword drawn and sliced off the lower part of al-Aswad's leg. Al-Aswad crawled to the cistern and threw himself upon it to fulfill his vow and was then killed by Hamza. After witnessing this, three men from Mecca stepped forward and challenged three of the Muslims to come out to fight them. Three of the helpers stepped up, but the Meccans did not accept them, wanting rather for Muhammad to send forward three from the emigrants. Hamza, Ali Ibn Abi Talib, and Ubayda Ibn al-Harith went forward to fight. Hamza and Ali quickly disposed of their opponents, but both Ubayda and his opponent severely wounded each other. As both lay on the ground suffering from their wounds, Hamza and Ali killed Ubayda's opponent and then dragged Ubayda back to their side of the battlefield. Ubayda, bleeding to death from an amputated leg due to a blow from his opponent, said to Muhammad, "Am I not a martyr, O apostle of God?" To which Muhammad replied, "Indeed you are."[902] Muhammad then allows Ubayda the honor of placing his cheek on his foot before dying.[903] These dialogues are pious inventions typical of heroic literature.

---

[899] Hamidullah, p. 19.

[900] Watt Montgomery, *Muhammad at Medina*, Oxford, London: Clarendon Press, 1956, p. 12.

[901] Ibn Ishaq, p. 299.

[902] Ibn Ishaq, p. 299.

[903] Ibn Kathir, *Al-Sira Al-Nabawiyya* Vol. 2 trans. Dr. Trevor Le Gassick, U.K.: Garner Publishing, 1998, p. 272.

These individual battles were followed by a few volleys of arrows shot by both sides and by Muhammad throwing a handful of dust at the Meccans[904] with the order to charge. A fierce melee ensued. During the battle, Muhammad retreated to a hut to pray while the battle raged, with his bodyguard Sa'd and several others standing at the door to protect him and fast horses nearby if an escape was necessary.[905] Muslim authors emphasize the bravado of the Muslims in the battle. One anecdotal report described a man, who in the thick of battle, was struck on the shoulder nearly severing his arm. He continued to fight until his arm became so painful that he stepped on his fingers and pulled off the hanging limb so that he could continue fighting without the hindrance.[906] Another anecdotal story describes the role that angels played in the Battle of Badr and reflects the polemic nature of the ancient Islamic sources. Ibn Ishaq gives the report of a Muslim warrior who was pursuing a Meccan during the battle in order to kill him, only to see the Meccan's head fall off, as a result of being decapitated by an angel.[907] Chapter 8 of the Qur'an, which deals with the battle also relates this idea and is the source of these later embellishments. The end result of the battle, nevertheless, was a decisive victory for the Muslims with fifty Meccans being killed[908] and forty-three taken prisoner,[909] whereas the Muslims only suffered the loss of fourteen men, six emigrants and eight helpers.[910] These small numbers indicate the relative accuracy of the early chroniclers of Islam. The numbers may vary and the names also, but all agree that the number was small and that the Muslims fared far better. These are not the embellishments of an invented drama from a later age.

When the fighting had ceased, Muhammad was anxious to know the status of Abu Jahl, so he gave the order for him to be found and slain. Abdullah Ibn Masud found Jahl writhing in pain and near death because of multiple wounds, including his leg being cut off. Jahl in Mecca had once mistreated Ibn Masud,[911] so Masud seized this opportunity to exact his revenge. He

---

[904]   Qur'an 8:17. See also Yusuf Ali, p. 418, note 1191.

[905]   Ibn Kathir, p. 272.

[906]   Ibn Ishaq, p. 304.

[907]   Ibn Ishaq, p. 303.

[908]   Ibn Ishaq, p. 338. Ibn Kathir states forty-nine were killed and thirty-nine taken prisoner, p. 310.

[909]   Ibn Ishaq, p. 339.

[910]   Ibn Ishaq, p. 337.

[911]   Ibn Ishaq mentions that Jahl had once punched Ibn Masud in Mecca, p. 304. Jahl, it is claimed, was one of a crowd that attacked and punched Ibn Masud in the face while he was reading the Qur'an out loud, pp. 141-2.

placed his foot on Jahl's neck, taunted him, and then cut off his head. He then brought it to Muhammad and said, "This, O Messenger of God, is the head of God's enemy" and threw it down before Muhammad. Muhammad then praised God[912] and made two prostrations in prayer.[913]

Muhammad gave an order for all the bodies of the Meccans killed in the battle to be gathered together and thrown into a pit. Muhammad then asked the dead bodies, "O people of the pit, have you found that what God threatened is true?"[914] apparently referring to whether they now recognized the reality of hell.

It is easy to find contradictions to these stories in the other Sira renditions of Badr. These are, as Rizwi has pointed out, often the result of stylistic selections or efforts to exalt one or another party within Islam. This is not the same as saying that Badr did not take place. Indeed Muslim historians are universal in their focus on this battle and on placing it first among the key engagements in which Muhammad took part. The event itself was not much more than a skirmish, which also shows the relative honesty of the Muslim historians. The tiny number of casualties listed and the relatively small size of the engaging groups indicate that not much embellishment has taken place, other than the typical heroic narrative-type material. Echoes of Badr are clearly seen in chapter 8 of the Qur'an, and clearly, this early victory sets the stage for Muhammad's aggressive posture throughout the final chapters of the Qur'an.

The Treatment of Prisoners of War

There remains a considerable amount of controversy regarding the treatment of the Meccan prisoners of war at the hands of the Muslims. It seems evident that there was a dual standard by which prisoners were handled. Those who had previously caused trouble for the Muslims were treated extremely harshly. Others, such as family members of Muhammad, were treated very leniently. Before the battle began, Muhammad ordered his men not to kill his uncle Al-Abbas. Upon hearing this, Abu Hudhayfa said, "Are we to kill our fathers and our sons and our brothers and our families and leave al-Abbas? By God, if I meet him I will flesh my sword in him!" This angered Muhammad, and Abu Hudhafya never felt safe afterward, concluding that the only way to

---

[912]   Ibn Kathir, p. 294.

[913]   Ibn Kathir, p. 296.

[914]   Ibn Ishaq, p. 305.

atone for this was to die as a martyr, which he did several years later in the Battle of al-Yamama.[915] Al-Abbas was captured as a prisoner, and Muhammad showed kindness to him by finding him a shirt[916] and by releasing the ropes that bound his hands.[917] Al-Abbas later became a Muslim and became a prominent figure in Islamic history.

Another example of favorable treatment extended toward a prisoner of war was Muhammad's son-in-law. Muhammad's daughter Zaynab was still living in Mecca with her husband, Abu al-As. Abu al-As was wealthy and one of the esteemed men of Mecca. He was the son of Halah, the sister of Muhammad's first wife Khadijah. Khadijah asked Muhammad to give their daughter Zaynab to al-As in marriage, and Muhammad consented.[918] When Zaynab learned that her husband was a prisoner of war, she sent Muhammad a necklace that her mother had given to her as a wedding present as ransom. He was so moved by this gesture that he gave Zaynab the necklace back and released al-As, but only on the condition that she move to Medina and their marriage be dissolved. Later, he became a Muslim, and Zaynab was then given back to him as his wife.[919]

In contrast to this kind treatment received by those who had gained the favor of Muhammad, those who were in bad standing with him or other Muslims suffered the full weight of their wrath. Muhammad ordered the execution of at least two prisoners. Uqba bin Abi Muait is reported to have thrown dung, blood, and intestines of a slaughtered camel on Muhammad's back while he was prostrating in prayer while still living in Mecca.[920] When Muhammad saw Uqba as a prisoner of war, he ordered him to be killed. Uqba pleaded for mercy, crying out, "Who will look after my children?"

Muhammad responded, "Hell!" and gave the order for his execution.[921] Muhammad also ordered a poet named Al-Nadr executed because he claimed that his stories about Persia were just as good as the Qur'an.[922] Al-Nadr's sister wrote a poem to Muhammad after the execution stating, "Muhammad, you

---

[915]   Ibn Ishaq, p. 301.
[916]   Bukhari, Vol. lV, p. 156.
[917]   Al-Tabari, *The Foundation of Community* ed. and trans. W. M. Watt and M. V. McDonald. Vol. 7, *The History of al-Tabari,* Albany, NY: State University of New York Press, 1989, p. 69.
[918]   Al-Tabari, p. 73.
[919]   Al-Tabari, p. 77.
[920]   Al-Bukhari, Vol. I, p. 295-6.
[921]   Ibn Ishaq, p. 308.
[922]   Watt, 1956, pp. 12-13.

the finest son of a woman noble . . . it would not have harmed you to forgive him, for a valorous man often forgives despite his anger or rage."

Muhammad responded by saying, "If only this had reached me before his death, I would have spared him!"[923]

Other Muslims followed the example of Muhammad in exacting revenge on their enemies who were prisoners of the Battle of Badr. Abdur-Rahman was hoping to get a sizeable ransom for his prisoner Umayya. When Bilal, a Muslim who was mistreated by Umayya in Mecca before fleeing to Medina with Muhammad,[924] saw Umayya, he cried, "The arch-infidel Umayya Ibn Khalaf! May I not live if he lives!"[925] Bilal and his friends began to chase Abdur-Rahman and Umayya. Abdur-Rahman's account of the event is preserved in the Hadith as follows:

> Being afraid they would catch us, I left Umayya's son for them to keep them busy but the Ansar killed the son and insisted on following us. Umayya was a fat man, and when they approached us, I told him to kneel down, and he knelt, and I laid myself on him to protect him, but the Ansar killed him by passing their swords underneath me, and one of them injured my foot with his sword.[926]

The treatment of these three prisoners may seem harsh to the modern reader, however, Muhammad was actually rebuked for letting any of the prisoners live according to Qur'an chapter 8, as we shall see later. His bodyguard, Sa'd, was blunt with Muhammad stating, "Yes, by God, O Messenger of God, this is the first battle God has waged against the polytheists and I would have preferred the men to be massacred rather than kept alive."[927] Later, Muhammad was to receive a revelation from Allah in regard to the taking of prisoners at Badr. "It is not fitting for a Prophet that he should have prisoners of war until he hath thoroughly subdued the land . . . Had it not been for a previous ordainment from Allah, a severe penalty would have reached you for the (ransom) that

---

[923] Ibn Kathir, p. 318.

[924] Ibn Ishaq records that Umayya used to torture Bilal by taking him out during the heat of the day, placing a large rock on his chest and telling him either to deny Muhammad and worship idols, or die, pp. 143-4.

[925] Ibn Ishaq, p. 303.

[926] Al-Bukhari, Vol. III, pp. 282-3

[927] Ibn Kathir, p. 290.

ye took."[928] Ibn Kathir states that Muhammad was sorry for ransoming them and that he should have put all of the prisoners of war to death.[929]

The Problem of Booty

One of the problems that resulted for the Muslims after the Battle of Badr was the division of booty. No doubt, there was disappointment over not capturing the caravan being led by Abu Sufyan, as was originally intended. Nevertheless, there was substantial booty to be found among the Meccan army that they defeated. Muhammad's uncle, al-Abbas, was one of the richest men in Mecca, and was forced to ransom himself and three cousins for a total of one hundred ounces of gold.[930] There were doubtless items necessary for battle among the booty, such as armor, weapons, and camels that would have been valuable to the Muslims. The issue of rightful ownership of this booty led to a dispute among the Muslim warriors. Those in possession of the booty claimed it belonged to them, whereas others argued that the booty should be divided equally among all of those who participated in the battle.[931] In this time of crisis, Muhammad received a revelation[932] from Allah on the handling of booty captured in war:

> And know that out of all the booty that ye may acquire (in war), a fifth share is assigned to Allah—and to the Messenger, and to near relatives, orphans, the needy, and the wayfarer—if ye do believe in Allah and the revelation we sent down to our Servant on the Day of Testing—the Day of the meeting of the two forces. For Allah hath power over all things.[933]

Yusuf Ali adds in a commentary footnote:

> The rule is that a fifth share is set apart for the Imam (the Commander) and the rest is divided among the forces. The fifth share reserved is

---

[928] Qur'an 8:67-68.
[929] Ibn Kathir, pp. 298ff.
[930] Bashumail, p. 177.
[931] Al-Tabari, p. 64.
[932] Muhammad received the revelation of surah 8, a full twenty pages in length, in response to the Battle of Badr, most of which deals with how to distribute the spoils of war.
[933] Qur'an 8:41.

expressed to be for Allah and the Prophet, and for charitable purposes for those to whom charity is due. Ultimately, everything is at the disposal of Allah and His Prophet: 8:1: but four-fifths are divided, and only one-fifth is retained for the special purposes. The Imam has discretion as to the mode of division. In the Prophet's lifetime a certain portion was assigned to him and his near relatives.[934]

It is interesting to note that another verse in the same chapter declares that all of the booty is "at the disposal" of Allah and the Prophet. This is interpreted as a general principle modified by the later principle of 20 percent to the army commander.

The Drunkeness of Hamza

One of the odd stories told both in the Hadith and the Sira literature is the celebration of the Muslims after the victory in which Hamza, one of the heros of the battle, gets roaring drunk and insults the Prophet. The story begins with Hamza stealing one of the camels from the booty in order to slaughter it and hold a celebration with his friends. He happens to take a camel allotted to Ali. In the midst of the celebration, Ali complains to Muhammad about the stolen camel and the Prophet goes in to speak to Hamza. Hamza by this time is quite drunk and in the altercation with the Prophet that follows he insults the Prophet. Hamza's physical strength is legendary and he was known as Muhammad's protector during his time in Mecca. The Prophet backs off from the confrontation. This story is so incredible in its content and so cross-grained with the lionization of Hamza, which is found in all the early Muslim histories that one must consider it to be historical. This event may have laid the foundation for Muhammad's later ban on alcohol. But one cannot imagine any reason for making up a story like this and getting it accepted by the larger Muslim community, concerning one of its great early heros and martyr at Uhud. This is history, not eulogy.

Assessment of the Muslim's Victory

Muslims have traditionally maintained that victory at the Battle of Badr where they were so greatly outnumbered, three hundred and fourteen against nine hundred and fifty, was achieved only by supernatural intervention by

---

[934]   Ali, Yusuf, p. 424, note 1209.

Allah, thus verifying that Islam is the one and only true religion. Yusuf Ali, in a commentary footnote, states, "It was impossible, without the miraculous aid of Allah, for such a small and ill-equipped force as was the Muslim band, to defeat the large and well-found force of the enemy. But their firmness, zeal and discipline won them divine aid."[935] The Qur'an has several descriptions of the supernatural help that Allah provided enabling the Muslims to win this improbable victory. Causing the Muslim army to appear twice their actual size in the eyes of the Meccans (3:13), the sending of three thousand angels to fight on their behalf (3:124; 8:9), rain that helped the Muslims (8:11),[936] drowsiness sent from God that enabled them to remain calm (8:11), and a dream where Allah showed the Meccan army to be few in number (8:43).

It is, however, possible to see many practical reasons for the Muslims victory without making an appeal to supernatural help. It is true that the original force of Meccans numbered around nine hundred and fifty men; however, when they received word that Abu Sufyan and the caravan were safe, many no longer felt the need to fight. In fact, at least one entire tribe, the Banu Zhrah, turned back to Mecca and did not fight in the Battle of Badr. It is not clear how many men this totaled, but some have estimated as many as 250-350.[937] Of those who remained, many were older,[938] whereas the Muslim fighting force appeared to be much younger.[939] Muhammad's strategy seemed to be to work with the disenfranchised and angry young men. Islam follows the same pattern in the prisons of the United States where in New York 30 percent of inmates are now Muslims. The Meccans were wealthy and soft, whereas the Muslims had been living in hardship for several years and had been toughened through the experience.

Not only were the Muslims younger and in better shape than the Meccans, but they also had an attitude more suitable for winning a battle. Muslim historians portray the Meccans as cocky and overconfident. When a messenger from the caravan came to the protecting force from Mecca to inform them that the caravan was safe and they were free to return to Mecca without fighting, they replied, "By God we will not go back without halting at Badr and staying there for three nights . . . for none of the Arabs will see

---

[935] Ali, Yusuf, p. 129, footnote 353.
[936] See Ali, Yusuf, p. 416, footnote no. 1187 for how rain helped the Muslims.
[937] Watt, 1956, p. 13.
[938] Ibn Ishaq, p. 291 and Bukhari, Vol. III, pp. 282-3
[939] Al-Tabari, p. 52-3.

us and our army and dare to fight us."[940] While the historicity of this account is negligible, since it is unlikely that the Muslims knew what the Meccans were discussing before the battle, it, nevertheless, illustrates the truth that the Meccans did not seem to have any real motivation to fight other than to maintain the status quo and personal honor. The Meccans had no desire to engage in a bloody battle to the finish, but rather simply wanted to protect their caravan and their trade route to Syria.

The Muslims, on the other hand, were more in a position of desperation with little to lose. They had a greater sense that their future was dependent upon this victory. A scout from the Meccans recognized this attitude of desperation and gave the following report when he returned to the Meccan camp, "The enemy are people who do not have any safe refuge or retreat except their swords. By God, I do not think a man of them will be killed until he has killed a man of you, and if they kill as many of you as there are of them, what will be the good of life after that?"[941] Muhammad had also effectively convinced his fighting force of the glories that awaited them in Paradise if they were to die in this *jihad*. After promising every man, he could keep all the booty he took, Muhammad said, "By him in whose hands Muhammad's soul rests, if any man fights them today and is killed, fighting steadfastly and with resignation, going forward, and not turning back, then God will cause him to enter Paradise." One man upon hearing this yelled, "Excellent! All that stands before me and entering Paradise is being killed by these people!" then he threw aside the dates he was eating, grabbed his sword and fought until he was killed.[942] Another man asked Muhammad, "O Messenger of God, what makes the Lord laugh with joy at his servant?" To which Muhammad replied, "Plunging his hand into the enemy without armor." The man then ripped off his armor, grabbed his sword and also fought until he was killed. This spirit of unity and devotion to Muhammad was a sharp contrast to the division that existed among the Meccans toward their leader Abu Jahl.[943] Whether or not these accounts are historically accurate, or later insertions for the purpose of glorifying the act of being martyred in *jihad*, in one sense is irrelevant, since the main function they serve is to provide motivation for Muslim men to engage in religious war with the hope of eternal life through martyrdom. We can see the power of that motivation in the twenty-first century.

---

[940]   Al-Tabari, p. 32.
[941]   Al-Tabari, p. 49.
[942]   Al-Tabari, p. 55.
[943]   Ibn Ishaq, pp. 296-8.

Muhammad also was clearly the greater strategist militarily. As mentioned previously, arriving at Badr first, stopping up the wells, and choosing where the battle would be fought gave them a great advantage. Muhammad also strategically made a treaty with the Banu Damra in August of 623 CE, just three months before the Battle of Badr.[944] The Banu Damra lived in the region of Badr, thus giving Muhammad a useful ally in the area, and more importantly, it put the Meccans on enemy territory.

Results of the Battle of Badr

There were many results from the Battle of Badr. The animosity between the Meccans and the Muslims grew to an irreparable level. Abu Sufyan had one son killed and another taken prisoner in Badr. He forbade any sign of mourning in order to minimize the rejoicing of the Muslims, and vowed revenge. He was the commander-in-chief against the Muslims in the upcoming Battle of Uhud.[945] It also had a devastating effect upon the power base of Mecca. Many of the leaders and most influential men in Mecca were killed on the battlefield at Badr creating a power vacuum that weakened Mecca, preparing it for its eventual fall.

On a much more profound level, the Battle of Badr had an impact upon Islamic thought, values, and practice that has extended to our modern day. The Battle of Badr was the first watershed event concerning *jihad* and martyrdom that entered the psyche of the Muslim mind. In what is probably an apocryphal story, the value Muslims place on *jihad* is illustrated by a conversation between the angel Gabriel and Muhammad, "How do you look upon the warriors of Badr among yourselves?" Muhammad answered, "As the best of Muslims."[946] The Qur'an itself from this point on extols the value of *jihad* and martyrdom in *jihad*. Another account from the Hadith shows Allah encouraging Muslims to be involved in *jihad*, as well as illustrating its twofold reward, booty in this life and Paradise in the hereafter.

"He (God) is committed to his care that He will either admit him to paradise or bring him back to his home from where he set out with a reward of his share of booty . . . if a person gets wounded in the way of Allah, he will come on the day of judgment with his wound in the same condition as

---

944   Al-Tabari, p. 12
945   Sell, Canon Edward, *The Battles of Badr and Uhud*, Madras, India: The Christian Literature Society, 1909, p. 33.
946   Al-Bukhari, Vol. V, p. 221.

it was when it was first inflicted; its color being the color of blood but its smell will be the smell of musk."[947]

Strongly linked with the valor of *jihad* is the glory of dying as a martyr in a religious war. The following story is recorded about a grieving mother speaking to Muhammad about her son who was killed in the Battle of Badr:

> "Haritha was martyred on the day (of the battle) of Badr, and he was a young boy then. His mother came to the Prophet and said, "O Allah's Apostle! You know how dear Haritha is to me. If he is in Paradise, I shall remain patient, and hope for reward from Allah; but if it is not so, then you shall see what I do?" He said, "May Allah be merciful to you! Have you lost your senses? Do you think there is only one Paradise? There are many Paradises and your son is in the (most superior) Paradise of Al-Firdaus."[948]

If the Western reader finds it difficult to understand the passion for which Muslims long for martyrdom, he or she must remember that it is the only way that a Muslim can be guaranteed forgiveness of sins and entrance into heaven:

> "Messenger of Allah, do you think that if I am killed in the way of Allah, my sins will be blotted out from me? The Messenger of Allah said: Yes, in case you are killed in the way of Allah and you were patient and sincere and you always fought facing the enemy, never turning your back upon him."[949]

The victory at Badr also greatly increased the prestige and political power of Muhammad. Defeat at this stage would have greatly hindered his ability to gather future followers, but this victory, especially while being outnumbered, allowed him to declare supernatural support from Allah, thus deepening his own faith and that of his followers. It had a profound unifying effect upon the *ummah* of Muslim believers in Medina. There was perhaps no greater way to convert the polytheists around him, in Medina and Mecca, to his cause than with the expectation of booty and the promise of honor in war.[950]

---

[947]   Muslim, Vol. III, p. 1043.
[948]   Bukhari, Vol. V, p. 318.
[949]   Muslim, Vol. III, p. 1047.
[950]   Arent Jan Wensinck, *Muhammad and the Jews of Medina*, Freiburg in Breisgau: K. Swartz, 1975, p. 105.

Edward Sell astutely observed that, "The die was now cast . . . Islam must now stand or fall by the arbitration of the sword."[951]

The Assassinations of Abu Afak and Asma bint Marwan

Riding the wave of rising power and prestige after the Battle of Badr, one of Muhammad's first actions[952] was to strengthen his position in Medina by turning his attention against his enemies. Abu Afak and Asma bint Marwan were both Jewish proselytes from the Arab tribe of Umayya b. Zayd[953] in Medina. Afak wrote a poem against Muhammad to show his disapproval of Muhammad's murder of al-Harith b. Suwayd b. Samit. Muhammad responded to this poem by asking, "Who will deal with this rascal for me?" Salim b. Umayr, a follower of Muhammad from Afak's same tribe, volunteered and killed Abu Afak who apparently was a very old man.[954] Similarly, Marwan displayed her displeasure with Muhammad and his followers for the murder of Afak by writing a poem criticizing them. Muhammad responded in a similar way as he did with Afak by again asking, "Who will rid me of Marwan's daughter?" Umayr b. Adiy al-Khatmi, a Muslim from the same tribe of Marwan, volunteered his services and went that very night and killed her while she was sleeping. Muhammad's response to this assassination was, "You have helped God and His apostle, O Umayr!"[955]

In our modern day, where political cartoons and satires are common, these actions may cause some to doubt the historical reliability of these accounts and to question whether it was possible for Muhammad to have responded so extremely. Ruven Firestone addressed this issue when he studied public satire in the Arabic culture of Muhammad's day and concluded the following:

> Pre-Islamic Arabian society in general placed great importance on the effectiveness of oral satire as a political weapon. This was usually accomplished through composition and recitation of poetry, which was used as much to discredit or humiliate enemies as to enhance the status and pride of one's own kinship group. Poetic satire to demean

---

[951] Sell, p. 35.
[952] Rubin, Uri, ed. *The Life of Muhammad*, Brookfield: Ashgate Publishing, 1998, p. 208. Jones bases the dating of the murder of Afak and Marwan on Al-Waqidi's account, which places it shortly after the Battle of Badr.
[953] Michael Lecker, *Muslims, Jews and Pagans*, Leiden: E. J. Brill, 1995, pp. 38, 52.
[954] Ibn Ishaq, p. 675.
[955] Ibn Ishaq, pp. 675-6.

or humiliate one's enemy was used in Muhammad's own day as well, and some of Muhammad's enemies in Medina are known to have used poetry as a weapon against him."[956]

It is also true that there is much disagreement in the Sira literature as to the chronology of these assassinations. Some have interpreted these events as heroic literature invented not real, or else ignored the stories completely. However, there is great consistency in the stories of assassinations, that they happened and in many cases who was murdered. It should not surprise us that one hundred and fifty years after the events there might be disagreement as to whether a murder took place after Badr or after Khandaq. No one doubted or questioned that assassinations were part of the political policy of the Prophet. This is historical reality, not fantasy. One would be very hard-pressed indeed to explain why such stories would be made up or how they could have gained credence in the Muslim world if false. At the time these materials were written, the writers were fully under the control of Muslim authorities.

These two assassinations show Muhammad's success in breaking down the tribal loyalties that were so strong in ancient Arabia and replacing them with allegiance to Islam. They also helped the spread of Islam in Medina. Ishaq informs us, "The day after Bint Marwan was killed the men of Banu Khatma became Muslims because they saw the power of Islam."[957] The power of coercion was to become a major tool of the Muslims in their rapid expansion during the following several centuries. Finally, these two assassinations illustrate Muhammad's increasing intolerance for any form of opposition to his role as prophet. Clearly, his focus is on the Jews as all of the assassinated individuals come from Jewish backgrounds. He now expands his intolerance for individual Jews to an entire Jewish tribe.

The Expulsion of the Banu Qaynuqa

Who Were the Banu Qaynuqa?

During the seventh century AD there was a large Jewish population living in the city of Medina, perhaps even constituting a majority. Estimates

---

[956] Reuven Firestone, "The Failure of a Jewish Program of Public Satire in the Squares of Medina," *Judaism 46*, 1997, p. 444.

[957] Firestone, p. 76.

vary from 10,000[958] to 36,000 or perhaps as much as 42,000.[959] Wensinck is pessimistic about these higher estimates, fearing they are inflated to demonstrate the power of Islam to overcome all odds; he, nevertheless, acknowledges that the Jews in Medina "constituted a formidable force because of both their numerical strength as well as their property."[960] As mentioned in the previous chapter, the Jewish population consisted of three tribes: the Banu Qaynuqa, Banu al-Nadir, and the Banu Qurayzah, as well as Jewish converts in many other tribes. The smallest of these three tribes was the Banu Qaynuqa, consisting of, at the most, seven hundred men.[961] Unlike the other two Jewish tribes, the Banu Qaynuqa owned no land or cattle; however, they owned two forts and made their living by trade and crafts. Many were goldsmiths, some manufactured armor[962] and weapons,[963] and they conducted a large and influential market in Medina.

The Expulsion

On March 27, CE 624,[964] four months after the Battle of Badr, Muhammad gathered the Banu Qaynuqa together in their market and ordered them to convert to Islam: "O Jews, beware lest God bring upon you the vengeance that He brought upon Quraysh (i.e., at Badr) and become Muslims. You know that I am a prophet who has been sent—you will find that in your scriptures and God's covenant with you."[965] The Qaynuqa responded emphatically that they would not accept Muhammad as a prophet nor convert to Islam. They apparently sensed his rage at this point for they fled to one of their towers where Muhammad had them placed under siege. After fifteen days had passed, they surrendered, had their hands tied behind their backs, and preparations were made for their execution. At this point, Abdullah Ibn Ubayy, a professing Muslim and a good friend of the Qaynuqa, made a passionate plea for Muhammad to be merciful and spare their lives. At first, Muhammad did not listen to him, upon which Ibn Ubayy thrust his hand into Muhammad's

---

[958]　Wensinck, p. 28.
[959]　Bashumail, p. 57.
[960]　Wensinck, p. 28.
[961]　Bashumail, p. 108.
[962]　Watt, 1960, p. 98.
[963]　Watt, p. 84.
[964]　Al-Tabari, p. 85.
[965]　Ibn Ishaq, p. 363.

collar, which caused Muhammad to become so angry that his face became discolored and he shouted, "Damn you, let me go!" Ibn Ubayy insisted that he would not let him go until he was merciful and spared the lives of the Qaynuqa. Muhammad finally responded, "Let them go; may God curse them, and may he curse (Ibn Ubayy) with them." Upon their release the entire tribe of the Banu Qaynuqa were expelled from the city of Medina.[966]

Reasons for the Expulsion

A common belief among Muslims is that there was an event at the market of the Qaynuqa that was the impetus to the expulsion of the Qaynuqa. According to this tradition, a Muslim woman was sitting in the market place of the Qaynuqa, and a mischievous Jewish goldsmith played a trick on her by attaching her skirt to a nail in such a way that when she stood up she was immodestly exposed. While the Jews were laughing at this event, an outraged Muslim man killed the Jewish goldsmith, and then the Jews retaliated by killing the Muslim.[967] This event then escalated to the eventual siege and expulsion of the Qaynuqa. However, there are several reasons to question the historicity of this account. First, it was not originally recorded by Ibn Ishaq in his account of the life of Muhammad, but rather was added almost one hundred years later by his redactor Ibn Hisham.[968] McDonald, in his preface to his translation of Al-Tabari, also questions the historicity of this event. He concludes that Al-Tabari, by his omission of the story, although he wrote after Al-Waqidi who included the event, showed that he judged it to be inaccurate.[969] This story of a woman being exposed due to a trick played on her in the market appears in legends of pre-Islamic Arabia.[970] Therefore, it seems best to conclude that this was a later insertion used to justify Muhammad's actions against the Qaynuqa.

Ibn Ishaq states another reason given for the expulsion of the Qaynuqa in his account. First, he gives the description of Muhammad's summon to the Qaynuqa to acknowledge him as a prophet and convert to Islam, followed by a verse from the Qur'an that was supposedly aimed at the Qaynuqa: "Those who reject Faith—neither their possessions nor their (numerous) progeny will

---

[966]   Al-Tabari, pp. 86-7.
[967]   Bashumail, pp. 55-6.
[968]   Bashumail, p. 19.
[969]   Al-Tabari, p. xxviii.
[970]   Watt 1960, pp. 130-1.

avail them aught against Allah; they are themselves but fuel for the Fire."[971] Ibn Ishaq then inserts a tradition that accuses the Qaynuqa of being "the first of the Jews to break their agreement with the apostle and to go to war, between Badr and Uhud."[972] There is a perplexing lack of detail given here. What was this agreement? How did the Qaynuqa violate it? Some have claimed that it dealt with the Jewish tribes not helping at the Battle of Badr;[973] however the Jews were only bound to protect Muhammad if he was attacked in Medina and was under no obligation to take part in campaigns outside of Medina.[974] No one has been able to produce evidence that any such rebellion by the Qaynuqa occurred. Wensinck is likewise suspicious and concludes the following:

> "This general tradition is ill-placed as far as the course of the account is concerned. Ibn Ishaq, of course, included the tradition at this place because he wanted to present the Jews as having committed some offense before Muhammad besieged them. The trick is obvious and on account of this failed-according to non-Islamic interpretation. The words inserted have no bearing on the context."[975]

It seems best to pursue other options for insight into possible factors that precipitated the expulsion of the Banu Qaynuqa.

After the Battle of Badr, Muhammad became concerned with consolidating his power and strengthening the *umma* that existed in Medina. As McDonald notes, "The very life of the Islamic religio-political community at Medina depended on the wholehearted belief that Muhammad was a prophet and the Qur'an the word of God."[976] There existed two main threats to these desires of Muhammad: the Jews and the *munafiqun* in Medina.[977] The most famous and purported leader of the *munafiqun* was Ibn Ubayy who was allied with Banu Qaynuqa.[978] Therefore, an attack on the Banu Qaynuqa would serve

---

[971]   Qur'an 3:10.
[972]   Ibn Ishaq p. 363.
[973]   Keshk, Muhammad Yusuf Ali, *The Conflict Between Muhammad and the Three Jewish Tribes of Medina* University of Utah, 1987, p. 52.
[974]   Hannah Rahman, "The Conflicts between the Prophet and the Opposition in Medina," *Der Islam 62*, 1985, pp. 2778.
[975]   Wensinck, p. 107.
[976]   Al-Tabari, p. xxviii.
[977]   Keshk, p. 51.
[978]   Keskh, p. 43.

two purposes by getting rid of one of the Jewish tribes and also striking out at the leadership of the *munafiqun*.

The market situation in Medina presents another important factor worth considering in the expulsion of the Banu Qaynuqa. There were four markets in Medina, two were owned by Jews and one by Ibn Ubayy.[979] When Muhammad and the other emigrants came to Medina, Muhammad took land near the Qaynuqa[980] and attempted to set up a market near the Qaynuqa;[981] however, it was unsuccessful, and Muhammad had to abandon this idea.[982] The market was important to Muhammad and the emigrants for two reasons. The emigrants made their livelihood from trade, unlike the helpers who mostly worked in fields. The inability of Muhammad to successfully establish a market left the emigrants largely without work and dependent upon the financial support of the helpers, which was becoming burdensome.[983] Another financial benefit of the market was the regular collection of taxes from all the merchants who sold goods in it.[984] The market was also strategic from a political standpoint:

In pre-Islamic Arabia as in the early days of Islam (and even in later periods or in the present) when tribal units continuously and persistently fought each other, formed and broke alliances, the market served as a common meeting place where any kind of social intercourse could take place without fear of acts of terror and violence . . . Control over the market involved not only economic advantages, but also political authority.[985]

Obtaining the market of the Qaynuqa and weakening of the two groups who posed the greatest threat to his religiopolitical reign, the Jews and the *munafiqun*, provided two powerful and persuasive reasons for Muhammad to expel the Qaynuqa.

A final reason really had to do with the ultimate threat to Muhammad, the content of his Qur'an, and his position as the new Prophet. Much of his material for the Qur'an was derived from Jewish oral traditions. But his material was mixed up, contradictory, and chaotic in such a way that the Jews

---

[979]   Michael Lecker, "On the Markets of Medina (Yathrib) in Pre-Islamic and Early Islamic Times" *Jerusalem Studies in Arabic and Islam 8*, 1986, p. 137.

[980]   Michael Lecker, "Muhammad at Medina: A Geographical Approach," *Jerusalem Studies in Arabic and Islam 6*, 1985, p. 38.

[981]   Lecker, 1986, p. 140.

[982]   Rahman, p. 279.

[983]   Watt, 1956, p. 251.

[984]   Keshk, p. 50.

[985]   Rahman, pp. 278-9.

could not have but rejected him. Once he realized this, Muhammad must have understood that the Jews, all the Jews, were the greatest potential threat to him, more than the Meccans. They were the ones who could demonstrate the inconsistencies, the anachronisms, and the contradictions in his text. They were the ones who could demonstrate that the Qur'an could not be the book of God, at least from a Jewish perspective. Thus did the people who Muhammad must have assumed would be his greatest allies, become his greatest enemies. The gradual expulsion and eventual extermination of the Jews in Hejaz must be seen as a deliberate policy of Muhammad around which apocryphal stories were invented to justify the actions.

Results of the Expulsion

The expulsion of the Banu Qaynuqa gave the first opportunity for the Muslim community to implement the law of the division of booty given after the Battle of Badr. Therefore, Muhammad received one-fifth of the booty and the rest of the Muslims received the other four-fifths.[986] The booty consisted of goldsmith's tools and armor, from which Muhammad claimed three bows, three swords, and two coats of mail.[987] This was minor, of course, compared with getting the market with all of its financial benefits.

The expulsion also had political ramifications. One Jewish tribe was eliminated from Medina. Ibn Ubayy's influence was reduced, which provided a warning to all of the other *munafiqun* to reconsider their lack of commitment to Muhammad. Finally, it showed the other two Jewish tribes the vulnerability of their position in Medina.[988]

The Raid on the Meccan Caravan at Qarada

What follows next is treated as a minor event in all of the ancient Islamic sources, and yet it was a strategically important event. The many raids before Badr and then the devastating defeat at Badr convinced the Meccans that they should no longer attempt to risk travel to Syria along the western trade route. After staying in Mecca for nearly a year following the Battle of Badr, Abu Sufyan began to reason that they needed to find an alternative route to Syria before they consumed all of their tradable items. They solicited the

---

[986] Al-Tabari, p. 87.
[987] Rahman, 271.
[988] Wensinck, p. 48.

help of an Arab guide, Furat Ibn Hayyan, who promised to take them along the Iraqi, or the eastern, route to Syria, on a path unknown to the Muslims. However, Muhammad received word of the planned trip and immediately sent out a force led by Zayd Ibn Harithah to intercept the caravan. Zayd captured the caravan at Qarada, a watering hole in Najd. All of the men of the caravan escaped with the exception of the guide, Ibn Hayyan. The caravan contained a large amount of silver, providing nice booty for Muhammad and his followers. His Muslims captors warned the prisoner, Ibn Hayyan, that if he converted to Islam, Muhammad would not kill him. When he was brought before Muhammad, he confessed faith in Islam and was released.[989]

This seemingly minor raid had two major implications. The trade route to Syria from Mecca was now completely sealed off. Clearly, this weakened Mecca and would soon bring them to the desperation of needing to come up with some sort of reprisal against Muhammad. The event at Qarada also provided the first example of forced conversion. Throughout history, as Islam spread, many would face the same choice as Ibn Hayyan, but not all would follow his example. Muhammad was gradually discovering that coercive violence works, not only in establishing political hegemony, but also in providing a way to motivate conversion.

Content of the Qur'an up to and Following the Battle of Badr

According to Islamic traditions, chapter 8 of the Qur'an entitled, "The Spoils of War," actually deals with the aftermath of the Battle of Badr. If this is true, then there are three other chapters according to Nöldeke's schema, which were revealed before Badr, and one other chapter revealed after but before the next major engagement at Uhud. In this section, I will consider the content of five chapters of the Qur'an in their assumed chronological order. These are chapters 98, 64, 62, 8, and 47.

Chapter 98: The Clear Evidence

Chapter 98 contains just 8 verses and is a reflection on who is righteous among the People of the Book and polytheists. Clearly, the divisions that Muhammad had established in the previous chapter were being questioned, probably by his own followers. His message is both conciliatory and condemnatory but establishes acceptance of his revelation as the benchmark.

---

[989] Al-Tabari, pp. 98-9.

This thrust is confusing and perhaps intentionally so. One can read the chapter in two quite different ways.

Verse 6 says that the People of the Book and the polytheists "will be in hellfire" because they "reject." The implication from verse 2 is that the rejection is of "a Messenger from Allah rehearsing scriptures." He calls such people, "the worst of creatures." Yet in verse 7-8 he says, "Those who have faith and do righteous deeds—they are the best of creatures. Their reward is with Allah, gardens of eternity." This sounds like a conciliatory statement meant to indicate that both polytheists and the People of the Book could go to heaven. Certainly, those who wished to could read the passage either as a condemnation or a potential vindication of those who were probably their own relatives. But the key to the passage is verse 5: "They have been commanded to do no more than this: To worship Allah . . . To establish regular prayer and to practice regular charity." Clearly, Muhammad has in mind those who convert to Islam and follow the laws of his new community. The "Bayyinah" of verse 4, Ibn Kathir interprets, is the Qur'an with the new revelation through Muhammad. It is the new "evidence."[990] The language is nevertheless politically clever and meant to inspire confusion and self-questioning in the minds of those who are not insiders to the movement and do not understand the code words of the new religion. The practice of regular charity, as we will note, means contributing to the Muslim war preparations. *Zakah* is primarily for the support of *jihad*. This chapter is an interesting brief vignette of the emerging political prophet. It also contains no information on warfare or booty distribution and thus may be seen as occurring before Badr.

Chapter 64

The 18 verses of chapter 64 continue in a similar sentiment. Muhammad reflects on the power and total knowledge of Allah, concerning both believers and unbelievers. Messengers have been sent with clear signs so at verse 8, he makes his command, "Believe, therefore, in Allah and his messenger and in the light which we have sent down," referring again to the "sign" which is the Qur'an. He declares that those who reject will be "companions of the fire." He warns the believers to beware even their wives and children and to practice charity by "loaning" to Allah. This is not what is usually meant by charity. This investment will be paid back. Perhaps the return is meant as

---

[990]   Ibn Kathir, *Tafsir*, Vol. 10, p. 550.

much to be the fruits of *jihad* as the "gardens beneath which rivers flow" in the next life. This brief chapter is preparatory to war but there is, again, no indication that any major struggle has taken place. It may also be seen as part of the ongoing sorting out of who is in Muhammad's camp and who is not.

Chapter 62: Friday

This chapter is a further condemnation of the Jews and a calling to Muslims to make Friday their holy day of prayer. It is both a demarcation against Judaism and a delineation of a new holy day. Muhammad directly compares himself to the Jewish followers of the Mosaic law. He speaks of himself as "the unlettered, a messenger from among themselves (i.e., the Arabs), to rehearse to them his signs, to sanctify them, and to instruct them in scripture." (verse 2) He compares the Jews who were charged with the "Mosaic law" with donkeys who cannot read the books they carry about (verse 5). Ibn Kathir explains that Jews were worse than donkeys because, though donkeys could never understand, the Jews could and yet refused. Yusuf Ali accuses them of blasphemy for disobeying God's law and indicates that this is typical of "Judaism."[991] We are approaching the kind of dehumanization that always proceeds hatred and oppression. He throws down his gauntlet again, declaring, "O ye that stand on Judaism, if ye think ye are friends to Allah, then express your desire for death." (verse 6) For Muhammad, the litmus test of true faith is the willingness to die in *jihad*. Ibn Kathir's interpretation of a challenge to call down curses upon oneself does not fit the context at all.[992] Muhammad's concern was his army. The Jews were unwilling to join Muhammad in *jihad* and are, therefore, among the condemned who stand outside of the kingdom of God. He concludes the passage with rules concerning the celebration of Sabbath on Friday. This must have been a further break with the traditions of Judaism that set Muhammad increasingly on a collision course with the Jews. Calling the Jews "donkeys" and demanding their rejection of their own religion indicates that Muhammad has already decided how this group is going to respond to him. Muhammad's ultimate dealing with the Jews of Al-Qaynuqa, Al-Nadir, and Banu Qurayza can be seen in the light of these powerful dehumanizing sentiments.

---

[991]   Ibn Kathir, *Tafsir*, Vol. 9, p. 635, Yusuf Ali, p. 1546, footnotes 5457, 5458.
[992]   Ibn Kathir, *Tafsir*, Vol. 9, p. 635.

Chapter 8: The Spoils of War

The 75 verses of chapter 8 ("The Spoils of War") are believed by Muslims to be the section of the Qur'an that directly reflects the events of the Battle of Badr. Badr is not named in the chapter, but the ethos of the entire chapter is the aftermath of a victorious battle. The chapter opens with the question of the division of the booty taken in battle. The spoils should be "at the disposal of Allah and the Messenger." (verse 1) The spoils of this battle is military equipment, and thus, they belong exclusively to the commander of the army. Muhammad is not just a Prophet, but the victorious commander in chief determining the division of the spoils.

Muhammad chides some of the believers for disputing with the Prophet when he ordered them out of their houses to battle. Verse 7 is crucial in fixing the chapter as regarding Badr. Muhammad declares that Allah promised one of two parties in the battle, and they wished for the unarmed one, but "Allah willed to justify the truth." The story as recounted in the Sira literature is that Muhammad's forces had sought to capture a Meccan caravan but had, instead, encountered a force of Meccans sent to protect the caravan. Thus, the raid became not a snatch and grab but a battle in the true sense, albeit on a very minor scale. Both Ibn Kathir and Yusuf Ali agree on these interpretations of the passage. Muhammad interprets this military victory as a victory of truth over falsehood. God himself fought on their behalf, says the Prophet, with "a thousand angels." This is the source of all the hagiographic material concerning angels fighting at the Battle of Badr. God strengthened their hearts and instilled "terror in the hearts of the unbelievers" (verses 9-12). The sin of the unbelievers was that "they contended against Allah and His Messenger" (verse 13). He goes on to declare, "for those who resist Allah is the penalty of the fire." Not just for the unbelievers, but those of the believers who turn their backs in battle (except in the case of a "stratagem of war") draws "the wrath of Allah, and his abode is hell." He concludes this section with a taunt to the unbelievers to desist in fighting. Their defensive warfare is interpreted as offensive because they are unwilling to submit to the messenger. The Prophet declares that the multiplication of their forces will do "not the least good" (verse 19).

Muhammad then calls the believers to "obey Allah and the Messenger" calling those who do not listen or obey "the worst of beasts." Muhammad's hand has been strengthened and now he is expecting implicit obedience on the part of the Medinan forces. This absolutist attitude becomes pervasive throughout the remaining chapters of the Qur'an. He reminds them that they were once "a small band despised through the land," but they have now received sustenance. They are called to be grateful and not betray "the trust of Allah and the Messenger" (verses 26-27).

In the following section, Muhammad reminds the believers of what has been plotted against them by the unbelievers and how Allah is the best of plotters on their behalf. This seems to me an interesting example of projection. Clearly, Muhammad is the one who has been conspiring against the Meccans, carrying out raids, plotting, and provoking warfare. Muhammad rehearses again the arguments that the Meccans had put to him during earlier times of dialogue, that the Qur'an is not unique, but a simple tale like those of the ancients. "Let Allah send down his judgments!" they say. Muhammad interprets that God would not do that as long as the believers lived in the midst of the unbelievers or "whilst they could ask for pardon" (verses 32-33). He goes on to justify the war on Mecca based on the Meccans keeping the believers from the "Sacred Mosque," which should only be guarded by "the righteous." Their prayers at the "Mosque" are "nothing but whistling and clapping" and a blasphemy (verses 34-35). Muhammad promises that they will be "gathered together to hell" and "cast into hell" (verses 36-37). Thus, in the thinking of Muhammad, their defensive actions are offensive. Their very presence at the sacred "mosque" is an offence worthy of war.

Muhammad makes a rhetorical invitation to the "unbelievers" to desist from resistance, and then commands the believers "fight them on until there is no more tumult and oppression and there prevails justice and faith in Allah." (verse 39) This is a war that demands conversion to Islam. He mentions another rule for booty that 20 percent should be assigned to Allah and the Messenger (verse 41). It is unclear how this relates to the previous command, but the mention of the caravan in the next verse indicates a different rule in regard to the capture of an economic prize.[993] He mentions again the "day of meeting of the two forces." This was predestined "that Allah might accomplish a matter already enacted" (verse 42). This section lists various signs indicating what God was about to do, a dream where the unbelievers were seen as few and their way of looking at each other on the battlefield. Why these should be considered "signs" is not clear from the text. The final sign is Satan's allurements, which failed because Satan himself turned and fled when the battle began, fearing Allah, and his judgment. Thus, the unbelievers of Mecca are demonized and the believers who fight the *jihad* without doubt are the righteous.

---

[993]   Perhaps this is in reference to the raid at Qarada where a caravan was captured.

A refrain occurs several times in this chapter; "for Allah is strict in punishment" (verses 13, 48, and 52). The next section elaborates on this theme describing the hypocrites and the unbelievers as the ones who will "taste the penalty of the blazing fire" (verse 50). The punishments are meted out for those who reject the "signs," which at this point seems to be a cipher for the Prophet himself and the revelations. The people of Pharaoh were destroyed for their lack of faith in the "signs of the Lord" (verse 54). Muhammad repeats an earlier analogy concerning them, "For the worst of beasts in the sight of Allah are those who reject him" (verse 55). There is also a sense of Muhammad lashing out at those in Medina who did not fully support this expedition. The focus on the hypocrites is a critical sign of this. He accuses some unnamed group of breaking "their covenant every time." Yusuf Ali interprets this as the Jews of Banu Qurayzah and, thus, sets the stage of righteousness for their slaughter.[994] Ibn Kathir makes no such connection, claiming that the passage refers to how Muslims should be treated who break their treaties, that is, with severe punishments. This seems to be the beginning of Muhammad dealing with the problem of hypocrites who claimed to be his followers but were not willing to engage in battle with him.[995] He says, "If ye gain the mastery over them in war, disperse . . . them." This passage shows how opaque the Qur'an is for Muslim interpreters. Ibn Kathir is certainly not shy to blame the Jews, especially of Banu Qurayzah, of every imaginable crime. But even he is not inventive enough to find them in this obscure reference. In this sense, the moderate and the radical Muslim are not qualitatively different in how they use the Qur'an. Muhammad instructs his followers to respond in kind to those who use "treachery" (verses 56-58).

Muhammad then focuses on the importance of striking terror into the hearts of enemies, both the ones you know and the ones you don't know. He emphasizes obtaining "steeds of war, to strike terror into the enemies." (verse 60) He calls for generous giving to enable the believers to obtain these means of warfare. Again, giving in the cause of Islam at this stage seems to be primarily for the purpose of funding *jihad*. There then occurs a more conciliatory verse, "if the enemy incline toward peace, do thou incline toward peace" (verse 61). The question again is under what conditions? The whole thrust of the passage would indicate that if the enemy capitulates to Islam then make peace and convert them. It has nothing to do with peace on an equal footing.

---

[994]   Ali, Yusuf, p. 429, footnote 1224.
[995]   Ibn Kathir, *Tafsir*, Vol. 4, p. 342.

The final section of the passage is a further battle cry. God calls to Muhammad, "O Prophet! Rouse the believers to the fight. "If there are twenty amongst you, patient and persevering, they will vanquish two hundred" (verse 65). Yet, God chides him, "there is a weak spot in you" such that one hundred "will (only) vanquish two hundred" (verse 66). God goes on to say, "It is not fitting for a Prophet that he should have prisoners of war until he hath thoroughly subdued the land" (verse 67). This is the weak spot. The rationale is that one should not "look for the temporal goods of this world" (verse 67). The implication seems to be that instead of taking hostages for ransom, Muhammad should simply have executed the prisoners he had taken. Ibn Kathir ignores this completely, probably because it implies some sort of sin on the part of the Prophet.[996] Yusuf Ali makes the passage refer to the captured idolators, which is absurd since the passage is addressed to the one who "took ransom."[997] It is the following verses that seem to be Allah's instruction on what to say to the ransomed captives. Indeed the Sira literature tells the story of several executions after the Battle of Badr, though most of the captives were ransomed. This turns into a criticism of the Prophet, which again affirms God's sovereignty. "Had it not been for a previous ordainment from Allah, a severe penalty would have reached you for the (ransom) that ye took." Yet Allah decides to condone this action, "Enjoy what you took in war, lawful and good." Thus does the inscrutable Allah affirm that the blameworthy behavior was according to his prior arrangement and is, therefore, lawful and good.

He then instructs the Prophet to address the captives, "If Allah findeth anything good in your hearts, He will give you something better" (verses 68-70). The implication seems to be that they can gain release through converting to Islam, a universal notion among the interpreters, and that this will set them free to also take part in the *jihad*. "And He will forgive you" must have seemed a bitter pill to swallow for people who had primarily come out to protect their own property. Muhammad then goes on to affirm that there was no "duty of protection" toward those who had been left behind in Mecca, even "those who believed" (verse 72). This would indicate that the killing of Muslims living in enemy territory is permissible. Muhammad seems to

---

[996]   Ibn Kathir, *Tafsir*, Vol. 4 pp. 354-355. It is very clear that Ibn Kathir is simply avoiding any interpretation of this supposed sin on the part of the Prophet. Allah wanted more violence not less.

[997]   Ali, Yusuf, p. 432, footnote 1235. Here also he skirts any sort of interpretation of what the Qur'an actually says.

define as true believers only those who have left Mecca and accepted exile to be part of his new Ummah. These are the ones who are "in very truth the believers." For them there is forgiveness and "a provision most generous" (verse 74). He defines the true believers as those who "fight for the faith" (verse 75).

Chapter 47: Muhammad

Yusuf Ali interprets *jihad* as primarily defensive warfare. In his introduction to this surah, he states, "The Muslims were under threat of extinction by invasion from Makkah." As we have seen, however, the Meccan response to Muhammad was entirely the result of Muslim aggression against Mecca. "Aggression" in the mind of the Prophet was any resistance to the hegemony of the Prophet. Peace is offered only to those who capitulate and convert to Islam. This is hardly defensive warfare. Further, the Battle of Badr was not a Meccan invasion of Medina, but an expedition to protect Meccan property. Yusuf Ali is a moderate interpreter of the Qur'an, but his ideas would not be acceptable to Muslim commentators familiar with the background of the passages. *Jihad* is offensive warfare for the purpose of the conquest and conversion of non-Muslims, period. Yusuf Ali dates the surah from before the Battle of Badr. But there are references to Muslim casualties and hostages. It is an ongoing meditation on the necessity and holiness of offensive *jihad* to conquer the polytheists, reflective of the period after Badr.

The chapter has thirty-eight verses divided into four sections. Muhammad begins by defining who is righteous and who is not. Those who hinder in the way of Allah by rejecting Allah will be led astray while those who believe in what is sent down to Muhammad and who do works of righteousness will have their "ills" removed by Allah and will "improve their condition" (verses 1-2). This is one of the few times where Muhammad is named directly in the Qur'an, and it is from this usage that the chapter is named. The remainder of the chapter goes on to describe what the works of "righteousness" are.

"Therefore, when ye meet the unbelievers, smite at their necks . . . when ye have thoroughly subdued them, bind a bond firmly: thereafter either generosity or ransom: until the war lays down its burdens." He goes on to say "those who are slain in the way of Allah—He will never let their deeds be lost . . . Soon will He . . . admit them to the garden." Warfare is necessary until the enemy is completely defeated, and the promise of the delights of heaven is oft repeated for those who are slain in the way of *jihad*. Muhammad points out the fate of all previous generations that "hate the revelation of

Allah." They are brought to "utter destruction," but Allah is the "protector of those who believe" (verses 8-11).

The second section is a familiar reflection on the contrast of the delights of heaven and the horrors of hell. In some ways, it reminds of the earliest chapters of the Qur'an where similar reflections are very common. Here, however, we are dealing with promises made to those in the aftermath of war. The similarity of these descriptions with those of the earliest chapters of the Qur'an indicates a continuity of authorship though now with a very different perspective. "Allah will admit those who believe and do righteous deeds, to gardens beneath which rivers flow . . . those who reject Allah . . . the fire will be their abode" (verse 12). Clearly, the righteous deeds envisioned here are the deeds of combat in holy war by which one has died. There is also a clear effort to dehumanize those who reject Allah, they "eat as cattle eat." This is similar to the phrase "worst of beasts," which occurs regularly in these chapters.

He mentions "thy city which has driven thee out" and how many larger cities than this "have we destroyed." Muhammad then compares the joys of heaven, "incorruptible rivers," "rivers of wine," and "rivers of honey" to "the fire . . . to drink boiling water so that it cuts up their bowels" (verse 15). This latter hell is the fate not only of those who resist the Prophet, but also of those who forget, "What is it he said just then?" (verse 16). At the end of this section Muhammad is commanded to ask forgiveness for "thy fault, and for the men and women who believe" (verse 19). It is not clear what this means, but the statement of culpability on the part of the Prophet could have at least some mollifying effect on the otherwise continual drumbeat that those who are believers are the "righteous ones" of whom Muhammad is the foremost as the Prophet and the Messenger. However, Yusuf Ali interprets this merely as Muhammad speaking as the representative of his people, not as someone with any sort of personal moral fault.[998] Ibn Kathir ignores the verse's clear meaning and deals only with the sins of believers.[999]

The third section introduces *jihad* as a kind of test of the sincerity of believers. When "fighting is mentioned" in a revelation, those who respond "in a swoon at the approach of death" are the ones in whose heart is "a disease." These are the ones that "Allah has cursed," they do not "earnestly seek to understand the Qur'an." They are the "apostates" whom "the evil one has instigated" (verses 24-25). These are the ones whom "the angels

---

[998]   Ali, Yusuf, p. 1383, footnote 4841.
[999]   Ibn Kathir, *Tafsir*, Vol. 9, pp. 102-105.

take . . . at death and smite their faces and their backs" because "they followed that which called forth the wrath of Allah." The unwillingness to engage in *jihad* is the test that separates false Muslims from true ones. Muhammad is declaring Muslims who are unwilling to fight in *jihad* to be *takfir*, not true Muslims. They are the same as infidels, and this forms the basis for modern Islamist terror against fellow Muslims. As one Pakistani jihadist put it when asked about killing fellow Muslims, "if they were true Muslims, they would be with us in the *jihad*."[1000]

In the final section of the chapter, God promises to "test those among you who strive (*jihad*)" to see who are "those in whose hearts is a disease." They are called "those who reject Allah" who "hinder from the path of Allah." Not engaging in violent *jihad* is apostasy. Thus, "Those who reject Allah and hinder from the path of Allah . . . Allah will not forgive them" (verses 32 and 34). The believers are encouraged to "Obey Allah and obey the messenger." "Be not weary and fainthearted, crying for peace," Muhammad declares as he urges them on in the holy war. They are also "invited to spend in the way of Allah." For those who do not, "He will substitute in your stead another people." Charity is for the purpose of enabling the warfare.

In conclusion, these five chapters clearly reflect the ethos both before the first major battle and the aftermath of that battle. There are no second thoughts, such as we might expect after the Battle of Uhud, which the Muslims lost. The attitude is a strident one of holy war that insists upon the utter defeat, subjugation, and conversion of those who resist the authority of the Prophet. It is doubtful that Muhammad had this power of control in the general affairs of Medina, even at this time. But here he is primarily addressing his own troops and his sense of where this struggle is going is palpable. The Jews are the enemy as are the Meccans. God promises final victory to those who demonstrate total obedience to Allah and the Prophet through engaging in the holy war.

[1000] Interview with a suicide bomber; JIRGA; http://www.youtube.com/watch?v=w8gu5Xfi_E4.

CHAPTER **8**

MIDDLE MEDINA PERIOD (CE 623-624)

Part 1: Muhammad after Badr

1.1. Muhammad's Power and Prestige Grows after Badr

As we discussed in the previous chapter, the Battle of Badr was the first significant military success of Muhammad's career in Medina. However, we may conclude that "the most important result of the battle was the deepening of the faith of Muhammad himself and his closest companions in his prophetic vocation,"[1001] which included a psychological aspect.[1002] There were strategic political considerations as well. Muhammad's political consolidation is one of the major factors answering the question, "why and how Muhammad was ultimately able to overpower the Meccans and other rivals in Arabia in the face of overwhelming odds against him."[1003] Muhammad's rise to power can be summarized in three themes according to Fred M. Donner: first, "the consolidation of his hold over Medina itself"; second, "his struggle against the pagan Quraysh of his native Mecca, who were for long his primary rivals"; and third, "his efforts to bring other tribal groups under his control."[1004] Muhammad made rapid and aggressive progress

---

[1001] Watt W. Montgomery, *Muhammad at Medina*, Oxford: Clarendon Press, 1956, p. 15.

[1002] Caetani's assumption quoted by Wensinck, A. J in *Mohammed en de Joden te Medina*, ed. and trans. W. Behn as *Muhammad and the Jews of Medina*, Freiburg in Breisgau: K. Schwarz, 1975, p. 105.

[1003] Fred M. Donner, "Muhammad's Political Consolidation in Arabia up to the Conquest of Mecca" in *Muslim World 69* (1979), pp. 229-230.

[1004] Donner, 1979, p. 230.

on power consolidation in Medina, in the midst of his ongoing struggling against the pagan Quraysh.[1005]

The Battle of Badr along with the later capture of the Meccan caravan at Qarada weakened the Quraysh of Mecca, just as it strengthened Muhammad's power in Medina. From this point on, the pagan population in Medina was easily won over to him. There remained some hypocrites (*munafiqun*) among them, but their power was limited.[1006] The only main potential resistance to his consolidation of power in Medina came from the three major Jewish clans—the Banu Qaynuqa, Banu al-Nadir, and Banu Qurayza.[1007] After Badr, Muhammad's first action was the expulsion of Banu Qaynuqa. Other Jewish clans remained silent, due to their internal divisions and allegiances to other Arab tribes allied with Muhammad. Muhammad targeted the weakest Jewish tribe first. According to Ibn Ishaq's account,[1008] Muhammad assembled the Banu Qaynuqa tribe in their market and urged them to accept Islam. While they refused to do so, he "besieged them until they surrendered unconditionally."[1009] Finally, they were expelled based on the intercession and pleading by Abdullah b. Ubayy. Hannah Rahman, an Islamic scholar, makes two significant political conclusions in regard to this expulsion. First, that Muhammad was now able to have better control over the market in Medina and second, that he managed to further reduce the influence and power of Abdullah b. Ubayy.[1010] On the other hand, for Muhammad, the neutralization of internal enemies in Medina was his prerequisite action to win over the external enemies. His victory at Badr provided him the great opportunity to realize this plan.[1011] The first achievement of this plan, undoubtedly, was the expulsion of Banu Qaynuqa, but clearly, the content of the Qur'an indicates that his ultimate goal was the elimination of the Jews.

Besides dealing with the collective opponents in Medina, Muhammad also developed a new strategy to deal with individual political opponents there. "There

---

[1005] Donner, 1979, pp. 230-231.
[1006] For example, Abdullah b. Ubayy, who was a hypocrite and the protector of Banu Qaynuqa. See Gil Moshe. "The Medinan Opposition to the Prophet" in *Jerusalem Studies in Arabic and Islam*, 10, 1987, p. 77.
[1007] Donner, 1979, p. 231.
[1008] Ibn Ishaq, Muhammad, *The Life of Muhammad*, ed. trans., and with an introduction by Alfred Guillaume, Karachi: Oxford University Press, 1955, p. 363.
[1009] Ibn Ishaq, 1955, p. 363. Also see Wensinck, 1975, p. 106.
[1010] Hannah Rahman, "The Conflict Between the Prophet and the Opposition in Medina" in *Der Islam 42*, 1985, p. 271.
[1011] A. J. Wensinck, *Mohammed en de Joden te Medina,* ed. and trans. W. Behn as *Muhammad and the Jews of Medina,* Freiburg in Breisgau: K. Schwarz, 1975, p. 105.

were some people in Medina of either Jewish or partly Jewish stock who had roused Muhammad's anger with satirical poems directed against him personally and the Muslims in general."[1012] To establish his status in Medina, the assassination of individual opponents would be an essential political strategy. We have considered the assassinations of both Asma bint Marwan and Abu Afak. Muhammad was fully aware of the importance of ideology and the power of poetry in that regard. The coercive use of religion in Muhammad's thinking became an excellent tool for empire building under the direct permission of God. We will now turn to see the murder of Ka'b b. al-Ashraf, the best known and foremost event of assassination of the satirists of Muhammad's political movement.

1.2.   The Assassination of Ka'b b. al-Ashraf

The assassination of Ka'b b. al-Ashraf took place after Badr and before the Battle of Uhud.[1013] There are disagreements about chronology and participants, but the historicity and importance of the story, which occupies about 5 percent of Ibn Ishaq's Medinan period text, is without doubt. Ibn Ishaq presents the assassination of Ka'b b. al-Ashraf as part of Muhammad's policy to remove political enemies in Medina.[1014] After the Battle of Badr, Muhammad sent Zayd b. Haritha to the lower quarter of Medina, and Abdullah b. Rawaha to the upper quarter of Medina to tell the Muslims of Medina about the victory of God. When Ka'b b al-Ashraf, the Jewish leader whose father was an Arab and mother was from Banu al-Nadir, heard the news he said,

> "Is this true? Did Muhammad actually kill these whom these two men mention? These are the nobles of the Arabs and kingly men; by God, if Muhammad has slain these people 'twere better to be dead than alive."[1015]

[1012] Wensinck, 1975, p. 110.

[1013] There are two different dates for the assassination of Ka'b b. al-Ashraf. In the Sira literature (Ibn Ishaq and Waqidi), his death is dated after the Badr and before the Uhud, while in the Tafsir literature, "the connection between Ka'b's death and the exile of Al-Nadir has been preserved in the commentaries on Surat al-hashr." See Uri Rubin's article, "The Assassination of Ka'b b. al-Ashraf," *Oriens 32* (1990) for a detailed discussion on this issue. We take the Sira literature's position for this dating based on the convincing argument in Uri Rubin's article. See also J. M. B. Jones, "The Chronology of the Maghazi," in *BSOAS* 1956, p 248. See also Wensinck, 1975, p. 113.

[1014] Ibn Ishaq, 1955, pp. 364-369.

[1015] Ibn Ishaq, 1955, p. 365.

Ka'b went to Mecca and encouraged the Quraysh to revenge. He wept with Quraysh and composed poetry to encourage them. Then he returned to Medina and composed a poem about Ummu'l-Fadl d. al-Harith:

> Are you off without stopping in the valley
> And leaving Ummu'l-Fadl in Mecca?
> Out would come what she bought from the pedlar of bottles,
> Henna and hair dye.
>
>> What lies 'twixt ankle and elbow is in motion
>> When she tries to stand and does not.
>> Like Umm Hakim when she was with us
>> The link between us firm and not to be cut.
>> She is one of B. 'Amir who bewitches the heart,
>> And if she wished she could cure my sickness.
>> The glory of women and of a people is their father,
>> A people held in honor true to their oath.
>> Never did I see the sun rise at night till I saw her
>> Display herself to us in the darkness of the night![1016]

Ummu al-Fadl bt. al-Hadith was the wife of Al-Abbas, who was captured at Badr. "She was from the important nomadic tribe of 'Amir b. Sa'sa'ah" and it is not clear why Ka'b should have praised her."[1017] Subsequently, Ka'b also composed love poetry of an insulting nature about the Muslim women. These poems finally led to the assassination of Ka'b.

We need to point out that there are many different versions of why Muhammad was angered with Ka'b, as describes by Rizwi:

One such story attributes their differences to the Prophet's desire to establish a market on the land of the Banu Qaynuqa, another, to the fact that Ka'b had joined with the Quraysh to plan an attack against Muhammad when he heard of the Muslim defeat at Uhud.[1018]

[1016] Poetry quoted from Ibn Ishaq, 1955, pp. 366-367; also found in Al-Tabari, *The History of al-Tabari*, Vol. VII, The Foundation of the Community, edited and trans. by W. M. Watt and M. V. McDonald, Albany: State University of New York Press, 1989, pp. 94-95.

[1017] Al-Tabari, 1989, p. 94, footnote 158.

[1018] Rizwi S. Faizer, "The Issue of Authenticity regarding the traditions of al-Waqidi as Established in his Kitab al-Maghazi" in *Journal of Near Eastern Studies*, Vol. 58, Issue 2, 1999, p. 102, which he quotes from M. J. Kister, "The Market of the Prophet" in *Journal of the Economic and Social History of the Orient 8* (1965): 272-76 and Uri Rubin, "The Assassination of Ka'b b. al-Ashraf" in *Oriens 32* (1990): 66

However, as Rizwi further describes, Al-Waqidi holds the same narrative and reason for Ka'b's murder with Ibn Ishaq: that "he was killed because he had insulted the Prophet after the Battle of Badr."[1019] Al-Waqidi's account is as follows:

> "Ka'b b. al-Ashraf, distraught over the news of the death of so many brave Meccans at the hands of the Muslims at the Battle of Badr, incited the residents of that city to assert themselves by hurling insults at the Prophet and his followers. Angered by these crude expressions of hostility, the Prophet decided to have Ka'b eliminated."[1020]

When Muhammad decided to get rid of Ka'b, Muhammad b. Maslamah was willing to take the challenge. With the permission of Muhammad, Maslamah together with another five Muslims devised a plot to kill Ka'b. Muhammad also permitted them to tell lies or any act of treachery in order to achieve the mission:

> "When the apostle was told of this [the fasting of Maslamah due to his lack of confidence to kill Ka'b] he summoned him and asked him why he had given up eating and drinking. He [Maslamah] replied that he had given him an undertaking and he did not know whether he could fulfill it. The apostle said, "All that is incumbent upon you is that you should try." He said, "O apostle of God, we shall have to tell lies." He answered, "Say what you like, for you are free in the matter."[1021]

With the help of Ka'b's foster brother, Abu Na'ilah, they managed to win Ka'b's confidence by telling a lie and giving the murderers an excuse to meet with him privately by night with their weapons. Ibn Ishaq describes the scene of murder:

> "[Abu Na'ilah invited Ka'b for a night walk] so they went off walking together; and after a time Abu Na'ilah ran his hand through his hair. Then he smelt his hand, and said, "I have never

---

[1019] Rizwi S. Faizer, "Muhammad and the Medinan Jews: A Comparison of the texts of Ibn Ishaq's Kitab Sirat Rasul Allah with Al-Waqidi's Kitab al-Maghazi" in *International Journal of Middle East Studies*, 28, 1996, p. 472.

[1020] Al-Waqidi's narrative quoted from Rizwi S. Faizer, "The Issue of Authenticity regarding the traditions of Al-Waqidi as Established in his Kitab al-Maghazi" in *Journal of Near Eastern Studies*, Vol. 58, Issue 2, 1999, pp. 102-103.

[1021] Ibn Ishaq, 1955, p. 367; See also Al-Tabari, 1989, p. 95.

smelt a scent finer than this." They walked on farther and he did the same so that Ka'b suspected no evil. Then after a space he did it for the third time, and cried, 'Smite the enemy of God!' So they [other murderers] smote him, and their swords clashed over him with no effect. Muhammad b. Maslamah said, 'I remembered my dagger when I saw that our sword were useless, and I seized it. Meanwhile the enemy of God had made such a noise that every fort around us was showing a light. I thrust it into the lower part of his body, then I bore down upon it until I reached his genitals, and the enemy of God fell to the ground . . . We carried him and brought him to the apostle at the end of the night."[1022]

Ka'b was finally killed, and his head was presented to Muhammad. Ibn Ishaq accurately noted the significance of this event among the Jews tribes:

"Our attack upon God's enemy cast terror among the Jews, and there was no Jew in Medina who did not fear for his life."[1023]

The terror raised among the Jewish tribes was the significant result and impact of this assassination. In the next morning after the assassination, Muhammad made a declaration to his people, "Kill any Jew that falls into your power."[1024] Ibn Ishaq's account about the affair of Muhayyisa and Huwayyisa was a good illustration of this point.[1025] Following the above declaration given by Muhammad, Ibn Sunayna, a Jewish merchant was killed by Muhayyisa. Ibn Sunayna, in fact, was having social and business relations with Muhayyisa and his family. Huwayyisa, the elder brother of Muhayyisa, who was not a Muslim at that time, was shocked with this murder, and started to beat his brother. Muhayyisa replied that if Muhammad commanded him to kill his own brother, he would have done so as well. Huwayyisa embraced Islam, as he was amazed with such a marvelous faith that superceded family loyalties. Again, these details are part of traditional heroic literature, but the historical reality lying behind this and reflected in the text of the Qur'an is unmistakable. The minimalist theories that try to use contradictions in these texts as a means for throwing them out as evidence of history, have themselves

---

[1022] Ibn Ishaq, 1955, p. 368. See also Al-Tabari, 1989, p. 97.
[1023] Ibn Ishaq, 1955, p. 368. See also Al-Tabari, 1989, p. 97.
[1024] Ibn Ishaq, 1955, p. 369. Al-Tabari, 1989, p. 97.
[1025] Ibn Ishaq, 1955, p. 369.

no way to arrive at any sense of history. History is written not by focusing only on the inconsistencies, but by focusing on the areas of consistency and understanding what they indicate.

In Al-Waqidi's account, however, he mentions that there was an agreement made between Muhammad and Banu al-Nadir after the murder of Ka'b; and "afterward the Jews were cautions and afraid and humiliated because of the murder of Ka'b b. al-Ashraf."[1026] Some scholars, such as Wensinck, view this narrative as a false report. He suspects that Al-Waqidi's personal view of Muhammad had caused him to loose sight of true history.[1027] Michael Lecker doubts Al-Waqidi's account on the assassination of Ka'b. He argues that Al-Waqidi combined three different traditions from earlier Muslim sources to generate a new version of the narrative, which is not historically true.[1028] However, Rizwi S. Faizer argues from another perspective. He believes that Al-Waqidi's account is correct and, in fact, is consistent with Ibn Ishaq's account. The reason why Ibn Ishaq did not mention the agreement between Muhammad and the Jews was due to his main theme of writing about Muhammad's prophecy and his prophetic calling, "whether an agreement was broken or not, as far as Ibn Ishaq was concerned, was beside the point."[1029] The important point we may observe is the emphasis on the coercive power of fear in all these accounts. This is the reconciling point between Ibn Ishaq and Al-Waqidi that the Jews were under tremendous fear and anxiety after the assassination of Ka'b. Assassination was a policy, which had its desired effect, whatever the particulars might have been.

In dealing with the cause of this assassination, Hannah Rahman comments that Muhammad definitely should have a legal ground to permit a death verdict for the member of the *ummah*. She suggests that the legal ground for this verdict was Ka'b's insulting poetry and his relationship with the Meccans.[1030] It is interesting that she uses legal terminology for an event that had nothing to do with courts of law. Rahman also points out that in Al-Waqidi's account, the assassination of Ka'b was viewed as a shameful deed in Medinan society,

---

[1026] Wensinck, 1975, p. 114.

[1027] Wensinck, 1975, p. 114.

[1028] Michael Lecker, "Waqidi's Account on the status of the Jews of Medina: A Study of a combined report" in *Journal of Near Eastern Studies* 54, Chicago, 1995, pp. 16-17.

[1029] Rizwi S. Faizer, *Muhammad and the Medinan Jews*, 1996, p. 480.

[1030] Hannah Rahman, "The Conflict Between the Prophet and the Opposition in Medina" in *Der Islam* 42, 1985, p. 281.

and some viewed it as an act of treachery (*ghadr*).[1031] Another distinguished scholar, Watt, makes the following conclusion concerning the assassination of Ka'b b. al-Ashraf:

> "Such measures made it clear that Muhammad was not a man to be trifled with. For those who accepted him as leader there were material advantages; for those who opposed him there were serious disadvantages. Thus, apart from Muhammad's preaching, men had many reasons for taking his side."[1032]

Muhammad's next move involved removing the second most powerful Jewish group in Medina. We have some evidences that the Banu al-Nadir was not expelled immediately after the assassination of Ka'b.[1033] However, there is a poem in Ibn Ishaq's account that linked these two events together. Ka'b was the leader of Banu al-Nadir, and his assassination was "considered later as the advent of the fate of his clan."[1034]

There are a few implications we can draw from this assassination. First, the policy of assassination had now become part of the strategic policy of Muhammad toward his enemies. As an empire builder, those who accepted and supported him would gain many material advantages, but he would deal ruthlessly with whoever resisted. Second, using coercion to induce people to convert to Islam became an acceptable part of Muslim policy where this was advantageous. Third, the use of deceit and treachery in Islam becomes permissible, where this can lead to success. The ends justify the means, and it is not without reason that three of the first four caliphs were murdered.

Part 2: The Event and Significance of the Battle of Uhud

2.1.   The Reason for the Battle

After the raid on the Meccan caravan at Qarada, the trade routes to Syria from Mecca were potentially cut off. Both the western and eastern trade routes to Syria were now within the reach of the Muslims. The Muslims used the Bedouin system of tribal raiding in a new way to bring Mecca to her knees.

[1031]   Rahman, 1985, pp. 281-282.
[1032]   Watt, 1956, p. 19.
[1033]   Wensinck, 1975, p. 115.
[1034]   Wensinck, 1975, p. 115.

Since all the materials about the battle are from the Muslims traditions, the Quraysh were always categorized as the aggressor of the battle. However, as the commercial community, the Quraysh had a justifiable reason to attack the Muslims in order to relieve the difficulty they faced in their trading business. "They had to fight for their very existence as a commercial community and for freedom to carry on their daily business."[1035] Certainly, the Quraysh also intended to take vengeance for their previous defeat at Badr.

2.2. The Preparation for the Battle

The Battle of Uhud took place on Shawwal AH 3 (625 CE) in the third year after the Hijrah and about a year after the Battle of Badr.[1036] We can only give a rough outline of this battle, as the collection of materials on this battle mainly emphasize individual hero's exploits and rebutting of accusations against them.[1037] Under the leadership of Abu Sufyan b. Harb, the Meccans were able to gather about three thousand warriors, and after marching about ten days, they reached the oasis of Medina. They camped at the oasis near the hill of Uhud, which was about three miles north of the city of Medina. Informed by spies, Muhammad held a war council early on Friday morning. Apparently, Ibn Abbas, who was Muhammad's uncle acted as a spy in the city of Mecca, following his release after Badr, and he informed Muhammad earlier about the movement of Quraysh.[1038] In the war council, Muhammad and other senior men decided to stay in Medina without fighting the Meccans at Uhud. They chose to deal with them through a house-to-house fighting in the city of Medina.[1039] Abdullah b. Ubayy b. Salul was one of those who supported this decision. Muslim traditions also tells us that Muhammad had a dream the night before, and he said to his followers,

> "I saw in a dream some cattle, and interpreted them as a good
> omen; and I saw that the blade of my sword was notched, and I
> saw that I had put on an invulnerable coat of mail and I interpreted

---

[1035] Sell, *The Battles of Badr and Uhud*, The Christian Literature Society, 1909, p. 69.

[1036] J. M. B. Jones, "The Chronology of the Maghazi" in *BSOAS,* 1956, p. 248; Watt, 1956, p. 21; Al-Tabari, 1989, p. 105; Wensinck, 1975, p. 115.

[1037] Watt, 1956, p. 21.

[1038] Muhammad Hamidullah, *The Battlefields of the Prophet Muhammad*, Deccan, 1973, p. 22, quoted from Ibn Sa'd, II/I p 25.

[1039] Al-Tabari, 1989, p. 108; Ibn Ishaq, 1955, p. 371.

that as Medina. If you see fit to remain in Medina and to leave
them encamped where they are, well and good; for if they remain
there, they will be in the worst possible place, and if they enter
Medina to fight us, we will fight them here."[1040]

As a result of this, the Prophet decided not to go out to face the Meccans at
Uhud. However, this defensive approach was opposed by the younger men.
They argued that to stay in the town would be seen as cowardly behavior
and would lower the Muslims' reputation in the eyes of surrounding tribes.
Since the people pleaded with him to go out to battle, he decided to go in
spite of his better initial judgment. Eventually, Muhammad put on his armor,
and decided to fight the Meccans at Uhud. Muslim sources then indicate that
the opposition regretted this decision, and were willing to accept the original
plan of Muhammad. Muhammad, however, stuck to his final decision by
saying,

"It is not fitting that a prophet who has put on his armor should
lay it aside until he has fought."[1041]

It is clear that these details are meant to excuse the Prophet for the defeat
that later takes place.

Leading one thousand Muslims, Muhammad set out for Uhud. Abdullah
b. Ubayy b Salul finally decided to flee from the battle. He brought back
about three hundred people, leaving only seven hundrerd people to fight three
thousand Meccans soldiers.[1042] Again, these numbers are probably skewed
to ensure that the Muslim position of weakness is emphasized. The actual
number of casualties in the battle are about the same as at Badr although this
time with higher casualties on the Muslim side. We are again dealing with
what would normally be regarded as a small skirmish. Abdullah b. Ubayy said
in regard to Muhammad's change of mind to go out and engage in battle,

---

[1040] Al-Tabari, 1989, p. 108.
[1041] Ibn Ishaq, 1955, p. 372.
[1042] The traditions suggests the flight of Abdullah b. Ubayy was due to his anger
toward Muhammad because Muhammad never listened to his opinion to fight
the Meccans in the town. Watt argues that "this is difficult to believe, since he
seems to have gone with Muhammad right to the site of the battle." Watt suggests
that the reason is "he retired, in agreement with Muhammad, in order to defend
the main settlement against a possible enemy attack." Watt, 1956, p. 22.

> "He obeyed them by setting out and disobeyed me. By God, we do
> not know why we should get ourselves killed here, men."[1043]

Although fleeing from war was a serious offence, Abd Allah b. Ubayy interestingly was not punished by Muhammad after the battle. This would seem to be a greater treason than anything that the Jewish tribes, including the Banu Qurayzah did. Nevertheless, Ubayy was not punished. This illustrates the selective and unpredictable nature of Muhammad's policies. His hostility to the Jews seemed much greater than toward other groups.

According to Muslim traditions, Muhammad rejected the help of a Jewish contingent because they were not believers.[1044] Ibn Ishaq describes this as follows:

> "On that day the Ansar said, 'O apostle, should we not ask help from
> our allies, the Jews?' He said, 'We have no need of them'."[1045]

Al-Waqidi has a similar account:

> "When the Prophet was on his way to the battlefield and had
> reached the outskirts of the town he saw a heavily armed
> detachment behind him that was making considerable noise. When
> he asked who they were he was told that they were the Jewish
> confederates of Ibn Ubayy. Muhammad, however, turned down
> their help saying that one should not solicite help from heathens
> to fight against heathens."[1046]

So we are very certain that the Jews did not take part in the Battle of Uhud.[1047] If these details are true, then Muhammad's position in Medina was still quite tenuous as he regarded the Jews as inherent enemies, no better than the polytheists.

Muhammad drew his troops up and positioned them with their backs to Uhud Mountain to provide a safe withdrawal position.[1048] In order to

---

[1043] Al-Tabari, 1989, p. 110.
[1044] Watt, 1956, p. 22.
[1045] Ishaq, 1955, p. 372. This is a tradition from Ibn Ishaq with the authority from al-Zuhri, but not from al-Bakka (Ziyad).
[1046] Al-Waqidi's account quoted from Wensinck, 1975, pp. 115-116.
[1047] Wensinck, 1975, p. 116.
[1048] Hamidullah, 1973, p. 22.

prevent his troops from being flanked, he ordered Abdullah b. Jubayr, who was distinguished with his white garments, to guard the passes in the hills at their back together with his best fifty archers. He strictly commanded them not to move from their position until he asked them to do otherwise. He thus instructed Abdullah b. Jubayr and the fifty archers,

> "Defend us against the cavalry with your arrows, and do not come
> up behind us whether the battle goes for us or against us. Hold
> firm to your position, so that we will not be attacked from your
> direction."[1049]

As the Muslim troops filed facing to the west, these archers were responsible for guarding the troops from being attacked from the rear and also to prevent the passage of Quraysh to the city of Medina.[1050] This explains why Muhammad had to give such a strict order, as this was really the most strategic location in the battle. Meanwhile, Abu Sufyan also arranged his troops. He himself took the center position, with Khalid leading the right flank and Ikrima b. Abu Jahl leading the left flank.

2.3.   The Battle

The battle commenced with the great success of Muslims in the first phase. Many Quraysh were killed. The standard-bearer of Quraysh, Talhah b. Uthman, was struck by Ali b. Abi Talib, and Muhammad was so delighted that he cried out *Allahu Akhar*! (God is great!).[1051] Hamza, uncle of Muhammad, also killed many Quraysh in the beginning of the battle. Ibn Ishaq describes the initial victory of the Muslims:

> "God sent down his help to the Muslims and fulfilled his promise.
> They slew the enemy with the sword until they cut them off from
> their camp and there was an obvious rout."[1052]

The Quraysh's lines were broken, and they were fleeing everywhere. Unfortunately, this initial success did not last long. Seeing the Quraysh's camp

---

[1049] Al-Tabari, 1989, p. 113; cf. Ibn Ishaq, 1955, p. 373.
[1050] Hamidullah, 1973, p. 25.
[1051] Al-Tabari, 1989, p. 115.
[1052] Ibn Ishaq, 1955, p. 379.

was unguarded, and looting was going on, the archers who were supposed to guard the flank of the Muslim troops desired to secure their share of the booty and disobeyed the command of Muhammad, leaving their strategic location and engaging themselves in the operation of looting.[1053] This disobedient behavior was described in the Qur'an:

> "Allah did indeed fulfill his promise to you when ye with his permission were about to annihilate your enemy, until ye flinched and fell to disputing about the order, and disobeyed it after he brought you in sight (of the booty) which ye covet. Among you are some that hanker after this world and some that desire the Hereafter, then did he divert you from your foes in order to test you. But he forgave you: for Allah is full of Grace to those who believe."[1054]

Khalid, the outstanding leader from Quraysh, took this opportunity and came through this opening with the Quraysh cavalry and managed to attack the disordered Muslims troops from the rear. Ibn Hisham describes the scene as follows:

> "The commander of the archers was left with only seven or eight men, when the inveterate Khalid attempted again and this time with easy success, to penetrate the battlefield from behind the Muslim army."[1055]

This action was the turning point for Quraysh troops, and they reorganized the ranks and overpowered the Muslim forces. The Muslims, once rushing for booty, were now fleeing in all directions. Muhammad himself was also hit on his face. He fell on his side, one of his teeth was smashed, and his lip was injured.[1056] When Muhammad fell on the ground, one Quraysh shouted that he had killed Muhammad, and the Muslims were in an even worst situation, despairing, fleeing, and crying out about Muhammad's death. "A small band of the faithful bravely defended the Prophet Muhammad till the last, and many

---

[1053] Al-Tabari, 1989, pp. 114-5.

[1054] Qur'an 3:152.

[1055] Hamidullah, 1973, p. 26, which he quoted from Ibn Hisham, p. 570.

[1056] Ibn Ishaq, 1955, p. 380. Also, according to Ibn Ishaq, the man who injured Muhammad was Utba b. Abu Waqqas.

of them sacrificed their lives in the noble task."[1057] Al-Tabari describes how the Muslims sacrificed their lives to rescue Muhammad:

> "When the enemy overwhelmed him, the Messenger of God said, 'Who will sell his life for us?' Then Ziyad b. al-Sakan rose up with five of the Ansar, and they fought to protect the Messenger of God. Man after man of them was killed in front of him until only Ziyad was left, and he fought until his wounds made him incapable of further fighting . . . he died with his cheek on the Messenger of God's foot. Abu Dujanah shielded the Messenger of God with his body, bending over him while arrows struck his back until it was full of them."[1058]

The group managed to get him up to the slopes of Uhud, and they did not disclose to Quraysh that Muhammad was still alive. On the slopes of Uhud, the Muslims were safe from further attack. Al-Tabari describes about the injury of Muhammad:

> "The Messenger of God's incisor was broken and he was wounded in the head. Blood began to pour down his face, and he kept wiping it away, saying, 'How can a people prosper who stain the face of their Prophet with blood while he is calling them to God? God revealed concerning this, 'It is no concern at all of thee (Muhammad), whether He relent toward them or punish them: for they are evildoers.'"[1059]

Finally, Abu Sufyan ordered a withdrawal, and the forces of the Meccans moved back to Mecca without further attacking the city of Medina. The Muslims were delighted by this unexpected decision. This strategic error snatched defeat from the jaws of victory, for the way had been cleared for an assault on Medina.

[1057] Humidullah, 1973, p. 27, which he quoted from Ibn Kathir, Vol IV, p 34 and Ibn Hisham, p 873.

[1058] Al-Tabari, 1989, pp. 120-121, according to Muhmud b. Amr b. Yazid b. al-Sakan's account. Also, some traditions say that it was Umarah b. Ziyad b. al-Sakan who rose up to protect Muhammad, but not Ziyad b. al-Sakan.

[1059] Al-Tabari, 1989, p. 120. The verse quoted is Qu'ran 3:128.

There were sixty-five Muslims and twenty-two Meccans killed in the Battle of Uhud.[1060] Among the Muslims killed was Hamza, the hero of the Battle of Badr and uncle of Muhammad. Before the withdrawal of Quraysh troops, the women who came along with the troops mutilated the dead bodies of the Muslims. They cut off their ears and noses and made them into anklets and collars.[1061] Hind d. Utba, wife of Abu Sufyan, found the dead body of Hamza, cut out his liver, and chewed it. She did so to take revenge for her father, uncle, and son, who were all killed by Hamza in the Battle of Badr. Abu Sufyan took the position that he neither prohibited nor ordered the mutilation of the dead bodies. Later, when Muhammad found that Hamza's body was mutilated, he was so angry and vowed that he would mutilate thirty members of the Quraysh if he had victory over them. It is told that the following verse was revealed to Muhammad in this incident:

"And do thou be patient, for thy patience is but from Allah; nor grieve over them: and distress not thyself because of their plots."[1062]

This is a direct command to Muhammad from Allah, and we are told that Muhammad finally forgave the Quraysh and forbade mutilation in Islam. But if we read the previous verse, it states the following:

"And if you punish (your enemy, O you believers in the Oneness of Allah), then punish them with the like of that with which you were afflicted. But if you endure patiently, verily, it is better for the patient."[1063]

If we read these two verses together, we may conclude that the retaliation was permitted, but only to the same extent, that is, only to one Quraysh, but not to thirty Quraysh. The question of torturing and mutilating one's enemies in war remains an open question in the Qur'an.

One of the questions this battle raises is why Abu Sufyan did not go further to attack Medina considering his clear victory in the battle and the supposed "death of Muhammad." In fact, Abu Sufyan apparently knew that the death

---

[1060] Ibn Ishaq, 1955, p. 403.
[1061] Ibn Ishaq, 1955, p. 385; Al-Tabari, 1989, p. 129.
[1062] Qur'an 16:127; cf. Ibn Ishaq, 1955, p. 387.
[1063] Qur'an 16:126; *The Noble Qur'an translation*, 1996, p. 352.

of Muhammad was false news before he left the battlefield. Al-Waqidi's account summarizes the standpoint of Meccans:

> When we renewed the attack against them, we smote a certain number of them, and they scattered in every direction, but later a party of them rallied. Quraysh then took counsel together and said, 'the victory is ours, let us apart. For we had heard that Ibn Ubayy had retired with a third of the force, and some of the Aws and the Khazraj had stayed away from the battle, and we were not sure that they would not attack us. Moreover we had a number of wounded, and all our horses had been wounded by the arrows. So they set off. We had not reached ar-Rawha until a number of them came against us, and we continued on our way'."[1064]

Watt's comments that the Quraysh were not in the position to take any further action against the Medinans because their horses were temporarily out of action, and morale for further military action was low.[1065] Another scholar, Donner, sees it as an evidence that Quraysh were satisfied that "they had adequately repaid the Muslims for their earlier discomfiture."[1066] In view of the more defensive approach of the tribal tradition and culture during Muhammad's period, this withdrawal is reasonable and understandable. The Meccan's philosophy was maintenance of the status quo. Muhammad's approach in his dealing with Quraysh and the Jews was laying the foundation of an empire; and this setback would not dissuade him.

As for the funeral of all the martyrs, al-Bukhari describes the following:

> "The Prophet collected every two martyrs of Uhud in one piece of cloth, then he would ask, 'Which of them had (knew) more of the Quran?' When one of them was pointed out for him, he would put that one first in the grave and say, 'I will be a witness on these on the Day of Resurrection.' He ordered them to be buried with their blood on their bodies and they were neither washed nor was a funeral prayer offered for them."[1067]

[1064] Al-Waqidi's comment from Amr' b. al-As, quoted from Watt, 1956, p. 28.
[1065] Watt, 1956, p. 28.
[1066] Donner, 1979, p. 232.
[1067] Sahih al-Bukhari, *The Hadith*, Volume 2, Book 23, Number 427, Medina: Islamic University, 1981.

2.4. The Aftermath of the Battle

The Battle of Uhud greatly weakened Muhammad's position politically, socially, and ideologically. Politically, the battle enhanced the position of Quraysh, but "lessened Muhammad's prestige among local nomadic tribes."[1068] A number of Muslims were killed at Bi'r Ma'una, and the betrayal of Muslims at al-Raji by the tribes of the Hijaz probably resulted from the loss of Muslim prestige.[1069] The *Ummah* had to deal with the loss of many of their own relatives and friends killed in the battle. Those killed were named as martyrs, and all their names were recorded.[1070] Many stories and poems were written to memorialize them.[1071] Furthermore, according to Donner, "we can assume that the defeat also gladdened the hearts of Muhammad's opponents in Medina."[1072] The Jews who did not take part in the battle made several remarks about Muhammad after the battle. Al-Waqidi describes the negative view of Jews toward Muhamamd:

> "Both Qurayzah and al-Nadir had made cynical remarks about the man who, in their eyes, had lost (reputation) on account of his defeat."1073

The most serious problem was the theological or ideological issue. If Badr was the clear signal of God's pleasure toward Muslims, then the defeat at Uhud would be viewed as divine displeasure. Also, the average Muslim, "who was more sharply aware of the loss of life than of the wider strategic context, was plunged into profound spiritual chaos, since some of his cherished beliefs had been shattered."[1074] Muhammad had no choice, but to resolve the above difficulties with immediate and decisive actions.

We will look first at how Muhammad dealt with the ideological issue, and then discuss his dealing with the political and social issues. In order to clear the doubts in the minds of his followers, Muhammad revealed the third sura, "Al Imran."[1075] The Muslim traditions normally explained the

---

[1068] Donner, 1979, p. 232.
[1069] Donner, 1979, p. 239.
[1070] Ibn Ishaq, 1955, pp. 401-3.
[1071] For example, Ibn Ishaq, 1955, p. 404f.
[1072] Donner, 1979, p. 232.
[1073] Wensinck, 1975, p. 116, which he quoted from Al-Waqidi.
[1074] Watt, 1956, p. 27.
[1075] Qur'an 3:121f.

defeat as the result of their own disobedience and as a test from God on their consistency.[1076] Ibn Ishaq concludes the Battle of Uhud thus:

> "The day of Uhud was a day of trial, calamity, and heart-searching on which God tested the believers and put the hypocrites on trial, those who professed faith with their tongue and hid unbelief in their hearts; and a day in which God honored with martyrdom those whom he willed."[1077]

The theological issue was dealt with intensively in the Qur'an, and we will just quote a few verses to illustrate:

> "And what you suffered (of the disaster) on the day (of the battle of Uhud when) the two armies met, was by the leave of Allah, in order that He might test the believers, and that He might test the hypocrites . . ." [1078]

> "And that Allah may test (or purify) the believers (from sins) and destroy the disbelievers."[1079]

> "Muhammad is no more than a Messenger, and indeed (many) Messenger have passed away before him. If he dies or is killed, will you then turn back on your heels (as disbelievers)? And he who turns back on his heels, not the least harm will he do to Allah, and Allah will give reward to those who are grateful."[1080]

[1076] Watt holds a different opinion that the Meccan success was largely due to their skillful battleship and excellent leadership under Abu Sufyan and Khalid, see his detailed discussion, Watt, 1956, pp. 23-5.

[1077] Ibn Ishaq, 1955, p. 391.

[1078] Qur'an 3:166-7. *The Noble Qur'an translation*, 1996.

[1079] Qur'an 3:141. *The Noble Qur'an translation*, 1996.

[1080] Qur'an 3:144, *The Noble Qur'an translation*, 1996. This verse "seems intended to allay anxiety after Muhammad had been wounded, for a short time word got about that he had been killed," Watt, *Companion to the Qur'an*, Oxford, 1967, 1994, p. 56. It may also intend to explain to the Jews that other prophets had suffered, and there would be no exception in Muhammad's case. However, the primary purpose of this verse is that even if Muhammad died in battle, Islam should continue. See also Al-Tabari, 1989, p. 125 for this verse.

Finally, the Qur'an asks the Muslims to stand firm, be patient, and to fear Allah, so that they may be successful.

> "O you who believe! Endure and be more patient (than your enemy), and guard your territory by stationing army units permanently at the places from where the enemy can attack you, and fear Allah, so that you may be successful."[1081]

Sura 61, which was most probably written after Sura 3, provided futher hope for Muslims that, though they had been defeated at Uhud, finally Allah would be triumphant, and Islam would be the universal religion that all will accept and obey.

> "He it is who has sent his messenger (Muhammad) with guidance and the religion of truth (Islamic Monotheism) to make it victorious over all (other) religions even though the Mushrikun (polytheists, pagans, idolaters, and disbelievers in the Oneness of Allah and in His messenger Muhammad) hate (it)."[1082]

The next critical issue Muhammad needed to deal with was the sociopolitical issue. The Battle of Uhud left Muhammad in a weakened position.[1083] His situation in Medina would become worse if he didn't act harshly toward his opposition, especially the Jews. We again see the interrelationship between his struggle with Quraysh and his power establishment in Medina.[1084] The Battle of Uhud "strained the relations between Muhammad and the Jews to such an extent that they were finally severed."[1085] In terms of political power establishment and also the establishment of a theocracy, the Jews, who were the ideological threat, had to be neutralized.[1086]

2.5. The Significance of the Battle

It is not true that the Battle of Uhud was a complete failure for the Muslims. In fact, Muhammad had turned this failure into an opportunity to

---

[1081] Qur'an 3:200, *the Noble Qur'an translation,* 1996.
[1082] Qur'an 61:9, *the Noble Qur'an translation*, 1996.
[1083] Donner, 1979, p. 232.
[1084] Donner, 1979, p. 232.
[1085] Wensinck, 1975, p. 115.
[1086] Wensinck, 1975, p. 116; Donner, 1979, p. 233.

strengthen the *Ummah* in the face of the relatively anemic Meccan follow-up. Watt accurately points out the actual situation: "It was not a great military disaster for the Muslims, though it caused them some theological heart searching."[1087]

We may conclude the Battle of Uhud with a few observations. First, the supremacy of Muhammad's infantry was demonstrated.[1088] Second, theologically, he managed to explain the situation through divine revelation and giving future hope for the expansion of Islam. Third, Muhammad continued steadily consolidating his sociopolitical position.[1089] Apparently, this power consolidation campaign led to the expulsion of the second Jewish tribe, Al-Nadir, which we will discuss in the following chapter. Fourth, a new concept of Muslim family was developed "to provide for the widows made by Uhud, Muslim men were encouraged to take up to four wives."[1090]

The Qur'an: The Aftermath of Uhud Up to Khandaq (the Battle of the Trench).

Five chapters of the Qur'an were written during this period. The first is chapter 3, which seems to deal directly with the aftermath of the defeat at Uhud. Two shorter chapters, 61 and 57, then follow that relate to the rebuilding of Muhammad's army and his dealings with the "hypocrites." The final two chapters, 4 and 65, contain extensive legislation for the Muslim community.

Chapter 3: The Family of Imran

Chapter 3 of the Qur'an is placed early as one of the crucial chapters of the book. Imran is the Muslim name for the father of Moses, and once again, Muhammad spends a great deal of time reflecting on the scriptures of the People of the Book, in this case addressing Christians more directly. In the aftermath of the defeat of Uhud, perhaps Muhammad is hoping for better assistance from the Christians. However, he is clear that the Christians, like the Jews, do not have the final version of "the Book" and that they also must turn

---

[1087] Watt, 1956, p. 34.
[1088] Watt, "Muhammad" in *The Cambridge History of Islam*, Vol. I A, Cambridge University Press, 1970, p. 47.
[1089] Watt, 1970, p. 48; see also Donner, 1979, p. 234.
[1090] Watt, 1970, p. 48.

to Islam as the new revelation. Those who refuse to do so are no longer part of the kingdom of God. Yusuf Ali sees the book as being primarily addressed to Christians just as chapter 2 was primarily addressed to Jews.[1091] It is also a book addressed to the Muslim community, which has just suffered its first major defeat in battle. This becomes very strong, beginning about verse 140, as Muhammad seeks to explain the defeat to his soldiers.

Section 1: The Qur'an Is the Completion of the Book of God

God begins by stating that "the Book" has been sent down confirming the law and the gospel. Muhammad begins with an apology for the Qur'an. Those who reject these "signs" will suffer "the severest penalty." The Qur'an is the final part of "the Book," but all the parts together are the "foundation." He says that the other parts of the Book "are not of well-established meaning," and those of perverse hearts follow the parts "not of well-established meaning" (verse 7). Perhaps this indicates that the other scriptures were not in Arabic and were thus hard to understand. People "seeking discord" search "for its hidden meanings." This indicates that the other holy books can only be interpreted into Arabic and "no one knows it's true meaning except Allah." Clearly, however, Muhammad affirms "We believe in the Book; the whole of it is from our Lord." So Muhammad affirms that all of the holy books are from God, but lays the foundation that his is now the key book because it is understandable.

Section 2: The Fate of Those Who Reject Faith and Those Who Accept Faith

"Those who reject faith" will be "fuel for the fire." They will be "gathered together to Hell" (verses 10-12). Muhammad uses the analogy of two armies, one fighting for "the cause of Allah" and the other fighting against. The Muslim commentators take this to be a reference to Badr, their previous victory. It would make sense to harken back to that after a defeat. He compares people who love "Gold, silver . . . horses . . . and cattle" to the "nearness to Allah." The good news for the "righteous are gardens in nearness to their Lord with rivers flowing beneath . . . with companions pure" (verses 14-15). As in chapter 2:25, the proper attention of the righteous is not the wealth of this world, but the sensual delights of the next world.

[1091] Ali, Yusuf, *The Meaning of the Holy Qur'an*, p. 125.

There is a stronger spiritual sentiment in the section. The believers cry out to God "forgive us . . . and save us from the agony of the fire." They are the one's "who pray for forgiveness in the early hours of the morning" (verses 16-17). There is an attitude of repentance on the part of the Muslims here that I think is exemplary of an attitude inspired by a setback. Muhammad concludes that the "religion before Allah is Islam (submission)," and he states that "The People of the Book" did not disagree except by way of "envy of each other." He tells the believers that if they dispute then, you say, "I have submitted (Islam) my whole self to Allah" and also say to "the People of the Book . . . do you submit (Islam) yourselves?" (verses 19-20). Yusuf Ali interprets this as a declaration of the name of the new religion (Islam). Clearly, Christians and Jews would regard themselves as being submitted to God, but would not regard that submission as being allegiance to a new religion. This sets the stage for the dividing line that Muhammad demarcates in the next section.

Section 3: The Rejection of Friendship with Unbelievers

Muhammad begins this section by condemning "those who deny the signs of Allah" and "slay the prophets." This is a cipher for Jews. These will suffer "a grievous penalty" (verse 21). Those who have been given "a portion of the Book" are now "invited to the book of Allah to settle their dispute," but they "turn back and decline . . . for their forgeries deceive them as to their own religion." Muhammad here assumes that the People of the Book have deceived themselves from following their own true religion, which was Islam by misinterpreting their own books. He seems to be dealing with the Christian concept of purgatory where "they say: The fire shall not touch us, but for a few numbered days" (verse 23-24). God's power is affirmed as if to say that such allies are not needed. Muhammad concludes, "let not believers take for friends or helpers unbelievers rather than believers." Muhammad here demarcates a line to separate his followers from the followers of the other monotheistic faiths, defining their relationship now as one of enmity.

Sections 4-12: The Story of Jesus and Muhammad's Appraisal of the People of the Book

In the next nine sections of chapter 3, Muhammad addresses the People of the Book directly with emphasis upon the Christians. The reading of this section reminds one immediately of the first one hundred verses or so of chapter 2, which was in essence an address to the Jews. Here Muhammad tries to show his mastery of the Christian story. If anything, he shows himself even more inaccurate from a Christian perspective. Clearly, Muhammad knew far more about the stories of the Jews than he did about the Christians, and this would indicate a much stronger presence of Jews in the region than Christians. Why would Muhammad then address a large section of this chapter just to Christians? Beyond the pale of the Hejaz lay the great empires of Rome, and Persia. There were undoubtedly followers of the Christian faith in both Mecca and Medina, but no clans or tribes in the immediate vicinity. But Muhammad knew that his faith ultimately had also to deal with the other great monotheism of the time. Perhaps his hope was that these would be more open to his message than the Jews had been. Knowledgeable Christians would be just as turned away as the Jews were by his skewed and fantastically mixed up rendition of their salvation history.

Muhammad begins by saying that God chose "Adam, and Noah, the family of Abraham and the family of Imran (the father of Moses) above all people—offspring, one of the other" (verse 33-34). Thus, his story begins as a geneology and tells the story of the People of the Book as it relates to the story of the birth of Jesus. A woman of Imran gives birth to a girl named Mary. The implication is the same as we saw earlier in the chapter entitled "Mary." Muhammad mixes up the Mary of the New Testament with the Miriam of the Old Testament. Mary is thus the sister of Moses. This chronological mix-up indicates that Muhammad is always seeing Christianity through the eyes of the Jewish community with which he had more contact.

Mary is then under the care of Zakariya, the father of John the Baptist! Here she receives special "sustenance." Zakariya prays for a child and the angels give him "glad tidings of Yahya" (John the Baptist) (verse 39). Zakariya complains that he is old and his wife barren. The angels give him a sign that he shall be mute "for three days" as a sign of what would happen (verse 41). The story follows somewhat the story of John the Baptist in the New Testament, but all the details are wrong. Elizabeth is not named and Mary's relationship to Zakariya is odd and undefined. This may be the result of certain Christian apocryphal stories about those who cared for Mary. The three days does not fit the description given in Luke at all.

The angels then address Mary calling her to worship Allah. Suddenly in verse 44, God seems to interject saying to the Prophet "This is part of the tidings of the things unseen which we reveal unto thee by inspiration." God intimates at the story of the casting of arrows to determine who would take care of Mary, also probably of apocryphal origin. Was Muhammad anticipating that some would say his story was mixed-up and that he would need to make reference to a completely new revelation from God to justify these new details? He then relates the angels' declaration "of a Word from Him: his name will be Christ Jesus." This "son of Mary" would "speak to people in the cradle" repeating an apocryphal story mentioned in chapter 19. Mary protests having a son "when no man hath touched me." The Lord responds "Allah createth what he willeth . . . He but saith to it, 'Be' and it is!" (verses 45-47). He is called to be a messenger "to the children of Israel" who is taught "the book and the wisdom and the Law and the Gospel." He would be accompanied by many signs, including turning clay birds into living birds, heal the blind and lepers, and "quicken the dead" (verses 48-49). There follows some odd verses about knowing what people eat and store and that God "made lawful . . . what was forbidden to you" (verse 50). When Jesus calls the disciples they "bear witness that we are Muslims." Plots against Jesus are mentioned, but Allah promises "O Jesus! I will take thee and raise thee to myself . . . and I will judge between you of the matters wherein ye dispute" (verse 55). This verse is elaborated on in chapter 4 indicating that Christ was not crucified, but taken up directly to God.

Once again, Muhammad sees himself as the arbitrator of disputes among the monotheists. God indicates that "those who reject faith shall suffer a "terrible agony in this world and in the hereafter." He also indicates that Jesus is just like Adam, God said to Him "Be, and he was" (verses 56-59). Muhammad invites those who dispute to gather together their sons and women apparently with the sons and women of the believers and "invoke the curse of Allah on those who lie!" "This is the true account" he concludes, "There is no God except Allah" (verse 62). There is a powerful confidence in Muhammad that he is actually speaking the revelations of God.

In the next section, Muhammad addresses the People of the Book directly, and this seems to be both Jews and Christians, that they worship only Allah and have no other partners. He asks them "why dispute ye about Abraham when the Law and the Gospel were not revealed until after him" (verses 64-65). This returns to a favorite theme of Muhammad that his religion is the original religion of Abraham distinct from Judaism and Christianity. To Muhammad has been revealed a secret knowledge not known to the Jews and Christians; "Abraham was not a Jew nor yet a Christian," Muhammad and his followers are "the nearest of kin to Abraham." He accuses the People of the Book of seeking to lead his followers astray. He responds by asking, "Ye people of the Book why reject ye the signs of Allah . . . Why do ye clothe truth with falsehood and conceal the truth while ye have knowledge?" (verses 66-71) Ibn Kathir notes, "Allah states that the Jews envy the faithful and wish they could misguide them."[1092] When Muslims impute motives into the hearts and minds of non-Muslims, they are simply imitating the Qur'an and its attitude to anyone who refuses to accept Muhammad as the Prophet of God. Their rejection of Muhammad "must" be the result of more nefarious motives.

Muhammad goes on to accuse "The People of the Book" of rejecting what has been revealed to the believers, of rejecting the revelation because it was not of "your religion" and was sent to "someone (else)" (verse 73). The People of the Book are not faithful with the money entrusted to them. They sell their own word for a trifling price. "There is among them a section who distort the Book with their tongues. You would think it is a part of the Book but it is no part of the Book." Muhammad's standard response to those who point out discrepancies between his revelations and previous revelations was to claim that the previous revelations were being deliberately misread or that things were being spoken that are not in the book at all. Muhammad had a deep respect for the books themselves, but could not perceive that the People of the Book regarded his "revelations" as a deviation from what they regarded as scriptural truth. He counters, "It is they who tell a lie against Allah, and they know it!" Here Ibn Kathir opines, "Allah states that some Jews, may Allah's curses descend on them, distort Allah's words with their tongues, change them from their appropriate places, and alter their intended meaning."[1093] In order to maintain his following, Muhammad had to show that his was the true book in contrast to what the Jews and Christians were teaching. He does not, however, claim that the books themselves are altered since this would indicate Allah's inability to preserve his own word (see 10:64, 6:34, and 6:115). Even Kathir does not seem to indicate that the actual holy book has been corrupted. The modern Muslim position that the Jewish and Christian scriptures have been corrupted is difficult to prove from the Qur'an itself.[1094] Muhammad's final argument seems to be addressed to Christians. How could someone with a prophetic office call the believers to worship

---

[1092] Ibn Kathir, *Tafsir*, Vol. 2, p. 187.

[1093] Ibn Kathir, *Tafsir*, Vol. 2, p. 195.

[1094] The only major Muslim group that denies the corruption of the Jewish and Christian scriptures is the African American Muslim movement, which even in its orthodox Sunni iteration regards the Bible as still the Word of God. They base their argument on the text of the Qur'an.

himself? How could he "instruct you to take angels and Prophets for Lords and patrons?" (verses 72-80).

The next section seems to indicate the covenant that Muhammad had with the Jews of Medina. He says that when the messenger comes to you confirming "what is with you" and Allah asks, "Do ye agree and take this my covenant as binding on you? They said: 'We agree'." Yusuf Ali takes this opportunity to cite all the places in the Bible where Muhammad is supposedly predicted including the distortion of the Greek *paracletos* and the gospel of Barnabas, which even in Ali's day was proven to be a Muslim forgery from fifteenth century Spain. But these distortions continue to appear in Muslim apologetic literature into our days. At least, Ibn Kathir is not able to descend into these inventions of a later age.

One can imagine that when Muhammad first came to Aqaba and sought helpers from among the Jews, they initially responded to him as a fellow monotheist and were willing to take him and his small community in. As they learned that what he brought with him did not correspond at all to their scriptures, a gradual divorce began. Muhammad blames them for faithlessness to the covenant. They regard him as being dishonest about who he really claimed to be. It was the tragedy of two authoritative scriptures hopelessly in disagreement with each other. That the Jews would reject Muhammad was inevitable. His response rejecting them as the people of God and accusing them of breach of faith was also inevitable. I imagine that the Jews also could not forsee that a fellow monotheist would eventually regard them as the worst enemy and work toward their final eradication in the Hejaz. When Muhammad affirms, "We believe in Allah . . . and what was revealed to Abraham, Ismail, Isaac, Jacob, and the tribes, and in (the books) given to Moses, Jesus and the Prophets . . . we make no distinction between one and another," he sounds like someone that a Jew might still be able to live together in peace with. This was not the case, for Muhammad's attitude now is that, "If anyone desires a religion other than Islam (submission), never will it be accepted of him; and in the hereafter he will be in the ranks of those who have lost" (verse 85). As Ibn Kathir puts it, "The only valid religion to Allah is Islam."[1095] The curse of Allah, the angels, and all mankind is on such a person who leaves Islam. Muhammad regards such people as apostates from the true faith, "those who reject faith after they accepted it." He concludes, "for such is a penalty grievous, and they will find no helpers" (verses 82-91). This concept will gradually grow in the remainder of the Qur'an into a vehement

---

[1095] Ibn Kathir, *Tafsir*, Vol. 2, p. 202.

rejection of the *murtad* or apostate from Islam. In all the books of Islamic law, a male apostate is to be put to death.

He goes on addressing the People of the Book. God gave the law at Sinai and called to follow the religion of Abraham. He established the first house of worship at Bakkah (which is probably a scribal error preserved in the Qur'an for Makkah).[1096] Pilgrimage is a duty to the "station of Abraham." Why then, he says, do the People of the Book reject "the signs?" Why do they seek to make "the path of Allah . . . crooked." He warns the believers, "If ye listen to a faction among the People of the Book they would render you apostates." We have seen this tendency earlier to attribute false motives to Jews and Christians that is pervasive in the Qur'an. Yusuf Ali makes no comment on this verse. Kathir, however, states, "Allah warns his believing servants against obeying the People of the Book, who envy the believers for the favor Allah gave them in sending His Messenger." He then cites the Qur'an 2:109, which speaks of this "envy"[1097] (verses 92-101). Clearly, a deep ideological struggle was taking place here, and Muhammad is fighting to keep his people faithful to the vision of the Arabian Prophet and his holy book, the Qur'an. What an incredible change this is from the types of messages we saw in Mecca where questions are continually put to the Prophet by his detractors. Here the battle lines are much more clearly drawn, and Islam has distinguished itself completely from both Judaism and Christianity. Muhammad's struggle is now primarily with other monotheisms. The pagan detractors and questioners have vanished from the text. This may explain Hawting's thesis we discussed earlier. So much of the volume of the Qur'an as found in the Medinan surahs has to do with criticizing other monotheisms that it could be easy to say that all the critiques found in the Qur'an ultimately address other monotheists. That is not the case. The emphasis has to do with the fact that Muhammad regards Judaism and Christianity as his primary enemies in the establishing of an Arab monotheism.

[1096] Normally, a minor point like that would be corrected in Jewish and Christian scriptures. This can even happen in larger portions such as the section of John 8, concerning the woman taken in adultery that is not found in the oldest manuscripts of the Bible and has now essentially been removed from the text. The Qur'an, however, claims to be "tanzil," literally "let down" from heaven. This exceedingly rigid conception of revelation makes any even slight variation in the Qur'anic text a major issue. The Islamic world has never allowed the science of textual criticism to develop as it has in the West.

[1097] Ibn Kathir, *Tafsir*, Vol. 2, p. 225.

Sections 11-20: Muhammad's Address to His Soldiers

There then follows several sections that extol the virtues of the believers and calls them to faithfulness to their Islam. He calls them to "fear Allah . . . and die not except in a state of Islam." They must not be "divided" and remember gratitude to Allah for saving them from "the pit of fire" even though "ye were enemies." They are called to be a "band of people" who call others to "what is right" and "forbidding what is wrong." He warns that some will have black faces on the day of judgment receiving the "penalty for rejecting faith." (verses 103-106) The rawness of what Muhammad is struggling with here seems to indicate the background of Uhud. Ibn Kathir seems also to shy away from the background. He describes events in the early civil wars of Islam and avoids completely an explanation dating from the Battle of Uhud. He makes it refer to the wars with the Kharijites and calls for the rejection of all *bid'ah* (innovation).[1098] The ideal had faltered, and this needed to be covered up by the later exegetes. Muhammad was struggling with the danger of some of his people falling away from the faith. This also could only be an attitude engendered by some kind of set back. He is arguing for them to stay loyal to their new religion.

Muhammad says of the believers "ye are the best of peoples . . . for mankind." Ibn Kathir proclaims, "The Good News that the Muslims will Dominate the People of the Book." And goes on to explain,

> "This is what occurred, for at the battle of Khaybar, Allah brought humiliation and disgrace to the Jews. Before that, the Jews in Al-Madinah, the tribes of Qaynuqa, Nadir and Qurayza, were also humiliated by Allah. Such was the case with the Christians in the area of Ash-Sham later on when the companions defeated them in many battles and took over the leadership of Ash-Sham forever."[1099]

Muhammad then contrasts them with "the People of the Book . . . most of them are perverted transgressors." They will do the Muslims no harm "if they come out to fight you." Yusuf Ali interprets the verse this way, "The People of the Book, if only they had faith, would be Muslims, for they have been prepared

---

[1098] Ibn Kathir, *Tafsir*, Vol. 2, p. 235.
[1099] Ibn Kathir, *Tafsir*, Vol. 2, p. 243.

for Islam."[1100] "Shame is pitched over them" Muhammad says, "They draw on themselves wrath from Allah." This is because they "slew the Prophets" and "rebelled." Nevertheless, Muhammad notes not all the People of the Book are alike. Some "rehearse the signs of Allah all night long . . . they believe in Allah and the last day . . . the good that they do, nothing will be rejected." But those who "reject faith" and do not follow Islam, "will be companions of the fire." In Muhammad's thinking it is still possible to convert some of these to Islam, or that they are already followers of Islam who will come out for Muhammad. Ibn Kathir lists all the "Virtues of the People of the Scriptures Who Embrace Islam," and Yusuf Ali agrees with him.[1101] Modern Western writers take these verses as indicating tolerance toward Jews and Christians, but it is really only tolerance toward Jews and Christian who convert to Islam. Then the Prophet warns, "Ye who believe! Take not into your intimacy those outside your ranks: They will not fail to corrupt you. They only desire your ruin: Rank hatred has already appeared from their mouths. What their hearts conceal is far worse (verse 118)." Yusuf Ali avoids commentary on this inflamed verse. Ibn Kathir generalizes from this that all Christians are untrustworthy because they seek to reveal Muslim secret military plans to unbelieving enemies. He uses the later Muslim caliphs to illustrate how "dhimmis" (subjugated People of the Book) should not be allowed as advisors to Muslims.[1102] This is a pathological religious stereotyping leading to a system of religious apartheid, which is the basis of Islamic law. Sharia is not just discrimination against women, but a generalized discrimination and imputation of evil motives against anyone not adhering to Islam. If President Obama wants to understand why they "hate us," he needs to look no further than the clear teaching of the Qur'an.

Muhammad goes on to say that the People of the Book are filled with rage at the believers "biting off the tips of their fingers at you" because they claim to believe, but only the Muslims believe "in the whole of the Book," including the Qur'an. In order to prevent the influence of the People of the Book that might lead to apostasy at this critical time after a defeat, Muhammad enjoins his people to have no relations with the People of the Book. He portrays them as enemies full of hatred and rage. They rejoice at the "misfortune" of the Muslims (verses 110-120). Muhammad reads his own motivations toward them into them. This is absolutely classic Freudian projection. Muhammad

---

[1100]   Ali, Yusuf, p. 155.
[1101]   Ali, Yusuf, p. 156, footnote 437; Ibn Kathir, *Tafsir*, Vol. 2, p. 246.
[1102]   Ibn Kathir, *Tafsir*, Vol. 2, p. 250.

is playing the blame game trying to find nefarious plots by the People of the Book as the excuse for his defeat.

In section 13, Muhammad turns his attention to interpreting the recent defeat of the Muslims at Uhud. He begins by reminding them of the earlier victory at Badr and this time he names Badr directly (verse 123). This is one of the few times that the Qur'an states something of a historical nature directly. Clearly, this initial victory has already become part of the Muslim historical consciousness, and it indicates the relative accuracy of the history provided by the Sira literature.

Muhammad shows that two parties at the time of Badr "meditated cowardice," but the Prophet reminds them of three thousand angels sent to fight with them (thus contradicting the one thousand angels mentioned in 8:9). He mentions that Allah can sometimes show mercy to the unbelievers and that "He forgiveth whom he pleaseth and punisheth who he pleaseth" (verses 121-129). This perhaps explains the inexplicable, how unbelievers defeated the believers.

The next section continues on this theme of forgiveness. Muhammad commands to give freely and to not practice usury. He calls men to "fear the fire" and "be quick in the race for forgiveness from your Lord." "Ask for forgiveness," he says, "who can forgive sins except Allah." There is a strong sense of humility and awareness of sin in this passage that is different from the previous Medinan surahs, and it indicates an awareness of fallibility that perhaps has come through a military setback. He urges his men, "so lose not heart, nor fall into despair . . . If a wound hath touched you, be sure a similar wound hath touched the others" (verses 139-140). These sound like the words of a commander to his dejected and injured troops. He speaks of this as Allah's test of the believers. "Did ye think ye would enter heaven without Allah testing those of you who fought hard and remained steadfast?" (verse 142). He goes on to speak of himself. "Muhammad is no more than a messenger: many were the messengers that passed away before him. If he died or were slain, will ye then turn back on your heels?" Although the passage is oblique, it certainly fits both the ethos and the time frame of the Battle of Uhud. Muhammad is preparing his troops for the possibility of his own death and declaring that Allah's purposes will nevertheless be fulfilled. This would seem to indicate that he really was wounded at the Battle of Uhud. He speaks of the prophets who "fought" and "never lost heart if they met with disaster." "Allah loves those who are firm and steadfast." He concludes, "Our Lord! Forgive us our sins and anything we may have done that transgressed our duty . . . help us against those who resist faith" (verses

146-148). Muhammad's explanation of the defeat seems to range between sin on the part of some of his soldiers and testing by Allah in determining their mettle for battle. He states, "He may take martyrs from among you. And Allah likes not the wrongdoers. And that Allah may test those who believe and destroy the disbelievers" (verses 140-141)

Muhammad goes on to rally his soldiers against their enemies. "If you obey the unbelievers, they will drive you back," "Nay, Allah is your protector." He demonizes them stating, "Soon we shall cast terror into the hearts of the unbelievers . . . their abode will be the fire" (verse 151). Muhammad uses the term *ra'aba* meaning here "to terrorize" or "cast fear." He then breaks into the explanation for their loss. "When ye . . . were about to annihilate your enemy . . . ye flinched and fell to disputing about the order and disobeyed it after he brought you in sight which ye covet" (verse 152). The passage is oblique and does not make clear what the transgression was that lead to their defeat. The Sira historians maintain that the Muslims became greedy for the booty they were about to capture and lost their discipline, allowing the Meccan calvalry to flank their line. This is the lengthy interpretation that Ibn Kathir provides as does Yusuf Ali.[1103] Muhammad does provide a few more specifics: "Ye were climbing the high ground, without casting a side-glance . . . and the Messenger in your rear was calling you back. There did Allah give you one distress after another." Again the wording is oblique and unclear, but does describe some kind of actions in battle that led to a defeat. He then pretends to read their thoughts, "Moved by suspicions of Allah—suspicions due to ignorance. They said, 'What affair of this is ours . . . we should not have been in the slaughter here. Say: 'Even if you had remained in your homes, those for whom death was decreed would certainly have gone forth to the place of their death" (verses 153-154). A defeated army was tempted to question the very God they were fighting for. He states that Allah was testing their hearts to purge them. He says that Satan caused them to fail on the day when the two hosts met, but that Allah is oft-forgiving. There is a highly political and careful narrative here that seeks to place blame for the failure while yet encouraging the faith for which they were fighting.

The next section is a reflection on death in war with the refrain, "if ye are slain, or die." He maintains that "It is Allah that gives life and death." When one is slain there is "forgiveness and mercy from Allah" and this is "far better than all they could amass." Verse 159 seems to be a direct address from God to the Prophet. He advises the Prophet on how to encourage his

---

[1103] Ali, Yusuf, p. 166, footnotes 462-464; Ibn Kathir, *Tafsir*, Vol. 2, pp. 287-294.

men. "Deal gently with them. Wert thou severe or harsh hearted, they would have broken away from about thee." God instructs the Prophet to "consult them in affairs." All of them should put their trust in Allah for "If Allah helps you, none can overcome you . . . Let believers put their trust." The fate of the believers is not like that of the unbelievers "whose abode is in Hell" (verse 162). God has shown "a great favor when He sent among them a Messenger from among themselves . . . sanctifying them . . . instructing them." He compares this "single disaster" with the view that "ye smote with one twice as great." It would seem that Muhammad is comparing this defeat as something minor compared with the earlier victory at Badr. He seems to also place blame for the defeat on the "hypocrites" who now claim "Had we known there would be a fight, we should certainly have followed you." Muhammad interprets, "they were that day nearer to unbelief than to faith, saying with their lips what was not in their hearts" (verses 165-167). Their sin was that they did not "fight in the way of Allah." Muhammad concludes, "Think not of those slain in Allah's way as dead. Nay, they live, finding their sustenance in the presence of their Lord." "On them is no fear . . . they glory in the grace and bounty from Allah" (verses 169-171). Out of these and many similar verses the doctrine is emerging that there is one sure way to heaven, the way of martyrdom in holy war. The passage also teaches the decrees of God, no one who is to meet death can avoid it, none who are meant to live could possibly die.

The next section is very oblique, and the commentators disagree on its meaning. He does speak of the messenger "even after being wounded" would "have a great reward" (verse 172). It is possible that this is a reference to Muhammad's being wounded at the Battle of Uhud.[1104] The threat made that "A great army is gathering against you" is oblique as are the following two verses. Muhammad does comfort his men not to grieve those "who rush headlong into unbelief" for there awaits them "a severe punishment" (verse 176). It appears that some left the ranks of the Muslims after this defeat. Muhammad calls the recent defeat a "respite" to the unbelievers, but that ultimately "they will have a shameful punishment" (verse 178). Those who refuse to give gifts for the support of the war, their necks will be tied "like a twisted collar" (verse 180). There seems to be a marked effort on Yusuf Ali's part to not connect these verses to the previous context. The passage is teaching that Zakah (almsgiving) is for the purpose of *jihad*. Ibn Kathir follows the same pattern. It is as if these verses were thought of as coming

---

[1104] This is universally accepted by Muslim commentators.

from a later time with no relation to the story of the battle. This is not a realistic division of the text, and clearly Zakah, in the Prophet's mind, was for the purpose of *jihad*, at least in this context. Charity is not the word we would normally use for this.

The next section seems to address scoffers who speak against Muhammad. They call Allah "indigent," which I would take to mean impotent in not giving the believers victory. Those who so mock will taste "the penalty of the scorching fire" (verse 181). These scoffers will not believe unless they see "a sacrifice consumed by fire." Muhammad claims, "There came to you messengers before me . . . why then did you slay them." This would seem to indicate Jewish scoffers. He responds with words that sound like Christ in the Gospel, "If they reject thee, so were rejected messengers before thee" (verse 184). He appeals to the "day of judgment" where there will be a "full recompense" . . . to those . . ."admitted to the garden." Muhammad again seems to comfort his followers against the taunts of the Jews, "Ye shall certainly hear much that will grieve you from those who received the Book before you." He counsels patient perseverance and then says, "Remember Allah took a covenant from the People of the Book to make it known and clear to mankind and not to hide it; but they threw it away behind their backs and purchased with it some miserable gain! And vile was the bargain they made!" (verse 187). His point is that the message of Islam was in their holy books, but they hid it and did not spread its message to mankind. The real book of Islam is in their books, but they are hiding it for personal gain. Muhammad concludes, "for them is a penalty grievous indeed" (verse 188). The Jews have mocked his God and his revelations and this battle seems to have proved them right. The Jews could hardly have interpreted it in any other way given the enormous discrepancies between what Muhammad was saying and what their scriptures said. So they had to be accused of covering up what was really written in their books. The picture of the greedy Jew, hiding the truth for financial gain, becomes Muhammad's way of dealing with the discrepancies in revelation and their mockery. One can see how the policy of assassination emerged directly out of this Qur'anic conception of the Jews. The mockers, Abu Rafi, Marwan, and Ka'b among others had to be put to death to silence their mockery. Critical scholars make much of the different dates for these assassinations, sometimes placed after Badr, other times after Uhud, still others after "Khandaq." This is meant to indicate that the events actually never happened. Clearly, the Qur'an provides a basis for such a policy. Muhammad's enmity for the Jews has degenerated into a seething hatred that would seek the right time to put an end to their viewpoint.

The differing details written 100-200 years later are simply a matter of differing authors with differing viewpoints using these stories to highlight their particular interpretation. The Qur'an provides the emotional backdrop to these events and indicates their veracity. These sentiments culminated in the policy of assassination, the driving out of two tribes, the final annihilation of a third, and the rape of the Jews of Khaybar.

The final section is Muhammad's appeal for the salvation of the believers. He cries out, "Give us salvation from the penalty of the fire . . . Our Lord! We have heard the call of one calling to faith, 'Believe ye in the Lord,' and we have believed. Our Lord! Forgive us our sins and blot out from us our iniquities" (verses 191, 193). God, as it were, responds to this appeal, saying, "Never will I suffer to be lost the work of any of you." Those that were slain in my cause, "I will blot out from them their iniquities, and admit them into gardens with rivers flowing beneath" (verse 195). He encourages his soldiers to not be deceived by the "strutting about of the unbelievers" for "their ultimate abode is hell." Perhaps seeing that his previous words were too harsh he states, "There are, certainly, among the People of the Book, those who believe in Allah, in the revelation to you, and in the revelation to them" (verse 199). However, this does not mean tolerance to those who remain Jews, for someone who believes "in the revelation to you" meaning Muhammad would be a Muslim who has left Judaism and confessed the Qur'an to be the new book of God. Very few Jews made that leap of faith.

Surah 61: The Battle Array

Chapter 61 of the Qur'an is dated by Yusuf Ali to the time shortly after the Battle of Uhud. It is a brief fourteen-verse celebration of *jihad*, which also makes Muhammad the true fulfillment of both Moses and Jesus. He begins by stating "Grievously odious is it in the sight of Allah that ye say that which ye do not." What is it that some are not doing? He explains, "Truly Allah loves those who fight in his cause in battle array, as if they were a solid cemented structure." (verse 4) Ibn Kathir notes, "Allah says here, 'The dearest of you to me, is he who fights in my cause.'"[1105] Yusuf Ali uses a description of this reminiscent of the "body of Christ" analogies of the New Testament: "The structure or building implies a more diversified organization held together

---

[1105] Ibn Kathir, *Tafsir*, Vol. 9, p. 614.

in unity and strength, each part contributing strength in its own way, and the whole held together not like a mass but like a living organism" (cf. 1 Cor. 12:12-27).[1106] For moderate Muslims, this kind of spiritualization is used to avoid the more obvious meaning. If any should question this call to holy war, Muhammad points out that Moses was his precursor and that Jesus predicted his coming. "Moses said . . . 'Why do you vex and insult me . . . I am the Messenger sent to you." Thus, Muhammad is in a similar position receiving criticism for the recent defeat even though Allah loves those who go out to war.

He then points out that Jesus predicted his coming. "Remember, Jesus, the son of Mary" said: "O children of Israel! I am the messenger of Allah to you, confirming the law before me, and giving glad tidings of a Messenger to come after me, whose name shall be Ahmad" (verses 3-6). Ibn Kathir quotes several traditions of Jesus from the Islamic literature predicting the coming of Muhammad.[1107] This verse has been the inspiration for many Muslim books on Jesus predicting Muhammad. We have already noticed Ibn Ishaq's use of this verse in explaining that the "comforter" Jesus promised to send was not the Holy Spirit, but Muhammad. This is accomplished by a distorting of the Greek word involved making it to mean "praised one" and connecting that to the root meaning of the name Ahmad. This is a stock in trade of Muslim apologetics to this day, and Yusuf Ali dutifully repeats it.[1108] Verse 7 is another example of projection. Having affirmed something that does not exist in the Christian New Testament he goes on to affirm that no one does a greater wrong than the person "who invents falsehood against Allah." From the Christian perspective, Muhammad is inventing falsehood against Allah. Muhammad then affirms that Allah has sent him as the Messenger of the "religion of truth" in order "that he may proclaim it over all religion" (verse 9). Thus, Islam is the original, best and only true religion. Ibn Kathir's commentary on this, also based on 9:33, is that for "those (Christians) who became Muslims among them acquired goodness, honor and might. Disgrace, humiliation and jizya befell those who remained disbelievers."[1109] Yusuf Ali's description sounds more tolerant but arrives at the same conclusion.[1110]

[1106] Ali, Yusuf, p. 1460, footnote 5433.
[1107] Ibn Kathir, *Tafsir*, Vol. 9, pp. 617-620.
[1108] Ali, Yusuf, p. 1461, footnote 5438.
[1109] Ibn Kathir, *Tafsir*, Vol. 4, p. 412, which is cited for the commentary on this verse in Vol. 9, p. 622.
[1110] Ali, Yusuf, p. 1462, footnote 5442.

Muhammad calls his people to a "bargain." If they follow "Allah and his Messenger and . . . strive (*jihad*) in the cause of Allah, with your property and your persons: that will be the best for you . . . He will forgive you your sins, and admit you to gardens beneath which rivers flow, and . . . Help from Allah and a speedy victory" (verses 11-13). In the final verse, Muhammad encourages his followers to be like the disciples of Jesus, who, at Christ's invitation, said "we are Allah's helpers." Israel was then split between those who believed Jesus and those who "disbelieved." Allah says, "We gave power to those who believed against their enemies and they became the ones that prevailed." Clearly, Muhammad is drawing a conclusion from the "Christian" empires of his day that had oppressed and conquered the Jews. That victory was a result of their being the true Muslims of their day. In the same way, the true religion of Islam would now gain the victory over all its enemies.[1111]

Surah 57: Iron: Muhammad's Call for New Military Resources

The twenty-nine verses of this short surah come next in Nöldeke's scheme. Yusuf Ali dates it after the conquest of Mecca, but the ethos is clearly after Uhud with the need for renewed giving of Zakah to rebuild the army after the plundering they had suffered at Uhud. In the first six verses, Muhammad exalts the all-knowing nature of God and his absolute power over all things. He corrects his earlier eight-day creation story here in verse 4 with a brief mention of creation in "six days." In verse 7, he launches into his call to faith on the part of his followers, "Believe in Allah and His Messenger, and spend out of that whereof he has made you" . . . for those who spend have, "a great reward."

He then asks why any "should not believe in Allah?" The messenger has "taken your covenant." This would seem to be a reference to Muhammad's earlier pledges at Aqaba, and this would indicate an earlier Medinan period. After the conquest of Mecca, Muhammad would have no cause to refer back to these old covenants. He is referring to those now because he needs to bolster his troops after the defeat of Uhud, by reminding them of their initial covenant with him. He says that the primary signs of this Prophet are "to lead you from the depths of darkness into the light" (verses 8-9). He then argues for the importance of giving *Zakah* for the *jihad*; "what cause have

---

[1111] Ibn Kathir relates this victory to the early Christian suppression of true Muslims after their victory over the Jews. Muhammad came, in his interpretation, to defeat the false Christians who had suppressed Islam. Cf. Vol. 9, p. 627.

ye why ye should not spend in the cause of Allah? . . . Not equal among you are those who spent and fought, before the victory." Yusuf Ali interprets "the victory" to mean the victory over Mecca.[1112] In the context, this doesn't make sense. Muhammad does not need to plead for more contributions after the great victory at Mecca, when there is plenty of booty to distribute from Muhammad's opponents who have been conquered. Ibn Kathir also claims that the conquering referred to in the passage is Mecca, but notes that there is a minority position that indicates an earlier time around the treaty of Hudaybiyya. [1113] Modern critical scholars place it earlier still, as do I. The context here is that Muhammad's own forces have been plundered after Uhud, and there is a need for new contributions to rebuild the army and its provisions. His reference to the "victory" is again a harking back to the glories of Badr in order to encourage the army to retake the initiative. "Who is he that will loan to Allah a beautiful loan? . . . He will have a liberal reward . . . Good news for you this day! Gardens beneath which flow rivers! To dwell therein for aye!" (verses 11-12). He speaks of the hypocrites coming to ask, "let us borrow from your light!" But . . ."All alongside will be punishment" (verse 13). The story reminds one of the parable of Jesus about the ten virgins who forgot to bring enough oil for their lamps (Matt. 25:1-13). These will be kept out of the wedding feast and Muhammad says the hypocrites will be separated "by a gate therein." Yusuf Ali makes his own connection to this parable.[1114] Of these Muhammad says, "No ransom be accepted of you, nor of those who rejected Allah. Your abode is the fire" (verse 15).

Muhammad then addresses the believers who "should engage in the remembrance of Allah" and not be "like those to whom was given revelation aforetime but long ages passed over them and their hearts grew hard?" (verse 16) Muhammad is explaining to his own believers how it has come to pass that the other monotheists among them are now rejecting their group and refusing to become part of the new monotheist army by confessing Allah and his messenger. The answer lies purely in their hardness of heart accumulated over the centuries. Thus, "Many among them are rebellious transgressors." There is not much here to encourage tolerance of Christians and Jews who refuse to convert to the renewal of their own faiths through accepting Islam. They can only be seen as rebellious perverters of their own truth, utterly without excuse.

[1112] Ali, Yusuf, p. 1422.
[1113] Ibn Kathir, *Tafsir*, Vol. 9, p. 473.
[1114] Ali, Yusuf, p. 1423, Footnote 5290.

Muhammad then returns to his theme of giving. "those who give in charity, men and women, and loan to Allah a beautiful loan, it shall be increased manifold and they shall have a liberal reward." (verse 18). There follows a self-definition of who the righteous are. "Those who believe in Allah and His messengers—they are the sincere and the witnesses in the eyes of their Lord" (verse 19). The use of the plural "messengers" here would seem to indicate that all those who followed the previous prophets are also part of this grand fellowship. However, remember that the previous prophets all preached the same message of Islam in Muhammad's conception. In this age, those of the Jews and Christians who refuse to confess Allah and his Prophet are not fellow believers, but "those who reject Allah and deny our signs—they are the companions of hell-fire." (verse 19). Muhammad defines the goods of this world as passing "chattels of deception" along with "pomp and mutual boasting and multiplying . . . riches and children." Those who seek Allah first receive forgiveness and a "Garden the width thereof is the width of heaven and earth." He cautions that "No misfortune can happen on earth or in your souls but it is recorded in a decree before we bring it into existence." (verses 20-22) The doctrine of the decrees of Allah which is the sixth major pillar of Islamic faith seems to have its origins in the way Muhammad explained the deaths of his followers in battle. This was a fate that they could not possibly have avoided, and therefore, it is to be accepted as from God by a decree before the foundation of the world. Death in battle is not to be feared for if it happens, it was already determined. Yusuf Ali passes over this critical verse without comment on its doctrinal content. Ibn Kathir is much clearer stating, "This great, honorable Ayah provides clear evidence to the misguidance of the cursed Qadariyyah sect, who deny Allah's Preordainment and His knowledge of everything before it occurs."[1115] Soldiers who truly believe this would be ferocious indeed. Muhammad, therefore, encourages them both not to despair and not to boast. They are not to be covetous, and if any be so, this is no concern to Allah for "Allah is free of all needs."

The passage reaches its climax in verse 25 as Muhammad makes his final appeal for physical support. God has sent down messengers with clear signs and God has also "sent down iron in which is mighty war." Muhammad's greatest loss at the Battle of Uhud was the iron weaponry, which the Meccans had collected off the battlefield after driving the Muslims into defeat. God through this "may test who it is that will help, unseen, Him

---

[1115] Ibn Kathir, *Tafsir*, Vol. 9, p. 495.

and his messengers for Allah is full of strength exalted in might" (verse 25). Muhammad is appealing for donations, perhaps even secret ones, to replenish his stores of weapons to prepare the way for the next battle. He concludes by reflecting on the other prophets before him. Noah and Abraham established the line of "Prophethood and Revelation," but their followers became "rebellious transgressors" (verse 26). After them Allah sent "Jesus the son of Mary, and bestowed on him the Gospel; we ordained in the hearts of those who followed him compassion and mercy but the monasticism they invented for themselves, we did not prescribe for them." Many of these are also "rebellious transgressors" (verse 27). The Jews have thus failed their calling in not recognizing the Prophet. The Christians have gone off into the peaceful pursuit of monasticism and that has led them astray of the violence Allah has called them to. Thus, the followers of the previous monotheistic traditions have gone astray from the noble task of *jihad* in bringing the nations into obedience to Islam, the one and only and original true faith. Muhammad concludes, "fear Allah and believe in His Messenger, and He will bestow on you a double portion of his mercy." What is Allah's intention by this? "That the People of the Book may know that they have no power whatever over the grace of Allah" (verses 28-29). The grace of God is no longer upon or controlled by these two earlier communities. It is now given to the community of Islam alone.

Chapter 4: Women: The Prophet's Legislation in the Light of Needs Arising Out of Uhud

One of the legacies of Uhud was the fact that a large number of Muslims were killed. Questions immediately arose concerning the equitable distribution of inheritance, what should be done with widows and orphans, and how to guide the community through this period of loss. Yusuf Ali agrees with Nöldeke's dating of this chapter and places it shortly after the battle of Uhud in chronology.[1116]

The chapter begins with a brief reflection that humankind was created from a single person and his mate by whom "countless men and women" have been "scattered." From this single verse introduction, Muhammad launches immediately into a discussion about orphans. Their property is to be restored to them when they achieve maturity, with nothing lost or substituted.

[1116] Ali, Yusuf, p. 182.

If the believers felt unable to treat the orphans equitably, they were to marry them, "two or three or four" though if they could not deal justly between wives, then they should only marry one and "that your right hands possess." This is a cipher for women captured in battle, and there is no limit on the number of them one may use sexually. This is how the Prophet desires to apportion the widows and female orphans from his slain soldier as Yusuf Ali notes.[1117] Women are to be given their proper dower and women who are of "weak understanding" are not to be taken advantage of in regard to their property, but should be supported in marriage. Yusuf Ali makes this apply only to minors, but Ibn Kathir indicates that it refers to "women" in general as people of "weak understanding."[1118] Orphan's goods may be used in their support, but not wastefully and well-off guardians should not seek remuneration. Parents' shares should be allotted to both men and women in inheritance. There is a specified differential not mentioned here. Those who dispose of estates should do so "as they would have for their own if they had left a helpless family behind" (verse 9). These words truly conjure the image of rules being laid out in the aftermath of a battle where many have died. Those who "eat up the property of orphans . . . will soon be enduring a blazing fire."

Section 2: The Laws of Inheritance

Muhammad then goes on to define the rules of inheritance. Males receive a portion equal to two females. If there are no sons, two females receive only two-thirds of the estate. If only one female, then she receives only half the estate. The assumption seems to be that other male relatives will take the rest. Parents receive one-sixth each for a deceased child who had children. Those without children, if there are no other heirs, the mother receives one-third and the father two-thirds. The general rule is that females receive half the inheritance of males in the view of Ibn Kathir.[1119] Yusuf Ali avoids deeper analysis referring readers to "legal treatises."[1120] Various other divisions are defined, and Muhammad concludes the section saying "those who disobey Allah and His Messenger . . . will be admitted to a fire."(Verse 14)

[1117] Ali, Yusuf, p. 184.
[1118] Ibn Kathir, *Tafsir*, Vol. 2, p. 378.
[1119] Ibn Kathir, *Tafsir*, Vol. 2, p. 389.
[1120] Ali, Yusuf, p. 188, footnote 521.

Section 3: The Laws on Sexuality

Lewdness on the part of women is proven on the testimony of four witnesses. The later Sunnah of the Prophet indicated one hundred stripes in the case of fornication and death by stoning in the case of adultery though the passage here is oblique and unclear. The sentence of confinement according to Ibn Kathir is later abrogated by the ruling of sura 24, which came just five chapters later, indicating that stoning is the proper punishment.[1121] Two men guilty of lewdness are to be punished, but if they repent, they are to be left alone. This seems to refer to homosexual behavior, but the passage is very unspecific (verse 16). Death is the only word concerning punishment used in the passage, and it refers only to the women. Ibn Kathir is quite specific that if this refers to homosexual behavior, then the clear teaching is that both parties must be killed, and this is still the practice in a number of Muslim countries.[1122] Repentance is of no value to those who "continue to do evil." Women should not have their inheritance stolen by men divorcing them unless they have been doing "open lewdness." A man should not take back the dower if he divorces one woman in order to take another. This obligation to give back stems from their sexual intimacy. Men should not marry their father's wives and a number of other relations. Of interest is that marriage is forbidden to wet nurses who have suckled the man in his childhood (verse 23). Muhammad seems to believe that this confers some kind of actual motherhood bond. In later Muslim law, marriages between a man and a woman suckled by the same woman were declared null and void because the boy and girl were considered to be siblings. Ibn Kathir presents arguments as to how many times of suckling was sufficient to establish this bond. The initial ruling was ten times and this was later abrogated to five.[1123] Having sex with women captured in battle is allowed even if they are married to someone else, "also women already married except those whom your right hands possess." Ibn Kathir clarifies, "those whom you acquire through war." He notes a story of some of Muhammad's followers who did not wish to have sex with captured women once they discovered that they were married. Muhammad, however, gave them permission through this verse and "Consequently we had sexual relations with these women."[1124] Yusuf Ali simply translates "captives in a

---

[1121] Ibn Kathir, *Tafsir*, Vol. 2, p. 400.
[1122] Ibn Kathir, *Tafsir*, Vol. 2, p. 402.
[1123] Ibn Kathir, *Tafsir*, Vol. 2, p 416.
[1124] Ibn Kathir, *Tafsir*, Vol 2, p. 422.

jihad" without further comment.[1125] Any female American soldier captured by Muslims on the battlefield may reasonably expect to be raped as the fulfillment of Islamic law. Those without means to marry free women are allowed to marry those captured in *jihad*. These would clearly be nonfree-will marriages. The punishment is lighter for transgressions of such women. The "taking of paramours" results in half the punishment due a free woman if they should engage in later licentiousness.

Muhammad then goes on to give various rules of life. He encourages traffic and trade, but forbids a man to kill himself (verse 29). Those who do injustice, "we shall cast into the fire" (verse 30). He forbids covetousness and states that if a portion of evil deed are "eschewed" then Allah will "expel . . . all the evil in you, and admit you to a gate of great honor" (verse 31). He concludes with general words about heirs and property.

Section 6: Rules for Husbands and Wives

In this time of social chaos with many new marriages established to deal with widows and female orphans, Muhammad sets out to establish rules for the relationships of the new husbands and wives. Husbands have advantage over wives because they are their "protectors," and the women have their "support" from the men. Women are to be "devoutly obedient" and guard what Allah would have them guard when the husband is absent. Those who are disloyal or show bad conduct, the husband should "admonish . . . refuse to share their beds, spank them" (verse 34). Yusuf Ali tries to interject mildness here claiming "slight physical correction may be administered."[1126] The word as it is used elsewhere in the Qur'an does not carry that meaning. The exegetes do not engage in that kind of analysis, and Ibn Kathir gives the general rule that the beating should not be "violent."[1127] Arbiters are recommended in the case of an ongoing dispute, "one from his family and the other from hers." Good behavior is enjoined toward all, including those whom "your right hands possess" (verse 36). Those who are miserly or who spend for vainglory have taken "the evil one for their intimate." Here Muhammad returns to the earlier fund-raising theme, "they spent out of what Allah hath given them for sustenance . . . He doubleth it and giveth from his own presence a great reward" (verses 35-40).

[1125] Ali, Yusuf, p. 192, footnote 537.
[1126] Ali, Yusuf, p. 195.
[1127] Ibn Kathir, *Tafsir*, Vol. 2, p. 446.

Section 7-8: On Prayer and the Perversity of the People of the Book

Muhammad begins by commanding his believers to not pray "with a mind befogged." Ali mentions that this rule was made before the drinking of alcohol was forbidden in Islam.[1128] When one is ceremonially impure, one must not pray until "after washing your whole body." He defines this as after toilet or sexual intercourse. Where there is no water, sand may be used. Those who were given a "portion of the book" (the ultimate book in heaven from which both the Qur'an and earlier revelations are taken) "wish that ye should lose the right path. But Allah hath full knowledge of your enemies" (verse 45). Muhammad here unequivocally defines any Christian or Jew who has not followed him to be the enemy. He gets more specific. "Of the Jews there are those who displace words from their places and say: 'We hear and we disobey and hear, may we not hear and raina (which Yusuf Ali explains as a respectful term used in mockery meaning "our bad one")'" (verse 46). Yusuf Ali describes this as the mocking words of the Jews in their interchanges with the Prophet. Given the impossibility of knowledgeable Jews accepting Muhammad's revelations as from God it does not seem unlikely that they might respond to his words with direct or indirect mockery. He responds, "Allah hath cursed them for their unbelief; and but few of them will believe."

Muhammad addresses the People of the Book, saying, "Believe in what we have revealed, confirming what was with you, before we change the face and fame of some beyond all recognition and turn them hindwards, or curse them as we cursed the Sabbath-breakers" (verse 47). Ibn Kathir states, "Allah commands the People of the Scriptures to believe in what he has sent down to His servant and Messenger Muhammad, the glorious book that conforms to the good news that they already have about Muhammad."[1129] Refusing this invitation means that Allah himself will disfigure them. The curse on the Sabbath-breakers was that they were turned into pigs and apes. Yusuf Ali translates literally "before we obliterate some features and turn them front to back."[1130] He smugly concludes that this is God fulfilling (Matt. 19:30) that the first shall be last (i.e., the Christians) and the last (i.e., Muslims) shall be first. God is threatening the People of the Book with obliteration

---

[1128] Ali, Yusuf, p. 198, footnote no. 562.
[1129] Ibn Kathir, *Tafsir*, Vol. 2, p. 479.
[1130] Ali, Yusuf, p. 200

if they do not believe in the Qur'an. Muhammad then goes on to state that there is only one unforgiveable sin "that partners should be set up with him." He denies that they can be "sanctified" for only Allah sanctifies whom he will (verses 48-9). It is unclear who he is referring to here. The Jews were as thoroughly monotheistic as the Muslims were, so who does he mean? It would be strange that he would throw in polytheists at this point. It may well be that this is an oblique reference to Christians, who are also People of the Book, and who worshipped Jesus, something Muhammad considered the worst of blasphemies. The idea of sanctifying oneself strengthens the notion that this refers to Christians. Muhammad's response to this is "they invent a lie against Allah! . . . a manifest sin!" (verse 50). Ibn Kathir makes it refer to both "Jews and Christians."[1131]

Muhammad accuses the people "who were given a portion of the Book" of believing in sorcery and evil. He seems to be referring to Jews as we will see later in the passage for they had received a portion of the original holy book. The word for evil, Yusuf Ali explains, is *taghut*, which is a reference to the evil one or Satan.[1132] He says, "they are whom Allah has cursed" and "whom Allah has cursed . . . have no one to help" (verses 51-52). They have no dominion or power for "they give not a farthing to their fellow men?" He then defines more specifically, who he means, "we had already given the people of Abraham the book and the wisdom. But for those who 'averted' . . . enough is hell for a burning fire." Muhammad strengthens this point indicating that all the Jews (and Christians ultimately) who reject him will burn in hellfire. "Those who reject our signs, we shall soon cast into the fire; as often as their skins are roasted through, We shall change them for fresh skins, that they may taste the penalty." (verses 54-56). Ibn Kathir spends six pages describing the "chastising" of the Jews, "Allah's curse on the Jews," "the envy and miserly conduct of the Jews."[1133] This culminates in a verse describing how these Jews will have their skins burned off and grown back and burned off again throughout eternity (verse 56). A God who takes delight in accomplishing such torture could only inspire his followers to do the same. By contrast, "those who believe and do deeds of righteousness, We shall soon admit to gardens with rivers flowing beneath . . . therein shall they have companions pure and holy." He concludes these two sections saying,

---

[1131]   Ibn Kathir, *Tafsir*, Vol. 2, p. 484.

[1132]   Ali, Yusuf, p. 201, footnote 573.

[1133]   Ibn Kathir, *Tafsir*, Vol. 2, pp. 484-490.

"obey Allah and obey the Messenger . . . if ye differ in anything . . . refer it to Allah and His Messenger" (verses 57-9). This final refrain is ubiquitous in this as well as the previous several chapters and shows the degree to which Muhammad felt the need to call his soldiers back to unquestioning loyalty to himself. Clearly, his leadership had suffered a severe blow and needed constant reinforcement from the "all-knowing Allah."

Section 9-12: Muhammad Deals with the "Hypocrites"

Muhammad now turns his attention to attacking those who claim "they believe in the revelations that have come to thee," but they actually "resort together for judgment to the Evil one." "Satan's wish," Muhammad states, "is to lead them astray." These are the "hypocrites" who "avert their faces from thee in disgust" (verse 61). What is their crime? It is simply that when "seized by misfortune" they come saying, "We meant no more than goodwill and conciliation." Apparently, there were those in Muhammad's camp who sought conciliation with the Meccan forces after the defeat of Uhud, and Muhammad wants nothing of that. His purpose is the military conquest and subjection of the Meccans. Thus, Allah says, "We sent not a Messenger but to be obeyed, in accordance with the will of Allah." "if we had ordered them to sacrifice their lives or to leave their homes, very few of them would have done it." Muhammad concludes, "All who obey Allah and the Messenger are in the company of those on whom is the grace of Allah—of the Prophets, the sincere, the witnesses, and the righteous" (verses 66-70).

Muhammad then goes on to condemn the hypocrites by describing the proper attitude of those who go out to holy war. "Let those fight in the cause of Allah who sell the life of this world for the hereafter . . . whether he is slain or gets victory—soon shall we give him a reward." The cause for the fight is rescuing the innocents still in Mecca: "why should ye not fight in the cause of Allah and of those who, being weak, are ill-treated—men, women and children, whose cry is: 'Our Lord! Rescue us from this town, whose people are oppressors" (verses 74-75). Muhammad's war is an offensive war for the conquest of Mecca, which he regards as a righteous war since Islam is not freely practiced in the city. Thus, "those who believe fight in the cause of Allah, and those who reject faith fight in the cause of evil: So fight ye against the friends of Satan." Muhammad's view is that if any other state exists where Islam is not in power, that state must ultimately be removed. Sayyid Qutb, the radical interpreter of Islam, states,

"Can anyone say that if Abu Bakr, Umar or Othman had been satisfied that the Roman and Persian powers were not going to attack the Arabian peninsula, they would not have striven to spread the message of Islam throughout the world? How could the message of Islam spread when it faced such material obstacles as the political system of the state, the socio-economic system based on races and classes, and behind all these the military power of the government?"[1134]

The Meccans were culpable and worthy to be conquered by simple virtue of the fact that they ran a non-Muslim government. The Christians and Jews were in the same category. Non-Muslims are considered incapable of self-governance.

There is another group among the hypocrites who perhaps have another reason for doubting the Prophet. His message over the past three years has changed radically. There are those among his closest compatriots who remember his calls for restraint in the Mecca period and are now astonished at the total transformation to a policy of war and killing requiring absolute obedience to the commands of the Prophet. Muhammad is commanded to "turn thy vision to those who were told to hold back their hands, but establish regular prayers and spend in regular charity? When the order for fighting was issued to them, behold! a section of them feared men . . . They said: 'Our Lord! Why hast thou ordered us to fight?'" Muhammad's response to this is to say "short is the enjoyment of this world." Further, death is unavoidable, no matter where one hides for Allah is the author of both good and evil and "all things are from Allah." Yet, "whatever evil happens to thee, is from thy soul." So, "enough is Allah for a witness. He who obeys the Messenger, obeys Allah" (verses 78-80). The message is to shut up and obey.

Muhammad reflects further on what may be troubling this group of his followers. "A section of them meditate all night on things very different from what thou tellest them." It is impossible from the text to tell what these things are exactly but the next verse gives a clue. "Do they not consider the Qur'an? Had it come from other than Allah, they would surely have found therein much discrepancy" (verse 81-82). It strikes me that it is precisely this discrepancy between a previously peaceful preaching and a present policy of all-out war that underlies the doubts some of his followers were feeling,

---

[1134] Qutb, Sayyid, *Milestones*, p. 62-63.

especially after a stinging defeat. Was God really with the Prophet and was this truly God's revelation? Typically, Muhammad strikes at the core of the argument by baldly claiming the unity of his revelation. In one sense, there is some truth to this. For the Meccan revelations, while not advocating violence, are rife with hateful characterizations of the Meccans. When one is used to calling people "friends of Satan," "wicked," "rebellious," "pigs and apes" it is not a very large step to move from preaching to warfare as the new way of establishing the hegemony of Islam. Herein, of course, lies the great failure of Islam and all religions that seek to establish themselves by physical violence. Muhammad does not realize that it is precisely his new policy of violence that creates the grounds for hypocrisy and falsehood based on the human desire for personal aggrandizement. His Meccan suras deal little with hypocrisy because the lure of political power and warfare's "booty" was not present. Ultimately, the idea that human physical violence can somehow achieve the utopian kingdom of God on earth is a falsehood that can only replace one form of oppression with another. Muhammad becomes the paradigm of the dictator who must be blindly obeyed and the political history of Islam has rarely been able to escape this paradigm of dictatorship.

Muhammad deals with his troubled believers by stating, "If they had only referred it to the Messenger or to those charged with authority" (verse 83), that is, one should share one's doubts and receive the proper correction. If one does not do so, "all but a few of you would have followed Satan." Ibn Kathir claims that this verse was in reference to a dispute among the Muslims in which there was "contradicting parts of the books with other parts." Muhammad became "so angry that his face was red."[1135] Creating holy words to deal with day-to-day political decisions leads inevitably to contradictions. Muhammad is bolstering his troops against the acid of doubt in his holy war. Allah responds, "The fight in Allah's cause—thou are held responsible only for thyself—and rouse the believers." There is no God, but God, and "He will gather you together against the day of judgment . . . and whose words can be truer than Allah's?" (verse 87) Thus does Muhammad deal with doubts concerning his revelations among those who are his true followers. Questioning is not allowed and contradictions are smoothed over by reference to an artificial system of abrogation of earlier revelations.

He then returns to the matter of the "hypocrites." He tells the believers not to divide into different camps over these hypocrites, but rather "take not

---

[1135] Ibn Kathir, *Tafsir*, Vol. 2, p. 526.

friends from their ranks." Muhammad's political response is to watch them closely. Some may eventually turn to Islam. Those who become true enemies: "If they turn renegades, seize them and slay them wherever ye find them." Those who join the Meccans in warfare should be rooted out completely. Those who make treaties and who are not actually attacking the Muslims, Muhammad should make peace with: "If they withdraw from you but fight you not, and send you peace, then Allah hath opened no way for you." But those who do not make peace, "seize them and slay them wherever ye get them; in their case We have provided you with a clear argument against them" (verse 91). Yusuf Ali provides no commentary to this part of the verse. Ibn Kathir provides thirteen pages on *jihad* and inciting the believers to fight, concluding with the necessity to kill anywhere those who resist the Islamic hegemony. However, he also points out grounds for making peace treaties with those who do not wish to resist the Muslims. These are different from the dealing with those who are hypocrites and who side with the unbelievers.[1136] Muhammad is developing his plans for peace treaties, in the face of his first defeat, in order to rebuild his position to renew hostilities against his enemies.

Sections 13-20: Further Rules for the Believers

Over the next eight sections, Muhammad outlines other rules for the community of Islam, some of which also stem from the events of the Battle of Uhud. The first section deals with believers who kill other believers. Although this is strictly forbidden and punishable by death, the passage recognizes that sometimes believers are killed in battle by mistake by other believers. Rules of compensation and the freeing of a believing slave as a sign of repentance are enjoined. But for those who kill a believer "intentionally, his recompense is hell" (verses 92-93). Ibn Kathir relates stories from the conquest of Mecca, where some confessed Islam at the point of the sword but were killed anyway. The "kaffarah" or fine for this was "to free a Muslim slave, not a non-Muslim slave."[1137] He cautions against accusing someone of not being a believer for the cause of plundering him. By corollary, if one is involved in *jihad*, it is fully correct to plunder any nonbeliever. Going out to *jihad* is encouraged for "Allah hath granted a grade higher to those who strive and fight with their goods and persons, than to those who sit," they are

---

[1136] Ibn Kathir, *Tafsir*, Vol. 2, pp. 52-42.
[1137] Ibn Kathir, *Tafsir*, Vol. 2, p. 544.

given "a special reward" (verses 95-96). Even Yusuf Ali is fully supportive of special privileges and rewards for those who fight in *jihad*.[1138]

The next section concerns the angels and the carrying of souls to judgment. Those who lived in areas of evil where they could move away and did not will be consigned to hell. But those who were truly too weak and oppressed to move away may be forgiven. Those who forsake their homes for Allah receive a "reward." Yusuf Ali points out that it is better to stay in danger so as to overthrow "the fortress of evil."[1139] Yusuf Ali, even as a "moderate" Muslim, argues that Muslims should impose their wills on other people, regarding anything that they regard as evil, as the Western world is gradually discovering.

There follow some rules of prayer. When one is travelling in enemy territory it is not wrong to shorten the prayers if there is fear that "the unbelievers may attack you" (verse 101). A rule is established that allows half of a Muslim war party to pray while the other half stands guard, and another where prayer is in any position because of extreme danger. Prayers should not be said when pursuing the enemy. Muhammad continues in the next section concerning the punishments of evil men and the potential of forgiveness if anyone seeks it. He discusses secret plotting as something evil though allowed for cases involving charity, justice, or conciliation. Also, "If anyone contend with the Messenger even after guidance has been plainly conveyed to him" . . . will "land him in Hell" (verse 115).

Muhammad then deals with the issue of unforgiveable sin. This is "joining other gods with Him." Those who call on "female deities" are really calling upon "Satan" (verses 116-117). Muhammad describes the temptation of Satan to deface animals and human nature. Satan's promises are deception, and those who follow him "will have their dwelling in Hell." Those who do good will be admitted "to gardens, with rivers flowing beneath." Neither Muslims nor the "People of the Book" shall receive anything other than what their deeds deserve. "If any do deeds of righteousness—be they male of female—and have faith, they will enter heaven." To make clear what he means, Muhammad adds, "Who can be better in religion than one who submits his whole self to Allah, does good, and follows the way of Abraham" (verses 123-125). Thus, ultimately, the reward of true faith belongs to the one who follows the original religion of Abraham, which is Islam.

[1138] Ali, Yusuf, p. 216, footnote 614.

[1139] Ali, Yusuf, p. 217, footnote 615.

Muhammad then takes up again the subject of rules for women. He mentions briefly again rules of marriage and "equitable" divorce, though he recognizes that "ye are never able to be fair and just as between women." Women should not be left "hanging" in any case. The final rule, including that for the "People of the Book" is that they should fear Allah. The believers are called to be just as witnesses, to "follow not the lusts" and to "believe in Allah and his Messenger." Muhammad concludes these sections with a final rendition of what Muslims must believe in. "Allah and His Messenger, . . . the scriptures which he hath sent to His Messenger, . . . His angels, His Books, His Messengers, and the day of judgment." All the hypocrites and those who deny faith in these things will be "all in Hell" (verses 136-140). The victory will always belong to the believers.

Sections 21-23: Return to the Theme of the Hypocrites and the People of the Book

"The Hypocrites," Muhammad says, "stand up in prayer . . . to be seen by men." The words here remind one of Jesus's sermon on the Mount concerning hypocrisy in prayer. They do not join either the enemies or the believers, and they will never find "the way." Believers are called to make only friends with other believers (verse 144). Yusuf Ali does not comment on this, but Ibn Kathir provides an interesting rationale for this. To befriend unbelievers is to offer Allah "a manifest sultan against yourself." The word *sultan*, he explains, means proof, in this case indicating that one is straying from the true faith and giving proof of this to Allah by these friendships.[1140] Isolation from other people and their viewpoints is an important way that radical ideas are fostered in a group. Muslim groups that are orthodox in the Western world follow this pattern of isolation and nonintegration because the Qur'an requires this. "The hypocrites will be in the lowest depths of the fire . . . except for those who repent." The Christians and Jews are also among these hypocrites because they "deny Allah and His Messengers, and wish to separate Allah from His Messengers, saying: 'We believe in some but reject others'." (verses 142-152) For such unbelievers Allah promises "a humiliating punishment."

Muhammad then turns his attention to the People of the Book again. He claims that they have asked that he "cause a book to descend from heaven."

[1140] Ibn Kathir, *Tafsir*, Vol. 2, p. 622.

This is the same as their sin against Moses when they demanded to see Allah, and then made the golden calf. He gave them the covenant of Sinai, but "they broke their covenant . . . rejected the signs . . . slew the messengers," and "uttered against Mary a grave false charge" (verses 153-156). They said "we killed Christ Jesus the son of Mary, the Messenger of Allah—but they killed him not nor crucified him, but so it was made to appear to them . . . They killed him not—nay Allah raised him up to himself" (verses 157-158). There is much controversy over the interpretation of these verses. Generally speaking, Muslims interpret these to mean that Jesus was not crucified, but someone else was substituted in his place.

Ibn Kathir provides nineteen pages of Hadith citations purporting to tell how Jesus was raised to heaven and someone else was crucified in his place as well as stories of his second coming. In one case, Jesus asks an unidentified young man to be his substitute. Nowhere does Ibn Kathir mention the modern interpretation of Judas Iscariot. In fact, Jesus assures the young man that he will gain paradise for being Jesus's substitute.[1141] Yusuf Ali follows the traditional position that "the Qur'an teaches that Christ was not crucified, nor killed by the Jews."[1142] A comprehensive discussion on this topic is available in Lawson's, *The Crucifixion and the Qur'an*. In the modern period, Muslims have come to identify this substitute with Judas Iscariot. There are at least eight different Muslim theories with regard to the substitute, and this chaos should be compared with the uniformity of early Christian, Jewish, and Roman writings that whatever they may have thought about Christ, all affirmed his crucifixion. With this verse and its traditional interpretation, Muhammad denies a key doctrine of the Christian faith. This seems to be Muhammad's way of appealing to the Christians by accusing the Jews of a terrible calumny. The remainder of the section condemns the Jews further for their "iniquity," which Allah punished by giving them more severe kosher laws, and their "usury," which will lead to "a grievous punishment." Some of them do believe in what was "revealed to thee," and they shall receive "a great reward" (verses 160-162).

In the final two sections, Muhammad addresses both Jews and Christians, but seemingly more the Christians. There must have been some sort of Christian group in Medina though there is no clear reference by which we can determine what sort of Christians they were. They did not seem to constitute a

---

[1141] Ibn Kathir, *Tafsir*, Vol. 3, pp. 25-42.
[1142] Ali, Yusuf, p. 236, Footnote 663.

community that resisted Muhammad the way the Jews did. Perhaps we should consider them various individuals mixed in with the tribes who, nevertheless, refused to accept Muhammad's revelations. Muhammad begins by saying that revelation has been sent down upon him as it was sent to Noah, the messengers, "Abraham, Ismail, Isaac, Jacob and the descendants, to Jesus, Job, Jonah, Aaron, and Solomon, and to David we gave the Psalms." He mentions that he has told some stories but others "we have not." Finally, he says, "to Moses Allah spoke direct" (verse 164). Muhammad here confesses the truth of the previous revelations and seems to be making the point that the followers of these revelations ought also to confess him as the newest "Messenger." Those who reject faith in him, Allah will show "the way of Hell." He then addresses the Christians directly, "O People of the Book! Commit no excesses in your religion: nor say of Allah aught but the truth. Christ Jesus the son of Mary was a Messenger of Allah, and His Word, which He bestowed on Mary, and a Spirit proceeding from Him: so believe in Allah and His Messengers. Say not 'Trinity': desist . . . for Allah is one God . . . above having a son" (verse 171). Islam thus denies most of the unique doctrines of Christianity while yet giving some remarkable titles to Christ, such as Word of God and Spirit of God, though these are interpreted by Muslims in a very different way that Christians would interpret these titles. The title of Jesus as a "Word" from God leads Ibn Kathir into a long discussion of how Jesus was not the Word of God, but was created "because of" the word of God.[1143]

In orthodox Islam, the Word of God, the Qur'an, is an uncreated coeternal reality with God. This distinction is not as clear in the Qur'an as Ibn Kathir makes it. Muhammad is appealing to the Christians, affirming something very unique for Christ even borrowing Christian "Word of God" terminology. His purpose is to come as close to Christian teaching as possible in order to attract while yet rejecting the actual content of Christian teaching. One can see this process at work among Muslim evangelists in the West seeking to convert Westerners to Islam. Muhammad concludes this chapter by telling Christians that Jesus served and worshipped Allah. A new straight pathway has come to them from Allah, and they should accept it. There will be a "grievous penalty" for those who do not. Strangely this final chapter ends on a verse dealing with a legal pronouncement about those who die without descendants ending with "the male having twice the share of the female." It

---

[1143] Ibn Kathir, *Tafsir*, Vol. 3, pp. 56-59.

is an odd ending and makes one think that it was added on later, perhaps as a verse left out of the earlier section on inheritance. (verse 176)

Chapter 65: The Divorce

In this final chapter of this period, Muhammad promulgates laws regarding the subject of divorce. It can be seen as a continuation of the previous chapter and is a brief twelve verses. God addresses the Prophet directly, "O Prophet! When ye do divorce women, divorce them at their proscribed periods." (verse 1) Yusuf Ali's interpretation seems to be the exact opposite of what God is saying to the Prophet. Yusuf Ali claims that divorce should not be pronounced during the period of menstruation but the point here is that the declaration occurs during the time of menstruation probably to ease the issue of waiting to see if there should be progeny.[1144] "Prescribed periods" are then "counted" meaning that a certain number of menstruations should pass insuring that no child has been conceived. Menstrual fluid in the Qur'an is considered a kind of female semen, which combines with male semen, both of which are unclean "nutfah." This explains the odd need to wait and see, the meaning of which Yusuf Ali completely ignores. His is a commentary for Westerners. Ibn Kathir notes that this is meant also to count for "a young wife who has not begun to have menses," that is, since her menstrual semen has not begun to flow yet it is harder to tell if she has become pregnant or not.[1145] Marriage to such young girls is perfectly halal (meritorious) since the Prophet sexually consummated his wife Aisha when she was nine years old according to all systems of Islamic law. Women are not to be thrown out of their house unless they have been "lewd." After the period of the courses are finished, one may take the woman back or finalize the divorce with two witnesses. Muhammad then goes on to define the periods for divorce. For women past menopause, three months are decreed, "and for those who have no courses." Here the point, again, is that girls who have been married before beginning menstruation should also wait three months. Here Muhammad is reflecting the Islamic view of child marriage in keeping with his own example. It is interesting that Ibn Kathir describes clearly this child marriage meaning while Yusuf Ali says not a word.[1146] The period for

---

[1144] Ali, Yusuf, p. 1483, footnotes 5505 and 5506.

[1145] Ibn Kathir, *Tafsir*, Vol. 10, p. 35.

[1146] Ibn Kathir, *Tafsir*, Vol. 10, pp. 32-47.

women who are pregnant is until after the birth of the child. Women are to be supported by their husbands during these periods, and when suckling the man's child, until the time of weaning. Children always belong to the man in Islam, and when a child is weaned, it is taken away from the mother. The man is to spend from his means to support the mother during that time. Muhammad concludes the section with a renewed call to faith in Allah and himself and with the promise that those who are obedient Allah "will admit to gardens beneath which rivers flow." (verses 1-12)

Final Conclusions

The Qur'an of this period clearly reflects the realities described by the Muslim historians. A battle has been lost and many Muslims have died. Muhammad must garner new resources to replenish his army and must work relentlessly to stave off disloyalty among his followers. Muhammad carefully reinterprets the events of the defeat as the fault of his own soldiers and yet also a test from Allah. He must deal with internal enemies whom he labels the "hypocrites" and external enemies among the Jews and the Christians. Most importantly, he must deal even with loyal followers who have begun to doubt him. As in the case of the "Satanic verses" and the mythical Miraj to the distant mosque, Muhammad is facing apostasy and these chapters attack that phenomenon ferociously. Finally, the sudden deaths require the promulgation of new laws to provide for remarriage, orphans, the treatment of women, and inheritance. Islam is now clearly defined as separate from (although the completion of) Judaism and Christianity, and Christians and Jews who now do not confess Muhammad and his Qur'an as from Allah are no longer part of the people of God. At best they are "hypocrites," and at worst enemies to be finally subdued by force. Muhammad's religion is now unequivocally defined as a force for *jihad* and coercive violence meant to establish a new kingdom of God on earth under the command of "Allah and his Messenger." Anyone calling this religion a "religion of peace" is engaging in absolute folly.

CHAPTER 9

WHAT HAPPENED TO
THE BANU QURAYZA?
THE BATTLE OF KHANDAQ
AND ITS AFTERMATH.

Introduction: The Jewish Problem

If the Jews of Medina had known how shrewd a strategist Muhammad was, they probably would have put up more of a resistance. However, by the time they began to understand his true purpose, it was too late. Two tribes, the Banu Quaynuqa and the Banu Al Nadir were besieged and then expelled from the city. The Banu Qurayza were not as fortunate. They were hoping for banishment, but instead they received death, at least for the 700 or so males who had gone through puberty.[1147] Why was Muhammad's judgment so harsh? Why could he not tolerate these Jewish tribes living among the growing Muslim population? And how did this fit into his overall strategy?

At first, when Muhammad came to Yathrib (later renamed "Medina," or city of the prophet), he sought support from the Jews and considered them to be "People of the Book."

> "Ibn Ishaq shows us that the Jews actually permitted Muhammad
> to participate in the activities of their community during the first
> few months after his arrival in Medina. The scenario presented by
> Ibn Ishaq shows Muhammad pass sentence on a Jewish couple,
> raise the value of the blood price of the B. Qurayza to equal that

---

[1147] Death sentences were given to all the males who had developed pubic hair.

of the B. Nadir and become involved in religious arguments with them. It suggests an atmosphere of integration and active proselytizing that is barely visible in the al-Waqidi text. Ibn Ishaq suggests that the better moments had encouraged Muhammad to believe that the Jews could be included in an Umma with the Muslims. Unfortunately, the activity led to much religious conflict . . . and . . . Jewish rejection of Muhammad."[1148]

He never did force them to convert to Islam, as he did the pagans, but he soon realized that if he were going to fulfill his empire-building plans for Medina and Arabia, the resistant Jews were going to have to be subjugated.[1149] Wellhausen points out at least three stages in this "drama." First there was the "acceptance stage" where Muhammad "had orientated himself on their religion, had repeatedly tried to win them over—but without avail." [1150] He had even oriented the qibla, or the direction of prayer toward Jerusalem, perhaps in the hope of winning over some of the Jews or at least linking Islam to Abraham and the accepted religions of Judaism and Christianity. Later, however, almost as a symbolic gesture of his change of opinion toward the Jews, seventeen or eighteen months after Muhammad's arrival in Medina[1151] he changed the direction of qibla to Mecca.[1152] Apparently, the treatment he had received from the Jews, rejection as a prophet and political leader, had continued to feed his anger and frustration, but at the same time had to be restrained until the time was right.[1153] In order to "achieve his ideal, the establishment of a theocratic monarchy at Medina . . . his field of operation had to be cleared first."[1154] He had to get rid of the Jews.[1155] At the heart of his plan was the formation of a new umma, or society, which in effect would transcend the political limitations tribal affiliation generated among the Arabs.

[1148] Rizwi Faizer, *Ibn Ishak and Al-Waqidi Revisited: A Case Study of Muhammad and the Jews in Bibliographical Literature*, McGill University Doctoral Thesis, p. 171.

[1149] John Glubb, *The Life and Times of Muhammad*, Chelsea, MI: Scarborough House Publishers, 1970. p. 221.

[1150] Julius Wellhausen, *Muhammad and the Jews of Medina*. Trans. A. J. Weinsinck, Freiburg: K. Shwarz, 1975, p. 105.

[1151] John Glubb, *The Life and Times of Muhammad*, p. 170.

[1152] Rizwi Faizer, *Ibn Ishak and Al-Waqidi Revisited: A Case Study of Muhammad and the Jews in Bibliographical Literature*, p. 171.

[1153] Julius Wellhausen. *Muhammad and the Jews of Medina.*, p. 105.

[1154] Ibid., p. 105.

[1155] Ibid., p. 105.

Keshk comments that "the problem for Muhammad was not that they were Jewish; the problem was that they remained tribal, and they remained for the most part antagonistic toward him." [1156] Since they would not relent to his political entreaties, the Jews had to be dealt with. According to Keshk, the problem was that

> "The three Jewish tribes of Medina were so adapted to their local environment and were deeply rooted in tribal traditions and customs that they could not accept or compromise with the new umma or the state that this umma was molding. The confrontation came because the Jews rejected Muhammad as an arbiter and not as a prophet, even though they had done both." [1157]

Keshk portrays only part of the story, however. The umma was very much a political concept,[1158] but it was also the basis of his budding theocracy. As the Jews continued to reject him as the prophet of the new umma, they posed a much greater threat by calling into question the theological foundations of Muhammad's system. Wellhausen suggests that

> "Muhammad had long realized that he could not achieve his ideal, the establishment of a theocratic monarchy at Medina, so long as he was surrounded by a party which almost equaled his own disciples numerically, upon whom he could not count, and who he previously had to fear. Thus, his field of operation had to be cleared first."[1159]

Muhammad's earlier treatment of the Jews was, therefore, merely part of the means by which he could attain his own goal. It should also be noted that the content of the Qur'an put Muhammad on a collision course with the Jews from the beginning. There was simply no way that the Jews could accept the confused (from their perspective) ramblings of Muhammad as being equal to their scriptures, indeed, as superceding their scriptures. Wellhausen

---

[1156] Khaled Muhammad Galal Muhammad Ali Keshk. *The Conflict Between Muhammad and the Three Jewish Tribes of Medina.* Master's Thesis: Department of Languages, University of Utah, December 1987, p. 67.

[1157] Ibid., p. 67-68.

[1158] Serjeant *The Sunnah Jamiah Pact,* p. 154.

[1159] Julius Wellhausen. *Muhammad and the Jews of Medina,* p. 105.

points out that Muhammad only had to wait "until his position had become sufficiently established so as not to need them any longer."[1160] The purpose of getting the Jews to agree to the Constitution of Medina and his earlier friendly treatment of the Jewish tribes was, perhaps, all part of biding his time. Later, the banishment of the two tribes and the massacre of the Banu Qurayza were necessary in order for Muhammad to become the *de facto* leader of Medina, and later of all Arabia. The tribal ties had to be eliminated in order for the new umma to rise up and create a greater loyalty to a greater cause.[1161] This became part of an unfolding plan whose basis was clearly theological.

Early Opportunities and the Expulsion of the Quaynuqa

Muhammad's first major opportunity to remove "liability groups," such as the Jews, came with the Battle of Badr. The earlier raids had brought funds into the coffers and men into the new umma, but Muhammad needed more legitimacy in the eyes of the Meccans and a greater call for his ideals. Thus, even though the actual military results of Badr were insignificant, the psychological repercussions were far-reaching. Wellhausen writes as follows:

> "Muhammad's prestige was considerably increased in all of Arabia, and his position at Medina put on solid foundation. The rest of the polytheists could probably in no way be converted more quickly than by Muhammad's success and the expectation of booty and honour in war. The Jews were weakened; they felt humiliated and disappointed now that the abused prophet had shown himself as a man of insight and energy in the eyes of Arabia."[1162]

Even though the battle was against the Meccans, the Jews in Medina would have felt the repercussions early on. Immediately after his success over the Meccans, Muhammad capitalized on his victory and turned his eyes toward the Jews. They were an obstacle to his plans, but they also could provide some of his material needs through their property, houses, and livestock. His followers, especially the ones who came from Mecca, had very few

---

[1160] Ibid., 104.

[1161] Keshk. *The Conflict Between Muhammad and the Three Jewish Tribes of Medina*, p. 68.

[1162] Julius Wellhausen. *Muhammad and the Jews of Medina*, p. 105.

possessions and a number of them were living on charity.[1163] Houses and lands would be a great reward and motivation for continued loyalty. He started, therefore, with the Qaynuqa because they were the weakest of the three main tribes and they lived the closest. He probably also realized that he would need to take one tribe at a time. Muhammad used the excuse that they had broken their agreement with the Muslims. It even seems that he had a revelation that prompted him to take action against them: "If you fear treachery from any people cancel (the agreement) in the like manner; Allah hates deceivers."[1164] Other stories are told of a Jew insulting a Muslim woman in the street by tying her skirt in a way that exposed her. This is a recurrent story in Arab poetry of the time and is clearly the invention of a later age. After besieging them for fifteen days, the Qaynuqa became prisoners in the hands of the Muslims. Wellhausen believes that, based on Al-Waqidi and Ibn Ishaq, it was Muhammad's intention to kill his captives.[1165] It was only after Ibn Salul stepped in and besought Muhammad to spare their lives that he finally relented.[1166] Perhaps he thought that banishment would still serve his purpose in removing the obstacle and providing material comforts for his men. Whatever his real motives were for sparing the Qaynuqa, their expulsion brought him greater respect and a more solid position militarily. Soon it would be time to deal with the next Jewish tribe, the Al Nadir.

The Banishment of the Al Nadir

Getting the true story behind the reason for the expulsion of the Al Nadir is not easy. The traditional reason given by Ibn Ishaq is that after having agreed to pay blood-money for two men of Beni Aamir, Muhammad went to the Jewish tribe of Al Nadir to seek funds to help in the settlement, apparently something that was commonly done at that time. The Jews agreed to help, but as they sought counsel privately among themselves, they determined that this would be an ideal time to kill Muhammad and be rid of his growing influence. One man, Amr ibn Jahash, agreed to go up to the roof and drop a large stone on the apostle. However, Muhammad found out about the plot and hastily retreated to Medina while some of his men waited, unaware of

---

[1163] John Glubb, *The Life and Times of Muhammad*, p. 198.

[1164] Qur'an, sura 8:60

[1165] Ibid., p. 108.

[1166] Ibn Ishaq, Muhammad. *The Life of Muhammad*. Ed. Alfred Guillaume. Karachi: Oxford University Press, 1955., p. 363.

his departure. Muhammad then returned with his followers in order to make war on the Al Nadir. Some say that the plot was overheard while Ibn Ishaq indicates that Muhammad received a warning from heaven.[1167] In September of CE 625 (AH 4),[1168] after a siege of less than three weeks, the Al Nadir surrendered on the condition that they would be allowed to emigrate to Syria. Muhammad agreed and the Muslims confiscated the houses, lands, and weapons of the Jews.[1169] Wensinck indicates that one of the reasons that Muhammad went up against the Al Nadir was because they were a wealthy tribe and had considerable landholdings. "It is no surprise that such property caused the envy of Muhammad, especially since he and his followers were dependent upon their fellow-townsmen, and because the muhajirun lived in poor circumstances."[1170] Wellhausen also points out the advantages accrued to Muhammad with the departure of the Al Nadir:

> "Extensive land became vacant which was distributed among the Muhajirun. Also the number of his opponents diminished noticeably which in turn curtailed the power of the munafiqun. Muhammad and his party no longer had to fear any strong resistance in Medina. The theocracy had become the only power and manifested itself in various expeditions which were launched."[1171]

McDonald seeks to answer the question of why Muhammad attacked the Al Nadir from a different angle. He says that the underlying cause "was the same as in the case of Qaynuqa, namely, that Jewish criticisms endangered the ordinary Muslim's belief in Muhammad's prophethood and in the Qur'an as revelation from God. It should be kept in mind that the attack was made only a few weeks after the Muslim loss of life at al-Raji and Bi'r Ma'unah (where 40 Muslims were killed)."[1172] Thus, McDonald feels that this attack was made to revive Muslim confidence and shore up flagging spirits due to the recent disappointments brought about by the reversals at Uhud, al-Raji, and Bi'r Ma'una. He claims, therefore, that the "story about someone in Nadir plotting to drop a stone on Muhammad's head was probably just a

[1167]   Ibid., pp. 437-8.
[1168]   John Glubb, *The Life and Times of Muhammad*, p. 224
[1169]   Ibid., p. 224.
[1170]   Julius Wellhausen. *Muhammad and the Jews of Medina*, p. 26.
[1171]   Julius Wellhausen. *Muhammad and the Jews of Medina*, pp. 121-2.
[1172]   McDonald, Vol. 7, Al-Tabari, xxxv.

pretext if not a later invention."[1173] Whatever the reason, another group of detractors was gone and Muhammad's new umma was growing, not only in numbers, but also in confidence. The Al Nadir had said that they would depart for Syria, and while many did emigrate to Syria, a number of others went north to Khaybar to join forces with the Jews there.[1174] In time, this would lead to a greater concern for Muhammad, for, as Wellhausen puts it, "together with the native Jewish population, they represented a formidable power that could exert considerable influence upon the events in the Hijaz. Medina was far from safe, hard-pressed by Mecca in the south and Khaybar in the north. Thus, it was not long until there was an attack."[1175] Muhammad would not make the mistake again of letting such a large force leave only to become part of a greater opposition. The fate of the Banu Qurayza was already locking itself into place. There was only one more major piece to be put on the board, the Battle of the Trench.

The Battle of the Trench (Khandaq)

After the Battle of Uhud, the leader of the Quraysh army, Abu Sufyan, had called for a "rematch" to take place a year later in Badr. Halfway to Badr, however, Abu Safyan decided that the conditions were not right and turned back. Apparently, because of the abnormally dry conditions there was not enough food for the horses. When Muhammad and his men arrived at Badr, his opponents were nowhere to be seen. They remained camped out for eight nights before they decided to return.[1176] Even though no battle took place, Muhammad and his men were greatly encouraged and began to see themselves as morally and militarily superior to the old order.[1177]

Within a year, however, the Quraysh began putting together another army to try to crush the growing threat of the Muslim blockades against the Meccan trading caravans en route to Syria. Ibn Ishaq claims that some of the Jews from Khaybar were responsible for instigating the Meccans and Bedouin tribes like the Ghatafan to put an end to Muhammad and his followers once and for all.[1178] Wellhausen discusses the efforts depicted in the

---

[1173] Ibid., xxxvi.
[1174] Julius Wellhausen. *Muhammad and the Jews of Medina*, p. 122.
[1175] Ibid., p. 122.
[1176] Ibn Ishaq, *The Life of Muhammad,* p. 447.
[1177] Ibid., p. 448.
[1178] Ibn Ishaq, *The Life of Muhammad*, p. 450.

Muslim sources by Huyayy ibn Akhtab to convince the leader of the Jewish Qurayzah in Medina, Ka'b ibn Asad, to break their treaty with Muhammad and join the Meccan confederation preparing to attack Medina.

> "Evidently Qurayzah decided only hesitantly to terminate the good understanding they had with Muhammad. Already during the siege they had refused to support al-Nadir. Therefore it was not easy for Huyayy ibn Akhtab to persuade Ka'b ibn Asad because to take sides for or against Muhammad was a matter of life and death. If after their defection Yathrib was not conquered and captured by Quraysh, the destruction of the Jews was certain."[1179]

It is clear from the older sources that the Jews did not take part in the siege of Khandaq.[1180] The Jews broke their treaty with Muhammad but did not actively support the Meccans. Wellhausen calls this, "certainly the least advantageous attitude they could have adopted"[1181] It is also possible that these supposed dialogues were simply made up at a later time to justify the actions that Muhammad took against the Jews. The main issue was their refusal to acknowledge Muhammad as the messenger of Allah as we have seen from the Qur'anic passages of this period. They were, therefore, automatically enemies who had to be subjugated whether they were loyal to their previous treaty or not.

When Muhammad received the news of the "grand alliance" assembled against the Muslims, he sought counsel with his leaders. This time they decided not to fight out in the open as they had done at Uhud. That would mean certain defeat, especially since the Quraysh alliance forces were ten thousand strong to Muhammad's three thousand.[1182] The Muslims were fortunate to have with them a convert who came from a Christian background in Syria and, after a number of misfortunes, became a fervent follower of Muhammad. He was the one who came up with the idea of digging a trench around the exposed part of the city.[1183] This proved easier to build than a wall. In fact, within six days of hard labor the ditch was finished. From estimates given by Ahmad Barakat, the ditch ran from Shaykhayn to the Mount of Banu

---

[1179] Julius Wellhausen, *Muhammad and the Jews of Medina*, pp. 122-3.

[1180] Ibn Ishaq, *The Life of Muhammad*, pp. 450-7.

[1181] Julius Wellhausen. *Muhammad and the Jews of Medina*, p. 123.

[1182] Ibn Ishaq, *The Life of Muhammad*, p. 452.

[1183] John Glubb, *The Life and Times of Muhammad*, pp. 243-4.

Ubayd, a distance of over two kilometers.[1184] Others say that it only filled in the gaps between the houses.[1185]

The confederacy led by the Quraysh began to arrive in early February of AD 627 (AH 5).[1186] The Qur'an describes the situation as follows: "When they come against you from above (referring to the Banu Qurayza) and from below you (referring to the Meccans and Bedouins), and when your eyes swerved and your hearts reached your throats, while you thought thoughts about God; there it was that the believers were tried, and shaken most mightily."[1187] Indeed, with the Meccans before him and the Banu Qurayza behind him, Muhammad was in a precarious position. If the Jews had decided to attack, it could have been the end of Muhammad and the Muslims. However, they chose to wait and watch. In the end, the ditch proved to be a divide that could not be breached and after twenty-seven days of small skirmishes and volleys of arrows, the confederacy had enough of Muhammad's war that brought no honor[1188] and left suddenly in the early morning. The retreat was also supposedly hastened by the cold wind that overturned their cooking pots and upset their once-determined spirits.[1189] Perhaps they realized that they were up against a new type of force that they were not prepared to conquer. Glubb says that,

> "If there were any difference in the fighting performance of the two sides, it was in the sphere of morale rather than in that of physical courage. Quraysh were waging a negative and, therefore, an uninspiring war. They did not want changes introduced into their way of life. The Muslims, on the other hand, were fired by the positive conviction that God had entrusted to them the task of reforming the world. It was in the spirit which inspired them that the two sides differed."[1190]

Perhaps the Jewish tribes in Medina also made the mistake of clinging to a past that was quickly blowing away with the strong winds whipping across

---

[1184] Ahmad Barakat, *Muhammad and the Jews*, New Delhi: Vikas Publishing House, 1979, p. 68.

[1185] John Glubb, *The Life and Times of Muhammad*, p. 245.

[1186] Ahmad Barakat, *Muhammad and the Jews*, 68; Ibn Ishaq, p. 450.

[1187] Qur'an, sura 33: 10-11.

[1188] John Glubb, *The Life and Times of Muhammad*, p. 244.

[1189] Ibn Ishaq, *The Life of Muhammad*, p. 460.

[1190] John Glubb, *The Life and Times of Muhammad*, p. 248.

the desert. Muhammad was that wind, and the new ummah he was creating was the sand that would reshape much of the world as it swept across many lands. On a different front, Watt has observed that the Banu Qurayza could have brought about the demise of Muhammad and his forces, but in the end, they did not fight.[1191] Perhaps their hesitancy to act brought about their own demise. People who only wish to maintain the status quo tend to behave in this restrained manner.

What Really Happened to the Banu Qurayza?

In March of the year AD 627 (AH 5),[1192] after the Quraysh retreated back to Mecca and the Battle of the Trench was over, Muhammad and his three thousand men turned their efforts toward the Banu Qurayza. After laying siege to their fortress for twenty-five days,[1193] the Banu Qurayza surrendered unconditionally, apparently hoping for the same sentence as two other Jewish tribes from the Medina area: banishment. However, Muhammad now had the power to make a bolder stroke and leave a more powerful impression. At the end of the next day, 600-900 males were beheaded and dumped into another ditch, and the women and children were taken as property and many were later sold into slavery in exchange for weapons and horses.[1194]

According to Ibn Ishaq, after it was discovered that the enemy had departed, "the apostle and the Muslims left the trench and returned to Medina, laying their arms aside."[1195] Muhammad realized the opportunity he now had to further his plan of shifting the loyalty of the people away from the tribes and toward the new universal ummah, that of Islam. The Jewish tribe of the Banu Qurayza was one of the major obstacles to the realization of that goal and now was the time to do something about it. Ibn Ishaq records that as Muhammad was making his way back from the battle line Gabriel came to him and urged him not to rest but rather continue the battle on a different front:

[1191] W. Montgomery Watt, *Muhammad at Medina*, Oxford: Clarendon Press, 1956, p. 39.

[1192] Julius Wellhausen, *Muhammad and the Jews of Medina*, p. 126

[1193] Ibn Ishaq, *The Life of Muhammad*, p. 461.

[1194] Ibid., p. 464.

[1195] Ibid., p. 460.

"According to what al-Zuhri told me, at the time of the noon prayers Gabriel came to the apostle wearing an embroidered turban and riding on a mule with a saddle covered with a piece of brocade. He asked the apostle if he had abandoned fighting, and when he said that he had he said that the angels had not yet laid aside their arms and that he had just come from pursuing the enemy. "God commands you, Muhammad, to go to B. Qurayza. I am about to go to them to shake their stronghold."[1196]

It is interesting to note that when Muhammad asked some bystanders if they had also seen the rider on the mule with a saddle covered with a piece of brocade they replied that they had seen a certian Dihya b. Khalifa al-Kalbi upon a white mule fitting that description. Muhammad was quick to assure them that it was really the angel Gabriel.[1197] These are the kinds of stories that are inventions of a later age.

Ibn Ishaq continues, "The prophet ordered it to be announced that none should perform the afternoon prayer until after he reached B. Qurayza. The apostle sent `Ali forward with his banner and the men hastened to it."[1198] One modern historian mentions that since some men did not perform their afternoon prayers until after their evening prayers that the trip from Medina to the village housing the Banu Qurayza must have taken four or five hours, but even on the map that he includes in his book the distance is shown as less than two kilometers.[1199] Surely, it would not take four or five hours to walk that distance (a little over one mile). When Muhammad and his men finally arrived Ibn Ishaq reports that "The apostle besieged them for twenty-five nights until they were sore pressed and God cast terror into their hearts." [1200]

During the siege, Ibn Ishaq relates how Huyayy b. Akhtab from the Al Nadir tribe, who had been banished previously, returned in order to fulfill his promise to the B. Qurayza. When they felt certain that Muhammad was not going to lift his blockade, Ka`b b. Asad surmised the situation and supposedly outlined their three possibilities: (1) accept Muhammad as a prophet and agree to follow him (2) kill their women and children and fight the Muslims to their

---

[1196]   Ibid., p. 461. See also Al-Bukhari, *Volume 4, Book 52, Number 6.*
[1197]   Ibid., p. 461.
[1198]   Ibid., p. 461.
[1199]   Ahmad Barakat, *Muhammad and the Jews*, 69, p. 84
[1200]   Ibn Ishaq, *The Life of Muhammad*, p. 461.

death, or (3) try to take Muhammad and his men by surprise on the Sabbath.[1201] The Jews did not want to accept Muhammad, even if it meant their death, and they felt even more strongly about killing their own women and children, for then there would be nothing left to fight for.[1202] I am not sure why they did not consider further the idea of a surprise attack on the Sabbath, for surely it was better than wasting away. Perhaps they were confident that Muhammad would find banishment a favorable sentence, and at that point, the loss of their houses and lands did not rate in the same category as saving their lives.

One of the questions that surfaces is how the Muslims would have known about these deliberations made behind the fortified walls of the Banu Qurayza so that later biographers such as Ibn Ishaq could include it in his narrative. These deliberations are merely words placed in the mouths of the Jews, as is often done in order to shed a more favorable light on the Muslims and their Prophet.[1203] Or could they at least contain a kernel of truth since the Jews knew that their lives were on the line? One phrase from the account does seem to prefigure the ultimate action of Muhammad, and the consequent sense of doom on the part of the Jews: "the apostle would not leave them until he had made an end of them."[1204] Would there still be hope of banishment?

The Jews ask for a trusted ally, Abu Lubaba b. `Abdu'l-Mundhir, to arbitrate a surrender for them, but when Abu Lubaba met with them his judgment that they should submit to Muhammad was accompanied with a gesture to his throat signifying slaughter.[1205] Apparently, Lubaba, who genuinely felt sorry for the plight of his friends, was so overcome with this divulgence of Muhammad's plan that he ran to the mosque and lashed himself to one of the pillars saying that he was not going to leave until Allah forgave him for what he had done.[1206] Fortunately, for him, Muhammad received a revelation in the morning that Abu Lubaba had been forgiven by Allah.[1207]

That same morning Ka'b b. Asad and the rest of the Banu Qurayza surrendered to Muhammad and cast themselves to his mercy. Al-Aus, an ally

---

[1201] Ibid., p. 461.

[1202] Ibid., p. 462.

[1203] Julius Wellhausen, *Muhammad and the Jews of Medina*, p. 123. Wellhausen often questions the probability of certain sayings when they show themselves to be highly improbable and conveniently slanted.

[1204] Ibn Ishaq, *The Life of Muhammad*, p. 461.

[1205] Ibid., p. 462.

[1206] Ibid., p. 462.

[1207] Ibid., pp. 462-463.

of the Banu Qurayza, leapt up and tried to persuade Muhammad to merely banish the Jews as he had done with the B. Qaynuqa and the Al-Nadir, but it seems that Muhammad had already made up his mind. It is important to remember that when Abdullah b. Ubayy b. Salul urged Muhammad to spare the Quaynuqa that Muhammad got angry with him, and it was only with great persistence that Salul was able to appease Muhammad and obtain a lifesaving order of expulsion for the Jews.[1208] It is also important to note that Wellhausen has argued it was Muhammad's original intention to kill the Banu Qaynuqa when they surrendered.[1209] This may help us understand Muhammad's next move of asking the Aus if they would be satisfied to submit to the judgment of one of their own leaders. After they agree, he names Sa'd b. Mu'adh as the one who would determine the fate of the Banu Qurayza.[1210] Ibn Ishaq indicates that it is Muhammad who chooses Sa'd for the job. Later writers, perhaps trying to wrench any of the responsibility of the massacre out of Muhammad's hand, argue that it was the Banu Qurayza themselves who asked for Sa'd to be their arbitrator.[1211] The choice of Sa'd b. Mu'adh was a shrewd move on the part of Muhammad. It would not only remove the burden of the ultimate responsibility off Muhammad's shoulders, but it would also prevent the Aus from applying too much pressure so that he would have to relent and let the Jews face only expulsion as had happened with the Qaynuqa previously.[1212] Ultimately, the destiny of the Jews had already been sealed with the selection of Sa'd because of his previous unpleasant experiences with the Banu Qurayza.[1213] Wellhausen adds, "That the Prophet appointed Sa'd ibn Mu'adh as judge is not objectionable for the older biographers. He was an Aws, the most respected Aws of the time. What better man could Muhammad have chosen."[1214]

Who Was Sa'd b. Mu'adh?

What do we know about Sa'd b. Mu'adh? And why did Muhammad choose this particular leader? Ibn Ishaq writes that when Muhammad

---

[1208] Ibid., p. 363.

[1209] Julius Wellhausen, *Muhammad and the Jews of Medina*, p. 104.

[1210] Ibn Ishaq, *The Life of Muhammad*, p. 463.

[1211] Ibn Kathir, *al-Sira al-Nabawiyya*, p. 463, cited in Keshk, p. 64. Also see Wellhausen, p. 125; also found in Al-Bukari, Vol. 8, Book 74, Number 278.

[1212] Ibid., p. 363.

[1213] Julius Wellhausen, *Muhammad and the Jews of Medina*, p. 125.

[1214] Ibid., p. 125.

sent Sa'd to test the loyalty of Ka'b b. Asad and the Banu Qurayza to the agreement that they had made with Muhammad, Sa'd showed that he was a man with a "hasty temper" and sought vengeance against the Jews for what he felt were disparaging words against the Prophet.[1215] We see this anger against the Jews in a number of other instances as well. For example, after the Battle of Badr

> "The foe was routed. God slew many of their chiefs and made captive many of their nobles. Meanwhile the apostle was in the hut and Sa'd b. Mu'adh was standing at the door of the hut girt with his sword. With him were some of the Ansar guarding the apostle for fear lest the enemy should come back at him. While the folk were laying hands on the prisoners the apostle, as I have been told, saw displeasure on the face of Sa'd at what they were doing. He said to him, "You seem to dislike what the people were doing." "Yes, by God," he replied, "it is the first defeat that God has brought on the infidel and I would rather see them slaughtered than left alive."[1216]

Muhammad noted Sa'd's attitude at that time and probably tucked it away for future reference.

In another incident, Aisha had been accused of immorality and after she was exonerated and the false accusers discovered, Muhammad came to her defense. In this Hadith, we also learn a little more about the loyalty of Sa'd bin Mu'adh and his readiness to shed the blood of anyone who would cast doubt on Muhammad and his family.

> "Narrated Aisha: . . ."
>
> So, on that day, Allah's Apostle got up on the pulpit and complained about 'Abdullah bin Ubai (bin Salul) before his companions, saying, 'O you Muslims! Who will relieve me from that man who has hurt me with his evil statement about my family? By Allah, I know nothing except good about my family and they have blamed a man about whom I know nothing except good and he used never to enter my home except with me.' Sa'd bin Mu'adh the brother of Banu 'Abd Al-Ashhal got up and said, 'O Allah's Apostle! I will

---

[1215] Ibn Ishaq, *The Life of Muhammad*, p. 453.
[1216] Ibid., p. 301.

relieve you from him; if he is from the tribe of Al-Aus, then I will chop his head off, and if he is from our brothers, i.e. Al-Khazraj, then order us, and we will fulfill your order.'"[1217]

After Sa'd was mortally wounded by an arrow striking the medial artery of his forearm during the Battle of the Trench, he made a comment that showed his true attitude toward the Jews: "O God, seeing that you have appointed war between us and them grant me martyrdom and do not let me die until I have seen my desire upon B. Qurayza."[1218] Again, this is dramatic oratory invented at a later time, but it may reflect a known attitude.

In time, he would die from the wound, but not before Muhammad gave him the opportunity to have his "desire" manifested upon the Banu Qurayza. Surely, Muhammad knew the mind of Sa'd, and his disdain for the Jews of Banu Qurayza. Could this be the reason that Muhammad chose Sa'd b. Mu'adh for the role of judge? It would be a brilliant move. The Aus would not object because Sa'd was well-respected among them. Also, they could not refute Muhammad's choice of judge since they had previously agreed to accept his choice beforehand.[1219] The judgment from someone other than Muhammad would also remove the ultimate culpability from Muhammad himself, and he could, therefore, distance himself from any possible criticism.

Finally, Sa'd was called for and came from the mosque where Muhammad had someone taking care of his wounds. The Aus entreated him to act kindly upon the Banu Qurayza, but his reply was a preview of the sentence to come: "The time has come for Sa'd in the cause of God, not to care for any man's censure."[1220] With those words, some already understood that the death sentence had already been pronounced upon the Banu Qurayza.[1221] When Sa'd entered the room to give his judgment he first asked the Aus

"Do you covenant by Allah that you accept the judgment I pronounce on them?" They said Yes, and he said, "And is it incumbent on the one who is here?" (looking) in the direction of the apostle not mentioning him out of respect, and the apostle answered Yes. Sa'd said, "Then I give judgment that the men

---

[1217] Al-Bukhari, Vol. 5, Book 59, Number 462.

[1218] Ibn Ishaq, *The Life of Muhammad*, p. 459.

[1219] Ibid., p. 463.

[1220] Ibid., p. 463.

[1221] Ibid., p. 463.

should be killed, the property divided, and the women and children taken as captives."[1222]

Upon hearing these words, Muhammad is quoted as saying, "You have given the judgment of Allah above the seven heavens."[1223] It is interesting that he included Muhammad as an outsider in the decision process. This distancing may have been something that Muhammad desired since it would not implicate him as much in the gruesome events that would soon follow. In this way, he could get away with the death of over six hundred men and *the blame would ostensibly go to a dying man.*

All of these events may be later inventions meant to dramatize, but history also teaches us that when loyalists tell unflattering stories about their heros, those stories have a strong element of historical credibility. One could hardly imagine, given the reverence for Muhammad in the entire Muslim world, that someone could make up such stories and gain acceptance for them in the Muslim community. The stories reflected a historical reality, and like the early stories of Jewish rabbis bemoaning the birth of Muhammad, they indicate the need the community felt to explain what might be seen as reprehensible actions. This designed explanatory matrix indicates that the basic story line of attacking and slaughtering a group of Jews is true, and that the narrators are attempting to put the best possible face on it. Given the attitude expressed toward Jews in the Qur'an during this period, it is also quite possible that the Banu Qurayza had done nothing more evil than to reject Muhammad's prophethood and insist on remaining Jews. This "crime," as we have seen in the Qur'an, is enough to justify their violent subjugation.

Muhammad then had trenches dug in the market of Medina and sent for the men of Banu Qurayza in batches. Many may not have realized what was taking place because they kept asking Ka'b b. Asad "what he thought would be done with them. He replied, 'Will you never understand? Don't you see that the summoner never stops and those who are taken away do not return? By Allah it is death!' This went on until the apostle made an end of them."[1224] The men would kneel beside the trench and some of Muhammad's men struck off their heads. In all between six hundred and nine hundred boys and men were brutally murdered. The women and children were sold into slavery, and the houses and lands were divided up by the Prophet.[1225] The

[1222] Ibid., p. 464.
[1223] Ibid., p. 464.
[1224] Ibid., p. 464.
[1225] Ibid., p. 464. See also Al-Bukhari, Vol. 5, Book 59, Number 362.

Banu Qurayza no longer existed as a tribe. Karen Armstrong's explanation that people used to behave in this way in those days deliberately neglects the fact that this behavior is considered canonical, it is what Muslims should do today in imitation of the Prophet[1226]. There are hundreds of videos online from televised mosque sermons available today calling for genocide against all Jews on planet earth. This is not an attitude of a small radical group but, in many places, a generally accepted opinion preached on television. This is because of the behavior of the Prophet himself.

As Muhammad was dividing the booty, he retained the Jewess Raihana bint Amr for himself. He desired to marry her, but she would not give up her faith and said to Muhammad, "Nay, leave me in your power, for that will be easier for me and for you."[1227] The fact that Muhammad's men had just put her father, husband, and relatives to death may have had something to do with her refusal to be married to the Prophet. Apparently, Muhammad was displeased with her behavior, but he let her live and made her his concubine.[1228] He seems to justify his action by the following verse:

> "O Prophet! We allow thee thy wives whom thou hast dowered,
> and the slaves whom thy right hand possesseth out of the booty
> which God hath granted thee."[1229]

The Critics Who Would Deny the Massacre

Even if Sa'd b. Mu'adh was the one who pronounced the sentence of death upon the Banu Qurayza, it is understood in the Muslim world that Muhammad could have chosen to override Sa'd's judgment and exile the Jews as he had done in two previous cases. Thus, Muhammad is still responsible for the death of over six hundred Jewish men and boys.[1230] For many Muslims, this conclusion is not acceptable. In this modern era of reconstructionist history,

---

[1226] Armstrong, Karen, Muhammad, *A Biography of the Prophet*, Harper, 1993, pp. 208-209.

[1227] Ibid., p. 466.

[1228] Ibid., p. 466.

[1229] Qur'an, sura 33:49. This is from the passage that Muslims generally agree deals with the story of the Banu Qurayza.

[1230] The Banu Qurayza actually forms a case for Islamic law. When the age of accountability for capitol punishment was to be determined the Banu Qurayza were used as the test case. Muhammad determined that those who had developed pubic hairs among the males would be executed, and this was then generalized as the Islamic ruling on the age of accountability.

there are scholars who will go so far as to deny the historicity of an event in order to "rectify" history so that it will fit their own presuppositions. Two Muslim scholars who attempt to rewrite the history of the Banu Qurayza are Ahmed Barakat and W. N. Arafat. Both men deny that a massacre took place. Can their arguments hold up under the scrutiny of the historical evidence that we already have, or are the sources that they attack, such as Ibn Ishaq's biography of the Prophet, flawed and filled with errors? Who has the correct handle on history?

Ahmed Barakat and the Failure of the Confederacy

Ahmed Barakat states that "it would be reasonable to consider Ka'b's speech to the B. Qurayzah on the eve of their surrender as mainly imaginary or distorted by later tradition."[1231] In other words, it would seem that he recognizes the event as having happened, but not that the speech as it is recorded is correct or accurate. When we analyze the three alternatives given by Ka'b to the Jews, we will notice that some of the words were probably added by later Muslim apologists, but the fact that he was present at the time and probably did say something to the B. Qurayzah remains possible. The first alternative supposedly given by Ka'b was that the Jews could follow Muhammad and "accept him as true, for by God it has become plain to you that he is the prophet who has been sent and that it is he whom you find mentioned in your scripture."[1232] Barakat points out that the Jews would not have recognized Muhammad as the true prophet, and they rejected him to a man, even when confronted with the sentence of death. Were this true, they would rather have accepted him and lived. Thus, since all of those who were taken out to die remained steadfast in their rejection of his prophethood, Barakat states that Ibn Ishaq's narrative at this point is "patently absurd."[1233] That the Jews would believe that Muhammad was a Prophet and yet cling to rejecting him in the face of death is an absurdity. The story of their recognition of the true nature of Muhammad's prophethood was undoubtedly added by later apologists to indicate the absolute perfidity of the Jews. The Jews simply could not accept Muhammad as a prophet due to the pervasive errors (from their perspective) in his Qur'an. None of this negates the fact that hundreds of men rejected Muhammad on that day and lost their lives.

[1231] Ahmad Barakat, *Muhammad and the Jews*, p. 76.
[1232] Ibid., p. 73.
[1233] Ibid., p. 74.

Barakat goes on to say that the second alternative given by Ka'b "shows Ibn Ishaq's ignorance of the Jewish law and history" because the Jews would not go against their law and commit suicide. However, what it does show is Barakat's failure to read carefully for Ibn Ishaq states clearly that the second alternative was for the male Jews to kill their wives and children and then fight to the death if need be, not commit suicide. Barakat is not consistent with the evidence at this point.[1234] He has also apparently forgotten Masada.

The third objection that Barakat has is in reference to Ibn Ishaq's account stating that the Jews would not accept Ka'b's suggestion to make a surprise attack on Muhammad on the Sabbath because the Jews would never fight on the Sabbath, even if it meant total annihilation. Support for Ibn Ishaq on this point would be weak because, as Barakat points out, "since the Maccabean revolt . . . All laws of the Sabbath or even the Day of Atonement can be overridden in the face of the sacred duty of preserving life."[1235] It is highly unlikely, then, that this third alternative was given by Ka'b.

Since Ibn Ishaq makes these elaborations in the alleged speech of Ka'b, Barakat claims that the whole exchange between Ka'b and the Jews must have been "imaginary."[1236] To claim that there are elaborations is one thing, but to claim that an entire incident never happened because the core content concerning the event has been appended is unfounded. If we took this approach to history, then we would have to throw out most of what we "know." Actually, in the case of Ibn Ishaq's account, the need to invent a dialogue to justify the controversial action is a testimonial to the historicity of the action. If anything, then, the report by Ibn Ishaq confirms the historicity of the capture of the Banu Qurayza and their subsequent demise. It may not have happened precisely as Ibn Ishaq details it, but the fact that Ibn Hashim, Al-Waqidi, and Ibn Sa'd all refer to most of the details involved shows that they all had a previous source or at least accepted the historicity of the event themselves.

To deny that something happened because there are conflicting accounts is not realistic. It is the job of the historian to get to the root of the story and outline at least the facts that can be agreed upon. For example, Barakat points out that Al-Bukhari and Muslim give contradictory accounts concerning Sa'd's appointment as *hakam* (judge). The former said that the B. Qurayza surrendered to Sa'd's judgment, and the latter said that they surrendered to the

---

[1234] Ibid., p. 74.
[1235] Ibid., p. 76.
[1236] Ibid., p. 76.

apostle's judgment, who in turn appointed Sa'd as judge. Actually, Ibn Ishaq reveals that the B. Qurayza did not accept *either* judgment. According to Ibn Ishaq, any acceptance of Sa'd as judge came from the Aws and Muhammad: "Sa'd asked the Aws and the Apostle if they would accept his judgment. They agreed."[1237] The Aws and Muhammad agreed that the B. Qurayza had *no* part in this agreement. Ibn Ishaq makes it clear that the B. Qurayza surrendered *after* this judgment was given.[1238] For Barakat to cast doubt on whether Sa'd pronounced the judgment detailed in Ibn Ishaq because of the contradictory statements of *later* commentators is misleading, to say the least. Right before this misrepresentation, Barakat infers that Ibn Ishaq's account must be flawed because Ibn Hisham (who produced the recension of Ibn Ishaq) quoted two verses from the Quran out of context when he referred to the actions of Abu Lubaba.[1239] Apparently, this is brought up in order to cast doubt upon the historicity of Ibn Ishaq's narrative.

Barakat's real intent is found several pages later when he reminds the reader that Ibn Ishaq's account was written two centuries after the fact so there was no way of "checking the numbers" (this is in reference to the number of B. Qurayza killed after their surrender).[1240] He then makes a misleading comparison to the contradictory reporting of men killed at Bi'r Ma'unah as if to say that since we know of other contradictory reports of casualties that the number of those killed concerning the B. Qurayza must have been falsely reported.[1241] Later, he issues an even stronger statement: "Ibn Ishaq's account of the punishment of the B. Qurayza is a plethora of self-contradictory statements. So are the accounts of al-Waqidi and Ibn Sa'd. The account as given by them is untrustworthy both in detail and substance."[1242]

I believe that Barakat's real reason in pointing out the discrepancies is the realization that if 600-900 Jews were massacred at that time, then it would accentuate the "moral failures" of Muhammad, since he would still be held culpable for the final outcome of that day.[1243] Thus, if Barakat can cast doubt on the historicity of Ibn Ishaq's account, then somehow it will exonerate Muhammad from retaining any blood on his hands. Caetani, in

---

[1237] Ibn Ishaq, *The Life of Muhammad*, p. 464.
[1238] Ibid., p. 464.
[1239] Ahmad Barakat, *Muhammad and the Jews*, pp. 76-7
[1240] Ibid., p. 87.
[1241] Ibid., p. 87.
[1242] Ibid., pp. 89-90.
[1243] Ibid., p. 86; also see Watt, Muhammad at Medina, p. 327.

his *Annali dell' Islam*, accuses reconstructionist historians like Barakat of trying to "remove from Muhammad the direct responsibility for the inhuman massacre of about 900 innocent persons . . . The sentence of Sa'd was in any case dictated and inspired by the Prophet, who certainly made him understand what was the decision required of him. The responsibility for the slaughter falls entirely on the Prophet."[1244]

Montgomery Watt, in the article entitled *The condemnation of the Jews of Banu Qurayza*, compares the various early sources concerning the events surrounding the massacre of the Banu Qurayza and concludes that Ibn Ishaq's account is not only historical, but also that he "may be regarded as the first of the succeeding group of 'scientific' transmitters of biographical material."[1245] What he means by this assessment is that Ibn Ishaq's biography qualifies as historical in that it carries a "solid core of undisputed material"[1246] and in the end, "nothing has been found to justify the complete rejection of Ibn Ishaq, al-Waqidi and their predecessors."[1247] History has shown us that when loyalists tell unflattering stories about their heros, these stories have a considerable level of credibility. The story of the Banu Qurayza is also woven into the historical narratives from the beginning in a pattern of justification. No one makes up stories like this to justify events that never took place. Finally, the massacre of the Banu Qurayza is also woven into the pattern of Islamic law and is at least obliquely mentioned in the Qur'an itself. The event is historical though the details may vary.

Some of the objections Barakat raised in order to support his denial are in themselves a denial of what were probably actual events. First of all, he argues that Medina was not equipped to imprison four to five thousand people (counting the women and children), and certainly it would have been impossible to execute 600-900 people in a day. As far as the need for facilities, however, the Muslims only needed a large courtyard area for holding the Jews. They did not need to feed them or house them; they only needed to retain them. The Jews were unarmed, fearful, and weak with hunger after the siege of over three weeks. They were not ready to put up much resistance. Also, several people would have been involved in the execution of the men. Barakat mentions at least two by name, Ali and Zubayr.[1248] With several executioners

[1244] cited in W. Montgomery Watt, *Early Islam: Collected Articles.* Edinburgh: Edinburgh University Press, 1990. p. 1.

[1245] W. Montgomery Watt, *Early Islam: Collected Articles*, p. 7.

[1246] Ibid., p. 12.

[1247] Ibid., p. 22.

[1248] Ahmad Barakat, *Muhammad and the Jews*, p. 85.

at work, it would not have taken that much time to have executed 600-900 Jews in one morning. Second, Barakat says that with so many dead bodies lying around, the town would have been made uninhabitable and a hotspot for all kinds of diseases.[1249] However, Ibn Ishaq's account points out that Muhammad's men dug trenches near the area of the town market to receive the bodies. The quick burial would have prevented the spread of disease.[1250]

Barakat deduces that the final number of men executed by Muhammad's men was quite small. After whittling down the number of those executed from the "600-900" given by Ibn Ishaq to the "moderate number" of two hundred given by Bell,[1251] Barakat settles on the final number as "sixteen or seventeen" based upon a Qur'anic injunction for just retribution that he says Muhammad would have been bound to: "an eye for an eye and a life for a life."[1252] Barakat derived the final number through a "formula" that goes something like this:

1. Take the four main leaders and execute them on the spot (Huyayy b. Akhtab, Ka'b b. Asad, Nabbash b. Qays, and Ghazzal b. Samaw'al).[1253] That would start us off with four people.
2. Execute two men for each of the six clans of the Aws represented. Since there were six clans represented, this would yield an additional twelve victims, or a total number of only "16 or 17."[1254]
3. Disregard the accepted traditional view that all males who had reached puberty were executed. Barakat wants to say that since the "Quran mentions only two groups which were punished: one was executed and the other taken captive,"[1255] Ibn Ishaq neglected to reveal the number of men who were not punished. But is it reasonable to believe that most of the men would have been allowed to "stay around or migrate"[1256] while all the women and children were sold into slavery. In the end, Barakat's "formula" does not align itself with the documents that we have which deal with the incident. The supposed aftermath described above is simply not credible.

[1249] Ibid., p. 86.
[1250] Ibid., pp. 85-86.
[1251] Ibid., p. 88.
[1252] Qur'an, sura 2:178.
[1253] Ahmad Barakat, *Muhammad and the Jews*, p. 91.
[1254] Ibid., p. 91.
[1255] Ibid., p. 92.
[1256] Ibid., p. 92.

W. N. Arafat and New Light on the Story of the Banu Qurayza

Another reconstructionist Muslim analyst, W. N. Arafat, contends that the details of the story, as told by Ibn Ishaq and those who followed his footsteps, were largely fabricated. He further states that, "It can be demonstrated that the assertion that 600 or 800 or 900 men of Banu Qurayza were put to death in cold blood cannot be true; that it is a later invention; and that it has its source in Jewish traditions."[1257] As usual, the Jews are the source of all evil on earth.

Arafat begins his critique by questioning the historicity of Ibn Ishaq's *Sira,* since it was written one hundred and forty-five years after the events in question. This gap in time would apparently allow for a number of changes and deletions. It is important to note, then, that the earliest full Qur'an that we have in existence is dated from AD 790, nearly one hundred and sixty years *after* Muhammad died.[1258] If Ibn Ishaq's account is on shaky ground, then the Qur'an itself comes under the same scrutiny.

One of the main problems that Arafat has with Ibn Ishaq's account is that Ishaq did not apply a strict chain of authority, called "isnads," in order to verify that the account given was based on reliable transmissions.[1259] Montgomery Watt shows, however, that many of these "isnads" were fabricated and could not be relied upon in any fashion.[1260] Also, Watt shows that Ishaq was at the forefront of the group of what he calls the "scientific" transmitters "who generally give authorities for their statements, but do not merely repeat the exact words they have heard and do not always give a complete chain of authorities back to the Prophet."[1261] The system of isnads was not fully developed in his time. This is perhaps why so many writers after Ibn Ishaq accepted his account as reliable. It is a strain, therefore, for Arafat to try to discredit Ishaq's account of the Banu Qurayza and other related ones as "odd tales" and "lies."[1262] The first statement, "odd tales," was made by Ibn Hajar, who rejected Ibn Ishaq because he allegedly received some of his information

---

[1257] W. N Arafat, *New Light on the Story of Banu Qurayza and the Jews of Medina.* Journal of the Royal Asiatic Society of Great Britain and Ireland, (1976), pp. 100-7, p. 1.

[1258] Jay Smith, *Uncomfortable Questions for the Qur'an.* www.debate.org/topics/history/home. htm. 1995.

[1259] W. N. Arafat, *New Light on the Story of Banu Qurayza and the Jews of Medina,* p. 2.

[1260] W. Montgomery Watt, *Early Islam: Collected Articles,* p. 7.

[1261] Ibid., p. 7.

[1262] W. N Arafat, *New Light on the Story of Banu Qurayza and the Jews of Medina,* p. 1.

from the descendants of the Jews of Medina. Apparently, truthful and relevant information cannot be ascertained from anyone associated with the Jews.

The other critic, Malik, was a contemporary of Ishaq who discredited the biographer because he did not contain complete *isnads*. In fact, *isnads* have been shown by modern scholarship to be almost completely useless in determining historicity. Most *isnads* are inventions of a later age and totally unreliable as determinants of historicity. These "chains of authority" are very important in the transmission of the law, especially in the Hadith, but if Montgomery Watt is correct, it was during the lifetime of Ibn Ishaq that this practice was coming into being. We would also need to question the historicity of Malik himself. How can we trust his words? Whatever the case, these are the two critics that Arafat mentions to cast doubt on Ibn Ishaq's account of the Banu Qurayza. Arafat also points out that Ibn Ishaq "was in fact subjected to devastating attacks by scholars, contemporary or later, on two particular accounts."[1263] The first account dealt with Ibn Ishaq's inclusion of spurious or forged poetry. The second account dealt with Ishaq's acceptance of the slaughter of the Banu Quarayza. It is interesting to note that Arafat's footnotes are the first point in regard to the poetry, but he does not give any source for his view on Ishaq's account of the massacre. It is also important to note that even though he makes reference to the "devastating attacks by scholars," he only mentions the two, Ibn Hajar and Malik. Are there any other critics? It would be a heavy hand indeed to cast aside the historicity of the account by Ibn Ishaq by the mere grievances of two other much later writers particularly when Al-Waqidi's account is substantially the same.

Let us now look at some of the criticisms that Arafat makes in regard to Ibn Ishaq's description of the events and then offer some possible explanations. First of all, Arafat states that the Qur'an was the only contemporary text, and it mentions that only "some were killed."[1264] Indeed, there were only two categories: those who were killed and those who were taken prisoner. Later, it is very clear that only the women and children were taken prisoner and then sold into slavery.[1265] This verse actually gives *greater* evidence that all the men were killed, since that was the only other category that the Qur'an mentions. Arafat tries to argue that the ones killed were only those who actually fought in the battle, and then all the other men were taken as prisoner:

[1263] Ibid., p. 3.
[1264] Qur'an, Sura 33:26.
[1265] Ibn Ishaq, *The Life of Muhammad*, p. 464.

"Exegetes and traditionists tend simply to repeat Ibn Ishaq's tale, but in the Qur'an, the reference can only be to those who were actually in the fighting. This is a statement about the battle. It concerns those who fought. Some of these were killed. Others were taken prisoner."[1266]

Again, this is contrary to what Ibn Ishaq states through Sa'd's judgment: "I give judgment that the men should be killed, the property divided, and the women and children taken as captives."[1267] Clearly, then, Arafat is in error in his analysis of the events. A better fit from the Qur'an would be as follows: "some were killed"—the adult males, and "some were taken captive"—the women and children. Even Yusuf Ali, in his commentary on this verse in the Qur'an, makes Muhammad out to be magnanimous because if he had followed Old Testament law (which Yusuf Ali believes that Sa'd was applying), then even the women and children should have been killed. However, Yusuf Ali concludes as follows: "The men of the Qurayza were slain; the women were sold as captives of war; and their lands and properties were divided among the Muhajirs."[1268] Thus, it seems that Arafat's views are contrary to the Qur'an.

Another argument that Arafat poses is that

"To kill such a large number is diametrically opposed to the Islamic sense of justice and to the basic principles laid down in the Qur'an—particularly the verse: "No soul shall bear another's burden." It is obvious in the story that the leaders were numbered and were well known. They were named."[1269]

First of all, it is important to realize that at this time the Qur'an was still in the process of being written. It would not be for years after the Prophet's death that his various practices would be mandated as Sunna and then written into law. The verse that Arafat alludes to is found in another chapter of the Qur'an.[1270] It was not written at the time of the incident with the Banu Qurayza, and therefore, cannot be linked to the motives or actions of the Prophet at

---

1266 W. N Arafat, *New Light on the Story of Banu Qurayza and the Jews of Medina*, p. 3.
1267 Ibn Ishaq, *The Life of Muhammad*, p. 464.
1268 Qur'an, Yusuf Ali's notes 3701-3704.
1269 W. N. Arafat, *New Light on the Story of Banu Qurayza and the Jews of Medina*, p. 4.
1270 Qur'an, Sura 35:18.

that time. In regard to the idea that only the named leaders would have been killed, we have to be realistic. If there were hundreds of common Jews killed that day, then it would not have been of interest to the Muslims to have a list of all their names recorded and it would not have been prudent. A list of the leaders would have been representative enough. After all, the names of most of the Jews were not listed in the Holocaust, nor were the thousands of political prisoners executed by Saddam Hussein. Why would we expect it in the past? Also, the concept of Ummah carried with it the idea of obliterating other tribal ties in favor of the new religious ties. Those who resisted faith in Allah and his Prophet could be given exemplary community-based punishments, since they adhered to a false sort of community. September 11 and other terrorist attacks are motivated by this principal of community-based punishments.

Arafat argues that "it is unlikely that the Banu Qurayza should be slaughtered when the other Jewish groups who surrendered *before* Banu Qurayza and *after* them were treated leniently and allowed to go."[1271] First of all, this assertion assumes the guilt of the Jews, and we have already shown that the charges brought against them seem invented. It is clear from the Qur'an that Muhammad regarded the Jews as a threat purely by virtue of the fact of their being Jews and not confessing his prophethood. However, based on the example of the Al-Nadir making their way up to reinforce the Jewish stronghold of Khaybar, if Muhammad let the Banu Qurayza go as well, then he would have had to deal with a much stronger force when he would eventually attack the Jews centered around Khaybar. He could later afford to be lenient with the Jews in Khaybar after their defeat and surrender because he already had made peace with Mecca and with the defeat of the Jews at Khaybar, he had the power and positioning to finally oust the Jews from Arabia. He did not need to resort to such an extreme tactic, as he felt was necessary with the Banu Qurayza. The mark of a good military tactician is to be flexible and make the best choices based on the present circumstances. Muhammad proved himself over and over to be versatile and shrewd when it came to battle. He was a master strategist, and his treatment of the Jews bears this out. Dead Jews don't produce abundant tributary taxes.

Another argument that Arafat brings up is in reference to the burial place of the Jews.

[1271] W. N. Arafat, *New Light on the Story of Banu Qurayza and the Jews of Medina*, p. 4 (italics in the original).

"If indeed so many hundreds of people had actually been put to
death in the market-place, and trenches were dug for the operation,
it is very strange that there should be no trace whatever of all
that—no sign or word to point to the place, and no reference to a
visible mark."[1272]

Again, the recent events in Iraq show the shallowness of this argument.
Thousands of mass graves are now being uncovered in the deserts of Iraq
revealing the meager remains of those who challenged Saddam Hussein after
the Gulf War in 1991. Even in only twelve years time, there was little left
to reveal that underneath the desert sands there would be so many to give
evidence to a brutal regime. In the same way, the burial place of the Banu
Qurayza would be quickly subsumed by the environment and the events
filed into Islamic law as righteousness. Have there ever been excavations
undertaken to prove or disprove the incident? Whatever the case, lack of a
present marker does not negate the reality of a past event.

One last argument that I will deal with concerns the issue of forming
legal precedents. Arafat postulates that

"Had this slaughter actually happened, jurists would have adopted
it as a precedent. In fact, exactly the opposite has been the case.
The attitude of jurists, and their rulings, have been more according
to the Qur'anic rule in the verse, 'No soul shall bear another's
burden.'"[1273]

Historically, then, we should see this Qur'anic injunction enforced throughout
the Muslim world, especially in the way that Muslims treat the non-Muslims
around them. This is not the case, however. We see that through history many
people have been forced into Islam by the sword and even today there are
countries like the Sudan in which Christians and animists in the southern part
of the country have been subjected to massacres, slavery and loss of property,
all because they would not submit to Islam. Hindus in Bangladesh have
been systematically robbed of their lands, murdered in communal riots, and
expelled to India. Turkish Muslims under a caliph slaughtered one and a half
million Armenians and Greeks in the first genocide of the twentieth century.

[1272] Ibid., p. 4.
[1273] Ibid., p. 4.

Ba't Yeor has documented the extensive programs of rulers in the Middle East toward their non-Muslim subjects. In fact, that slaughter of the Banu Qurayzah does provide legal precedents in the Islamic writings, particularly the age of accountability when capitol punishment may be applied. It is cited as precedent in numerous Hadith and lawbook writings.

Conclusion

In conclusion, Arafat cannot support his stance that Ibn Ishaq was inaccurate and that the Banu Qurayza males did not face execution. In regard to Ibn Ishaq's *Sira*, his central theme seems to be that

> "The sources of the story are, therefore, extremely doubtful and the details are diametrically opposed to the spirit of Islam and the rules of the Qur'an to make the story credible. Credible authority is lacking, and circumstantial evidence does not support it. This means that the story is more than doubtful."[1274]

As we have seen, however, Arafat's credible logic is lacking and the evidence does not support his various points. In fact, some of his arguments against Ibn Ishaq actually end up supporting the earlier account, especially as he brings the Qur'an into the argument. In the end, both Arafat and Barakat fail to shake the core historicity of Ibn Ishaq's account, primarily because the evidence is exclusively on the side of Ibn Ishaq.

Qur'anic Passages from This Period

Up to this point, we have only looked at passages clearly written in the ethos of the failure of the Battle of Uhud and Muhammad's efforts to stabilize his situation and rebuild his army. According to all Muslim commentators, chapter 33 deals with the slaughter of the Banu Qurayza, among other things. According to Nöldeke, there is only one other passage intervening between the aftermath of Uhud and the victory of Khandaq and that is chapter 59. It should be very interesting to see the ethos of this chapter as we approach (or perhaps have already passed) the climactic battle for Muslim defense against the counterattack of Mecca.

[1274] Ibid., p. 5.

Chapter 59: The Mustering

Initially, it is worth mentioning that the number of revelations given between the Battle of Uhud and the Battle of Khandaq seems quite limited. Perhaps the struggle to stabilize Muhammad's army and to renew its military campaigns against the Meccans took most of his time. There was left little room for Allah's revelations apart from those that dealt directly with the rebuilding of the army and the community as well as moving against the Jews and other "hypocrites" who threatened Muhammad's growing hegemony. Chapter 59, which we have designated as a transitional chapter is of just twenty-four verses. Muslim commentators, including Yusuf Ali, maintain that the chapter deals with the expulsion of the Al-Nadir Jewish tribal group. If true, this certainly fits the pattern of the Prophet's consolidations and ridding himself of the questioning Jews. Before we enter into this chapter, it is worthwhile to ask the question, at this point in time, how much of the content of the Qur'an were the Jews aware of?

The Qur'an still seems to indicate that questions are being put to the Prophet, but certainly in no way as frequently as we saw in the Meccan surahs of the Qur'an. Those few questions that do come forward have an almost rhetorical sense, as if Muhammad is putting into the mouths of his enemies the kinds of questions he thinks they ought to be asking. We know that there are many Hadith, austensibly from this period, which instruct Muslims not to discuss the Qur'an or share its contents with outsiders. The Qur'an itself seems to hint at this. It would seem extremely unlikely to me that the Jews and Christians, so specifically addressed in chapters 2 and 3 of the Qur'an early on in this period, could have mistaken Muhammad's ultimate intentions for them. His words leave little doubt of his intentions even though occasionally softened by stating that some of the Jews and Christians were indeed good Muslims who were doing good deeds. Muhammad's rage was not ethnically or racially based, but ideologically based. Those who followed his ideological faith were automatically righteous, whether Jewish or Christian or pagan in background. Those who refused to follow him, whether Jewish or Christian or pagan, were perverts worthy to be militarily subjugated, if not ultimately annihilated. It would seem to me that Muhammad, at this stage, was circulating his revelations only to his own people and instructed them to treat them like military intelligence, not to be spread to the Ummah's enemies. This pattern existed for decades, perhaps even a century or more before the Qur'an began to be written down. Indeed, we have no copies of the Qur'an earlier than one hundred and eighty years after the time of the Prophet.

Given the thoroughly militaristic intentions of the Muslim community, it would seem that covering up the Qur'an was a means to prevent the enemies of Islam from knowing what their ultimate intentions were at a time when Muslims were only a small percentage of the population in the Middle East. It is perhaps also this secrecy that explains the paucity of early information in the writings of non-Muslims in the Middle East of this time concerning Muhammad and the Qur'an. The initial Muslim invasion as late as AD 660s was described as groups of bandits with very little connection to an ideology. There is also another reason for this secrecy.

In my opinion, Muhammad was open about his revelations in his initial dealings with the Jews in Medina. As we have already noted, Muhammad probably found himself the focal point of intense criticism by the Jews who could not have found his writings anything other than thoroughly ludicrous. Once burned, the Prophet quickly understood the danger to the faith of his own troops if his revelations were questioned. Interestingly, there are few attempts at telling lengthy stories about the previous Prophets in the Medinan surahs with the exception of the earliest, chapter 2. From that point on, Muhammad's references are cursory and keep to major themes that he already understood from Jewish salvation history. He does not want to introduce any more self-contradictory material to his own soldiers. His references to Christians, similarly, are restricted to polemic against certain Christian beliefs presented in such a way as to be easy for his troops to memorize and use to fend off any approaches made to them on a religious basis by the Christians. Islam is, to this day, a religion that defines itself primarily in anti-Christian and anti-Jewish slogans that are very easy for Muslims to learn by rote as any Christian who has tried to speak about Christian beliefs to a Muslim has quickly learned. Clearly, the Jews of Medina did not fully appreciate where Muhammad was headed and therefore reacted, if at all, far too late.

Chapter 59 of the Qur'an is really about the "treachery" of the Jews and their just punishment. Of course, we don't get to hear the other side of the story.

Muhammad starts by saying that God "is He who got the unbelievers among the People of the Book from their homes" (verse 2). Muhammad is here celebrating a driving out of the Jews as something that Allah himself has accomplished. "They thought their fortresses would defend them from Allah!" But Allah came at them "from quarters from which they little expected, and cast terror into their hearts so that they destroyed their own dwellings by their own hands and the hands of the believers." The message here is not of a slaughter of the Jews, but some kind of betrayal or unexpected attack to which they were forced to surrender and give up all their possessions. Ibn Kathir claims that the Jews began a conspiracy with the Meccans after the Battle of Badr to betray Muhammad and that is why Muhammad had to drive them out of Medina.[1275] Perhaps, after rebuilding his army, Muhammad decided to surprise attack this weaker group of Jews, both for the plunder opportunity and to rid himself of people knowledgeable enough to question his revelations. There is nothing in the Qur'an about the Jews being unfaithful to their earlier "defensive" covenant. They are simply spoken of as being driven out "at the first gathering." Their sin was that they refused now to acknowledge the Prophet and that was treachery enough for them to be expelled.

Muhammad's darker intentions are clear. "Had it not been that Allah had decreed banishment for them, He would certainly have punished them in this world: and in the hereafter they shall have the punishment of fire. That is because the resisted Allah and His Messenger: and if anyone resists Allah, verily Allah is severe in punishment." Clearly, Muhammad's ultimate intentions were for the annihilation of the Jews as a threat to his revelations and political power. He seems to regret that Allah only called for banishment. It is unimaginable that the other Jews in Medina could have heard these passages and been unaware of what was in store for them. They must have been for internal consumption only as part of the strategems of war. This kind of behavior is seen today when Muslim representatives will speak of peace in English, and then call for *jihad* in Arabic when addressing their own congregations. We must constantly remind ourselves that we are hearing only one side of the story and not a rendition of historical reality. Muhammad goes on to describe the destruction of tender palm trees, perhaps as a way of forcing the Jews to surrender because their means of livelihood were being destroyed during the siege. Muhammad excuses this, "it was by leave of Allah and in order that He might cover with shame the rebellious transgressors." The nature of their rebellion, as we have seen in all the previous passages, was not military resistance to Muhammad, but refusing to accept him as the new Prophet of God. In a word, desiring to remain Jews was an unspeakable crime of rebellion. Their existence would only be tolerated if they were politically subjugated "dhimmis" providing special tax revenues to the Muslims.

[1275] Ibn Kathir, Vol. 9, pp. 543-8.

In verse 6, Muhammad begins to boast about how little this expedition cost and how much wealth they have gained by it. "What Allah has bestowed on His Messenger from them—for this ye made neither expedition with either cavalry or camelry." He states that it was the "terror," which God put in their hearts that drove them out. He makes it clear who owns this material that has been stolen from the Jews. "What Allah has bestowed on His Messenger from the people of the townships—belongs to Allah—to his Messenger and to kindred and orphans, the needy and the wayfarer . . . so take what the Messenger assigns you . . . to the indigent Muhajirs, those who were expelled from their homes" (verses 6-8). Here Muhammad reveals the real reason for the attack on Al-Nadir. As we noticed in the earlier post-Uhud chapters, Muhammad's greatest concern is the restoration of the economic fortunes of his army. The Muhajirs from Mecca were the core of that army. It may well be that Muhammad simply decided to pillage a tribe of Jews with this in mind. If the early Muslim historians are correct and the Al-Nadir were goldsmiths, attacking their market provided a bounty of wealth to distribute to the more indigent of his army, the talk of orphans and wayfarers notwithstanding. This would also remove that group of Jews who lived closest to Muhammad's camp, and thus the one's who might have done the most questioning of his revelations. Muhammad seems to make an excuse in verse 9 as to why the local Medinan believers do not seem to receive any of this booty, for they "had homes" already. The indication is that the Jewish homes, or what was left of them, were given to the Muhajirs. Yusuf Ali justifies this plunder by saying the Jews had come and taken the land from the Arabs originally and had refused to assimilate to the culture of Arabia.[1276]

The second section of the chapter deals with the behavior of the "hypocrites" and "their misbelieving brethren among the People of the Book." He quotes them as saying, "if ye are attacked we will help you." He concludes, "they are indeed liars." I think this brief critique of the Prophet helps us to establish closely the dating of the passage. It would seem strange to bring up the subject of lack of participation in battle concerning Uhud again. Further, Uhud was fought well outside of Medina and perhaps would have fit under a category other than an attack on Medina itself. But the Battle of Khandaq was by any measure a direct assault on Medina by the Meccans. This would be a good reason indeed to accuse the "hypocrites" of disloyalty in not aiding in the defense of the city, which the constitution seemed to call

---

[1276] Ali, Yusuf, *The Meaning of the Holy Qur'an*, p. 1446.

for. Muhammad goes on to attack them, not so much for their disloyalty as for their disunity within themselves and fear of the Muslims. The wording is very confusing, but he says in verse 12, "If they are expelled, never will they go out with them; and if they are attacked, they will never help them." The Prophet seems to say that it is safe to attack the People of the Book because the hypocrites will not support them, either in their expulsion or in battle. Ibn Kathir presents this as his interpretation of the text.[1277] Muhammad says of the hypocrites, "Ye are more feared in their hearts than Allah . . . strong is their fighting amongst themselves . . . their hearts are divided." Muhammad is rallying his troops at this opportune moment to attack their enemies because the Meccans have turned away, and they are divided among themselves. Muhammad understood that the Jews were his greatest threat. The hypocrites among the Arabs would eventually come over to his side since they were pragmatists, so there is no plan for attacking them. The plan is to wipe out the Jews who are the real ideological threat. He responds, "The end of both will be that they will go into the fire, dwelling therein forever" (verses 12-17). Muhammad's plan is simple, wipe out the Jews, since the hypocrites among the Arabs will never fight for them in reality, and then with no other recourse, the Arab hypocrites will join themselves to the Muslims.

Muhammad concludes this short rallying cry to the new war to eradicate the Jews with reminders to "fear Allah" and exalt the Qur'an; "had we sent down this Qur'an on a mountain, verily thou wouldst have seen it humble thyself and cleave asunder for fear of Allah." The final three verses extol Allah: "Allah is He . . . there is no other God . . . the sovereign, the holy one . . . guardian of faith, . . . the exalted in might, irresistible, . . . the creator . . . bestower of forms, . . . the most beautiful names, . . . He is exalted in might, the wise" (verses 22-24). With such exultations, Muhammad concludes this revelation.

Chapter 33: The Slaughter of the Banu Qurayza in Qur'anic Perspective

Chapter 33 is entitled, "The Confederates," and deals with the aftermath of Muhammad's rape of the Banu Qurayza. In this passage, we see the mind of a man who has conquered his enemies, and how he treats them in victory. Further, we see the religious justifications for these actions in the clear word

---

[1277] Ibn Kathir, *Tafsir*, Vol. 9, pp. 568-71.

of approval from Allah. Indeed, Allah himself is speaking in exultation at the annihilation of a group of Jews. The Prophet's marriages, as well as his rape of a captured Jewess also figure in the justifications for his behavior that Allah provides.

The passage begins with Allah commanding the Prophet not to listen to "the unbelievers and the hypocrites," but rather to "follow that which comes to thee by inspiration" (verses 1-2) The issue here is Muhammad's marriage to his adopted son's wife Zaynab for which he is being criticized. His logic in verse 4 is that just as women divorced by the practice of *Zihar*[1278] are not "mothers," so the "son" by adoption is not a son at all, and therefore, it is legal for Muhammad to take his "son's" divorced wife as his own. In Arab culture of the day, this was considered incest. Allah here rewrites Arab culture to the Prophet's benefit. However, it does have a consequence. The verse completely denies the legal relationship of adoption, and thereby consigns orphans in the Muslim world to a legal no-man's land. Even the liberal Yusuf Ali admits that "Adoption" in the technical sense is not allowed in Muslim law.[1279] How ironic that the Prophet who was an orphan himself, because of his desire to take his adopted son's wife to himself, consigned all orphans to a status of alienation within their own culture. One can see the results of that pillar of Islamic law throughout the Muslim world today. Allah is the one who "shows the way." The names of all Muslims who were adopted at this time were changed back to the biological father's names.[1280] Muhammad points out that blood ties are more important than even the relations of different groups of Muslims, "Blood relations have closer ties in the decree of Allah than believers and Muhajirs" (verse 6). What an odd contrast to his attempts to eradicate blood ties in favor of the Ummah of faith. When it comes to his own convenience all rules seem to be negotiable with Allah's help. Traditionally, verse 6 is also interpreted to mean that Muhammad's wives, as "mothers to the believers" were not allowed to remarry after the Prophet's death.

In section two, Muhammad reflects on the events of the Battle of Khandaq. This is clear because he refers to a direct attack on "Yathrib" the original name of the town, and he does not exalt in any sort of actual physical victory, but that the attackers did not attain their goal. There is no complaint of loss of life so the ethos is clearly of the "siege" of Khandaq. Muhammad

---

[1278] A form of divorce in that the man retains his wife as a sort of slave without conjugal rights.

[1279] Ali, Yusuf, p. 1056.

[1280] Ibn Kathir, *Tafsir*, Vol. 7, p. 635.

claims that the enemy was turned back not by battle, but by "forces that ye saw not." Ibn Kathir claims a large conferated army had been gathered by the Jews of Al-Nadir in Khaybar in collusion with the Meccans.[1281] The forces of the Muslims had been shaken by fear of this large army. "Behold!" they came from on you from above you and from below you . . . the believers "were . . . tried: They were shaken" (verse 9). He goes on to describe a party of "Hypocrites" who said, "Ye men of Yathrib ye cannot stand! Therefore go back! And a band of them ask for leave from the Prophet saying, 'Truly our houses are bare and exposed.'" He accuses them of wanting to "effect . . . an entry . . . from the sides of the (city) . . .'" and that they had been "incited to sedition." All of this clearly reflects the ethos of a siege around Medina. Muhammad accuses them of turning their backs on their covenant with Allah, probably referring to the earlier constitution of Medina. He very effectively questions their loyalty in a way that creates social pressure to hold the army together. He goes on to accuse them of cowardice. "Running away will not profit you . . . nor will they find for themselves, besides Allah, any protector or helper" (verses 16-17). Muhammad has not won a victory in this sense for fear clearly still exists in the army. He goes on to say, "they think the Confederates have not withdraw." The Muslim forces were still afraid of a possible return of the Meccan army, which Muhammad refers to as "the confederates," an indication that the army was a conglomeration of many groups opposed to the Prophet.

Muhammad then begins to speak words of encouragement to his troops that he regards as loyal. Of these he says, "When the believers saw the confederate forces . . . it only added to their faith and their zeal in obedience . . . they have never changed in the least . . . Allah may reward the men of truth" (verses 22-24). He points out that the Meccan attack was futile. "Allah turned back the unbelievers for their fury: No advantage did they gain" (verse 25). This again speaks of the ethos of Khandaq, a battle that had no clear result, but which in essence was a defeat for the Meccans because all their efforts accomplished nothing. Now Muhammad turns to the key point.

"Those of the People of the Book who aided them—Allah did take them down from their strongholds and cast terror into their hearts, some ye slew and some ye made prisoners. And he made you heirs of their lands, their houses, and their goods . . . Allah has power over all things" (verses 26-27). Ibn Kathir describes at length the slaughter of all the Jewish males (7-800

[1281] Ibn Kathir, *Tafsir*, Vol. 7, pp. 646-7.

in his estimation) who had attained puberty (had visible pubic hair).[1282]
Muhammad uses the term *ra'aba* for the "terror" infused in the hearts of
the Jews (33:26). He indicates that these "People of the Book" had been
treacherous and had "aided" the confederates. It is strange, however, to note
that none of the Muslim writers actually accuses the Jews of taking part in the
attack. Ibn Kathir, who is most predisposed to accuse Jews, mentions nothing
of any actual Jewish attack, only that there were conspiracies being led by the
Jews. It is also interesting to note that this passage follows immediately after
the chapter describing the ouster of the Jewish tribe of Al-Nadhir. It would
seem that these two events occurred in relatively quick succession. I would,
therefore, posit that Muhammad's intention throughout his sojourn in Medina
was to get rid of the Jews, the one potentially dangerous ideological threat to
his new Kingdom. Qaynuqa and Nadir fell before Khandaq. Muhammad's
attacks on the Jews led the Banu Qurayza to withdraw their treaty with
Muhammad since his intentions toward them were obvious. They did not
actually attack him. Once Khandaq had ended essentially in victory for the
Muslims, Muhammad was now free and had an excuse to finish off the last
and largest group of Jews in Medina.

He slaughtered all the males who had passed through puberty as the
Muslim texts relate, and gave the women for his men to rape, reserving
Raihana bint Amr, the daughter of the leader of Banu Qurayza, to rape himself
as a way of demonstrating his absolute conquest of this last Jewish tribe. From
here on, the Jewish women would make Muslim babies and the stories about
the Prophet forbidding his troops to practice "al-Azl" (coitus interruptus) with
their captives probably dates from around this time. The different datings
for these events that postmodernist writers make such a point about is not
an indication that the stories are made-up. The stories are clearly historical
and are reflected everywhere in the Islamic sources, Qur'an, Hadith, Tafsir,
and Fiqh literature. That the writers may have mixed the stories in different
ways to illustrate different ideas is clearly true. Spreading the dating out over
a longer period may have been a way to demonstrate the ongoing perfidity
of the Jews, or to demonstrate how long-suffering Muhammad was before
he finally dealt with them. The Qur'an indicates that these events happened
quickly, perhaps only a few weeks apart when the moment was opportune
to drive out and finally destroy the Jews. That Muhammad's sole intention,
from the time the Jews of Yathrib rejected him, was their destruction is seen
in all the Medinan chapters up to this point and further seen in the treaty of

---

[1282] Ibn Kathir, *Tafsir*, Vol. 7, pp. 667-1.

Hudaybiyya concluded with Mecca shortly after Khandaq. What was the purpose of this treaty? It was to give Muhammad free hands to destroy the Jewish enclave at Khaybar, the last outpost of those whose ideology was a genuine threat to Islam.

Muhammad now switches topics and begins to address his wives. He offers them a choice between the "glitter" of this world and the rewards of the next, which come from following Allah and His Prophet. He calls them to live exemplary lives stating that "unseemly" behavior on their part will lead to a "doubled" punishment. Those who are "devout in the service of Allah and His Messenger" will receive "her reward twice" (verses 28-31). He encourages them not to speak in a way that would awaken a disease in those "moved with desire." He goes on to say that they should "stay quietly in your houses" while practicing prayer, charity, and obedience. From these words, the system of seclusion of women begins to emerge in Islam. Some Muslim historians explain this as resulting from Muhammad seeing Zaynab when she was scantily clad and feeling desire for her. This led him to influence his adopted son to divorce her so that he could marry her. Apparently, this was some matter of conscience to Muhammad who dealt with this, not by admitting fault, but by blaming women for his problem and secluding them as a way of dealing with it.

In the next section, Muhammad begins to praise the men and women who are worthy of praise and sets out to define who they are. The "believing . . . devout . . . true . . . patient . . . constant . . . humble . . . men and women" . . . are those "who give . . . who fast . . . who guard their chastity . . . and . . . engage . . . in Allah's praise—for them Allah has prepared forgiveness and a great reward" (verse 35). In the next verses, he defines what this means. "It is not fitting for a believer, man or woman, when a matter has been decided by Allah and His Messenger, to have any option about their decision: If anyone disobeys Allah and His Messenger, he is indeed on a clearly wrong path." What occasion has afforded this absolutistic declaration of the Prophet's authority? "When Zayd had dissolved with her, with the necessary, we joined her in marriage to thee: In order that there may be no difficulty to the believers in marriage with the wives of their adopted sons, when the latter have dissolved . . . with them. And Allah's command must be fulfilled" (verse 37). Muhammad's marriage to his adopted son's wife had occasioned criticism in the community, and this is put down with a direct revelation of Allah. Muhammad was not to be questioned or troubled about this. "There can be no difficulty to the Prophet in what Allah has indicated to him as a duty" . . . for this is "a decree determined" (verse 38). Muhammad is "The Messenger of Allah and the Seal of the Prophet's" (verse 40). He is not to be questioned in anything he does. He has become a very different Muhammad from the Muhammad of Mecca. He is now a totalitarian dictator whose mouth is the mouthpiece of God himself.

Section six is an exultation of the Prophet by Allah that ends with some rules about his marriages more or less completing the previous set of thoughts. "Oh Prophet! Truly we have sent thee as a witness, a bearer of glad tidings and a warner . . . as a lamp spreading light. Then give the glad tidings to the believers, that they shall have from Allah a very great bounty" (verses 45-47). One is to "trust in Allah" and "obey not the unbelievers." Muhammad then launches into some rules for marriage, some addressed to himself. For the first time, he mentions his own women "whom thy right hand possesses." As we have noted several times before, this phrase refers to women captured as booty, who are free to be enslaved and utilized, sexually. So God declares to the Prophet, "Oh Prophet! We have made lawful to thee thy wives to whom thou has paid their dowers and those whom thy right hand possesses out of the prisoners of war whom Allah assigned to thee; and daughter of the paternal uncles and aunts and daughters of thy maternal uncles and aunts who migrated with thee; and any believing woman who dedicates her soul to the Prophet if the Prophet wishes to wed her—this only for thee, and not for the believers: We know what we have appointed for them as to their wives and the captives whom their right hands possess . . ." (verse 50). Thus, Muhammad receives special revelation that he is allowed to marry as many women as he likes, whereas common believers are only allowed four. The rule for captives of war remains the same for all, as many as you like. It is in this context that Aisha, Muhammad's child bride is recorded as saying, "I see that your Lord Hastens to confirm your desires."[1283]

This first reference to Muhammad having sex with a female captive must be a reference to Raihana bint Amar for the massacre of the Banu Qurayza was the first occasion during which large numbers of non-Muslim women were captured. There are hundreds of Hadith that define legal principles in regard to this. Because Muhammad is the perfect exemplar for all time, and this is the foundational document for Islamic law, we may assume that this is considered the right of all Islamic armies into our day. That rape is a common feature of war is nothing new. Making permission for it as a religious sanction, however, goes a long way in explaining the mass rapes committed by Muslim armies in Bangladesh in 1971, south Sudan for a thirty-year period, Darfur

---

[1283] Ibn Kathir, *Tafsir*, Vol. 7, p. 722.

more recently, the extensive and rarely prosecuted kidnappings of Christian women in Egypt, Hindu women in Pakistan and Bangladesh, and the fact that every female American soldier captured by Muslims has been raped. "Allah," of course, "is oft forgiving, most merciful" (verse 50).

The Prophet's sexual rounds with his women are also set free by Allah. "Thou mayest defer any of them that thou pleases, and thou mayest receive any thou pleases: it is no sin on you" (verse 51). Yusuf Ali uses this occasion to teach on how Muslims are required to treat all of their wives equally in the matter of conjugal rights but, of course, the Prophet is above that sort of thing. "His marriages, after he was invested with the Prophetic office, were mainly dictated by other than conjugal or personal considerations."[1284] This is the exact opposite of what the passage actually says and shows how liberal Muslims attempt to explain away the behavior of the Prophet. Men are hereby invested with absolute control over their women's sexuality. Strangely, God seems to set a stop for further marriages at this point for the Prophet (he is variously spoken of as having nine, eleven, and thirteen wives at this point). "It is not lawful for thee women after this, not to change them for wives, even though their beauty attract thee, except any thy right hand should possess." Ali notes that Muhammad only married one other woman after this, Mary the Copt. In any case, the option to continue raping new captured women was entirely permissible from Allah's perspective.

The Prophet then begins to isolate himself from the common believers. "O ye who believe! Enter not the Prophet's houses until leave is given you . . . when invited, enter; and when ye have taken your meal, disperse without seeking familiar talk. Such annoys the Prophet" (verse 53). It is often the case when men become all-powerful they shun the company of commoners and their problematical questions and small talk. When approaching wives of the Prophet, men should ask them "from before a screen" indicating the seclusion of women. They should not be recognizable to unrelated men. Allah also forbids anyone to marry Muhammad's widows after he dies. For Aisha, who was consummated at age nine, early in the Medinan period this must have been an odious fate indeed. There is something increasingly perverse about a man who insists that even after his death, the women he has had sex with should never be allowed to have sex with anyone else, no matter how young they are. Moderate Muslims today call these women "Mothers of the Believers" as if to give them some special exemplary role after the death of the Prophet. This, however, is not mentioned in the Qur'anic passage and

---

[1284] Ali, Yusuf, p. 1073.

represents the attempts of later Muslims to mollify the picture. Yususf Ali uses the expression "Mothers of the Believers," but simply does not comment on this prohibition at all.[1285] Ibn Kathir states that they cannot be married to others because they are married to the Prophet "in the hereafter."[1286] Clearly, neither Muhammad nor the Qur'an mentions any other special role for these women other than that they would be sequestered for the rest of their lives.

Muhammad then defines which male relatives a woman may expose herself to: "Fathers, . . . sons . . . brothers . . . brother's sons . . . sister's sons and women in their household, including slavegirls." It is from this and similar verses that the idea of niqab or face mask, which completes a total covering of a woman has emerged. The "screen" referred to above would keep any part of a woman from being seen by a visiting man and thus, when a women is outside the home she should also be covered in such a way that nothing of her is visible to outside men. Women working with men outside the home would be close to impossible. Yusuf Ali tries to make this apply only to the Prophet's household, but Ibn Kathir makes it clear that "Allah commands women to observe hijab in front of men to whom they are not related."[1287] Muhammad elaborates on these requirements in the next section.

There then follow various other rules of salutation and respect to the Prophet. "Allah and his angels send blessings on the Prophet: O ye that believe! Send ye blessings on him, and salute him with all respect" (verse 56). From this has come the custom that Muslims always repeat the formula "Sallalahu wa-allehiy wa-sallam" (peace and blessings of Allah be upon him) whenever stating the name of the Prophet. For, "Those who annoy Allah and His Messenger—Allah has cursed them" (verse 57). Ibn Kathir relates that this was the same blessing as God had bestowed upon Abraham.[1288] This is understood as a messianic title. Those who bless Muhammad, God will bless. All of these rules are meant to establish the separateness and infallibility of the messenger of Allah. He is now above critique and requires absolute obedience on the part of his followers. His rules are akin to the rules of etiquette of an oriental court. He is the blessed of God. Yusuf Ali makes the

---

[1285] Ali, Yusuf, p. 1124.

[1286] Ibn Kathir, *Tafsir*, Vol. 8, p. 28.

[1287] Ibn Kathir, *Tafsir*, Vol. 8, p. 29.

[1288] Ibn Kathir, *Tafsir*, Vol. 8, p. 31. Here from a Jewish and Christian perspective Muhammad appropriates a messianic title for himself, making himself the blessed of God and the Blesser of the nations (Gen. 12:1-3). There follows in Ibn Kathir's commentary eleven pages on blessing the Prophet.

messianic connection: "We are asked to bless and honor him all the more because he took upon himself to suffer the sorrows and afflictions of this life in order to guide us to God's mercy . . ."[1289] This implies the preexistence of Muhammad and his choice to come down to earth as messiah.

Muhammad's final two sections complete his thoughts on the seclusion of women, speak of the coming day of judgment on the unbelievers, and hypocrites, and likens himself to Moses. Women are first encouraged to "cast their outer garments over their persons" . . . so as not to "be known and not molested." Ibn Kathir makes clear that they should be totally covered, "leaving only one eye showing."[1290] The only way to be kept "unknown" in public would be by means of a total covering including the face. Thus, Saudi and Taliban rules find a clear foundation in the Qur'an. It is an interesting reversal that any woman not so dressed can virtually expect to be "molested" for her lack of covering is an invitation to it. For non-Muslim women not accustomed to such coverings the implications are clear.

Muhammad turns then to the judgment on the hypocrites, "They shall have a curse on them: Wherever they are found, they shall be seized and slain" (verse 61), he claims this has always been the law of God. Ibn Kathir explains these as "those who make an outward display of faith while concealing their disbelief."[1291] Yusuf Ali attempts to exaggerate the nature of their crimes stating, "capitol punishment is the only adequate punishment for crimes of treason."[1292] But it is not clear what their "treason" is other than resistance to Muhammad's plans for war. In the final chapters 9 and 5, Muhammad will declare what this hypocrisy is; their unwillingness to die in *jihad*. Muhammad is here declaring Muslims "takfir" when they behave as hypocrites and do not obey his call to war. They are "no longer Muslims," and they may be safely killed.

Men ask him about "The hour" referring to the timing of the final judgment and he responds, "Perchance the hour is nigh!" (verse 63). He

---

[1289] Ali, Yusuf, footnote 3761, p. 1125.

[1290] Ibn Kathir, *Tafsir*, Vol. 8, p. 45. Yusuf Ali tries to mollify this by saying, "This rule is not absolute: If for any reason it could not be observed, God is oft-returning, most merciful" (p. 1127). It is hard to understand what circumstances are required to make such observance impossible. In Saudi Arabia, a fire occurred in a girl's school. The doors were barred less they go out and be seen without their jilbabs. Hundreds burned to death.

[1291] Ibn Kathir, *Tafsir*, Vol. 8, p. 46.

[1292] Ali, Yusuf, footnote 3769, p. 1127.

then describes the judgment on the unbelievers, they are cursed to "a blazing fire . . . their faces will be turned upside down in the fire, they will say: Woe is us! Would that we had obeyed Allah and obeyed the Messenger" (verse 66). Finally, he addresses the believers "be not like those who vexed and insulted Moses, but Allah cleared of the (calumnies) they had uttered" (verse 69). Thus, all of Muhammad's activities, his marriage to his adopted son's divorced wife, his rape of female prisoners, his slaughter of a tribe of Jews, and his multiple marriages, all are justified by the direct revelation of Allah. At this stage in his life, the only time Allah chides his Prophet is when he is not severe enough. This is hardly the picture of a man gaining greater religious sensitivity later in his life. Rather it is the picture of a man gradually being corrupted by his worldly exploits and power and making his Allah a personal mouthpiece of permission and justification for his every action. Unfortunately, this is the period from which all of Islamic law derives.

CHAPTER 10

THE TREATY OF HUDAYBIYA
AND THE DESTRUCTION OF
THE JEWS OF KHAYBAR

A. The Biographical Literature for This Period

Following the defeat of the Meccan attack on Medina, Muhammad began to make a new strategy with the Meccans. Rather than pursue a direct assault on Mecca, he sought to establish a truce of sorts that would allow him freedom to deal further with potential enemies in his vicinity, in this case, the Jews of Khaybar. Part of his purpose, as well, was to demonstrate the central role that Mecca and the Ka'ba had now come to take in his new religion. The Muhammad that had left Mecca six years earlier was a man still oriented to Judaism as his paradigm and praying toward Jerusalem as the Jews did. He has now made a total break with Judaism and regards them as his greatest enemies. Muhammad completes his career, killing far more Jews than pagans according to the Muslim records. The fact that Mecca has now taken a central place in his religious system, including praying in that direction is a powerful appeal to the Meccans. His teaching now includes and honors the system of Meccan pilgrimage incorporating most of the pagan elements under new Abrahamic names. In fact, one of the chapters from this period is specifically about pilgrimage. All of this is appealing to the hearts of the Meccans to consider the advantages of throwing their lot in with Muhammad.

The religion of paganism had no future in Arabia. As I and other writers have pointed out, Arabia in the early seventh century seemed destined for conversion to one or another form of monotheism. One might ask the question, why was Judaism so prevalent in Arabia at this time when it had virtually no political power elsewhere. It would seem to me that this is just the point. Conversion to Christianity meant political domination by either Abyssinia or the Eastern Roman Empire, as indeed was occurring with the Arab tribes bordering Persia. Conversion to Zoroastrianism meant domination by the Persian Empire. I would posit the Arab attraction to Judaism was exactly because it implied no domination by any outside power. Muhammad quite plainly regarded himself in Mecca as a new Prophet in the style of the Prophets of the Old Testament. He was the new iteration of Judaism that would stand its ground against the predations of both Byzantium and Persia. His stinging rejection by the Jews of Medina meant he had to find a new basis for his monotheism, completely distinct from Judaism. Combining it with the cult of Mecca provided him with a powerful appeal to the Arab tribes. Muhammad did not need to be brutal with the pagans. A careful combination of coercion and diplomacy pointing to a new unity that would benefit all financially would convince them to leave behind their dying paganism in favor of this new religion that exalted their warlike characteristics and maintained their cherished cultus in only slightly altered form.

With this in mind, Muhammad decides to demonstrate his devotion to Mecca by attempting a pilgrimage to the city. He approaches Mecca with a sizeable group at the time of the lesser pilgrimage dressed in pilgrim's garb, not for war. It is a brilliant strategic move. If he is refused, it is an insult to the religion of the Arabs, if he is admitted, his influence increases significantly in Mecca itself, and the tribes will now get to see his sanctification of their rites. His party advanced as far as al-Hudaybiya. There are many and often contradictory tales told of the nature of the negotiations between Muhammad and the Meccans. The end result was that Muhammad concluded a treaty with them for a ten-year period that involved the Muslims turning back this year, but returning the next for pilgrimage. According to the Muslim sources, Muhammad accepted a wording for the treaty that left out both the name of his God and his title as Prophet. This kind of detail, which is clearly humiliating to the Prophet, has the same claim to historicity as the Constitution of Medina. There can be no other explanation for the inclusion of such a detail other than that it was historically true. Muhammad's appeal at this point is brilliant for it sows discord in the Meccan camp while at the same time not significantly reducing his own power. Some of Muhammad's followers were discomforted in Mecca, but Muhammad wants the inclusion of the Meccans, not their destruction. Ibn Ishaq notes that more and more Meccans began to join Muhammad's camp. With this treaty completed, he is now in a position to deal with the Jews, whom the Meccans will no longer support due to their treaty with Muhammad.[1293]

There is one element of the story that bears greater consideration since it figures greatly in both the Qur'an and the traditional literature. This was the so-called pledge of the tree. This took place supposedly, when Othman, the Prophet's representative, was sent to Mecca to negotiate the truce and was delayed in returning. The delay fanned doubts about his fate and some kind of military pact was sworn between Muhammad and his followers to avenge Othman if he should be harmed. The event is supposedly recorded in 48:18, which states the following: "Allah's good pleasure was on the believers when they swore fealty to thee under the tree. He knew what was in their hearts, and he sent down tranquility (sekinah) to them; and he rewarded them with a speedy victory." There is something strange about this story, since we also know that some followers were discouraged by the treaty, or even opposed it as denigrating to their honor. The issue in the Qur'anic passage is not the safety of Othman, but "fealty" or a "pledge" to Muhammad. It may well be that this pledge was Muhammad's way of enforcing discipline upon his troops by insisting they pledge loyalty to him in the matter of this treaty. Perhaps the more violent of Muhammad's followers found it hard to understand how a peace treaty with the despised pagans could further the cause of Islam. The Qur'anic passage I have dated as after the conquest of Mecca for the verse concludes, I think, with hindsight, "He rewarded them with a speedy victory." In other words, the Qur'an affirms that the Prophet's strategy of peace with Mecca worked.

Muhammad's very next move according to the Muslim historians is to attack the Jews of Khaybar to the north of Medina. It is his final move to eradicate the only group in Arabia knowledgeable about where Muhammad's ideas had come from and able to point out its inconsistencies. Muhammad had earlier sent out a squad of soldiers to murder one of the key Jewish leaders of Khaybar, Abu Rafi. He now marched by rapid forced march from Medina in three days and was able to surprise most of the Jews outside of their fortresses. There ensued at one of the fortresses a brief battle in which the Jews were finally defeated. Muhammad was able to plunder freely and the captured the Jewish leader, Kinana. According to the biographers, when Kinana hid some of his possessions, he was tortured to reveal their location before being killed. Muhammad takes the wife of Kinana, Safiya, to be his

---

[1293] Ibn Ishaq, pp. 499-507.

new concubine. She proved to be more amenable than Raihana and consents to convert to Islam in order to be a proper wife and not merely a slave. She has to pay a price for this and forfeits her demand for a dowry. The conversion and marriage notwithstanding, one of his soldiers in his army is claimed to have stood guard outside the wedding tent in case the damsel tried to do the Prophet harm. Muhammad did not kill all the Jews of Khaybar, but reduced them to status of sharecroppers on their land, and his subjugation of this group is regularly cited in the Islamic books of law as an example of how Jews and Christians may be allowed to exist as subjugated people under the hegemony of Islam. Muhammad had defeated his final group of Jewish enemies.

B. Content of the Qur'an during This Period

Five chapters of the Qur'an seem to reflect the period of Hudaybiya and the conquest of Khaybar. These are chapters 63, 24, 58, 22, and 60. Interestingly, the "People of the Book" virtually vanish in these four chapters. Perhaps the threat the Muhammad had felt in Medina had now been removed and he could concentrate on other things.

1. Chapter 63

Chapter 63, entitled "the Hypocrites," is a brief eleven-verse attack on those who feign faith and obedience to Muhammad. The People of the Book are nowhere mentioned as was the general case in the earlier chapters. Muhammad is now powerful enough after the discomfiture of the Meccans to put real pressure on anyone not wholeheartedly aligned with the Prophet. Was it still possible to be a non-Muslim in Medina at this stage? There still are references to those who "resist," but their identity is far less clear. However, it is precisely this kind of coercive environment that encourages the very hypocrisy that Muhammad rails against. Muslim interpreters believe that verse 8 refers to the attack on the tribe Banu al-Mustaliq. Al-Waqidi dates this raid shortly before the siege of Medina.[1294] According to Ibn Ishaq, it took place just after the slaughter of the Jews, and this would fit the chronology just after the slaughter of the Banu Qurayza and just before Hudaybiya.[1295] Muhammad begins, "When the hypocrites come to thee they say, 'We bear witness that thou art indeed the Messenger of Allah . . . They have made their

---

[1294]   Muir, p. 295.
[1295]   Ibn Ishaq, pp. 490-493

oaths a screen . . . because they believed, then they rejected faith . . . the curse of Allah be upon them" (verses 1-5). Allah tells Muhammad that it doesn't matter if he prays for their forgiveness for "Truly Allah guides not rebellious transgressors." Muhammad concludes his reflections by calling the believers not to be diverted from their "remembrance of Allah" by their riches and their children. Giving to the cause of Allah for the expansion of His Kingdom is an essential task of the believers (verses 6-11).

2. Chapter 24

Chapter 24 is entitled, "The Light" and supposedly is written in the light of accusations of immorality on the part of Muhammad's wife Aisha shortly after the attack on Al-Mustaliq. She was apparently separated from the Muslim column and was found by a Muslim soldier who returned her to the Prophet. The assumption was that they had sexual relations and the scandal caused Muhammad to put Aisha aside for a time. Finally, Allah revealed this passage indicating the innocence of Aisha and revealing various laws about marriage and punishments for sexual sins. He begins by defining the punishments for adultery, one hundred stripes, and a punishment of eighty lashes on those who falsely accuse without four witnesses (verses 1-4). He does not name Aisha in the passage, but refers to the accusation of adultery as "the lie." Later, the believers are chided for not putting "the best construction on it" for the charge was "an obvious lie." He rebukes them for the "most serious slander," and he threatens those responsible with "A grievous penalty in this life and in the hereafter" (verses 11-19). Clearly, the accusation of whatever type deeply disturbed the Prophet. However, he bears part of the blame. The assumption created by veiling and seclusion is that women left in the presence of men without these precautions automatically fall into immorality. It certainly fits the pattern of Muhammad's own construction in previous passages that one of his wives could be accused of immorality because of the failure of the system of seclusion. All Muslim commentators agree on the background of this story, though its chronology is differing. How would one make up such a story like this and get it accepted by the Muslim community? Clearly, the event, or something like it actually happened. Ibn Kathir spends some fifteen pages, explaining the background of the story and using various means aside from the Qur'anic revelation to demonstrate the innocence of Aisha. It is also worth noting that Aisha makes a distinction between the time when seclusion was required and the time prior to the commandment for the seclusion of women. She was recognized by the slave boy because he had seen her during the time before seclusion was required. Women were not only forced to be covered up, including their faces by this new rule, but even the sound of their voices and the very act of discussion between unrelated males and females became forbidden.[1296]

After turning to the subject of generosity to those still lacking in means, Muhammad returns to the subject of the accusation against "chaste women." Here we find a small concession on the part of the Prophet, he calls them "indiscreet but believing." Nevertheless, those who criticize them "are cursed in this life and in the hereafter" (verse 23). He establishes rules for social intercourse, apparently to prevent further scandals like this. One is not to enter a home unless invited in. Men and women are encouraged to: "lower their gaze and guard their modesty" when in each other's presence. Further, women are instructed not to display their beauty to anyone except their husbands, fathers, sons, and so forth . . . This passage also allows for small children to be able to see women. One is allowed to marry slaves, and Muhammad encourages the manumission of slaves who are Muslims. He also encourages his followers not to force female slaves into prostitution, however, he concludes Allah is oft-forgiving "if anyone compels them" (verses 27-34). The enforced prostitution of slaves is allowed by the Prophet though not encouraged. Ibn Kathir considers such prostitution to be forbidden though it is not clear what consequences are to be applied.[1297] Yusuf Ali tries to make the Qur'an sound utterly condemnatory calling this "white slave traffic . . . absolutely condemned." But the Qur'an does not condemn the practice "absolutely," because it enjoins no consequences to these actions and indeed indicates that Allah will forgive this. It would be interesting to research the return of slavery to Sudan and Somalia to see if it involves elements of prostitution. One lily white convert to Islam has issued a published call for the reestablishment of slavery.[1298]

Section 5 of the Qur'an begins with a meditation on the "light of Allah" and the celebration of his praises. Allah gives great rewards to the believers, but the unbelievers "are like a mirage in sandy deserts." Those to whom Allah does not give light, "there is no light" (verse 40). He reflects on the birds who offer praise to Allah by their flight; the clouds, mountains and flashes of lightning do the same. God has created "night and day" and every

---

[1296] Ibn Kathir, *Tafsir*, Vol. 7, pp. 33-48, see particularly page 34.
[1297] Ibn Kathir, *Tafsir*, Vol. 7, p. 80.
[1298] Shaykh Abdalqadir as-Sufi, *The Return of the Califate*, Madinah Press, 1996, pp. 4-5.

animal. This passage in many ways reminds one of the more lyrical writings of the Meccan period of the Qur'an. However, the passage really refers to judgments on the unbelievers who will not receive this light. Ibn Kathir is quick to point out that this refers to the Jews who worshipped Uzayr (Ezra) as a son of God and will be cast into the fires of hell.[1299]

Muhammad returns quickly to the subject of those who are hypocrites. They say, "We believe," but they do not submit to the judgment of the Messenger (verse 48). True believers, when called by the Messenger say "we hear and we obey: It is such as these that will attain felicity." Muhammad promises them that peace and security will come. The abode of the unbelievers "is the fire" (verses 51-57). In the final section, Muhammad defines three times when one may remove one's clothes, and during those times, children and slaves should not come into the private rooms. Elderly women do not have to follow the rules of veiling, although it is best if they do. Clearly, the rules imply that unrelated males and females should not be able to recognize one another. This would certainly justify the modern use of the "niqab," which completely disguises the identity of females in public. Some provision is also made for the blind or those with other hinderances in regard to who may see whom without violating privacy. He concludes that obedience to the Prophet is absolutely necessary, no pretext can be used to escape the necessity of obedience. "Those of you who slip away under shelter of some excuse: Then let them beware who withstand the Messenger's order, lest some trial befall them or a grievous penalty be inflicted on them" (verse 63). Muhammad has now traveled far down the road to dictatorship. The corrupting influence of this kind of power is evident everywhere in these later passages of the Qur'an. Unlike secular dictators, however, Muhammad is the very mouthpiece of God.

3. Chapter 58

Chapter 58 is a short chapter that deals primarily with the issue of a certain kind of divorce mentioned earlier, the so-called Zihar where a man divorces his wife sexually, but retains her as a domestic servant/slave. The chapter is entitled, "The Woman Who Pleads," and purports to report Allah's judgment for a woman who had been so divorced and came to plead her case with the Prophet. The Prophet does not seem to forbid the practice, but claims one may not call such women "mothers" and that they should be

---

[1299] Ibn Kathir, *Tafsir*, Vol. 7, p. 99.

a "free slave" or feed "sixty indigent ones" if one commits this sin (verses 1-3). The remainder of the passage concerns those who resist the Prophet by means of "forbidden secret counsels" (verses 7-13). Muhammad had engaged in many conspiracies of his own, so it is not surprising that he was constantly on the lookout and warning against conspiracies against himself. He also instructs his followers to not befriend those "as have the wrath of Allah upon them?" Such people are "companions of the fire." These are the ones "who resist Allah and his Messenger." For, "Those who resist Allah and His Messenger will be among those most humiliated" and those who hate the ones who resist Allah and his Messenger will be admitted to "gardens beneath which rivers flow" (verses 14-22).

Chapter 22

We conclude this section with chapter 22. There is some debate among Muslims as to when this passage was revealed. Some claim that it was revealed late in the Meccan period.[1300] A careful study of the content, however, excludes this possibility as many Muslim scholars also state. It is probable that it includes some brief verses dating from the Meccan period, and this is the conclusion of Yusuf Ali.[1301] Most of the passage is from mid- to late-Medinan and is entitled "The Pilgrimage." It includes reflections on the last days, the duties of pilgrimage, and the importance of fighting for the cause of Islam. I think that it reflects Muhammad's turn toward Mecca reflected in the peace of Hudaybiyya. Muhammad is pursuing a strategy to turn the Meccans by appeal and not merely by physical violence and coercion. The passage has plenty of reflections on the need for violence showing that Muhammad believed in the carrot-and-stick strategy in establishing the political supremacy of Islam. The passage also reflects the later emphasis on Mecca as the center of pilgrimage and rejects the claims of the Jews, indicating a late-Medinan provenance.

[1300]　This is Ibn Kathir's position. It is clear that such a position is held in order to make the concept of pilgrimage to Mecca central in the earlier revelations, as if this was Allah's revealed form of the religion from the beginning. Such is not the case. Why did Muhammad mix two groups of verses? Perhaps it was meant to indicate how Allah's thinking had changed, or perhaps it was even an attempt to make the practice of Hajj to Mecca seem like an older tradition. C. f. *Tafsir*, Vol. 6, p. 516.

[1301]　Ali, Yusuf, p. 820.

Chapter 22 opens with an apocalyptic vision of future judgment reminiscent of Matthew 24. There are woes declared on "every mother giving suck" and upon "every pregnant female." It will be the time of the "wrath of Allah" and Satan will guide people "to the penalty of the fire" (verses 1-4). He then launches into an argument, which we have not seen since the Meccan period. He argues for the reality of resurrection based on the proofs of the creation of human infants and the verdancy of the earth, "Allah is the reality . . . who gives life to the dead . . . Allah will raise up all who are in the graves." (verses 6-7). The one who disagrees with this is one "without a book of enlightenment" meaning either the Jewish, Christian, or Muslim scriptures. This is clearly addressed to pagan Arabs. In the following section, the Prophet seems to address those who are believers but "on the verge," who are tempted to "call on such deities besides Allah." The ethos of this passage seems also to be Meccan for Muhammad's words here are warnings, not threats. The deities "can neither hurt nor profit them." He goes on to state that those "who believe and do righteous deeds" will be admitted "to gardens beneath which rivers flow" (verses 11-14).

Muhammad then goes on to question the followers of other revelations. "Those who believe, those who follow the Jews, and the Sabians, Christians, Magians, and polytheists—Allah will judge between them on the day of judgment" (verse 17). Muhammad seems to be lumping these groups together and he goes on to describe the judgments that befall those who resist Allah, "for them will be cut out a garment of fire: Over their heads will be poured out boiling water." He seems to be making a distinction between "those who believe" meaning Muslims and the other groups whom Allah will judge. This rejection of the believers in earlier revelations would indicate a later Medinan period for the surah, even though some stylistic elements seem earlier. Perhaps certain verses that were Meccan have been appropriated and augmented here to provide a new interpretation. He threatens the Jews, Christians, and Sabians with "taste ye the penalty of the burning." He goes on to explain who the genuine believers are, and what they would receive "of gold and pearls; and their garments there will be of silk." These are the ones who "have been guided to the purest of speeches . . . guided to the path of him who is worthy of praise" (verses 23-24). This seems to be a play on the Prophet's name, which can be interpreted as the "praised one." Thus only the followers of Muhammad will be admitted to "gardens beneath which rivers flow" while the followers of the other religions will "taste of a most grievous penalty" (verses 23, 25). His complaint is specifically against those who "would keep back from the way of Allah, and from the sacred mosque" (verse 25). This establishes the chapter as Medinan, and specifically after the switch to Mecca as the center of the cultus and before the Muslim conquest of the Meccan sanctuary. The next section focuses on the nature of the Meccan sanctuary.

Muhammad now continues his reinterpretation of the Meccan sanctuary as the center of the Abrahamic cult. He states, "we gave the site to Abraham, of the house." Further God says, "proclaim the pilgrimage among men" . . . to . . ."celebrate the name of Allah . . . and circumambulate the ancient house" (verses 26-29). Believers are allowed to eat off the "cattle" but to "shun the abomination of idols." Muhammad seems to be sifting the rites of the Ka'aba and preparing his followers to accept some of them, but refuse those that speak of the idolatrous past. He then goes on to describe the rite of sacrifice. God has appointed rites of sacrifice "to every people." Animals are to be lined up for slaughter and their meat enjoyed while being also distributed to the poor. Piety is the source of God's honor, not the "meat" and "blood" themselves (verses 34-37).

The passage then switches abruptly to the subject of *jihad*. Allah gives "permission" for making "war" based upon the injustices done to "those who have been expelled from their homes." He argues that this must be done against the unbelievers. Otherwise, "there would surely have been pulled down monasteries, churches, synagogues, and mosques in which the name of Allah is commemorated." His argument seems to be that Allah had earlier given permission to Jews and Christians to fight against the desecration of their holy sites as now Allah was doing for the Muslims. God seems here to address the Prophet, "if they treat thy (mission) as false, so did the peoples before them." God boasts, "how many populations have we destroyed, which were given to wrongdoing?" Thus, if injustice exists among the Jews and Christians by virtue of their rejection of the Prophet, then holy war is called for to establish the true faith. Apparently, some questioned why the Prophet had not conquered all the lands in order to "hasten on the punishment," to which he replies that "a day in the sight of the Lord is like a thousand years" (verse 47). This is very close to a direct citation of Psalm 90:4, which is repeated even more closely in the New Testament in 2 Peter 3:8. Muhammad's ethos was inclusive of these previous traditions and deeply influenced by their eschatology.

Having set out the precepts of holy war, Muhammad then goes on to state a seeming contradiction. "Say: O men! I am (sent) to you only to give a clear warning." What then is the nature of the *jihad*? It does not seem to be that Jews and Christians would be forced to accept Islam. What they must accept is the political hegemony of Islam, which is necessary to remove all obstacles to anyone becoming a Muslim. This is the law of social righteousness that Muhammad seems to advocate here. The actual decision to follow Islam must still be one of the heart. Muhammad is still only a warner of the judgment to come. However, the military and political coercion used to establish the hegemony of Islam cannot but distort the genuineness of heart, which the Prophet argues for. His means ultimately destroy his ends.

The passage turns almost confessional. God seems to be excusing the behavior of the Prophet stating:

"Never did we send a messenger or a prophet before thee, but, when he framed a desire, Satan threw some (vanity) into his desire: But Allah will cancel (yansakh) anything that Satan throws in" (verse 52).

Yusuf Ali reads this seeming confession as merely the weakness of the "human perspective." The word for "cancel" here is the Arabic "Yansakh" derived from the root word "naskh" (abrogation) where God cancels out one revelation in favor of another.[1302] Muhammad is apparently trying to explain changes that are being made in the revelations he has received and is essentially confessing that sometimes Satan's words have been mixed up in his mind with God's words. Needless to say, none of the commentators try to tackle that question.

Ibn Kathir, to his credit, mentions the possibility of this referring to the "gharaniq," a reference to the Satanic verses, but he claims that the isnads (transmitters) for these traditions are "mursal," and do not go back to the companions of the Prophet.[1303] Mistakes notwithstanding, God is behind his Prophet ensuring that "Allah will confirm his signs." God does this in order "that he may make the suggestions thrown in by Satan, but a trial for those in whose hearts is a disease" (verse 53). The terminology here is very oblique. What were the suggestions that the Prophet made and how were Satan's words mixed up in them. Two possible contexts come to mind. One is the already above mentioned terms of the treaty of Hudaybiyya where the Prophet was not given his full due in the terms of the agreement. This might have been the Prophet's way of explaining this seeming humiliation to his followers. As such, this could be seen as an immediate post-Hudaybiyya chapter meant to explain God's strategy to the believers.

[1302] Ibn Kathir, *Tafsir*, Vol. 6, p. 598.

[1303] Ibn Kathir, *Tafsir*, Vol. 6, p. 597. As we will note in chapter 13 most of the isnads are inventions of a later age and have nothing whatsoever to do with issues of historicity.

It must also be admitted that this passage uses terminology reminiscent of the "Satanic verses" revealed through Satan in the early Meccan period of the Prophet's work. Ibn Kathir alludes to this connection.[1304] However, the overall content of the passage is Medinan and seeks to establish the new sanctuary myth of Mecca. It is also possible that verse 52 refers to previous practices in prayer toward Jerusalem that have been abrogated. There are many verses in the Qur'an chapter 2 that refer to that practice, but perhaps, like the Satanic verses, other verses have been removed and these fragmentary Meccan verses have been relocated with the new sanctuary myth placed where the Jerusalem verses used to be. That is, of course, conjecture. Chapter 60 which follows also raises the issue of *naskh* as we shall see later. The Prophet seems to use this excuse as a way of explaining all events in such a way that they are seen as advantageous to the emerging Islam. A written treaty with the Quraysh might have been seen as a sort of revelation agreed to and signed by the Prophet and Muhammad makes clear that any such word is easily erased by the almighty Allah. He concludes that those who "reject faith and deny our signs (ayats or verses of the Qur'an)" will endure "a humiliating punishment" (verse 57).

In the following section Muhammad gives comfort to those who have lost their homes and also have been slain or died without ever returning. This seems to be addressed to those who thought Muhammad's concessions to the Meccans at the treaty of Hudaybiyya would thereby lose their opportunity of returning. This firmly fits the passage to this historical context because only in such a context would this question have arisen. As long as the Muslim community was on the warpath with Mecca, the possibility of return remained. Taken at face value, Muhammad's concessions at Hudaybiyya and his turning back from the pilgrimage must have deeply dismayed some of his closest followers who had faithfully emigrated with him. Muhammad argues for a magnanimous approach. Those who have died "have a goodly provision" and those who have fought have, "retaliated to no greater extent than the injury he received." Muhammad directs his followers to find solace for the time being in Allah who is "free of all wants and worthy of all praise" (verses 58-64). Allah is in absolute control of all events, so there is no reason for discontent.

Muhammad goes on to address those who are disputing over these events. It seems that some were followers of other traditions. Muhammad claims that God has given traditions to all people: "To every people have

---

we appointed rites and ceremonies which they must follow: Let them not then dispute with thee on the matter." Perhaps some Arab adherents to either Judaism or Christianity were still among his followers, and the occasion of the seeming defeat of this peace treaty occasioned further critique concerning traditions to be followed. God reassures the Prophet "but do thou invite to thy Lord for thou art assuredly on the right way." At a critical juncture like this, Muhammad seems to appeal to all members of his movement to retain unity and to remember that his way is the "right way." He accuses those who resist this of worshipping things "beside Allah." They nearly threaten to "attack" the Prophet "with violence" (verse 72). Their destiny is "the fire, Allah has promised it" (verses 67-72). With a heavy hand, the Prophet silences his critics within the movement. Anything other than obedience is idolatry. He concludes the passage by calling on the Muslims to worship Allah. Here for the first time, he names them as "Muslims," which name, he claims, was established by Abraham himself: "It is the cult of your father Abraham. It is he who has named you Muslims, both before and in this (revelation) that the Messenger may be a witness for you, and ye be witnesses for mankind!" (verse 78). Here Islam is finally defined as a separate religion, with a separate name, scripture, and identity. What was merely a term of piety (submitted one) has now become the name and identity of a new religion, though defined as the original religion of God. The essence of that new religion is to "Strive (*jihad*) in His cause" (verse 78). Thus the religion of Abraham is the religion of *jihad*, which Ibn Kathir interprets, calls for striving with your wealth, your tongues, and your bodies."[1305]

4. Chapter 60

The final chapter of this period is chapter 60, which deals with the issue of having friends among the unbelievers. This was an issue raised by the treaty of Hudaybiyya and was supposedly revealed some time before the final attack on and conquest of Mecca. Chapter 60 opens with these ominous words: "O ye who believe! Take not my enemies and yours as friends." (verse 1) Ibn Kathir quickly explains that this means not only the pagans who resist Islam, but also the Jews and Christians. He cites chapter 5, considered the final chapter of the Qur'an: "Take not the Jews and Christians as protecting friends, they are but protecting friends of each other. And if any among you takes them, then surely, he is one of them." To do so is virtually a declaration of apostasy

---

[1305] Ibn Kathir, *Tafsir*, Vol 6, p. 622.

from Islam and Kathir calls this "a stern warning and a sure threat."[1306] What is interesting is the use of the term "protecting." This does not indicate people who are making war on Islam. Yusuf Ali in his commentary tries to make a distinction between unbelievers who oppress and make war on Islam and those who don't.[1307] But the Qur'an is clear at this point. Anyone who does not accept Muhammad as the Prophet, that is, anyone who does not convert to Islam is an enemy to be shunned and eventually subjugated. Kathir cites three other late-Medinan verses stating the same thing and each uses the word "protecting" as the adjective for the "friend." In other words, even those who would protect you as a friend are really enemies to be shunned and subjugated.[1308] The efforts of the United States to win friends by protecting Muslims is pointless for this reason.

The remainder of the verse indicates that to befriend such people is to stray "from the straight path." Here Muhammad rails against those who had "driven out the Messenger and yourselves." In essence, everything in the Prophet's life becomes a paradigm of the future. Wherever Islam goes, if there is resistance to the political hegemony of Islam, this is a crime equivalent to driving out the Prophet from his homeland. Anyone who resists the message of the Prophet is to be shunned and eventually crushed by military means. He has made a treaty with Mecca, but this is not where the story will end. The story of the Prophet's letters to the great world leaders takes place about this time and, even if this is purely mythical, it has its foundation in the Qur'an. Unbelievers may be initially invited to Islam. Muhammad had even made a treaty with the unbelievers in Mecca. But this was temporary and was intended to be eventually replaced by full Islamic hegemony. Resistance on their part to that call constitutes a "crime" worthy of attack. Muhammad goes on to impute evil motives to the unbelievers, "If they were to get the better of you, they would behave to you as enemies, and stretch forth their hands and their tongues against you for evil; and they desire that ye should reject the truth" (verse 2). Kathir emphasizes that they would use "every type of harm in their disposal to hurt you."[1309] This kind of universal imputation of evil motives to anyone not believing in Islam serves to isolate the Muslim community from interaction with other communities. I have sat in many a mosque and listened to impassioned renditions of various conspiracy theories; the CIA

[1306]   Ibn Kathir, *Tafsir*, Vol. 9, p. 586.
[1307]   Ali, Yusuf, p. 1531.
[1308]   Ibn Kathir, *Tafsir*, Vol. 9, pp. 586-587.
[1309]   Ibn Kathir, *Tafsir*, Vol. 9, p. 588.

lead the attacks on September 11, Jews were warned to leave the towers before the attacks, Jews spread the AIDS virus, polio vaccines are meant to sterilize Muslim men . . . etc . . . etc . . . The Muslim world is awash in this kind of nonsense, and its foundation is the Qur'an itself, which requires and engenders an attitude of distrust toward all non-Muslims.

The next few verses claim that nonbelieving relatives will be "of no profit to you . . . on the day of judgment." Muhammad cites Abraham and his dealing with his own unbelieving relatives. Supposedly Abraham said, "We are clear of you and whatever ye worship . . . we have rejected you, and there has arisen between us and you, enmity and hatred forever—Unless ye believe in Allah and him alone" (verse 4). Kathir translates this "hostility and hatred."[1310] Yusuf Ali tries to mollify the picture by generalizing that those to be so hated are the enemies of Allah who "hate the righteous," as if that is anyone other than those who refuse to accept Islam. His definition is telling; "the righteous must cut themselves off eternally from them, unless they repent and come back to Allah."[1311] Thus anyone who does not believe in the Allah of Islam is someone who "hates the righteous" by definition. The passage then goes on to say that Abraham "said to his father: 'I will pray for forgiveness for thee'." This is an injunction which the Qur'an later revokes. Ibn Kathir is quick to point out that the later chapter 9, verses 113-114 abrogates (*naskh*) this earlier revelation allowing for prayer for unbelieving relatives. He cites, "It is not for the Prophet or those who believe to ask Allah's forgiveness for the idolators, even though they be of kin."[1312] To pray for unbelievers is even discouraged by Yusuf Ali who states that his prayer, "was a special case, and is not to be imitated by weaker men, who may fall into sin by thinking too much of sinners."[1313]

The next section of the passage would seem to negate what I have said to this point. In the second section of the passage Muhammad states, "It may be that Allah will grant love between you and those whom ye hold as enemies . . . Allah forbids you not with regard to those who fight you not for your faith nor drive you out of your homes from dealing kindly and justly with them" (verses 7-8). This would seem to say that it is all right to befriend those who do not fight you. But there is a key difference here. It is assumed that they have now placed themselves under the political power of Islam. Ibn

[1310] Ibn Kathir, *Tafsir*, Vol. 9, p. 590.
[1311] Ali, Yusuf, p. 1453.
[1312] Ibn Kathir, *Tafsir*, Vol. 9, p. 591.
[1313] Ali, Yusuf, p. 1455.

Kathir makes this very clear as he relates the supposed background to the verse. After the treaty of Hudaybiyya, an idolatrous woman came to visit her daughter in Medina and the Prophet allowed this. As long as the unbeliever lives in treaty with the Muslims, and this comes increasingly to mean a treaty that subjects the person to the political hegemony of Islam, then friendship is allowed.[1314] Those who resist Islam's political hegemony, verse 9 goes on to explain, Allah "forbids" friendship with.

The final four verses of the passage discusses the problem of what to do with women who have left Mecca to come and live with the Muslims in Medina. I had initially thought this passage to be after the conquest of Mecca, but the sending back of women refugees who were still pagan to their husbands in Mecca does not make sense in a postconquest context. Muhammad tells his men to "hold not to the guardianship of unbelieving women" (verse 10). The implication is that they should be sent back. Verse 11 is even more startling; Muhammad states that "if any of your wives deserts you to the unbelievers" then they are allowed to take the pagan wives who come over to them. This kind of exchanges of people could only make sense if the terms of the treaty were still in effect. Muhammad goes on to say that any woman who deserts to Medina and gives the confession of faith in Islam and fealty to the Prophet should not be sent back. Ibn Kathir derives from this the principle that a believing Muslim woman must never under any circumstances be married to a non-Muslim man, and this has become universal in Islamic law.[1315] Men, of course, may marry non-Muslim women, the purpose of which is to increase the demographic power of Islam over the unbelievers. The Prophet concludes by again foreswearing any kind of friendship with unbelievers upon whom abides "the wrath of Allah." (verse 13). Thus concludes this section on the period of the Hudaybiyya peace treaty.

[1314] Ibn Kathir, *Tafsir*, Vol. 9, p. 596.
[1315] Ibn Kathir, *Tafsir*, Vol. 9, p. 600.

CHAPTER 11

THE CONQUEST OF MECCA

A. The Biographical Traditions

In January 630 CE, Muhammad finally achieved what he had been striving for during his years of exile in Medina. The Muslim army had marched into Mecca without a military struggle. He was able to visit his home again, the sacred center of both his culture and his faith. His big political enemies in Mecca had either died in the meantime, or had joined his ranks, such as Abu Sufyan, right before the invasion force had entered the city. The previous eight years had witnessed a power struggle between the two urban centers of the Hijaz, pitting polytheist Mecca against Muslim Medina. What were Muhammad's next steps going to be? What were his long-term goals? This chapter covers the time period around the conquest of Mecca and, describes how Muhammad essentially consolidated the Islamic community (*umma*) in Arabia internally, and defined relations with those outside of the *umma*. That would include, for the most part, those individuals, tribes, and empires of the pagan, Jewish, Zoroastrian, and Christian faiths.

There was a significant change in the nature of the *umma* gradually occurring after the conquest. Peters states that the Constitution of Medina, perhaps the first formal definition of the community including the emigrants (*muhajirun*) and the Medinans (*ansar*), was a political agreement for the situation in Medina, as it included both Muslims and polytheists (and perhaps Jews). After Mecca was taken, however, membership in the *umma* automatically meant adherence to the Muslim faith and allegiance to Muhammad as the ruler.[1316] The sense of an exclusive Muslim community seems to have emerged in the Qur'an about the time of the peace of Hudaybiya

---

[1316] F. E. Peters, *Muhammad and the Origins of Islam, Suny Series in Near Eastern Studies,* New York, pp. 242, 243.

as noted in the previous chapter. Although Muhammad, as Watt has remarked, was not yet the sole ruler in Arabia, nor even in the *Hijaz*, or even Medina, after the Battle of Hunayn (which will be discussed shortly) none dared to challenge him openly anymore.[1317] He no longer had to avoid offending the polytheists in the region, and he was free to establish his rule on his own terms. At the same time, he started paying greater attention to regions outside of Arabia proper, thus setting the precedent for the great Arab-Muslim conquests. The basis for this inward consolidation and outward expansion was set in the conquest of Mecca and its aftermath.

Events That Led to the Conquest

After the conquest of Khaybar, Muhammad returned to Mecca to celebrate the lesser pilgrimage. According to the treaty from the previous year, the Quraysh withdrew from the city and allowed Muhammad to have access with his followers for three days. Seven years had passed since the hijra to Medina, and Muhammad was now in a position of parity with regard to political influence and military power. In reality, however, his position was now far stronger than the Meccans. By means of this pilgrimage, he made abundantly clear that Mecca would now be the center of his cultus. Islam was now an Arabian religion incorporating much of what the Meccan's held most dear and completing the transition to a form of monotheism that had already seemed inevitable, perhaps for several centuries. Most importantly, this new religion was completely distinct from the religions and empires surrounding Arabia and incorporated as an aspect of its faith, the martial arts of Arabia. The Meccans themselves were gradually moving in the direction of adopting Mumammad's paradigm.

In this context, Muhammad took a peaceful and conciliatory approach. At this point, there was no further need for unnecessary bloodshed. His goal was within his grasp, and he had the patience to wait for the right timing. At the insistence of the Meccans, he left the city after the agreed three days had passed. There is mention that he asked to stay a fourth day in order to celebrate his latest wedding, and he even invited the Meccans to take part. The conciliatory gesture was brushed aside but the impact remained; Muhammad was among his own and anticipated that his own would shortly see the light.

[1317] W. Montgomery Watt, *Muhammad: Prophet and Statesman*, Oxford: Oxford University Press, 1974, pp. 212, 213.

In the meantime, Muhammad's prestige grew among the Arabian tribes. Though his forces suffered one major defeat at Al-Muta in Syria, generally he gained the allegiance of an increasing number of Arab tribes, which greatly increased the potential size of his army. As Mecca's strength waned, the Prophet's star was on the rise. All he needed was a convenient excuse to bring about the final fall of the pagans at Mecca. This opportunity was not long in coming.

The pretence for Muhammad's march on Mecca was provided by a formal breaking of the treaty that occurred when a group in Mecca known as the tribe of Khoza'a that had made favorable allegiance to Muhammad was attacked by another Meccan tribe, the Beni Bekr. Our only source for this explanation is Islamic, so there may be reason to doubt the account. But the general strategy of the Prophet could easily have led to this kind of altercation that then became the excuse for a general invasion of Mecca. Muhammad must have been aware that victory was highly likely now that his enemies, the keepers of the *status quo*, were in general retreat. Muhammad saw his chance for a final, relatively bloodless coup d'etat. The Meccan commander Abu Sufyan apparently had some complicity in the final collapse of Meccan resistance. The handwriting on the wall for Arabian paganism was finally fulfilled, not by an outside religion, but one native to the soil and affirming the traditions of the Arabs.

Inner Consolidation: Conquest and Conciliation

In keeping with the usual historical practices of the conqueror, one could have expected widespread purging of Muhammad's longtime opponents in Mecca, and a substitution of leadership of the city in favor of some of his most trusted companions. Certainly, some of the previous precedents Muhammad set could have led one to such a conclusion. That course of events, however, did not occur. There were no widespread political executions in Mecca, nor did Muhammad attempt to change the political hierarchy that existed in the city. What were his motives in acting in this manner? Some authors, such as Inamdar, go so far to say that Muhammad was genuinely attempting to reconcile with his enemies and even with his own past, thus setting an example to follow and breaking the usual pattern of destructive fratricide and civil war.[1318] This conclusion cannot be reconciled with other, less benevolent, actions taken by Muhammad in the aftermath of various victorious battles.

[1318] Subhash Inamdar, *Muhammad and the Rise of Islam: The Creation of Group Identity*, New York: Psychosocial Press, 2001 p. 181.

The answer to this question, it seems, lies in political expediency: Muhammad, himself of the tribe of Quraysh, knew that this tribe would constitute the core of the future movement in Islam. The Meccans had the organizational skills and widespread prestige in Arabia that Muhammad wanted to incorporate into Islam. And this he did: not long after the conquest of Mecca, the leaders of pre-Islamic Mecca represented a large segment of the ruling elite in the Islamic *ummah*.[1319] According to Isaac Hasson, Muhammad pursued a policy of making his enemies of yesterday as some of the most active participants in the new Islamic movement. In the Battle of Hunayn, he took his first active step of incorporating the Meccans into Islam.[1320]

Battle of Hunayn:

The Battle of Hunayn, which took place in January 630 CE,[1321] played a major role in integrating the Meccans into the *umma*, while at the same time setting the stage for the many tribes of Arabia to join the Islamic movement. Some have simply attributed Muhammad's success in this integration to the fear of the Meccans, or Muhammad's promises of booty. Watt remarks that these reasons might have played a part, but the chief factor was that the Prophet of Islam took on the role as the hero of the Meccans by facing urban Mecca's archenemies: the Bedouin federation of *Hawazin* and the inhabitants of the Meccan rival city Al-Ta'if, the people of *Thaqif*.[1322] Indeed, although the trade in Al-Ta'if had been controlled by Mecca, once the "sacred city" began losing its influence due to the conflict with the Muslims, anti-Meccans took over the town, thus setting the stage for a showdown.[1323] It appears that this conflict was not primarily due to the challenge of Islam, pitting Muslim Mecca against the pagan *Hawazin* and *Thaqif*. Rather, as stated above, it was a conflict between Mecca (*Quraysh*) and its rivals. Several factors in Ibn Ishaq's account corroborate this, as shall be seen.

[1319] Fred Donner, "The Early Islamic Conquests," *ACLS Humanities E-Book*, 2008 p. 77.

[1320] Isaac Hasson, *La Conversion de Mu'awiya ibn Abi Sufyan*; p. 215: "*Cela montre que nous sommes face a une politique systematique, a savior faire des ennemis d'hier les meilleurs agents et partisans du nouveau regime, donc une politique fructueuse a long terme.*"

[1321] According to Watt, p. 207.

[1322] Watt, p. 211.

[1323] Watt, p. 207.

The course of events commenced when Malik b. Awf, the leader of the Bedouins (*Hawazin*), organized an anti-Mecca alliance, which was twice the size of Muhammad's army. Muhammad prepared his army for battle as well, adding the Meccans to his previous alliance of Medinans and emigrants. It is clear from the story as told by Ibn Ishaq that these Meccans, although formally surrendering themselves to Muhammad, had not yet given up their pagan roots. Muhammad himself sought material help from Safwan, an influential man in Mecca, even though he was still a pagan:

> "When the apostle decided to go out against the Hawazin he was told that Safwan b. Umayya had some armour and weapons, so he sent to him though he was at that time a polytheist, saying, 'Lend us these weapons of yours so that we may fight our enemy tomorrow.' Safwan asked, 'Are you demanding them by force, Muhammad?' He said, 'No, they are a loan and a trust until we return them to you.' He said that in that case there was no objection and he gave him a hundred coats of mail with sufficient arms to go with them. They allege that the apostle asked for transport to carry them and he provided it."[1324]

On the way to battle the following event occurs, which clearly indicates that Muhammad's new Meccan allies had not completely accepted the new faith yet:

> "Ibn Shihab al-Zuhri from . . . told me that al-Harith b. Malik said: We went forth with the apostle to Hunayn fresh from paganism. The heathen Quraysh and other Arabs had a great green tree called Dhatu Anwat to which they used to come every year and hang their weapons on it and sacrifice beside it and devote themselves to it for a day. As we were going with the apostle we saw a great lote tree and we called out to the apostle from the sides of the way, 'Make us a tree to hang things on such as they have.' He said, 'Allah akbar! By Him who holds my life in His hand, You have said what Moses' people said to him.' "Make us a god even as they have gods." He said, "You are an ignorant people. You would follow the customs of those who were before you."[1325]

[1324] Ibn Ishaq, *Life of Muhammad*, trans. Alfred Guillaume, p. 567.
[1325] Ibid, p. 568.

Initially, the battle did not go well for Muhammad's forces, as they were ambushed in a ravine at Hunayn. Many of the "Muslim" army fled, and only the *ansar* (helpers) of Medina and his companions of the *muhajirun* (emigrants) stuck with him. Abu Sufyan, the Meccan leader who supposedly had converted to Islam right before the conquest of Mecca, commented on the events in the following manner, which again clearly shows that the Meccans were not yet Muslims, and religion was not the cause for this battle: "*Abu Sufyan b. Harb said, 'Their flight will not stop before they get to the sea!' He had his divining arrows with him in his quiver.*"[1326] In other words, Abu Sufyan was still a practicing animist. Safwan, the pagan who supported Muhammad and now was fighting with the Muslims, responded with these words to a defeatist and pessimistic Meccan: "*Shut up! God smash your mouth! I would rather be ruled by a man of Quraysh than a man of Hawazin.*"[1327] Here we have the root of the issue: Muhammad was a man of Quraysh, a Meccan by origin, and was thus supported by the Meccans against the hated Bedouin *Hawazin*.

The tide of the battle eventually turned in favor of Muhammad, after he appealed to the *ansar* and his companions on the basis of the oath of allegiance underneath the tree at Hudaybiya:

> "The apostle was saying when he saw the army in confusion, 'O Abbas cry loudly, "O Ansar, O comrades of the acacia tree"', and they answered 'Here we are'; . . . Finally a hundred were gathered by him and they went forward and fought. At first the cry was 'To me, Ansar!' and finally 'To me, Khazraj!' They were steadfast in the fight and the apostle standing in his stirrups looked down at the melee as they were fighting and said, 'Now the oven is hot.'"[1328]

One notes here how the same stories often appear in several locations. This story which the Qur'an mentions refers to an earlier situation and is merely being appropriated here for dramatic effect. Muhammad's army won the battle and the people of *Hawazin* and *Thaqif* fled, but he was not eager to exact revenge upon the vanquished as some of his compatriots seemed to be. One pregnant woman admonished Muhammad to go after the fleeing enemy: "'*Kill those who run away from you as you kill those who fight you, for they*

[1326] Ibid, p. 569.
[1327] Ibid, p. 569.
[1328] Ibid, p. 569/570

are worthy of death!' The apostle said, 'Rather God will save (me the need),
O Umm Sulaym!'"[1329] Apparently Muhammad might have already foreseen
that the Bedouin tribes and Al-Ta'if would join him, and there was no need
to alienate them now. Later on, however, some Meccans did slaughter about
seventy of their enemies from Al-Ta'if, among them a certain Uthman b.
Abdullah. Muhammad certainly was not sad to see him killed: *"God curse*
him! He used to hate Quraysh." Muhammad's main criterion for disliking this
man was not his denial of the Islamic faith. Rather, it was his hatred for the
dominant tribe in Mecca. Although the verses in the Qur'an[1330] concerning
Hunayn make it out to be a battle for faith against the unbelievers, the course
of events as described by Ibn Ishaq suggests otherwise.

In the Battle of Hunayn, the Bedouin tribes of Arabia put up their last big
challenge to Muhammad, under the leadership of Malik b. Awf.[1331] After this
battle, tribal deputations started to trickle into Medina to seek Muhammad's
alliance and mediation. What would happen next? *"When the polytheists*
were routed they came to al-Ta'if. Malik b. Auf was with them and others
were encamped in Autas."[1332] The Bedouin chieftain had fled to his allies
in Al-Ta'if, and Muhammad moved to besiege this city in order to clean up
what he had started.

Siege of Ta'if:

As at Hunayn, this military undertaking did not start off well. Even
depriving *Thaqif* of their livelihood would not weaken the city's resolve to
hold out.

> "The apostle besieged them and fought them bitterly, and the two
> sides exchanged arrows, until when the day of storming came at
> the wall of Al-Ta'if, a number of his companions went under a
> testudo and advanced up to the wall to breach it. Thaqif let loose

---

[1329] Ibid, p. 570

[1330] Qur'an 9:25-26 "Assuredly Allah did help you in many battlefields and on the
day of Hunayn: behold! your great numbers elated you, but they availed you
naught: the land, for all that it is wide, did constrain you, and ye turned back
in retreat. But Allah did pour His calm on the Messenger and on the Believers,
and sent down forces which ye saw not: He punished the Unbelievers: thus doth
He reward those without Faith."

[1331] Watt, p. 209

[1332] Guillaume, p. 574

on them, scraps of hot iron, so they came out from under it and Thaqif shot them with arrows and killed some of them. The apostle ordered that the vineyards of Thaqif should be cut down and the men fell upon them cutting them down."[1333]

Indeed, more Muslims were killed during the siege of Ta'if, which took place in February 630 CE, than in the open battle of Hunayn.[1334] After a few weeks, Muhammad decided to break off the siege. Ibn Ishaq cites the following dream as the cause, although he himself is not sure of the reliability of the source:

> "I have heard that the apostle said to Abu Bakr while he was besieging al-Ta'if, 'I saw (in a dream) that I was given a bowl of butter and a cock pecked at it and spilt it.' Abu Bakr said, 'I don't think that you will attain your desire from them today.' The apostle said that he did not think so either."[1335]

Muhammad knew that he would be able to conquer Al-Ta'if eventually, in a peaceful manner, and must have seen further bloodshed as unnecessary. Tabari cites the following conversation between him and an adviser:

> "The messsenger of God consulted Nawfal ibn Mu'awiyah al-Dili and asked his opinion about continuing (the siege). He replied,' oh messenger of God, they are like a fox (hiding) in its den. If you persist (in your siege), you will capture it, and if you leave it, it will not harm you."[1336]

Muhammad took a long-term view on this matter—he could afford to bide his time. But many in Muhammad's army were not happy with this decision. Some of them could not wait to see the forces of Islam conquer the pagans. Others, however, had quite different motives:

[1333] Ibid, p. 589.
[1334] Watt, p. 576, 591. Twenty-four Muslim martyrs are recorded by Ibn Ishaq on account of the siege of Ta'if, whereas only four Muslim deaths occur due to the Battle of Hunayn
[1335] Guillaume, p. 590.
[1336] Poonawala: translation of al-Tabari, vol. 9; p. 24

"When the army moved off Sai'd b. Ubayd . . . called out,'The tribe is holding out.' Uyayna b. Hisn said, 'Yes, nobly and gloriously.' One of the Muslims said to him, 'God smite you, Uyayna! Do you praise the polytheists for holding out against the apostle when you have come to help him?' 'I did not come to fight Thaqif with you,' he answered, 'but I wanted Muhammad to get possession of al-Ta'if so that I might get a girl from Thaqif whom I might tread (Tabari:make pregnant) so that she might bear me a son, for Thaqif are a people who produce intelligent children.'"[1337]

Although dialogue recorded by the early Muslims like Ibn Ishaq must usually be regarded as later addition, this particular verbal exchange still reveals a general attitude at the time: the prospect of booty, and women was a powerful force in gaining the support of the new Muslims. After the siege, Muhammad's army turned its attention back on the Battle of Hunayn, for much booty had been gained as a result of it, and many women had been captured.

Division of Spoils/Reconciliation with Hawazin:

As mentioned earlier on in the chapter, Muhammad had a great desire to integrate the Meccans into the Islamic system, due to their prestige and organizational skills. By representing Mecca against the Bedouins and Al-Ta'if, he definitely gained their appreciation. To a greater extent, however, booty gained from battle and generously distributed among the new converts served to strengthen Meccan loyalty to his leadership. In fact, Muhammad gave the Meccans more booty than he distributed to many of his longtime companions. This was how he defended his decision:

" . . . a companion said to the apostle:'You have given Uyayna and al-Aqra a hundred camels each and left out Ju'ayl b. Suraqa al-Damri!' He answered,'By Him in whose hand is the soul of Muhammad, Ju'ayl is better than the whole world full of men like those two; but I have treated them generously so that they may become Muslims, and I have entrusted Ju'ayl to his Islam.'"[1338]

[1337] Guillaume, p. 590
[1338] Ibid, p. 594/595.

Not long after this, a delegation from *Hawazin* came to Muhammad to request he give back their women, children, and material goods. Muhammad made them choose between their families and their belongings, and the Bedouins chose their families. Somewhat grudgingly, the Muslims agreed to give back the women and children.[1339] After reconciling with the Bedouins, Muhammad successfully enticed Malik b. Awf, the Bedouin chieftain, to join him as well by offering to not only return his family and property, but also give him an additional one hundred camels. Malik's reaction was swift, as he immediately left Al-Ta'if to join Muhammad. Ibn Ishaq records him praising Muhammad for his graciousness: "*I have never seen or heard of a man like Muhammad in the whole world; faithful to his word and generous when asked for a gift, and when you wish he will tell you of the future.*" Almost immediately Malik was put in command of troops to harass the holdovers at Al-Ta'if.[1340] It is astonishing how quickly Malik b. Awf managed to change sides. In Tabari's work, Muhammad had a particular phrase for this strategy: "*Those whose hearts were to be reconciled.*"[1341] According to Poonawala, "*this term is applied here to certain tribal chiefs and influential men whose loyalty the Prophet endeavored to secure by lavish gifts.*"[1342] Malik was not the only man this strategy succeeded with.

Inner Consolidation: Quelling Religious Dissent

Muhammad put a great deal of effort into strengthening his coalition by incorporating the Meccans, the Bedouins, and later on also the people of Al-Ta'if. He was willing, at times, to accept initial lukewarm attitude toward Islamic monotheism in order to gain victories and improve the chances for long-term commitment to the Muslim faith. He was not prepared, however, to accept religious pluralism among the Arab tribes for very long. Immediately following the conquest of Mecca, Muhammad sent out various messengers to the surrounding tribes, inviting them to Islam. At times his messengers, like the newly converted Meccan Khalid b. al-Walid, were a little too zealous.

> "The apostle sent out troops in the district round Mecca inviting men to God: he did not order them to fight. Among those he sent

---

[1339] Ibid, p. 593.
[1340] Ibid, p. 594.
[1341] Poonawala, Vol. 9, p. 31.
[1342] Ibid, Vol. 9, p. 32.

was Khalid b. al-Walid whom he ordered to go to the lower part of the flat country as a missionary; he did not send him to fight. He subdued the B. Jadhima and killed some of them."[1343]

In this particular case, Muhammad felt compelled to send Ali in order to pay the blood money for those killed by Khalid. In another instance, Muhammad sent Khalid to destroy the shrine of Al-Uzza, one of the three main goddesses. The guardian of the shrine tried to ward off Khalid with a curse.

> "O Uzza, make an annihilating attack on Khalid, Throw aside your veil and gird up your train. O Uzza, if you do not kill this man Khalid then bear a swift punishment or become a Christian".

Khalid, however, would not be deterred: *"When Khalid arrived he destroyed her and returned to the apostle."*[1344]

The Opposition Mosque:

Muhammad did not restrict his actions only to idol worship and paganism. In an interesting incident on the way home from the expedition to Tabuk, which occurred in late AD 630 and will be discussed shortly, Muhammad was confronted with the so-called "Mosque of Dissent," which had been built with the supposed intention of providing temporary shelter for the homeless, sick, and needy.

> "When he stopped in Dhu Awan news of the mosque came to him and he summoned Malik b. al-Dukhshum, . . . , and Ma'n b. Adiy . . . , and told them to go to the mosque of those evil men and destroy and burn it. They went quickly to B. Salim b. Auf who were Malik's clan, and Malik said to Ma'n,'Wait for me until I can bring fire from my people.' So he went in and took a palm-branch and lighted it, and then the two of them ran into the mosque where its people were and burned and destroyed it and the people ran away from it."[1345]

[1343] Guillaume, p. 561.
[1344] Ibid, p. 565.
[1345] Ibid, p. 609.

Muhammad was not prepared to allow separate religious initiative, not originating with himself, even though the founders of the mosque purported to be Muslims and thus part of the *umma*. Such actions were regarded as treason, striking at the heart of Islam: namely undermining allegiance to Muhammad. The following verses in the Qur'an are said to have been revealed regarding this incident:

> "And there are those who put up a mosque by way of mischief and infidelity—to disunite the Believers—and in preparation for one who warred against Allah and His Messenger aforetime. They will indeed swear that their intention is nothing but good; but Allah doth declare that they are certainly liars."[1346]

It seems quite possible as Muhammad's influence grew that there would be imitators. Muslim sources refer to false prophets that arose at this time, which we shall note below. The Qur'an seems to indicate efforts by the Prophet to reign in religious innovation on the part of his own followers.

Conversion of Al-Ta'if:

When the people of Al-Ta'if finally agreed to accept Islam, toward the end of AD 630, they attempted to coax Muhammad into giving them some flexibility regarding their idols. When he refused, they asked to be relieved of the somewhat stringent Islamic requirements to perform prayer, but were refused again.[1347] Muhammad acted in response in order to forestall any future loyalty problems in Al-Ta'if.

> "When they embraced Islam, and the Messenger of God had drawn up their treaty for them, he appointed Uthman b. Abi Al-As to be their leader, although he was the youngest among them. This was because he was the most zealous in his desire to study Islam and to learn the Qur'an."[1348]

[1346] Qur'an 9:107.
[1347] Guillaume, p. 615.
[1348] Poonawala, Vol. 9, p. 45.

False Prophets:

Among the most serious challenges to Muhammad's position as the sole authoritative prophet (and thus also ruler) were some of the claims made toward the end of his life by "false" prophets like Musaylima and al-Aswad. The former lived at Al-Yamama, claimed to be a co-prophet with Muhammad, and started composing verse and rhyme similar in style to the Qur'an. When two messengers of Musaylima gave Muhammad a letter in which he proposed a division of Arabia between the two prophets, Muhammad was rather outraged, especially after finding out the messengers were in agreement with Musaylima.

> "By God, were it not that heralds are not to be killed I would behead the pair of you!' Then he wrote to Musaylima: 'From Muhammad the apostle of God to Musaylima the liar. Peace be upon him who follows the guidance. The earth is God's. He lets whom He will of His creatures inherit it and the result is to the pious." [1349]

His reaction to al-Aswad, who was active in Southern Arabia and Yemen, turned out to be more drastic:

> "The Messenger of God waged war against the false prophets by sending messengers. He sent a messenger to some of the descendants of the Persian soldiers in the Yemen instructing them [to get rid of] al-Aswad by artful contrivance . . . Al-Aswad was killed while the Messenger of God was [still] alive . . . Despite his illness, the messenger of God was not distracted from the command of God and the defense of His religion."[1350]

In the long run, Muhammad was not prepared to tolerate religious dissent. He knew that the consolidation of the *umma* depended on absolute loyalty to his leadership, which included his mandate as the last and foremost Prophet. Once his unifying presence was gone later on, the question of political succession

---

[1349] Guillaume, p. 649.
[1350] Poonawala, Vol. 9, p. 167.

arose, eventually leading to rifts within the Islamic movement during and after Ali's caliphate.

The Break with and Ultimatum to the Pagans:

It is clear from the previous accounts that many of the newly converted Muslims were only halfheartedly committed to the new faith. It is also clear that Muhammad permitted quite a number of the Meccans to stay polytheists for a while. Safwan presents a prominent example—he fought with Mecca against the Bedouin tribes. In another case, Muhammad sent a raiding party that was at least partly pagan against an obstinate tribe who would not pay their taxes (*zakah*[1351]). The leader of that party was Uyayna b. Hisn, the same man who expressed his desire for women during the siege of Ta'if. His tribe was still pagan at the time of this retaliatory raid.[1352] Muhammad gave the Meccans (as well as the new converts from *Hawazin* and *Al-Ta'if*) some time to adjust and these stories have a good claim to historicity. This clever carrot-and-stick approach, as well as allowing time for adjustment goes a long way in explaining the later unity and military power of the Arab tribes as they spread out from Arabia and conquered the Near East.

However, after Al-Ta'if surrendered and his army returned from Syria on the expedition to Tabuk, Muhammad sent Abu Bakr down to Mecca to lead the *Hajj*. It was at this time, in early AD 631, that the death knell was rung for limited tolerance toward non-Muslim Arabs in the *Hijaz*. Originally, Muhammad had made an agreement with the pagans, letting them stay non-Muslim for a limited time, but no longer:

> "A discharge came down permitting the breaking of the agreement between the apostle and the polytheists that none should be kept back from the temple when he came to it, and that none need fear during the sacred month. That was a general agreement between him and the polytheists; meanwhile there were particular agreements between the apostle and the Arab tribes for specified terms."[1353]

[1351] Here again what is normally translated in the west as charitable contributions refers actually to state taxes, primarily for the support of the Muslim army.

[1352] Ella Landau-Tasseron, *Processes of Redaction: The Case of the Tamimite Delegation to the Prophet Muhammad*, p. 254.

[1353] Guillaume, p. 617.

Ibn Ishaq associated the following verse from the Qur'an with this incident, at which time Muhammad reportedly received this "revelation":

> "And when the sacred months are passed,' He means the four which he fixed as their time, 'then kill the polytheists wherever you find them, and seize them and besiege them and lie in wait for them in every ambush. But if they repent and perform prayer and pay the poor-tax, then let them go their way. God is forgiving, merciful."[1354]

The polytheist option was now closed for the Meccans. They were no longer just politically aligned with Muhammad, but also religiously and spiritually. The pilgrimage in Mecca had become solely a Muslim affair, and Muhammad commanded Ali to pass this on to the assembled pilgrims.

> "No unbeliever shall enter Paradise, and no polytheist shall make pilgrimage after this year, and no naked person shall circumambulate the temple. He who has an agreement with the apostle has it for his appointed time (only)."[1355]

Furthermore, Muhammad issued a ban on intercalation, an old pagan Arabic custom of adding an extra "sacred" month to the lunar calendar. Peters says that the lunar calendar did not make sense for the agricultural setting of Arabia, thus the traditional addition of extra months. Also because of this ban, there exists today a great deal of confusion as to the exact dates of events occurring between the *Hijra* (emigration) and Muhammad's death. In the words of Peters: " . . . *there is more calendrical confusion connected with these 10 years of Muhammad's mission in Medina than with any other decade in human history either before or after this period.*"[1356] This inherent confusion goes a long way in explaining the differing chronologies for this period presented by the early Muslim Sira authors. Rather than providing a basis for negating

---

[1354] Ibid, p. 619. This is a quote from surah 9:5; Guillaume's version is used rather than Yusuf Ali's because the latter considerably alters the meaning of the verse by translating *zakah* as practicing general charity, and not as paying the poor tax. This tax was a clear sign of the acceptance of Islam and Muhammad's rule and membership in the gradually increasing empire.

[1355] Ibid, p. 619.

[1356] Peters, p. 253.

their version of history. I think this explains why differentiations of dating would occur. What is interesting is that the names of expeditions or events, even if differing in their chronology, are usually the same. This is not an invented history, but a history confused by differing systems of chronology, and primarily confused in relatively minor details, not major events.

Contents of the Qur'an during This Period

We now enter the next to final period of the Qur'an. The period from Hudaybiyya to the conquest of Mecca is one of momentous events, many military campaigns and not many revelations. It is a two-year period which, if my chronology is correct, only saw the revealing of four brief chapters of the Qur'an. It is probably the least amount of revelatory production for any period in the life of the Prophet. I will consider the final two chapters of the Qur'an in the next chapter dealing with the final days of the Prophet. These, in my opinion, are his summaries of what was important to Islam, the newly minted religion. They strike me as final words of exhortation as the Prophet prepared his people for his own departure from earthly life.

The four chapters we will look at are 48 (The Victory), 66 (Prohibition), 110 (The Help), and 49 (The Private Apartments). Yusuf Ali refers to chapter 48 as the primary passage concerning the peace of Hudaybiya.[1357] Ibn Kathir presents various traditions including that it was revealed at the minor pilgrimage stating that the passage was recited by the Prophet as he marched into the city of Mecca and that it reflected the treaty. I disagree with both interpretations. I have noted the passage in the previous chapter which reflects the questions and issues raised in the minds of Muhammad's followers after the concessions of the treaty of Hudaybiya. This passage clearly reflects a major victory, and one could easily imagine the Prophet reciting this exaltingly as he achieved the prize of seven years of warfare. There is nothing else in the life of Muhammad that could have motivated so powerful an initial verse, "Verily we have granted to thee a manifest victory." This could not refer to the largely controversial treaty or the draw of Khandaq. There is nothing here about victory through slaughter, so it could hardly refer to Muhammad's victory over the Jews. The passage is clearly charged with a sense of peaceful victory not involving bloodshed, "It is He who sent down tranquility into the hearts of the believers, that they might add faith to their faith" (verse 4). The believers after Hudaybiya were anything but tranquil

---

[1357] Ali, Yusuf, p. 1328.

and believing. The word used is a cognate to the Hebrew related "Sakinah," literally the glory of God had come down into the hearts of the believers.[1358] These are the words of a man whose controversial strategy had worked, the plum of his desire fell into his hands without need for massive bloodshed with resulting blood feuds and weakening of his growing military power. I would argue against both Yusuf Ali and Ibn Kathir that this reflects the Prophet's actual march into Mecca at the head of a victorious invading army.

There is a sentiment of entry into heaven that marks the chapter. "That he may admit the men and women who believe, to gardens beneath which rivers flow." An opposite fate remains for "the hypocrites, men and women, and the polytheists, men and women . . . He has cursed them and got hell ready for them" (verses 5-6). This is an entry to paradise and an entry to hell narrative reflecting the Prophet's entry into Mecca. His enemies at are his feet, and he breathes the fire of hell at them that they might turn now and give him their total obedience. Allah himself has brought this to pass confirming Muhammad as the Messenger of God, "We have truly sent thee as a witness as a bringer of glad tidings and as a warner: In order that ye may believe in Allah and his Messenger" (verses 8-9) This is not worship to Muhammad but, "Verily those who plight their fealty to thee do no less than plight their fealty to Allah" (verse 10). The Meccans did not show fealty to Muhammad in the treaty. If anything, the Meccan terms were an insult. Here Muhammad and his behavior is now established as the true paradigm of a faithful Muslim. His enemies have fallen at his feet and given him their fealty, which Muhammad recognizes as fealty to Allah. Whatever doubts may have existed before this, Muhammad's every action now becomes the paradigm, the pathway, the *sunna* to be imitated in every way. Fealty here also means loyalty to the Muslim army. From this point on, confessing Muhammad as the Prophet of God means that you are joining his army for the establishment of Islam as the new religio-political kingdom of God on earth.

In the next section, Muhammad addresses directly for the first time the "desert Arabs." He is expressing threats against the Bedouin tribes who did not take part in his successful campaign. He says "They say with their tongues what is not in their hearts." Again Yusuf Ali and Ibn Kathir relate this to their not taking part in the Hudaybiya treaty, but this again does not make sense. The reason for their failure is stated "ye thought that the messenger and the believers would never return to their families" (verse 12). This is precisely what happened at Hudaybiya, but here Muhammad is stating that

---

[1358] Kathir, *Tafsir*, Vol. 9, p. 127.

their desire for repatriation has been fulfilled. It is interesting to note that one of the Prophet's first campaigns after the conquest of Mecca was against the Bedouin tribe of Hawazin who had resisted the Prophet's growing power.

The summons that these desert tribes had resisted was a summons to war. Muhammad rhetorically states, "Ye shall be summoned against a people given to vehement war." Coming afterward to request a share in the booty without taking part in the war is the same in the Prophet's eyes as a "wish to change Allah's decree" (verses 15-16). Ibn Kathir in his Tafsir indicates that participation in violent *jihad* is what separates true Muslims from the hypocrites.[1359] Hudaybiya was established not on the pretext of war, but on the pretext of engaging in pilgrimage. One may ask why the Muslim commentators want to associate this passage with Hudaybiya and not with the conquest of Mecca? It would seem that this is an attempt to read back into history a sense of victory before it had actually occurred, and perhaps also to cover up the level of discontent that the original treaty created.

Muhammad goes on to say that the sure way to paradise is *jihad*, and this concept becomes pervasive in this and all the remaining chapters of the Qur'an. Those who are blind, or ill are not blamed for not attending the *jihad*, but those "who obey Allah and his Messenger—(God) will admit him to gardens beneath which rivers flow." Ibn Kathir goes on to explain that this passage indicates that all able-bodied Muslims must take part in *jihad*.

Much is made in the Tafsir literature of verse 18 which states, "Allah's good pleasure was on the believers when they swore fealty to thee under the tree . . . and he rewarded them with a speedy victory." The tree has become in the traditional literature a symbol of the pact which Muhammad made with his followers at the treaty of Hudaybiya. I noted in the previous chapter how this is traditionally interpreted, and what it may actually mean. Clearly this passage is written after the conquest of Mecca, and the Qur'an is celebrating the wisdom of the Prophet through this strategy, which lead to complete victory over the Meccans in just two years. Muhammad's detractors within his own camp have been proven wrong. His power and the loyalty of his troops are now sealed. The passage goes on to mention new conquests in the offing for the future, "And many gains will they acquire . . . Allah has promised you many gains which ye shall acquire . . . He has restrained the hands of men from you . . . and other gains which are not within your power, but which Allah has compassed" (verses 19-21). This future tense is in marked contrast to the past tense of the initial verse. According to Ibn Kathir, Muhammad is

---

[1359] Kathir, *Tafsir*, Vol. 9, p. 146.

promising to those who took the hard pledge of Ridwan that they will now experience much booty and spoils, although he interprets that as the coming conquests of Khaybar and Mecca.[1360] My conclusion is that he is now pointing them in the direction of conquering the remaining Arabian tribes, and perhaps even looking beyond to things now seen as "not within your power." This verse indicates to me that Muhammad had a strategic sense of the potential power of the Arabian army to move beyond Arabia itself in conquest.

The passage goes on to celebrate how the victory was achieved. He states, "He who has restrained their hands from you and your hands from them in the midst of Makkah, after that He gave you the victory over them" (verse 24). Muhammad points out that his strategy prevented unnecessary bloodshed and yet provided victory. He goes on to point out in verse 25 that secret believers in Islam might have been killed by a more general war with Mecca, "Had there not been believing men and believing women who ye did not know that ye were trampling down." This verse indicates that Muhammad knew he had deeply infiltrated the camp of the Meccans and that he had many secret sympathizers there. Given the deceptions and spying that went on between the two camps this is highly likely. This intelligence probably provided him with the confidence that a less strident approach would win the day with far more resources intact for new campaigns elsewhere. Muhammad continues, "Allah sent down his tranquility (sekinah) to his Messenger and to the believers, and made them stick close to the command of self restraint . . . Truly did Allah fulfill the vision for His Messenger: Ye shall enter the sacred mosque . . . and He granted besides this, a speedy victory" (verse 26). The future tense used here I think refers to the upcoming pilgrimage season when Muslims for the first time would take part in the Hajj "without fear." The consequence of this is far reaching; "It is he who has sent His Messenger with guidance and the religion of truth to prevail it over all religion . . . Muhammad is the Messenger of Allah; and those who are with him are strong against unbelievers" (verses 28-29). The victory over Mecca is merely a precursor to Islam's ultimate victory over all the other religions on earth, for all religions other than Islam are ultimately unbelief. He concludes by demonstrating that Islam is now the fulfillment of both Judaism and Christianity; "This is their similitude in the Tawrah; and their similitude in the Gospel is like a seed which sends forth its blade, then makes it strong" (verse 29). This is an allusion to Christ's parable of the sower, which though not accurate to the biblical narrative reflects well Muhammad's self-conception.

[1360] Kathir, *Tafsir*, Vol. 9, p. 149.

Chapter 66 is a brief twelve verse revelation dealing with a domestic dispute that occurred in Muhammad's family between several of his wives that led him to renounce conjugal relations with all of his wives for a time as a punishment. The Hadith literature indicates that the Muslim women were learning bad habits of talking back to their husbands, and Aisha and Hafsa, two of the Prophet's wives, had rebuked him for spending too much time with another wife while enjoying some honey with her. Muhammad responded to this by putting aside all of his wives for a time and swearing off the eating of honey. The passage was apparently revealed to allow the Prophet to reject his oath to never again eat honey and to put his wives in their places.

The passage opens, "O Prophet! Why holdest thou to be forbidden that which Allah has made lawful to thee? Thou seekest to please thy consorts . . . Allah has prescribed for you method for absolution from your oaths" (verses 1-2). So the Prophet is absolved from his oath, and he goes on to describe in oblique terms the altercation. "The Prophet disclosed a matter in confidence to one of his consorts, and she then divulged it." The passage then describes his interrogation of the woman and the calling for "ye two turn in repentence." He then threatens them with divorce, "It may be, if he divorced you, that Allah will give him in exchange consorts better than you—who submit" (verses 3-5). Muhammad then goes on to challenge the men to control their families, just as the Prophet has done, "O ye who believe! Save yourselves and your families from a fire whose fuel is men and stones over which are angels stern, severe." After a further call to repentence the passage concludes, "O Prophet! Strive hard against the unbelievers and the hypocrites, and be firm against them. Their abode is hell—an evil refuge." His final example is of two wives of the Prophets Noah and Lot who were condemned for their unbelief while the daughter of Pharaoh and "Mary the daughter of Imran" are held up as examples of true faith. This again indicates that Muhammad thought that Mary was the sister of Moses. He was never able to figure out the two Marys in his own text, and they are the only women mentioned by name in the Qur'an!

It is impossible to determine exactly what the nature of the altercation was in the Qur'an. The Hadith stories may simply represent pious legends invented to explain an opaque Qur'an. The triviality of the issue and offence (staying too long with one wife and eating honey) would argue in my mind for the truthfulness of the story. What would motivate someone to make up a story so trivial and indicating such a mean-spirit in the Prophet of God? The key issue and result is clear. Even trivial household arguments can be reason for God to send down revelation to his Prophet. Further, control and disciplining of women is a primary function for the man as the leader of the household. Muhammad here illustrates applying the very progression of disciplinary techniques described earlier in 4:34, although actual physical punishment is not mentioned. He returns from this domestic affair to what is a virtually constant drumbeat in all these late chapters of the Qur'an, the military defeat and eternal punishment of the unbelievers.

Chapter 60 entitled "That Which Examines" is also a brief thirteen verse sura concerning how Muslims should not befriend unbelievers even from their own families. It is a chapter meant to finalize the breaking off tribal ties in favor of ties of allegiance to Islam. The passage rejects a notion of praying for unbelieving relatives, which was enjoined during the Meccan period of the Qur'an and thus it forms one proof text for the Muslim belief in "*naskh*" or the abrogation of older revelations in the Qur'an by newer ones. The background of the text concerns a Muslim named Hatib who was supposed to have warned the Meccans of the impending Muslim attack on Mecca after the breaking of the treaty of Hudaybiya. His rationale was that some of his family had been left behind as unbelievers in Mecca, and he was concerned for their safety. While Muhammad pardoned the man for his providing the Meccans with intelligence, the chapter was revealed to complete the break within families over issues of religion.

This break with the pagans marked a significant shift that had been taking place in the *umma*. Primary loyalty was no longer due to the tribe and clan, but submission to God and the Prophet now constituted the foundations of society.[1361] Tabari records the following commands of Muhammad to his followers:

> "Forbid them from appealing to tribes and kinsfolk when there is
> a dispute among them, but let their appeal be to God alone who
> has no associate . . . He who does not appeal to God but [instead]
> to tribes and kinsfolk should be smitten with the sword."[1362]

[1361] Inamdar, p. 226. "There were important differences that the *umma* fashioned. Religion replaced blood as the defining social bond. The *umma* banned blood feuds and settled disputes by arbitration, which increased unity. The Sheikh of the umma, Muhammad, had absolute religious authority given by the people to God who had conferred them onto his messenger and chosen apostle; his powers were not conditioned by the tribe's approval or easily revoked. Muhammad was the head of a new supertribe, a religious 'tribe'."

[1362] Poonawala, Vol. 9, p. 86.

After the conquest of Mecca and until his death, Muhammad sought to consolidate the Islamic community and bring the tribes of the *Hijaz* under his control. The break with the pagans presents the most distinct and obvious move in this direction. At the same time, however, Muhammad was also defining his community toward the outside, particularly toward the Christian tribes to the North and the Byzantine Empire. During the *hajj* of AD 631, in which the break with the pagans was formally announced, Muhammad (in absentia) also formally defined relations with Jews and Christians. First, however, the focus was turned back in time toward the expedition of Tabuk.

Chapter 110 is very brief and is essentially a three verse celebration of the victory of Allah over the pagans. Muslims are enjoined to celebrate Allah's praises when they see "the people enter Allah's religion in crowds." Muhammad's viewpoint was that coercive violence works. Before the call to war was given, few people became Muslims. Now that the sword is being used, people come to Islam in "droves." Osama bin Laden exulted in the same way after September 11 when it was reported that 35,000 Americans had converted to Islam after the attack. In the minds of radical Muslims, coercive violence truly works, and the foundation for their belief is Muhammad himself.

Chapter 49, called "the Chambers," is the longest, though also brief, production from this period. There are just eighteen verses. It is, in essence, a definition of the court etiquette which Muhammad was now requiring of his followers. We have seen elements of this in earlier passages. The passage opens directly with, "O ye who believe! Put not yourselves forward before Allah and his Messenger." The passage goes on to say, "raise not your voices above the voice of the Prophet, nor speak aloud to him in talk, as ye may speak aloud to one another." Those who lower their voices in the Prophet's presence are considered to be people of "piety" (verses 1-3). Clearly Muhammad is taking on here the airs of a king in his court, whose word is law and whose presence should inspire an awed silence and full submission. Those outside his apartments should also not shout out loud to get his attention. Clearly the stratagem to overcome Mecca had now placed Muhammad in the position of kingship, and he was concerned to establish the etiquette thereof.

There follows a number of verses that call first for careful examination of news from unreliable people lest revenge be taken in a way that would "harm people unwittingly." This is a camp that lives on the edge of military campaigns and this carried with it the possibility of both misunderstanding and unnecessary violence. This extended even between groups of believers.

He goes on to say, "If two parties among the believers fall into a quarrel, make ye peace between them: but if one of them transgress beyond bounds against the other, then fight ye against the one that transgresses" (verse 9). The problem becomes where to draw such "bounds?" Is it Sunni bound or Shia bound? Is it radical bound or moderate bound? Is it Sufi bound or Wahhabi bound? Is it black Abid Darfuri bound or light-skinned Sudani Arab? Ibn Kathir notes that this verse became an excuse to the Khawarijites and Mu'tazilites to carry out violent campaigns against Muslims they considered to be in sin. He reflects on this as going too far.[1363] However, in a religion which exalts coercive violence as the final arbiter of truth, once the non-Muslims are eradicated, the purification process needs a new focus against all contrarian behaviors and viewpoints. It becomes a vectoring in downward spiral of endless legalism.

"The believers are but a single brotherhood" he intones. How far does the uniformity of that "singleness" extend? What place does non-Arab culture have in that "singleness?" This is the foundation for declaring "*takfir*" in the Muslim world today that defines various Muslim groups as "non-Muslim" and makes their violent eradication permissible. When the Pakistan parliament declared Ahmadiyyas to be non-Muslims they essentially gave permission for the bombings and shootings in Ahmadiyya mosques that we have seen in recent years. The foundation for Muslim suicide bombers to blow up other Muslims is found in the words of the Prophet himself.

The final section of the passage deals with various forbidden behaviors. Men are not allowed to laugh at other men, nor women laugh at women. Sarcasm and nicknames are similarly forbidden. Muslims are not to be suspicious of one another, nor to gossip. Ibn Kathir tells the story of a Muslim convicted on his own testimony of adultery and being stoned to death. The Prophet forbade anyone gossiping about him as he was now purified and enjoying heaven.[1364] All of this seems to be in distinction to how one should look upon those outside of the community.

Verse 13 is enigmatic. I have often looked in Islamic texts for some understanding of the meaning and purpose of cultures and cultural differences. Verse 13 seems to be one of the few in the Qur'an that recognizes these differences. It starts with the biblical story of creation. "O mankind! We created you from a single pair of a male and a female, and made you into nations and tribes, that ye may know each other." The passage goes on to

---

[1363] Ibn Kathir, *Tafsir*, Vol. 9, p. 194.

[1364] Ibn Kathir, *Tafsir*, Vol. 9, p. 204.

say that the best of all peoples, even among the "desert Arabs" are those who "obey Allah and his Messenger." I had hoped to find some notion that God himself was glorified by this subdivision of humanity into tribes and nations; something that would allow for an aspect of multiculturalism in Islam. Muhammad's understanding as described by Ibn Kathir is that these distinctions are merely for the purpose of being able to identify where people are from.[1365] Yusuf Ali also describes this as "labels by which we may know certain differing characteristics." There seems to be no understanding of the richness of human culture or of incorporating human cultural diversity into the purposes of God. Unity is enjoined at the cost of a uniformity of cultural expression. Islam is a monocultural system, a deified Arabism that enjoins the slavish imitation of even the most minor aspects of the Prophet's cultural behavior, ritual prayers in Arabic, and a single nation state to rule the world. Ibn Kathir goes on to say that this uniformity is so absolute that even the idea of compatibility of couples for marriage is of no concern in establishing marriage contracts.[1366] It is interesting to me that Europe under Christianity retained its linguistic diversity. The linguistic diversity of the "Arab" Middle East has been largely eradicated under Islam.

Muhammad returns at the end of the passage by defining again what it means to be a believer. "Only those are believers who have believed in Allah and his Messenger, and have never doubted, but have striven with their belongings and their persons in the cause of Allah: Such are the sincere ones" (verse 15). It is clear the kind of striving (*jihad*) mentioned here is not warring with evil desires in one's own heart. *Jihad* involves one's wealth and physical body in the purpose of warfare. It has no other meaning in the Qur'an. Only Muslims who engage in violent *jihad* are "sincere ones."

[1365]   Ibn Kathir, *Tafsir*, Vol. 9, p. 206.
[1366]   Ibn Kathir, *Tafsir*, Vol. 9, p. 209.

CHAPTER 12

MUHAMMAD'S CONQUESTS, DEATH, AND THE FINAL TWO CHAPTERS OF THE QUR'AN

Outward Expansion: Defining the Relationship between Muslims and "the People of the Book" Expedition of Tabuk:

In October of AD 630, Muhammad started preparing his troops for an expedition north toward Syria, which was Christian Byzantine territory. This was not the first time Muhammad had ventured north: the disastrous affair at Mu'ta, before the conquest of Mecca, took place even further north into Syria. This particular undertaking, however, seemed to have involved more deliberate planning and effort.

> "Now the apostle nearly always referred allusively to the destination of a raid and announced that he was making for a place other than that which he actually intended. This was the sole exception, for he said plainly that he was making for the Byzantines because the journey was long, the season difficult, and the enemy in great strength, so that the men could make suitable preparations. He ordered them to get ready and told them that he was making for the Byzantines."[1367]

The Muslims at Medina were generally not very excited about Muhammad's plan, particularly because of the hot weather and lack of water. Apparently, Muhammad did not force them to go, but later on he gave those who stayed

---

[1367] Guillaume, p. 602.

behind some scathing rebukes, which are recorded in the Qur'an. "Fighting in the way of God" had indeed assumed the position of a sacred duty—to not participate in military action was to risk eternal punishment, so it seems, according to the Qur'an.

> "Among them is (many) a man who says: 'Grant me exemption and draw me not into trial.' Have they not fallen into trial already? And indeed Hell surrounds the Unbelievers (on all sides)."[1368]

> "Those who were left behind (in the Tabuk expedition) rejoiced in their inaction behind the back of the Messenger of Allah: they hated to strive and fight, with their goods and their person, in the Cause of Allah: they said, 'Go not forth in the heat.' Say, 'The fire of Hell is fiercer in heat.' If only they could understand!"[1369]

What were Muhammad's motives in this expedition? Why did he put so much effort into it? Was there really a large Byzantine army gathering to confront the Muslim forces? Peters does not think this very likely. The emperor would not have been paying much attention to events in the Arabian Desert at that time. Rather, because the tribes of the *Hijaz* no longer opposed him, Muhammad was forced to look elsewhere for booty, on which his army depended.[1370] Indeed, in Al-Tabari's account of the events, some of Muhammad's men came to him weeping, for they didn't have any mounts to go on the expedition, and Muhammad had none to give them. The *umma* was not economically self-sufficient and needed a source of income, which the previous raids in Arabia had provided. The earliest Christian sources when referencing the Arab invasions refer to them as "bandits," and it seems likely that the pattern Muhammad initially set was to force the paying of tribute and then withdraw. We are a long way from the administration of an Islamic empire.

Many of the *Quraysh* were quite familiar with Syria due to their vast trading experience. Abu Sufyan, the leader of the Meccans, even owned property in Syria, according to Donner. And not to be forgotten, the Islamic faith put great importance in Jerusalem as a holy site, and would thus be

---

[1368] Qur'an 9:49.
[1369] Qur'an 9:81.
[1370] Peters, pp. 240-241.

interested in moving north.[1371] There were many reasons for this expedition, as is seen. Perhaps of greatest importance was the fact that many Christianized Arab tribes lived in Syria, and Muhammad would have been more than interested in incorporating them into his empire. According to Donner, however, he was not very successful, generally speaking, in converting them in his lifetime.[1372]

In any case, Ibn Ishaq does not report any major clash at Tabuk, a city in northern Arabia. Instead, some leaders of Christian tribes came to him, most notably the governor of Ayla in southern Palestine, in order to make an agreement with him. Others like Khalid of the Kinda were captured, but spared on an agreement to pay the poll tax. Muhammad established a precedent by putting them under his protection and making them pay this poll tax (*jizyah*), which would come to characterize Muslim-Christian/Jewish relations in the Middle East for centuries to come.[1373]

Apparently, Muhammad saw no need to linger up north, although no conquests are reported. *"The apostle stayed in Tabuk some ten nights, not more. Then he returned to Medina."*[1374] What had he accomplished, other than a few treaties with smaller tribes and cities? Perhaps quite a bit, when seen in the context of the Byzantine-Persian power struggle. The emperor had just managed to regain Syria and Palestine from the Persians, which they in turn had conquered in AD 610. The Byzantines had lost connection with their Ghassanid allies, and probably would have been in the process of reestablishing alliances with these Arab "buffer" tribes in protection against the hostile southern Bedouins and the Persian army to the east. Muhammad, however, was getting ready to unite the Arab tribes, and there is a chance he knew about this window of opportunity to gain the allegiance of the northern tribes against the weakened Byzantines. Over time he managed to accomplish this.[1375]

Slowly, but surely, the groundwork for Muhammad's invasion of the northern lands was being laid. In Arabia itself, however, many tribes still were not entirely committed to the Islamic movement, and especially in

---

[1371] Donner, pp. 96-98.

[1372] Ibid, p. 105.

[1373] Guillaume, p. 607, 608. This poll tax was not removed from the non-Muslim populations of the various Islamic empires until the coming of Western colonial powers.

[1374] Ibid, p. 608.

[1375] Donner, p. 99, 100.

the southern and eastern parts many of them adhered to Christianity and Judaism.

Tribal Delegations and Muhammad's Messengers:

After Muhammad had returned from the expedition to Tabuk in late 630, and *Thaqif* had finally submitted to him in January of 631CE, most of the tribes of Arabia started sending delegations to Medina, clearly signaling Muhammad's preeminence.

> "When the apostle had gained possession of Mecca, and had finished with Tabuk, and Thaqif had surrendered and paid homage, deputations from the Arabs came to him from all directions. In deciding their attitude to Islam the Arabs were only waiting to see what happened to this clan of Quraysh and the apostle . . . ; and when Mecca was occupied and Quraysh became subject to him and he subdued it to Islam, and the Arabs knew that they could not fight the apostle or display enmity toward him they entered into God's religion 'in batches' as God said, coming to him from all directions."[1376]

Judging from Ibn Ishaq's account above, perhaps the attraction of Islam as a religion was not the primary reason for this sudden rush of converts. The Kings of Himyar sent a messenger to Muhammad as well, telling him of their acceptance of Islam. These seem to have been Persian Satraps who switched allegiance as the Sassanid empire at this point was tottering on the verge of collapse. There must have been many Jews or Christians still unconverted among them, for in his response, Muhammad further defined their rights and obligations toward Islam.

> "If a Jew or a Christian becomes a Muslim he is a believer with his rights and obligations. He who holds fast to his religion, Jew or Christian, is not to be turned from it. He must pay the poll tax-for every adult, male or female, free or slave, one full dinar calculated on the valuation of Ma'afir or its equivalent in clothes. He who pays that to God's apostle has the guarantee of God and His apostle, and he who withholds it is the enemy of God and his apostle."[1377]

[1376] Guillaume, pp. 627-628.
[1377] Ibid, p. 642.

Not only did Muhammad receive many tribal delegations, but he also sent out many messengers into the surrounding regions. Many of these missions were of a peaceful beckoning nature, but no doubt many of them had an element of coercion, as in the following account.

> "Then the apostle sent Khalid b. al-Walid . . . to the B. al-Harith b. Ka'b in Najran, and ordered him to invite them to Islam three days before he attacked them. If they accepted then he was to accept it from them; and if they declined he was to fight them."[1378]

Naturally, the Banu al-Harith of Najran submitted to Islam, but certainly not from a heart conviction of the rightness of this new faith. Interestingly, the city of Najran was a Christian enclave.[1379] This is, therefore, an incident not of pagans but of Christians submitting to Islam under the threat of death. It may well be the first instance of a direct Islamic subjugation of a Christian group and indicates that Muhammad now regarded his faith as demanding the subjugation of Christians. As we shall see, the Qur'an of this period certainly indicates that as well. Muhammad has declared war on the entire non-Muslim world including all other monotheists.

Ibn Ishaq also includes accounts of messengers sent to the Byzantine Emperor, the Negus of Abyssinia, and Chosroes, the ruler of Persia.[1380] These accounts are not reproduced in this chapter, mainly because of their hagiographic and contrived nature. According to Ibn Ishaq, both the emperor and the Negus accepted Islam, a turn of events that is doubtful when compared to the progression of history.[1381] The Persian ruler, however, rejected Islam, and sought to capture and kill Muhammad. This action, according to Ibn Ishaq, supposedly led to his death by divine retribution. He was succeeded by his son, the ruler who would lose the Persian Empire to the forces of Islam.

In any case, by the year 632 CE, Muhammad had control, more or less, over all of Arabia. He may not have been actively ruling whole of the region,

---

[1378] Ibid, p. 645.

[1379] Poonawala, Vol. 9, p. 24.

[1380] Guillaume, pp. 652-659.

[1381] The East Roman Empire never did fall to the Arabs, and the Turks did not conquer Constantinople until the fifteenth century. The Christian populations of Asia Minor have been almost completely ethnically cleansed and eradicated. Also, Abyssinia, which is today's Ethiopia, is still a culturally Christian country to this day.

but through stronger and weaker alliances he had succeeded in unifying all of the Arab tribes, thus readying the *umma* for the great outward invasion, which was to follow spanning the century after his death.[1382]

Abu Bakr's Pilgrimage in 631 CE

Again the attention moves back to the *hajj* in 631 CE, led by Abu Bakr in Muhammad's absence. In the previous expedition to Tabuk, Muhammad had already set a precedent for Muslim-Christian relations by entering into agreements with various tribes, pledging to protect them if they submitted to him and paid the *jizyah*, the poll tax. According to Ibn Ishaq, at the same time the formal break with the pagans occurred through Ali's announcement of Muhammad's "revelation," the relationship between Muslims and "People of the Book" (Jews and Christians) was formalized as well. Ibn Ishaq associates the following Qur'anic verse with this incident:

> "Fight those who do not believe in God and the last day and forbid not that which God and His apostle have forbidden and follow not the religion of truth from among those who have been given the scripture until they pay the poll tax out of hand being humbled, . . ."[1383]

What is the motive behind this poll tax on the Christians and Jews? Was it merely a sign of submission to Islam, or perhaps even payment for protection? Or was it merely of symbolic value, as many claim today, signifying the tolerance of the Islamic regime? Ibn Ishaq again clarifies the exact motive behind this move, which came in the context of the break with the pagans, as must be remembered. *"God gave them compensation for what He cut off from them in their former polytheism by what He gave them by way of poll tax from the people of scripture."*[1384] Polytheism had been a lucrative business for the Meccans, and Muhammad knew that his move to ban idol worship at the Ka'ba would not be appreciated. Being the astute businessman he was, he realized that an alternative source of income would be necessary. Simultaneously, through the poll tax, Muhammad created the basic foundation

---

[1382] Watt, pp. 224-226.

[1383] Guillaume, p. 620. Ibn Ishaq quotes 9:29 here; again, this version is preferable to Yusuf Ali's.

[1384] Ibid, p. 620.

that would serve as the model for the relationship between Muslims, the Jews, and Christian minorities in the Middle East for centuries to come.[1385]

Preparing for Life after Muhammad:

Farewell Pilgrimage:

By the spring of AD 632, Muhammad had created a system that Watt aptly calls *Pax Islamica*, a system with vast potential for growth. Here was a budding empire that proved to be quite attractive to the neighboring Arab tribes, pulling them away from Persia and the Byzantines, and thus contributing to the weakness of the latter empires. Booty gained from invasion and outward expansion provided the economic fuel. The lack of dependence on a foreign ruler (instead, Islam promised relative equality among the tribes) served as the political impetus of this genuinely Arab movement. And finally, unity among the tribes was established through Islam, which served as the core and glue of the community, and substituted clan loyalty with commitment to the *umma*.[1386]

In March 632 CE, Muhammad led what was to be his last pilgrimage (*hajj*). Although he might not have been aware of his impending death, he had already taken many steps necessary to prepare the Islamic community for his absence. In his last time at Mecca, Muhammad finalized some of the rituals of Islam, deciding to incorporate some pre-Islamic elements, and getting rid of others.[1387] Peters notes that here Muhammad fused the previously separate greater (*hajj*) and smaller (*umra*) pilgrimages into one.[1388] Islam was not a coherent whole when Muhammad left Mecca for Medina ten years before, and as we can see here, it was still changing its shape at the end of the Prophet's lifetime. Some scholars even believe that Muhammad began to finalize an edition of his revelations and that the ambiguous letters at the start of many chapters are actually an organizational system set up by the Prophet.[1389]

[1385] This raises the following question: Was Muhammad all that eager about winning the hearts of men, or was this just a method to subdue potential irritants on the way to political power?

[1386] Watt, pp. 224-226.

[1387] Guillaume, p. 651. Ibn Ishaq again mentions the ban on intercalation. This raises the question whether the practice was forbidden the year before when Abu Bakr led the *hajj* or the following year. Perhaps Ibn Ishaq was somewhat confused himself.

[1388] Peters, p. 248.

[1389] This is according to Bell's analysis of the Qur'an.

Death of Muhammad: June, 632 CE

There has been much speculation surrounding Muhammad's death concerning the causes, the length of his illness, and the final moments before his death. Particular attention has been given historically by both Muslim and non-Muslim writers to the "poison" theory. According to this, Muhammad had been given a poisoned sheep's shoulder to eat by a Jewess in the aftermath of the successful attack on Khaybar (629 CE). He bit into it, but noticed something was wrong and did not swallow his bite, unlike his unfortunate companion. However, over time, he developed his fatal illness due to this incident, and he died three years later. This account does seem somewhat unlikely, however. One way or another, Muhammad did develop a serious illness that led to his death. His last command, according to Al-Tabari, bore particular importance for both Jews and Christians, for it was going to determine their future on the peninsula:

> "The last injunction enjoined by the messenger of God was that no two religions be left in the Arabian Peninsula. The messenger of God died on the 12th of Rabi, the very day on which he came to Medina as an emigrant."[1390]

Muhammad had cleared the sacred city of Mecca of polytheists and pagans. Now he wished to do the same for all of Arabia. His wish was fulfilled during the Caliphate of Umar when the movement had gained enough political power that it did not need to rely on the support of Christian or Jewish tribes. To this day, the presence of non-Muslims in Arabia (mainly Saudi Arabia) is regarded with great suspicion. His actions typified the ethnic cleansing that is typical of all countries where Islam has become the majority religion. There is no majority Muslim nation that treats its non-Muslim minorities with equity.

According to a tradition recorded by Bukhari, Muhammad asked to be with his favorite wife, Aisha, as his time was nearing.

> "Narrated Aisha that during his fatal ailment, Allah's Apostle used to ask his wives, 'Where shall I stay tomorrow? Where shall I stay tomorrow?' He was looking forward to Aisha's turn. So all his wives allowed him to stay where he wished, and he stayed at Aisha's house till he died there. Aisha added: He died on the day

---

[1390] Poonawala, p. 206.

of my usual turn at my house. Allah took him unto Him while his head was between my chest and my neck and his saliva was mixed with my saliva."[1391]

And so died Muhammad, the founder of Islam. The movement he established was destined to soon conquer the lands from Spain to Central Asia.

The Final Two Chapters of the Qur'an

The final two chapters of the Qur'an are chapter 9 (entitled "The Repentance") and chapter 5 (entitled "The Repast"). Chapter 9 comprises 129 verses and chapter 5, 120. They are placed early in the Qur'an indicating their importance, but are relatively short in length. Chapter 9 is the most violent chapter in the Qur'an and contains the so-called "Sword verse," which according to some Islamic scholars has abrogated (*naskh*) hundreds of more moderate verses in the Qur'an. The Qur'an has been far from a peaceable book up to this point. Unlike other religions that ultimately rejected the idea of establishing a kingdom of God on earth by human hands, these final two chapters constitute a clarion call to establish God's kingdom on earth by means of coercive violence. The chapter roundly condemns all Jews and Christians who do not confess Muhammad as the Prophet of God. There are repeated calls for the killing or subjugation of Jews and Christians who are condemned in the most extreme wording one can imagine. Further, the chapter declares repeatedly that the only genuine Muslims are those who engage in violent *jihad*. The chapter constitutes a declaration of war on the non-Muslim world.

Yusuf Ali, in his commentary, regards chapter 9 as a continuation of chapter 8, which was the chapter on the spoils of war. He notes that the passage is one of the last of the Qur'an and may be subdivided into two parts, verses 1-29 and verses 30-129, the former being revealed somewhat later than the latter, and the first group of verses dealing with a "declaration of state policy."[1392] The latter supposedly deals with the Prophet's reflections on the raid to Tabuk. The dating is around 630 CE. Ibn Kathir claims it is the last surah of the Qur'an while others maintain that surah 5 was last.[1393] Chapter 9 cannot be interpreted in any other way than that of a manifesto of

---

[1391] Bukhari, Vol. 7, p. 105, n. 144.

[1392] Ali, Yusuf, p. 435.

[1393] Ibn Kathir, *Tafsir*, Vol. 4, p. 369.

unending holy war against pagans, Christians, Jews, and all others who do not accept Muhammad as the Prophet of God.

Chapter 9 opens with Muhammad revoking his treaty of some sort toward some of the pagans of Arabia. He issues an ultimatum that they must all convert to Islam within the next four months, "freedom from obligations from Allah and his Messenger to those of the Mushrikin (idolators), with whom you made a treaty. So travel freely for four months throughout the land, but know that you cannot escape Allah; and Allah will disgrace the disbelievers" (verse 2).[1394] After this four-month period, which Ibn Kathir interprets as a time for them to seek refuge from attack, a new rule would come into being. There is mention of some tribes having other treaties that would still be in effect if they did not do anything hostile to the Muslims. Then in verse 5, the new rule is enunciated, "So when the sacred months have passed, then fight and slay the pagans wherever ye find them, and seize them, beleaguer them, and lie in wait for them in every stratagem (of war); but if they repent and establish regular prayers and practice regular charity, then open the way for them." Muhammad declares open season on the remaining pagans not under any specific treaty with the Prophet, and this verse is referred to as "the verse of the sword." They are to be annihilated unless they convert to Islam.

Al Bukhari's Hadith contain an entire book of *jihad* that explains this concept in various ways; "Get ready against them all you can of power forces including steeds of war to strike terror into the enemy of Allah and your enemy."[1395] The Hadith expands the target for *jihad* beyond the pagans to the Jews and the Christians, "The hour will not be established until you fight with the Jews, and the stone behind which a Jew will be hiding will say, 'O Muslim! There is a Jew hiding behind me, so kill him."[1396] There are innumerable similar references in all the canonical Hadiths. Ibn Kathir concludes, "This way they will have no choice but to die or embrace Islam."[1397] Muhammad mollifies this somewhat by stating that those who seek asylum with the Muslims should be granted asylum in order that they might learn about Islam. This is another way of saying that conversion is inevitable. Ibn Kathir interprets this as a right of safe passage for pagans to come to

---

[1394] The translation in Ibn Kathir's *Tafsir* is more clear at this point than Yusuf Ali's which is why I have used it.

[1395] al-Bukhari, Vol. 4, pp. 96-97, (78).

[1396] al-Bukhari, Vol. 4, p. 110, repeated twice.

[1397] Ibn Kathir, *Tafsir*, Vol. 4, p. 376.

Muhammad to hear about Islam.[1398] The Prophet is at the pinnacle of his power and his tolerance level is zero.

In the next section of the chapter 9 Muhammad goes on to explain the rationale for this change of policy. He asks, "How can there be a league before Allah and His Messenger with the pagans, except those whom ye made a treaty near the Sacred Mosque?" He goes on to explain, "with their mouths they entice you, but their hearts are averse . . . rebellious and wicked . . . evil indeed are the deeds they have done. In a believer they respect not the ties either of kinship or of covenant! It is they who have transgressed all bounds" (verses 8-9). Once again Muhammad is accusing those who are the focus of his hatred of the very thing he is doing himself. He is the one revoking a peaceful approach and rejecting ties of kinship and covenant, now to be replaced by Islam. His behavior is paradigmatic for the blame game that the Muslim world plays with the non-Muslim world to this day. Muslims are righteous and holy, non-Muslims are "evil," "wicked," "rebellious," and "enticing."Ibn Kathir comments the following:

> "Allah mentions the wisdom of dissolving all obligations to the idolators and giving them a four month period of safety, after which they will meet the sharp sword wherever they are found."
> He affirms "that they do not deserve a covenant of peace, because of their shirk in Allah and disbelief in Allah's Messenger."[1399]

This rule certainly applies to Christians who affirm that Jesus is God and refuse to confess Muhammad as a Prophet. Thus, their theological beliefs are reason enough to declare war. Warfare is unavoidable unless one converts to Islam or submits to Islamic rule. Muhammad later accuses the Jews of worshipping "Uzayr" (Ezra) in this same passage showing that this new covenant of warfare really extends to all non-Muslims. Of course, those who convert to Islam and keep the prayers and donate to the *jihad*, "They are your brethren in faith" (verse 11).

Muhammad's rationale for this warfare is the sufferings he encountered at the hijra, "Will ye not fight people who violated their oaths plotted to expel the Messenger and took to aggression . . . ? . . . Fight them and Allah will punish them by your hands, cover them with shame." He reminds of previous injustices of eight years earlier as an excuse for all-out war in the

---

[1398] Ibn Kathir, *Tafsir*, Vol. 4, p. 378.
[1399] Ibn Kathir, *Tafsir*, Vol. 4, p. 381.

name of religion. He promises victory "to those who have (striven hard and fought)[1400] and take none for friends and protectors except Allah, His Messenger and the believers" (verses 13-16). Muhammad dichotomizes the world into Muslim and non-Muslim and affirms that the only true friends Muslims have are within their own community. All others are enemies to be conquered, killed, or converted. The Islamic concept of the world divided into two houses, the Dar-ul Islam or house of Islam and the Dar-ul Harb or house of war, finds its basis here. Muhammad goes on to say that those who fight in *jihad* are the highest of all Muslims using the phrase "striven hard and fought" over and over. "Those who believe, and suffer exile, and strove hard and fought in Allah's cause with their wealth and their lives, are far higher in degree with Allah. They are the successful." They are the ones who will receive the "gardens . . . wherein are delights that endure" (verses 19-21). Their deeds in *jihad* are considered higher than those who maintain mosques. Furthermore, "Take not for protectors your fathers and your brothers if they love infidelity above faith." He states that they should hold Allah, his Messenger and waging war for Islam, "dearer" than "your fathers, your sons, your brothers, your mates, or your kindred" (verses 23-24). Ibn Kathir holds up as example Abu Ubaydah who killed his own father Al-Jarrah because of his idolatry at the Battle of Badr.[1401]

The final section of the Prophet's declaration of war contains a brief mention of the Battle of Hunayn, one of the few historical events in the Prophet's life that the Qur'an speaks directly about, "Assuredly Allah did help you in many battlefields and on the day of Hunayn." This battle did not go well initially, but the Prophet states that "*sekinah*"[1402] or "tranquility" was sent down by Allah on the Messenger and the believers and Allah "sent down forces which ye saw not" (verses 25-26). The point seems to be that Muhammad's general declaration of war on all pagans was the cause of some discomfort amongst the Muslims, pointing to a whole new set of battles and warfare in the future. Muhammad is pointing his men in the direction of an ongoing *jihad* that really has no end until the world is ruled by Islam. The final

---

[1400] I insert here the translation from Ibn Kathir since it shows more clearly what the passage actually means. The phrase "striven hard and fought" occurs over and over in the passage.

[1401] Ibn Kathir, *Tafsir*, Vol. 4, p. 395.

[1402] This is a clear borrowing from Hebrew and indicates Muhammad's roots in Jewish conceptions. This is the word for the "glory" of God, which came down on the tabernacle and led the Israelites in their wars to conquer the promised land.

two verses of this declaration of war are telling. First, "truly the pagans are unclean; so let them not after this year of theirs, approach the sacred mosque. And if you fear poverty, soon will Allah enrich you" (verse 28). Muhammad's attitude toward unbelievers could not be more plain in this verse. "Believers" are "pure," states Ibn Kathir, and "idolators are impure."[1403] Muhammad seems to be responding to a fear on the part of the Muslims that this will lead to a decrease of pilgrimage to Mecca and thus potential poverty. Verse 29 solves this problem; "Fight those who believe not in Allah nor the last day, nor hold that forbidden which hath been forbidden by Allah and His Messenger, nor acknowledge the religion of truth, from among the People of the Book, until they pay the jizya with willing submission, and feel themselves subdued." Ibn Kathir states, "This ayah means, 'this will be your compensation for the closed markets you feared would result.' Therefore Allah compensated them for the losses they incurred because they severed ties with the idolators, by the jizya they earned from the People of the Book."[1404] Muhammad has now established the kingdoms of the Christians and the Jews as the new focus for offensive *jihad* in order to fill the coffers of the Muslim state. Yusuf Ali's explanation of this as "symbolic," "insignificant," and "a commutation for military service" is an effort to downplay the hostile intent and warfare as-means-of-profit attitude that this verse engenders.[1405]

Ibn Kathir's interpretation of the text is closer to reality. They are to be conquered because "Had they been true believers in their religions, that faith would have directed them to believe in Muhammad, because all Prophets gave the good news of Muhammad's advent and commanded them to obey and follow him."[1406] As McAuliffe points out, true Christians and Jews are really just Muslims who haven't heard about Muhammad yet. "Qur'anic Christians, then, are Christians who either accepted the Prophethood of Muhammad and the revelation entrusted to him or would have done so had their historical circumstances permitted."[1407] The larger group of Christians in the Qur'an "is excoriated, subjected to a broad range of religious accusation and denunciation." Ibn Kathir calls the Jews and Christians people of the "Dhimma" who via the jizya "are miserable, disgraced and humiliated." The

---

[1403] Ibn Kathir, *Tafsir*, Vol. 4, p. 403.
[1404] Ibn Kathir, *Tafsir*, Vol. 4, p. 405.
[1405] Ali, Yusuf, p. 447, footnote 1282.
[1406] Ibn Kathir, *Tafsir*, Vol. 4, p. 405.
[1407] Jane Dammen McAuliffe, *Qur'anic Christians*, Cambridge: Cambridge University Press, 1991, p. 287.

jizya was intended to "ensure their continued humiliation, degradation and disgrace."[1408] Muhammad has set his forces on an all-out war against anyone who will not confess him as the final Prophet of God. To confess Muhammad as Prophet is synonymous with conversion to Islam.

Section five of this chapter deals with the rationale for attacking the Jews. As we have seen Judaism and Islam were more closely related than Christianity and Islam. In many ways their conceptions of God were very similar. One might have thought of Muhammad virtually as a quasi-Jew during his time in Mecca. How are Muslims to explain this apparent similarity and the vituperous hatred for Jews that all the sira, tafsir, and Medinan Qur'anic surahs reflect? Muhammad clearly had this anomaly in mind in the revelation that follows. "The Jews call Uzayr (Ezra) a Son of God, and the Christians call Christ the Son of God . . . Allah's curse be on them: How they are deluded away from the truth" (verse 30). This criticism is correct for the Christians. But the Jews did not regard Ezra as a Son of God. Yusuf Ali tries to explain away this obviously inaccurate portrayal of Judaism in several footnotes (Section 718, p. 252, section 1283, p. 446). Ibn Kathir states, "As for the Jews, they claimed that Uzayr was the son of God, Allah is free of what they attribute to Him. As for the misguidance of Christians over Isa, it is obvious. This is why Allah declared both groups to be liars."[1409] The criticism of the Jews is entirely unfair and distorted and reflects a Qur'anic attitude that is both intolerant and violent and dishonest. It is making a false excuse for Muhammad's persecution of Jews.

There is a distinction between the various *tafsirs* at this point. Yusuf Ali attempts to explain away and justify verses that call for violence. Ibn Kathir simply emphasizes the call for violence and hatred that is endemic to the text. This would, perhaps, be the distinction between moderate and fundamental Islam. Neither would engender an attitude of tolerance toward people of different religious viewpoints, and the moderate could easily be attacked by the fundamental Muslim for not being faithful to the clear thrust of the Qur'anic text. Perhaps this is why moderate Islam has so little voice in the Muslim world today.

Muhammad then goes on to attack the Christian priests and rabbis who set themselves up as "Lords" as well as "Christ the son of Mary." He imputes to them the worst possible motives, "They want to extinguish Allah's light with their mouths, but Allah will not allow except that his light should be

---

[1408]   Ibn Kathir, *Tafsir*, Vol. 4, p. 406.
[1409]   Ibn Kathir, *Tafsir*, Vol. 4, p. 408.

perfected even though the disbelievers hate (it)" (verse 32). Christians have, to this point, had little contact with Muhammad or Islam. The Prophet here anticipates their rejection and calls that anticipated rejection "hatred" as an excuse to fan the fires of hatred in his followers toward those who follow Christ. It seems to me that it is precisely the attitude that allows Muslim governments to publish books like *The Protocols of the Elders of Zion*, a forgery of the nineteenth century concerning a Jewish conspiracy to take over the world, and also encourages Muslims that I have met in mosques in the United States to claim that the CIA is responsible for 9/11. For to impute such attitudes in people that one has not yet met in any appreciable sense is nothing other than a lie, and a lie designed as an excuse for war. What does God intend by this according to the Prophet? "It is He who hath sent His Messenger with guidance and the religion of truth to prevail it over all religion, even though the pagans detest (it)" (verse 33).

Here there is no difference between "moderate" and "radical." Yusuf Ali states, "so will Islam outshine all else." Ibn Kathir is more to the point; "Tamim Ad-Dari" (who was a Christian before Islam) used to say, "I have come to know the meaning of this hadith in my own people. Those who became Muslims among them acquired goodness, honor and might. Disgrace, humiliation and Jizyah befell those who remained disbelievers."[1410] The priests and rabbis are described again by Muhammad as those who "devour the wealth of mankind in falsehood, and hinder from the way of Allah . . . who hoard up gold and silver . . . announce. A painful torment on that day when that will be heated in the fire of Hell and with it will be branded on their foreheads, their flanks and their backs, 'this is the treasure that you hoarded for yourselves. Now taste of what you used to hoard'" (verses 34-35). This is nothing other than hate speech designed to inspire hatred, distrust, and warfare against Jews, Christians, and anyone else who does not confess that Muhammad is the Prophet of God. This is a manifesto of unending holy war. The irony is that Muhammad condemns the "greed" of Jewish and Christian priests while planning to fill his own coffers with their gold. The gold would also be used by God as a branding iron to sear into their flesh the punishment for their rebellion in not confessing the Prophet of Islam. Here is the source book for the violent screeds of al-Qaida.

The end of this section deals with the holy months when fighting was prohibited. Muhammad forbade the type of intercalation used by the Arabs of the time to extend the period of peace. He concludes that this "transposing

---

[1410] Ibn Kathir, *Tafsir*, Vol. 4, p. 413.

is an addition to unbelief." Thus, "wrong not yourselves therein and fight the pagans" (verses 36-37). This unclear change in dating made the accurate dating of the Medinan history of the Prophet impossible as no one is quite sure when this ruling occurred and when it was put into effect. It also has the effect of removing legislation that encouraged periods of peace. He is calling for *jihad* 24/7, fifty-two weeks of the year. Muhammad goes on to chastise the Muslims for not being more enthusiastic for holy war. He asks, "Do you prefer the life of this world to the hereafter?" (verse 38). Thus, in a common parlance of the Muslim world today, a Muslim is someone who loves death more than the unbelievers love life. He declares, "If you march not forth, he will punish you with a painful torment" (verse 39). Then Muhammad turns autobiographical, using himself as an illustration at the time of *hijra*. "When the unbelievers made him leave: He had no more than one companion" (verse 40). Though alone, in essence, the Prophet triumphed because God was with him. So "March forth whether you are light or heavy, and strive hard with your wealth and your lives in the cause of Allah" (verse 41). Light or heavy are variously interpreted by Ibn Kathir as levels of armaments, age, strength, or numbers in the force. Muhammad is motivating his army to march. He derides those who delay in joining the *jihad* as those who "would destroy their own souls, for Allah doth know that they certainly are lying" (verse 42).

Section seven of the chapter deals again with the subject of the hypocrites who did not participate in the *jihad*. Allah apparently rebukes the Prophet for granting an exemption to some from the fighting. "Those who believe in Allah and the last day ask thee for no exemption from fighting . . . only those ask thee for exemption who believe not in Allah and the last day" (verses 44-45). Thus *jihad* becomes the test of whether one is a true Muslim or not. Here lies the foundation for the contempt that radical Muslims feel for nominal/moderate Muslims who are not engaged in the *jihad*. This is the foundation of the call of *takfir*! A Muslim who is not willing to die in *jihad* is not a Muslim. Ibn Kathir notes that this was a moderate rebuke of the Prophet prefaced with prior forgiveness for the wrong, "May Allah forgive you."[1411] Muhammad was never criticized by Allah for too much warfare, only for too little. Even this mistake on the part of the Prophet is controlled by God who by this insured that the hypocrites were not present "sowing sedition among you . . . indeed they had plotted sedition before, and upset matters for thee—until the truth arrived, and the decree of Allah became manifest" (verses

---

[1411] Ibn Kathir, *Tafsir*, Vol. 4, p. 437.

47-48). This becomes an opportunity to reflect on the absolute sovereignty of Allah whose decrees really establish everything. "Say, nothing will happen to us except what Allah has decreed for us." Despite this sovereignty, human behavior is still reprehensible. "The only reasons why their contributions are not accepted are: That they reject Allah and His Messenger; that they come to prayer without earnestness; and that they offer contributions unwillingly." The hypocrites are criticized also for being displeased with the "alms" (zakah) distributed to them (verses 51-59).

In the next section of the chapter, Muhammad defines what zakah or "alms" are for. Among the categories are "al-mu'allafatu qulubuhum" or "those who are given alms to embrace Islam."[1412] From the Hadith stories Ibn Kathir provided, it is clear that these "alms" are really war booty used to attract individuals and tribes to adopt Islam. Yusuf Ali ignores this use of bribery in conversion to Islam in his commentary. Jihadists are also mentioned by Ibn Kathir as receiving of the "charity." Other categories for zakah are better known to Westerners, such as the poor, sick, and for the freeing of slaves. In the next verse, Muhammad picks up on a phrase apparently circulating concerning the Prophet as "He is (all) ear," which was apparently sarcastic. Muhammad calls this "mockery" "molesting" the Prophet. Sarcasm as a disguised critique Muhammad regards as rebellion and he says, "Know they not that for those who oppose Allah and his Messenger is the fire of Hell?—wherein they shall dwell. That is the supreme disgrace" (verse 63). This leads Muhammad into an ongoing meditation on the fate of the hypocrites and the disbelievers. He says of the hypocrites, "You have rejected faith after you had accepted it . . . they have forgotten Allah; so He has forgotten them."

Ibn Kathir interprets their "rejecting faith" as their unwillingness to engage in the *jihad* of the Tabuk campaign.[1413] He then declares, "Allah has promised the hypocrites men and women, and the rejecters of faith, the fire of hell" (verses 67-68). He returns in one brief verse to an old homily from the Meccan period concerning "Noah, Ad and Thamud; the people of Abraham, the men of Midian and the cities overthrown" (verse 70). The example of their judgment is then contrasted with the believers who "obey Allah and His Messenger." These will receive "gardens under which rivers flow, to dwell therein, and beautiful mansions in gardens of everlasting bliss." (verses 71-72)

1412 Ibn Kathir, *Tafsir*, Vol. 4, p. 455.
1413 Ibn Kathir, *Tafsir*, Vol. 4, p. 463.

This homily continues in the next section which opens with, "O Prophet! Strive hard against the unbelievers and the hypocrites, and be firm against them. Their abode is hell . . ." They are condemned for claiming "they said nothing" when in fact they "blasphemed." The word Yusuf Ali translates as "blasphemed" is the word for "disbelief." Thus, disbelieving Muhammad's call to *jihad* is "blasphemy" (verses 73-74). This is a powerful argument for a radical to throw in the face of a moderate Muslim. To not believe in the necessity of violent *jihad* to establish the political hegemony of Islam over the world is "blasphemy." This is made the worse because "they did it after accepting Islam" and particularly "after he bestowed on them of His bounty," which would seem to be the largess of the war booty. Ibn Kathir explains that after these gifts were given the hypocrites were "stingy" in the giving of gifts of alms, contributing to the Islamic war treasury.

Muhammad declares war on these false Muslims, "Strive hard against the disbelievers and the hypocrites . . . their abode is hell" (verse 73) This is the foundation of "takfir," the declaring of a Muslim to be a non-Muslim, which makes them legitimate targets for *jihad*. Chapter nine has thirty references to "not believing" (kafara) and "unbelief" (Kufr) or "unbelievers" (kafir, kafirun, kuffar, kawafir), and most of these references are to those who called themselves Muslims.[1414] Confession of faith is to join the Islamic army with total fealty to the Prophet or his emissary as military leader. This is why the confession of faith is so short and to the point. It is an oath of allegiance to the Islamic army. Prayer gatherings in the mosque are essentially the muster ground for the army, which is why the lines are straight, exclusively male and there are no seating materials to hinder the army from marching out of the mosque to battle. Almsgiving is directly involved in the financing and rewards for military campaigns. When the Holy Land Foundation "charity" in the United States provides financing to Hamas for suicide bombers (which they would call freedom fighters) they are being fully obedient to the "sunnah" or practices of the Prophet as clearly enunciated in the Qur'an itself. It is

---

[1414] Chapter nine of the Qur'an including the following verses: (kafara): Verses 3, 26, 30, 37, 40, 54, 66, 74, 80, 84, 90, (kufr): Verses 12, 17, 23, 37, 74, 97, 107, and (kafir, kafirun, kuffar, kawafir): Verses 2, 26, 32, 37, 49, 55, 68, 73, 85, 120, 123, 125. This is the foundation to declaring Muslims to be non-Muslims (takfir), and the attitude towards such is abject hatred. Anyone truly believing this would feel fully justified in Pakistan to go into an Ahmadiyya or Shia mosque and begin shooting people or even blow themselves up as happens on a regular basis.

interesting to note that a "moderate" like Yusuf Ali makes fewer and fewer comments in this chapter, and what comments he makes are increasingly obscure and generalizing as if this were merely a homily on the hypocrisy of not giving "alms."[1415] A Muslim unwilling to contribute to a *jihad* is worthy to be attacked.

A Muslim suicide bomber named Punjabi Talib whose vest failed to detonate was interviewed in Pakistan after his capture and questioned as to why he would blow himself up in the midst of fellow Muslims. This is the excerpt of that interview:

> "S: In suicide bombing innocent Muslims and even those who hate America are killed; therefore, are you not killing those for whom you are fighting?
>
> P: No. Those who are not taking part in jihad are not innocent. Only those are innocent who are taking part in the jihad in Miranshah etc.
>
> S: Is there no one innocent in the entire Pakistan?
>
> P: No. We have no repentance, no sorrow for killing. If our leader orders us to kill two people and hundreds are killed in this process even then we will do so."[1416]

The point here is that anyone not taking part in the *jihad* is not a true Muslim and is, therefore, worthy to be killed. The foundation for this belief is in the Qur'an itself.

Ibn Kathir uses the background of the campaign of Tabuk as the rationale for the Qur'anic statements, and he even includes a long story about a supposed plot to assassinate the Prophet that lies behind certain verses.[1417] In the context of a military campaign, financing of warfare, strategies, plots and counterplots, assassinations and murder, and threatening those unwilling to fight become the name of the game. How is Osama bin Laden disobedient to this vision of Islam? Muhammad concludes that those who have lied and showed hypocrisy in the matter of this military campaign can never be forgiven; "Whether thou ask for their forgiveness, or not: If thou

---

[1415] Ali, Yusuf, pp. 462-463.

[1416] Interview with a suicide bomber. "JIRGA; http://www.youtube.com/watch?v=w8gu5Xfi_E4.

[1417] Ibn Kathir, *Tafsir*, Vol. 4, pp. 476-480.

ask seventy times for their forgiveness, Allah will not forgive them: because they have rejected Allah and his Messenger" (verse 80). This is in reference to people who call themselves Muslims! This level of vituperation can only be explained in the context of a military campaign. In modern parlance, these soldiers have gone AWOL in time of war in their disobedience to the Prophet. This is why male apostates from Islam are executed according to all books of Islamic law. A Muslim male who converts to another religion deserts the Muslim army in time of war. That war is conceived of as perpetual, so the punishment of death on apostates is also perpetual.[1418] Frankly, this goes far beyond those who convert to other religions. Any able-bodied Muslim not willing to take part in *jihad* is essentially an apostate and worthy to be put to death.

The next section goes on to explain the deeds of the hypocrites in clearer terms. "Those who were left behind (in the Tabuk expedition), rejoiced in their inaction behind the back of the Messenger of Allah: They hated to strive and fight, with their goods and their persons in the cause of Allah. They say, 'Go not forth in the heat'. Say, 'the fire of hell is fiercer in heat'" (verse 81). Yusuf Ali and others claim that there was a great Roman army preparing invasion of Arabia and that this campaign was thus defensive.[1419] The campaign may have been made to avenge an earlier defeat at the hands of Roman provincial officers after the Muslims attacked them at Muta. As we see today, an attack by the Muslims that draws a defensive response from non-Muslims in battle is considered an "attack" against which the Muslims are defending themselves![1420] This conception is axiomatic in Muslim dealings with the media in the west. The West is always at fault, no matter how outrageous Islamist terrorist attacks. No matter who attacks first, whether Saddam Hussein in Kuwait, or Osama bin Laden in New York, the Western response is considered "The U.S. killing Muslims." When Faisal Shahzad tries to set off a bomb in Times Square, exclusively to kill civilians and children, his argument is "The drones don't know if they kill

---

[1418] Women, since they are not members of the army, are not executed for apostasy in Islamic law. They are to be imprisoned for life or until they repent and return to Islam.

[1419] Ali, Yusuf, p. 464, footnote 1335.

[1420] The unprovoked assault of five Muslim nations against Israel in 1948 is now presented as a catastrophe that is utterly the fault of the "racist" Jewish state. The media in the West has largely swallowed this line looking with great concern at 600,000 Palestinians who left Palestine in the conflict but ignoring 900,000 Jews who fled Muslim lands at the same time.

children."[1421] Thus, attacks on Muslim terrorists planning atrocities that kill civilians inadvertently are equivalent and justify deliberate attacks on purely civilian targets. This is the blame game that the Qur'an establishes. More attacks will take place even if Western powers do nothing. Their non-Islamic stance makes them a worthy target.

Allah raves on, "When a Surah comes down enjoining them to believe in Allah and to strive and fight along with His Messenger, those with wealth and influence among them ask thee for exemption, and say: 'Leave us: We would sit with those who sit'. They prefer to be with (the women)" (verses 86-87). He goes on to excoriate the "desert Arabs" who were "false to Allah and his Messenger" because they "sat inactive." He declares them directly to be "kufr" people of unbelief and this is the same word used for polytheists who are to be exterminated. He states that weak and infirm Muslims, or those without means to obtain weapons are free of guilt, but that the condemnation "is against such as claim exemption while they are rich." God seems to rave in the Prophet's ear, "they will present their excuses to you . . . say thou: 'Present no excuses: We shall not believe you . . . They will swear to you by Allah, when ye return to them, that ye may leave them alone. So leave them alone: For they are an abomination, and Hell is their dwelling place—a fitting recompense for the (evil) that they did" (verses 91-95). Here Yusuf Ali mistranslates the Qur'an. "Leave them alone," would normally be interpreted by English speakers as indicating that these unbelievers should be left by themselves in peace. In actual fact, the verse really means total ostracism from the community with the clear possibility of a death sentence; one "turns away from them" in total rejection.

Ibn Kathir makes this clear when describing the condition of those so rejected by the community until they repented, and even then were made to wait for a pardon from God and his Prophet.[1422] There is clearly no place for conscientious objection in the worldview of Muhammad or of his God. This raving ends with, "The Arabs of the desert are the worst in unbelief and hypocrisy, and the most fitted to be in ignorance." Yet he seems to regain his composure stating, "But some of the desert Arabs believe in Allah and the last day and look on their payments as pious gifts bringing them nearer to Allah" (verse 99). Virtually all the verses here are interpreted by Ibn Kathir in terms of various rules of *jihad* and forms of condemnation for the hypocrites

---

[1421] ABC news quotations from Shahzad's admission of guilt in a New York courtroom, June 21, 2010.

[1422] Ibn Kathir, *Tafsir*, Vol. 4, pp. 512-513.

who did not take part in it.[1423] Against Ibn Kathir's Qur'an and Sunnah-based interpretation, Yusuf Ali makes no arguments. He simply tries to cover up the actual meaning. None of his footnotes on the references to *Zakah* ever refer to their purpose in supplying finances for *jihad*.

The next three sections of the book continue this ongoing comparison of the righteous believers who joined Muhammad in the *jihad*, and the unrighteous hypocrites who did not. "The Vanguard" of Islam, the Prophet states, are the immigrants from Mecca and the Ansar who supported them. They were the first to join the war. They will receive "gardens under which rivers flow" (verse 100). Muhammad then states in contrast, "the desert arabs . . . are hypocrites . . . obstinate in hypocrisy" and "we shall punish them." Some have admitted their fault and so Allah advises the Prophet, "Of their goods take alms, that so thou mightest purify and sanctify them . . . know they not that Allah doth accept repentance from his votaries and receives their gifts of charity" (verses 101-103). It seems that Allah's wrath can be bought off with charity bribes that finance the next military campaign.

Muhammad goes on to discuss a rival mosque in Medina. He states that those who wait on the judgment of God are not like those who spread disunity in the mosque "in preparation for the one who warred against Allah." The latter who do so stand on a crumbling sand precipice which will "crumble to pieces with him into the fire of hell." Those with such hearts will have their hearts "cut to pieces" (verses 107-110). Ibn Kathir associates these verses with the story of a rival mosque established in Mecca that questioned the authority of Muhammad and was later destroyed. The story goes that a Christian Arab in Medina rejected the Prophet and was behind the establishment of the rival mosque. This may be a pious legend meant to discredit Christians, but it could also be an example of the religious ferment going on in Medina, where various groupings were struggling for and against the Prophet even at this late date.[1424] Muhammad continues this comparison in the next section by likening his revelation to the Jewish law and the Gospel as a calling for war. "Allah has purchased of the believers their persons and their goods; for theirs is the garden: They fight in His cause, and slay and are slain: A promise binding on Him in truth, through the law, the Gospel, and the Qur'an: And who is more faithful to his covenant than Allah?" (verses 107-111). Muhammad seems to think that the great similarity between his message and the previous holy books is their emphasis on *jihad*.

[1423] Ibn Kathir, *Tafsir,* Vol. 4, pp. 492-501.

[1424] Ibn Kathir, *Tafsir*, Vol. 4, pp. 514-516.

In verse 113 Muhammad again declares that there should be no prayer of forgiveness for pagans, again revoking an earlier verse of the Qur'an during the Meccan period. His rationale is that they are irredeemable "companions of the fire" whom even Abraham disassociated himself from, including his own father. The passage seems to indicate that some of the Muhajirs who emigrated from Mecca and some of the Ansar were swayed away from their commitment to *jihad*. Three individuals are mentioned, though not named, as being particularly complicit. These are offered forgiveness by Allah once they had perceived that "there is no fleeing from Allah." Both Ibn Kathir and Yusuf Ali associate this repentance with Ka'b, Marar, and Hilal, three well-known Muslims. These three were disciplined by total ostracism of the Muslim community for fifty days, even their wives being forbidden to lay with them.[1425] They were considered no longer Muslims, and therefore, their wives became no longer their wives.[1426] Their repentance was considered exemplary as they remained faithful throughout their period of ostracism. This story may also be a pious legend seeking to explain the Qur'an at this very ambiguous point. Yet it illustrates in the combination of Qur'anic text and tafsir commentary what the ideal Islamic society should look like. Everyone functions as police, and values such as *jihad* should be strictly enforced. It reminds one of a totalitarian state where individual freedoms are completely subjugated to the purposes of the dictator. To not take part in *jihad* is akin to apostasy. Muhammad concludes this section stating, "It was not fitting for the people of Madinah and the Bedouin Arabs of the neighborhood, to refuse to follow Allah's Messenger, nor to prefer their own lives to his: Because nothing could they suffer or do but was reckoned to their credit" (verse 120). *Jihad* has an automatic reward, whether of booty taken in victory or Allah's pleasure and heavenly rewards in defeat or death.

In the final section Muhammad commands: "O ye who believe! Fight the unbelievers who gird you about." Ibn Kathir's tafsir translation is probably more accurate as fighting the "nearby" unbelievers. His tafsir explains this as the nearby Romans who were the target of the Prophet's Tabuk campaign. Once the pagans had been subdued in Arabia, Muhammad was setting his

---

[1425] Ibn Kathir, *Tafsir*, Vol. 4, pp. 530-538, and Yusuf Ali, p. 473.

[1426] In Islam, a Muslim woman must under no circumstances whatsoever be married to a non-Muslim man. Many Western women who convert to Islam do not realize that if their husbands do not also convert, Islam requires them to divorce their non-Muslim husbands. I have met women in the United States heavily pressured by the Muslim community to divorce their husbands for this very reason. Some have left Islam as a result.

troops in the direction of new conquests. Ibn Kathir explains this saying as follows:

> "The Messenger of Allah started fighting the Idolators in the Arabian peninsula . . . When he finished with them . . . he then started fighting the People of the Scriptures. He began preparations to fight the Romans who were the closest in area to the Arabian peninsula, and as such, had the most right to be called to Islam, especially since they were from the People of the Scriptures."[1427]

Far from showing respect for other monotheistic religions, Muhammad felt a particular burden to attack them because they, in his view, had been prepared for his message by the predictions about him, which he supposed to be in their scriptures. To refuse his call to Islam was tantamount to a declaration of war. Muhammad also condemns the hypocrites as "those in whose hearts is a disease" who "are tried every year once or twice" yet "turn aside." Yet even if they turn away, Muhammad says, "Allah sufficeth me" (verse 129). Thus ends Muhammad's declaration of war on the non-Muslim world, and on those of his followers who would shrink back from his pathway of violent *jihad*.

Muhammad's Final Rejection of the Jews and the Christians

Chapter 5 is considered by many Muslims to be the final chapter of the Qur'an. Ibn Kathir believes chapter 9 is the final chapter.[1428] The exact order does not matter as the attitudes expressed are virtually the same. In many ways the chapter is an address to the Jewish and Christian communities. It resembles chapter 2 in this regard, though the Christians are now as equally prominent in the Prophet's address as the Jews. Numerous apocryphal stories are told in a final attempt to show that true Christians and Jews would be followers of the Prophet of Islam. It also contains a set of laws concerning foods, ritual purity, and religious practices. It functions very well as a summary of Muhammad's views of the People of the Book that has come to be axiomatic of Muslim treatment of non-Muslim religious minorities to the present day. This chapter details Islam in its final form

---

[1427] Ibn Kathir, *Tafsir*, Vol. 4, p. 546.
[1428] Ibn Kathir, *Tafsir*, Vol. 4, p. 369.

with regard to the Prophet's relations with the People of the Book and his interpretation of their identity.

Chapter 5 opens with rules concerning foods that are permissible and those that are forbidden. This includes injunction about hunting during the time of pilgrimage. "Dead meat, blood and the flesh of swine" and any meat slaughtered in other than in the name of Allah are forbidden. Rules are also stated forbidding the use of certain forms of divination (with arrows). In the midst of these rules the Qur'an exclaims, "This day have I perfected your religion for you, completed my favour upon you, and chosen for you Islam as your religion" (verse 3). As we noted in the previous chapter, it is only at the very end of the Qur'an that Muhammad fully comprehends that he has established a new religion and that this religion is called "Islam" for "submission" which word was originally merely an attitude descriptor. He states that the food of "the People of the Book" is lawful for Muslims and that it is also lawful to take Christian women as wives. They follow rules regarding ritual cleansing before prayer or "wudu." Particular attention is paid to those ritually unclean through sexual activity or the call of nature. The use of sand in place of water is enjoined where necessary. The Prophet concludes this legal section with a call to obedience to Allah, justice and "deeds of righteousness." Those who reject the faith "will be companions of hell-fire" (verse 11).

In the next section Muhammad begins to address the Jews and the Christians. He describes the twelve captains (tribes?) of Israel as establishing regular prayers, charity, and "loans" to Allah as if they were Muslims. But they breach their covenant and "change the words from their places and forget a good part of the message that was sent them." Allah curses them. Thus they are "ever bent on deceits," but Allah commands to "forgive them" as well, all in the same verse (verse 14). The verse is chaotic and self-contradictory. Ibn Kathir maintains that some Muslims consider this verse to forgive the Jews abrogated (*naskh*).[1429] This explains why he considers chapter 9 to be the final chapter of the Qur'an. Similarly the "Christians" also "forgot a good part of the message that was sent to them" (verse 15). Thus Muhammad recasts himself as the restorer of these abandoned parts of the revelation; "O People of the Book! There hath come to you our Messenger, revealing to you much that ye used to hide in the Book and passing over much (that is now unnecessary)" (verse 16).

[1429] Ibn Kathir, *Tafsir*, Vol. 3, p. 129.

Yusuf Ali interprets this as the charge that Jesus gave his disciples to welcome the new Prophet Ahmad and uses Ibn Ishaq's John 15:26 as the "glimpse" of this in the Bible. By contrast, Muhammad calls his book "light and a plain book" that is the new revelation of God that guides easily to the "straight" pathway. He goes on to condemn the Christians for "blasphemy" in saying that "Allah is Christ, the son of Mary" (verse 19). God has the power "to destroy Christ" he says. Ibn Kathir responds to this "blasphemy" by stating "This refutes the Christian creed, may Allah's continued curses be upon them until the day of resurrection."[1430] Then lumping the Jews and Christians together he says, "the Jews and the Christians say: 'we are sons of Allah, and His beloved'" to which Muhammad replies, "why then doth he punish you for your sins?" Even the title of "Sons of God" is seen as blasphemous. Perhaps Muhammad felt that his conquest of the Jews and anticipated conquest of the Christians was the demonstration of the superiority of his system, and the fact that they were in sin and thus were punished by God for their blasphemies? This is an argument which Muslims have used against Christians for centuries; why would God allow the Christians to be conquered by the Muslims if they were the true followers of God? Muhammad invites the "People of the Book" to take faith in "our Messenger after the break in our Messengers," i.e., Muhammad is now the new messenger after Christ and their false creeds are now superceded (verses 14-19).

Muhammad then speaks of Moses who called his people to enter into the promised land. He briefly tells the story of the two spies (unnamed) who wished to enter the promised land while the rest of the nation was "rebellious" and wandered "for forty years." Ibn Kathir opines that this is due to their refusal to engage in *jihad*.[1431] Those who refuse to engage in *jihad* are called the "losers," and loss in the task of warfare seems to be the Prophet's litmus test of whether one is a true Muslim or not. Ibn Kathir goes on to describe the Jews as being hated of Allah for their refusal of *jihad*, and he concludes "May Allah curse their faces that were transformed to the shape of swine and apes, and may Allah's curse accompany them to the raging fire."[1432]

Muhammad then tells the story of the two sons of Adam (also unnamed) where one presented an acceptable offering and the other did not. The righteous son did not resist the wicked as he was being murdered but declared that the place of his brother would be "among the companions

---

[1430] Ibn Kathir, *Tafsir*, Vol. 3, p. 134.
[1431] Ibn Kathir, *Tafsir*, Vol. 3, p. 143.
[1432] Ibn Kathir, *Tafsir*, Vol. 3, p. 149.

of the fire." Allah sends a raven to scratch the surface of the ground to cover the body of Abel. Yusuf Ali interprets this to mean "cover the shame of his brother" (verses 30-34). Ibn Kathir interprets it to mean that one raven covered the body of another raven and this showed Cain what to do in covering the body of his brother.[1433] The story is derived from the Babylonian Talmud in the Midrash of Pirke Rabbi Eleazer. Verse 32 is often cited by moderate Muslims as the message of the Qur'an stemming from the murder of the righteous brother, namely; "On that account: We ordained for the Children of Israel that if anyone slew a person—unless it be for murder or for spreading mischief in the land—it would be as if he slew the whole people: And if anyone saved a life, it would be as if he saved the life of the whole people." This also is a Talmudic reference from the same story.[1434] The passage is referring to the ill-treatment of "Messengers" and it concludes, "Then although there came to them our Messengers with clear signs, yet, even after that, many of them continued to commit excesses in the Land." Thus this passage refers to those whom the Qur'an considers righteous. Yusuf Ali puts it this way, "To kill or to seek to kill an individual because he represents an ideal is to kill all who uphold the ideal."[1435] The key concept is killing "without justification." Ibn Kathir puts it this way, "He who allows himself to shed the blood of a Muslim is like he who allows shedding the blood of all people."[1436]

This verse really only affirms the tolerance of Muslims toward other Muslims. Those who resist the message of the Messenger may be duly slaughtered as the next verse affirms; "The punishment of those who wage war against Allah and his Messenger, and strive with might and main for mischief through the land is: Execution, or crucifixion, or the cutting off of hands and feet from opposite sides, or exile from the land" (verse 33). In other words, a non-Muslim who resists the political hegemony of Islam may be duly executed, crucified, mutilated, or driven out of the country. To resist the hegemony of Islam is, in the Qur'an's view, to wage war against Allah and his Messenger.[1437] This is hardly a verse that shows the Qur'an's high view of the value of human life, only the value of Muslim human life.

[1433] Ibn Kathir, *Tafsir*, Vol. 3, p. 155-156.
[1434] This is found in the Mishnah Sanhedrin. In that text it is the killing of an Israelite that is equated with killing all of Israel.
[1435] Ali, Yusuf, p. 257.
[1436] Ibn Kathir, *Tafsir*, Vol. 3, p. 159.
[1437] Ibn Kathir, *Tafsir*, Vol. 3, p. 161.

It is to be admitted that Muslims who commit "mischief" may be punished in a similar way if they kill Muslims or refuse to take part in *jihad*.

Ibn Kathir tells the story of some men of the tribe of Ukl, who after killing some fellow Muslims were captured, had their eyes burned out with heated iron, their hands and feet chopped off, and were left to bleed and dehydrate to death in the desert sun.[1438] Yusuf Ali does not give the explanatory Hadith background to this verse. Astonishingly, he tries to present the Qur'an as advanced at this point, and contradicting the Hadith, he states that "Piercing the eyes" and "exposure to the tropical sun" was forbidden even though the Hadith teach clearly both of these practices. Apparently crucifixion is a humane practice, since it is advocated in the Qur'an. All of this is of little comfort to non-Muslims who could be treated in a similar fashion simply for defending their homes against a Muslim attack. This seems to be a major problem throughout the Qur'an. The occasional verses that seem to advocate tolerance or human rights of some sort seem always to be surrounded by contexts that negate their meaning. In this case the context is downright gruesome in its advocacy of vicious torture.[1439] One may also add that Muslims unwilling to engage in *jihad* are also guilty of a "crime" worthy of ostracism and death.

The next section of the Qur'an is a brief meditation on the value of *jihad* and the condemnation of the unbelievers (who are Muslims) that refuse to engage in it. Allah commands the believers to strive (*jihad*) with their physical power and goods that they "may prosper." Unbelievers cannot be redeemed even if they give twice the value of the earth. They may wish to "get out of the fire, but never will they get out therefrom" (verses 35-36). Ibn Kathir adds numerous gruesome stories of the torments of hell to enlighten this perspective.[1440] Yusuf Ali simply ignores the passage. There is no foundation here for "moderate" Islam so the moderate Muslim is reduced to silence. Perhaps this explains the silence of moderate Islam in the Middle East today. Moderate Islam is just simply not Islam.

[1438] Ibn Kathir, *Tafsir*, Vol. 3, p. 162. The story is also told in most of the canonical Hadiths.

[1439] This reminds me of the Jewish young man who was kidnapped in France and gradually tortured to death over a period of several weeks while his kidnappers attempted to extort money from his family using numerous citations from the Qur'an over the phone as justification for their actions.

[1440] Ibn Kathir, *Tafsir*, Vol. 3, p. 171.

Thieves, whether male or female, shall have their hands cut off. Ibn Kathir explains the minimum amount of theft to require cutting off the hand as being a quarter dirhem. He states, "This meager amount was set as the limit for cutting the hand, so that the people would refrain from theft" and states that this is a "wise decision."[1441] Ever ready to make the Qur'an seem superior, Yusuf Ali states that "petty thefts were exempt from this punishment" which is clearly not what the Hadith teach, and then cites Jesus apparently as an advocate of such punishments because of Matthew 27:38![1442] It is clear that the moderate Muslim interpreter of the Qur'an simply has to lie in order to twist the text to make it seem like something other than what it is. When the verse is beyond twisting, as we noted earlier, they simply ignore it perhaps hoping it will go away.

The section ends with Allah reflecting on the behavior of the wicked unbelievers, their hypocrisy, and lies. Exemplary amongst them are "the Jews—men who will listen to any lie" . . . and "change the words from their times and places" (verse 44). Ibn Kathir says that the context of this verse concerned the Jews hiding the ruling in the Taurat concerning the stoning of adulterers.[1443] For the Jews there would be "a heavy punishment." He remarks that some Jews come to him "for decision, when they have law before them." He concludes, "They are not people of faith" (verse 46). This is the only reference I can find in the Qur'an to Jews coming to the Prophet for his adjudication. It would seem that he expects them to adjudicate themselves within their own community and that he is irritated that they are still not converting to Islam.

What to do with those who are forced to confess the hegemony of Islam but continue to cling to their own beliefs? They are allowed to exist in communities isolated from the Muslims and clearly despised by them in imitation of the Prophet's own hatred of anyone not confessing his Prophethood. This is the origin of the "dhimma" concept. The non-Muslims from recognized religions are allowed to exist as a subjugated community under special taxation and various other rules to demonstrate their "humiliation." Islam at this point has become religious apartheid, the separate and unequal treatment of people depending upon their religious beliefs. As bad as the Qur'an is in its condemnation of Jews, the tafsir literature is

---

[1441] Ibn Kathir, *Tafsir*, Vol. 3, p. 174.
[1442] Ali, Yusuf, p. 254, footnote 742.
[1443] Ibn Kathir, *Tafsir*, Vol. 3, p. 180.

even worse with endless tales of the infidelity, dishonesty, wicked intent, rebelliousness, trickery, lustfulness, etc . . . A typical heading in Ibn Kathir reads, "Chastising the Jews for Their Evil Lusts and Desires, While Praising the Tawrah."[1444] It is interesting to note that while the Jews are considered the epitomy of evil, their Torah is still respected as God's Word. The next verse states, "Verily, we did send down the Tawrah: Therein was guidance and light" (verse 47). He claims that the Jews were entrusted "the protection of Allah's book" and the implication is that they did so, for, "whosoever does not judge by what Allah has revealed, such are the disbelievers." Thus not judging by the Torah is tantamount to disbelief. It is interesting that almost all later Islamic apologetics emphasize the corruption and abrogation of the previous scriptures. Yusuf Ali states, "the taurat mentioned in the Qur'an is not the Old Testament: nor is it even the Pentateuch."[1445] This does not seem to be the attitude of Muhammad or the Qur'an. This argues for the relative age and reliability of the transmitted Qur'anic text. He goes on to affirm, "We ordained therein for them, 'Life for life, eye for eye, nose for nose, ear for ear, tooth for tooth" (verse 48). This affirms the Jewish injunctions of Exodus 21:23-25 in the law of lex talionis.

Muhammad then turns to the story of Jesus. As in the case of Moses and Adam, his main point seems to be that he and his Qur'an are now the fulfillment of these earlier revelations. Jesus was sent "confirming the law

---

[1444]   Ibn Kathir, *Tafsir*, Vol. 3, p. 183.

[1445]   Ali, Yusuf, p. 257, footnote 753. Yusuf Ali seems happy to cite Western critical scholars with regard to the Bible to support his assertion stating that the Taurat is embedded in "semi-historical and legendary narrative." This is not the Qur'anic attitude at all and Yusuf Ali is not willing to subject the Qur'an to the same critical scrutiny. Whereas the Old Testament stands up very well to the archeological findings and linguistic usages that are contemporaneous with the time frame of the Bible, the Qur'an is full of anachronisms and linguistic anomalies from an archeological perspective. One simple example will suffice as a comparison. The Bible states that "Haman" was the prime minister in Persia in the fifth century BCE. The Qur'an states that he was the prime minister to Pharaoh in the time of Moses 1200-1400 BCE. It should be fairly easy to compare linguistically if the name Haman is typical for one or the other place and time period. A. R. Millard in his article on "Persian Names in Esther . . . " concludes: "Finding several names in Hebrew letters reflecting Persian ones so closely rules out any likelihood of corruption accidentally reaching a true form. That they occur whether the LXX is close to the MT (as for Hammedatha), or very different, suggests the MT has the superiority. Thus we conclude the Hebrew text of Esther can be trusted to give non-Hebrew names accurately." *Journal of Biblical Literature*, Vol. 96, 1977, p. 485.

that had come before him." Jesus was sent the scripture "confirming the scripture that came before it, and guarding it in safety: So judge between them by what Allah hath revealed" (verses 49-50). In this sense the Bible is still considered to be authoritative and revealed by Allah. However, the Qur'an now functions as the confirmation of what was sent earlier, and it is now the arbiter between the Jewish and Christians scriptures as to what truth is. It is "muhayminan" or "trustworthy" over every other holy book.[1446] The strong implication is that Muhammad has now come as the Messenger confirming what was sent to Jesus. Muhammad is now reinterpreting the worldviews of Judaism and Christianity in terms of his own self-perception. The People of the Book must now follow him, if they are to be on the pathway of truth. He warns his followers not to be "beguiled" by the Jews and the Christians concerning anything "of that which Allah hath sent down to thee" (verse 49). The actual word according to Ibn Kathir is "turn you far away from some of what Allah has sent down to you."[1447] The passage is a strange mishmash of conflicting ideas. Yes, the Jewish and Christian scriptures are authoritative and come from God. Yes, Jews and Christians should judge their own communities by the law present in their holy books. Thus those books are still the unchanged Word of God according to Muhammad. Yet Muhammad has nothing to learn from Jews and Christians. Their knowledge will only lead true Muslims away from devotion to Allah and his Messenger. Thus he concludes at the start of the next section, "O ye who believe! Take not the Jews and the Christians for your friends and protectors" (verse 51). Isolation from the influence of Jews and Christians is essential to preserving the Muslim community from any undue questioning of the truths handed down by the Prophet. Allah wanted his people to stay away from the Jews who could show them where Muhammad's Qur'an came from and what was wrong with it. Having borrowed much from these traditions he must now close the door to further influence lest doubt result, for doubt is a "shaytan" (Satan).

Muhammad then begins to accuse the Jews and Christians of having "a disease" in their hearts. This disease is precisely doubt inspired by the warfare of the Prophet. "We do fear lest a change of fortune bring disaster. Ah! Perhaps Allah will give victory." These are the Words God puts in the mouths of the hypocrite Jews and Christians who are doubtful in the face of warfare. What is God's true intention? "Allah will produce a people whom He will love . . . mighty against the rejecters, fighting in the way of Allah" (verse

---

[1446] Ibn Kathir, *Tafsir*, Vol. 3, p. 196.

[1447] Ibn Kathir, *Tafsir*, Vol. 3, p. 195.

57). It would seem that the Christians and the Jews were primarily doubtful about the concept of violent *jihad* and coercive violence in spreading the new message. The new community of believers would love God and establish the kingdom of God on earth by means of coercive violence. The only ones the true Muslim can trust are "Allah, His Messenger, and the believers" who engage in *jihad* (verse 55).

The next section begins with the same admonition as the previous. "O ye who believe! Take not for friends and protectors those who take your religion for mockery or sport—whether among those who received the scripture before you or among those who reject the faith" (verse 60). Ibn Kathir explains, "Allah forbids his believing servants from having Jews and Chrsitians as friends because they are the enemies of Islam and its people, may Allah curse them."[1448] Yusuf Ali, the moderate Muslim, does not spout curses like Ibn Kathir, but agrees with these isolating sentiments, for one who associates with these people "must be counted as of them."[1449] This is not a particularly "moderate" sentiment. Muhammad's threat is that anyone who befriends them will become part of them. He emphasizes, these are the ones who are "the losers." He then addresses the Jews and Christians, "Say: O People of the Book! Do ye disapprove of us for no other reason than that we believe in Allah and the revelation that hath come to us and that which came before, and that most of you are rebellious and disobedient?" (verse 62). The Jews and Christians are not allowed to respond to this convoluted rhetorical question, which both presupposes the disobedience of the People of the Book and mixes up scriptures they do accept with scriptures that they do not. It is pure circular reasoning, the assumptions justify the conclusions.

What is Muhammad's word to these "disobedient" People of the Book? "Shall I point out to you something much worse? . . . Those who incurred the curse of Allah and His wrath, those of whom some he transformed into apes and swine" (verse 63). He cannot develop a logical argument to justify his own claim to be a Prophet of God other than the threat of hell and the punishment of transformation into apes and swine. It should not be surprising that a God who enjoins the crucifixion and mutilation of people who resist his "Messenger" would also delight in engaging in mutilation himself. This also explains why Muslims, when given the opportunity, seem to enjoy mutilating the bodies of Americans they have killed. Thus Ibn Kathir rages in his subtitle, "The People of the Scriptures Deserve the Worst Torment on the

---

[1448] Ibn Kathir, *Tafsir*, Vol. 3, p. 204.
[1449] Ali, Yusuf, p. 259, footnote 764.

Day of Resurrection."[1450] He then goes on with various accusations against the Jews and Christians. They say "we believe" but they lie. They are "racing each other in sin and transgression." They eat things forbidden. They utter sinful words. The Jews claim that God's hand is tied. "The Jews are indeed miserly, envious, cowards, and tremendously humiliated" opines Ibn Kathir regarding this phrase.[1451] They are in "obstinant rebellion and blasphemy." Their hearts are full of enmity and hatred for each other. The Jews "kindle the fire of war." An odd projective accusation, since Muhammad has declared war himself on anyone who refuses to confess his role as the new Prophet. "They strive to do mischief on earth." (verses 61-64). Yusuf Ali tries to mollify this picture by pointing out how Jesus sent demons into pigs! He opines that perhaps this should be interpreted allegorically.[1452] There is no indication in literary form of this being intended as an allegory.

Muhammad concludes by appealing rhetorically to them, "If only the People of the Book had believed and been righteous, we should indeed have blotted out their iniquities and admitted them to gardens of bliss. If only they had stood fast by the law, the Gospel, and all the revelation that was sent to them from their Lord, they would have enjoyed happiness on every side" (verses 65-66). Muhammad's self-conception here is complete. True Jews and Christians would have recognized his book as the completion of their revelations. Then they would have joined his community and the worldwide *jihad* and been admitted to the "gardens of bliss." Notice that the Qur'an here continues to affirm that the law and the Gospel are God's Word, albeit a word Muhammad still thinks is the same as his Qur'an. Those Jews and Christians who continue to resist conversion to the one and only true religion, the true Judaism and Christianity which Islam is, must now be subjugated by that same *jihad*.

In the two following sections Muhammad continues his address to the Jews and Christians, condemning them for their lack of faith in him and illustrating their iniquity from theological beliefs they hold which Muhammad regards as anathema. He defines what it means to be a true Jew or Christian. Repeating the earlier "O People of the Book!" he contends that faith in "the law, the Gospel, and all the revelation that has come to you" (meaning the Qur'an) is necessary and those who reject it are "people without faith" (verse 68). He reiterates in the next verse, "those who believe" (a constantly

---

[1450] Ibn Kathir, *Tafsir*, Vol. 3, p. 215.

[1451] Ibn Kathir, *Tafsir*, Vol. 3, p. 222.

[1452] Ali, Yusuf, p. 262, footnote 770.

recurring phrase that means those who believe in the Qur'an) are the ones in whom there "shall be no fear." This verse is often cited by multiculturalists as a great verse of tolerance declaring that Jews, Sabians, and Christians will have hope in the next life. But the key proviso is that such people must also accept the Qur'an in order to avoid judgment. Ibn Kathir makes this clear in his subtitle for the verse, "*There is no Salvation Except through Faith in the Qur'an.*"[1453] Yusuf Ali is a bit more circumspect but his commentary makes it clear that in order to be a truly righteous follower of Allah, of any religion, one must accept the Prophethood of Muhammad. Belief in Muhammad is thus "an essential test of the genuineness of such belief."[1454] To be a genuine Christian you must believe that Muhammad is the Prophet of God. To be a genuine Jew you must believe that Muhammad is the Prophet of God. Moderate Muslims and radical Muslims are in complete agreement on this point. The next two verses speak of how Allah sent messengers to the Jews, some of whom they rejected and others they "slay." The clear implication of the text is that Muhammad is a part of that train of Prophets that the Jews must accept.

In verse 72, he attacks the Christian belief in Jesus as the Son of God. "They blaspheme who say: 'Allah is Christ the son of Mary.' But said Christ: 'O Children of Israel! Worship Allah, my Lord and your Lord.' Whoever joins other gods with Allah—Allah will forbid him the garden, and the fire will be his abode . . . They do blaspheme who say: Allah is one of three in a trinity: For there is no god except one God . . . Christ, the son of Mary was no more than a Messenger . . . His mother was a woman of truth. They had both to eat their food . . ." (verses 75-78) A more thoroughgoing denial of the basic beliefs of Christianity could not be formulated than this. Jesus himself is employed as a witness against such beliefs. The quote seems to be a vague reminiscence of John 20:17. The idea of trinity is completely rejected in favor of Tawhid, the absolute unity of God. Thus also denied is the idea of relationship within the nature of God. A God of no internal complexity is also a God beyond the possibility of relationship, either with himself or with humankind. Clearly Muhammad misunderstood the trinity, thinking that it referred to God, Jesus, and Mary. Nevertheless, tawhid would also forbid the more orthodox Christian belief. The humanness of Mary and Jesus in needing food is emphasized and may reflect certain debates about the nature of Christ that were evident in Christian communities at this time.

[1453] Ibn Kathir, *Tafsir*, Vol. 3, p. 231.
[1454] Ali, Yusuf, p. 271.

He declares, "O People of the Book! Exceed not in religion the bounds" (verse 77). His final thoughts can best be described as a sort of imprecatory psalm calling down the curses of Allah upon the Jews and speaking of the Christians as being perhaps a bit less evil. "Curses were pronounced on those among the Children of Israel who rejected the faith, by the tongue of David and of Jesus the son of Mary . . . in torment will they abide . . . strongest among men in enmity to the believers wilt thou find the Jews and pagans; and nearest among them in love to the believers wilt thou find those who say 'we are Christians'" (verses 78-82). This is another verse that secular multiculturalists will cite as exemplary of Islam's tolerance. Clearly it is not tolerant toward Jews and polytheists.

However, it is important to read the context and see what sort of Christians Muhammad is referring to. These are the Christians who "when they listen to the revelation received by the Messenger, thou wilt see their eyes overflowing with tears, for they recognize the truth: They pray: 'Our Lord! We believe; write us down among the witnesses'" (verse 83). Again, this tolerant verse really only refers to Christians who are converting to Islam because they see that Muhammad's new scripture is the new Word of God. Ibn Kathir explains the supposed background of a group of Abyssinian Christians who came as a delegation to the Prophet, and when they heard the recitation of the Qur'an, "They embraced Islam."[1455] Yusuf Ali is of the same opinion, "They are Muslims at heart whatever their label may be."[1456] Again, ultimately there is no difference in the view of the radical Muslim and the moderate Muslim at this point. Christians who refuse to confess Muhammad as the Prophet of God are to be militarily subjugated. Ibn Kathir also mentions that the Christians were easier to deal with because "fighting was prohibited by their creed."[1457] Radical Muslims seem to understand the difference between Christianity and Islam in a way that modern secular multiculturalists do not. Most of the issues of hypocrisy and double-mindedness that Muhammad rails against are the direct result of his policy of using coercive violence to establish the kingdom of God on earth. Muhammad concludes that those who belie or reject his signs "shall be companions of hell-fire."

The last five sections of chapter 5 may be divided into two parts. The first three are a collection of rules for the Muslim community. The last two seem to be a final address to the followers of Christ. He begins by criticizing

---

[1455] Ibn Kathir, *Tafsir*, Vol. 3, p. 245.
[1456] Ali, Yusuf, p. 268, footnote 789.
[1457] Ibn Kathir, *Tafsir*, Vol. 3. p. 246.

"deliberate oaths" and how one may escape their consequences. He forbids intoxicants, gambling, divination by arrows and consecrated "stones." Believers are called to "Obey Allah and obey the Messenger." He forbids the hunting of game in the sacred precincts of Mecca. Muhammad also forbids asking questions about unclear parts of his revelation. He opines, "Some people before you did ask such questions, and on that account lost their faith" (verses 102-103). If ever there were verses against critical thinking, it is these. Ibn Kathir goes on to describe those who asked such questions and "became disbelievers because of that."[1458] Muhammad's writings had already shown many areas of inconsistency and contradiction. This is meant to put the lid on anyone asking hard questions about the text. The Hadith include several stories about Muslims who abandoned Islam because of issues they had with the Qur'an. Yusuf Ali opines that one may "reverently" ask questions but never "beyond the bounds," which seems to indicate any question that might raise doubt in the believer.[1459]

The Prophet goes on to forbid various uses for camels that had a connection to idolatry. Ibn Kathir's lengthy explanations of these obscure names[1460] indicate that there was very little understanding of what they actually meant. This would indicate the genuineness of the text. One would hardly preserve such obscure things in an edited and revised Qur'an. Muhammad gives rules for hearing the final will and testament of Muslims who are dying. This would be necessary in the case of Muslims dying of wounds in battle far away from their homes. Various oaths are prescribed.

The final two sections of the chapter concern Allah's word to Jesus. He begins, "One day will Allah gather the Messengers together, and ask: 'What was the response ye received'" (verse 109). God then commands Jesus to "recount my favor to thee." God's boons on Jesus include being strengthened with the Holy Spirit, speaking in his infancy,[1461] receiving the law and the Gospel, and making clay birds which he breathed upon and they became living birds. This story is a direct borrowing from the gnostic "Infancy Gospel of

---

[1458]   Ibn Kathir, *Tafsir*, Vol. 3, p. 282.
[1459]   Ali, Yusuf, p. 274, footnote 807.
[1460]   These names are Bahirah, Saibah, Wasilah, and Ham, Vol. 3, p. 283.
[1461]   The stories of Jesus speaking at birth are found in the "Gospel of Nicodemus" and the "Infancy Gospel of Thomas." Both of these texts date from the fourth and fifth centuries. It is interesting to note that the "Infancy Gospel of Thomas" is available in an actual fifth century manuscript housed in California demonstrating that the stories preceeded the writing of the Qur'an and were borrowed into the Qur'an from Christian sources.

Thomas," an apocryphal Gospel of the second to fourth century. Jesus heals the blind and lepers and raises people from the dead. Jesus was protected from the Children of Israel, a seeming denial of the crucifixion.[1462] The disciples believe in Jesus and "bow to Allah as Muslims." Yusuf Ali points out that everyone who bows to Allah is a Muslim, whatever their outward religious label may be.[1463] The disciples then ask for a "table set" (Al-Maidah) which provides the name for the chapter. This seems to be an obscure reference to the Lord's supper, and the word itself is probably derived from old Ethiopic language. Jesus prays to Allah to provide this table as "a sign from thee; and provide for our sustenance" (verse 117). Allah concludes the chapter by asking Jesus, "Didst thou say unto men, 'Worship me and my mother as gods in derogation of Allah?'" (verse 119). The response of Jesus is predictable, "never could I say what I had no right." Jesus points out that he was taken up to heaven as a result of his confession to "worship Allah, my Lord and your Lord." For those who make such confession there are "gardens, with rivers flowing beneath" (verse 122).

So ends the Qur'an and Muhammad's revelation to mankind. In summary one can only say that this is a book which establishes Islam as the only true religion, and that this is a book where *jihad* against pagans, Jews and Christians is the method by which Muslims are tested as to their sincerity, and it is the method whereby Islam's political kingdom of God on earth is established. The pathway to Islamic radicalism will always go through deeper study of the Qur'an and the Sunna of the Prophet. The twenty-first century will be a century of blood as a result.

[1462] Ibn Kathir, *Tafsir*, Vol. 3, p. 298.
[1463] Ali, Yusuf, p. 284.

CHAPTER 13

THE HISTORICAL RELIABILITY
OF THE SOURCES

During the last twenty-five years, the study of the early history of Islam has been a lesson in stark contrasts. It would be hard to imagine a chasm in scholarship greater than the one that exists between those who believe that the Muslim documents are, with many reservations, sources of early Islamic history, as does this writer (with great reservations), and those who believe that those same documents are essentially useless. As an example of these two viewpoints consider the following quotes, first from one of the contemporary historians of early Islam, W. Montgomery Watt:

> "The Crone-Cook rejection of the Muslim sources for the early history of Islam thus appears to be contrary to sound historical methodology. When one further considers the vast amount of material involved—many thousands of interlocking items—it is incredible that some person or group about the eighth century could have invented all these details and got them universally accepted. It is also incredible that some one at that date should have been so sophisticated as to realize that invented material tends to be wholly consistent, and then to introduce discrepancies and corrections in order to put twentieth century investigators off the scent! Most incredible of all is that no traces have been left of the process of invention."[1464]

[1464] W. Montgomery Watt, *"The Reliability of Ibn-Ishaq's Sources,"* in *La Vie du Prophete Mahomet*, Strasbourg: Presses Universitaires de France, 1980, p. 39.

In contrast, Patricia Crone, of the above named school of thought, states:

> "For over a century the landscape of the Muslim past was thus exposed to a weathering so violent that its shapes were reduced to dust and rubble and deposited in secondary patterns, mixed with foreign debris and shifting with the wind . . . The religious tradition of Islam is thus a monument to the destruction rather than the preservation of the past."[1465]

These two mutually exclusive positions seem to be based upon opposing assumptions which, as one researcher noted, readily lend themselves to circular reasoning: The assumptions justify the documents and the documents prove the assumptions.[1466] It is the purpose of this final chapter to examine the arguments concerning the historical sources of early Islam. We shall attempt to show that the assumption which was foundational to this study, that the early documents are, with great reservations, historical, is accurate.

The Crone-Cook thesis grew out of a radically new perspective on the Qur'an and traditions of Islam put forward by John Wansbrough, a researcher in early Islamic studies at Oxford. Their thesis was that the Islamic "historical" documents are useless for the reconstructing of Islamic history. Wansbrough in his *Qur'anic Studies* rejected the concept of the unity of the Qur'an as the book of Muhammad and attempted to show through literary criticism and typology that the book was a composite produced by the early Muslim community over a period of at least a generation or more. This study was followed up with a second book, *The Sectarian Milieu*, which explained the rise of Islam out of a Judeo-Arab milieu that only later coalesced into the forms we understand as classical Islam. Implicit in these theories was a denial of the historicity of Muhammad, at least as

---

[1465] Crone, Patricia, *Slaves on Horses*, Cambridge: Cambridge University Press, 1980, pp. 6-7.

[1466] Herbert Berg, *The Development of Exegesis in Early Islam*, Curzon Press, 2000, pp. 49-50. Berg goes on to say, "Once one accepts the framework of one of these two groups, one's understanding of early Islamic texts and the conclusions one is able to draw from them seem to be predetermined" (p. 93).

presented in the early Muslim literature, as well as the entire structure of the early history of Islam.[1467]

With this foundation, Patricia Crone and Michael Cook set out to write a new history of Islam, not based on Muslim sources, but non-Muslim. Their assumption was that the Muslim sources were polemic and represented how the Muslim community of the second century AH had constructed history out of their own self-perception at that time. Their writings were in no sense a reflection of what had happened two centuries earlier. To reconstruct that history, contemporary non-Muslim sources, in their opinion, were the only good sources. The reconstruction which Crone and Cook wove out of non-Muslim sources has been largely rejected by Western scholarship, and completely by Muslim scholars. Nevertheless, there is much to be gained from the perspectives of Crone, Cook, and Wansbrough, even if their thesis is rejected. This chapter will look at the evidence that Crone, Cook, and Wansbrough brought to light in their radical reinterpretation of Islamic history. We will show the reasons why we have accepted, with many reservations, the picture of Muhammad and his development presented in the early Muslim sources. But we will also show, in the light of the Crone-Cook thesis, how Western scholarship is shying away from critical study of the life of the Prophet.

As noted in our introduction, in one sense this issue is irrelevant. From the point of view of Muslims, the historical traditions of early Islam are factual and explicitly accepted as the basis for their faith in the behavior, "sunna," of the Prophet. This behavior is normative for all Muslims. The outside observer must take these traditions at face value in order to understand Muslim belief and practice. This is not, however, an acceptable answer to skeptical Westerners. For that reason, in this chapter, we will delve into some of the issues relating to the historicity of these texts. We shall not attempt a comprehensive study in this regard; that would result in a massive volume in its own right. Our purpose in this chapter is to survey the kinds of problems and evidence that have been put forward in support of the two

---

[1467] Some writings in this genre go even further. Karl-Heinz Ohlig in the recent volume *The Hidden Origins of Islam* makes the radical statement, "Indeed, the Umayyad leaders and even the early Abbasids were Christians" (p. 10). A more radical reinterpretation of the history of early Islam could not be imagined. While I do not agree with these fantastic claims, the authors do a good job of illustrating how dishonest modern scholarship is in parroting the orthodox Islamic version of history. *The Hidden Origins of Islam*, Karl-Heinz Ohlig and Gerd-R. Puin, editors, New York: Prometheus Books, 2010.

opposing viewpoints mentioned above. On that basis we will state again the reasons for our assumptions that provide the basis for answering the primary questions of this book.

Problem 1: The Lack of Historical Documents

One of the most counterintuitive facts of early Islamic history is that we have few surviving documents from the first two centuries of Islam. The very earliest probably date at least a full century after the time of the Prophet, though an argument from silence, it is still remarkable that an empire that conquered much of the known world in a region both literate and having a climate that easily preserves documents, nevertheless has left us little by way of Qur'anic manuscripts. Hawting put it this way:

> "We have no biography of Muhammad, no commentary on the Qur'an, no law book, no collection of Hadiths, no history of early Islam, etc., which can be said to predate, in the forms in which we have it, the beginning of the third Islamic century."[1468]

Neither do we have any complete copies of the Qur'an which date any closer than about 250 years after the death of the Prophet. The earliest fragments and segments of it date no earlier than 150 years after the Islamic expansion.[1469] These fragmentary texts "attest to an arrangement of the texts different from the one we find in the definitive corpus." Thus, "not only the writing of the Qur'an, but also the organization of its contents, were not yet stabilized" more than a century after the death of the Prophet.[1470] This is astonishing given that Muslims had, within twenty years of the death of the Prophet, gained the financial and organizational means to make and preserve thousands of copies of their holy book. The question is why didn't they?

Crone and Cook, as well as John Wansbrough before them, argued that the earliest documents were not preserved because the documents never

---

[1468] G. R. Hawting, "John Wansbrough, Islam and Monotheism," in *Method and Theory in the Study of Religion*, Lisse: Swets & Zeitlinger, 2002, p. 29.

[1469] John Gilchrist, *The Qur'an*, South Africa: Mercsa, 1995, pp. 135-136.

[1470] Ohlig and Puin, editors, *The Hidden Origins of Islam*, New York: Prometheus Press, 2010, p. 194. The article by Premare further points out the variations in the early Qur'anic text that are preserved in the earliest Christian responses to the Qur'an by St. John of Damascus and the Monk of Beth Hale (pp. 194-197)

existed. The Qur'an as well as the historical traditions are essentially the invention of a later age written to justify Muslim rule through reading back into history. Ibn Rawandi[1471] expresses the theory:

> "Once the Arabs had acquired an empire, a coherent religion was required to hold that empire together and legitimize their rule. In a process that involved a massive backreading into history, and in conformity to the available Jewish and Christian models, this meant that they needed a revelation and a revealer (prophet) whose life could serve . . . as a model."[1472]

Thus early Muslim history is "a purely literary artifact." In an effort to explain the emergence of Islam, Crone and Cook developed a theory, based on non-Muslim sources that Islam emerged as a Jewish messianic movement. They termed this movement "Hagarism."[1473] Rawandi states: "Hagarism was a Jewish Messianic Movement intent on reestablishing Judaism in the promised land, with little Arabic about it apart from the language."[1474]

This explanation seems inadequate for several reasons. First of all, it is totally based on the polemic writings of non-Muslims hostile to Islam. It does not seem

---

[1471] The writer is an apostate from Islam who utilizes the pseudonym of a tenth century Muslim rationalist for personal safety.

[1472] Ibn Rawandi, "Origins of Islam: A Critical Look at the Sources," in The *Quest for the Historical Muhammad*, Amherst: Prometheus Books, 2000, p. 104.

[1473] After Hagar the Egyptian concubine of Abraham.

[1474] Rawandi, 2000, p. 95. There have been recent even more fanciful theories that the early Muslims were all really Christians, that Muhammad was actually a name for Jesus, and that the early coinage of the Muslim area contained Christian symbols because these early rulers were actually not Muslims, but Nestorian Arab influenced Christians. (Ohlig and Puin, 2010, pp. 10-11). It seems to me that these are misunderstandings of the nature of numismatic and epigraphic evidence. For example, in the United States several years after the conclusion of the war of independence, States were minting copper coins with the bust of George III and his name appearing! That clearly did not mean that the British were still ruling in the United States. The early Muslim conquests did not involve the taking over of the realm of administration and only gradually do we see Islamic influence in the area of minting coinage and in inscriptions on monuments. One also wonders at what point all these Christian ideas, rulers, coins and symbols suddenly got massively reinterpreted in a new paradigm that accomplished sudden total control with no significant disagreements from those who must have understood what these symbols originally meant. The theory is simply not credible.

plausible that one set of polemic writings (by non-Muslims) should somehow be more reliable than another set (by Muslims). In fact, Hoyland, after an extensive survey of all the writings of this period from Greek, Armenian, Georgian, Coptic, Chinese, and other less significant sources concludes "non-Muslim sources cannot provide a complete and coherent account of the history of early Islam."[1475] James Howard-Johnston has just released a book, as this book is going to press, entitled *Witnesses to a World Crisis*, in which he compares the Muslim and non-Muslim documents. He arrives at a depiction of early Islamic history which largely affirms the historical pattern of the Muslim writings.[1476]

Of particular interest is the connection to Judaism in this theory based on the many Christian texts, which tend to lump early Islam and Judaism together. This is not, however, the result of an integral link between the two religions, but rather results from Christian polemic that tended to blame all problems on the Jews. Hoyland notes that initially the Muslims were not perceived as anything more than raiders. Thus while the "people of the desert" are mentioned incidentally in Christian polemic writings, the authors of these writings place their emphasis upon the Jews. After a brief note condemning the "barbarous people of the desert," Maximus the Confessor, writing in the mid-600s, states:

> "To see the Jewish people, who have long delighted in seeing flow the blood of men, who know no other means of pleasing God than destroying his creation . . . who deem themselves to be serving God well, by doing precisely what he detests, who are most deprived of faith in the world and so the most ready to welcome hostile forces."[1477]

This passage, and so many others like it, reflects not a unity between Muslim and Jew, but rather a hope on the part of some Jews that perhaps the Muslim invasion would provide the Jewish community relief from Christian persecution. In the mind of the Confessor, the Jews were separate from the "hostile forces." They were lumped together with the early Muslim raiders merely as a paradigm of their supposed perniciousness.

Furthermore, it is hard to imagine how a movement with integral links to Judaism could produce a Qur'an which is so overtly hostile to the Jews. Even a

---

[1475] Robert G. Hoyland, *Seeing Islam as Others Saw it*, Princeton: The Darwin Press, 1997, p. 598.

[1476] Howard-Johnston, Witnesses to a World Crisis, Oxford: Oxford University Press, 2010.

[1477] Hoyland, 1997, p. 78.

cursory reading of the Qur'an shows little that is positive about the Jews. They are described as becoming apes and swine (surahs 2:65, 5:60, 7:166); being cursed of God (surahs 2:87, 4:45-47, 5:78, 9:30); full of hatred (surahs 5:64, 5:82); slayers of the prophets (surahs 2:91, 3:21, 3:181, 4:155); unbelievers and blasphemers (surahs 5:41, 5:64, 59:2-11); workers of iniquity (surahs 5:78-81, 59:2-17); falsifiers of God's book (surahs 2:79, 3:78, 5:14, 7:162); compared to donkeys (surah 62:5); treacherous (surahs 33:26-27, 59:2-4); and its rabbis are false to God's Word (surah 5:44, 63).[1478] In a general sense, if the Qur'an was compiled much later, reflecting the needs of the Muslim community in the late first and early second century of Islam, it is hard to understand why there is more anti-Jewish polemic than anti-Christian polemic in the Qur'an. During most of that time, the major political foe which the Muslims faced was Christian Byzantium. Why would a document produced late include so much condemnation of the Jews who were by that time an insignificant factor? The Crone-Cook thesis regarding the rise of early Islam out of a "sectarian milieu" of Judeo-Islam does not seem reasonable. Rather it seems much more plausible to view the above cited content in the Qur'an in the light of an early struggle between Muhammad and the Jews of Medina. This confirms the pattern found in the Muslim biographical literature.

How then are we to explain the lack of early manuscripts? A possible explanation lies in the early Muslim preference for oral tradition. The Arabs had a well developed oral literary tradition extending back well before the beginnings of Islam. The content of the Qur'an and traditions of the community were preserved through memorization, and through what Fazlur Rahman calls the "silent transmission of prophetic tradition":

> "That is, many early Muslims simply lived out the words and acts of Muhammad. And this silent living tradition, the tradition of what Muslims actually did, is the sunna . . . the very charge made by Western skeptics, that Hadiths are merely an attempt to give the actual practice of the Community prophetic authority is irrelevant. The actual practice of the community was already prophetic, at least in spirit if not in detail."[1479]

[1478] On March 22, 2004, *Sheikh 'Atiyyah Saqr, former head of the Al-Azhar Fatwa Committee'* in an online chat declared twenty bad traits of Jews based on the Qur'an, which mirrors this list and adds further negative traits. His published reflections were translated by MEMRI.ORG, April 6, 2004.

[1479] Fazlur Rahman, quoted by Herbert Berg, *The Development of Exegesis in early Islam*, Richmond, Surrey,U.K.: Curzon Press, 2000, p. 34.

There are problems with Rahman's viewpoint. Donner points out that:

> "There is mounting evidence that the Qur'an text, or parts of it at least, must, at some stage in its history have been transmitted in purely written form, without the benefit of a controlling tradition of active recitation. This evidence takes the form of recognizing in the Qur'anic text misunderstood words, hyper-corrected words (the lectio facilior), or stray marks which then became incorporated into the recitation, something that could only happen, if the oral recitation were derived from the written text, rather than the other way around.[1480]

Hoyland also points out from pre-Islamic Arabic inscriptions that there was a literary tradition existing in Arabic that had a strong written element.[1481] These elements are significant, demonstrating a textual tradition, but they do not negate a strong oral tradition in conjunction with a textual transmission, just whether that oral tradition was completely fixed or not. Most of the issues raised are fairly minor as Donner himself indicates when he points out "we do not find long passages of otherwise wholly unknown text claiming to be Qur'an, or that appear to be used as Qur'an—only variations within a text that is clearly recognizable as a version of a known Qur'anic passage."[1482] Indeed, the presence of unknown words is often associated with the age and genuineness of the transmission, indicating that words were maintained even when they were not understood. In many ways, the early interaction of oral and textual is symptomatic of the transition represented in the Qur'an itself from oral traditions to textual. Bowering notes:

> "As the first book length production in Arabic literature, the Qur'an stands at the crossroads of the oral, and highly narrative and poetical, tradition of pre-Islamic Arabic on the one hand and the written, and increasingly scholarly, Arabic prose tradition of

---

[1480] Fred M. Donner, "The Qur'an in Recent Scholarship," in *The Qur'an in its Historical Context*, edited by Gabriel Said Reynolds, New York: Routledge, 2008, p. 40.

[1481] Robert Hoyland, "The Linguistic Background to the Qur'an," in *The Qur'an in its Historical Context*, edited by Gabriel Said Reynolds, New York: Routledge, 2008, p. 65.

[1482] Donner, 2008, p. 43.

the subsequently evolving civilization of Islam on the other. The beginnings of this transition from the oral to the written can be pinpointed to the time of Muhammad and are clearly reflected in the rhymed prose style of the Qur'an. This rhymed prose, the mode of speech of the pre-Islamic soothsayer's oracles, is a characteristic mark of the Qur'an, the first sizeable Arabic document to depict this form in writing."[1483]

Premare in his article, "Abd al-Malik b. Marwan and the Process of the Qur'an's Composition" combines the textual variations recorded by both Muslims and Christians and indicates that "the Qur'anic passages can be seen as the result of mental labor aimed at the redaction, selection, and stylistic reorganization of the text . . . based on various preexisting texts not yet formally fixed and rendered immutable."[1484] The texts, however, are not later inventions. They bear very close resemblance to the actual contents of the present Qur'an.

The charge by Crone that after two or three generations "nobody remembered any of these events"[1485] seems absurd, particularly in the light of studies done on the reliability of oral tradition. Vansina, in his study on oral tradition, states:

> "Oral traditions should be treated as hypotheses, and as the first hypothesis the modern scholar must test before he or she considers others. To consider them first means not to accept them literally, uncritically. It means to give them the attention they deserve, to take pains to prove or disprove them systematically for each case on its own merits.[1486]

Sweeping generalizations rather than the painstaking analysis of individual traditions seems to characterize the Crone-Cook thesis. Studies have shown that oral transmission over even a period of several hundred years can convey

---

[1483] Gerhard Bowering, "Recent Research on the Construction of the Qur'an", in *The Qur'an in its Historical Context*, edited by Gabriel Said Reynolds, New York: Routledge, 2008, p. 71.

[1484] Ohlig and Puin, 2010, p. 197.

[1485] Quoted by Rawandi, 2000, p. 102.

[1486] Vansina, Jan, *Oral Tradition as History*, Madison: The University of Wisconsin Press, 1985, p. 196.

significant historical facts. Vansina goes on to say, "One cannot emphasize enough, however, that such (oral) sources are irreplaceable, not only because information would otherwise be lost, but because they are sources 'from the inside'."[1487] The oral tradition of Islam which is alive and well today is reflective of that process. In the Crone-Cook thesis this inside perspective is lost entirely.

When Islam first emerged as a military force, oral tradition would have been sufficient to hold the Muslim armies together in a shared sense of purpose. Probably written documents also existed and were transcribed with inclusions as Donner has noted. The texts were of close resemblance to what finally emerged in the Qur'an, but they were unedited and organized differently from the modern Qur'an. Over time, however, as the empire developed, a written literature became necessary. This is partly because the Muslims became heirs to the literary traditions of Judaism and Christianity, and particularly the polemic traditions of Christianity. However, the greatest impetus must have come from the necessity of administering an empire. In that context, written documents as a basis of law were required, and that is why a written tradition emerged toward the end of the first century of Islam. That written tradition gradually replaced the oral traditions, at least in the Islamic courts of law. One can easily see that oral Qur'anic recitation existed side-by-side with a written text, and that there was fluidity in their mutual influence, probably more in the early period, less as the text became more standardized.

Transmissions of Islamic Traditions Outside of the Qur'an

It is worthwhile here for a moment to look at the subject of the Muslim traditions in this process. The process of moving from oral to written tradition was a gradual one. As experts in various aspects of Islamic tradition emerged, they passed on their learning, as Schoeler notes, primarily through a "lecture" format that emphasized "hearing" rather than "reading." These lectures could be based on written notes, or memory, but the authoritative "transmission" was only considered complete if the student actually "heard" the traditions from his teacher. This was partly a result of the mistrust of written sources due to the unpunctuated nature of early Arabic writing.[1488] The potential for distortion, particularly in cases of a legal nature, was clear.

[1487] Vansina, 1985, p. 197.
[1488] Gregor Schoeler, "Die Frage der schriftlichen oder mundlichen Uberlieferung der Wissenschaften im fruhen Islam," in *Der Islam*, Vol. 42, 1985, pp. 223-229.

The earliest questions concerning the historicity of the traditions of Islam emerged through the studies of Ignaz Goldziher regarding the legal traditions of Islam. Joseph Schacht notes that one of Goldziher's great discoveries was:

> "That the traditions from the Prophet and from his companions do not contain more or less authentic information on the earliest period of Islam to which they claim to belong, but reflect opinions held during the first two and a half centuries after the hijra."[1489]

Muhammad was a warrior and an empire-builder, not an administrator. The Qur'an itself is sparse in its administrative pronouncements. As Islam moved from a period of conquest to the task of ruling an empire, the need emerged for a whole new set of legal traditions, never dreamed of by the Prophet. His name or the name of his close companions was necessary in order to lend an air of authority to those traditions. Further, in order to show that the traditions had been correctly transmitted, a rather artificial system of transmitters' names, known as "isnads" was developed to indicate the reliability of the traditions. The earliest documents use this system sparsely and inconsistently because the system had not been fully developed. Most of these traditions were undoubtedly fabricated. J. H. A. Juynboll notes that there is a "blossoming point" when a particular tradition suddenly has numerous transmitters, and that point is probably where the tradition was invented. Prior to that point the traditions generally only have a single strand of transmitters, and it is likely that these were invented to supply an air of authority. As Juynboll puts it, "the saying that he [the blossoming point transmitter] claims was uttered by the Prophet is in reality his own words."[1490] The time point for most of these traditions is in the third or later generation of Muslims after the Prophet. Some traditions, as we shall see below, seem to be obtusely derived from stories which have little or no connection to the legal point being made. This is not fabrication but twisting of known material to fit a need. This is a far cry from saying that the entire early history of the religion was fabricated.

[1489] Joseph Schacht, "A Revaluation of Islamic Traditions," *Royal Asiatic Society of Great Britain and Ireland*, 1949, p. 143.

[1490] J. H. A. Juynboll, "Some Isnad—Analytical Methods Illustrated on the Basis of Several Woman—Demeaning Sayings from Hadith Literature," in Harald Motzki (Ed.), *The Formation of the Classical Islamic World*, Ashgate, 2004, p. 185.

Many of the legal traditions seem to be based on events in the Prophet's life that have little or nothing to do with the principle being argued for. This seems to indicate people taking events in the Prophet's life that are probably true and forcing them, like square pegs into round holes, to justify some legal principle which is really unrelated to the event described. Surely if the event described was entirely made up, why wouldn't one design a story that at least fit the basic parameters of the legal question? As an example of this, consider the Muslim traditions about how Muhammad frowned on his soldiers practicing coitus interruptus (al-azl) with captured non-Muslim women seemingly encouraging that they try to impregnate their captives. These historical events, while really dealing with the permissibility of raping and the desirability of impregnating non-Muslim women captured in war, is made in the traditions to be Muhammad's pronouncement on the permissibility of birth control.[1491] This is almost the exact opposite of what the story actually means. This convoluted reasoning indicates that the lawyers of Islam were extracting legal principles from stories generally unrelated to the principles they were trying to derive. Why do this except that the stories were true? It would have been far easier to invent a story about the Prophet having a conversation with his followers in the mosque about the permissibility of practicing coitus interruptus with their wives.

Also, as the social circumstances of the Muslim empire changed, the same events in early Muslim literature could be interpreted very differently. To illustrate this, consider the comparison which Faizer makes between Ibn Ishaq's description of the aftermath of the Muslim conquest of the Jewish enclave at Khaybar and a similar passage in the writings of Al-Waqidi a generation later. After the Jews are defeated and many are slain in battle, the following event involving some of the captured Jewish women occurs:

[1491] Sahih Al-Bukhari, *The Translation of the Meanings of Sahih Al-Buhkari,* Vol. 7. Muhammad M. Khan, trans. (Al Medina Al Munawwara, Islamic University. Hilal Yayinlari Beirut: Dar Al Arabia, 1981), p. 103. The Islamic legal literature deals with this subject in a highly oblique way. The Shafi'i legal manual *Reliance of the Traveler* only mentions this in the context of Islamic views of contraception. In two places it retells the story of companions of the Prophet asking about the permissibility of *azl.* The context dealing with captured women prisoners of war is left out. The law manual describes the practice as "*makruh,*" permissible but not meritorious: "It is of the etiquette of intercourse not to practice coitus interruptus, there being disagreement among scholars as to the permissibility or offensiveness of doing so, though the correct position in our opinion is that it is permissible."

"Bilal who was bringing them led them past the Jews who were slain; and when the woman who was with Safiya saw them she shrieked and slapped her face and poured dust on her head. When the Apostle saw her he said, "take this she devil [emphasis mine] away from me." He gave orders that Safiya was to be put behind him and threw his mantle over her, so that the Muslims knew that he had chosen her for himself.""

The parallel passage in Al-Waqidi reads:

"The Messenger of God had sent her [Safiya] ahead with Bilal to his camel. And he passed with her and her cousin by the slaughtered. And Safiya's cousin screamed a loud cry. The Messenger of God hated what Bilal did . . . The Messenger of God said to the cousin of Safiya: This is only the devil [referring to Bilal. [emphasis mine]]."[1492]

Faizer goes on to compare these two passages saying:

"The simple but obvious transference of imagery is delightful. It certainly establishes the image of the Prophet as kinder and more tolerant than what Ibn Ishaq would have us believe. It is possible, however, that al-Waqidi was reacting to the information communicated by Ibn Ishaq and adjusting the tradition in an honest attempt to be faithful to his interpretation of the nature of the Prophet.[1493]

It seems strange at the outset that the prelude to rank sexual activity should be described in terms that make it seem more like literature than history, and this is part of Faizer's thesis. It also appears that Faizer's analysis has not gone far enough. It is clear that these two passages are describing the same historical event, but interpreting it according to the circumstances of their own time. Ibn Ishaq is the older of the two, coming at the end of the first period of Muslim military expansion. For obvious reasons stories of the military exploits of

---

[1492] Rizwi S. Faizer, *Ibn Ishaq and al-Waqidi Revisited: A Case Study of Muhammad and the Jews in Biographical Literature*, Doctoral thesis, Montreal: McGill University, 1995, pp. 183-184.

[1493] Faizer, 1995, p. 184.

the Prophet were of prime importance during this period. They provided the precedents for Muslim actions in war. It is likely that Ibn Ishaq is not at all hostile to the Prophet's actions as Faizer implies. In an age of conquest, where women were part of the spoils of battle, it was general practice of the soldiers to use these non-Muslim women sexually. Rules regarding this are clearly stated in the Qur'an.[1494] The Jews had resisted Muhammad and in the course of battle, the leader of the tribe as well as Safiya's husband were killed. Safiya, as the daughter of the leader of the Jewish tribe, would naturally be selected by Muhammad for himself, symbolically demonstrating, through his sexual intercourse with her, the total subjugation of the Jewish tribe. Al-Waqidi, writing during a later, more settled age, tries to find a way to mollify this picture, by postulating the "romance" theory that Safiya was attracted to Muhammad through his magnanimous behavior. A visit to Muslim Web sites today under Safiya bint Huyayy, demonstrates that this thesis has been enthroned as the reigning paradigm. Even Western writers are carried away by this interpretation:

> "The Prophet married a Jewish widow from the Bani Quraydha in 627 CE and a little more than a year later married another Jewish woman of the vanquished Khaybar tribe, who accepted him even though her father, brother and husband had lost their lives to the Muslims."[1495]

It is clear that Ibn Ishaq's version, for several reasons, is the more accurate. First, his description of Jewish mourning, shrieking, slapping the face, and pouring dust on the head depicts accurately Jewish culture of the day whereas Al-Waqidi's single loud cry does not. Further, it does not make sense to call Bilal a "devil" for doing what the Prophet in the previous verse had just told him to do. Finally, the reversal of imagery by Al-Waqidi is a typical form of literary transformation that attempts to make it appear Ibn Ishaq got his account mixed up when, in fact, Al-Waqidi is the one doing the mixing.

Numerous examples could be shown from other Muslim texts that borrow well-known phrases or materials from older texts in ways that convey the modernized viewpoint of the author. This changing of traditions to fit the

---

[1494] Qur'an 33:50, 4:33.
[1495] Emory C. Bogle, *Islam Origin and Belief*, Austin: University of Texas Press, 1998, pp. 18-19.

times is going on at present in Muslim publications. In Bukhari's Hadith
we read:

> "The Prophet wrote the (marriage contract) with Aisha while she
> was six years old and consummated his marriage with her while
> she was nine years old and she remained with him for nine years
> (i.e. till his death)."[1496]

The same story is told in Ibn Ishaq, Al-Waqidi, and Sahih Muslim, indeed
in all of the early Muslim sources. However, most modern Islamic online
versions of the Hadith have deleted this tradition. In modern Islamic books
this is transformed into a teenaged wedding for Aisha:

> "Aisha became the Prophet's wife in Makkah when she was most
> likely in the tenth year of her life but her wedding did not take
> place until the second year after the hijra when she was about
> fourteen or fifteen years old."[1497]

Aside from the fact that this new version of history denies all the early Islamic
sources, it is also an example of transposing of facts. It uses her age at the time
of her wedding consummation (plus one year) as the date of her engagement
and then pushes the actual consummation ahead four to five years to make it
seem acceptable to a Western audience. This creates impossible problems in
chronology, including having Aisha engaged to Muhammad before Khadija
had died, something which all Islamic sources deny. In fact, radical Muslim
governments continue to interpret these texts literally. When the government
of Ayatollah Khomeini took control of Iran in 1979, one of their earliest acts
was to reduce the legal age of marriage for women from eighteen years to
nine, in keeping with the literal practices of the Prophet as affirmed in all
canonical sources of Islamic law.

It is of particular importance to note that though the interpretation of the
events varies from author to author in these older sources, the basic form of
the stories remains remarkably similar in all of the early Muslim literature.
There is no reason to doubt the historicity of these events. Muslims had every
reason to expunge them from the history of the Prophet. That they did not

---

[1496] Sahih al-Bukhari, trans. Dr. Muhammad Khan, Medina: Islamic University,
1979, Vol. 7, p. 65.
[1497] Abdul Wahid Hamid, *Companions of the Prophet*, London: MELS, 1998, p. 243.

is a tremendous testimony to the honesty of their texts. It seems unlikely, in the light of this, to believe that Muslims made up these stories, or that they emerged out of a "sectarian milieu." When loyalists tell unflattering stories about their heroes, those stories have a strong claim to credibility.

Returning to the Text of the Qur'an

This brings us to the third potential answer to the lack of early Muslim texts; the deliberate destruction of early manuscripts, particularly of the Qur'an. This is a radical contrast to the entire history of Judaism. The Jewish tradition was a "profoundly textual"[1498] one, in which books were never destroyed, instead, old manuscripts were preserved by giving them funerals in genizas (storage niches) in the synagogue. This has created a remarkably rich textual tradition as old copies of the Torah have been retrieved and compared with other versions. The case of the geniza of the Cairo synagogue which contained early Common Era documents as well as the Dead Sea Scrolls are just two of the more notable examples of text retrieval in the Jewish tradition. The story of Muslims burning manuscripts of their own holy book is a recurring one, and certainly sets them apart from the Jewish tradition. Al-Bukhari states in his Hadith:

> "Uthman sent to every Muslim province one copy of what they had copied, and ordered that all other Qur'anic materials, whether written in fragmentary manuscripts or whole copies be burnt. Zaid bin Thabit added, "A verse from Surat Ahzab was missed by me when we copied the Qur'an and I used to hear Allah's Apostle reciting it. So we searched for it and found it with Khuzaima bin Thabit al-Ansari. (That verse was): 'Among the believers are men who have been true in their covenant with Allah.'" (33:23)

This tradition originated 250 years after the events it purports to describe. Are we to trust this as describing an actual process? Some Western scholars would say no. No copies or even fragments of Uthman's "recension" have survived. We do have traditions from the second and third Islamic centuries that even Uthman's recension had been lost. "Malik also said: 'Uthman's mushaf has disappeared. And we have found no information about it among

---

[1498] DeLange, 2000, p. 1.

the authoritative writers."[1499] John Wansbrough, whose theories on the origins of the Qur'an set the stage for the Crone-Cook thesis, attempts to show that the Qur'an is a compilation of sectarian views of Jewish origin. Based on a literary analysis of the text he arrives at some tentative conclusions:

> "taken together, the quantity of reference (to Judaeo-Christian scripture), the mechanically repetitious employment of rhetorical convention and the stridently polemical style, all suggest a strongly sectarian atmosphere, in which a corpus of familiar scripture was being pressed into the service of as yet unfamiliar doctrine."[1500]

Wansbrough denies an Uthmanic recension stating "One is compelled to assume either the suppression of substantial deviations was so instantly and universally successful that no trace of serious opposition remained, or that the story was a fiction designed to serve another purpose."[1501] Following this thesis, Rawandi states:

> In short the Koran as we have it, is not the work of Muhammad or the Uthmanic redactors, much less the immaculate word of God, but a precipitate of the social and cultural pressures of the first two Islamic centuries.[1502]

The problem with Wansbrough's point is that there have been substantial deviations in the Qur'anic text. Muslims have been involved for 1,400 years in a process of purging the text of the Qur'an to remove all variations. During much of that period they had the full power of the state to aid in the process. Arthur Jeffery's studies in the *Materials for the History of the Text of the Qur'an*, as well as recent discoveries of old manuscripts in Yemen, indicate this process.[1503] Devin Stewart covers a number of the textual variations found in the Qur'an that Muslim scholars in the medieval period sought to emend and correct in his article "Notes on Medieval and Modern Emendations of

---

[1499] Ohlig and Puin, p. 205.
[1500] John Wansbrough, *Quranic Studies*, Oxford University Press, 1977, p. 20.
[1501] Wansbrough, 1977, p. 45.
[1502] Rawandi, 2000, p. 111.
[1503] Arthur Jeffery, *Materials for the History of the Text of the Qur'an*, E. J. Brill, 1937.

the Qur'an."[1504] That there has been conflict over the text of the Qur'an is a fact also suppressed in the Muslim world, despite quiet Islamic scholarship through the centuries, for it calls into question the nature of the Islamic revelation, and thereby the very structure of the Islamic state.[1505] Wansbrough himself stopped writing on this subject because of threats to his life.

The problem lies in the Islamic conception of revelation. One of the most confusing aspects of the Qur'an is the fact that both context and the identity of the one who is speaking is seldom clear. Wansbrough's description of the text at this point is correct:

> "The fragmentary nature of Muslim scripture can nowhere be more clearly observed than in those passages traditionally described as narrative. These consist in fact not so much as narrative as of exempla . . . the exempla achieve a kind of stylistic uniformity by resort to a scarcely varied stock of rhetorical convention . . . while the effect is tedious in the extreme, by means of this deictic formula . . . a number of disparate topics, abruptly introduced and just as abruptly dismissed, is mechanically linked."[1506]

Based on this description, Crone and Cook make the following conclusions about the origins of the Qur'an:

> The book is strikingly lacking in overall structure, frequently obscure and inconsequential in both language and content, perfunctory in its linking of disparate materials and given to the repetition of whole passages in variant versions. On this basis it can plausibly be argued that the book is the product of belated and imperfect editing of materials from a plurality of traditions.[1507]

[1504] Devin J. Stewart, "Notes on the Medieval and Modern Emendations of the Qur'an," in *The Qur'an in its Historical Context*, edited by Gabriel Said Reynolds, New York: Routledge, 2008, pp. 225-247.

[1505] Part of the uproar in the Muslim world today is the fact that Western critical theories are calling into question the very foundations of Islam, and this has political, not merely religious significance.

[1506] Wansbrough, 1977, pp. 18-19.

[1507] Patricia Crone and Michael Cook, *Hagarism, The Making of the Islamic World*, Cambridge: Cambridge University Press, 1977, p. 18.

We would, in fact, argue for the exact opposite conclusion based on this very same evidence. The idiosyncratic nature of this text points to a single author whose materials were so respected that, even when they made no sense, they were maintained as they were. The idiosyncrasy is that God is speaking through the Prophet in response to questions or issues and events either brought to mind or put to the Prophet. The fragmentary nature of his responses is a testimony to this process. One can hardly imagine a redactive effort producing so little semblance of organization and unified train of thought. It is inherently confusing for a person to be speaking in the first person for a third person. Add to that the fact that we are hearing only one half of the dialogue. Without knowing the questions, the answers often make no sense.

It is inconceivable that the knowledgeable Muslims of the second century after hijra would include in a redacted Qur'an, such glaring historical errors as Mary the mother of Jesus being the sister of Moses![1508] Muhammad tells the story of Moses and Pharaoh twenty-seven times, and leaves out the story of the Passover every time! Not to mention that many of the details and the whole thrust of the story is different from the Torah. One could hardly imagine a Jewish sectarian milieu maintaining such inaccuracies. One could also argue that, if the Qur'an is merely the product of later community polemics against Christianity, then the inclusion of the virgin birth and miracles of Jesus are unnecessary concessions to an enemy faith. This is precisely what does not make sense in Wansbrough's argumentation. He notes this fact in *The Sectarian Milieu:*

> "It may be worth mentioning that within the Islamic lexicon such eccentricities as the virgin birth and the messiah epithet of Jesus are also found. Originally quite alien to the formulation of doctrine, these eventually generated a kind of subsidiary imagery to discussions respectively of divine attributes and apocalyptic."[1509]

[1508] Qur'an 19:28, Muslims have attempted to explain this mixing of the Miriam of Exodus 20:15 with Miriam the mother of Jesus by claiming that Mary was of the lineage of Aaron which is, of course, also false, since Mary was of the lineage of Judah, Luke 1:27. It is clear that Wansbrough is far off in saying that the Qur'an uses "familiar" sectarian documents in the service of as yet unfamiliar doctrine. The doctrine was familiar; it is the sectarian documents which were unfamiliar for Muhammad, and this explains the many historical errors in the Qur'an.

[1509] John Wansbrough, *The Sectarian Milieu*, Oxford: Oxford University Press, 1978, p. 100.

These facts do not fit his system because these are the very idiosyncratic elements that point to an individual whose unique teachings were moving in a historical progression concerning his relationship with Christians and Jews. Clearly Muhammad was eclectic, picking up oral traditions here and there and fitting them, where acceptable into his system. Griffith points out:

> Genuinely Christian, even biblical lore, no doubt retold in Arabic from Syriac originals for the benefit of Arabic speaking Christians, is sometimes deployed in the Qur'an for the purpose of purchasing credibility for the Qur'an's own teachings among the Arabic speaking Christian members of its audience.[1510]

Bowering notes this eclectic almost piecemeal aspect when he states, "Not a single written source, whether scriptural or liturgical, however, has been identified that would satisfy the search for an underlying Ur-Qur'an, whether postulated as a Christian hymnal or a Syro-Aramaic lectionary, that served as a written source book for the Qur'an."[1511] The Qur'an, Western scholarship is increasingly coming to admit, is the product of Muhammad. This is why one can find in the same text verses that praise Christians and other verses that call for their total subjugation.[1512] F. E. Peters states:

> "The Qur'an was regarded not as preaching or "proclamation" but as revelation pure and simple, and thus was not so inviting to redaction and editorial adjustment as the Gospels. Indeed, what was done to the Qur'an in the redactional process appears to have

---

[1510] Sydney Griffith, "Christian Lore and the Arabic Qur'an," in *The Qur'an in its Historical Context*, Surrey, UK: Routledge, 2008, p. 115.

[1511] Bowering, 2008, p. 83.

[1512] Compare Qur'an 5:82 which says that closest to the Muslims are the people who call themselves "Christians," and Qur'an 9:29 which calls upon Muslims to fight against the Christians until they feel themselves to be thoroughly subdued and pay the jizya poll tax to the Muslims as a sign of their subjugation. Ibn Kathir in *Al-Sira al-Nabawiyya* mentions that the occasion for the first mentioned revelation was when Muhammad criticized Christians to Salman the Persian who had been a Christian, and Salman disagreed. After the verse was revealed Muhammad went on to explain that all good Christians are actually Muslims. Ibn Kathir did not consider this a strong tradition, Vol. 1, p. 222.

been extremely conservative. The materials were kept, in the words of one modern scholar, "just as they fell."[1513]

Clearly it is this very brittle concept of revelation which both insists on retaining the text the way it is (in spite of incomprehensibility), and also creates the need to destroy documentation to cover up variations in the text. The Qur'anic text, according to Jeffery, contains a small percentage of interpolations based upon comparisons of early manuscripts.[1514] As in the example of the retrieved verse 33:23 mentioned above, the variations are of a very insignificant nature, and do not alter any major doctrines of Islam. But for Muslims this does not solve the problem. As the word-for-word dictation of God, the Qur'anic revelation cannot stand the slightest variation in its text. Changes either by addition or subtraction call the entire revelation into question. Al-Tabari notes the following about one of the early scribes of Muhammad:

> "Abdallah b. Sa'd . . . used to write for him. He apostatized from Islam on the day of the conquest of Mecca . . . He is supposed to have arbitrarily altered the revelation, or to have boasted for doing so after his apostasy from Islam."[1515]

According to the text, after Sa'd is captured, Muhammad wishes to put him to death, but his relative Uthman intercedes for him, and he is spared on condition of his reconversion to Islam. Such was the seriousness with which Islam regarded anything which denigrated or called into question the text of the Qur'an. A similar case is the assassinations carried out by Muhammad's agents against Jews who dared to make a mockery of the Qur'an in satirical poetry.[1516] Hence, variations in manuscript materials must be expunged from the record. Jeffrey notes examples of the suppression of variant readings:

> "With regard to such variants as did survive there were definite efforts at suppression in the interests of orthodoxy. One may refer, for instance, to the case of the great Baghdad scholar Ibn

---

[1513] F. E. Peters, "The Quest of the Historical Muhammad," in *International Journal of Middle East Studies*, Vol. 23:3, 1991, p. 299.

[1514] Jeffrey, 1937, p. 9.

[1515] Al-Tabari, Vol. 9, pp. 147-148.

[1516] Reuben Firestone, "The Failure of a Jewish Program of Public Satire in the Squares of Medina," *Judaism*, Vol. 46, 1997, pp. 439-452.

Shanabudh (245-328 AH), who was admitted to be an eminent
Qur'anic authority, but who was forced to make public recantation
of his use of readings from the Old Codices."[1517]

It is interesting to note that certain traditions of Islam indicate that textual
variation was a cause for questioning of the Islamic faith, and thereby
the allegiance to the Muslim army. Such questioning was, consequently,
severely punished. We read the following account from the Hadith about
a Muslim man Sabigh, who went around the early Muslim military camps
asking divisive questions about the Qur'an. The Caliph Umar deals with
him severely:

> "Late in the second and early third decade of Islam, religious
> information and instruction in the newly conquered province of
> Iraq, Syria and Egypt was to be had only in the large military
> camps and the newly established settlements, such as Basra and
> Fustat, where many of the companions of Muhammad, some of
> whom were eager to instruct the people, were to be found. Sabigh,
> according to the earliest Iraqi and Egyptian sources, sought out
> men in these provincial military camps and raised questions about
> the ambiguous (mutashahib) and difficult (mushkilat) passages
> of the Qur'an in a foolish and stubborn way."[1518]

This eventually led the Caliph Umar to administer two hundred lashes to the
man. The nature of his questions is never defined, though the implicit threat
to Muslim military unity is obvious. Abbott goes on to comment:

> "Before we pass judgment on Umar's severity, it is fitting to consider
> not only the offense itself but also its probable consequences under
> the then existing religio-political situation. Sabigh's activity
> was not private or casual. Its extent and persistence presented a
> double threat. Theologically, it held the danger of spreading doubt,
> disbelief and heresy. Politically it could, by undermining the new
> faith, undermine also the allegiance of the military forces whose

---

[1517] Jeffrey, *Materials for the History of the Text of the Qur'an*, E. J. Brill, 1937, p. 9.

[1518] Nabia Abbott, *Studies in Arabic Literary Papyri*, Chicago: University of Chicago Press, 1967, p. 108.

loyal support was so essential to the success and stability of the newly established religio-political community."[1519]

It is for this same reason that Muslim males who left the faith were put to death. It was considered to be treason and equivalent to deserting the army in time of war. Women apostates are not executed because they are not members of the armed forces.

There are other curious Hadiths about the text of the Qur'an such as the following from Sahih Muslim:

> "The Messenger of Allah forbade that one should travel to the land of the enemy taking the Qur'an with him . . . The enemy may seize it and may quarrel with you over it."[1520]

It appears certain that this Hadith was not enforced during the second century after hijra and indicates an early fear which I suggest was generated by an implicit awareness of text variations in the Qur'an. Clearly political motivation was involved. As the basis for an empire, the Qur'an needed to be protected from outside scrutiny until the text had been standardized. This is why, in my opinion, the Qur'an gets very little mention in early non-Muslim writings about Islam.

To summarize, the lack of early Muslim documents does not indicate that the Qur'an did not exist or that the early historical traditions were fabricated. There were clear political and military reasons why early documents were not widespread, and those documents that were written down were probably deliberately destroyed. Further, Muslim emphasis on oral tradition and memorization, which continues in some ways to this day, is an adequate secondary explanation for the lack of documents. This brings us to a second set of questions.

Problem 2: The Question of the Historical Value of the Qur'an

It is clear from even a cursory reading of the Qur'anic text that if one is looking for historical data, there is not much to be found here. Apart from a few references to Muhammad and his companions, and a place-name or

---

[1519] Abbott, 1967, p. 110.
[1520] Sahih Muslim, Vol. 3, Lahore: Muhammad Ashraf Publishers, 1990, p. 1040. Also found in Bukhari, Vol. 4, pp. 146-147.

two, the only thing we can associate with the text is based on later Muslim exegesis of the Qur'an. F. E. Peters has the following to say about the Qur'an as a historical/biographical source:

> "Have we grounds for a biography? We have none in the Qur'an, it would appear, since its form is that of a discourse, a divine monologue or catechism so to speak, that reveals little or nothing about the life of Muhammad and his contemporaries."[1521]

It is this aspect of the Qur'an that must control our analysis. This is not a book that was laid down with any sort of historical or biographical purpose. It is a book purporting to be God's guidance to humankind, his direct words. Further, it is not a book that comes out of a neutral mass of tradition. It is clearly a polemic work that argues for God's nature and purpose, argues for the Prophet and his example, argues against what other people believe, and answers other people's criticisms of the new faith. Most importantly, it is a book of liturgical poetry meant to train an illiterate populace in the basic confessions of the new faith, in distinction to all other available faiths. Norman Calder notes one of the great contributions of Wansbrough's work: "Most illuminating of all to my mind is the observation, essential to *The Sectarian Milieu*, that Muslim scripture is liturgical." Based on the rhythmic and poetic elements of the Qur'an, Calder states:

> Few books are so obviously unified, so obviously demand to be experienced as a whole.[1522]

Thus, the fragmentary nature of the Qur'an stems from its very purpose. It is a collection of stories meant to be retold in poetic liturgical form, which demonstrate the truths of the faith. It is a collection of slogans to be used to reinforce the faith and to attack those who would criticize it, recorded in an easily memorized format for an illiterate population. It is a collection of arguments for a faith in conflict with other persons and faiths, arguments worked out in the heat of actual discussions that became a poetic course in apologetics for the faith. It is a collection of the oral traditions of other faiths appropriated and transformed into proof texts for the new faith, sometimes

---

[1521] Peters, 1991, p. 299.

[1522] Norman Calder, "History and Nostalgia," in *Method and Theory in the Study of Religion*, Swets & Zeitlinger, 2002, pp. 53-54.

by agreement and sometimes by disagreement, and all recorded in a format that millions of Muslims to this day memorize. In the Qur'an we find a religion battling for its very existence and using every device and technique in the Arabic poetic tradition to sway a still doubting Arab population to its side. The unity of poetic form, and style as well as purpose, does not answer the question of the historicity of the document, but it certainly points to a different milieu than that of second century Islam. It seems to reflect a milieu very similar to that described in the Muslim documents on early Islam.

Tafsir: Exegesis of the Qur'an

Another area of concern for our study of early Islam is the analysis of the early Muslim exegesis of the Qur'an. Patricia Crone points out just how important these exegetical materials are:

> "For practical purposes, our sources are thus exegetical Hadith plus Hadith of other kinds. It is not generally appreciated how much of our information on the rise of Islam, including that on Meccan trade, is derived from exegesis on the Qur'an."[1523]

One of the foundations of this study has been Nöldeke's chronological ordering of the surahs of the Qur'an, which is entirely based on Muslim exegesis of the "occasions of revelation." Wansbrough explains:

> "It is the relation of event to scripture which requires to be examined: in the Muslim haggadah the exegetical device known as *ta 'yin al-mubham* (identification of the vague and ambiguous) served to establish a connection between scriptural phraseology and external referent, in the interest of narrative continuity. In halakhic exegesis the device was extended to become a kind of chronological grid known as *asbab al-nuzul* (occasions of revelation), employed to promote some and eliminate other verses as the alleged bases of juridical decisions."[1524]

[1523] Patricia Crone, *Meccan Trade and the Rise of Islam*, Princeton University Press, 1987, p. 204.
[1524] Wansbrough, 1978, p. 7.

The question that emerges from these materials is whether this exegesis is based upon the actual background of the Qur'an, or are the authors reading back into the ambiguous text of the Qur'an what they want to find there? Ibn Rawandi says:

> "The numerous purported historical events that are supposed to have occasioned a revelation (Badr, Uhud, Hudaybiyya . . .) owe many of their features, and often their very existence to the Koran itself . . . that is to say, wherever the Koran mentions a name or an event, stories were invented to give the impression that . . . someone knew what they were about . . . much of the classical Muslim understanding of the Koran rests on the work of popular storytellers, such storytellers being the first to propose particular historical contexts for particular verses."[1525]

If this were true, we could expect a great deal of debate between various viewpoints on the background of many verses in the Qur'an. There is some, but nothing like what we would expect if the Qur'an was truly completely ambiguous, and all the interpretations were invented. Rawandi here represents an oversimplification of Wansbrough's thesis. Wansbrough is much more tentative at this point and speaks of the relationship of revelation and exegesis as ambivalent:

> "One is tempted, if not quite constrained, to see in those sanctuary traditions the origin of the isra/miraj story, imposed upon Q. 17:1 in much the same way Surat al-Fil was made the peg for a similar sanctuary tradition concerning Mecca. If, indeed, the exegesis did not in both instances precede the revelation, it would none the less appear to have originated independently of the verses it purported to explain. That same ambivalent relationship between scripture and interpretation holds for much of the content of the Muhammadan evangelium."[1526]

This particular passage of the Qur'an and its exegesis is suspicious for several reasons. Muslims made something of a policy of building their mosques in the captured or destroyed remains of the temples of other religions; Hagia

---

[1525] Rawandi, 2000, p. 101.
[1526] Wansbrough, 1977, p, 69.

Sophia in Istanbul and the Babri Masjid in Ayodhya are just some of the more prominent. This was an aspect of the militarism of Islam, meant to demonstrate their hegemony. These particular verses of the Qur'an have been interpreted to refer to the Prophet's miraculous night journey, first by the winged horse Buraq up to the temple mount in Jerusalem, and then by ladder up to the highest heaven where Muhammad received some of the major regulations for Islamic ritual prayer and fasting. The verse itself is quite oblique. It simply states: "Glorified be he who took his servant for a journey by night from Al-Masjid Al-Haram to Al-Masjid Al-Aqsa, the neighborhood whereof we have blessed, in order that we might show him our ayat."[1527] There is no clear reference to Jerusalem at all. Yet Jerusalem is included in the Muslim triad of holy cities, and the Muslims laid claim to the Jewish temple mount based upon the exegesis of this verse. Herbert Busse notes:

> "The Muslim exegetes used, as is well known, rabbinical and Christian sources to explain the Qur'an, and to supplement the text which is, in their opinion, difficult to understand. One, if not the main, purpose of the materials used in commentaries on Sura 17:2-8 was to bring forward arguments in favor of the Muslim claim to the Temple Mount."[1528]

Muslim exegesis, when it relates to some of the biblical passages found in the Qur'an, is particularly fanciful, and rife with historical inaccuracies. Busse notes a few examples:

> "The Muslim exegetes came to the conclusion that the Philistines conquered Jerusalem with Goliath as their leader, destroyed the Temple and took away the Ark of the Covenant."[1529]

Further details emphasize the lack of historical awareness in these early authors. They have little knowledge of the destruction of Jerusalem in AD 70, some attributing it to Antiochus Epiphanes and others to Khardaus, king of Babylon, others still to Constantine! Names are regularly mixed up with

---

[1527] As translated in Ibn Kathir, *Tafsir*, Vol. 5, p. 550.
[1528] Herbert Busse, "The Destruction of the Temple and its Reconstruction in the Light of Muslim Exegesis of Sura 17:2-9," in *Jerusalem Studies in Arabic and Islam*, Vol. 20, 1996, p. 3.
[1529] Busse, 1996, p. 7.

resulting historical confusion, as when Zechariah, the son of Jehoiadah, is mixed up with the Zechariah, father of John the Baptist. Busse remarks:

> "Once the latter was identified as John the Baptist's father the way was paved for similar transfer of elements from the story of Nebuchadnezzar to that of Titus, and the story of Zechariah to that of John the Baptist . . . Tabari combines the stories of John the Baptist and Nebuchadnezzar."[1530]

What are we to say, then, concerning the exegetical literature and its interpretation of the Qur'an with regard to the life of the Prophet? Are these interpretations equally fanciful? Wansbrough would see this material as part of Muslim "salvation history," which is really not history at all, but a form of polemic meant to convince others of the truth and triumph of the religion. Berg notes that Wansbrough sees all the biographical literature as essentially salvation history and concludes, "In other words, the sira (biographical literature) is tafsir (exegesis) and cannot be used to determine the real events during the life of the Prophet."[1531]

Berg attempts to evaluate the exegetical traditions through an analysis of their "isnads." The isnad was a listing of the transmitters of a tradition used by Muslims to demonstrate authenticity through validating the sources. We have already noted the critique of isnads for the legal traditions of Islam, which began with Goldziher. They proved to be inventions of a later age as were some of the traditions, though certainly not all as we have noted earlier. There was a clear political motive for inventing traditions in order to provide a legal basis for an empire. Berg selects the twelve exegetical devices described by Wansbrough and uses them in a computer-based study of the exegetical traditions attributed to Ibn Abbas. He concludes that the isnads of this type of literature are equally as unreliable as the legal traditions.

> "The use of exegetical devices was very inconsistent, suggesting that the isnads were fabricated haphazardly. Each fabricator had a pool of exegetes names at his disposal and he merely selected one to place in the isnad . . . It is as a group that the Hadiths appear to be fabricated.[1532]

[1530] Busse, 1996, pp. 13-14.
[1531] Berg, 2000, p. 107.
[1532] Berg, 2000, p. 207.

He goes on to suggest that Ibn Abbas himself is a selection based on historical proximity to Muhammad and relation to the Abbasid dynasty which bears his name, rather than any actual connection of the historical figure to the transmission of Quranic interpretation. Berg sees a possible source of these fabricated exegetical Hadith in a reaction against "subjective exegesis" (tafsir bil-ra'y).[1533] Total freedom to read into the text could lead to the disintegration of the foundations of the Islamic state. Once again there was a compelling political reason to establish a form of orthodoxy and to defend it by whatever means. Given the political and military power of the Islamic state, it is not surprising that this effort was successful, however dishonest it may have been. Berg concludes his study on the exegetical tradition as follows:

> "Wansbrough's doubt about the origin of tafsir seems confirmed: the earliest names given in the isnads do not seem to have consistent or discernible connection to the exegetical material in the corresponding matns. Moreover, it seems that exegetical hadiths were subject to the same processes as their legal and historical counterparts . . . It is a strong argument in favor of skepticism toward the isnads of exegetical hadiths in particular, and of other genres of hadiths in early Islamic texts in general."[1534]

Isnads were an artificial addition to the oral culture of the Arabs. Indeed their use was only gradually adopted to provide a sense of authority to the oral traditions being passed down. It is worth noting that in Ibn Ishaq's text, one of the earliest, isnads are only inconsistently used. Ibn Ishaq represents a transitional phase in the movement from oral to written form in the Islamic biographical tradition. The lack of concern for isnads in the earlier historical writings may indicate that the events were so well known that there was no need for accompanying artificial authoritative props. Watt argues that because the historical writings dealt with events which were generally well agreed upon and which seldom had a legal bearing, they were an entirely different category from the Hadith literature in general.[1535] The connection of an artificial isnad to an oral tradition does not necessarily disprove the tradition. It merely shows the need at a later time for an authoritative structure. The key to solving the issue of the historical value of the exegetical Hadith and

---

[1533] Berg, 2000, p. 214.
[1534] Berg, 2000, p. 228.
[1535] Watt, 1980, p. 42.

thereby of the historicity of the Qur'an, in our opinion, lies in a thoroughgoing analysis of all of the historical traditions. There is simply no substitute for a case-by-case study of these materials.

I do not have space in this brief chapter to do more than introduce a few of the studies, which have been done to determine the historicity of those Muslim traditions which relate to events in Muhammad's life. In contrast to the isnads, studies of individual historical traditions have tended to show a core of historically valuable information. We will consider this first from the viewpoint of an admittedly rather minor tradition analyzed by Harald Motzki concerning the murder of Ibn Abi al-Huqayq. All the early histories of the life of Muhammad discuss his use of assassination to remove his political and ideological enemies. Among these stories is the planned murder of a Jewish tribal leader in Khaybar, north of Medina.

Motzki compares the literary content as well as the isnads of each of the traditions that relate to this event. He finds four separate strands of tradition, each with slightly different content and occurring in such a way that they cannot be seen as dependent upon each other. Further, there do not appear to be any exegetical, theological, or legal needs associated with these traditions, which might have distorted their content. Most importantly, at least two of the traditions represent two tribal groups whose members took part in the "expedition." Not surprisingly, some of the major differences among the traditions can be explained in terms of one tribal tradition arguing against the other concerning who was to have the glory for dealing al-Huqayq the fatal blow. Motzki concludes:

> These stories are much older than one would expect . . . They certainly received their stories during the last third of the first/ seventh century . . . it is not only possible but probable, that their common elements reflect, at least in part, historical reality.[1536]

Motzki then goes on to summarize the common content of all four traditions:

> "This historical kernel is, however, rather meager. It consists of the information that the Prophet sent a few men under the command of 'Abd Allah b. Atik to Abu Rafi b. Abi al-Huqayq who lived outside of Medina in order to kill him. The assassin (or assassins)

[1536] Harald Motzki, "The Murder of Ibn Abi al-Huqayq: On the Origin and Reliability of some Maghazi Reports," in *The Biography of Muhammad*, p. 232.

had to ascend to his apartment and when descending he or another man missed a step and hurt his foot. They did not leave until the death of the victim had been verified. It does not make sense to assume that someone would have invented such a story at a time when many eyewitnesses of the Prophet's Medinan period were still alive . . . We can only ask ourselves again how different people came to invent independently the same details of a story narrating the murder of al-Huqayq."[1537]

What we find particularly interesting is the conclusion which Motzki comes to as a result of his study:

"What is the impact of our results on the study of the Prophet's biography in general? First of all, it is obvious that the biographies of the Prophet written by Western scholars do not give a historically reliable picture of his life. Their eclectic use of the sources, due to the lack of source-critical studies, prevents it. These books . . . are nothing more than arbitrary summaries of the Muslim tradition on their Prophet."[1538]

This conclusion is undoubtedly true, but in a way very different from what Westerners might anticipate. In fact, very few modern biographies mention the Prophet's policies with regard to assassination. They seem to assume that these events are not historical, or not worth repeating, even though they occupy considerable space in the Muslim sources (e.g., 5 percent of Ibn Ishaq's Medinan period text). The assumption that some things are unhistorical has led these writers to leave out most of the uncomfortable material regarding the Prophet's life. This is ironic, because the biographical literature is polemic, and meant to present the Prophet in the best possible light. It is a literature that probably presents Muhammad as far better than he really was. Yet Western writers present him in a far better light than the Muslims themselves. Source-critical studies, far from decreasing what we know about the Prophet, may show many stories to be true which Western writers tend to avoid.

On reading through the early documents of Islam, one often comes across descriptions of events that simply defy any rationale of invention. Islam

---

[1537] Motzki, p. 232.
[1538] Motzki, p. 233.

has always been, and remains to this day, highly intolerant of conversion from Islam to other faiths. Yet we find recorded in the early sources stories of Muslims who apostatized from Islam. Tabari records the apostasy of Abdallah b. Sa'd one of Muhammad's scribes.[1539] Ibn Kathir records the apostasy of one of the emigrants to Abyssinia and his attempt to convert his wife to Christianity:

> "As for Abd. Allah b. Jahsh, he stayed in Mecca until the Prophet (saas) was sent. He left thereafter with the others who went to Abyssinia. Once there he became a Christian and abandoned Islam. He remained there till he died, still a Christian."[1540]

After his death, his widow returned to Arabia and married the Prophet! By means of this direct connection, little noticed by scholars, Muhammad could have obtained information about Christian sectarian beliefs and may lie behind the story of the table (maidan) mentioned in chapter 5, which includes Ethiopic language. One cannot imagine any reason to invent this particular incident.

A similar example is the story of Hamza's drunkenness. Hamza is an uncle of Muhammad renowned for his physical strength and early conversion to Islam. It is said that his conversion to Islam greatly lifted the spirits of the persecuted Muslim community in Mecca because Hamza acted as a protector. Hamza is present at the Battle of Badr and distinguishes himself by valor in battle. It is he who slays the first polytheist in this battle. He is later martyred at Uhud. Hamza is lionized in all the early Muslim writings. Nevertheless, a curious story is told of his drunken celebration after the victory at Badr. Ali had received two camels as booty from the Battle of Badr, which he planned to use for his wedding dowry. Hamza "was in that house drinking wine and a lady singer was reciting, 'O Hamza, kill the fat old she camels and (feed them to your guests).'" After Hamza had done so, Ali complained to Muhammad who "went to Hamza and spoke harshly to him. Hamza looked up and said, 'Aren't you only the slaves of my forefathers?' The Prophet retreated and went out. This incident happened before the prohibition of drinking."[1541] Surely

---

[1539] Al-Tabari, Vol. 9, p. 148.
[1540] Ibn Kathir, Vol. 1, p. 258.
[1541] Bukhari, Vol. 3, pp. 329-330, Section 563, and Muslim, Vol. 3, p. 1096. These Hadiths are interpreted as meaning that those who are drunk are not responsible for their words.

Muslim writers did not need to invent a story besmirching the reputation of Hamza solely for the purpose of devising a rationale for the forbidding of alcohol?!

Another example is the way in which Muslim authors are prone to stereotyping. Abu Jahl is always presented in the worst possible light as one of the opponents of Muhammad, and the primary polytheist leader killed at the Battle of Badr. Nevertheless, Ibn Kathir records an event of reconciliation between him and Muhammad in Mecca. However, Ibn Kathir, for his part, questions the veracity of the tradition stating "equally strange are the comments of Abu Jahl."[1542] Kister notes that some traditions told of the Prophet taking part in pagan rituals, which was a major problem for Muslim theologians. They attacked these traditions as untrustworthy, or claimed that the Prophet only attended to rebuke the idolaters. Al-Haytham reported Muhammad as giving two of his sons by Khadija pagan names, "al-Uzza" and "Abd Manaf," though later writers expunged this.[1543] Islamic traditions tended to be highly male oriented, nevertheless Ibn Kathir records the death of a Muslim slave girl named Sumayya at the hands of Abu Jahl and calls her the first martyr of Islam.[1544] Why record the obscure name of such a person, particularly a woman, if the event is not historical?

Some Muslim traditions, which serve no purpose in their own context, strangely confirm the research of later Western writers, even those doubtful of the historicity of the documents! Patricia Crone attacks the notion of Mecca as a center of trade noting that there were no significant trade routes overland, "All routes went through either the Red Sea or the Persian Gulf . . . just as there was no South Arabian trade, so there was no overland spice route for the Meccans to take over."[1545] Curiously, Ibn Kathir seems to confirm this view with an odd notation about a pre-Islamic rebuilding of the Ka'aba. He relates how the roof of the Ka'aba was rebuilt using timber from a shipwrecked Byzantine merchant ship from Jidda on the Red Sea that was sent to Abyssinia with building materials for a Church the Persians had burned. Interestingly, the carpenter who helped rebuild the Ka'aba was a Coptic Christian![1546] In another instance, Crone shows that the Meccans did not trade in any outside

---

[1542] Ibn Kathir, Vol. 1, p. 368.
[1543] M. J. Kister, p. 75.
[1544] Ibn Kathir, Vol. 1, p. 357.
[1545] Patricia Crone, *Meccan Trade and the Rise of Islam*, pp. 44-45.
[1546] Ibn Kathir, Vol. 1, p. 199.

valuables besides perfume.[1547] This seems also confirmed by Ibn Ishaq's brief notation of the struggle of the "scented ones."[1548]

Some traditions seem designed to frustrate the interpretations of Western writers. Relating traditions of pre-islamic conversions to other faiths, Wansbrough states:

> "The facility with which three of the four celebrated God-seekers (hanif) could be accommodated by conversion to Christianity emerges neither from the nature of their quest nor the structure of the tale, the real substance of which is the odyssey of the fourth: Zayd b. Amr. He became neither Jew nor Christian, but did abandon the religion of his people.[1549]

Ibn Kathir, however, states in no uncertain terms "how Zayd ben Amr became a Christian before the coming of Islam."[1550] Some traditionalist may have used this story as an opportunity for anticipatory polemic for Islam, but the very fact of disagreement, particularly where the debate is not helpful for Islam, is an indication of historicity.

Other Islamic traditions show remarkable honesty in the face of what surely must have been an enormous pressure toward political correctness. Horovitz notes that one aspect of Ibn Ishaq's work that was criticized early on was his inclusion of numerous poems of doubtful authenticity particularly in citations from Ibn Sa'd. Horovitz argues:

> "There is no reason to doubt the authenticity of many of the poems cited by Ibn Sa'd, especially such as relate to the events of Madinah, and many also in the time of Ibn Hisham were acknowledged authentic by the connoisseurs of poetry."[1551]

He goes on to say that Ibn Ishaq shows an unusual impartiality in the introduction of poems; he even allows the opponents of the Prophet, by

---

[1547] Crone, 1987, p. 83.

[1548] Ibn Ishaq, *The Life of Muhammad*, Alfred Guillaume, trans . . . , Oxford: Oxford University Press, p. 57.

[1549] Wansbrough, 1978, p. 103.

[1550] Ibn Kathir, Vol. 1, p. 278.

[1551] J. Horovitz, "Earliest Biographies of the Prophet and Their Authors," *Islamic Culture*, April, 1927, p. 181.

inserting the verses uttered by them, to speak unhindered, and in some cases Ibn Hisham has deemed it necessary to tone down too sharp expressions used by these poets.[1552] The honesty of Ibn Ishaq is also seen in the fact that he maintained that the ancestor of the Abbassid Caliphate, Ibn Abbas, fought on the side of the polytheists at the Battle of Badr despite living in Baghdad under the Abbassids. This fact was later suppressed in the writings of Al-Waqidi and Ibn Hisham.[1553] To these many traditions may be added the innumerable instances where one author corrects another in an area where no theological or legal issues were at stake. Faizer notes that Al-Waqidi interjects in one minor Hadith, "do not listen to this tradition about their fighting . . . this was in Khaybar (not an event with the Banu Qurayza)."[1554]

The Muslim sources do include many obviously apocryphal, polemic, and miraculous stories that are not historical. These materials do have value, however, in indicating the attitude that Muslims developed toward their Prophet and toward the followers of other religions. One aspect of this is the transference of the imagery of other religious leaders to Muhammad. This was part of a historical process, after conquest, to aid in the maintenance of Islamic political power. Horovitz notes that when St. John of Damascus debated with Muslims in the late seventh century, he could argue that Muhammad had done no miracles, and his learned Muslim opponents could not disagree with him. This problem was already being rectified by the time the first Siras were being written down. Horovitz states:

> "Consciously and deliberately the theologians transferred to Mohammad what they had heard in the miracle-legends related by those of other faiths . . . many of these controversies set the stage for the transference of Christian imagery to Muhammad . . . those very controversies must have encouraged them to put on the missing colors all the more heavily."[1555]

Thus, in the aforementioned tradition of the murder of al-Huqayq, some add the story of Muhammad miraculously healing the foot of the man who was injured escaping. Ibn Kathir describes the story of Halima's pilgrimage to Mecca when Muhammad was lost and his uncle found him

---

[1552] Horovitz, 1927, p. 181.
[1553] Horovitz, 1927, p. 173.
[1554] Faizer, 1995, p. 183.
[1555] Horovitz, in *The Life of Muhammad*, Uri Rubin, ed., pp. 270, 277-278.

in the Ka'aba. The story is highly reminiscent of Jesus in the temple at age twelve.[1556] The preliminary chapters of Ibn Ishaq, Ibn Kathir and al-Tabari are full of stories of signs of the advent of the Prophet. Ishaq in particular finds materials in the writings of the Jews and Christians to demonstrate their foreseeing of the coming of Muhammad. He quotes the geneology of Ishmael from Genesis 18 verbatim and uses the reference to the paraclete in John's gospel as a prophecy of the coming of Muhammad. Many of these interpretations are still the stock in trade of Muslim apologists to this day. It is at this level that Muslim historians wrote down what they "thought had happened or wanted to believe had happened or wanted others to believe had happened."[1557]

Muhammad's treatment of the Jews is also justified by a similar appeal to what Muslims suppose must be found in the Jewish scriptures. Wellhausen nearly a century ago noted that there are many Muslim references to Jewish prophecies concerning Muhammad:

> "A great many of these accounts owe their origin to the direct accusation against the Jews who, although they saw the long expected prophet live before them, refused to believe. That these obstinant people received their just punishment on account of this attitude was no more than proper."[1558]

Into this category may be placed all the records of dialogues between Jews that inevitably demonstrate their prior knowledge of the coming Prophet and their culpability in not accepting him. In this way they essentially function as mouthpieces for the Muslim apologists. Clearly this is polemic literature at its worst. Nevertheless, the very fact that Muslims feel constrained to invent dialogue of this type to justify Muhammad's actions against the Jews, is an indication of the historicity of those actions. No one invents justifications for actions that never took place. This was also necessitated by the growing Islamic conviction concerning the sinlessness of Muhammad.[1559] Every action

---

[1556] Ibn Kathir, Vol. 1, p. 166.

[1557] Herbert Berg, 2002, p. 6.

[1558] Wellhausen, *Muhammad and the Jews of Medina*, trans. Jan Arent Weinsinck, 1975, p. 39.

[1559] Kister notes: "The Prophet, like other prophets, was protected from any sin whatsoever both before and after being granted prophethood." It is this overall viewpoint that constrains much of the content in Muslim historical literature. M. J. Kister, *Life of Muhammad*, ed. Uri Rubin, p. 74.

of the Prophet, no matter how questionable, had to find its justification, either by the wickedness of those killed, or by the clear direction of God himself.

In one sense, the Muslim sira literature gives testimony to an aspect of the early struggle of Islam, which Wansbrough, Crone, Berg, and Cook as well as most other historians do not seem to perceive. The sectarian milieu is a milieu in which polytheism is clearly dying. Not only do we have large tribes, either partly or entirely, converted to either Judaism or Christianity, but also we have individual converts to these religions mentioned amongst virtually all the Arab tribes. Polytheism in most of the Middle East was essentially dead by the seventh century. It lingered on as a fading phenomenon in remote areas of Arabia and in the mountains. Most historians have been fooled by the stories about battles with polytheists into thinking that Islam's primary struggle was with them. The polytheists are most likely a straw man set up to disguise the real struggle; Islam's battle against other monotheistic faiths. Muhammad killed many more Jews than polytheists.[1560] His policies are clearly more vindictive and violent toward the members of these rival faiths than toward the Meccans. Compare Muhammad's lenient response to Ibn Ubayy who deserted him before the Battle of Uhud with his slaughter of the Banu Qurayza, merely on the accusation of their plotting against him. The Hadith seems to emphasize this at times. According to Sahih Muslim, when a woman was searching for her son who was killed, the Prophet congratulated her saying:

> "'You will get the reward of two martyrs for your son'. She asked: 'Why is that so, Apostle of Allah?' He replied: 'Because the people of the Book have killed him'. This shows that fighting with the people of the Book (ie. Christians and Jews) carries more reward than fighting with others."[1561]

I do not agree, however, with Hawting's assertion that the Qur'an is only written as a polemic against other monotheists. There are some interesting points to be made from his thesis, but the presence of the names of Arab

---

[1560] Ibn Ishaq mentions six to nine hundred Jewish males past puberty who were executed after their surrender to Muhammad. This total alone is far more than the combined total of pagans killed which are listed in his biography of the Prophet. To that total must be added the Jews of Khaybar and individual Jews killed or assassinated in other tribal groups.

[1561] *Sunan Abu Dawud*, Vol. 2, New Delhi: Kitab Bhavan, 1993, p. 688.

deities in the Qur'an, the large amount of polemic against Jews and Christians, which seems to set them up as a different category, in my mind makes his thesis less than convincing.[1562]

The treaty of Hudaybiyya, in many ways, also demonstrates this. In this sense, Crone's idea of a nativist movement among the Arabs is probably accurate:

> "An alternative hypothesis would be that Islam originated as a nativist movement, or, in other words as a primitive reaction to alien domination of the same type as those which the Arab conquerors were themselves to provoke in North Africa and Iran . . . Muhammad mobilized the Jewish version of monotheism against the dominant Christianity and used it for the self-assertion, both ideologically and militarily, of his own people."[1563]

Muhammad could hardly align himself with the Jews. They had no state and could not give him a power base. Their rejection of him sealed their fate. If he became Christian, he was in danger of being absorbed into the Christian Byzantine Empire. If he became Zoroastrian, he would be similarly absorbed into the Persian Empire. To establish a truly Arab Empire he needed to reform and to woo the Arabs with a monotheism of their own. This political strategy, developed in Medina, was brilliant, and it succeeded.

Even contradictions in the historical traditions offer opportunities for discovering more accurate historical accounts. Lecker notes this:

> "Paradoxically, contradictions in our sources have their benefits, they not only highlight the matters which the early Islamic community considered worth disputing, but they often provide us with information which, because it is shared by otherwise conflicting sources, has a strong claim to historical veracity."[1564]

An example of this is Uri Rubin's discussion of the assassination of the Jewish poet Ka'b b. al-Ashraf. There are two datings given in the early Muslim

---

[1562] G. R Hawting, *The Idea of Idolatry and the Emergence of Islam*, Cambridge: Cambridge University Press, 2006, see particularly his section of Allat, Manat and al Uzza pp. 130-149.

[1563] Crone, 1987, pp. 247-248.

[1564] Lecker, in *The Life of Muhammad*, ed. Uri Rubin, p. 37.

sources for this event, after Badr, and after Uhud. The disagreement even extends to the exegesis of Surat al-Hashr in the Qur'an, which traditionally refers to the period after Uhud. Rubin notes:

> "Al-Tabari, however, forms an interesting exception. In his commentary on Surat al-Hashr the name of Ibn al-Ashraf is not mentioned at all . . . It seems, that having a sharp historical sense, al-Tabari was aware of the 'fact' that Ka'b had been killed already after Badr . . . It seems that for this reason he avoided mentioning Ka'b's name in his comments on a sura which is related to an event believed to have happened rather later."[1565]

The Muslim sources disagree about the reasons for Ka'b's murder as well as many of the circumstances. Far from causing us to doubt the historicity of the event, these disagreements reinforce its historicity. None of the Muslim sources doubt that the event happened, but in many ways they are at pains to explain it. There can be no doubt that assassination formed an integral part of the Medinan policies of Muhammad. This reality has haunted Muslim culture and politics down to the present day. It may be argued that Wansbrough stopped writing on early Islamic history, and Rawandi and Warraq took their pseudonyms for this very reason. Ideas and actions have consequences, particularly when they are elevated to a policy of God.

The slaughter of the Banu Qurayzah is a similar case in point. Modern Muslim authors invariably argue either for the non-historicity of the account, often with ingeniously foolish arguments such as there not being enough rope with which to tie up the Jewish prisoners (yet they had captured a caravan with one thousand camels, all with tethers!) or they argue for the viciousness of the Jews who deserved what happened to them. Western authors have, on the other hand, ignored these events. Bogle's aforementioned "marriage" between the Jewish widow, Raihana bint Amr, neglects to point out why she was a widow and ignores the fact that even the Muslim sources agree that she never married Muhammad, though she was sexually consummated by the Prophet after he supervised the execution of her father, husband, brothers, and sons over age twelve, and then sold her minor children into slavery to buy arms for the Muslim army. This event is called by Muhammad himself in Ishaq's sira, "a judgement from God." It is remarkable that Western writers ignore such

---

[1565]   Uri Rubin, "The Assassination of Ka'b b. al-Ashraf," in *The Life of Muhammad*, ed. Uri Rubin, p. 70.

material from the historical writings of Muslims or try to explain them away with lame arguments such as "This was a very primitive society" forgetting that these actions are elevated to the policy of God.[1566] These narratives form a significant portion of the early biographical writings. It is equally remarkable that they do not notice the principle established by these events: collective punishment of a community for the supposed sins of its leaders. This principle perfectly justifies the events of 9/11.[1567] Further, the Banu Qurayzah incident has many precedents for Islamic law. In determining which of the males of the Banu Qurayzah would be killed the Muslim soldiers examined them to see if they had pubic hair. The presence of the initial signs of puberty were sufficient for a child to have his head chopped off. This became a precedent within Islamic law concerning the age of accountability and when capital punishment could be applied. This is why the event of the Banu Qurayza is found in all the Hadith literature and in the later books of Islamic law (Fiqh). Karen Armstrong's argument that this is how people behaved in those days in Arabia studiously avoids its present day legal ramifications.[1568] It is this astonishing combination of Western relativism combined with doubt as to the historical veracity of the early Muslim documents that has allowed the transformation of Muhammad into the story of a man of peace. It is surely one of the great cover-ups of world history.

Conclusions

Based on our review of the arguments, we have felt that the Muslim historical documents, the exegesis of the Qur'an and the Qur'an itself, provide a framework that is partly historical. Certain elements are clearly not historical, but these can be identified through the purposes they express: miracles, polemic, and later, legal needs. Those who criticize these documents tend to ignore the fact that the documents are highly consistent with regard to major events. No Muslim author doubts or questions the dating of hijra, the Battles of Badr, Uhud or Khandaq, no one significantly questions the chronology of the treaty of Hudaybiya or the conquest of Mecca. Though the framework is largely historical, each individual tradition must be passed

---

[1566] Karen Armstrong, *Muhammad, A Biography of the Prophet,* San Francisco: Harper, 1993, p. 207.

[1567] It is also mentioned in the Hadith that killing of women and children of non-Muslims is permissible when their identity is unknown, something that justifies the anonymous bomb attack (Bukhari, Vol. 4, p. 159).

[1568] Karen Armstrong, 1993, p. 208.

through a source-critical grid before being accepted. In the few cases where this has been done, far more material has emerged as historical than actually has been used by Western scholars. Further, if the materials that have emerged thus far are representative, they will surely challenge the liberal interpretation of the life of Muhammad so popular just now.[1569] Berg's words seem a fitting conclusion:

> "Today's Islamicists seem on the whole very reluctant to say anything which might be interpreted as critical of Islam, including its own sacralized "origins" and "history" . . . Wansbrough's greatest contribution to Islamic origins may be his summons for Islamicists to return to scholarship."[1570]

[1569] It is disturbing to note how many of the liberal interpretive books on the life of Muhammad are available for purchase on Islamist Web sites.

[1570] Herbert Berg, "The Implications of and Opposition to the Methods and Theories of John Wansbrough," in Method and Theory in the Study of Religion, Kentucky: Swets and Zeitlinger, 2002, p. 19.

CHAPTER 14

THE REJECTION OF

AL 'AZL IN THE PROPER TREATMENT

OF NON-MUSLIM CAPTIVE WOMEN

In a recent edition of the magazine, *National Review,* Raymond Ibrahim, highlighted the activities of an exiled Coptic priest by the name of Father Zakaria, who has been named "Islam's 'Public Enemy #1'" by the Arabic newspaper *al-Insan al Jadid.*[1571] Father Zakaria runs a Web site and a television program where he illustrates some of the more arcane aspects of Islamic law which he then challenges the doctors of Islam to discuss with him. All of this takes place in Arabic, making the show highly accessible to Arabic-speaking Muslims. Some of the material is down-right funny, such as the issue of breastfeeding adult males as a means to avoid adultery. Some of this, however, relates to far more significant concerns. Father Zakaria discussed the sex-slave issue of Islam, which sanctions the use of non-Muslim women, primarily war captives, as concubines. This comes at a time when the West is debating the issue of *sharia* (Islamic law) and the degree to which it should be applied in Western societies. The archbishop of Canterbury, Rowan Williams, recently wrote a scholarly article calling for the limited application of *sharia* in England.[1572] He was backed up here in the United States by a Harvard law professor who argued for the same idea in the *New York Times.*[1573] This article will address the background to this

---

[1571] National Review, March 25, 2008.
[1572] Archbishop's Lecture—Civil and Religious Law in England: a Religious Perspective, Thursday, 07 February, 2008.
[1573] New York Times, March 17, 2008

particular aspect of Islamic law and attempt to answer the question of how this should be considered in the twenty-first century.

One of the more controversial topics in the modern study of Islam, concerns the relative status of women and the treatment and civil rights of non-Islamic minorities within the context of Islamic law. This qualitative research project will look at a very narrow topic within Islamic law which addresses both issues. The aim of the research is to bring to light Muhammad's teaching and practice on this subject through reading and analysis of primary source document references to *al 'azl* and its rejection in the proper treatment of non-Muslim captive women. If *sharia* is to change in the modern context, it must surely begin with the more problematical pronouncements found in the foundational texts of Islam. The purpose of this study is to illustrate one such practice while attempting to answer the question, how is this aspect both of Quranic teaching and of the Prophet's behavior (*sunnah*) to be interpreted in the modern age? Our hope is that this study will benefit liberal Muslims who seek to reform Islam for the twenty-first century context. It is not our purpose to offend any Muslim readers by this project, but to illustrate that all religions must find a way to deal with their darker texts in a globalized world where universal human rights across cultural and religious barriers will become one of the most important issues of the twenty-first century.

Literature Review:

In this project we will use of five types of primary source documents. The first is the holy book of Islam, the Qur'an. This is believed to be the very words of Allah, and the primary source for all aspects of Muslim faith and practice. The Qur'an was "revealed" between the years CE 610 and CE 632. For the purposes of this study the integrity of the text of the Qur'an is assumed, even though there are many reasons to question this. The Qur'an remains for Muslims the coeternal Word of Allah, and must be respected as such.

The second source will be the collections of traditions (*hadith*) of the Prophet. As John Esposito points out in his book *Islam, The Straight Path*, "Muhammad has served as the ideal model for Muslim life, providing the pattern that all believers are to emulate. He is, as some Muslims say, the 'living Quran.[1574]'" The *hadith* collections form the foundation for Islamic

---

[1574] John Esposito, *Islam, The Straight Path*, New York: Oxford University Press, 1991, p. 13.

law. Three of the most reliable collections of *hadith* from the perspective of Sunni Islam have been chosen for this study. These "traditions" comprise the early reports of the companions of Muhammad concerning his teachings and practice. I assume once again the relative integrity of these texts though there are even greater reasons to doubt the historicity of many of them. These texts remain the most important source in Islam for s*haria*, and must be respected as such. The *hadith* are second only to the Qur'an as the basis for *sharia*.[1575]

One of the primary justifications for following the *hadith* is found in the Qur'an in Al-Ahzab 33:21 "Ye have indeed in the Messenger of Allah a beautiful pattern (or noble example of conduct) for any one whose hope is in Allah and the Final Day . . ."[1576] In a recent personal interview with a Saudi Arabian Imam I was told that without the *hadith* one could not understand the Qur'an, know how to perform prayers, or any other religious duties.[1577]

The *hadith* were compiled some 200-300 years after Muhammad and their veracity was demonstrated through a criterion considered valid by the scholars at the time. The two most famous of the collections and the most authoritative of the six accepted *hadith* are Sahih Muslim and Sahih Al-Bukhari.[1578] We will also consider the third most reliable collection of Abu Dawud.

[1575] Glasse Cyril, *The Concise Encyclopedia of Islam*, New York City, NY: HarperCollins Publishers, 1989. 141.

[1576] *The Meaning of the Holy Qur'an*, trans. Ali Abdullah Yusuf, Beltsville, MA: Amana Publications, 2003.

[1577] Private Interview with Imam Ali, August 20, 2004.
I asked him what importance he placed on the hadith and what their purposes are. Ali went into a long explanation of history and definitions of *sunnah* (way of, sayings and actions of Muhammad) and hadith. But he said that "Without the *sunnah*, you could not understand the Qur'an," He said you must have the *sunnah* and follow it, he said, "without it, how would we know how to properly perform the prayers, or do anything" He did go into the art and science of the *isnad* and how we can trust it. It is significant to note in this context that nowhere in the Qur'an are the specific practices of *Shahada* (confession), *Saum* (fasting), *Salat* (prayer), *Zakah* (almsgiving) and *Hajj* (pilgrimage) clearly and completely defined. These most essential practices of Islam are all defined in their specific details in the *hadith*.

[1578] Glasse, *The Concise Encyclopedia of Islam*, p. 141.

The *hadith* are structured into two components, the *matn* (text) and its *isnad* (chain of narrators).[1579] The *matn* contains: 1. God's own words (*qudsi*), 2. Muhammad's words that are attributed as recitations of Allah's words, and 3. A saying or action of Muhammad or his approval or disapproval of someone else's. The *isnad* contains a chain of transmitters which makes it, according to the scholarship of the time, reliable[1580] The *hadith* are also ordered by their reliability, and the most reliable have received the title "*sahih*" or correct. This class of *hadith* is considered the most reliable and, therefore, canonical as defining correct behavior for Sunni Muslims.[1581] All of these *hadith* are available in English translation.

The third category of literature utilized is the *Sira*, or biographical stories of the Life of Muhammad. The earliest preserved biography, entitled *The Life of the Prophet of God* (*Sirat Rasul Allah*) is available in translation by Afred Guillaume. The writer, Ibn Ishaq, was born in Medina about 707 CE and wrote this biography around the year 750 CE. It is told of Ibn Ishaq that he was a man of good reputation, great memory, and as a young man his veracity in hadith was self-evident.[1582] The translator states that, "For the most part the stories rest on the account of eyewitnesses and have every right to be regarded as trustworthy."[1583] This biography was also edited by a well-known scholar named Abdul-l Malik Ibn Hisham who gives genealogical footnotes and critical observations.[1584] The book only survives in this edited form. Ibn Ishaq's work is foundational to all the later writers of *sira* works, such as Al Tabari and Ibn Kathir. Tabari is the most famous of the early biographers, and he restored certain parts of Ibn Ishaq's work that Ibn Hisham had edited out as too controversial. This study will center on Ibn Ishaq's work as one of the earliest and most reliable. Brief mention will be made of the other second earliest biography of Al-Waqidi.

A fourth category of Islamic literature will be briefly consulted to show later Islamic treatments of this topic. This is the "*fiqh*" literature, or books of Islamic law. I have chosen Ibn-al-Naqib al-Masri's (d. 1368) *Reliance of the*

[1579]   Kazi Mazhara, *Treasury of Hadith and Sunnah, 551 Hadith*, Claymont, DE: Amana Publications, 1997, p. 23.
[1580]   Mazhara, p. 27.
[1581]   Mazhara, p. 28.
[1582]   *Ibn Ishaq, The Life of Muhammad,* trans. Guillaume. Karachi, Pakistan: Oxford University Press, 2004. xxxv.
[1583]   Guillaume, xix.
[1584]   Guillaume, xli.

Traveler.[1585] This is a manual of Shafi'i jurisprudence recently translated into English. It shows the very oblique way that this topic tends to be interpreted, a manner which modern writers have adopted.

Finally, there are several commentaries (*tafsir*) on the Qur'an which have also been consulted in preparing this paper. The most popular is Yusuf's Ali's commentary which is incorporated in the text of his translation of the Qur'an. This may be regarded as a modern interpretation of the text although it incorporates insights from much older works. As a balance to this, Ibn Kathir's commentary, from the sixth century AH, was also consulted.

Terms Defined:

Al-'Azl. "Dismissal, separation, withdrawal, coitus interruptus"[1586] "to part, to separate,"[1587] and "he put it aside, or he "separated." In a technical sense it implies incomplete sexual intercourse.[1588] Withdrawal of the penis from the vagina before ejaculation as a means of birth control.

'Iddiah. "Waiting period" "a woman's menstrual period," which was from thirty to forty-five days to see if a woman was pregnant or not. Inclusive of the period of waiting after the dissolution of a marriage.[1589]

Istilad. "The offspring's claim" that signifies a man having a child born to him of a female slave, which he claims and acknowledges as his own, this acknowledgement causes the freedom of the slave woman and her title is changed to:

Ummu 'l Walad "the mother of the offspring," and relation to her master as his wife and the child as free.[1590]

[1585] Al-Misri, Ahmad ibn Naqi', *Reliance of the Traveler*, trans. Nu Ha Mim Keller, Maryland: Amana Publications, 1994 edition.

[1586] Gibb Kramers, *The Encyclopedia of Islam New. Ed Vol. 1,* Netherlands: Leiden Brill, 1960, p. 826.

[1587] Yeshil Shemseddin, *Hazret-i Muhammad.* Topkapi, Istanbul: Yaylacik Matbaacilik Ltd., 2005.

[1588] A. H. Siddiqui, *Sahih Muslim Vol. 1-4.*, trans. Dr. Muhammad Muhsin Khan. Hilal Yayinlar Ankara, Turkey. Indianapolis: MSA, 1990, p. 733. See footnote.

[1589] J. H. Kramers, H. A. R. Gibb, ed. *Shorter Encyclopedia of Islam*, Leiden E. J. Brill\London Luzac and Co. Netherlands: Leiden Brill, 1961,. p. 448.

[1590] Thomas P. Hughes, *Library of Religious and Philosophic Thought "A dictionary of Islam."* Clifton, New Jersey: Reference Book Publishers, Inc., 1965, p. 598.

Jihad. "Effort, struggle, holy war," a divine institution of warfare to extend Islam into the non-Islamic territories and/or to defend Islam from danger.[1591]

Nikah. Literally, "Sexual intercourse," but in the Qur'an used as a legal institution implying marriage.[1592] Sexual intercourse then would imply a legal marriage.

Sunnah. "Custom usage." This term is applied to the speech and example of Muhammad.[1593]

The practice of taking captives from among civilians during wartime was normal in ancient cultures. In the last two hundred years, rules of warfare have changed and captives generally tend not to be civilians but the opposing soldiers taken in battle. The Geneva Convention established laws for the protection of any captive during wartime. Some of these laws pertain particularly to the treatment of women. According to the general protection of prisoners of war in articles thirteen and fourteen:

> "Likewise, prisoners of war must at all times be protected, particularly against acts of violence or intimidation and against insults and public curiosity. Measures of reprisal against prisoners of war are prohibited. *Prisoners of war* are entitled in all circumstances to respect for their persons and their honour. Women shall be treated with all the regard due to their sex and shall in all cases benefit by treatment as favourable as that granted to men. Prisoners of war shall retain the full civil capacity which they enjoyed at the time of their capture. The Detaining Power may not restrict the exercise, either within or without its own territory, of the rights such capacity confers except in so far as the captivity requires."[1594]

It might seem that comparing the laws of Islam to these modern texts is unfair; times and cultures have changed immensely since the seventh century. However, if the *sunnah* of the Prophet of Islam is normative for all Muslims even in the modern age, and virtually all Muslim experts on Islamic law would

---

[1591] Glasse, *The Concise Encyclopedia of Islam,* p. 210.
[1592] Kramers, *Shorter Encyclopeadia of Islam*, p. 447.
[1593] Glasse, *The Concise Encyclopedia of Islam,* p. 381.
[1594] http://www.unhchr.ch/html/menu3/b/91.htm

claim this, then we must compare the two systems if we are to understand the nature of the conflict.

The subject of women taken captive during *jihad* was addressed in the Qur'an, and since these were almost always non-Muslim women, these brief notations became extremely important with regard to understanding how canonical Islam treats non-Muslims. The *hadith* also sheds much more light on this subject as a commentary to the Qur'an.

In the section called Al-Nisa referring to accepted *nikah,* it is prohibited that Muslim men marry women already in *nikah* status, except if they happen to be captive women.

> "Also (prohibited are) women already married, except those whom your right hands possess. Thus hath Allah ordained (prohibitions) against you. Except for these . . ."[1595]

The translator and commentator comment correctly when explaining the term "those whom your right hands possess" refers to the captives in *jihad,* specifically women.[1596]

Chapter 23 *Al-Mu'minun* of the Qur'an also comments on treatment of captive women during *jihad.*

> "The believers must win through those who humble themselves in their prayers, who avoid vain talk, who are active in deeds of charity; who abstain from sex, except with those joined to them in the marriage bond, or (the captives) whom their right hands possess, for (in their case) they are free from blame,"[1597]

This verse establishes that sexual intercourse with a captive in *jihad* is not sin or *haram* but *halal* (what is meritorious in Islam), as the aforementioned verse that said one could *nikah* with a married captive, and in gratefully doing so free her from her slave status if she bore a child. (Law of *istilad.*) Ibn Kathir comments on this passage that Allah has made permissible sexual intercourse with those "their right hand possessions from among the captives."[1598] It is

---

[1595] *Quran,* trans. Yusuf Ali, 4:24, p. 192.

[1596] *Quran.* 192. see footnote.

[1597] *Quran.* 23:1-6, p. 844.

[1598] Ibn Kathir Hafiz, trans. Sheikh Safiur Rahman Al-Mubarakpuri. *Tafsir,* Vol. 6, p. 631. Riyadh: Dar us salam Publishers and Distributors, 2000.

interesting to note that passages of this type are found in all periods of Quranic revelation, the above chapter having been revealed in the middle Meccan period of revelations (613-614 CE). They are more frequent, of course, in the chapters dating from the Medinan period (622-632 CE).

In Al Ahzab, chapter 33, which dates from the mid-Medinan period, Allah gives Muhammad captive women as booty.

> "O Prophet! We have made lawful to thee thy wives to whom thou hast paid their dowers, and those whom the right hand possess out of the prisoners of war whom Allah has assigned to thee;. Allah is Oft-Forgiving, Most Merciful."[1599]

Also it was written that Muhammad had a limit on the number of wives that he was allowed by Allah, but the exception was with the female captives of *jihad*. He could have as many of those as he wanted.

> "It is not lawful for thee (to marry more) women after this, nor to change them for (other) wives, even though their beauty attract thee, except any their right hand should possess (as handmaidens)."[1600]

Ibn Kathir explains "The slave girls whom you took from the war booty are also permitted to you."[1601] Even in Yusuf Ali's more sanitized *tafsir* he quotes Al Maarij speaking again to the subject of not guarding the chastity or virginity of captured wives and (captives) their right hands possess.[1602] There seems to be a strong precedent from the Qur'an, which allows the Muslim jihadists to not guard the virginity of captive women, and it is also clear that married captive women are not exempt from this law of Allah. There are many other passages in the Qur'an that relate to the rape of female prisoners, but we need to turn our attention to a particular detail that emerges in the *hadith* literature.

Al-'azl is not mentioned in the Qur'an, but the Qur'an gives the precedence for the need of *al-'azl*. If one did not want to keep a women captive or set her free from her captive state *'azl* was ideal for a Muslim soldier. If a Muslim soldier wanted to have lawful sex with a captive woman and at the same time ransom her

---

[1599] *Quran*, Yusuf Ali. 33:50-51, pp. 1071-1073.
[1600] *Quran* 33:52, p. 1074.
[1601] Ibn Kathir, Vol. 7, p. 720.
[1602] *Quran*, Yusuf Ali., 70:29-30, pp. 1528-1529.

back to her relatives *al-'azl* was the best option in their mind for contraception. If one of the captives came to be with child, her status would change according to the law of *istilad,* and she would become the *ummu 'l walad.* The ransom also would be lost by the birth of a child.[1603] The context also to when these laws were given is extremely important in understanding why Allah would allow one to have sex with a captive. Both Dawud and Bukhari, record the story of a Muslim soldier who entered a Mosque to ask Muhammad a question regarding withdrawing the penis (*al-'azl*) and it was answered accordingly:

> "We went out with the Apostle of Allah on the expedition to Banu al Mustaliq, and took some Arab women captive, and we desired the women, for we were suffering from the absence of our wives, and we wanted to ransom; so we intended to withdraw the penis (while having intercourse with the slave-women). But we asked ourselves: 'Can we draw the penis when the Apostle of Allah is among us before asking him about it?' So we asked him about it. He said: 'It does not matter if you do not do it, for every soul that is to be born up to the Day of Resurrection will be born."[1604]

Ibn Ishaq explains that this took place in the year AH 6 when Muhammad attacked the Banu Mustaliq. The Muslims took the wives, children, and property as booty. Muhammad himself distributed the captives among his fellow jihadists.[1605]

Another example was when a man came to Muhammad and asked about *al-'azl* concerning his slave because he did not want her to conceive. Muhammad replied, "Withdraw your penis from her if you wish, for what is decreed for her will come to her."[1606]

Another example of Muslim jihadists wanting to practice *al-'azl* is recorded for us in a *hadith* by Sahih Muslim.

> " . . . and there is another person who has a slave-girl and he has sexual intercourse with her, but he does not like her to have conception so that she may not become *Umm Walad,* whereupon

---

[1603] Dawud Sunan Abu, *Sunan Abu Dawud. Vol. 1-3.* trans. Ahmad Hasan, Daryaganj, New Delhi: Nursat Ali Nasri Publishers for Kitab Bhavan, 1993, p. 582. See footnote.

[1604] Sunan abu Dawud, p. 582 and Sahih Muslim, p. 733.

[1605] Ibn Ishaq, *Life of Muhammad,* pp. 490-493.

[1606] Sunan abu Dawud, p. 582.

(Muhammad) said: 'There is no harm if you do not do that, for that (the birth of the child) is something preordained."[1607]

More examples of *'azl* from Sahih Muslim:

"Abu Said al Kudri reported: We took women captives and we wanted to do *al 'azl* with them. We then asked Allah's messenger about it, and he said to us: 'Verily you do it, verily you do it, verily you do it, but the soul which has been born until the Day of Judgment must be born'."[1608]

"Abu Said al Kudri reported that mention was made of 'azl in the presence of Allah's Apostle whereupon he said: Why do any one of you practice it? For there is no created soul whose Creator is not Allah'?"[1609]

"Abu Said al Kudri reported that Allah's Apostle was asked about *'azl*, whereupon he said: 'There is no harm if you do not do that, for it (the birth of the child) is something ordained.' Muhammad (one of the narrators) said: 'La 'alaikum (there is no harm) *implies its prohibition*."[1610] (Italics mine)

Although it does not seem that the practice of *al 'azl* is directly prohibited, but it is looked at unfavorably according to Muhammad because of his view of the cosmology of the soul where existence is predestined no matter the "precautions," such as *'azl* that are taken.

Another example that shows Muhammad's dislike of this practice is recorded for us in this following Hadith in Sahih Muslim:

"They asked him about *'azl*, whereupon he said: 'That is the secret (way of) burying alive', and 'Ubaidullah has made this addition in the hadith transmitted by al Muqri and that is: 'When the one buried alive is asked."[1611]

[1607] Sahih Muslim, p. 734.

[1608] Muslim, p. 733.

[1609] Muslim, p. 735.

[1610] Muslim, p. 734.

[1611] Muslim, p. 736.

The footnote in Sahih Muslim on this Hadith helps us understand this more fully as it explains that Muhammad was referring to the pre-Islamic practice of burying female children alive for fear of hunger or disgrace. "The question is this: And when the one buried alive is asked for what sin she was killed." Muhammad appears to equate *'azl* with the practiced of burying children alive.[1612]

This means that *'azl* although not fully prohibited is considered *makruh* (neither *haram* nor *halal*) and is not looked at as a good thing for jihadists to do. The issue here is not the fact of intercourse but the prevention of conception. Nothing in these texts indicates that it might be wrong to rape a female captive, that practice is fully *hallal*.

Another battle was fought by Muhammad and his followers at Hunayn, after the battle Kudri records this for us in Sahih Muslim:

> "Having overcome them and taken them captives, the Companions of Allah's Messenger seemed to refrain from having intercourse with captive women because their husbands being polytheists. Then Allah, Most High, sent down regarding that: 'And women already married, except those whom your right hands possess' . . . They took captives (women) on the day of Autas who had their husbands. They were afraid (to have sexual intercourse with them) when this verse was revealed: 'And women already married, except those whom your right hands possess'."[1613]

This verse is from Sura Al-Nisa 4:24 from the Medinan period. Ibn Kathir goes on to explain this:

> "We captured some women from Awtas who were already married, and we Disliked having sexual relations with them because they already had husbands. So we asked the Prophet about this matter, and this Ayah was revealed, 'Also (forbidden are) women already married, except those whom your right handspossess'. Consequently, we had sexual relations with these women."[1614]

Abu Sunan Dawud gives us more detail concerning this battle and the treatment of these captive women, and the reason that they did not want to

---

[1612] Muslim, p. 736.
[1613] Muslim, p. 743.
[1614] Ibn Kathir, Vol. 2, p. 422.

have sexual intercourse with them was because it was "in the presence of their husbands who were unbelievers."[1615]

The husbands were present as captives in the camp. Al-Bukhari records for us this story:

> "We got female captives in the war booty and we used to do *'azl* with them. So we asked Allah's Apostle about it and he said, 'Do you really do that?' repeating the question thrice, and then said, 'There is no soul that is destined to exist but will come into existence, till the Day of Resurrection'."[1616]

According to Ibn Ishaq, the battle was fought in the year AH 8 when 12,000 Muslims went to Hunayn. There was a slaughter of those in the settlement, and the captives of Hunayn were brought to Muhammad with their property. They were brought to Al Jirana, and at Al Jirana 6,000 women and children were held captive there. These women were returned to their husbands later for a price of six camels each for ransom.[1617] These were ransomed after the fact was determined that *Al-'azl* was practiced. In other words, the husbands were unwilling to ransom a wife who could be pregnant with another man's child.

Muhammad set an example for his followers as he took women prisoners during *jihad* as his booty. He had the first pick of the most beautiful of the women as it was his right from Allah called *safi* "special portion of booty or property of choice."[1618] One example is after the Battle of Khaybar (a siege and defeat of a Jewish tribe) it was recorded that Muhammad had desired a Jewish woman whose husband had been killed in the battle. It was reported by Anas b. Malik:

> "We came to Khaibar. When Allah bestowed the conquest of fortress (on us), the beauty of Safiyyah, daughter of Huyayy was mentioned to him (the Prophet). Her husband was killed and she was a bride. The Apostle of Allah chose her for himself. He came

---

[1615] Sunan abu Dawud. p. 577.

[1616] Sahih Al-Bukhari, *The Translation of the Meanings of Sahih Al-Buhkari vol. vii.* trans. Muhammad M. Khan, Al Medina Al Munawwara, Islamic University. Hilal Yayinlari Beirut: Dar Al Arabia, 1981, p. 103.

[1617] Ibn Ishaq, *Life of Muhammad*, pp. 566-593.

[1618] Sunan Abu Dawud, pp. 847-848.

out with her till we reached Sadd al Sahba, where she was purified. So he cohabited with her."[1619]

In Islamic history, it is said that Safiyah became his wife referring back to this point of "cohabiting" with her. In Bukhari, it is recorded that it was three days later that he cohabited with Safiyah, and that there was much interest among Muhammad's followers: "The Muslims wondered, is she considered as his wife or his slave girl?" Then they said, "If he orders her to veil herself, she will be one of the mothers of the Believers, but if he does not order her to veil herself she will be a slave girl."[1620] Does this imply that the Muslims wondered if Muhammad would practice *azl* with her? The passage shows later that Muhammad had decided to keep her as a wife and not allow her to be ransomed by the surviving Jews. In such a case, since he would not be seeking ransom, *azl* would not be practiced. The rape is carried out with intention to impregnate. This is fully *hallal*, sanctioned by both the teaching and actual practice of the Prophet.

The same events in early Muslim literature could be interpreted very differently at different stages in history. To illustrate this consider the comparison made between Ibn Ishaq's description of the aftermath of the Muslim conquest of the Jewish enclave at Khaybar and a similar passage in the writings of Al-Waqidi, a generation later. After the Jews are defeated, the following event involving some of the captured Jewish women occurs:

> "Bilal who was bringing them led them past the Jews who were slain; and when the woman who was with Safiya saw them she shrieked and slapped her face and poured dust on her head. When the Apostle saw her he said, 'take this she devil [emphasis mine] away from me.' He gave orders that Safiya was to be put behind him and threw his mantle over her, so that the Muslims knew that he had chosen her for himself."

The parallel passage in Al-Waqidi reads:

> "The Messenger of God had sent her [Safiya] ahead with Bilal to his camel. And he passed with her and her cousin by the slaughtered. And Safiya's cousin screamed a loud cry. The

---

[1619] Ibid. p. 848.
[1620] Sahih Al-Bukhari, Vol. vii, p. 14.

Messenger of God hated what Bilal did ... The Messenger of
God said to the cousin of Safiya: This is only the devil [referring
to Bilal. [emphasis mine]."[1621]

Rizwi Faizer goes on to compare these two passages saying:

"The simple but obvious transference of imagery is delightful.
It certainly establishes the image of the Prophet as kinder and
more tolerant than what Ibn Ishaq would have us believe. It is
possible, however, that al-Waqidi was reacting to the information
communicated by Ibn Ishaq and adjusting the tradition in an
honest attempt to be faithful to his interpretation of the nature of
the Prophet."[1622]

It seems strange that the prelude to rank sexual activity should be described in
terms that make it seem more like literature (delightful?) than history, and this
is part of Faizer's thesis. It also appears that Faizer's analysis has not gone far
enough. It is clear that these two passages are describing the same historical
event, but interpreting it according to the circumstances of their own time. Ibn
Ishaq is the older of the two, coming at the end of the first period of Muslim
military expansion. For obvious reasons stories of the military exploits of
the Prophet were of prime importance during this period. They provided
the precedents for Muslim actions in war. It is likely that Ibn Ishaq is not at
all hostile to the Prophet's actions as Faizer implies. In an age of conquest,
where women were part of the spoils of battle, it was common practice of
the soldiers to use these women sexually. The Jews had resisted Muhammad,
and in the course of battle the leader of the tribe as well as Safiya's husband
were killed. Safiya, as the daughter of the leader of the Jewish tribe, would
naturally be selected by Muhammad for himself symbolically demonstrating,
through his sexual intercourse with her, the total subjugation of the Jewish
tribe. Al-Waqidi, writing during a later, more settled age, tries to find a way
to mollify this picture, by postulating the "romance" theory that Safiya was
attracted to Muhammad through his magnanimous behavior. A visit to Muslim
Web sites today under Safiya bint Huyayy, demonstrates that this thesis has

---

[1621] Rizwi S. Faizer, *Ibn Ishaq and al-Waqidi Revisited: A Case Study of Muhammad
and the Jews in Biographical Literature*, Doctoral thesis, Montreal: McGill
University, 1995, pp. 183-184.
[1622] Faizer, 1995, p. 184.

been enthroned as the reigning paradigm. Even Western writers are carried away by this interpretation:

> "The Prophet married a Jewish widow from the Bani Quraydha in 627 and a little more than a year later married another Jewish woman of the vanquished Khaybar tribe, who accepted him even though her father, brother and husband had lost their lives to the Muslims."[1623]

It is clear that Ishaq's version, for several reasons, is the more accurate. First, his description of Jewish mourning, shrieking, slapping the face, and pouring dust on the head depicts accurately Jewish culture of the day whereas Al-Waqidi's single loud cry does not. Further, it does not make sense to call Bilal a "devil" for doing what the Prophet in the previous verse had told him to do. Finally, the reversal of imagery by Al-Waqidi is a typical form of literary transformation that attempts to make it appear Ibn Ishaq got his account mixed up when in fact Al-Waqidi is the one doing the mixing.

Al Bukhari explains in more detail the treatment of "slave girls."

> "Ibn 'Umar said, 'If a slave girl is suitable to have sexual relations is given to someone else as a gift, or sold or manumitted, her master should not have sexual intercourse with her before she gets one menstruation so as to be sure of absence of pregnancy' . . . Ata said, 'There is no harm in fondling with one's pregnant slave girl without having sexual intercourse with her'. Allah said: 'Except with their wives and the (women captives) whom their right hands possess (for in this case they are not to be blamed). (70:30)."[1624]

[1623] Emory C. Bogle, *Islam Origin and Belief*, Austin: University of Texas Press, 1998, pp. 18-19. Emory Bogle's rendition of this event is symptomatic. In his 1998 book, *Islam Origin and Belief*, he refers to the above event as follows: "The Prophet married a Jewish widow from the Banu Quraydha in 627, and a little more than a year later married another Jewish woman of the vanquished Khaybar tribe, who accepted him even though her father, brother and husband had lost their lives to the Muslims" (Bogle, 1998, pp. 18-19). This in spite of the fact that even the Muslim documents admit that Rayhana never married the Prophet. The coercive nature of these relationships is obvious. Modern Western literature clearly whitewashes these events.

[1624] Sahih Al-Bukhari, Vol. iii, p. 240.

Another attack on a tribe called the Fazarah was recorded and the treatment of captive women is explained for us in Al Bukhari:

> "We attacked Fazarah and took them from all sides. I then saw a group of people which contained children and women. I shot an arrow toward them . . . I brought them to Abu Bakr. There was among them a woman of Fazarah. She wore skin over her and her daughter who was the most beautiful of the Arabs with her. Abu Bakr gave her daughter to me as a reward. I came back to Medina. The Apostle of Allah met me and said to me, 'give me the woman, Salamah.' I said to him: 'I swear by Allah, she is to my liking, and I have not yet untied her garment.'"[1625]

It is reported later that these women were used as ransom for other Muslim prisoners in Mecca and needed to be traded for them.

The final story for us to consider concerns the case of Muhammad's treatment of the Jewish tribe of Banu Qurayzah. The tribal elders of the group were accused of having conspired against the Muslims during the Battle of the Trench in AD 627. After besieging the Jewish tribe for several weeks, an agreement was reached for their surrender. Following this the order was given to systematically execute the men (all who had developed pubic hair) of the tribe (numbering from 600-900) by beheading.[1626] Shares of this Jewish tribe were divided up such as the women and children. Rayhana, daughter of the leader of this Jewish tribe was taken as slave girl by Muhammad She showed "repugnance" for and refused to convert to Islam and thereby be considered legally married after the Prophet consummated her sexually.[1627] She was never married to the Prophet and remained his slave girl until her death, although modern Western writers refer to her relationship to the Prophet as a "marriage."

The Islamic legal literature deals with this subject in a highly oblique way. The Shafi'i legal manual *Reliance of the Traveler* only mentions this in the context of Islamic views of contraception. In two places it retells the story of companions of the Prophet, asking about the permissibility of *azl*.[1628]

[1625] Bukhari, pp. 749-750.

[1626] From this event is derived the Muslim view of the age of accountability, when one can be liable to capital punishment. Once pubic hair has developed, one is considered fully accountable for one's actions.

[1627] Ibn Ishaq, *Life of Muhammad,* p. 466.

[1628] Al-Misri, 1994, pp. 526, 949, 950.

The context dealing with captured women prisoners of war is left out. The law manual describes the practice as "*makruh*," permissible, but not meritorious:

It is of the etiquette of intercourse not to practice coitus interruptus, there being disagreement among scholars as to the permissibility or offensiveness of doing so, though the correct position in our opinion is that it is permissible.[1629]

Conclusions and Further Questions:

From this research it appears that the practice of *al 'azl* was neither rejected as *haram* (sin) nor was it accepted as *halal* (acceptable practice), but it was *makruh* which is put at the same level as using tobacco or caffeine products. The practice of taking female captives was common place and is halal, and we have many examples of their treatment and status. If a captive woman became pregnant, she would by the law of *istilad* become *ummu l walad,* and therefore not be able to be ransomed, nor would she have the status of a slave. The practice of *al 'azl* was therefore needed and practiced, so there could be ransom. Muhammad seemed to disapprove of the practice of *al 'azl* by teaching the doctrine of creationism of the soul, predestination, and the sovereignty of Allah, albeit not condemning *'azl* as *haram*. It is clear that there was no problem with non-interruptus relations with enslaved non-Muslim women.

Modern research that has been done concerning the practice of *al 'azl* discusses only women's rights concerning their choice of birth control and issues of sexual fulfillment. This is not the issue according to the above research. The issue is whether or not Muslim men have the right to rape non-Muslim captive women as taught by Islamic primary sources. *Al 'azl* was a practice that was done to prevent pregnancy and allow for a good ransom price.

There are several examples of modern research which totally misses the point. Carla Obermeyer, D.Sc., a professor at Harvard deals with "reproductive rights" in Islam. Obermeyer mentions the practice of *al 'azl* as the only method of contraception in Islamic literature, but ignores the reasons why it was practiced.[1630] Another writer relating to this subject, Basim Musallam, refers to the practice of *al 'azl* as to whether it was

---

[1629] Al-Misri, 1994, p. 950.

[1630] Obermeyer, Carla Makhlouf. *Reproductive choice in Islam: Gender and state in Iran and Tunisia.* Studies in Family Planning; Jan/Feb94, Vol. 25 Issue 1, 41. See also: Human Rights Quarterly 17.2 1995, 366-381. *A Cross Cultural Perspective on Reproductive Rights.*

allowed by various schools of Islamic law (*fiqh*), and that it should not be practiced without the wife's consent because it would deprive her of sexual fulfillment![1631] The only extensive article dealing directly with al '*azl* was written by Donna Lee Bowen which stated "the women's rights in question were those of progeny and sexual fulfillment." She goes on to explain that various Islamic jurists have pronounced '*azl* as *makruh, haram,* or *halal,* according to the level of status of the women that are in relation to the man committing the act.[1632] What is overlooked is the treatment of non-Muslim women and its direct relationship to the practice of al '*azl*.

It is remarkable that this issue is ignored in all Western writings on *sharia*. The only place where the subject is taken up seems to be in reference to birth control, and whether it is allowable under Islamic law. This line of reasoning is absurd because the important issue here has nothing to do with birth control, nor sexual fulfillment of the woman. It is an issue of women's rights, and what may be expected of Islamic armies in war. The issue here is the system of religious apartheid, which prevails in Muslim societies, denying non-Muslim populations of basic human rights and equal protection for all citizens under law. Religious background should have absolutely nothing to do with whether one is subject to rape or not. Al '*azl* is one of the many, many problems in Islamic law. If there is to be a true liberalization in Islam, then laws and traditions of this type simply must be repudiated by the Islamic Ulemma. Rayhana's "repugnance" for Islam is the natural reaction of any woman to being raped because of her religion.

Modern Use of Rape in Muslim Government Practice

On August 11, 2009, a crowd gathered at Jamkaran just outside of Qom, Iran. The crowd had come together to listen to Imam Ayatollah Mohammad Taqi Mesbah-Yazdi and Ahmadinejad, president of Iran, discuss the use of rape by the Islamic regime. Earlier it seems that Mesbah-Yazdi had made a statement that following the president was next to following Allah. They had

---

[1631] Issawi, Charles. Book review: *Sex and Society in Islam. Birth control before the nineteenth century.* By Basim F. Musallam. (London, New York Cambridge University Press, 1983), Found in the Journal of the American Oriental Society 105.2, 1985, 362.

[1632] Bowen, Donna Lee, *Muslim juridical opinions concerning the status of women as demonstrated by the case of '*azl.* Journal of Near Eastern Studies 40 No. 4. 1981, 323-328.

gathered for a question and answer type session and responded to the issues that were being presented. One person asked if they could consider any confessions from people being tortured as real evidence, the response was simply, "Getting a confession from any person who is against the Velayat-e Faqih ('Guardianship of the Islamic Jurists,' or the regime of Iran's mullahs) is permissible under any condition."[1633] The concept of *takfir* also lies at the core of this practice. Any Muslim resisting the "Guardianship of the Islamic Jurists" is not a true Muslim and therefore becomes subject to punishment by rape.

A follow-up question asked if it was permissible for a jailor to obtain information from a prisoner by use of rape. The Imam answered with, "the necessary precaution is for the interrogator to perform a ritual washing first and say prayers while raping the prisoner. If the prisoner is female, it is permissible to rape through the vagina or anus. It is better not to have a witness present. If it is a male prisoner, then it's acceptable for someone else to watch while the rape is committed."[1634] In fact, the Imam goes even further and asserts that there are rewards waiting for men who rape the women in these circumstances by stating, "if the judgment for the [female] prisoner is execution, then rape before execution brings the interrogator a spiritual reward equivalent to making the mandated Hajj pilgrimage [to Mecca], but if there is no execution decreed, then the reward would be equivalent to making a pilgrimage to [the Shi'ite holy city of] Karbala."[1635]

This speech shows the disturbing opinion of the leaders of the country of Iran that rape is permissible, and in fact even rewarded by heaven, when it comes to prisoners that have been taken captive. The specific use of rape here is to force a confession out of a person by the means of torture. It is interesting to note that there seems to be government sanctions for these actions and the foundation of this is the Qur'anic concept of "women whom your right hand possesses."

In an article written by Dr. Sayyed Al-Qimni on "Muslim Intellectual Doublespeak" he quotes an American shiek who denied that slavery ever existed in Islam and is most definitely not permissible. He then went on to say that two days later, he heard the Imam of the Great Mosque in Basra giving out a fatwa that permitted any man taking a Western female soldier

---

[1633] Nissan Ratzlav-Katz, "Ahmadinejad's Imam: Islam Allows Raping, Torturing Prisoners," Published on September 9, 2009. Accessed May 18, 2010, URL: http://www.israelnationalnews.com/News/News.aspx/133214

[1634] Ratslav-Katz.September 9, 2009.

[1635] Ratslav-Katz, September 9, 2009.

or an Iraqi woman suspected of aiding the American troops captive he was allowed to "lie with her."[1636] He also accuses CAIR, an American-Islamic organization, of denying the tradition that Muhammad married a woman after killing her family because of the war at the time and of permitting the women on the defeated side to be taken as captives.[1637]

It is interesting that this article notes the general non-consensus in the world of Islam. The extremists go from outright denying that such things are allowed or that they even happen to the opposite extreme of imams calling for the rape of women that have been taken hostage.

In the year of 1988, several thousand Kurds died in a campaign war with Iraq named the Anfal operation. It was the final campaign against the Kurdish people who had wished to become their own state and have independence. The issue of a Kurdish national state had come out of the ruins of the Ottoman Empire. The Kurds found themselves running across newly drawn borders of Turkey, Iran, Syria, and Iraq, and because of this they started to fight for a state of their own. In September 1980, Iraq invaded Iran and Iraq became quite engrossed in fighting against Iranians. The Kurdish people took the opportunity to begin fighting as well against the Iraqis along with the Iranians. The Iraqis saw this as capital treason and decided to squash this treason, and Saddam Hussein appointed Al Hassan al-Majid to oversee the operations. He ordered the use of poisonous gas that affected mostly civilian populations and then began to destroy villages. However, the fate of women and children that were captured during this time would depend on where they were located. If they were located in the area of Anfal VIII, they were sent to prison camp at Sulaymaniyeh.[1638]

It was at this torture camp in Sulaymaniyeh that many detestable acts were carried out. There is now a Torture Museum located at Sulaymaniyeh where these acts are immortalized in photos and plastic replicas of what happened to these people. There were about four hundred different officers who saw to this prison with many different ranks and orders. According to

---

[1636] Al- Qimni, Sayyed. "Egyptian Progressive Criticizes Muslim Intellectual Doublespeak," published on 14 January 2005, accessed on 23 February 2010. URL: http://www.memri.org/report/en/0/0/0/0/0/0/1297.htm

[1637] Al-Qimni.as above.

[1638] Joost R. Hiltermann, "The 1988 Anfal Campaign in Iraqi Kurdistan, Online Encyclopedia of Mass Violence," [online], published on 3 February 2008, accessed 30 April 2010, URL: http://www.massviolence.org/The-1988-Anfal-Campaign-in-Iraqi-Kurdistan, ISSN 1961-9898.

Hewa Aziz in the article written on the museum, it is stated that one area's identity card clearly had "rapist" written upon it as the job of the worker who carried the card. One woman stated that there were over five hundred women and girls in an underground chamber being tortured and humiliated because they were Kurdish women.[1639]

In Anthony Mascarenhas' book *The Rape of Bangladesh* he states, "When Pakistan became an independent country in August 1947, it was created with built-in conflict . . . East and West Pakistan were different in every way." He goes on to say that both sides had different ways of thinking and speaking, dressing, and even the sports they enjoy are different, West Pakistan considers itself to be apart of the Middle East while East Bengal finds more connection with people in Southeast Asia.[1640]

It would seem that some attempt was made to unite the Muslims from both East and West under the banner of Islamic brotherhood, but Mascarenhas quotes the leaders of Bangladesh saying, "the compulsions of economic development were too strong to be sidetracked by the slogan of Islamic solidarity and brotherhood. It would regard the bonds of Islam so strong that they would be expected to forget their economic exploitation and backwardness.[1641]" However, there remained the vast majority of Muslims in West Pakistan, while the East had a sizeable amount of Hindus.

Mascarenhas goes on to say that:

> "There is a general knowledge of the unspeakable cruelties visited on thousands of defenseless men, women and children in the violent upsurge of the East Bengalis that followed the campaign of genocide launched by the Pakistan army on 25 March 1971. These horrifying acts—killings, rape and the mutilation of women and children—are understandably an embarrassment to the sensitive people of Bangla Desh now locked in a battle for their homeland."[1642]

[1639] Aziz, Hewa. "*Saddam's House of Horrors*," published on Saturday 19 January 2008, accessed on 26 April 2010. Asharq Alawsat, URL: http://kurdishinstitute. eu/en/info/saddam-s-house-of-horrors-1201099356.html

[1640] Mascarenhas, Anthony. *The Rape of Bangla Desh*. London: Vikas Publications, 1971, p. 9.

[1641] Mascarenhas, p. 12.

[1642] Mascarenhas, p. 18.

There are several stories that have been documented in the book *Against Our Will: Men, Women and Rape* by Susan Brownmiller. She tells one story of a young couple who were newly married when six Pakistani soldiers came into their house and raped the young woman. Due to the nature of honor in this area of the world, the young woman left for a shelter for rape victims and did not think she would ever return to her home. Her reasons were that her husband refused to see her, her father was ashamed of her, and the village did not want her.[1643]

She tells another story of a girl named Khadiga who was thirteen and walking to school one day when she was kidnapped by soldiers and forced into a military brothel. There were several other girls there, but she stated that she was abused daily by at least two men, some of the other girls were abused much more often.[1644] However, young women were not the only ones assaulted. A woman named Kamala Begum lived in Dacca and stayed behind because she assumed that she was "too old" for any men to take notice of her. However, she too found herself the victim of assault when three Pakistani men attacked her in her home.[1645] After the war with Pakistan was over, it was reported that anywhere from 200,000 to 400,000 women were raped.[1646] The Prime Minister Mujibur Rahman then declared that all of the victims of rape were heroines and tried to reintegrate them into society with little success.[1647] The intense nature of honor embedded in the culture and psyche of the people and connected to a woman's virginity and chastity cannot easily be erased.

In Africa there are similar stories found in the Darfur area. There has been conflict here for a number of years. The central government in Khartoum has been working to squash "rebellions" and has turned to recruiting from Arab nomad militia that is called the Janjaweed.[1648] One article reports on a Janjaweed runaway who tells his story in the militia. He mentions that he thinks the Sudanese government was tricking Arabs into joining the group

---

[1643] Susan Brownmiller, *Against Our Will: Men, Women and Rape*. New York, NY: Simon and Schuster, 1975, p. 81.
[1644] Brownmiller, p. 81.
[1645] Brownmiller, p. 82.
[1646] Brownmiller, p. 81
[1647] Brownmiller, p. 82.
[1648] Center on Law and Globalization. "Arab Women Play a Role in War-Related Rape in Darfur." Smart Library on Globalization. 2010 CLG Portal (copyright). URL: http://clg.portalxm.com/library/keytext.cfm?keytext_id=137

stating that they had a duty to defend their communities against any attack that could come from the black rebel groups.[1649] The men were then trained by the soldiers, ordered to attack at certain areas, and given any military support that they would need. He said the attacks would start early in the morning and usually last most of the day. He said other men would take women out of sight and rape them, and if the women refused, they would be shot.[1650]

In a report given by Ann McFerran, she tells the story of a young woman named Nafisa who lives in a camp named Kalma. She was attacked one day while collecting firewood. She was thirty years old and already had two children. When she was raped, her greatest worry was that she was pregnant and could not afford another child to feed. She also feared her family would be shamed by this baby. She soon found out she was pregnant, and at first she hated herself and her baby. However, she later decided that the child was a precious gift, and she wanted to love the child instead of killing it like she has seen other women do to their babies.[1651]

Though the government denies that they are encouraging these acts, they do not seem to make it any easier for women in these situations. Laws on rape in Sudan make it more likely that a woman would be charged for inappropriate sexual conduct than the man who raped her. In a report given by Refugees International, they state that the laws simply expose victims to more abuse. Under the governmental law, a woman must be able to prove that she did not consent to the rape, and if she cannot prove this, she could be charged with unlawful sexual intercourse. Along with this judges will often ask for these women to produce four men who witnessed the penetration, which is nearly impossible. Apart from these laws, men involved in the military and government cannot be prosecuted unless a senior officer denounces them. The janjaweed are considered part of the defense forces and are thus exempt from any prosecutions (Fricke).[1652]

Rape in time of war is a common occurence, and certainly not the exclusive domain of the Muslim world. These are cases, however, where

---

[1649] Martin Fletcher, "Janjaweed defector confesses Sudan's atrocities in Darfur." Published on Thursday 19 October 2006, accessed on 17 May 2010. URL: http://www.sudantribune.com/spip.php?article18203

[1650] Fletcher.

[1651] Ann Mcferran, "Curse of the Janjaweed," published on 23 September 2007, accessed on 19 May 2010. URL: http://www.timesonline.co.uk/tol/news/world/africa/article2489206.ece

[1652] Center on Law and Globalization.

Muslim governments have been explicitly involved and justifying their actions in terms of Islamic law. No other religion on the planet provides such extensive rationale for the use of rape against non-Muslims or Muslims that have been declared to be non-Muslims. No other region of the world has so many examples of religious and secular leaders willing to encourage such behavior. If Islam is to be considered a tolerant religion, then there must be a worldwide reformation that explicitly identifies, criticizes, and rejects this and many other inhumane practices. Sharia law at its core is religious apartheid, the separate and unequal treatment of people based on their religious beliefs. Neither Muhammad nor his law is the perfect exemplar for the twenty-first century.

GLOSSARY

Abdul Manaf: Illustrious great-great-grandfather of Muhammad.

Abdul Muttalib: Grandfather of Muhammad who cared for him briefly after the death of his father Abdullah and mother Amina.

Abdullah Yusuf Ali: Translator the the Qur'an whose copious footnotes amount to a commentary on the text of the Qur'an.

Abraha/Abreha (Abramos): Axumite king of Yemen, ruled 536-555 CE.[1653]

Abu Bakr: Father of Aisha, close companion of Muhammad and the second Caliph.

Abu Jahl: "Father of lies" is the meaning of this epithet given by the Prophet to his most vociferous opponent in Mecca Amir bin Hesham bin al-Mughira. He was killed at the Battle of Badr.

Abu Sufyan: Military leader of the Quraysh in the conflicts with Muhammad eventually converted to Islam after the conquest of Mecca.

Abu Talib: The uncle and protector of Muhammad during his time in Mecca.

Abyssinia/Axum: Christian kingdom centered in modern Eritrea and Ethiopia where the Muslims took refuge around 615 CE.

AH: "After Hijra." The Islamic dating system starts with Muhammad's migration to Medina in 622 CE.

[1653] The last epigraphic evidence for Abraha/Abreha is 553 CE. K. A. Kitchen (*Documentation for Ancient Arabia*, Liverpool University Press, 1994, p. 9), follows the Islamic dating of 570 CE for the death of Abraha after his invasion of the Hejaz. There are reasons to debate this and a date of 555 CE is accepted here as the terminus for his reign.

Al-Aws and Khazraj: The two primary tribal groups in Medina under the Banu Qayla.

Al 'Azl: Coitus interruptus, a practice frowned upon by the Prophet of Islam who preferred completed rape of female prisoners.

Ali bin Abi Talib: Muhammad's nephew and perhaps the first male convert to Islam.

Ansars: Believers in Muhammad who originated in Medina.

Aqaba Treaty: This treaty between Muhammad and certain parties in Medina set the stage for Muhammad's hijra to Medinan and the military conflict with Mecca.

Badr: Muhammad's first major victory in battle over the Meccans in 624 CE.

Bahira: Christian monk who supposedly predicted Muhammad's prophethood.

Banu Nadir: One of the key Jewish tribal groups in Medina driven into exile by the Prophet.

Banu Qaylah: The overarching tribal group of Medina.

Banu Qaynuqa: One of the key Jewish tribal groups in Medina driven into exile by the Prophet.

Banu Qurayza: One of the key Jewish tribal groups in Medina slaughtered by Muhammad.

Bilal: African slave converted to Islam who reputedly led the first calls to prayer in Islam.

Byzantines: The eastern Roman empire centered in modern Turkey and controlling much of the Middle East during this time. Constant war with Sassanids during much of this period.

Dhu Nuwas/Yusuf Asar: King of the then Jewish dynasty of Yemen who supposedly persecuted the Christians of Najran, South Arabia. Approximate dates 517-525 CE.[1654]

Furqan: Salvation or deliverance, a title of revelation as well as a title for one chapter of the Qur'an.

[1654] Debate about the exact dates have been rife due to the uncertainty of the exact dating of the "Himyaritic Era." This debate has been more or less settled and the dates provided here are in accordance with K. A. Kitchen, *Documentation for Ancient Arabia*, Liverpool University Press, 1994, p. 3.

Gabriel: The angel who conveys heavenly books to their prophetic recipients in Islamic theology.

Gharaniq: High flying cranes associated with the deities of the Ka'aba in the pagan period.

Ghassan: Arab tribal kingdom located in the region of modern Syria. Nominally Christian and controlled by the Byzantines. Often in conflict with the Lakhmids of al-Hira.

Hajj: Pilgrimage to Mecca in the sacred month of Ramadan. The greater pilgrimage.

Hadith: Tradition, collections of stories concerning primarily Muhammad's behavior and teaching that form the foundation of Islamic law.

Hamza: Muhammad's uncle and an early convert to Islam "martyred" at the Battle of Uhud.

Hanif: A class of Arab monotheists not connected with either Judaism or Christianity seen as forerunners of Muhammad's Arab monotheism.

Hassan b. Tiban/Abu Karib: Known from an inscription dated 516 CE as Ma'ad-Karib II Ya'hur. He was the ruler of Yemen/Himyar and is thought to have been Jewish. His son, Dhu Nuwas, was Jewish. Approximate dates 505-517 CE.

Hijaz: The Western coastal region of modern Saudi Arabia where Mecca and Medina are located.

Hijra: Muhammad's "emigration" to Medina in 622 CE.

Himyarites: The ruling dynasty/people group of Yemen, South Arabia. Displaced by the Abyssinians/Axumites in 525 CE.

Hira: Capitol city of Arab tribal kingdom of the Lakhmid dynasty located in southern Iraq bordering Ghassan and at times a tributary to the Sassanid Persian Empire often at conflict with Ghassan. This kingdom and its name has been connected to the cave where Muhammad supposedly received his first revelations by those who claim that the birthplace of Islam is really Mesopotamia and that in its origins it was largely a Christian movement.[1655]

[1655] See Volker Popp, "The Early History of Islam Following Inscriptional and Numismatic Testimony," in, *The Hidden Origins of Islam*, Karl-Heinz Ohlig and Gerd R. Puin, New York: Prometheus Press, 2010, pp. 17-33.

Houris: the celestial virgins of the Qur'an who are the reward of faithful Muslims in heaven.

Ibn Ishaq: Author of one of the early biographies of Muhammad.

Ibn Kathir: Writer of a ten-volume commentary on the Qur'an foundational to this study as well as a biography of the Prophet of Islam.

Ibn Sa'd: Seventh or eighth century historian of Islam and the life of Muhammad.

Ifrit: A spirit (jinn) considered to be of high position or authority.

Ka'ba: The central shrine of the Meccan sanctuary.

Khadija: The first wife of Muhammad who died in the Meccan period of the Prophet. Reputed to be his first follower.

Lakhmids: Arab dynasty, probably Christian in the pre-Islamic period centered in modern Iraq with capitol at al-Hira. Tributary to Sassanids and often in conflict with the Ghassanids.

Lat, Uzza, and Manat: The three daughters of Allah, idols of the Ka'aba.

Miraj: Muhammad's night journey to Jerusalem and heaven mentioned in Qur'an 17:1.

Munafiqun: Hypocrites, Muslims who feigned loyalty to Muhammad but were unwilling to engage in *jihad*.

Muhajirun: Those believers who emigrated from Mecca to Medina.

Najran: Christian city in South Arabia supposedly conquered by the Jewish king of Himyar/Yemen, Dhu Nuwas, followed by a general massacre of the Christian population in 523 CE.[1656] Led to Axumite Christian invasion of Yemen.

naskh: The doctrine of abrogation which allows Muslims to reconcile contradictory passages in the Qur'an by means of a chronological system that negates earlier verses by later revelations.

Nutfah: The combination of male and female semen that results in conception in the view of the Qur'an. It is considered a filthy fluid which renders sexual partners unclean.

Theodore NÖldeke: German scholar of the nineteenth century who helped to delineate the chronological order of the chapters of the Qur'an.

[1656] Kitchen, p. 4.

Qarina: The demonic alter ego that abides as a familiar spirit within every human being.

Qiblah: The Muslim direction for prayer (toward Mecca).

Quraysh: Primary tribal group of Mecca, generally opponents of Muhammad.

Qur'an: The Muslim holy book revealed through Prophet Muhammad.

Ruh-ul Quddus: The spirit of God in the Qur'an, a concept which Muhammad refrains from explaining.

Sana'a: Capitol city of Yemen.

Sassanids: Dynasty of the Persian Empire of this time centered in the region of modern Iran. Constant warfare throughout this period with Byzantines.

Sayyid Qutb: The father of the modern Islamist and terrorist movements.

Sharia: Islamic law and in many ways the core conception of Islam. God's law (Fiqh) is the king of the Islamic sciences.

Sira: Muslim historical writings specifically biographies of the Prophet of Islam.

Sunnah: The pathway or behavior pattern of the Prophet of Islam to be imitated even down to the way in which he brushed his teeth.

Tafsir: Commentary literature that interprets the Qur'an.

Taqwa: Fear or awe of God.

Tamatha: "to deflower" or "expand the hymen through intercourse."

Thaqif: An Arab tribal group that controlled the city of Ta'if in the highlands above Mecca.

At-Tirmidhi: A collector of traditions of the Prophet Muhammad.

Ummah: Community, Muslim conception of the unified nation of Islam related to the early concept of Hums.

Umra: Pilgrimage to Mecca at times other than the sacred month, the lesser pilgrimage.

Uqbah bin Abi Mu'ayt: Meccan opponent whom Muhammad had killed after he was captured at the Battle of Badr.

Urub: literally horny, a woman desirous of intercourse with her husband.

Waraqa: A cousin of Muhammad's first wife, Khadija, reputedly a Christian who encouraged Muhammad to accept his calling as a Prophet.

Yathrib: The original name of the city to which Muhammad emigrated. He changed its name to Medina.

Yemen: Mountainous region of south west Arabia adjacent to the Hijaz. Also known as "Himyar" in pre-Islamic times.

Zorastrians: Followers of Zoroaster the national religion of the Persians before their conquest by the Arab Muslims.

BIBLIOGRAPHY

1. Nabia Abbott, *Studies in Arabic Literary Papyri*, Chicago: University of Chicago Press, 1967.
2. Abdalqadir as-Sufi, *The Return of the Califate*, Madinah Press, 1996.
3. Abu Dawud, *Sunan*, Vols. 1-4, New Delhi: Kitab Bhavan, 1993.
4. W. N. Arafat, New Light on the Story of Banu Qurayza and the Jews of Medina. *Journal of the Royal Asiatic Society of Great Britain and Ireland,* 1976, pp. 100-107.
5. Karen Armstrong, *Muhammad, A Biography of the Prophet,* San Francisco: Harper, 1993.
6. Ahmad Barakat, *Muhammad and the Jews*. New Delhi: Vikas Publishing House, 1979.
7. Muhammad Bashumail, *The Great Battle of Badr,* Delhi: Islamic Book Service, 1997.
8. Herbert Berg, *The Development of Exegesis in Early Islam*, Curzon Press, 2000.
9. Herbert Berg, "The Implications of and Opposition to the Methods and Theories of John Wansbrough," in *Method and Theory in the Study of Religion*, Swets and Zeitlinger, 2002.
10. Emory C. Bogle, *Islam Origin and Belief,* University of Texas Press, 1998.
11. Gerhard Bowering, "Recent Research on the Construction of the Qur'an," in *The Qur'an in its Historical Context*, ed. Gabriel Said Reynolds, New York: Routledge, 2008.
12. Al-Bukhari, *The Translation of the Meanings of Sahih Al-Buhkari volumes 1-9,* trans. Muhammad M. Khan, Al Medina Al Munawwara, Islamic University. Hilal Yayinlari Beirut: Dar Al Arabia, 1981.
13. Herbert Busse, "The Destruction of the Temple and its Reconstruction in the Light of Muslim Exegesis of Sura 17:2-9," in *Jerusalem Studies in Arabic and Islam*, Vol. 20, 1996.
14. Norman Calder, "History and Nostalgia," in *Method and Theory in the Study of Religion*, Swets & Zeitlinger, 2002.
15. Canon Sell, *The Battles of Badr and Uhud*. The Christian Literature Society, 1909.

16. Patricia Crone, *Meccan Trade and the Rise of Islam*, Princeton University Press, 1987.

17. Patricia Crone, *Slaves on Horses*, Cambridge: Cambridge University Press, 1980.

18. Patricia Crone and Michael Cook, *Hagarism, The Making of the Islamic World*, Cambridge University Press, 1977.

19. Ali Dashti, *Twenty-three Years*, Mazda Publishers, 1992.

20. Fred M. Donner, Muhammad's Political Consolidation in Arabia up to the Conquest of Mecca, *Muslim World*, 69 (1979): 229-247.

21. Fred M. Donner, "The Qur'an in Recent Scholarship," in *The Qur'an in its Historical Context*, ed. Gabriel Said Reynolds, New York: Routledge, 2008.

22. Fred Donner, *The early Islamic Conquests*.

23. Rizwi S. Faizer, Muhammad and the Medinan Jews: A Comparison of the texts of Ibn Ishaq's Kitab Sirat Rasul Allah with al-Waqidi's Kitab al-Maghazi, *International Journal of Middle East Studies,* 28 (1996): 463-489.

24. Rizwi S. Faizer, *Ibn Ishaq and al-Waqidi Revisited: A Case Study of Muhammad and the Jews in Biographical Literature*, Doctoral thesis, Montreal: McGill University, 1995.

25. Rizwi S. Faizer, The Issue of Authenticity Regarding the Traditions of al-Waqidi as Established in His Kitab al-Maghazi, *Journal of Near Eastern Studies,* 58(2) (1999) pp. 97-114.

26. James Howard-Johnston, *Witnesses to a World Crisis*, Oxford: Oxford University Press, 2010.

27. Isma'il R al-Faruki, *Islamic Da'wah Its Nature and Demands*, American Trust Publications, 1986.

28. Reuben Firestone, "The Failure of a Jewish Program of Public Satire in the Squares of Medina", *Judaism*, 46 (1997).

29. Abraham Geiger, *Judaism and Islam*, New York: KTAV Publishing, 1970. This is a reprint of a nineteenth century work.

30. Moshe Gil, The Medinan Opposition to the Prophet, *Jerusalem Studies in Arabic and Islam*, 10 (1987): 65-96.

31. Moshe Gil, "The Constitution of Medina: a Reconsideration" in *Israel Oriental Studies*, Volume IV. Tel Aviv University. Jerusalem, Israel: Central Press, 1974.

32. John Gilchrist, *The Qur'an*, South Africa: Mercsa, 1995.

33. Ginzberg, *Legends of the Jews, Volumes 1-4,* Johns Hopkins University Press, 1998.

34. John Glubb, *The Life and Times of Muhammad*, Chelsea, MI: Scarborough House Publishers, 1970.
35. Sydney Griffith, "Christian Lore and the Arabic Qur'an," in *The Qur'an in its Historical Context*, Routledge, 2008.
36. Abdul Wahid Hamid, *Companions of the Prophet*, London: MELS, 1998.
37. Muhammad Hamidullah, *The Battlefields of the Prophet Muhammad*, Deccan, 1973.
38. Isaac Hasson, La Conversion de Mu'awiya ibn Abi Sufyan, *JSAI 22*, pp. 214-242.
39. G. R. Hawting, "John Wansbrough, Islam and Monotheism," in *Method and Theory in the Study of Religion*, Lisse: Swets & Zeitlinger, 2002.
40. G. R Hawting, *The Idea of Idolatry and the Emergence of Islam*, Cambridge: Cambridge University Press, 2006.
41. J. Horovitz, Earliest Biographies of the Prophet and Their Authors, *Islamic Culture*, April, 1927.
42. Robert G. Hoyland, *Seeing Islam as Others Saw it*, Princeton: The Darwin Press, 1997.
43. Robert Hoyland, "The Linguistic Background to the Qur'an," in *The Qur'an in its Historical Context*, ed. Gabriel Said Reynolds, New York: Routledge, 2008.
44. Muhammad Ibn Ishaq, *The Life of Muhammad*. Ed. trans. and with an introduction by Alfred Guillaume. Karachi: Oxford University Press, 1955.
45. Ibn Kathir, *Al-Sira Al-Nabawiyya Volumes 1-4*, trans. Dr. Trevor Le Gassick, U.K.: Garner Publishing, 1998.
46. Ibn Rawandi, "Origins of Islam: A Critical Look at the Sources," in *The Quest for the Historical Muhammad*, Amherst: Prometheus Books, 2000.
47. Raymond Ibrahim, "Jihad, Martyrdom, and the Torments of the Grave," *Pajamas Media*, March 14, 2009.
48. Subhash Inamdar, *Muhammad and the rise of Islam: the Creation of Group Identity*, New York: Psychosocial Press, 2001.
49. Interview with a suicide bomber "*JIRGA*; http://www.youtube.com/watch?v=w8gu5Xfi_E4.
50. Arthur Jeffery, *Materials for the History of the Text of the Qur'an*, E. J. Brill, 1937.
51. J. M. B. Jones, "The Chronology of the Maghazi," *BSOAS,* 1956.
52. J. H. A. Juynboll, "Some Isnad—Analytical Methods Illustrated on the Basis of Several Woman—Demeaning Sayings from Hadith Literature,"

in Harald Motzki, Ed., *The Formation of the Classical Islamic World*, Ashgate, 2004.

53. Hanna Kassis, *A Concordance of the Qur'an*, Los Angeles: University of California Press, 1983.

54. Khaled Muhammad Galal Muhammad Ali Keshk, *The Conflict Between Muhammad and the Three Jewish Tribes of Medina*. Master's Thesis: Department of Languages, University of Utah, December 1987.

55. M. J. Kister, "The Market of the Prophet," *Journal of the Economic and Social History of the Orient,* 8 (1965).

56. K. A. Kitchen, *Documentation for Ancient Arabia*, Liverpool University Press, 1994.

57. Todd E. Klutz, *Rewriting the Testament of Solomon*, New York: T & T Clark International, 2005.

58. Manfred Kropp, "Beyond Single Words," in *The Qur'an in its Historical Context*, Routledge, 2008.

59. Henri Lammens, "Fatima and the Daughers of Muhammad," in *The Quest for the Historical Muhammad by Ibn Warraq*. Amherst, NY: Prometheus Books, 2000.

60. Ella Landau-Tasseron, "Processes of Redaction: the case of the Tamimite Delegation to the Prophet Muhammad", *www.jstor.org/stable/618597, 1986*

61. Jacob Lassner, *Demonizing the Queen of Sheba,* Chicago: University of Chicago Press, 1993.

62. Todd Lawson, *The Crucifixion and the Qur'an*, Oxford: One World Press, 2009.

63. Michael Lecker, "Waqidi's Account on the Status of the Jews of Medina: A Study of a combined report," *Journal of Near Eastern Studies,* 54 (Chicago, 1995): 15-32.

64. Michael Lecker, *Muslims, Jews and Pagans, Studies on Early Islamic Medina*, Brill, 1995.

65. Michael Lecker, *Jews and Arabs in Pre-and Early Islamic Arabia.* Ashgate, 1998.

66. Michael Lecker, "On the Markets of Medina (Yathrib) in Pre-Islamic and Early Islamic Times," *Jerusalem Studies in Arabic and Islam* 8 (1986), pp. 133-147.

67. Michael Lecker, "Idol Worship in Pre-Islamic Medina (Yathrib)." *Le Museon* 106 Louvain-la-Neuve, 1993.

68. Michael Lecker, "Muhammad at Medina: A Geographical Approach," *Jerusalem Studies in Arabic and Islam* 6 (1985), pp. 36-51.

69. Bernard Lewis, *The Jews of Islam,* Princeton, NJ: Princeton University Press, 1984

70. Jane Dammen McAuliffe, *Qur'anic Christians,* Cambridge University Press, 1991.

71. McDonald and Watt, Vol. 7 *Al-Tabari,* SUNY series in Near Eastern Studies.

72. Gertrude Melamede, "The Meetings at Al-Aqaba," in Uri Rubin, ed., *The Life of Muhammad,* Brookfield, VT: Ashgate, 1998.

73. Harald Motzki, editor, *The Biography of Muhammad,* Brill, 2000.

74. Harald Motzki, "The Murder of Ibn Abi al-Huqayq: On the Origin and Reliability of some Maghazi Reports," in *The Biography of Muhammad,* Brill Academic Publishers, 2000.

75. Muhammad Hamidullah, *The Battlefields of the Prophet Muhammad,* Hyderabad: Deccan, 1973.

76. Muhammad Taqi-ud-Din Al-Hilali and Muhammad Muhsin Khan. *The Noble Qur'an.* Islamic University, Al-Madinah Al-Munawwarah: Darussalam Publishers and Distributors, 1996.

77. William Muir, *The Life of Mohamet,* London: Smith Elder & Co., 1877.

78. Miklos Muranyi, "The First Muslims in Mecca: A Social Basis for a New Religion?" in Uri Rubin, ed., *The Life of Muhammad.* Brookfield, VT: Ashgate, 1998.

79. *Muslim,* Volumes 1-4, Lahore: Muhammad Ashraf Publishers, 1990.

80. Ohlig and Puin, ed., *The Hidden Origins of Islam,* New York: Prometheus Press, 2010.

81. F. E. Peters, "The Quest of the Historical Muhammad," *International Journal of Middle East Studies,* 23(3) (1991), pp. 291-315.

82. F. E. Peters, *Muhammad and the Origins of Islam,* Suny Series in Near Eastern Studies.

83. Poonawala, *Translation of al-Tabari,* Vol. 9, SUNY Series in Near Eastern Studies.

84. Seyyid Qutb, *Milestones,* The Mother Mosque Foundation, 1986.

85. Hannah Rahman, "The Conflicts between the Prophet and the Opposition in Medina," in *Der Islam,* 42, 1985.

86. Uri Rubin, "The Assassination of Ka'b b. al-Ashraf," *Oriens* 32 (1990).

87. Uri Rubin, ed. *The Life of Muhammad,* Brookfield: Ashgate Publishing, 1998.

88. Sahih al-Bukhari, *The Hadith, 9 volumes,* Medina: Islamic University, 1981.

89. Joseph Schacht, "A Revaluation of Islamic Traditions," *Royal Asiatic Society of Great Britain and Ireland,* 1949.

90. Gregor Schoeler, "Die Frage der schriftlichen oder mundlichen Uberlieferung der Wissenschaften im fruhen Islam," in *Der Islam,* 42, 1985.

91. R. B. Serjeant, "The Sunnah Jami'ah, pacts with the Yathrib Jews, and the Tahrim of Yathrib: analysis and translation of the documents comprised in the so-called "Constitution of Medina"" in *The Life of Muhammad* by Uri Rubin. Brookfield, VT: Ashgate, 1998.

92. Jay Smith, *Uncomfortable Questions for the Qur'an.* WWW.debate. org/topics/history/home. htm. 1995.

93. Devin J. Stewart, "Notes on the Medieval and Modern Emendations of the Qur'an," in *The Qur'an in its Historical Context,* ed. Gabriel Said Reynolds, New York: Routledge, 2008.

94. Abu Al-Tabari, "The Foundation of the Community," Ed., trans. W. M. Watt and M. V. McDonald. Vol. 7, *The History of al-Tabari.* Albany: State University of New York Press, 1989.

95. Roberto Tottoli, *Biblical Prophets in the Qur'an and Muslim Literature,* Routledge, 2002.

96. Jan Vansina, *Oral Tradition as History,* Madison: The University of Wisconsin Press, 1985.

97. John Wansbrough, *Quranic Studies,* Oxford University Press, 1977.

98. John Wansbrough, *The Sectarian Milieu,* Oxford University Press, 1978.

99. W. Montgomery Watt, *Muhammad at Medina,* Oxford: Clarendon Press, 1956.

100. W. M. Watt, "Muhammad," in *The Cambridge History of Islam.* Ed. P. M. Holt and Bernard Lewis. Cambridge: Cambridge University Press, 1970, pp. 30-56.

101. W. Montgomery Watt, "The reliability of Ibn-Ishaq's Sources," in *La Vie du Prophete Mahomet,* Strasbourg: Presses Universitaires de France, 1980.

102. W. Montgomery Watt, *Companion to the Qur'an,* Oxford, 1967, 1994.

103. W. Montgomery Watt, *Early Islam: Collected Articles.* Edinburgh: Edinburgh University Press, 1990.

104. W. Montgomery Watt, "Muhammad" in *The Cambridge History of Islam,* Vol. I A, Cambridge University Press, 1970.

105. W. Montgomery Watt, *Muhammad: Prophet and Statesman*, Oxford: Oxford University Press, 1960.

106. Wellhausen, *Muhammad and the Jews of Medina*, trans. Jan Arent Weinsinck, 1975.

107. A. J. Wensinck, Mohammed en de Joden te Medina. Edited and translated by W. Behn as *Muhammad and the Jews of Medina*. Freiburg in Breisgau: K. Schwarz, 1975.

108. A. Yusuf Ali, *The Holy Qur'an: Text, Translation and Commentary*, Leicester: The Islamic Foundation, 1975.

INDEX

A

Aaron (Harun), 86, 128-29, 217
Abbassids, 510
Abbott, Nabia, 497
Abdallah b. Sa'd, 496, 507
Abd Allah b. Salam, 237
Abdullah b. Jahsh, 243, 507
Abdullah b. Jubayr, 314
Abdullah b. Rawaha, 305
Abdullah b. Ubayy b. Salul, 288-90, 292, 304, 311-13, 318, 361, 369, 512
Abdullah Ibn Masud, 276
Abdullah Yusuf Ali, 46, 49, 51, 55-56, 61-62, 77, 85, 93, 124, 204, 219, 255, 258, 269, 298-99, 323-24
on Abraham's sacrifice, 127
accusation on Jews, 295
on adoption, 390
on the Battle of Badr, 282
on the beast of the end times, 111
on the birthplace of Jesus, 143
on borrowing the custom of fasting, 239
on the crimes of Meccans on the raid to Naklah, 267
on crimes of treason, 397
distinction between unbelievers, 412
on division of humanity into tribes and nations, 438
on the division of war booty, 280
on husbands and wives, 344, 395
on Islam establishing its political power, 270
on Jesus's death, 353
on jihad, 300, 336, 351
making references to the Bible, 133-35, 142, 264
on Muhammad being tutored, 96, 158-59
on Muhammad's messianic title, 396
on Muhammad's night journey, 94
on Muhammad's plunder against Jews, 388
on the nearness of God, 102
on prayers, 119
on the prophethood of Ismail, 120
on the return of Jesus, 145
on the Samiri, 129, 217
on slave trade, 404
on Solomon, 136-37, 139-40
on the split moon, 93
on surah 4, 341
on surah 7, 216
on surah 9, 447
on surah 48, 430
on surah 57, 338
on surah 72, 104
on the unity of God, 100
on women captives, 121
Abdul-l Malik Ibn Hisham, 8, 289, 315, 376, 510, 520
Abdul Manaf, 541
Abdul Muttalib, 21, 33, 42, 541
Abdul Shams, 68
Abdur-Rahman, 279
Abel, 465
Abraha (Abyssinian king), 17-18, 21-22, 127, 541
attempting to conquer Mecca, 17, 21
dam inscription of, 17
Abraham (Ibrahim), 60, 63-64, 104, 126-27, 165, 169, 215, 218, 224,

Edwards Brothers, Inc.
Thorofare, NJ USA
June 24, 2011